Image and Mind

STEPHEN MICHAEL KOSSLYN

Harvard University Press
Cambridge, Massachusetts
and London, England
1980

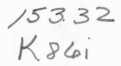

Library of Congress Cataloging in Publication Data
  Kosslyn, Stephen Michael, 1948–
    Image and mind.

    Bibliography: p.
    Includes index.
    1. Visualization. 2. Imagery (Psychology)
3. Memory. I. Title.
  BF367.K67   153.3'2   80-10329
  ISBN 0-674-44365-9

To my parents

Preface

The research program I describe in this book began quite inadvertently, during an experiment on the organization of "semantic memory," when I noticed that two people in a row had judged as false the statement "A flea can bite." I made it a habit to talk to the subjects after each session and to review with them any peculiar responses. When asked about this strange mistake (I was convinced that everyone, even people who had never owned a dog or cat, knew fleas could bite!), one subject said something like "I looked for a mouth, but couldn't find one." The other subject said "I looked, but couldn't see any teeth." Looked? See? What is this, I wondered, this talk about visual imagery? Imagery did not seem to fit in at all with the semantic net models I had been thinking about, and it was not clear how factors that should affect the organization of such a net would affect using imagery. Thus, I asked all my subjects whether they had tended to use mental imagery in deciding whether the statements presented to them were true or false, and I graphed the results separately for people who claimed to use imagery and for those who did not. Amazingly, the patterns were wildly different. For those who professed not to use imagery, decision times decreased with increasing association strength between a noun and a property, as I had expected (if association strength reflects "distance" between two representations in some kind of net). But for those who used imagery, times were not affected by association strength at all! (Years later I found out why: In this earlier experiment less strongly associated properties also tended to be larger, and larger properties are more easily seen on images—as is discussed in chapter 7). In the next experiment, Keith Nelson and I tested two groups of subjects, asking one group to use images in evaluating statements and giving the other group no instructions about strategy. These results again showed different effects of association strength depending on whether imagery was used. It was not clear to me where to go from there, but three other fortuitous

vii

events came together and ended up defining the present research program.

At the same time I was measuring people's reaction times and asking about the bases for their decisions, I was pursuing my long-standing interest in developmental psychology. I read Bruner, Olver, and Greenfield's book, in which the authors claimed that young children rely on imagery in their thinking more than adults do. This was an interesting idea but seemed hopelessly intractable given our dearth of knowledge about imagery. To track the bear, one needs to know what its footprints look like; without knowing what it means to "use imagery," how can one know what would be the behavioral consequences of using imagery in one's thinking? In chapter 10 I discuss the literature on this "representational-development" hypothesis and argue that the present enterprise not only has clarified the nature of the question being asked but has provided the beginnings of an answer to it.

The second major root of the present project was a single line in Gordon Bower's paper, "Mental Imagery and Associative Learning," which was later published in a highly revised form in 1972. In the early version, Bower was describing some of his introspections: "Frequently only part of the scene is 'focussed' as figure, the rest being indeterminant ground until we fill in or generate another part of the scene, much as we move our eye over actual scenes." (This line was altered beyond recognition [p. 57] in the final version.) When I read this sentence, an experiment immediately sprang to mind: If Bower's observations were true, it should require more time to "see" parts of images that were not in focus at the time of query than parts that were in focus. I was struck by the idea that if images were in some sense structurally like pictures, then they should depict spatial extent and more time should be required to traverse greater distances across them. Oddly enough, when I designed and conducted my first scanning experiment (described in chapter 3, section 2.1), I was only vaguely aware of the stunning work on mental rotation that Roger Shepard and my fellow students Jacky Metzler and Lynn Cooper were conducting right down the hall.

After publishing the scanning experiment in 1973 I lost direction; it was not clear to me where research on imagery, either mine or that of the field in general, was leading. The catalyst that truly launched the present project was the idea that images are like displays a computer can generate on a cathode-ray tube. On this view, images are "surface representations" that are generated from more abstract underlying representations. Although this idea was inspired in part by Chomsky's work in linguistics, it was primarily a simple extension of a class assignment in my first computer programming course, taught by Jerry Feldman. We were asked to write a program to draw various geometric figures using a set of shapes. The shapes themselves were generated by sets of procedures, and the figures were composed by printing out different shapes in various combinations and relative positions. It gradually dawned on me that I had the beginnings of a model of human mental imagery in my class project.

Thus, the earlier work provided a set of techniques for studying imagery, primarily based on simple extensions of the kinds of sentence verification tasks used to study semantic memory. Further, my early interest in semantic memory shaped the kinds of questions I wanted to answer, questions about how images serve as repositories of information, about how we extract information from images, and about the situations in which it is advantageous or necessary to use mental imagery. The cathode-ray tube metaphor provided a way of thinking about these questions and the kinds of answers one might find. This metaphor also guided and directed the research strategy that has structured the project to date.

I have dedicated this book to my parents, and I mean this in the broadest sense of the term. I cannot thank my biological parents, S. Duke and Rhoda Kosslyn, enough for all they have done to shape me and hence my work. I also am at a loss to extend adequate thanks to my "intellectual parents." In particular, I owe more than I could ever express to John P. Seward, who employed me in his animal lab during my undergraduate years and showed me what it is to be a scientist and a truly civilized human being. Edward Sadalla also was a source of intellectual stimulation during my undergraduate days. During graduate school Gordon Bower, Herbert Clark, and Edward Smith all spent generous amounts of time with me and much of my education occurred during informal interactions with these gentlemen, as well as with other members of the Stanford University community, notably Susan Haviland, Dan Osherson, John Anderson, Keith Holyoak, Arnold Glass, and Eve Clark. Many of my current ideas are direct outgrowths of discussions and arguments with these people.

I also wish to extend my deepest appreciation to George E. Smith, who meticulously read an early version of the book and devoted one evening a week to me for months on end. George asked hard questions and helped me struggle with the answers. I am also indebted to R. Duncan Luce for carefully reading the entire manuscript and offering deep and penetrating comments. Duncan pointed out conceptual, stylistic, and organizational problems, and deserves credit for helping make the book more coherent and readable. Keith Holyoak, Steven Pinker, and Steven Shwartz performed similar services, and did not spare me when they spotted a factual or a conceptual error. Discussions with Steven Pinker proved especially helpful when I was beset by conceptual confusions, and I wish to thank him for his time, energy, and insights. Conversations with Jerry Fodor also proved very stimulating, and chapter 11 is written around some of his illuminating ideas. Eric Wanner, my editor and friend, more than once forced me to see the error of my ways and is responsible for improving the book greatly over its earlier form. Eric helped me figure out how to put first things first, and I am much appreciative. Camille Smith proved patient and tolerant in editing the manuscript.

I also want to thank all of my collaborators, who are cited in the appropriate places in the text. Without their help, I could not have accomplished a tenth of what is described herein. I am especially grateful to my research assistants Brian Reiser, Martha Farah, and Sharon Fliegel (who have since gone on to bigger and better things), who came through when it counted. Bill Shebar and Roger Wallach helped me dig out references and forced me to think about them. Steven Shwartz, my collaborator in the simulation project, deserves much of the credit for the elegance of the model. Willa Rouder, Debbie Lathrop, Angela O'Neill, and Loretta Czernis suffered through typing the manuscript into the computer and altering it too often to count. Scott Bradner was absolutely invaluable in getting the book off of my computer tapes and onto these pages.

Finally, I want to thank the institutions that nurtured and supported my work. The National Science Foundation, primarily through the good offices of Joseph Young, has been magnanimous in providing me with support (Grants BNS 76–16987, BNS 77–21782, and BNS 79–12418). Stanford University, Johns Hopkins University, and Harvard University have generously given me space and support. Further, in each university I have found the kind of intellectual and emotional environment conducive to the kind of research I do and the kind of life I live.

S.M.K.

Cambridge, Massachusetts
1980

Contents

Figures

Image and Mind

1. A Research Program

To get an intuitive feeling for the topic of this book, try to answer the following questions: What shape are a German Shepherd's ears? Is a tennis ball larger than a pear? Does a bee have a dark head? Is a Christmas tree a darker green than a frozen pea? Most people report that they mentally picture the named objects in the course of trying to answer these questions. For example, a typical respondent will tell me that he or she pictured the dog's head and "looked at" the ears in order to assess their shape. Further, if asked something like "Do frogs have lips or stubby green tails?" people sometimes report first "looking" at the mouth of an imaged frog, then "mentally rotating" the image, and then "zooming in" on the rear in order to have a "close look" before answering. My research program is an effort to discover what images are, how they arise, when they are used, and what it means to "look at" and "manipulate" visual mental images.

The putative role of imagery has varied historically from being an absolutely essential element of thought to being incidental and of little importance. Why has interest in imagery waxed and waned over the years? As I shall discuss in detail in chapter 11, imagery was most popular when the notion of an "idea" was given center stage in psychological theorizing. Since the most elementary "ideas" have to be represented by something that itself does not need to be described in terms of yet more basic representations, "ideas" could not, at root, be represented by words. Not even the most radical nativist believed that words themselves are innate. The only alternative usually countenanced, and one that to many had introspective validity, was mental images. Thus, it is not surprising that since the notion of "idea" was central to the original conception of a scientific psychology, so was the notion of mental imagery. In fact, Wilhelm Wundt, the father of modern experimental psychology, seemed to maintain that all thought processes were accompanied by images (albeit somewhat subtle ones, at times). This extreme claim led to a furious debate,

1

known today as the imageless thought controversy, when other researchers found that subjects did not always report experiencing images
when reasoning about some problem. But the Wundtians consulted their
introspections, and begged to differ. The real problem here was not the
fact of disagreement, but the fact that until very recently there were no
good ways of empirically studying claims about any kind of mental representations. Thus, when disagreements arose, they could not be resolved
to the satisfaction of all or most parties.

John Watson stepped into this impasse and rejected the whole notion
that mental events are the proper subject matter of psychology. Watson
nudged psychology in a new direction, and soon most psychologists were
studying behavior in its own right, self-consciously eschewing any attempts to draw inferences about internal events from observed behaviors.
Thus, imagery—along with the notion of mental representation in general
—fell into disrepute and was largely ignored from 1915 to the early 1960s.
The recent resurgence of imagery research is due in part to widespread
appreciation of the limitations of behaviorism (in providing explanations
of language acquisition, perception, and the like) and to recent conceptual
innovations in linguistics and artificial intelligence, which have allowed us
to return to the study of imagery with new perspectives. In addition, new,
more sophisticated methodologies have enabled researchers to externalize mental events in more objective ways. Thus, there has been a rebirth
of interest in imagery, again inextricably tied to an interest in mental representation in general. As a consequence of this renewed interest, new
empirical findings about imagery have accumulated rapidly.

The recent studies of imagery have taken four basic forms. Most research has centered on the effects of the use of imagery on a person's ability to perform various tasks. This kind of research has focused on the usefulness of imagery as a mnemonic technique and on the effects of the
quality of a person's imagery (for example, its vividness) on a variety of
cognitive functions. A good example of research in this vein is Bower's
(1970) experiments on imagery as a memory aid. Bower's subjects were
asked to remember pairs of concrete nouns (such as "dog-bicycle"). A
group asked to form mental images of the named objects interacting in
some way (a French poodle riding a bike) recalled the pairs far better than
did a group asked simply to repeat the pairs over and over or a group
asked to form separate, noninteracting images of the pairs. Similarly,
Marks (1972) reports that people experiencing more vivid images (as measured by a questionnaire) recall more details of pictures than do people
experiencing less vivid images. Notably, the main thrust of this kind of
research is the study of the role of imagery in affecting some behavior in
its own right, without very much (if any) effort being expended to make
inferences about the nature of images per se. The problem here, however,
is that there is no independent evidence that the imagery itself is what pro-

duces the effects. In fact Bower later decided that it is the additional structure in an abstract encoding of the relationship to be incorporated in an interactive image—and not the image itself—that is responsible for the observed memory improvement (see Anderson and Bower, 1973).

The second kind of recent research consists of attempts to demonstrate a functional equivalence between imagery and like-modality perception. For example, Segal and Fusella (1970) asked subjects to form either a visual or an auditory mental image, and then to try to detect a very faint visual or auditory signal. They found that sensitivity to the visual signal was impaired more if one was simultaneously maintaining a visual image than if one was maintaining an auditory image, whereas the auditory signals were impaired more if one was simultaneously holding an auditory image. To date, however, these findings have done little to illuminate the actual nature of the modality-specific mechanisms shared in perceptual and imaginal processing.

The third approach has focused on trying to discover tasks in which people spontaneously use imagery. For example, Huttenlocher and Higgins (1972) argue that people use imagery when performing some kinds of simple deductive reasoning. When people are presented with pairs of relative statements (for example, "John is smarter than George," and "Bill is dumber than George"), they purportedly integrate the information into an imagined spatial array that depicts the relationships among all the items along the relevant dimension. The difficulty in constructing the spatial array is thought to underlie subjects' difficulties in performing deductions about relationships among the items (such as who is smartest). Unfortunately, without an understanding of the nature of imagery per se, one cannot predict with confidence the consequences of using imagery. Thus, the data taken to support image use in a given situation are often open to multiple plausible interpretations (see, for example, Clark, 1972).

The fourth tradition in the study of imagery has dealt with what seems to be the logically prior question to be addressed before one can study the role of imagery in cognition, namely the structure of imagery per se. Wundt, whose original project falls in this tradition, approached this problem via trained introspection. Workers in his laboratory learned to be sensitive to the nuances of their internal lives and spent many hours performing relatively simple tasks, repeating actions and experiences over and over as they honed their attention down to a few critical details. In addition to the notorious unreliability of this method, and the problem of how to resolve differences in observations, history has taught us to attend to another problem: The discovery of "imageless thought" underscores the fact that even if people's introspections were consistent and reliable, there is a limit to how much we can gain from simple introspection. This observation applies not only to "abstract" cognitive processing (such as often occurs when one is trying to make a decision), but to imagery itself.

That is, much processing must occur before we are aware of an image in order to bring stored information into consciousness. Almost by definition, we cannot fathom the workings of these nonconscious processes via introspection. Further, even when we are trying to interpret data that are available to introspection, we may simply not be sensitive to many revealing aspects of our imagery, like relatively small variations in time to perform different imagery operations. The rebirth of interest in the general topic of imagery has been accompanied by improved methods of studying it.

Most of the recent work investigating the structure of images involves "the quantification of introspection." That is, researchers have tried to externalize mental events, tried to discover and measure the behavioral consequences (often in terms of performance time) of internal processing. If a given introspection is not spurious, then there ought to be externally observable consequences of the observed internal state or event. The experimenter does not spend too much time concentrating on the introspection itself, but quickly leaps to the observable ramifications and tries to document these. Shepard and Metzler's (1971) experiment on "mental rotation" of geometric shapes is a good example of a study in this tradition. These researchers noted introspectively that images seem to be able to rotate, appearing much as would the corresponding objects if they were rotated. If this introspection is valid, one might expect that more time should be required to rotate images farther, if images pass through intermediate positions when they are rotated. And in fact Shepard and Metzler found that the time necessary to compare two forms increased linearly with the angular disparity between their orientations—suggesting that subjects did indeed "mentally rotate" an image of one of the forms into congruence with the other. It is important to note that these results go beyond the simple introspection that images seem able to "rotate": There was no reason to believe that time would increase *linearly* with amount of rotation (images could possibly have mimicked acceleration, "drag," and so forth). The "quantification of introspection" technique provides not only more reliable data than that obtained via simple introspective reports, but more fine-grained information as well. Thus, not only did these sorts of findings begin to tell us something about imagery, but they seemed to lend credence to the claim that images are indeed "psychologically real" entities, that they are something worthy of being studied.

My research program falls into this fourth camp, in that it is an effort to understand the structure of visual mental images. In this book I will try to specify how images serve as data-structures in human memory. That is, the central concern here is with how images serve as repositories of information in memory, and how they may be used in answering questions about properties of imagined or recollected objects, in spatial reasoning, and the like. This approach to imagery is distinctly different from any of its forebears in an important regard: The focus here is not on the nature of the image itself, but on the nature of the imagery representation *system*. It seems clear that the properties of a representation arise only in the context of how that representation is processed. For example, consider a case where some items are ordered into a list in a computer's memory. Say that the only way one can examine this material and its order is via the retrieval processes of the machine. Now, if these items could be retrieved only in one order on one day, and only in another order on another day, for all intents and purposes the order of the list itself would have been changed. But it could be that only the way in which the items were retrieved, not the actual order of the items, had been changed. The functional ordering of the list, then, arises from properties of the data-structure and the process that operates on it. In studying imagery, one can investigate the data-structures, the images themselves, only in the context of having people do something with them. Thus, by its very nature, we can never isolate an image in the pure, but can study it only in relation to the processes that operate on it. In order to understand how images serve as internal representations, then, we must study the image processing system as a whole. Obviously this is easier said than done.

1.0 A TWO-PHASE STRATEGY

There is no set answer to the question "How does one formulate a scientific theory?" One option is simply to use intuition as a guide; this "rationalist" approach has been fruitful in other sciences. However, it seems to me that the intuitions of the successful rationalist usually were grounded in a rich body of data about the subject matter. This does not bode well for such an approach in contemporary cognitive psychology. At the present juncture, too many different sorts of theories seem consistent with the data at hand; we simply do not know enough to get off on the right foot.

The approach I use is first to collect data that make it possible to narrow down the class of acceptable models. This is the goal of research in what I will call Phase I. Only after accumulating some information about the basic characteristics of the imagery representation system did we attempt to formulate a detailed theory and model in Phase II.

1.1 Phase I: Discriminating among Classes of Theories

The purpose of research in Phase I was to formulate issues, the resolution of which would narrow down the class of acceptable theories. I began with a particular preconception of the imagery system and used this as a heuristic for generating central issues. This preconception rested on a metaphor, the essence of which is simply put: Visual mental images are

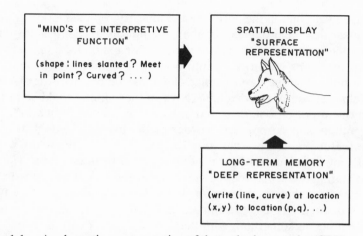

Figure 1.1.   A schematic representation of the cathode-ray tube (CRT) metaphor.

hypothesized to be like displays on a cathode-ray tube (CRT) that are generated by a computer program (plus data), as is schematized in figure 1.1. This metaphor has several components:

First, the quasi-pictorial "surface images" we experience are distinct from underlying "deep representations." Surface images occur in a spatial display medium. This medium allows parts of images to portray the corresponding portions of the imaged object such that the interpoint distances among the portions are implicit in the representation. The metaphor leads one to expect that images will be subject to the limitations of the medium in which they occur. For example, images should have a limited spatial extent (should "overflow" the screen if made too large), should fall prey to resolution limitations imposed by the "grain" of the display medium, should fade over time, and so on. My notion was that this display medium corresponds to a kind of visual short-term memory buffer.

Second, the display is processed by a "mind's eye" that "looks" at the display. This mind's eye is an interface with a conceptual system and serves to classify portions of the spatial image in terms of semantic categories. There is nothing intrinsic in the pattern "∧" that indicates that it is "pointed"; this requires processing by some kind of interpretive mechanism that makes contact with the appropriate representations in long-term memory. Obviously, the "mind's eye" is not a real eye (no metaphor, by definition, is meant to be taken literally!) but corresponds to a set of procedures that serve as an interface between spatial images and more abstract discursive ("semantic," if you will) representations. These procedures register the presence of particular patterns (lines, angles, and so on), and the output of these procedures serves as the input to a semantic classification mechanism.

Third, in the metaphor the deep representations consist of information stored in long-term memory that can be converted into a surface image. The metaphor leads us to hypothesize that the surface images we experience are actively generated from information stored in long-term memory. Further, since images fade over time, the metaphor implies that they must be continually activated in order to be maintained. Finally, in the metaphor the underlying data-structures *may* be decidedly nonpictorial in form; an image could be generated from sets of descriptions, lists of vectors, or the like.

The CRT metaphor was appealing to me for a number of reasons. Perhaps most important, it seemed to capture the correct aspects of the traditional notion that images are like "mental pictures." That is, images seem to depict information (as opposed to describing it; the notions of "depict" and "describe" will be characterized more formally in chapter 3) similarly to the way information is depicted on a CRT display screen. In addition, however, the CRT view avoided the problem associated with a strict "picture theory" notion of imagery (see Woodworth and Schlosberg, 1954), in which images are simply likened to "pictures in the head." On this view, images are often construed as mental photographs, hanging before the "mind's eye." Common introspection (and much data, as we shall see) suggests that images are not static, wholistic entities, but rather have parts that fade in and out and require effort to maintain. In the context of the CRT metaphor, images are actively constructed, dynamic displays—and hence need not be photographically accurate. Further, unlike a picture, images seem to be composed of relatively interpreted, previously processed units. This makes sense if the long-term memory encodings that underlie surface images are representations of "gestalt wholes" corresponding to parts of an object or scene. If so, this would also explain the introspection that when we omit something from an image it tends to be an interpreted part or property thereof, rather than an arbitrary portion "torn off" or the like (see Pylyshyn, 1973). Thus, the CRT notion seemed to hold promise of leading to the formulation of an account not only of the spatial properties of imagery (for example, as evinced when images are transformed) by reference to the surface representation, but also of the nonpictorial aspects of imagery (such as its fleetness, degradation, and prior interpretation into parts and properties).

In addition to the appeal of the CRT metaphor in the face of the available research findings and commonly reported introspections, there were more formal reasons why I found it an attractive tool for use in guiding a research program. Although any sort of model could serve to direct one toward basic issues, the CRT metaphor had three important properties that made it especially useful.

First, the metaphor specified a number of individual *components*, each of which could serve as a focus of study. For example, it led me to investigate whether there is a structure like the putative "display," and then to ask about its properties (such as its grain, its shape, and its "size"). This helped make the problem tractable. The thought of studying the entire imagery representation and processing system all of a piece is overwhelming (something like trying to bite into a huge apple, far too large to get one's mouth around) and a sure source of discouragement. Taken a piece at a time, the enterprise becomes more manageable.

Second, the metaphor suggested a *computational system*. It led me to ask how the components interact and work together. For example, it led me to ask about how underlying deep representations are mapped into the "display" and then "inspected." These questions are concerned with the properties of mechanisms, and hence seemed likely to foster the development of a full-fledged, explicit computational theory and model, which is the primary goal of the present research enterprise. It was relatively clear from the beginning that working from the metaphor could lead to the development of a detailed model.

Finally, I intentionally began with only the barest, most unadorned version of the metaphor. The CRT metaphor is not so much a model as the beginnings of a model, a "protomodel." It seemed counterproductive to begin with a detailed model for two reasons: First, many of the details of the model would be filled in arbitrarily, and this extra work would be for nothing if the basic assumptions of the model were found to be awry. Second, the additional detail could seduce one into studying noncentral questions (for instance, estimating the parameter values of that particular model) which would not help one define the class of acceptable models. This tendency is not unknown in cognitive psychology and seems the next worst thing to an out-and-out "confirmation bias," wherein one merely seeks data consistent with one's model or merely formulates a post hoc explanation for data (especially a verbal protocol) without concern for the predictions of competing conceptions.

The goal of research in Phase I was to derive a set of constraints that would define a prima facie class of acceptable theories of image representation and processing. The CRT metaphor served this end by highlighting key issues about the nature of the representation and processing system and suggesting alternative positions on each issue. The major thrust of Phase I, then, was to design and conduct experiments that would allow one to discriminate among these alternative positions. An important characteristic of Phase I research is its *capacities orientation*. That is, I was not at this point concerned with how people "naturally" perform some task outside the laboratory. Rather, I wanted to know the properties of imagery representations and processes that people can make use of, that people do have at their disposal. If people are capable of making use of some kinds of representations and processes, one's theory will have to account for this range of phenomena. In addition, I was loath to rest the fate of the project on the outcome of single "critical experiments." The results of any given experiment always can be explained in a number of different ways—and sometimes reflect more the influence of extraneous uncontrolled variables than the ones of interest. Thus, I adopted a method of *converging evidence*. That is, my colleagues and I conducted a series of different experiments, the results of which converge in being more consistent with one position on an issue than with the alternative positions. Whereas it is relatively easy to concoct alternative accounts for any given result, it becomes increasingly more difficult to formulate alternative models as more findings must be explained together. This technique, obviously, provides no guarantee of discovering the truth, but if we err in how we resolve a given issue, we are likely to discover this soon enough when we test predictions derived from the theory based on these constraints. On cracked and crumbling foundations stands a shaky house.

It is important to note, then, that in Phase I of the research program I did not attempt to derive an explanation for a given finding or phenomenon, except in the crudest way. Instead, the idea was to show that *whatever* sort of straightforward explanation one offers for some results, it will probably have to include a given structure-process component. For example, I will argue that a given set of results seems to indicate that a spatial "surface" image can be scanned across; I will not immediately attempt to explain exactly how such processing occurs, but will merely build a case that any reasonably straightforward explanation of image scanning will have to postulate a functional spatial image (of the sort suggested by the CRT metaphor). Only in Phase II, after beginning to formulate a theory, will I offer detailed accounts of performance of imagery tasks, including those reported in the literature as well as those used in Phase I.

1.2 Phase II: Constructing a Model

Metaphors and protomodels have only limited use as guides to theory-construction. In this project the protomodel began to lose force, to dry up, after a short while. After I had considered the obvious contrasts among several general notions, it was no longer clear how to proceed. Further central issues did not present themselves. At this point it made sense to begin considering the details of how a real system might operate within the constraints formulated during Phase I. The goal was to develop a *theory* of imagery via working with and elaborating a *model*. As I use the terms, "theory" refers to a set of abstract principles that can be embodied in a model; a "model" is a particular statement or material instantiation of a theory and often includes properties that are not theory-relevant (for example, the fact that a CRT screen is made of glass and phosphor is not a theory-relevant property of the protomodel). (This theory/model distinction will be developed further in chapter 5.) The idea here was to use the detailed model in much the same way that the protomodel had been used earlier—as a means of raising issues, the resolution of which would further constrain the theory itself. Many new questions arose in the course of trying to develop a model that would account for all of the empirical findings. Instead of filling in details of the model arbitrarily, experiments were performed to narrow down the acceptable options—again producing more constraints on the theory proper. For example, images could have been rotated in the model by moving portions of the surface image directly, or by transforming the underlying representation—which in turn would update the surface image. Experiments were designed and conducted to distinguish among these alternative implementations. This is the *directive* function of the present model-building enterprise. In an important regard, I take this property of raising new questions, the answers to which will accumulate, as the primary motivation for trying to construct a model of the imagery system. In addition, unanticipated properties of the model occasionally emerged that led to new predictions, which were then tested. This is the *deductive* function of the model. The results from these experiments not only provided new data to be explained, but served as a check on whether progress was really being made; if too many predictions failed, a wrong turn obviously had been made somewhere.

To summarize, development of the model and theory was initially motivated by results from experiments conducted during Phase I. But more data were required to constrain the details of the model and theory. Data from subsequent experiments then had to be accounted for, requiring further development that in turn produced more issues to be resolved and predictions to be tested, and so on. It is only via this kind of pulling ourselves up by our bootstraps that we can gain a clear conception of the representation and processing system as a whole.

2. The Debate about Imagery

The construct of imagery has a long and tortuous history in philosophy and psychology. One consequence of all this discussion has been a set of a priori arguments that would seem to stand in the way of the present enterprise. These arguments have two thrusts: that imagery as a construct is incoherent and logically flawed, and thus should not be treated as a bona fide psychological entity; and that even if imagery phenomena exist, imagery should not be treated as a separate cognitive domain. The latter class of arguments centers around attempts to show that so-called imagery phenomena are best explained using more general cognitive principles. That is, it is asserted that the functional component of imagery is just a special aspect of, no different in kind from, the representational system used in other domains (like language); hence, the experience of imagery is relegated to the status of an "epiphenomenon," if it is discussed at all.

In 1973 Zenon Pylyshyn published a highly influential paper, revitalizing the old anti-imagery arguments in the context of contemporary work in artificial intelligence, computer simulation, and general theories of human information processing. As a response to this and other papers in the same vein, James Pomerantz and I endeavored to summarize and critique the anti-imagery arguments (Kosslyn and Pomerantz, 1977). In this chapter I will expand the line of argument developed earlier, now offering a point-by-point response to the anti-imagery arguments (which are gleaned primarily from Anderson and Bower, 1973; Clark and Chase, 1972; Dennett, 1969; Pylyshyn, 1973, 1975, and in press; and Reid, 1974).*

The present debate has four primary foci. First, there are arguments against using the construct of imagery at all. Second, there are a number of reasons offered why imagery is not a distinct domain, but simply another realm where "propositional representation" occurs. The concept of

---

*Much of this chapter is built around the Kosslyn and Pomerantz paper, and Jim Pomerantz deserves credit for helping develop the arguments offered here.

"propositional representation" will be formally defined in the next chapter; for present purposes it is enough to note that these representations are abstract language-like entities that describe or assert facts. Third, there are the corresponding pro-imagery arguments, which counter the purported problems with the construct. And finally, there are arguments that imagery need not necessarily be considered a special type of "propositional" processing, but may sensibly and usefully be regarded as a relatively distinct class of cognitive phenomena.

1.0 ATTACKS ON IMAGERY

1.1 Problems with the Construct

The anti-imagery arguments primarily consist of attacks on the idea that visual images are stored in memory much as a snapshot is stored in a photograph album.* It is important to realize that the "images" being discussed are likened to "mental photographs" that are treated as replicas of previous patterns of sensory activity at or near the receptor level. These patterns purportedly are stored in a relatively undifferentiated form. Experiencing an image consists of retrieving and examining one of these mental photographs.

1.1.1 Misleading Properties of the Metaphor

Imagery and seeing. The "picture metaphor," as it has been called, introduces a host of inappropriate analogies between seeing and imaging. For example, a "mind's eye" is often said to "see" images internally. This notion seems to require a second processing system, or "mind's eye's brain," to interpret information from the mind's eye, which in turn would require another eye to interpret the images projected onto this internal brain, and so on in an infinite regress.

Further, when asked to image something like a tiger and count its stripes, most people report having difficulty. It is not as if a picture is present and merely waiting to be viewed. The picture metaphor also leads us to speak of perceptual events like scanning and focusing in relation to image processing. These analogies are difficult to reconcile with the fact that no mind's eyeballs exist to do the scanning.

Interpretation and organization. The picture metaphor wrongly implies that images are perceived much as pictures are perceived. The error lies in the fact that images, unlike pictures, are not in need of much fundamen-

---

*Most of Pylyshyn's arguments are addressed to the topic of visual imagery. I will follow suit, although the reader should keep in mind that parallel arguments also may be levied for and against imagery in other modalities.

tal perceptual processing such as contour sharpening or figure-ground segregation. Rather, images are preorganized into objects and properties of objects. Further, when we forget part of an image, it is not a random part. It is not as if a corner is torn from a photographic picture in the head; if our image of a room is incomplete, for example, it is not missing half a sofa or half a lampshade. Rather, images seem to be organized into meaningful parts, which in turn are remembered in terms of spatial relations among them (see Reed, 1974).

Physical properties. Much of the appeal of the idea of mental images comes from mistaken identification of internal representations with physical objects. To say that an image "rotates," for example, is incoherent. Images are not physical objects. Unlike a picture, an image cannot be dropped, carried under one's arm, and so on. Images do not automatically obey the laws of physics or assume physical properties, like rigidity and spatial extent. If images pass through intermediate orientations when they seem to "rotate," for example, they do not do so for the same reasons that a rotating physical object passes through intermediate states. Researchers in the field have erred in acting as if physical properties came "free" with the imagery format.

1.1.2 Inefficiency

Capacity limitations. Pylyshyn argues that processing and storing of information in image form would be cumbersome, if not totally unworkable, because a huge storage capacity would be necessary to preserve all the information transmitted by the retina. The amount of stored information would soon exceed the capacity of the brain if people did indeed store the wealth of images they commonly claim to remember.

Accessibility. Even if all the unanalyzed images could be stored, it would be virtually impossible to search for one particular image among them, since uninterpreted images could not be organized into a format facilitating their retrieval. But people who experience imagery report no awareness of such searching: The desired image seems to come to mind directly and quickly. Thus it seems necessary to assume that some sort of "interpretation" is stored in memory along with each image. If this is granted, it would seem more economical to store only the interpretations and dispense with the images entirely.

1.1.3 Introspective Evidence

Pylyshyn suggests that the commonly reported *experience* of imagery should not be given much weight in theorizing. As compelling as imagery may be to some of us through our introspections, this does not justify the use of the concept in an explanatory way. The mere experience of imagery, as vivid and undeniable as it may be, does not imply that imagery plays any causal (as opposed to merely epiphenomenal) role in cognition. Moreover, not everyone reports experiencing images, and those who do cannot always agree on the nature of their experience.

1.1.4 Problems of Definition

The "image" is an ill-defined construct which is in need of further explication. Theorizing about imagery has involved much vagueness and many glosses, and the actual operational definitions used in experiments have not followed explicitly, or always even implicitly, from theory. Furthermore, the operational definitions of imagery vary so widely from experiment to experiment as to obscure the common construct being addressed.

1.1.5 The Factual Nature of Knowledge

Pylyshyn and others argue that "propositional" representation is appropriate for representing knowledge. Propositions, as noted above, are abstract language-like representations that assert facts about the world. This sort of representation is required to store information because what we know about the world is a set of facts or assertions that are necessarily either true or false. Part of what it means to say a "proposition" is "abstract" is to say that it is amodal, and hence can be used with equal facility in representing information encoded via the senses and via language. For example, the representation of a red ball on a box next to a tree might be a set of elementary descriptions, like "ball on box," "ball is red," and so on. Mental pictures, on the other hand, do not assert anything, and hence are neither true nor false; they merely exist, with no truth value (although propositions about a picture's correspondence to an object or scene do have truth value). Thus, images, if considered to be mental pictures, are inadequate for representing knowledge of the world.

1.2 The Lack of a Distinct Domain

On this view, talking about "imagery" as a distinct entity reflects an incorrect parse of the cognitive system, an incorrect way of dividing up the system into component subsystems. Certainly, all subsystems, like the language and perceptual systems, are to some extent interactive. But genuine subsystems have separate operating principles that distinguish them from one another. Not so with imagery. To the contrary, imagery is simply a facet of a more general cognitive faculty which is best characterized as using only propositional representation. Thus, imagery is not properly treated as a distinct domain worthy of a special theory.

1.2.1 Structure and Process

The real issues in the field concern specification of the properties of internal structures and the processes that operate on them. Because properties of structures can be understood only with respect to the processes that operate on them, one must always specify structure/process pairs when proposing an explicit account of some data. If imagery is viewed as a data-structure which is processed in specifiable ways, it is not any different from other data-structures in kind—and hence is not to be treated within a distinct theory.

1.2.2 Necessity of a Third Code

It has often been assumed that there are only two kinds of internal codes. *Verbal* codes must exist at some level simply because we can transmit and receive verbally encoded messages. Similarly, *perceptual* (for example, visual) codes are necessary to account for our perceptual capacities. There is, however, good reason to postulate a third coding system, which is abstract (amodal), propositional, and not externalizable. According to Pylyshyn and others (for example, Clark and Chase, 1972; Moscovitch, 1973), our ability to translate or exchange information between verbal and visual codes (as when we describe a picture) requires the existence of a third "interlingual" code, because the structural differences between visual and verbal representations preclude direct translation:

> But the need to postulate a more abstract representation—one which resembles pictures nor words and is not accessible to subjective experience—is unavoidable. As long as we recognize that people can go from mental pictures to mental words or vice versa, we are forced to conclude that there must be a representation (which is more abstract and not available to conscious experience) which encompasses both. There must, in other words, be some common format or interlingua. (Pylyshyn, 1973, p. 5)

Because images will necessarily be reduced to a third code during processing, and hence are inextricably bound to the general processing system, it makes no sense to construct a separate imagery theory, distinct from theories of other forms of representation.

1.2.3 Efficiency

Since eventual translation into a third code is thus necessary, it would be more efficient simply to encode all information into the common format to begin with. Use of a single amodal representational format would result in a considerable simplification of the mental machinery needed for retrieving information. The need for a pictorial interpretive device (a "mind's eye") in addition to devices needed to retrieve nonpictorial information would be eliminated if information were represented in a single format. This suggests that all knowledge is coded in an abstract propositional format, from which translation into verbal or perceptual structures can be made as needed. If so, then there is no cause for a distinct theory of imagery.

1.2.4 Reduction to Primitives

Even given a consistent operational definition of imagery, imagery cannot serve in an explanatory role because it is not a primitive construct. We want our explanations to involve only the most primitive, atomistic, and mechanistic elements possible. Imagery, however defined, is not a primitive construct and ought to be further reduced.

1.2.5 Elegance

Finally, it is more aesthetic and parsimonious to posit only a single form of internal representation for all knowledge. We should try to posit only a single format if at all possible not only to maintain parsimony, but because such a system is more elegant.

The foregoing claims all rest on the assumption that the available data can be accounted for by appeal to a single amodal language-like representational system. But is this assumption warranted? Perhaps the most compelling data to the contrary are the results on "mental rotation." Consider these findings and the way a "propositional theory" might easily account for them.

Cooper and Shepard (1973), Cooper (1975), Cooper and Podgorny (1976), and Shepard and Metzler (1971) report experiments on the mental rotation of imaged objects (letters, digits, Attneave figures, or block-like forms). In a typical experiment they asked subjects to judge whether or not a test figure was the same as a standard figure, or different from it (for example, whether it was a mirror-reversed version of the standard). The test figure was presented at one of several orientations and the angular disparity between test and standard figures was systematically varied. The major finding was that the farther the test figure was rotated from the upright orientation of the standard, the longer were subjects' decision times. Furthermore, in some experiments, subjects were preinformed as to the identity and orientation of an upcoming test figure. They were asked to indicate when they were "ready" for presentation of the test figure, and preparation time was measured. These times showed the same basic pattern as the decision times obtained when subjects were not preinformed: The time people required to prepare increased linearly with the angular disparity between the cue and the standard upright orientation.

Interestingly, once a person had prepared, the orientation of the test figure no longer affected decision times.

An image of an object may be represented in terms of a network of propositions that describes how lines and arcs are interrelated. A letter A, for example, might be described (using abstract propositions) as two lines meeting at the top to form a vertex and bridged about halfway down by a short horizontal line. Rotation proceeds by replacing all relations with new ones, systematically altered in regard to spatial reference. When the letter A is rotated 45 degrees clockwise, for example, "top" might be replaced by "45 degrees right of vertical," and "horizontal" by "tilted at a 135-degree angle." Presumably the underlying "mental language" has a vocabulary rich enough to represent many shades of orientation. Rotation involves a series of modifications, each one representing the object at a slightly different orientation. Hence, the further the rotation, the more operations are required and the more time is necessary. Further, prior adjustment of the relations will allow direct matching to a test figure at the specified orientation.

The main question here is why gradual rotation is necessary at all; that is, why is the image of the test figure not transformed in a single operation into the proper orientation for comparison with the standard? A possible answer rests on the claim that evolution produced the constraint that images behave like the analogous physical transformations. One often-cited use of imagery, after all, is as a model for anticipating the effects of physical manipulations. Thus, it is plausible that the propositional representation system would have evolved to mimic the sorts of gradual transformations that occur when one physically manipulates objects. Other explanations involving specific mechanisms are possible, and will be discussed in chapter 8. Anderson (1978) offers a somewhat different and more detailed propositional account of the mental rotation data, but the foregoing serves to convey the form of this kind of explanation. The problem is not that the mental rotation results are difficult to explain without recourse to imagery: To the contrary, too many alternative accounts are viable. I will attempt to discriminate among some of these accounts empirically in later chapters.

2.0 THE IMAGERY POSITION

2.1 Critique of Arguments against the Construct

Pylyshyn's attacks are based on a particular conception of imagery, namely, the "picture in the head" hypothesis. Clearly, this approach is untenable. But few—if any—active researchers subscribe to such a simple view. No researcher in the field would seriously argue that images are pictures; pictures are concrete objects that exist in the world, while images are ethereal entities that occur in the mind. We refer to the properties of images as "quasi-pictorial" because images lack some of the properties of pictures: Obviously, people do not have CRT tubes in their heads (no matter how hard you hit somebody's head, you won't hear the tinkle of breaking glass). Nor do we have any other kind of actual picture in our heads: Pictures are objects that can be hung on walls, dropped on toes, and so on. To have a picture in one's head would be very uncomfortable. What researchers usually mean when they talk of having pictures in one's head is that one has retrieved, or generated from memory, representations like those that underlie the experience of seeing. That is, when we see something, some characteristic internal representations must be formed; some of these representations may underlie emotional reactions, some may be formed as one describes the object or scene, and so on. Image representations are like those that underlie the actual experience of seeing something, but in the case of mental imagery these representations are retrieved or formed from memory, not from immediate sensory stimulation. There is nothing incoherent or paradoxical in this kind of conception of imagery.

2.1.1 Misleading Properties of the Metaphor

Imagery and seeing. Many of the visual metaphors used in theorizing about imagery are not as ill-conceived as it might seem. For example, the fact that mobile eyeballs are not available for viewing images poses no insurmountable problems. In Sperling's (1960) famous experiments on scanning afterimages (or "icons"), eye movements were clearly irrelevant. Furthermore, Kaufman and Richards (1969) showed that where one's eyes are directed and where one thinks one is looking are not necessarily the same. What is required for scanning an image is a shift of attention from one part of the image to another. This no more requires physical motion than does the shift of a "pointer" within a data structure in a computer memory.

It is important to realize that there is nothing paradoxical or incoherent in the notion of a "mind's eye". We can think of the mind's eye as a processor that interprets quasi-pictorial representations (that is, those underlying visual perceptual experiences) in terms of "conceptual" categories. For example, the array of points depicting blocks in a computer program designed to recognize patterns (see Winston, 1975) may be thought of as a "perceptual" representation, which then may be categorized (via "feature" extraction, template matching, and the like) into conceptual categories (such as "block"); this classification stage is equivalent to inspection by a mind's eye. When these interpretive processes are applied to remembered perceptual information instead of information that comes from the senses, an image rather than a percept will be experienced. Sophisticated computer programs (such as those described by Boden, 1977; Winston, 1975) have demonstrated that a homunculus is not required for an effective perceptual system (see Neisser, 1967). The routines used in these programs could, in principle, operate just as well on information being fed in from the computer's memory (imagery) as from a TV camera (perception). In fact, most of these programs dispense with external input and work only with memory representations.

In addition, it is important to note that the fact that all details of an imaged object are not present or perceptible (for example, the number of stripes on a tiger) is not to the point. Even if images were perfectly photographic, one might not have encoded this information in the first place. Even an actual painting, such as an impressionist work, need not have distinct, countable details. In addition, people sometimes have trouble counting the precise number of parts (such as a tiger's stripes) even if each part is in fact included in a picture of an object (try counting the number of dots on an acoustic tile of a ceiling sometime; for data, see Kowler, Benson, and Steinman, 1975). Further, images may be pictorial but not photograph-like: If images are like displays on a CRT, parts may fade in and out, making some information difficult to "read."

Interpretation and organization. It does not seem fruitful to suppose that images are simply reembodiments of stored sensations. Although storage of primitive sensations is possible (as in afterimages), the products of higher perceptual activity can be stored as well. Perception is a process of information reduction whereby a welter of sensations is reduced into a simpler and more organized form. These organizational processes result in our perceptions being structured into units corresponding to objects and properties of objects. It is these larger units that may be stored and later assembled into images that are experienced as quasi-pictorial, spatial entities resembling those evoked during perception itself (as was discussed in the previous chapter). It is obviously wrong to consider the representation of an object during perception as photographic; by the same token, it is erroneous to equate image representations with mental photographs, since this would overlook the fact that images are composed from highly processed perceptual encodings.

Physical properties. It is certainly true that a literal "picture-in-the-head" notion is incorrect. However, it is not difficult to formulate representational systems that embody the laws of physics. There is no paradox here: One system need not be a *copy* of another in order to mimic it. Although we should not be satisfied with an unanalyzed term like "rotation" being used as an explanation, the task is to discover the ways in which certain image transformations are like rotations—not to deny that imagery can in fact mimic physical processes. To be sure, images are not actually rotated—but they certainly behave as if they were! If propositional theories had held sway, who would have thought to collect the data, to document the phenomena, that are now in need of deeper explanation?

2.1.2 Inefficiency

Capacity limitations. Pylyshyn claims that image representations would strain the limited capacity of the brain. This point remains moot because (1) we do not know what the capacity limitation of the brain is, or even if for all practical purposes it has one; and (2) we have no good measure of the amount of information contained in an image or a percept of a scene. Furthermore, the capacity-limit argument would be effective only against the most primitive picture theory, in which the image is thought to consist of relatively unprocessed sensations. If we treat images as being composed of relatively large, interpreted, perceptual "chunks," like the arms, legs, head, and trunk of a person, the number of informational units to be encoded may not be so great.

Accessibility. Pylyshyn's claim that an enormous amount of time would be necessary to retrieve a particular image assumes that images (1) are uninterpreted, and thus cannot be "content addressed," and (2) have no other information associated with them in memory that could be used to "look them up." It seems entirely possible that verbal labels or other codes associated with images could serve this purpose. If images are analogous to the displays generated on a cathode-ray tube by a computer program, for example, different data files (which store different images) can be named and later called up by name. In addition, it remains possible that all images are in fact randomly searched whenever a particular one is sought, just as Pylyshyn suggests. We have no way of knowing what the speed of such a search might be and need not assume that the search would be apparent to consciousness (see Sternberg, 1966).

2.1.3 Introspective Evidence

Three points should be made concerning introspective data:

A source of corroborative data. Introspections are not adequate in and of themselves to attest to the functional role of imagery in cognition. However, they are one source of evidence which, when taken together with behavioral performance data (such as the time necessary to make certain introspections), can assist in demonstrating that images have distinct functions in cognition. Certainly, much progress has been made in the study of perception and psychophysics by considering "objective" data in conjunction with subjects' introspections about the qualities of their experiences.

Generality. Although a theory that deals with publicly observable behavior alone may be adequate for understanding a class of behaviors, one that can explain introspective evidence as well with no added complexity certainly is to be preferred.

Phenomenology. The experience of imagery is undeniable, even if its functional role is in doubt. This experience must arise as a consequence of some psychological processes; simply labeling it as "epiphenomenal" will not make it go away. The study of phenomenology is a legitimate enterprise in its own right, and any theory that serves to illuminate phenomenological issues achieves added value.

2.1.4 Problems of Definition

Fuzziness of concept. The absence of a precise definition of "image" at present hardly constitutes grounds for deciding on the ultimate ontological status of imagery or its role as a theoretical construct. Pylyshyn expresses concern that different theorists and experimenters operationalize imagery in different ways and that there is no single operation that can uniquely define the existence or functioning of the image. This is common in psychology and far from being undesirable. Most psychologists have become comfortable with the use of "converging operations" in attempts to define entities that are not subject to direct observation. Garner, Hake, and Eriksen (1956) argue that unitary operational definitions should be avoided when dealing with inferred constructs, since such definitions confound the entity being measured with the instrument used in making the measurement. Rather, a number of independent operations should be devised to "converge" on the construct. In fact, there is no greater problem with imagery in this regard than with any other unobservable construct in science. The construct of an "electron" suffers from similar problems, but it has long held a place in physical theories. In addition, I would like to point out that we should not make the mistake of identifying operational definitions—no matter how many or how cast—with the actual psychological entities of interest. The meaning of "electron" did not change with the advent of new measuring instruments (although the description of it did change as new information was gathered). At best, operational definitions may be necessary precursors of more precise formulations of the internal structures and processes that are the actual objects of study. As research proceeds and results accumulate we will eventually find ourselves in a position to begin formulating a viable, detailed theory of image representation and processing, as I hope this book will show.

2.1.5 The Factual Nature of Knowledge

Mere possession of representations in propositional format does not constitute knowledge, any more than a page has knowledge because a sentence is written on it. It makes sense to speak of knowledge only in the context of some processes that make use of internal representations. If not a mind's eye, some sort of "mind's frontal lobe" is necessary to interpret even abstract propositions (and yet we do not feel in danger of an "infinite regress" of propositions and "mind's frontal lobes"!). If knowl-

edge is viewed in terms of active processes performed on data structures
rather than in terms of the static structures themselves, then using propositions instead of images as the format for these structures does not necessarily gain us anything. In either case, processors must be postulated that
operate on the data structures. The power of any representational format
can be assessed only by considering its compatibility with these processors.

Thus, a person does not have knowledge when he or she has a mental
image any more than a camera has knowledge when it contains exposed
film (see Wittgenstein, 1953). Nevertheless, images may contain information from which knowledge can be derived. If images are sensory patterns
that have been partially processed and stored, the question of how knowledge can be derived from images is quite similar to the question of how
knowledge is derived from ongoing sensory activity. Knowledge obviously is derived from perceptual representations, and there seems to be
no reason why it should not also be gleaned in similar ways from mental
images.

2.2 Critique of Arguments against a Distinct Domain

There is no dispute that virtually any information can be represented in
terms of propositions. The invention of the "proposition" originally was
motivated in part by a desire to capture the common "idea" underlying
synonymous statements, even if they are expressed in different languages. Consequently, the construct of the proposition was formulated to
be as powerful and flexible as possible, with the goal of utilizing it to
represent all knowledge. The issue here is not whether some system using
only propositional representations can be formulated to account for imagery phenomena. That seems trivially true (see Anderson, 1978). But *sufficiency* obviously does not imply *necessity*. Thus, even if some sort of (arbitrarily complex) propositional theory may be possible for "imagery
phenomena," this need not be the correct theory. At the present juncture,
then, we want to know whether there are strong a priori concerns that
should dissuade us from formulating a separate imagery theory, even if a
separate imagery theory could in fact more parsimoniously account for
the data and have greater value in leading us to predict new and interesting results. If there are no compelling reasons against the plausibility of
such a distinct theory, then it makes sense to try to cast one and discover
whether this is a useful way to proceed.

2.2.1 Structure and Process

If we regard properties of the image as properties that are "apparent to
the mind's eye," we seem to be following the Opposition's admonitions

and studying structure/process pairs. The issue now becomes whether this kind of structure/process pair is different in kind from those underlying more general cognitive functions. If the representations are in a distinct format, then a different kind of processing system as a whole will be necessary. That is, given the existence of representations with particular functional properties, there are constraints on the possible nature of the processes in the system. The "mind's eye" interpretive procedures like those posited by the CRT protomodel are very different from the procedures that interpret linguistic strings. For example, they do not have to enter a lexicon to identify the "form class" of a symbol. As will be developed in chapter 3, quasi-pictorial representations do not bear an arbitrary relation to the thing represented, unlike discursive representations. Information about an object is inherent in the pattern of the representation itself, is "worn on its sleeve," as it were. The issue then becomes an empirical one, whether this kind of distinct format does in fact occur in memory. If imagery makes use of a distinct kind of representation and accompanying processes, it is fallacious to claim that a single theory ought to subsume imagery and other forms of processing merely because structure/process pairs are used throughout.

2.2.2 Necessity of a Third Code

Those who have claimed that translation between verbal and perceptual codes requires a separate propositional representation system have never specified how this translation would be accomplished. It appeared to Pomerantz and me that this assumption simply pushes the problem back a step. How is translation to be accomplished between images and propositions? Between propositions and verbal codes? Translation problems exist if one stores images and verbal material or if one stores only propositions, and may be more difficult for the latter procedure if the two translational steps required (versus one for "dual-code" representations) are based on different operations. Furthermore, as Anderson (1978) points out, if all translation requires an intervening code, then we are faced with an infinite regress: To translate between a visual code and a propositional one requires yet another code, but to translate to this code again requires another code and so on. However translation between verbal and imagery codes is achieved, it is not clear that an intermediate propositional representation would aid in this process.

To solve the translation problem, one must have a set of transformational rules that specify how one format is represented in, or mapped into, another. It would be a mistake, however, to equate these transformational rules with specific world knowledge as Pylyshyn appears to do. These rules would not represent information about the world, but only about the codes between which translation is required. These rules would take the

form of processes or routines, which when applied to information codes in
one format, would produce a corresponding representation in another format. No intermediate third form of representation need be involved.
Thus, the translation problem does not imply that imagery is merely one
aspect of a more general processing system, which itself is the only appropriate object of study.

2.2.3 Efficiency

Will processing really be easier if all knowledge is stored in a propositional format? Depending on the task, the different characteristics of representation systems can lead to differences in the nature, speed, and efficiency of the processing they support. Consider two formats for
representing geographical information: a map and a chart of intercity distances. These two systems may be completely isomorphic to each other in
all important respects since either one can be generated from the other.*
Nevertheless, they have obviously different properties. The map is an analog (or "depictive," as will be characterized in chapter 3) representation,
which makes it suitable for rapid geometrical computations; the chart of
intercity distances is digital, which makes it suitable for rapid arithmetic
computations. If we want to know quickly whether there are any three
cities in some region that fall on a straight line, we consult the map; if we
want to know the total distance of an air flight from New York to Los
Angeles to Miami, we consult the chart. Clearly other forms of external
representation besides these two are possible: lists of sentences
expressing propositions such as "Miami is south of Atlanta," for example, or tree structures containing similar propositional information. It is
likely that each of these formats would be optimal for some purposes but
not for others. The "efficiency" of a representation, then, depends in part
upon the purposes to which one puts that representation.

Given that different types of external representation formats have different characteristics, the same may apply to internal representations. As
I shall argue in the next chapter, there is good evidence that information
can be represented internally in at least two different formats, which differ in their suitability for different tasks. Thus, it is neither necessary nor
obviously desirable to assume that information must always be recoded
into a common, propositional format. Even if images were generated or
derived from propositional representations, the information they contain

*Anderson (1978) claims that a map will have additional information indicating absolute
orientation. Usually this is indicated explicitly by a compass or direction arrow, however; if
a "north point" is placed top and center and this point is included in the intercity distances,
a Multidimensional Scaling solution will then also recover this orientation information. In
any event, it is not clear whether the absolute orientation information is a property of the
map itself or of how the reader can process it.

might be more readily accessed from the emergent image rather than from the underlying structure.

Furthermore, before we can compare the economy of representation systems including a distinct image representation subsystem with the economy of those relying solely on propositional representation, it is necessary to know how many propositions are necessary to represent an object, scene, or event. This question is difficult to answer because (1) we lack the means to measure the amount of information in a percept of an object, scene, or episode, and (2) we do not know which of a (probably infinite) number of sets of propositions best represents an object, scene, or event. In any case, when one considers the models proposed to date (for example, Baylor, 1971), one is impressed with the sheer number of propositions needed to represent even relatively simple objects. These numbers become even greater if one assumes, with Pylyshyn, that propositions are constructed to represent knowledge at several different levels of hierarchy at the same time. Thus, it might be much more wasteful to generate hordes of propositions at the time of encoding than to store a smaller number of perceptual units which could then be used at a later time for making deductions. If limited encoding or memory capacity is an important factor in internal representation, then it is advantageous to encode and store as little as possible and to deduce as much as possible when more detailed information is required. Although propositions could also be used for deduction, certain implicit relations may be derived much more easily from images.

Since the storage capacity of the brain and its encoding systems is unknown, not much weight should be given to these considerations. However, it is clear that capacity arguments levied against positing a distinct imagery representation system can be wielded with equal force against formulating a general propositional theory.

2.2.4 Reduction to Primitives and Levels of Analysis

It seems likely that imagery can be described in terms of more elementary components, perhaps including propositional representations. But will this exercise increase our understanding of mental phenomena or merely cloud important distinctions? As Putnam (1973) points out, we must take care to distinguish explanations from "parents of explanations." Consider Putnam's example of the appropriate explanation for why a certain square peg will not fit into a certain round hole. The proper level of analysis would not entail discussion of subatomic particles, but would make use of emergent properties like "rigidity" and "contour," properties that are not necessarily derivable from a knowledge of the molecular constitution of the objects involved. Similarly, one would not learn much about architecture simply by studying bricks, mortar, and other building materials. Thus, if images are functional internal representations different in format from other representations, it makes sense to study imagery per se, rather than to study only the most "basic" irreducible representations. The issue here is not whether images may be derived from more primitive "propositional" or "symbolic" representations. Rather, it is whether a quasi-pictorial image—however derived—has distinctive characteristic properties and so can serve as a distinct form of representation. If so, then images deserve a role in psychological explanations, and it makes sense to have a separate theory of image processing.

2.2.5 Elegance

At a very abstract level of analysis it does seem more elegant to postulate only a single form of internal representation. I have two comments to make on this point: First, it is true that on the face of things a theory positing only one type of representation seems simpler than a theory positing more than a single type of representation—all other things being equal. And this is why the onus is on the pro-imagery camp to argue that images could be a distinct format and to provide data supporting this position. But this metric of parsimony may be misguided. Propositional accounts are not particularly straightforward or simple for many imagery results. In chapter 3 we will see some of the convolutions necessary for a propositional theory to account for data that are easily and naturally explained if images are a distinct quasi-pictorial format. Essentially, then, we have a tradeoff between the parsimony of the theory (determined in part by the number of different formats posited) and the parsimony of the accounts. A balance must be struck between the two; as more parameters are added to a theory, the accounts become simpler but less informative. But positing only one format at the expense of very unwieldy accounts may not really be more parsimonious than positing two formats if much simpler and more straightforward accounts of data are forthcoming. Second, sufficiency does not imply necessity: The fact that one might be able to formulate accounts of all data using a single representation does not eliminate the possibility of alternative mechanisms. For example, even though a propositional account of "mental rotation" is possible, it is not necessarily correct. This is an empirical question (to which I will return in chapter 8). It is not surprising that *some* propositional model (albeit ad hoc) can usually be offered for any given result: Current propositional theories do not possess strong inherent constraints; thus, some variant of a propositional model usually can be formulated, with equal ease, it would seem, to "explain" any empirical finding or its converse. One consequence of this is that even though it seems likely that some kind of post hoc propositional account of imagery data is always possible, these accounts are virtually always sterile. Unlike the imagery accounts, no new predictions or insights have followed from them. A model must lead one to ask further questions if it is to play any real role in a research program.

3.0 CONCLUSIONS FROM THE DEBATE

Imagery is not an inherently flawed concept. There are no compelling reasons to reject the use of imagery in psychological explanations. Only the most primitive "picture metaphor" conception of imagery can be rejected outright. The essential claim that imagery is a distinct representation system, utilizing data-structures of a special quasi-pictorial format, is neither internally inconsistent, incoherent, nor paradoxical. The CRT protomodel escapes this line of attack unscathed.

Imagery is not necessarily only a special aspect of a more general propositional representation system. There is nothing inherently inconsistent or incoherent in the notion of a distinct imagery processing system, nothing that would demand that proposition-like representations in fact do most of the real work, as Pylyshyn maintained. Although some sort of propositional system probably could be formulated to account for data on imagery, it is not clear that this is desirable. A special imagery representation system could have evolved, and positing one may be empirically fruitful. If this turns out to be true, the wisdom of developing a separate imagery theory will have been vindicated.

Explicit theories are needed. The foregoing discussion underlines the need to specify exactly how particular sets of processes work over representations that have particular characteristics. Without such specification, we have great liberty in the sorts of properties that follow from a given form of representation, and we can continue to offer arguments and counterarguments on both sides indefinitely. What is needed is explicit theories that fall in each class, imagery and nonimagery, that can be empirically tested and evaluated in terms of generality, parsimony, and so on. As it now stands, there are simply too many possible varieties of "imagery" and "propositional" theories, theories that have appreciably different properties, to allow any sort of evaluation of relative efficacy on purely rational grounds.

Images are not pictures. The simple picture metaphor is clearly inadequate. We cannot simply assume that images are like pictures, and go on from there. But we already knew that images are not *exactly* like pictures, or they would *be* pictures! Given that the two are not identical, it becomes critical to specify the respects in which they are alike and those in which they differ. The traditional conception of imagery is not very helpful in this regard, however, precisely because the claim that images are like percepts that arise from memory fails to pick out the properties of images that distinguish them from distinctly nonimagistic representations. We need an independent characterization of what it means for a representation —arising from long-term memory *or* the senses—to be "quasi-pictorial." Only after we pick out at least some of the "privileged properties" of these kinds of representations, those which distinguish this class of representations from other classes, will we be in a position to study the psychological reality of the mental images we experience. And only through the interplay of data-collection and theory-formulation can we eventually specify the relationship between "mental pictures" and real ones. Clearly, theories that posit that people can use quasi-pictorial mental representations will be very different from ones that do not. This, then, is the first issue at hand: Should we treat the quasi-pictorial images we experience as a special kind of functional representation in human memory, or as an incidental concomitant or special property of more general abstract processing?

3. Validating the Privileged Properties of Imagery

Are the spatial, picture-like images most people report experiencing a functional part of mental life? On one view, there are no special image representations that play a causal role in cognitive processing. There are three versions of this position: First, images may not be "mental objects" at all. That is, the word "image" may not *refer* to any entity; utterances about mental images may have the same function as utterances like "For Pete's sake," where there is no "Pete" actually being referred to (see Wittgenstein, 1953). Instead of being a distinct kind of data-structure that gives rise to certain experiences, the image is here considered to be a fabrication that is imposed on, or created from, a set of beliefs about internal processing (see Dennett, 1969; Ryle, 1949). In the second version, it is conceded that the experience of mental imagery may in fact be genuine (I find it hard to believe that most people could seriously maintain otherwise), but this experience itself is thought to be just a way of "talking about" a process to ourselves, merely one form of interpretation of the same kind of mental events that occur when we do not experience images. Schacter and Singer (1962) showed that the same physiological state (arousal) apparently is experienced radically differently depending on how the state is interpreted. In the third version, introspection does in fact reveal some of the properties of an underlying data-structure, but this data-structure is itself an incidental by-product of the processing of more abstract representations. On this view, then, the image representations are merely "along for the ride" and themselves play no part in cognitive processing. Whether or not we experience images, then, is beside the point. Images could be analagous to the lights flashing on the outside of a computer while it is adding: There is a systematic relationship between the internal operations and the flashing lights, all right, but one could smash the bulbs and the computer would happily go adding along.

Alternatively, mental images could be distinct kinds of data-structures which can be used in the course of cognition. Further, the quasi-pictorial properties of images apparent to introspection may in fact reflect functional properties of the underlying representation, properties that affect how image representations may be processed.* It is important to realize that the issue here concerns the *format* of image representation. The idea of format is perhaps best understood by first drawing a distinction between an *inscription*, a *character*, and a *compliance class*, to use Goodman's (1968) terminology. An inscription is a physical mark of some kind, such as a configuration of points like "A." A character class defines which groups of inscriptions will be classed as equivalent, such as "A" and "a." The compliance class is the "content," the meaning, of the character (for example, "first letter of the alphabet"). The format specifies the nature of the inscriptions used in a given code and how these inscriptions are mapped into (are used to represent) compliance classes. In some cases, like pictorial formats, it is not clear that there is an intermediate "character class"—differences in how the same object is drawn convey different information, whereas differences in how a particular letter is drawn do not affect how that inscription serves as a representation. The format is not to be confused with the *content* of the representation. A given content can be represented in a number of different formats (this sentence, for example, could be represented using the formats of spoken English, Morse code, magnetic fluxes on a tape, squiggles on a page, and so on). The question is whether we should posit that image representations have a different format from that used in other representations, like those which underlie language. This, in a nutshell, is the most fundamental issue in the field; we obviously must resolve this question before trying to formulate a theory of imagery.

Before we can begin to decide whether the available data about image processing settle this issue, we must first have a clear conception of the defining characteristics of a quasi-pictorial imagery format and the characteristics of the most viable no-imagery alternative, a "propositional" format. It is important to consider the so-called propositional format because in the current breed of no-imagery models, *all* internal representation in memory is assumed to be in this format. Imagery models do not necessarily reject the claim that *some* information may be represented in a propositional (or verbal, or motoric, and so on) format in human memory, but rather assert that there are also quasi-pictorial imagery representations which are structurally distinct from propositional representations.

---

*Note that the word "image" is here used to refer to a data-structure that happens to give rise to the experience of perceiving in the absence of appropriate sensory stimulation, and does not refer to the experience itself. As a working hypothesis I began with the notion that the characteristics of an image evident in the experience of imagery did in fact index characteristics of the underlying data-structure, but this need not be so.

1.0 TWO FORMATS

Consider the two representations of a ball on a box illustrated in figure 3.1, which correspond to externalized quasi-pictorial and propositional representations. Although these physical representations on a page share only some properties with the mental representations, they may help to contrast the two formats. The key distinction here rests on the difference between *description*—as is accomplished with propositions—and *depiction*—which is achieved with pictorial representations. The following properties characterize a propositional representation, but not a quasi-pictorial image representation.

A propositional representation has five key properties, as illustrated in figure 3.1: (1) a relation, (2) at least one argument, (3) a syntax (rules of formation), (4) a truth value, and (5) the property of being "abstract." Although propositions are not linguistic structures, and hence may not always be readily externalized using words, they often can be approximated with simple sentences and expressed with a predicate calculus. The example in figure 3.1 is a hybrid, using English words but nonstandard syntax. In this case, "on" is the relation, "ball" and "box" are the arguments, the syntax requires two arguments ("on [ball]" is an unacceptable fragment), the proposition is true or false, and it is abstract. By "abstract" I

"A BALL IS ON A BOX"

Propositional Representation (Description)	Quasi-pictorial Representation (Depiction)
ON (BALL, BOX)	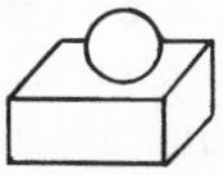
1. Relation	1. No distinct relation
2. Argument(s)	2. No distinct arguments
3. Syntax	3. No clear syntax
4. Truth value	4. Truth value only when under a particular description
5. Abstract	5. Concrete
6. Not occur in spatial medium	6. Occurs in spatial medium
7. No abstract spatial isomorphism	7. Abstract spatial isomorphism
a) No necessary part/whole relations	a) Necessary part/whole relations
b) Size and orientation optional	b) Size and orientation necessary
c) Arbitrary marks	c) Non-arbitrary marks
8. No abstract surface-property isomorphism	8. Abstract surface-property isomorphism
a) No necessary part/whole relations	a) Necessary part/whole relations
b) Shape not necessary	b) Shape necessary
c) Arbitrary marks	c) Non-arbitrary marks

Figure 3.1. Properties of propositional and quasi-pictorial formats.

mean two things: First, it can be used to make statements about classes, independent of reference to particular instances. Second, this kind of representation could just as easily be used to store the information in an English, French, American Sign, or semaphored communication as to store the information in a picture. It is important to note that propositions can be concatenated (using connectives, like "or," and using the same arguments in multiple relations, as will be illustrated later). This sort of concatenation can result in very complicated data-structures, including all graph structures (for example, hierarchies, heterarchies, all manner of lists). Minsky and Papert's (1972) notion of "symbolic" representation is equivalent to propositional representation as here described.

Now, to contrast propositional representations with quasi-pictorial image representations:

1. Images do not contain identifiably distinct relations; relations only emerge from the conglomerate of the components being represented together. Thus, one needs two components before a relation like "on" can be represented.

2. Images do not contain discrete primitive arguments. The components of an image are not discrete entities that can be related to one another in precise ways. An image of a box, for example, can be decomposed into faces, edges, and so on—and these are certainly not elementary arguments in and of themselves. Further, these components attain their status as parts of a box only in one another's company, unlike a propositional argument, which in and of itself has a particular interpretation.

3. Images do not seem to have a syntax (except perhaps in the roughest sense). Any syntax dictating "well-formedness" of pictures or images will probably depend on some sort of interaction with a "semantic component," that is, what an image is supposed to be an image of. As we all know, "impossible pictures" are created regularly (by Escher, for example), and rules that govern the nature of objects in the world (such as the rule that gravity operates in only one direction) may not necessarily constrain the things that one can depict in a picture.

4. Unlike a proposition, an image does not have a truth value. In fact, as Wittgenstein (1953) pointed out, there is nothing intrinsic in a picture of a man walking up a hill that prevents one from interpreting it as a picture of a man sliding downhill backward. The meaning of an image, and hence its truth value, is assigned by processes that work over the representation and are not inherent in the representation itself.

5. Finally, images are not abstract in the way propositions are. Images can be used to represent classes only with great difficulty, and even then not all classes can be depicted (as discussed at length in chapter 11). Further, an image of a picture will be different from an image of any spoken description of the picture, or even the same material pictured differently.

Quasi-pictorial images are special in that they seem to *depict* information. The following are the "privileged properties" that images possess by virtue of the way they depict information.

1. Images occur in a spatial medium that is functionally equivalent to a (perhaps Euclidean) coordinate space. This does not mean that there is literally a screen in the head.* Rather, locations are accessed such that the interval properties of physical space are preserved in at least two dimensions (possibly three; this is an empirical question). A perfect example of this is a simple two-dimensional array stored in a computer's memory: There is no physical matrix in the memory banks, but because of the way in which cells are retrieved, one can sensibly speak of the intercell relations in terms of adjacency, distance, and other geometric properties.

2. Images are patterns formed by altering the state of local regions in the internal spatial medium. The pattern formed in the spatial medium is a topographic mapping from the represented object such that (*a*) each local portion (set of contiguous points) of the image corresponds to a portion of the represented object as seen from a particular point of view, and (*b*) the interval relations among the portions of the image implicitly represent (vis-à-vis the processes that assess "distance" in the medium) the interval distances among the corresponding portions of the represented object. This property has been described by Shepard (1975) as an "abstract first-order isomorphism," and I will call it an "abstract spatial isomorphism" to distinguish it from the following property.†

There are three formal corollaries to this claim: (*a*) Any portion of an image is a representation of a portion of the represented object. For example, any portion of an image of my grandmother's car is an image of a portion of the car. (*b*) It is impossible to depict a shape in an image without also depicting some orientation and apparent size (that is, visual angle subtended). (*c*) The internal symbols used to represent an object in an image are not arbitrarily related to the object. If the internal "space" is 2-dimensional, for example, once patterns in two local regions of the space are used to depict two portions of an object, the regions where patterns can be placed to depict the rest of the object are then determined. That is, mapping two portions into the medium establishes how distance on the object is mapped into distance in the internal medium, and pro-

*Although there could be, if images occur as topographic projections on the surface of the cortex; this kind of space is a subset of the one I am referring to here, however.

†Note that because of the vagaries of attention and the accuracy of visual encoding, the mapping here is from image to object: (*a*) the image need not represent all of the portions of an object as seen from a particular point of view; the requirement is only that each portion of the image correspond to a portion of the object (if that image is to be an image of the object, although perhaps a degraded one); and, (*b*) the interval relations among the portions are those that were encoded when viewing the object, and hence need not perfectly reflect those of the portions of the actual object, although if they are too far off (and how far remains an open, probably empirical, question), the image will cease to be a representation of *that* object.

vides anchor points that constrain the possible regions at which patterns can be used to depict other portions of the object—given that every portion of an image must correspond to a portion of the represented object or objects such that the interportion intervals are implicit in the image. The same point is true if images occur in a 3-dimensional functional space, but now at least three portions must be represented before the symbols used to depict the rest of the object are fixed.

3. Images not only depict information about spatial extent, but also depict information about the appearance of surface properties of objects, such as texture and color. (Note: because of the vagaries of lighting and the like, objects may appear different from the way they actually are; an image represents the object as it appeared at the time of encoding, which may not necessarily faithfully depict the actual surface properties themselves.) Thus, although the image itself is not mottled, or green, or bright, or faded, it can attain states that are interpreted as evincing these properties. I will refer to this as the property of "abstract surface-property isomorphism." The three implications of the claim that images depict shape information have corresponding implications for these visual properties: (*a*) A portion of an image of a green thing, for example, is an image of a portion of a green thing. (*b*) It is impossible to represent color or texture or intensity without also representing some shape (albeit perhaps ill-defined and bloblike). (*c*) The pairing of a representation of a given level of intensity with a given intensity of sensory stimulation is not arbitrary. If two representations correspond to two levels of intensity, intermediate levels of intensity must be represented within the interval scale as defined.*

It is important to note that the foregoing claims not only posit properties of the representation per se, but also posit that we have the interpretive processes to "see" these properties. The descriptive, propositional format differs from the depictive, imagery one with respect to each of the properties just described:

1. Propositional representations do not occur in a spatial medium. In fact, it is not necessary to talk of them occurring in any medium at all, as they need not derive any of their properties from the structures that support them.

2. Propositions are in no sense topographic representations, as described above: (*a*) parts of a proposition need not correspond to parts of the represented object or scene, and (*b*) distance between portions of a represented object or scene is not implicit in the representation. Rather, distance information must be represented explicitly.

*My hunch is that one can prove formally that the corollaries noted above follow from the initial claim. It may even be possible in the case of abstract spatial isomorphism to derive all of the claims from the part/whole condition.

To further emphasize the difference between the two formats, consider each of the three properties that are implied by an "abstract spatial isomorphism": (a) In contrast to an image, a part of a propositional representation need not be a representation of a part of the represented object. For example, although "grandmother" is part of "my grandmother's car," "grandmother" does not represent a part of the car.* (b) Shape, size and orientation are independent parameters in a propositional representation; it is possible to represent shape without also representing size and orientation. (c) The pairing between symbol and represented object is completely arbitrary in a propositional format, unlike in an imagery one.

3. Similarly, propositions must describe the properties of an object's appearance; the form of a proposition (without looking up the meanings of the symbols) does not convey information about the pictorial properties of an object. As above, none of the three corollaries of the claim that images depict texture, color, intensity, and the other visual properties is true of propositional representations: (a) A part of a representation of a green thing, for example, need not be a representation of part of a green thing. (b) Visual properties may be represented independently of shape, size, and/or orientation. (c) The symbols used to represent visual properties are arbitrary. "Anchoring" a scale with two or more representations does not constrain what symbols may be used to represent other values.

2.0 INVESTIGATING THE PRIVILEGED PROPERTIES OF IMAGERY

My collaborators and I collected four classes of data in order to counter the image-as-epiphenomenon view. The logic of these experiments hinges on the notion that if images are functional, quasi-pictorial representations, the properties inherent in, and peculiar to, images should influence information processing when people use imagery. There are two important aspects of the experiments: First, people were asked to use imagery; if the data are to reflect the properties of imagery, we must be confident that images were in fact used in the performance of some task. Second, the experiments were designed so that the "privileged" properties, those that seem to distinguish an image from other forms of representation, should affect information processing—if those properties are in fact components of a functional representation. If we can produce data that follow in a straightforward way from our conception of an image (as characterized in the foregoing discussion), and if these data are difficult to explain without

*This distinction between quasi-pictorial and propositional representation was originally pointed out to me by Ned Block.

positing a functional image, then we will choose the more straightforward account and proceed as if images are a distinct form of internal representation.

2.1 Scanning Visual Images

If images depict spatial extent, then they should preserve relative interval distances among portions of an object (or among objects, in a scene.)* In these experiments time to scan images was used as a kind of "tape measure," as a way of assessing whether images depict spatial information. If distance per se regulates time to scan between portions of an image but does not regulate time when an image is not scanned, this is one source of evidence that images are functional quasi-pictorial representations in human memory.

The first experiment on scanning visual images was reported in Kosslyn (1973). There were four groups of subjects in this experiment. Two of the groups were shown ten line drawings like those in figure 3.2 and were asked to encode an image of them. That is, we asked these people to study each drawing, shut their eyes and image it, and then compare their image with the drawing. This procedure was repeated until they claimed to be able to mentally picture the drawing as accurately as possible. Subjects then participated in a reaction-time experiment. In this task, the name of a given drawing was presented and then followed five seconds later by a

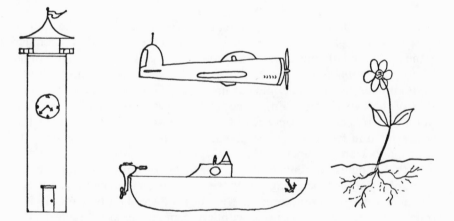

Figure 3.2. Examples of the line drawings used as stimuli by Kosslyn (1973).

*Assuming the distances between portions of an object are encoded with a relatively high degree of accuracy. The exponent in Stevens' Power Law for length is 1, indicating that it is safe to assume that no systematic distortions of interportion distances occur at the time of encoding.

possible property of the portrayed object. Half the time the named property had in fact been included in the drawing, and half the time it had not been present. So, for example, the subject might hear "speedboat" and then "motor" or "mast." The imagery groups were asked to "look at their images," and push one button as soon as they could "see" the named property or push another when they "looked" and could not find it. These people were told that this was not a test of how quickly they could decide whether the probed part had been included on the drawing; rather, we were concerned with how long it took to examine the image for the property. If the picture had the property, the subject was told, he or she should be able to find it on the image.*

The two imagery groups differed in only one respect. The Image Focus group was asked to mentally stare at one end of the image right after evoking it. Half of these subjects were asked to stare at the left end or top (depending on the object's orientation), and half the right or bottom. When they heard the probe word, these subjects were to look for the queried part on the image. If images actually do depict objects in a spatial medium, then the farther one must scan from the focus point to see a property, the more time should be required. For example, if one were focusing mentally on the left end of the speedboat, we would expect it to take less time to see the motor than to see the porthole, and less time to see the porthole than the anchor. Subjects in the other imagery group, the Image Whole group, were not asked to focus on a given end of the image but were told to keep the whole image in mind at once, and then to look for the property when it was presented. I hoped that there would be no effects of spatial location of parts on these data. Care was taken to ensure that half the subjects focused at one end and half at another end of each imaged stimulus. This prevented the results from being attributable to a confounding between the particular items that appeared at either end and distance from the point of focus.

Members of the other two groups were not asked to use imagery in performing the task. Instead, they were asked to describe the pictures and memorize descriptions. When the probe word appeared, they were simply to decide as quickly as possible whether the named property was on the picture. The Verbal Focus group was analogous to the Image Focus one: Subjects were asked to describe a given end of the drawing prior to receiving the probe. In the Verbal Whole group, the subjects were asked to describe the whole drawing before receiving the probe. This control was

---

*A good argument can be made that words like see, look, inspect, and other visual terms always should be put in quotes when referring to imagery, since imagery is not vision. However, as I shall argue later, imagery and like-modality perception utilize many of the same structures and processes, on my view enough to justify omitting the quotation marks when using visual terms to refer to image processing.

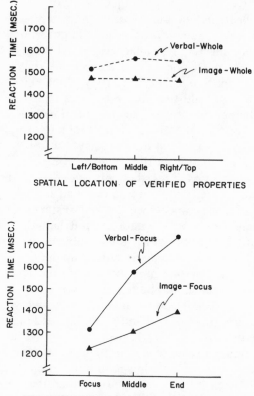

Figure 3.3. Time to verify properties of pictures at different locations and distances from the point of focus in the Kosslyn (1973) experiment.

introduced in an effort to demonstrate that a simple verbal-list model would not explain the imagery data.

The results of this experiment are illustrated in figure 3.3. As hoped, more time was taken to scan longer distances across the images. Also, this scanning effect was distinguished from scanning a verbal representation in two ways: First, the effects of distance were much more pronounced in the Verbal Focus condition than in the Imagery Focus one. Second, whereas it was equally easy to scan left-right or right-left in the imagery condition, it was much harder to scan right-left in the verbal condition (difficulty in this condition largely contributed to the relatively large increases in scanning time with increased distance evident in figure 3.3). In addition, there were no effects of property location in the Image Whole and Verbal Whole conditions. Ideally, the time taken to scan the whole image should have been equal to the time necessary to scan halfway across the image in the Image Focus condition (since half the image presumably would be scanned, on the average, in the Image Whole condition). This is not evident in figure 3.3, but it should be noted that there was not a significant difference between the mean time to scan half way across an image and the mean inspection time when subjects were not asked to focus initially—the visible difference ascribed to noise resulting from the fact that different people participated in the two groups.

Does the finding that time increased with distance scanned, and that this effect is not identical to one obtained with verbal processing, provide support for the claim that images depict information about spatial extent? Sadly, it is possible to argue otherwise. After publishing the paper reporting the foregoing results I received a telephone call from Danny Bobrow, a respected researcher in the field of artificial intelligence. Danny presented me with a counter-interpretation of my findings. On this view, my subjects encoded propositional representations of the drawings, like the one illustrated in figure 3.4 for the speedboat. When asked to focus, a subject simply activated a portion of the graph, say the portion representing things on the left end. In this case, time to locate a given property depends on how many links must be traversed to reach the representation of the property—and the longer the distance on the object, the more links must be traversed in the graph. The difference between the Image Focus and Verbal Focus groups can be explained here by assuming that more properties were encoded into the representation in the verbal condition (since people explicitly attempted to categorize parts), and hence more links had to be traversed in searching the graph. The asymmetries due to left-right, right-left scanning can be attributed to the details of organization: As in Anderson's (1972) FRAN model of free recall, two nodes may be connected by two links, one pointing in each direction. When describing a picture, one may "read" it from left to right (because of practice in reading English prose), and the internal representation may become structured with a predominance of pointers going only one way; when learning

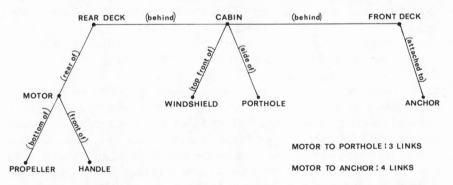

Figure 3.4. A propositional structure representing the information encoded from a picture of a motorboat.

to image the drawing, in contrast, one may set up symmetrical pointers between adjacent nodes, making it equally easy to search the graph either way. So, in the Verbal Focus condition where the right end is fixated, one may sometimes not be able to traverse the graph, may have to exit from it and re-enter at a new point—a process that consumes far more time than would simply traversing the graph. This explanation follows quite naturally from the sort of model offered by Anderson and Bower (1973).

This sort of propositional list-structure interpretation of my original scanning results received what appeared to be support from some experiments by Lea (1975). In a typical experiment, people evaluated from memory the relative locations of objects in a circular array. Lea asked his subjects to learn the array via imagery, then gave them the name of one object and asked them to name the first, second, or *n*th item (which could be an object or something the subject was taught to associate with an object) in a given direction. Lea found that the time to respond depended on the number of intervening items between an initial focus point and the target, but not on the actual distance separating a pair of objects in the array. This is exactly as would be expected if subjects simply traversed links in a network or searched through a list of items. The interpretation of these results is muddied, however, because Lea never insisted that his subjects base all judgments on actual processing of the image itself. That is, subjects were not told to count the items as they appeared in their images, but only to count the appropriate number of steps to the target. It is reasonable to suppose that these people encoded the circular array both as a list and as an image. Given that imagery tends to require more time to use in this sort of task than do nonimaginal representations (as we shall see shortly), subjects may have actually arrived at most judgments through processing nonimaginal list structures. If so, then it is not surprising that the actual distance separating pairs did not affect retrieval times.

In response to Lea's results, and in recognition of the propositionalist counter-interpretation of my earlier findings, my collaborators and I performed a series of experiments to test the claim that images depict distance, as reflected in distance per se affecting the time to scan images. The propositional account of my earlier data rests on a flaw in the design of the experiment, namely that in the course of scanning larger distances people also passed over more parts of the imaged object. Thus, in our subsequent experiments we removed this confounding and varied separately the distance a subject scanned and the number of intervening items scanned across (see Kosslyn, Ball, and Reiser, 1978, for further procedural details). If images really do depict interval spatial information, and if images themselves can in fact be scanned, then interval distance between parts of an imaged object should affect scanning time. If the apparent effects of distance observed in my earlier experiment were in fact due to accessing some sort of ordered list or propositional graph structure, however, then only ordinal relations between parts—not actual interval distances—should affect time to shift one's attention from one part of an image to another.

In the first experiment of this series subjects saw simple drawings which contained a line with three letters staggered along it. Two of the letters were in one case (for example, *A* and *R*), and the other in the remaining case (for example, *e*). Subjects studied a drawing, it was removed, and they were asked to mentally image it. Following this, they were asked to focus either on the right or on the left end of their images. Shortly thereafter, the name of one of the letters on the line was presented. The subject's task was to scan to the named letter, and as soon as he or she arrived there to push one button if it was capital or another button if it was lower case. The stimuli were constructed such that in the course of the experiment subjects had to scan three different distances while passing over zero, one, or two intervening letters. Each distance occurred equally often with each number of intervening items, allowing us to consider each variable separately.

The results of this experiment are illustrated in figure 3.5. Interestingly, time increased systematically with both distance and number of intervening letters. The distance effect follows if people really do scan a quasi-pictorial image, and the effect of intervening letters is not surprising if people look at each letter as they pass over it (perhaps momentarily slowing down in their scanning as well), which requires an additional increment of time. Our findings argue against the idea that people were not really scanning a quasi-pictorial image, but rather simply processing a serially ordered list of letters. If so, we should have found only an effect of number of intervening items (if scanning the list was self-terminating); there is no reason to expect such a list to have interval distance from each end associated with each letter. Furthermore, we found effects of distance even when the target letter was not separated from the focus point by any intervening letters. Finally, we found that it took about the same amount of time to scan right to left as to scan left to right. This result replicates that of the Image Focus group in my earlier experiment on image scanning, when subjects were asked to remember images and focus on one end prior to query, as opposed to the verbal condition of that experiment, in which left-to-right scanning was easier. Thus, image scanning seems to involve processes or mechanisms different from those highly practiced ones used during reading.

Given the two independent effects of distance and number of intervening letters, one might be tempted to ask which factor is the more important. This is a nonsensical question: By increasing the range of distances, we could increase the importance of this variable. In addition, we could probably manipulate the importance of number of intervening items by making the distractors more or less difficult to discriminate from the

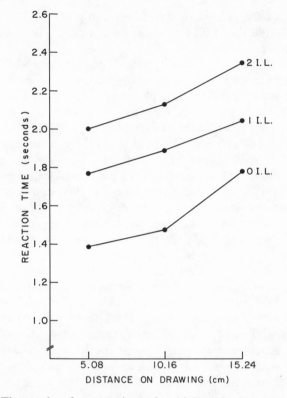

Figure 3.5. The results of an experiment in which subjects scanned different distances along an imaged line and classified the case of an imaged letter; subjects scanned over zero, one, or two intervening letters (I.L.'s) before reaching the target letter.

targets. Furthermore, the claim here is not that distance is more important than other variables but only that images do preserve distance information—and that such information can be used in real-time processing, affecting the operation of cognitive processes.

One might argue that the effects of distance on scanning time really reflect nothing more than the enthusiastic cooperation of our subjects, who somehow discerned the purpose of the experiment and manipulated their responses accordingly. Although two of our subjects in this experiment did hypothesize distance effects, they claimed to do so by introspecting upon their performance during the task; no subjects confessed to having consciously manipulated their responses. Nevertheless, we would be more comfortable with a task that was harder to second-guess and manipulate.

The second experiment involved scanning between the 21 possible pairs of 7 locations on an imaged map. Each of the distances was different, and the task seemed sufficiently complex to thwart any attempts to produce intentionally a linear relationship between distance and reaction time. Since the critical question is whether images preserve interval information, it is important that scanning time can be taken to reflect amount of distance traversed. Thus, to ensure that subjects scanned only the shortest distance between two points, we altered the instructions slightly and asked these people to image a black speck moving as quickly as possible along a direct path between the focus and target objects.

Subjects were shown the map illustrated in figure 3.6. They were told that there were seven key locations on the map, each of which was indicated by a small red dot (an *X* in the illustration presented here). These people were asked to study the map, close their eyes and mentally picture it, and then compare the image with the map, correcting the image accordingly. This procedure was repeated until the subject claimed to have a good image of the map. He or she then was asked to indicate where the dots were, and which objects they marked, by drawing them on a blank sheet of paper. When finished, this page was placed over the map and the subject noted where his or her drawing was awry. This procedure was repeated until the subject was accurate to within .25 inches of each of the actual locations.

Next the subject was asked to image the map and mentally stare at a named location. A word was then presented that either did or did not name

Figure 3.6.   The fictional map that subjects later imaged and scanned across.

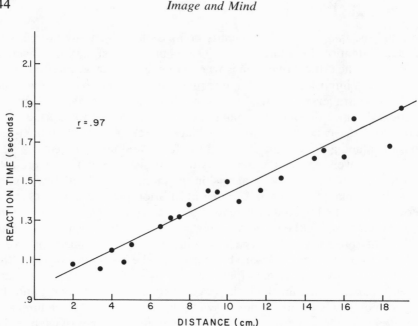

Figure 3.7. The time to scan between all pairs of locations on an image of the map illustrated in figure 3.6.

another location on the map. The subject was to scan to the object if it was on the map and push a button when he or she arrived, or was to examine the map and push another button if the named object could not be found. Every location served equally often as a focus point and target. As mentioned above, scanning was to be accomplished by imaging a flying black dot.

The results from the "true" trials of this experiment, in which subjects scanned a known distance between points, are illustrated in figure 3.7. As is evident, the farther the subject scanned between a pair of locations, the more time was required. In fact, once again time to scan increased linearly with the distance to be scanned. This demonstration supports the claim that images are quasi-pictorial entities that can be processed and are not merely epiphenomenal. One of the characteristic properties of such a representation is that interval distances between portions are depicted, and these data suggest that functional representations underlying the experience of visual mental images do have this property.

Interestingly, a number of subjects reported that they had to slow down when scanning the shorter distances, because the four objects at the lower left of the map were "cluttered together." The data showed no sign of this, however, providing further grounds for taking with a grain of salt subjects' own interpretations of their introspections. This experiment seems immune to the potential failings of the first experiment; somewhat surprisingly, no subject reported suspecting the hypothesis when it was explained afterward.

Given the results of the two experiments just described, how can we explain Lea's (1975) failure to find increases in reaction times as distances increased? I earlier suggested that this failure was a consequence of his instructions: Subjects were not told to base all judgments upon consultation of their images, only to start off from an imaged location and "to scan" a certain number of objects from there. Although these people began with an image, the actual decisions could have been generated by processing items in a list. If so, only ordinal—and not interval—relations among items (objects in the array) should have affected time to sort through the list. Effects of actual distance ought to occur only when one scans the spatial image itself, which depicts interval information about distance.

A second hypothesis of why Lea failed to obtain effects of distance on time to scan also involves his instructions. Lea did not insist that his subjects always construct the entire array ahead of time; instead, subjects were told simply to image a starting place, and then to decide which object was some number of locations away. Perhaps distance affects time to shift attention between locations in an image only when the locations are both "in view" simultaneously. That is, if an entire image is not kept in mind at once, the distance relations between visible and invisible locations may not be represented; these relations could be an "emergent" property of constructing the whole image from its component parts. One might shift to an invisible part by generating a sequence of individual images representing intervening locations, and not by actually scanning across an image. In this case, interval distance would not be expected to affect time to shift attention between parts.

We performed an additional experiment to examine the hypotheses described above. This experiment included two groups which received different instructions. In both groups, subjects learned to draw the map as did those in the previous experiment. In the control condition, subjects were then asked to image the map and focus on given locations just as in the previous experiment. Now, however, no mention was made of scanning the image. Instead, people were simply to decide as quickly as possible whether the probe word named an object that had been included in the drawing. Thus, if the scanning results were due to local activation of some sort of underlying abstract structure (perhaps a graph with dummy nodes interposed to "mark off" increasing distance), then we should find distance effects here. If the scanning results were due to scanning a spatial image that depicted extent, however, then we should not find distance effects with this control. If we did find in this experiment that distance affects decision times, we would be in trouble: We could not then infer that effects of distance implicate scanning of quasi-pictorial images.

In the second group (the overflow condition) subjects performed the same basic task, but with one modification: When focusing on the initial location in their image, these people were asked to "zoom in" on it until that object filled their entire image, causing the remainder of the island to "overflow." My introspection was that I could only get so close, as it were, to an imaged object before parts began to overflow. This introspection is shared by everyone with whom I've talked who "has" imagery (experimental validation of this introspection will be presented later in this chapter). Further, all subjects in this task understood the instructions and claimed to be able to comply. After zooming in on the focus location, the subject was to wait for the probe word. At this point, he or she was to see an image of the object if it was in fact present on the map, and then push one button; if the named object could not be imaged as it appeared on the map, the subject was to simply push the other button. No mention was made in this condition of scanning the image or of imaging flying specks.

The two groups of this experiment, then, were intended to simulate the possible spontaneous behavior of subjects in Lea's task. In the first group, people did not really use the image; in the second group, distances were not explicitly present in the image. If scanning is in fact a consequence of traversing "observed distances" across an image, distance should not influence performance time in either of these conditions.

The results are illustrated in figure 3.8. As is evident, we did not find distance effects in the no-imagery control condition, in which subjects simply answered without reference to the image. Contrary to our initial hypothesis, however, we did find that time increased systematically with distance between the focus and target locations in the overflow condition. For present purposes, the important point is that the observed effects of scanning longer distances do seem to reflect a property of image processing per se, and can be taken as support for the claim that images depict spatial extent. Lea's results, then, may simply reflect the fact that his subjects were not told to respond only after seeing the probed object in their image. Clearly, before we draw inferences about image processing from given data, we must be certain that when the data were produced people did in fact use images. The instructions administered in our experiments seem capable of inducing subjects to use imagery—even if other means of performing a task are available.

Lea's results were probably not a consequence of his subjects' failing to keep the entire array in their images prior to processing it, as witnessed by the results in the overflow condition. Although people in this condition were asked to include only the focus location in their initial images, times

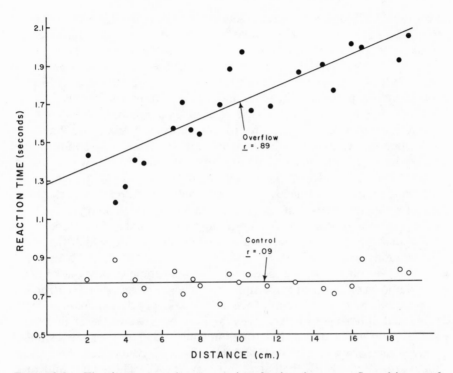

Figure 3.8. The time to scan between pairs of points in an overflowed image of the map in figure 3.6 (top) and the time to verify locations when subjects began by focusing on a location but did not scan their images (bottom).

nevertheless increased with distance to a probed object. We were somewhat surprised by this finding, which may indicate that one may construct images such that portions are "waiting in the wings," ready to be processed if necessary. I will discuss actual accounts of this finding in chapter 8.

There is one hitch in the foregoing explanation of the data obtained from the overflow group: If these people "zoomed in" closer to the imaged map than did those in the initial map-scanning experiment, the subjective distances between parts should have been greater in the overflow condition. If so, then it is reasonable to expect that more time should have been required to scan these enlarged images, which was not the case. One explanation of this disparity rests on a procedural difference between the overflow condition and the first map-scanning experiment: Subjects in the first experiment were instructed to image a small black speck flying between parts. This task may have required more effort than the simple shift-of-attention instructions used in the present experiment, and thus slowed down scanning. In addition, it is possible that subjects in the two experiments simply scanned at different rates: If people in the overflow condition scanned relatively quickly, perhaps because distances traversed were on the average relatively large, then we would not necessarily expect any differences in scanning times between the two conditions. We eliminated the difference in instructions in the next experiment and also tested all people in all of the conditions, hoping that a given person would adopt a constant scanning rate for different materials.

The final experiment in this series was an examination of the effects of subjective size of an image on time to scan across it. We worried that if we used stimuli as complex as those included on the map, people might have to "zoom in" (if the image was small) or "pan back" (if it was large) in order to see parts clearly. Not only could difficulty in identifying parts of relatively complex images obfuscate effects of scanning images of different subjective sizes, but people might adjust their scanning rates in accordance with the difficulty in identifying parts. Pilot data lent credence to these fears, encouraging us to use simpler stimuli, on which the parts were readily identifiable.

Thus, we conducted an experiment in which people imaged one of three schematic faces at one of three subjective sizes. The faces were extremely simple and the target property (eye color) was very discriminable. These faces had either light or dark eyes, and the eyes were one of three distances from the mouth, as illustrated in figure 3.9. These subjects studied a given face, it was concealed, and they then received one of three cues, the words "full size," "half size," or "overflow." These cues indicated the relative subjective size at which the subject should image the face just

Figure 3.9. The schematic faces that subjects imaged at one of three sizes.

seen. "Full size" indicated that the face should be imaged as large as possible while still remaining entirely "visible at a single glance of the mind's eye." After forming an image of the face, the subject was then to focus on the mouth. "Half size" directed the subject to image the face at half the full size, and then to focus on the mouth. And "overflow" directed the subject to image the face so large that only the mouth was visible in the image, the rest having overflowed. When the subject had imaged the face at the correct subjective size and was focusing on the mouth, the word "light" or "dark" was presented. The subject was then told to "glance up" at the eyes in the image and to push one button if the eyes were the color described and another button if they were not. These instructions made no mention of imaging a flying speck or the like. As usual, subjects were urged to perform the task as quickly as possible while keeping errors to a minimum.

If distance is in fact depicted in visual images, and if more time is required to scan longer distances (and if subjects maintain a reasonably constant rate of scan for different-sized images), then subjectively larger images ought to require more time in general to scan than subjectively smaller images. Further, the effects of increased distance between mouth and eyes should become more pronounced with larger images, since when size is multiplied, so are the distances.

The results of this experiment are evident in figure 3.10. As expected, people again required more time to scan longer distances across their images. This was reflected in three results: First, times increased with further separation between the mouth and eyes of the imaged stimuli (again note that there were exactly the same number of intervening items between the focus and target locations). Second, more time was generally required to scan across subjectively larger images. Third, there were increasingly large effects of increased distance between mouth and eyes for subjectively large images. This last result was not as neat as it could have been, however. As is evident in figure 3.10, the "fanning effect" indicating multiplication of distances with increased size was evident only for the true responses. Further, although there was some difference in slope (that is, the effects on scanning time of increased distance between the mouth and eyes) between the full-size and half-size conditions, this difference was not as large as would be expected if length had been varied, and was larger than would be expected if area had been varied (see Kosslyn, Ball, and Reiser, 1978, for details of size of the predicted effects in both conditions). There are three possible explanations for these results: (1) people may have sometimes varied length and sometimes varied area; (2) "half size" was a compromise between half the area and half the length; or, (3) people may not have needed to scan the face with the shortest distance between mouth and eyes when it was imaged at half size. In this case, the eyes may have been visible even when the person focused on the mouth.

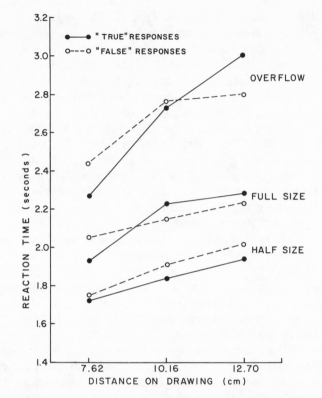

Figure 3.10. The time required to classify the eyes of the imaged faces illustrated in figure 3.9 when subjects initially focused on the mouth. Three different distances were scanned, and subjects imaged the faces at three different sizes.

Hence, there would be a larger slope (that is, a larger increase in time necessary to scan to eyes at different distances from the mouth) than we expected—and less of a difference in the slopes between the half-size and full-size conditions.

At the time this experiment was done, the failure to find slope differences for images of different sizes on false trials was inexplicable. Later in this book (see chapter 8) a partial explanation will be forthcoming which hinges on the notion that there are two distinct ways in which images can be transformed.

Finally, it is worth noting that the results of this experiment allow us to eliminate one more possible no-imagery interpretation of the scanning effects. That is, it could be claimed that the closer together two objects or parts are, the more likely it is that they will be grouped into the same "chunk" during encoding. Presumably, parts in the same chunk are retrieved in sequence more quickly than parts in different chunks. In this experiment, size of an image was not manipulated until after the drawing was concealed, precluding systematic differences in encoding among the three size conditions. Thus, the fact that subjectively larger images generally required more time to scan than did smaller ones seems to run counter to the notion that spatial extent affected scan times only because of a confounding between distance and the probability of being encoded into a single unit.

2.1.1 Conclusions from the Scanning Experiments

The experiments just described converge in demonstrating that people can scan the distances embodied in images. More time was required to scan longer distances, even when the same number of items fell between the focus and target locations. In addition, subjectively larger images required more time to scan than did subjectively smaller ones. Somewhat surprisingly, the effects of distance persisted even when a person "zoomed in" on one part so that the remainder of the image seemed to "overflow." Finally, there were no effects of distance on decision times when people did not actually use their images, even though an image had been generated and focused upon. These results taken together indicate that images are pictorial in at least one respect: Like pictures, images seem to depict information about interval spatial extents. The scanning experiments support the claim that portions of images depict corresponding portions of the represented objects, and that the spatial relations between portions of the image index the spatial relations between the corresponding portions of the imaged objects. These qualities are apparent in our introspections, and the experiments suggest that people can operate upon the representations that are experienced as quasi-pictorial mental images.

Given these results, how do we account for Lea's (1975) finding no systematic effects of distance on evaluation times? First, the control experiments suggest that Lea's results may simply reflect his failure to ensure that subjects responded only after "seeing" the target in their image. If left to their own devices in making decisions, subjects might find a no-imagery strategy faster, and a no-imagery strategy would not result in distance influencing decision times. Second, Lea's task was so difficult (the mean reaction times reached as high as 8 seconds) that effects of distance (which are measured in milliseconds, not seconds) may simply have been drowned out by the nonscanning components of this task. Finally, even if imagery was used, Lea's metered search task, which involved counting successive items, may have induced subjects to form a sequence of separate images, each representing an object in the array, rather than attempt to hold and then scan a complex image (which may be difficult to maintain). As will be described in chapter 6, Weber, Kelley, and Little (1974) report that people can "verbally prompt" sequences of images, and something like this may have occurred in Lea's metered search task. If so, then we have no reason to expect distance to affect response times in his experiment.

2.2 Inspecting Images at Different Apparent Sizes

Our protomodel suggests that images depict visual information, and that this information is interpreted by some of the same sorts of classificatory procedures used in classifying sensory input during vision. If so, we might expect some of the same constraints that affect ease of categorizing percepts to affect ease of classifying parts of mental images. An obvious candidate for such a variable is apparent size: Parts of "subjectively" smaller objects (those subtending smaller visual angles) are "harder to see" in perception. If this difficulty is in part a consequence of properties of the central medium in which percepts are represented (for example, perhaps the medium has a "grain"), then we might expect parts of subjectively smaller objects to also be harder to see in a mental image. I have reported a number of experiments designed to demonstrate that this is in fact true (see Kosslyn, 1975, 1976a). These experiments all make use of an "imagery detection task" in which subjects are asked to image some object and then try to see some named property on the image. The measure of interest is the amount of time required either to see a given property or to inspect the appropriate region and be certain that the object does not possess the named property.

I was initially worried that if we simply asked people to vary subjective size directly, they would easily discern the predictions of the experiment. Thus, innocent subterfuge seemed in order. In my first experiment, I attempted to manipulate size indirectly by making use of the introspection that images could be only so large subjectively before they seemed to overflow. It is as if the CRT screen is only so big, and a display overflows when it is too large. Thus, size was manipulated indirectly by asking people to image relatively small "target" animals (such as a rabbit) as if they were standing next to either an elephant or a fly. If there is only a fixed amount of "space" within which to image and most of this space is taken up by the elephant, then an adjacent correctly scaled image of a rabbit should seem subjectively small. In contrast, if a rabbit is imaged next to a correctly scaled image of a fly, the rabbit should seem much larger. Thus, in the first experiment, I asked people to image pairs of animals, one member of which was always an elephant or a fly. Shortly thereafter, a probe was delivered and the subject was to see whether the target animal (not the elephant or the fly) had the property. Subjects were told that we were interested in how long it took to see properties of animals on images, not simply in how quickly the subject would decide by any means whether the property was appropriate for the animal. Further, the subjects were told that if the animal had the property, they should be able to find it on their images. Subjects were asked to keep the images of both animals clearly in mind up until the probe word was presented. At this point, the subjects were not required to maintain the image of the context animal (elephant or fly) if they did not want to. I counterbalanced such that every target animal and probed property occurred equally often in both contexts (next to the elephant and next to the fly).

The results of this experiment were clear-cut: People did in fact require more time to see parts of animals imaged next to elephants. Introspective reports offered after the experiment often included references to having to "zoom in" to see properties of subjectively smaller images.

One obvious problem with this finding is that I confounded the size of the context animal with its identity. Perhaps people have a favorite elephant, like Dumbo, but no favorite fly (it's a very discriminatory culture in which we live). So, more time and effort may be spent in elaborating the image of an elephant than the image of a fly. If so, then the results may be due to distraction from the target animal, rather than to size per se. There seemed a straightforward way around this problem: We brought in a new group of people and asked them to do something a little odd. We wanted them to do exactly the same task as before—except to image giant flies and tiny elephants next to the target animals. Somewhat surprisingly, subjects seemed to have little trouble in complying with these instructions. As before, the subjects were asked to see parts of the target animals imaged next to the elephant or fly; again, time to inspect the image was measured. The results of this variation and the original experiment are illustrated in figure 3.11.

As is apparent, asking subjects to reverse the sizes of the context animals had the desired effect. It now required more time to see parts of target animals imaged next to a fly. Further, it required more time in general to see properties in the second version of the experiment. This last result could indicate that it requires time to transform the sizes of the context images, and hence less time is available for constructing good images of the target animals. It could also be due to differences in the subject population, however, since the first experiment was conducted during the regular school term whereas the second was done during summer session (and thus some of these subjects were visiting high school students).

These two experiments seem to show that the apparent effects of size were not due to the identity of the context animal per se. But consider a propositionalist account of these results: The functional component of "imaging" actually corresponds to activating properties on lists associated with concepts in memory. Because of processing capacity limitations, only a limited number, n, of properties may be activated at once. Because people know they should be able to see more on larger images, they activate more properties in the elephant list than in the fly one (if

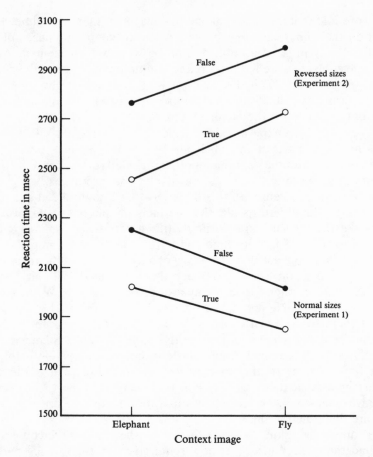

Figure 3.11. The time to see properties of target animals when they were imaged standing next to an elephant or a fly. The elephant and the fly were imaged either at their normal sizes relative to the target animal or at reversed sizes.

these animals are imaged at normal sizes; if reversed, vice versa). If k properties are activated on the context list, then as k gets larger $n - k$—the number that can be activated on the target animal's list—decreases. Hence, when a relatively large context image is present, fewer properties are activated on the target animal's list, and the probability of a given probed property being activated decreases. If the queried property is not activated prior to probe, it must be retrieved from long-term memory, requiring an additional increment of time. Thus, ''smaller'' context images result in a greater probability that a probed property of the target image will be activated—and hence verified quickly—than occurs when large context images are included.

I performed two experiments in an effort to eliminate this sort of coun-

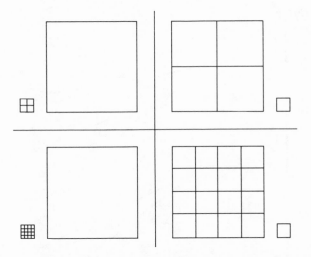

Figure 3.12. The four possible combinations of relative size and complexity of the imaginary matrices subjects were asked to image painted on a wall to an animal's left. The right square represents the relative size of the imaged animal.

terexplanation. In the first experiment the context animals were replaced by matrices. The matrix was either relatively simple—containing only four cells—or relatively complex—containing sixteen cells. Further, each matrix was large or small relative to an adjacent image of a "target" animal. Subjects were asked to image target animals as if they were against a wall, with an imaginary matrix painted to the animal's left on the wall. Figure 3.12 illustrates the four conditions of the experiment, the right box in each pair indicating the relative size of the imaged animal. Each person received each condition equally often, and counterbalancing over four groups of subjects ensured that each probe occurred equally often in each condition. After imaging a matrix-animal pair, the subject received a probe and again indicated as quickly as possible whether or not he or she could see the property on the animal.

The results of this experiment are shown in figure 3.13. First, people required more time to see properties of relatively smaller animals. Second, people needed more time to see properties of animals imaged next to the more complex matrix. These two effects were independent, indicating that the size effect is not simply an artifact of complexity (as measured here) of the adjacent figure.

I also performed a second version of this experiment to eliminate a potential flaw in the previous ones. In the three previous experiments using context images, we never asked the subject to do anything with the context image. Thus, nothing but the subject's good will stood between us and utter disaster. Given the inherent limitations of the methodology, this

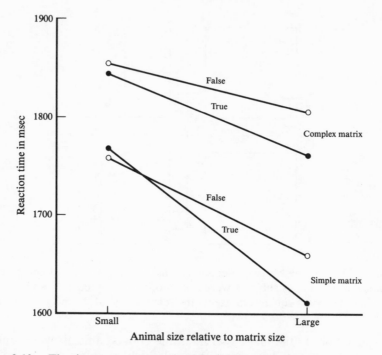

Figure 3.13. The time to see properties of animals when they were imaged next to large or small matrices that were relatively simple or complex.

will always be true to some extent (we cannot directly observe a person's mental events). But it seemed wise to replicate this last result with a more constraining methodology. In this experiment I simply substituted two different digits (randomly chosen) for the four-cell matrix and four digits for the sixteen-cell matrix, again asking subjects to image an animal as if these stimuli were painted on a wall—at one of two relative sizes—to the left of the animal. Thus, the animal could be relatively large next to two or four digits (arranged in two rows of two) or could be relatively small next to two or four digits. Half of the trials queried properties of the animal, and half queried the presence of a given digit. Subjects were to look at the image and see whether a given digit was in fact present or whether a part was characteristic of an animal (as before), pushing one of two response buttons as quickly as possible.

The results of this experiment are illustrated in figure 3.14. The data nicely replicate those of the previous experiment with the matrices. More time was required to see properties of animals when they were imaged next to four digits instead of two—and more time was required to see digits in more complex images. Furthermore, it took more time to see parts of smaller animals, or smaller digits, and this effect was independent of how many digits were present in the image.

Figure 3.14. The time to see properties of animals or to identify digits when they were relatively large or small and when two or four digits were included in the image.

The foregoing two experiments demonstrate that the effects of size were not merely a consequence of increased numbers of units when larger context images were included. Unfortunately, one could argue that number of units is the wrong variable: Perhaps amount of area is critical. Consider the CRT metaphor: As a display is enlarged, more dots must be filled in by the electron gun in order to "draw" the picture. Thus, it could be argued that the apparent effects of the size of the image subjects examine are really due to the effort to display a larger context image. As more effort is expended in maintaining the larger context image, less is left over to display the target image. In this case, the size of the target image would not really be responsible for the observed effects. To get around this objection I performed another experiment.

In the next experiment of this series subjects were asked to image items in isolation. In an attempt to parry "demand characteristic" explanations (that subjects know they should be able to see parts of larger images more easily, and hence respond more quickly), I was exceptionally careful in the postsession interviews of subjects and did not include subjects who deduced the predictions. Comfortingly, most subjects were too busy performing the task to worry about the point of the experiment (see Kosslyn,

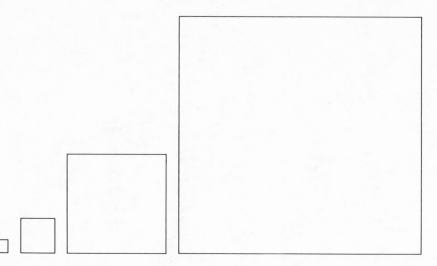

Figure 3.15.   The relative sizes at which subjects imaged animals. Each square is one sixth the area of the square to its right. The largest square was 14 cm/side in the original illustration.

1975 for details). Subjects first learned to draw four colored squares, each a different size. The relative sizes are illustrated in figure 3.15. Four groups of subjects were used so that each color indexed each size equally often. After learning to draw the squares, the subject was told that the largest size corresponded to "as large as the object could be imaged without it overflowing," and the rest were scaled down accordingly. The subject then heard a series of trials in which a color name was followed shortly by an animal name (which cued him or her to image the animal at the corresponding relative size), and then by a probe word (half of which were true of the animal and half false, as in the previous experiments). As usual, the subject was to look at his or her image and try to find the probed part as quickly as possible. The results of this experiment are illustrated in figure 3.16. As hoped, people found it more difficult to see parts of subjectively smaller images. Unlike the previous experiments, however, there was no effect of subjective size on time to see that a queried part was not present. This result may have been due to a procedural difference among the experiments; before, subjects were asked to "put the probed property on the animal and see how it looked" before deciding that the animal did not have it. In this experiment, this requirement was eliminated and people were asked simply to look where it ought to belong. As we shall see (in chapter 7), there are good reasons why size need not have affected these "false" responses.

I devised two more experiments in an attempt to nail down the claim that parts of subjectively smaller objects are more difficult to see in an

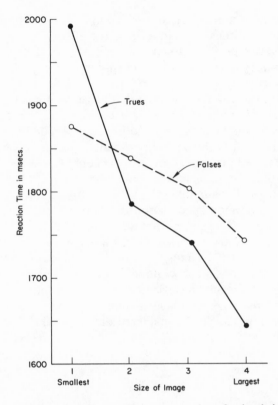

Figure 3.16. The time required to evaluate properties of animals imaged at one of the four relative sizes illustrated in figure 3.15; the largest size was to be as large as possible without overflowing and the rest scaled down accordingly.

image. One could argue that the effects of size are really due to the time required to adjust the image to the correct size: The more time required, the less time remains to construct a well-detailed image prior to query. There are two variants of this hypothesis: One notion is that a subject always begins with as large an image as possible and then shrinks it to the correct size. The more shrinking required, the more time is consumed prior to completion of the image. And the less time available to fill in the details, the more likely it is that the probed detail will not be present on the image and will require time and effort to retrieve from long-term memory. The other notion is that because we have practice in constructing images at normal, "large" sizes, more effort is required to construct images at nonstandard sizes. The greater the disparity between the size of the image and its "standard internal size," the greater the effort to construct it. Thus, it might be claimed that as an image decreases in size it becomes increasingly difficult to construct. And an image that is more difficult to construct is more likely to be incomplete at the time of test. Both variants of this hypothesis, then, ascribe the effects of image size not to difficulties in seeing parts but to how likely it is that the probed property is "activated"—not necessarily on a quasi-pictorial experienced image— prior to query.

A contrasting hypothesis would be that larger, not smaller, images will take more time to evoke if images are constructed, since one can see where more parts ought to belong and hence will spend more time filling out the larger images. In the next experiment, subjects began by memorizing the squares used in the previous experiment. The subjects then heard a color name followed immediately by an animal name, at which time they formed an image of the animal at the subjective size corresponding to the square of that color and pushed a button when the image was completed. We urged subjects to be sure to form all images at equal clarity and vividness. The time necessary to evoke images was measured; these results are presented in figure 3.17. Times increased as subjective size increased. These results are inconsistent with the predictions of the counterexplanation of our previous results described above. Some subjects reported that large animals were easiest to image at large sizes and small animals easiest to image at small sizes. So, I considered data from the seven largest and

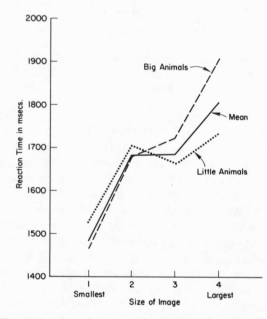

Figure 3.17. The time to form images at the four relative sizes illustrated in figure 3.15; the largest image was to be as large as possible without overflowing and the rest scaled down accordingly.

seven smallest animals separately. The effects of image size, however, were consistent for both sets of animals. Perhaps these results are not surprising, given that the animals varied in size only from a mouse to a collie. Nonetheless, this is another instance where people's untutored interpretations of their introspections proved faulty.

Finally, I investigated one other counterinterpretation: On this view, the initial effects of size might be due to differences in opportunity for fading of the large images relative to the small ones. That is, if small images are constructed sooner, perhaps they have decayed more at the time of probe than the more recently completed larger images. I reasoned that if there is no appreciable difference in the size effect when properties are probed six or ten seconds after the animal name is presented (and image construction initiated), then we can conclude that differential fading is not an important variable in this situation. Thus, we asked subjects to image animals at two different sizes (those represented by the largest and smallest squares used in the previous experiment). There were two blocks of trials: one in which the delay between hearing the animal name and the probe was only six seconds, and another in which the delay was ten seconds. The results of this experiment are presented in figure 3.18. As is evident, for true responses there was no real difference in the effects of subjective size in the two conditions; false responses once again showed only marginal effects of size, although this was not reflected in a significant interaction between size and truth value (see Kosslyn, 1975, for statistical analyses). Thus, we can conclude that differential fading is not an important variable in this situation.

2.2.1 Countering a Propositionalist Account

Size per se seems to influence time to verify properties in an "imagery detection task." The next question concerns the role of the quasi-pictorial image in the causal sequence underlying these effects of size. The foregoing experiments were motivated by the notions that (a) images are quasi-pictorial internal representations that are processed by a "mind's eye," and (b) this mind's eye is subject to some of the same constraints that affect interpretation of sensory input during perception. One could argue, however, that these results have nothing to do with the resolution or quality of a quasi-pictorial image but rather are a consequence of the way propositional representations are processed. That is, perhaps the representation of the concept of an animal includes a list of properties that can be activated prior to the probe. According to this view, people realize that they should see more things on a larger image, and hence move farther down (activate more entries on) the property list. Thus, the probability of a given probed property being activated prior to query will be higher when subjects are asked to form subjectively larger images. And verification

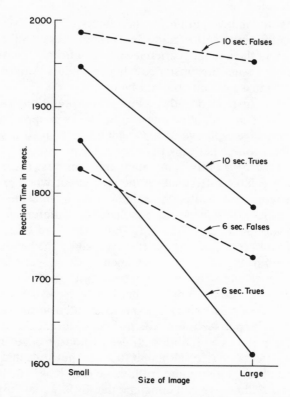

Figure 3.18. The time to evaluate properties of subjectively large and small images after retaining them for six or ten seconds.

time is faster when a sought property is already activated than when it must be searched for in long-term memory. Thus the effects of size are explained without positing functional quasi-pictorial representations.

I did two experiments to distinguish this conception from my own, which posits that size qua size is responsible for the observed effects on verification time. If the effects of subjective size are simply a consequence of probability of activation on a list, then subjects should be faster in verifying properties stored near the "top" of the list because these properties are most likely to be already activated at the time of probe. Some psychologists have claimed that the ordering of such lists is reflected by association strength, frequency of co-occurrence between a noun and property, or the like. This inference is based on the observation that an object's highly associated, frequently co-occurring properties are verified most quickly in standard sentence verification tasks, in which a subject is asked to judge as quickly as possible whether a given property is appropriate for a given object (see Collins and Quillian, 1969; Conrad, 1972; Smith, Shoben and Rips, 1974). For example, the finding that the assertion "A lion has a mane" is affirmed more quickly than "A lion has a tail" could be taken to imply that "mane" is stored higher than "tail" on the "lion property list." If lists are so ordered, then the association strength of a property—not its size—should dictate the time needed to see the property on an image. But if images are quasi-pictorial representations that depict information, and if smaller properties are more difficult to classify, then the size of a property per se should influence image-inspection time.

To test the claim that image-inspection time is affected by size per se, I first selected items like "cat-claws" and "cat-head," where the smaller property was also more associated with the noun (as determined by normative ratings; see Kosslyn, 1976a, for details). This experiment had two parts. In the first part people received a set of trials consisting of names of animals followed by names of possible properties (half true and half false, as usual) and were to decide as quickly as possible whether the property belonged to the animal. Subjects were given five seconds after hearing an animal's name to "think of properties" of that animal. No mention of imagery was made in this condition. In the second part, the subjects received a new set of trials and were now asked to use imagery in making the judgment; as in the earlier experiments, the subject was to form an image of the animal upon hearing its name, and then to look for the named property on the image. Two groups of subjects were tested, and the set of items preceded by imagery instructions for one group was not preceded by the imagery instructions for the other group and vice versa, ensuring that every item appeared in both conditions equally often. The items are listed in table 3.1.

Table 3.1. The animals and properties used in an experiment in which smaller properties were more highly associated than larger ones.

	Set 1: True properties			Set 2: True properties	
Animal	High association/ small	Low association/ large	Animal	High association/ small	Low association/ large
Mouse	whiskers	back	Shark	teeth	tail
Alligator	teeth	tail	Monkey	hands	shoulders
Bear	claws	legs	Rat	eyes	fur
Bee	stinger	wings	Iguana	tongue	legs
Cobra	fangs	tail	Panda	paws	chest
Owl	eyes	chest	Billygoat	beard	back
Lion	teeth	legs	Raccoon	mouth	stomach
Frog	tongue	back	Rabbit	nose	back
Cat	claws	head	Horse	hooves	stomach
Duck	feet	feathers	Octopus	suckers	skin
Rattlesnake	rattle	belly	Beaver	teeth	back

The results are illustrated in the left-most panel of figure 3.19. Three findings are of interest here: First, with no imagery instructions we replicated the usual finding that verification times decrease for more strongly associated "true" properties. Second, this effect was turned on its ear when subjects were asked to use imagery: The larger—although less strongly associated—properties now were verified more quickly. Finally, using imagery required more time than did the no-imagery verification procedures. This last result could indicate that imagery requires more operations (for example, formation of the image, retrieval of the definition of the part, inspection of the image) than does simply looking up a representation in a list or the like. I will provide a detailed account of these findings in chapter 7—for present purposes it is sufficient to note that these results allow us to argue that imagery is a distinct form of representation.

One could argue that people participating in the above experiment scanned down the same property lists when preparing for the query under both sets of instructions, but that with imagery instructions they passed over small properties and activated only large properties, since they knew that large properties should be most visible if images were like percepts. This interpretation seems countered by the results of two variations of the foregoing experiment, in both of which subjects formed the image only at the time of probe. If people really do scan serially down a list when

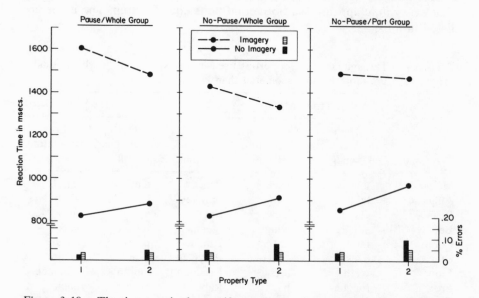

Figure 3.19. The time required to verify two types of properties in three different conditions when imagery was or was not used. Type 1 properties are high association/small area and Type 2 properties are low association/large area.

searching for a property in both imagery and no-imagery conditions, we should find the same pattern of response times in the imagery and no-imagery conditions here. In the first variation, a new group of subjects was asked to image the property on the entire animal; in this case, because part size was relative to the entire animal, the subjective size of the property would be relatively large when the part was not highly associated (as in the previous experiment). No pause was inserted between the animal and property names in either the imagery or the no-imagery condition, so the subject was forced to form the image at the time of inspection. As is evident in the middle panel of figure 3.19, the results of this variation were virtually identical to those from the first group of subjects. As before, the small, highly associated items took less time when imagery was not required but more time when it was required.

In the remaining variation of this experiment, again a pause was not inserted between presentation of the animal and property names. Now, however, the subjects were asked only to image the property or the relevant portion of the animal's body. Thus, size did not have to be preserved in the image, as subjects could normalize the smaller parts so they seemed to fill as much of the "image space" (more on this notion shortly) as did the larger parts. And in fact, in the imagery condition there were no effects of association strength or of size—as is evident in the rightmost panel of figure 3.19. This is not surprising, given the finding that images of different-sized animals could be formed equally easily at different subjective sizes. In all three variations, effects of the two types of properties were significantly different for the different instructions. Thus, even when people are asked to form an image on the spot, it is clear that "inspecting" a mental image is different from evaluating properties without using imagery.*

The findings from the no-pause conditions indicate that the effects of size are not an artifact of the probability that a part was activated in a list prior to probe (if the no-imagery verification times reflect list ordering), since presumably none of the relevant properties could have been activated before the stimulus was presented. But one could argue that these results are somehow an artifact of the odd items I used. After all, it is unusual for smaller properties to be more strongly associated with an object (the stimulus items were in fact very difficult to construct). Therefore, another experiment seemed warranted. Actually, the experiment itself had been done years before, when I was still a graduate student, for a different purpose (some of the data are reported in Nelson and Kosslyn, 1975). In

---

*Note that the no-imagery instructions did not instruct the subject not to use imagery; I feared this would be like asking someone "not to think of a pink elephant"—which virtually guarantees that they will. Postsession discussion revealed, however, that the vast majority of these subjects did not use imagery spontaneously in the no-imagery condition. Some of these data will be discussed in chapter 10.

this experiment people verified sentences about animals of the form "A lion has a tail" or "A bee can eat." Half the subjects were asked to use imagery in reaching their assessments, and half were simply asked to answer as quickly as possible. There was a brief pause after the verb in which the subject recalled properties or formed an image. I took the data from the "has" statements and calculated means for each item in the two instructional conditions. I then asked a new group of people to rate how associated the properties were with the animal (on a standard seven-point rating scale) and how large the property was relative to the animal. These ratings (along with others to be discussed later) were entered as independent variables in a regression analysis of the reaction times. Interestingly, in the imagery condition, significant amounts of variance in the reaction-time data were accounted for by size and none to speak of by association strength. Just the reverse held true for the no-imagery data, size being inconsequential but association strength proving very important. Since these items were not selected with size in mind at all, and since size and association strength were only haphazardly related, one cannot object here on the basis of item selection.*

One could argue that these results simply indicate that more than one list is stored, and that different lists are differently ordered. Given all the ways in which we can order things (for example, for parts of an animal, in terms of softness, nearness to the ground, edibility, reflectivity, and so on)—including some ways that involve hitherto unencountered dimensions (like how useful a dried part would be as writing paper)—it is absurd to suggest that all possible orderings are stored. Given the capability of generating new orderings as they are needed, why should we store more than one list-ordering, which is presumably indexed by reaction times in a standard semantic memory task? And if we compute new orderings only when needed, why should subjects bother to reorder properties in terms of size in the present imagery task? Reordering is unnecessary to perform the task correctly. Certainly, it is possible that we store a few orderings that are used frequently (to save the effort of continually recomputing the same thing). But there is no compelling evidence or argument that people do in fact store a list of each animal's properties ordered in terms of size.

---

*In addition to a condition in which a pause was inserted, we also included a no-pause condition. Now size did not account for significant variance in the imagery condition but association strength did. The lack of effects of size was not surprising, given that the instructions were like those given to the third group in the other experiment (the results from which are illustrated in the right-most panel of figure 3.19), but the effects of association strength were not easily explained at the time the experiment was conducted. After the present theory was developed, however, not only was it explained but it was expected—see chapter 7.

2.2.2 Conclusions from the Imagery-Detection Experiments

It seems to me that the most straightforward interpretation of these results is that subjective image size affects the ease of seeing parts in an image. Each particular result could have been explained in other ways, but taken as a whole I find the imagery interpretations more convincing than the no-imagery alternatives. One interesting thing about these findings is that they seem to contradict the ones on imagery scanning: Now less time is required to inspect larger images. I will consider this apparent paradox, the interaction of the two properties—distance and resolution—after I begin to flesh out the details of a model.

2.3 Effects of Subjective Size on Later Memory

When a person uses imagery to learn associations between words, the images evoked to represent the words may themselves be encoded into memory. Alternatively, perhaps the images are sloughed off and all that is stored in memory is an abstract, sentence-like proposition expressing a relationship between the words. If the quasi-pictorial image people claim to experience is in fact functional and can be re-encoded into memory, then its properties—like its apparent size—should influence the amount and quality of information encoded into memory. Presumably, if one encodes a subjectively small image into memory, this representation will be more impoverished than if one encodes a larger (but still entirely visible) image—and hence later memory for the object imaged small will suffer.

This expectation is exactly the reverse of that of Neisser and Kerr (1973), who argued that images represent the "layout" (Gibson, 1966) of perceived space directly, rather than depicting objects as seen from a particular point of view. They expected that differences in how parts of an image were pictured would not influence memory for those parts. In two experiments, they asked subjects to image objects either engaged in a visible, pictorial interaction (for example, "x is sitting on top of the torch held up by the Statue of Liberty"), engaged in an invisible, concealed interaction (for example, "x is hidden inside the torch held up by the Statue of Liberty"), or in a visible but not interactive, separate relationship ("looking from one window, you see the Statue of Liberty; from a window in another wall, you see x"). Neisser and Kerr found no differences in memory for objects imaged Pictorially or Concealed, although in both of these conditions memory was better than it was in the Separate condition. They took this finding to support the notion that only the spatial information was important, and how objects appeared in the image was irrelevant. This interpretation is muddied, however, by the fact that not all subjects followed instructions all of the time in the concealed condition. In fact, on only 27 of the 144 trials did subjects report really forming concealed images in the concealed condition. When subjects in this condition in Experiment 1 imaged the response item so it was not concealed at all, they later remembered it 95 percent of the time; when they did not see the response object in their image, they later were correct only 85 percent of the time. Although this difference was not significant, the possibility of a ceiling effect should dissuade us from affirming the null hypothesis.*

The following experiments provide a more stringent test of the claim that quasi-pictorial, and not merely spatial (in Gibson's sense or in Anderson and Bower's, 1973, propositional sense) information is encoded when one forms visual mental images (see Kosslyn and Alper, 1977, for procedural and statistical details). We asked people to image pairs of test items interacting in one of two ways. The second object named in a pair either was to be imaged appropriately scaled for size or was to be imaged shrunken in size. If the special properties of the quasi-pictorial images people report experiencing are encoded into memory, it should be more difficult later, upon recall, (1) to *identify* the second imaged object of a pair if it initially was imaged tiny, even when the first word's referent image is retrieved successfully, and (2) to *retrieve* an imaged object of a pair if few of its perceptual characteristics were encoded into memory, as seems likely if it was encoded in a greatly reduced size. If Neisser and Kerr (1973), Simon (1972), Byrne (1974), and others who imply that images are not quasi-pictorial representations that depict information are correct, of course, there should be no effects of how hard it is to see an imaged object. The following experiments are concerned with the effects of the quality of an image on later memory for the image's referent.

It seemed likely that if we simply asked subjects to remember words via imagery they would utilize other strategies also; this would obscure effects of imagery differences on memory. Pilot data lent support to this fear: In our pilot procedure, we asked subjects to try to remember each word by imaging it (at one of two subjective sizes); we explicitly requested that they eschew alternative learning methods. After the experiment, we queried these people regarding their ability to use *only* imagery in encoding pairs of words. Sadly, our subjects confessed to making use of a whole host of mnemonic techniques (such as rehearsing or making connecting sentences). These pilot subjects were not trying to be uncooperative, apparently, but claimed to find themselves compelled to encode material to the best of their ability in the face of foreknowledge of an impending test. Neisser and Kerr had adopted an incidental-learning tech-

---

*Keenan and Moore (1979) provide further cause for approaching the Neisser and Kerr results with caution; in their experiments, Keenan and Moore did find effects of visibility in an image on later memory for the imaged items.

nique in order to avoid this sort of problem, and we decided to follow suit.

In the first experiment of this series, subjects heard pairs of words and formed visual mental images of the named objects interacting in some way; half of the pairs were imaged with both objects at normal relative sizes, and half were pictured with the second object imaged at a tiny size. In this second condition, the subject was told that although he or she would know what the image of the second object represented, it should be reduced in size "so small as to appear as a dot." After constructing the images at correct relative sizes, the subjects simply rated the vividness of each of their images (using a standard seven-point scale). Following this, we surprised the subjects by either giving them the first word of each pair and asking for recall of the second or giving them the second word of each pair and asking for the first. (As usual, each pair occurred in each condition equally often over counterbalancing groups.) The results were straightforward: When the name of the tiny image was used as the recall cue, the normal-sized one was more poorly recalled than when both images were normal-sized; when the normal-sized image of a pair was the recall cue, memory was worse if the other image in the pair had been tiny than if it had been normal. The magnitude of the size effect was the same when either member of the pair was used as the recall cue.

In this first experiment we also analyzed the vividness ratings. Pairs including a reduced image were rated as being less vivid than pairs in which both objects were imaged at normal sizes. But, for some reason, subjects who were given the second item of the pair as the retrieval cue rated pairs as being less vivid in general than did subjects who received the first word as the recall cue. As the procedure for the two groups was identical until after all pairs had been rated, this finding is inexplicable. Further, we attempted to discover whether vividness was the cause or the effect in this situation, that is, whether the observed memory differences were caused by the differences in vividness, which were altered indirectly by manipulating size, or by differences in recognizing objects that are small per se (regardless of their vividness). We attempted to distinguish between these alternatives by performing a stepwise multiple-regression analysis. We entered cue type (first or second word), counterbalancing group, size, and vividness as independent variables, on which were regressed the memory data. The results were clear-cut: Only cue type and size accounted for respectable shares of the variance. Notably, when all other factors were partialed out, vividness had virtually no correlation with memory performance. In fact, vividness accounted for the least variance of any of the four independent variables (whereas cue type—first or second word—accounted for the most, with size coming next in importance).

These results support the notion that a property of quasi-pictorial images, their apparent size, has a functional role in memory. Smaller things seem to be more difficult to identify, in imagery as well as in perception. This conclusion is consistent with the earlier finding that more time is required to see properties of subjectively small, as compared with large, visual images. Another property of quasi-pictorial images, their apparent vividness, seems here to have no real memorial consequences in and of itself. Although smaller images tended to be reported as being less vivid, it was not this lack of vividness that was responsible for subsequent recall difficulties. This finding is not surprising given some of the subjects' remarks after the experiment. Some subjects interpreted vividness to mean something like "brightness"; others seemed to ignore brightness and assess vividness by the number of visible details on the image. While we predict that the latter sort of vividness ought to covary with size, we have no reason at present to make the same prediction for the former sort.

Interpretation of the vividness findings is further complicated by the disparity between the two groups, which differed only in the type of recall cue; both groups rated the pairs according to exactly the same instructions. Sheehan and Neisser (1969) discovered that the reported vividness of imagery can be manipulated by a number of subtle factors, such as who is the experimenter. Thus, I do not wish to attach too much importance to the difference in mean reported vividness between the two groups. Rated vividness seems to be a particularly sticky measure, for reasons that will be discussed in chapters 9 and 10.

One who does not believe that functional (nonepiphenomenal) quasi-pictorial representations underlie the experience of imagery might offer the following criticism: When the subject is told that one of the objects in an imaged pair is reduced in size, the relationships between the objects is very different from those produced when no size reduction is called for. For example, if one is to image a woman and a rock interacting in some way, the relationship one forms between the two may be quite different if the rock is supposed to be imaged appropriately scaled (she might be sitting on it) than if it is supposed to be imaged at a tiny size (it might be a dot in her hand). A tiny version of almost anything could be represented by the latter predicate, but only a limited number of things are likely to be supporting a sitting woman in the first—making it easier to guess what was a forgotten word. Memory differences, then, might be attributable to differences in the relationship encoded between objects when the second is small or large, and not to differences in size as such. The next experiment controlled for this possibility by specifying the relationships to be imaged.

Subjects in the second experiment first read sentences, each describing an interaction between two objects; their task was to image each scene or event and rate the vividness of each image. For half of the sentences, the second object was to be imaged at a tiny size, whereas for the other half of the sentences it was to be imaged at a normal size relative to the first object; as usual, each sentence occurred in each condition equally often across counterbalancing groups.

Consistent with our previous findings, more words were recalled when they were imaged at a normal relative size than when they were pictured at a tiny size. Do the results of this experiment sew up the argument that size qua size is the critical determinant of memory in this situation? A critic might still balk at this conclusion, and offer a straightforward counterinterpretation: Our subjects might have decided not to image an object at the size of a dot, but instead simply to forget about the object as such and just image a dot. Even if this situation occurred, it seems hardly different from Neisser and Kerr's Concealed condition, in which one of the objects was not supposed to be visible in any form in the image. This point is debatable, however, and seems best resolved via empirical means rather than through force of argument.

In the third experiment of this series, we took pains to ensure that both objects of an imaged pair were in fact present in the image. Instead of asking people to image smaller objects at a "dot" size, we now asked them to image the objects at the relative sizes of a nickel and a pie plate. It was stressed that subjects should always image each object, even if the image was very small. Otherwise the method and procedure were identical with those used in the first experiment for the group receiving the first words of the pairs as recall cues.

The results were straightforward: Even when subjects are told to be sure that a smaller image is still identifiable, it is later recalled more poorly. Unfortunately, this result still does not guarantee that the memory deficits were due to problems in later recognition of a poorly encoded subjectively small image. In one of the experiments described in the previous section we found that subjectively smaller images were formed more quickly than larger images. Thus, one could argue that less work, less "depth of processing," is involved in imaging pairs that include a smaller member. Since less effort in encoding is associated with poorer memory (see Craik, 1973; Craik and Lockhart, 1972), we need not appeal to properties of quasi-pictorial images to explain these results. The next experiment was an attempt to eliminate this alternative explanation.

In this experiment, subjects first imaged both objects at normal sizes. On half of the trials, subjects then reduced the size of one of the images of the pair (to the relative size of a nickel compared to a pie plate). On the remaining trials, in contrast, the sizes of the images were not altered. After adjusting the size, if need be, subjects again rated the vividness of the images. Thus, *more* effort now was associated with pairs that included smaller images. In addition to working harder to produce smaller images, subjects now imaged reduced sizes only for a portion of a trial. Even when one member was ultimately reduced in size, the first, larger image should have left a memory trace, but a relatively "diluted" one since the larger image was preserved only for a short time. Both of these factors should have reduced the effects of image size. Thus, if subjects still remembered pairs with small images more poorly than pairs with normal images, we would have reasonably firm grounds for concluding that size qua size of images does in fact affect memory.

The results of this experiment were not very dramatic but clear: Although only a small difference was obtained, pairs including a reduced image again were statistically significantly more difficult to recall. We were not surprised that size had a relatively small impact on memorability in this experiment, for the reasons noted above. The results suggested, however, that fewer details of an image were effectively encoded if it was reduced instead of retained at a larger size. When an image was not reduced, more details may have been available for encoding for the full amount of time the image was maintained, thus making the image more easily identifiable when later retrieved.

2.3.1 Conclusions from the Memory Experiments

Objects imaged at subjectively small sizes were more difficult to remember. This effect was not due to differences in the encoded relations, nor was it an artifact of ease of forming the image. Subjects in these sorts of experiments often claim to retrieve the image and inspect it when attempting to recall the encoded word. If so, then it is not surprising that people have more difficulty in recalling items encoded as small images: these images are harder to see, to identify, at the time of retrieval. The present findings, then, seem to contradict the claim that images are not quasi-pictorial representations that depict information. If objects one cannot even see in one's images are nonetheless fully represented propositionally, or "spatially"—as Neisser and Kerr claim—it would seem reasonable to suppose that the same should be true of objects one can barely see. And if the properties of the quasi-pictorial images we experience (such as "introspective visibility") are irrelevant for retrieving concealed objects, then we have no reason to expect diminished size to affect retrievability of imaged objects. The current findings, then, seem to run counter to the notion that the functional component of imaging is an abstract spatial representation. Neisser and Kerr could attempt to explain these results by claiming that smaller images are "less noticeable features of a layout" than larger ones. One's "plans" for searching such a layout presumably result in "overlooking" objects encoded as smaller images (Neisser, personal communication; see Neisser, 1976). It is not clear, however, why one should not encounter the same sorts of difficulties when retrieving encodings of images of concealed objects. This expectation is, of course, exactly contrary to Neisser and Kerr's predictions.

I wish to leave the reader with one caveat: The effect found in the foregoing experiments is not a large one. It was overwhelmed when pilot subjects intentionally tried to encode the items in anticipation of a memory test. Further, in an additional experiment not described here we combined all of the controls used in the last three experiments; although we found a trend in the right direction (pairs including a reduced image being recalled more poorly), the effect was not significant. This finding was not surprising, as we had stacked the cards strongly against ourselves (requiring shrinking induced greater depth of processing, reading sentences may have produced auxiliary encodings, and so on); the combined "noise" induced by each manipulation may have simply overshadowed the effect. Thus, although the present results support the claim that quasi-pictorial image representations are not simply epiphenomenal, they do not allow us to conclude that these representations normally play a major role in memory for verbal material (as will be discussed later). Nonetheless, our findings do tell us something about how images represent information, and what they tell us places constraints on theories of imagery and of memory in general.

2.4 Measuring the Visual Angle of the Mind's Eye

Probably the most important property of images is their purportedly spatial structure, which is usually described as being like that of a percept. That is, spatial information is supposedly represented in the same way in perception and imagination. If so, then it makes sense to think of visual images as having only a limited spatial extent. This is an especially reasonable conjecture if images do in fact occur in the same central structures that represent what we see (see Paivio, 1971; Segal and Fusella, 1970), since these internal structures need only represent input from a limited arc (delineated by the limited scope of the eyes). The following experiments investigate the idea that images are limited in spatial extent, and that the "maximal subjective size" of images is constrained by the spatial medium that supports imagery representations.

Although it is not clear what it would mean for images to extend indefinitely, the only earlier evidence that they do not is very indirect. This evidence comes from the first experiment described in section 2.2, in which I asked people to image an animal, such as a rabbit, as if it were next to an appropriately scaled elephant or fly. People reported later that the elephant "took up most of the room," leaving only a little for a tiny image of a rabbit; the fly, in contrast, took up relatively little room, leaving plenty for imaging a seemingly larger rabbit. As described earlier, these people required more time to see properties (such as, the nose) of an imaged rabbit when it was next to an elephant than when it was next to a fly, reportedly because properties were harder to see on subjectively smaller images. This finding was reversed when people were asked to image the fly huge and the elephant tiny. These introspections and consistent reaction time data suggest that the medium in which one forms visual images is spatially bounded; if it were not, the rabbit could have been the same subjective size independent of the relative size of the adjacent image.

Most of the experiments in this series make use of a variation of the same task: People were asked to shut their eyes and form a visual image of a given object (which was either named or shown) as if it were being seen far off in the distance. They then were requested to imagine that they were moving toward the object, and asked whether it seemed to loom larger as they moved closer; all subjects included in the experiments said that it did. The subject was then asked whether there came a point when he or she could not see all of the object at once; all subjects reported this effect. The subject was then requested to "stop mentally walking" at just the point at which the object seemed to begin to overflow, where not all of its parts were clearly "visible at a single glance of the mind's eye." At this point, the subject was asked to estimate how far away the object would be if he or she were actually seeing it at that subjective size. That is, I wanted to know at what distance a real object would subtend the same visual angle as the imaged object seemed to subtend at the "point of over-flow." This estimate of distance was the dependent measure.

If the spatial extent of images is in fact limited by the structure in which they occur, which presumably has a constant "size," then the larger the actual size of the imaged object, the farther away it should seem at the point of overflow. This prediction was tested by first discovering which of a set of variables (such as the height, width, longest axis) correlated most highly with the distance estimates. I expected that the largest obtainable measure of extent would correlate most highly (for example, longest axis instead of height). Furthermore, I expected a linear relationship between this measure and the distance estimates. In addition, if images are spa-tially constrained by the representational structure, then the "visual angle" at the point of overflow should remain constant for different-sized objects. This claim was examined by calculating the "visual angle" at points along the best-fitting function relating actual size of the stimulus and distance at the point of overflow.

Each subject was interviewed after participating, and no subject in any of the following experiments deduced the purposes of the experiment. Some subjects did realize after participating that larger objects seemed to overflow at greater distances, but no subject inferred or realized through introspection that the experiment was designed to measure the angle sub-tended by images at the point of overflow. This experimental task was dif-ficult, and not all subjects tested felt they could perform this task reliably; data were discarded from subjects who claimed they could not complete the experiment (see Kosslyn, 1978a, for procedural and statistical details as well as further information about numbers of subjects discarded and the like).

In the first experiment of the series, people were simply handed a list of animals with their respective heights and lengths. These people per-formed the "mental walk" task described above, and simply wrote down estimated distance, in feet and inches, at the point of overflow. The fifteen stimulus animals were selected so that a range of sizes was represented

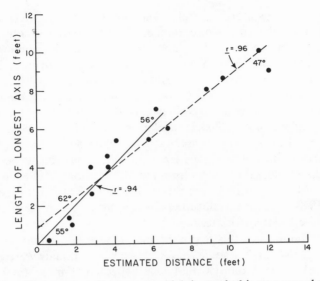

Figure 3.20. The average distance at which imaged objects seemed to overflow when subjects imaged animals from long-term memory.

(from mouse to elephant); animals were chosen so that heights and lengths were not highly correlated (for example, alligator, giraffe, turtle, kangaroo, goat, boar). The names of these animals were listed in a random order on a sheet; to the right of each name was listed the height and length of the exemplar we wanted the subject to use in the task. The sizes listed were those thought to be typical for the beasts, as assessed by informal consensus among four people.

A mean distance for each stimulus item was calculated. These means were treated as the dependent variable in a step-wise multiple-regression analysis. The height, length, and longest axis (the height or length, whichever was largest) were entered as independent variables on which were regressed the distance estimates. The results were as follows: First, the longest axis accounted for more variance in the distance estimates than did the other two variables. Second, the correlation between the longest axis and distance estimates was very high, $r = .96$; as expected, distance estimates increased with increasing size of the longest axis. As is visible in figure 3.20, however, the angle calculated along the best-fitting function (the dashed line) did not remain constant, but was smaller for larger animals. This effect seemed entirely due to the very largest animals, however; when only the smallest eleven animals were analyzed, the angle along the best-fitting function (the solid line) did remain constant.*

*The angle was calculated twice along each function, once at the upper end and once at the lower end; on all graphs in this section, angles were calculated at the nearest integer distance greater than that for the smallest object and at the nearest integer distance smaller than that for the largest object.

In order to assess more carefully whether the angle in fact varied systematically with the size of the animals, I performed a second analysis.
First, the mean angle for each animal was calculated (by pooling the subjects' estimates), and then these angles were simply correlated with the
length of the longest axes. This correlation was only $r = .21$; angles did
not systematically vary with the size of the imaged object. Finally, separate correlations were calculated between the longest axes and each subject's distance estimates. These correlations ranged from .78 to .97 with a
median of .90. Further, although the individual data were noisy, the shape
of the function did not vary systematically from person to person. The
averaged data reflect the results from individual subjects in a similar fashion for all of the experiments in this series, and the reader is referred to
Kosslyn (1978a) for data about the range of variability in correlations and
angles for the following experiments.

The basic findings of this first experiment were consistent with my expectations. However, for some reason, the largest animals were estimated
as being farther away than I would have expected. Three straightforward
explanations of this came to mind: First, it could be that the angle is
smaller for larger animals, perhaps because people know more details
about these beasts and hence they are more difficult to image. The low
correlations between animal size and angle counter this conjecture,
however. Second, perhaps there is some kind of systematic error in using
feet and inches to estimate distance—people do not necessarily use the
number scale in a linear manner (see Banks and Hill, 1974). Third, perhaps the problem lies in differences in memories for different-sized animals: Large beasts are almost always seen from a relatively long distance
(in zoos or circuses), and this fact may affect distance estimates somehow
(for example, they may be imaged with fuzzy borders, making it difficult
to make sure the imaged animal is the size indicated; if subjects imaged
overly large animals, the angle calculated would underestimate the actual
angle). If any of these factors is important, the estimate of the maximal
angle could be awry. The next experiment eliminates the last two of these
possible sources of error.

This experiment differed from the first one in two major ways: First,
subjects were shown pictures drawn at different sizes, and asked to image
these pictures in the mental-walk/distance-estimation task. Second, subjects were not asked to make verbal estimates of distance at the point of
overflow. Instead, they indicated distance by positioning a tripod apparatus the appropriate distance from a blank wall. These methodological
changes remove possible sources of error due to understanding and estimating size in terms of feet and inches; in addition, the borders of the stimuli were all sharply defined.

Line drawings of thirteen different animals were used as stimuli. The
longest axis that could be drawn across these animals varied from fifty

inches (for the elephant) to seven inches (for the rabbit). The drawings were done with a black felt pen on white paper and contained all of the obvious features of the animal, but were only minimally shaded. Larger animals were drawn larger than smaller ones, although the actual proportional sizes were not preserved (for example, the elephant was only about twice as large as the lion). As before, the stimuli were selected such that height and width varied considerably and were not highly correlated with one another. In addition, a tripod apparatus was constructed for this experiment. This apparatus had a chin rest on a tripod that was adjustable for height; a plumb line hung down directly below the edge of the subject's chin, allowing easy measurement of how far his or her eyes were from a wall.

Subjects were shown the drawings one at a time (in a random order) and were asked to study each picture until they could form a vivid mental image of it with their eyes closed. Subjects were to learn to image a picture by studying it, imaging it, and then comparing their image to the picture; this procedure was to be repeated until the subject's mental image was as vivid and accurate as possible. Following this, the drawing was removed from sight and the subject was asked to perform the mental-walk/distance-estimation task with it. That is, the subjects were asked to image walking toward the drawing and to stop when the image of it seemed to overflow. Subjects externalized their estimates of distance at the point of overflow by positioning the tripod the appropriate distance from a white wall.

Data were analyzed as before. In addition to height, length, and longest axis, the "greatest extent" was now also included as an independent variable in the regression equation. The "greatest extent" was the single longest line that could be drawn through a picture; since this line always was a diagonal, I shall refer to it as the "diagonal" in order to keep it distinct from longest axis (height or length, whichever was longer).

The diagonal proved to account for the most variance in the distance estimates, and the correlation between the two was $r = .95$; as before, distance increased linearly with size (in this case, as measured by the diagonal). In addition, as is evident in figure 3.21, the angles calculated along the best-fitting function remained fairly constant at around 20 degrees. It was a surprise that this angle was about half the size of the angle estimated in the first experiment. This was true even though the lengths of the diagonals were used in calculating the angles, which were larger than the corresponding "longest axis" measure used before; if longest axes had been used here, an even smaller (although only slightly smaller) estimate of the size of the angle would have been obtained. There are numerous possible explanations for the discrepancy in obtained angles. The next experiment was designed to investigate two of the more straightforward accounts.

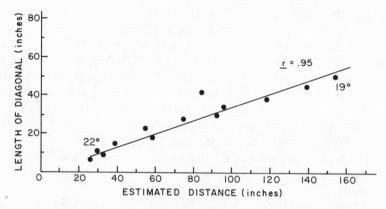

Figure 3.21. The average distance at which imaged objects seemed to overflow when subjects imaged line drawings of animals.

The drawings used in the previous experiment were of familiar objects. These drawings, however, tended to be smaller than the actual objects. Thus, the subjects' world-knowledge may have intruded into this task, causing the animals to be imaged larger than drawn. If so, then the size of the angle at the point of overflow would have been underestimated by using the actual sizes of the drawings. In addition to this possibility, these line drawings may have required more material to be "filled in" than did ordinary images evoked from long-term memory, such as were used in the first experiment of the series; the ordinary images of real animals may have been fuzzier, either because of the longer elapsed time between seeing the animal and imaging it, or because properties of real animals simply are not as sharply delineated as were the details of the line drawings. Thus, if there is only a limited amount of energy or "processing capacity" with which to form images, more filled-in images may not be able to be displayed over as large an area. If so, then we might expect blank, featureless figures to be imaged at relatively large sizes. Further, if amount to be filled in is in fact the key variable, then we might expect area—not greatest extent—to constrain subjective size.

Thus, in the next experiment the procedure of the previous experiment was repeated, but featureless black rectangles of various dimensions were used as stimuli instead of line drawings of animals. These objects had no prior semantic reference to systematically distort their imaged sizes, were utterly without detail, and allowed assessment of the role of area in determining the distance estimates in our mental-walk task.

Data were analyzed as in the previous experiment, except that area was now entered as another independent variable in the regression equation. The results were virtually identical to those obtained with line drawings as stimuli: The diagonal again correlated most highly with distance estimates, and distance increased linearly with the size of diagonal, $r = .96$. In addition, the angles calculated along the best-fitting linear function remained constant at around 20 degrees. These findings are evident in figure 3.22.

These results seem to indicate that intrusion of real-world knowledge did not cause the smaller size of the angle measured in the experiment in which subjects imaged line drawings. Nor was the number of details responsible for the disparity in angles; the rectangles were entirely homogeneous and without detail, but nonetheless subtended the same angle at the point of overflow as did the line drawings. One could argue, however, that "number of details" is the wrong variable. The amount of surface to be filled or the like may be more appropriate; however, this kind of metric would lead us to expect the rectangles to be imaged smaller—not larger—than the line drawings, which was not true. In addition, the finding that the diagonal—not area—accounted for the most variance in the distance estimates is inconsistent with such a capacity-limit explanation.

There are at least six plausible explanations for the disparity in the size of the angles obtained in the different experiments. The following experiment included controls for three possible sources of variation, and was designed to investigate the remaining three. The three factors controlled were are follows:

1. The previous experiments involved different subjects and experimenters; perhaps the experiments unwittingly encouraged different criteria for overflowing, or perhaps due to the luck of the draw the people in the different experiments had very different mental visual fields. There is evidence that different experimenters sometimes inadvertently influence subjects' ratings of image vividness (see Sheehan and Neisser, 1969) and

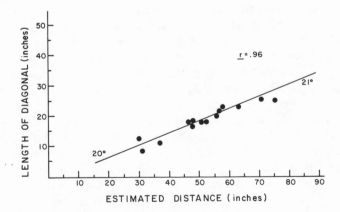

Figure 3.22. The average distance at which imaged objects seemed to overflow when subjects imaged black rectangles.

that subjects vary along a number of other imagery dimensions (see Richardson, 1969). So, stimuli were now used from each previous experiment with the same subjects and experimenter.

2. Different estimation procedures were used in the previous experiments. In the present experiment, people were trained on distance estimation first, and then reported distances as in the first experiment of the series. This procedure eliminated any opportunity to use possible visual cues on the wall as an aid in making distance estimations.

3. The different materials in the previous experiments may have led subjects to adopt different criteria for deciding when an image had "overflowed." Because, for example, images of remembered real three-dimensional animals may have fuzzier edges than drawings, people may have allowed three-dimensional images to overflow more before deciding that the image had in fact overflowed. In this experiment, subjects were urged to use the same criterion of "overflow" for each set of stimuli.

The three factors investigated were as follows:

1. Subjects in the first experiment of the series had to adjust the size of the imaged animal from written specifications. Perhaps subjects tend to systematically underestimate the extent of a "foot" when forming images, but do not underestimate extent when assessing distance. If so, then we should also find a relatively large angle when subjects are shown a small drawing with its dimensions labeled in terms of feet and inches and are asked to image this drawing at the indicated size. The following experiment included a new set of stimuli like these; these stimuli differed from the line drawings of animals used in the second experiment only by being smaller and having labeled size dimensions. If these stimuli seem to be imaged the same size as the stimuli of the first experiment (names of animals and associated sizes) at the point of overflow, then the familiarity of the "real images" of the first experiment, their three-dimensionality, the amount of elapsed time since seeing the referent, and so on probably were not the critical variables that resulted in the larger "visual angle."

2. The images in the second and third experiments may in fact have been more difficult to form. If so, then perhaps less processing capacity was available for imaging larger extents. The fact that area and number of details seemed irrelevant may only show that these measures do not really reflect psychological complexity (for example, perhaps the additional work of filling in the rectangles completely just compensated for the additional work required to delineate the lines of a drawing). This problem is circumvented in the next experiment by simply asking the subjects to rate the complexity of each image and the difficulty of using it in performing the mental-walk task. If we find smaller angles for stimuli rated high in complexity and/or difficulty, this would suggest that something like processing-capacity limitations may constrain the subjective extent of images.

3. Finally, I speculated that the earlier size specifications were systematically too large for most people's conceptions of the animals. If so, then the size of the objects may have been overestimated when the angle was calculated, resulting in an overestimate of the size of the "visual angle of the mind's eye." Thus, these subjects were asked simply to indicate whether the sizes were too large, too small, or about right for each stimulus where sizes were specified in feet and inches.

This next experiment also was designed to test two possible reasons why the angle at the point of overflow did not remain constant for different-sized animals in the first experiment of the series. Recall that larger beasts seem to overflow at greater-than-expected distances (see figure 3.20). In the subsequent experiments the stimuli by necessity were appreciably smaller than the largest animals named in the first experiment; perhaps large things per se overflow at smaller angles. In order to investigate this, the new small labeled drawings were constructed to cover the same range of sizes as the stimuli used in the first experiment. In addition, in the first experiment distance was analyzed as a function of the longest axis, since the greatest extent could not be calculated. In this experiment both variables could be considered separately with the small labeled drawings; perhaps the difference between greatest extent and longest axis increases dramatically for larger animals, and the angle seemed to become smaller with larger animals in the first experiment simply because the longest axis was used in the analysis.

In this experiment, ten stimuli were selected from each of the previously used stimulus sets, with the full range of sizes represented. In addition, ten new stimuli were constructed, consisting of small line drawings of animals, each drawn on a separate white sheet with a black felt pen. The drawings were all about the same size, no more than about six inches per side, and included arrows indicating specifications, in feet and inches, labeling the vertical and horizontal axes of the animal. These new drawings included about the same amount of detail as did the drawings used in the second experiment of this series.

Before beginning the experiment proper, the subjects were trained in distance estimation. This task proved to be surprisingly easy for most people, leading me to suspect that errors in distance estimation probably were not very extreme in the earlier experiments. After estimation training, the subjects were given the standard instructions on how to perform the mental-walk/distance-estimation task. Following the instructions, however, it was emphasized that "overflow" meant being unable to see all edges of the entire imaged object in sharp focus at the same time. If the edges became at all fuzzy, the subject was to consider that the image had "overflowed." "Fuzzy" was defined as being akin to falling into peripheral vision, as occurs when an object moves from the front to the side; subjects agreed that at some point the object is not as sharply in focus as when it is straight ahead. It was this point, the subject was told, that the image should be taken to have begun to overflow. Thus, an extremely rigorous criterion for "overflowing" was stipulated, based on any part of the periphery of the image becoming indistinct. The subjects were urged to use this criterion in the same way for all of the different kinds of stimuli about to be presented.

Following this, the subjects were asked to perform the mental-walk/distance-estimation task with each of the stimuli in each of the four sets. As before, subjects were allowed to set their own pace proceeding through the items. After the stimuli were presented, the subjects were asked whether the specified sizes for each animal were too large, too small, or about right. I was interested in the possibility that I had previously systematically overestimated the sizes and subjects had imaged the animals smaller than I thought, resulting in an erroneous inference of a larger angle. Finally, after the subjects had performed the mental-walk task with all forty stimuli, they were presented the stimuli again in the same order, and were asked to image each stimulus and to rate the complexity of the image. In addition, these people were asked to rate how difficult it was to perform the mental-walk task with each stimulus.

As is evident in figure 3.23, the results essentially replicated the previous findings, again demonstrating that the estimated distance at the point of overflow increases linearly with the size of the imaged object. There were five important results of this experiment:

First, even with distance-estimation training, using the same subjects and same experimenter, and a presumably constant criterion for what it means to "overflow," the memory images used in the first experiment of the series again seemed to overflow at larger angles than did the images of large drawings or rectangles.

Second, the small labeled drawings also overflowed at a larger angle than did the large drawings or rectangles. Interestingly, the angle at the point of overflow obtained for the small labeled pictures was the same as that obtained with the memory images. The failure to find a difference in overall angle here argues that the disparity observed previously was not due to differences in the dimensionality (two dimensions versus three), familiarity, or color of the stimuli, nor to anything peculiar to long-term-memory versus short-term-memory images. The data argue that something about having to adjust an image in accordance with written size specifications results in larger angles; this could be due to people underestimating the size of a foot, problems in adjusting images and keeping the edges clear-cut, and so on.

Third, simply having to image an object in accordance with a written size specification did not result in the angle changing for different-sized animals; this did occur again with materials from the first experiment of the series, but not with the small labeled drawings. In addition, graphing

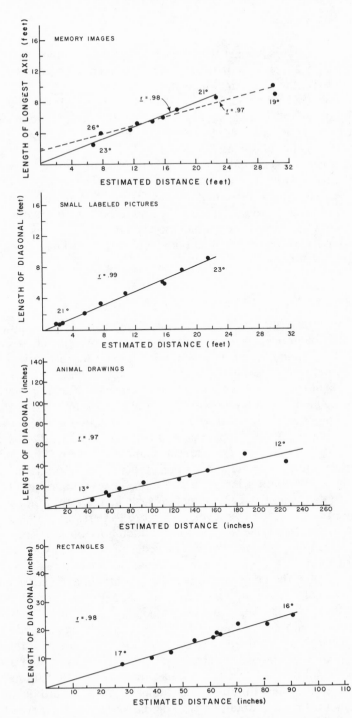

Figure 3.23. The average reported distance at which imaged objects seemed to overflow when subjects imaged four types of stimuli.

the distance estimates against the longest axis instead of the greatest extent (not shown here) did not result in the angle changing for different-sized animals (in the new small labeled drawings).

Fourth, the size of the angle did not decrease systematically with rated complexity or difficulty. Thus it seems unlikely that the maximum subjective size of the angle subtended by an imaged object is constrained by processing-capacity limitations as discussed earlier.

Finally, when subjects adopted the rigorous criterion of "overflowing," the angles estimated were generally smaller than those obtained before. Thus, it seems clear that "overflowing" is not an all-or-none thing, such as happens when a picture runs over the edge of a cathode-ray tube. Instead, images may fade progressively toward the edges until they are not evident; the point at which one decides that an imaged object is not apparent is not sharply defined.

2.4.1 Estimating the Shape of the Image Field

Images of large animals retrieved from long-term memory (stimuli from the first experiment of the series) have consistently overflowed at smaller subjective sizes than expected. These animals tend to be relatively tall, which could possibly have something to do with this finding. That is, although height alone did not account for an important share of the variance in distance estimations in the previous experiments, people did occasionally report having less "vertical room" than "horizontal room" in which to construct images. A very simple experiment was performed to examine this possibility and to attempt to infer the shape of the mental image field.

A group of additional students participated in the experimental task, using an imaged one-foot ruler as the stimulus. These people were to perform the mental-walk/distance-estimation task imaging the ruler as if it was mounted on a wall at eye level; they were to perform the task three times, once imaging the ruler as if it was mounted horizontally, once vertically, and once at a 45-degree angle. The order of condition was counterbalanced over subjects. Obtaining the same angles in all three conditions would indicate that the image space is circular; obtaining the largest angle in the horizontal condition, followed by diagonal and vertical, would mean that the space is like an oval on its side; an ordering of diagonal, horizontal, vertical would mean that the space is rectangular and so on.

The angles actually obtained were of 30, 27, and 28 degrees for the horizontal, vertical, and diagonal rulers, respectively. Although the horizontal angle is slightly larger than the vertical, the standard deviations were so large as to render this difference insignificant (the standard deviations of the angles for the horizontal, vertical, and diagonal rulers were 15, 14, and 13 degrees, respectively). Thus, the image field appears to be roughly round in shape. Even if the differences observed here were significant (say with the inclusion of vastly larger numbers of subjects), they were not large enough to account for the disparities in angle size found with images of real, remembered animals. Thus, at present there is no ready explanation of the variability in angle size found when people are asked to image named animals.

2.4.2 Validating the Methodology

Given the inconsistencies in the measurements of the visual angle of the mind's eye, one could wonder whether the technique itself is valid. Perhaps these results have nothing to do with processing a quasi-pictorial image, but merely are somehow based on people's "abstract knowledge" of the visual system. If this is true, it is not clear why there were differences in angles among the different materials nor why stimuli from the first experiment of the series continue to behave differently from the other materials. Nevertheless, it seemed important to control for this possibility. In an initial control, people were simply asked to estimate, without using imagery, how far away objects would be when they could no longer be seen at a single glance. Subjects found this a difficult task. Even if the objects themselves were not imaged, people reported imaging the extents "in the air," and using these images. Thus, this task was abandoned and I decided to validate the technique by obtaining converging results from other tasks. In one task subjects were asked to image a set of lines of known length and a line mentally constructed to be as long as possible without either end overflowing. The time required to scan the lines of known length was then used to calculate how many milliseconds were required to scan each additional degree of visual arc along an imaged line. These data were then used to infer the length of the longest nonoverflowing imaged line. Thus, because we know from previous experiments that scan time is a good indicator of spatial extent, scan time can be used here as a kind of "tape measure" to estimate the extent of the longest nonoverflowing imaged line. Because of the finding that the size of the angle varies with the definition of "overflow," care was taken here to define "overflow" in a stringent manner, attempting to induce these subjects to adopt the same strict criterion used by the people performing the mental walk task with an imaged ruler in the previous experiment. In addition, after they performed the scanning task, subjects were asked simply to motion with their hands how long the longest nonoverflowing line would have been had it actually been drawn on a surface a given distance away. By measuring the distance between the subject's hands, and knowing the distance from the hands to the face, it was easy to calculate a "visual angle." If it makes sense to suppose that the extent of mental images is limited by the structure in which they occur, similar estimates of the maximal extent should be obtained with all three techniques (given that the same criterion of "overflow" is used).*

The scanning experiment made use of the task requiring scanning an imaged line and classifying the case of an imaged letter (see the second experiment described in section 2.1). In this version of this task, subjects imaged a line with a different letter of the alphabet placed on each end; these letters were in upper or lower case or a combination of the two. The subject mentally focused on one end of the imaged line, and then "looked at" one of the two letters and categorized it according to case. If the letter was on the end of the line not being focused on, the subject was to scan across the line until it was clearly in view before responding. The effects of distance on scan time were calculated simply by subtracting categorization times obtained when the subject was focusing on the queried letter initially from those where the subject was initially focused on the wrong letter and had to scan across the image before responding.

The subjects first heard a number on a tape, at which point they saw two letters of the alphabet; they were to study the letters and try to remember them well enough to be able to make a visual mental image of them. Next, the subjects heard the word "cover," at which point the letters were concealed, and the subject positioned his or her chin in the chinrest mounted facing an array of four lines of different lengths and different colors. The color name presented next directed the subjects to study the line of that color. If none of the lines was drawn in that color, the subjects were to image a line "as long as possible without the ends overflowing the image." The word "image" directed the subjects to close their eyes and image the two letters as if they were placed on the respective ends of the line (the right letter of the pair on the right, and the left on the left). The subjects were asked to image the line at the length it had appeared when they had studied it. Next, the word "right" or "left" indicated on which end the subjects should mentally focus; they were to fixate on the letter on that end of the imaged line until hearing the final word of a trial. This word named one of the two letters in the image. The subjects were asked to look at the named letter, and see whether it was upper or lower case. They were to push one button if it was upper case, and another if it was lower case. If the letter was not on the end of the line they were focusing upon, they were to scan to the other end and to see the letter clearly before responding. To encourage actual scanning along the

*In point of fact, this experiment was conducted after we began to construct the model. Although all of the issues raised in chapters 3 and 4 were in fact formulated and studied (that is, the "decision tree" to be developed in chapter 4 was constructed and descended) before Phase II began, this history is not particularly important: the distinction between Phase I and Phase II is primarily a conceptual one, data collected in Phase I being used to delineate the broad class of acceptable models formulated during Phase II.

entire extent of the line, the subjects were asked to image a tiny black speck flying as quickly as possible along its length to the other end. They were instructed to perform this task as quickly as possible while keeping errors to a minimum.

After the test trials were presented, the subjects were asked to indicate with their hands held out at 45 centimeters how long their imaginary line would have been had it actually been drawn in the array. This length was measured by the experimenter.

As expected, people required more time to classify a letter they were not focusing upon at the time of probe. Mean scan times for each of the lines were obtained by subtracting the amount of time required to make classifications when no scanning was necessary from the time required when subjects had to scan. The left panel of figure 3.24 illustrates these data with the best-fitting linear function (calculated on the basis of the four known distances, using the method of least squares). As is evident, time to scan increased linearly with distance, replicating our previous experiments. (Actually, time increased with degrees of arc scanned, not with distance per se; but in this experiment there was only a negligible deviation from linear increases in distance with linear increases in arc.)

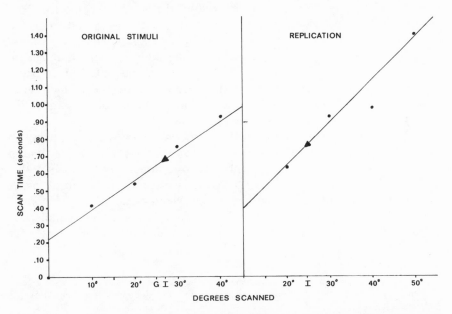

Figure 3.24.   Time to scan lines subtending different visual arcs. The mean scanning time for the longest possible nonoverflowing line is indicated by the filled triangle. The inferred angle is indicated by an *I* along the abscissa, and the *G* indicates the angle calculated from the subjects' gestures. The left and right panels illustrate data collected with different ranges of line lengths and different subjects.

The amount of time necessary to scan the longest nonoverflowing line is plotted at the appropriate point on the function, indicated by the filled triangle. Given that 17 milliseconds were required to scan each additional degree in this experiment, and that the intercept was 225 milliseconds, the fact that a mean of 682 milliseconds were required to scan the longest non-overflowing line implies that this line subtended approximately 27 degrees of "visual" arc. This estimate is quite close to the 30 degrees obtained in the mental-walk task with the horizontal ruler in the previous experiment. In addition, a "visual angle" was calculated on the basis of each person's gestured line length; the mean angle here was 25 degrees. These estimates were also very close to those obtained by extrapolating from the scan times. In fact, both estimates of the angle calculated here fall within the 99 percent confidence interval of that obtained previously with the mental-walk task with an imaged horizontal ruler.*

I worried that subjects in the scan task estimated their mean scan times for the actual lines and simply waited a mean amount of time before responding for the "longest nonoverflowing imaged line," or did indeed scan a longest nonoverflowing line but formed it to extend over a medium distance in response to demand characteristics. That is, the expected angle essentially was "bracketed" by making the physical lines extend over an equal range of arcs to either side of the angle expected from the results of the overflow task performed earlier with an imaged ruler. To eliminate this possible source of error the experiment was simply repeated, but now a new group of subjects imaged lines subtending 20, 30, 40, and 50 degrees of visual arc. The results are illustrated in the right panel of figure 3.24. The angle estimated here was 25 degrees, which replicates the earlier results beautifully, even with different subjects and a different range of stimulus lines actually presented.

Thus, the angle estimated from the previous mental-walk task using an imaged horizontal ruler was very similar to that derived from the time to scan an image of the longest possible nonoverflowing line. Further, this estimate was in close accord with that derived from the gestural task.† The results of the present experiment, then, lend credence to the mental-walk technique used previously. Whatever the faults of the mental-walk technique may be, it does not seem to have led us too grievously far astray.

---

*This experiment also provides further evidence that people can scan to overflowed parts of their images, replicating the findings reported above. I shall consider an account of this finding in chapter 8.

† It is interesting to note that about half of the subjects made their gestural estimates not by first moving their hands out to the specified distance from the face and then adjusting the distance between them, but instead by holding their hands up near the sides of their heads, at a given distance from their temples, and then simply moving their hands forward to the specified distance.

2.4.3 Conclusions from the Visual Angle Experiments

These experiments yielded five basic findings. First, larger objects seem to overflow at subjectively greater distances. This result supports the notion that there is only a limited "image space" in which visual images may be formed. This spatial medium might best be regarded as a kind of short-term-memory "visual buffer." Second, the absolute size of the angle varies depending upon the exact instructions and stimuli. Images seem to overflow gradually; the spatial medium may have the highest resolution near the center and become progressively coarser toward the edges. Third, given the same criterion of "overflow," very similar measures of the visual angle of the mind's eye are obtained from the mental-walk/distance-estimation task, a gestural estimate, and time to scan along an image of the longest possible nonoverflowing line. The two latter measures, then, serve to validate the mental-walk/distance-estimation task. Fourth, the maximal subjective size of images does not seem to be dictated by limited processing resources, as indicated by the failure of area, difficulty ratings, or complexity ratings to predict size of angle. Fifth, a given extent seems to overflow at about the same distance in a horizontal orientation as it does when imaged vertically or at an oblique angle (when a relatively strict criterion of "overflow" is used). This suggests that the shape of the highest-resolution portion of the image space is roughly circular, which was an unexpected finding (my intuition ran counter to this result when it was published, and later work by Finke and Kosslyn, 1980, demonstrated this intuition was not entirely spurious, as will be discussed later).

There were two major surprises in this series of experiments: First, the actual size of the angle was different for different stimuli. Larger angles were obtained when subjects were asked to form an image in accordance with a description than when they simply "internally reproduced" the appearance of an object shown at the beginning of the task. This was true if subjects were given only the names and sizes of stimulus animals or were shown small drawings with the to-be-imaged sizes indicated along the axes. Further, asking subjects to use an imaged one-foot ruler (which had not been shown immediately prior to the task) resulted in larger angles, as did asking subjects to image the longest possible nonoverflowing line (the extent of which was later inferred from scanning times and gestured extent). This result may be due to people systematically distorting the extent of a "foot," which might account for all results except those from the experiment in which people simply imaged the longest nonoverflowing line. I shall turn to this notion in some detail shortly. Alternatively, perhaps one simply forms sketchier images when the stimuli are described than when one "internally reproduces" previously seen stimuli without having to make any adjustments. Perhaps it is simply more difficult to discern the edges of sketchier images evoked by descriptions, and so it is difficult to tell when they have just begun to overflow; if so, then for these sketchier images a subject may adopt a less stringent criterion for deciding when the image has "overflowed." The way in which "overflow" was defined effectively shifted this criterion in our experiments, and it is possible that subjects in the second and third experiments set more strict criteria because the edges of the line drawings and rectangles were so sharply defined.

The second problem with the results was that the angle calculated along the best-fitting function relating size and estimated distance did not remain constant in experiments using images of animals retrieved from long-term memory (stimuli from the first experiment). It seemed possible that this result was due to the properties of the imagery-formation procedure and/or the distance-estimation task. Stevens (1975) reports that the exponent for length estimation in the Power Law is 1, indicating that people do not systematically distort length estimates with different extents. This may suggest that our subjects did not systematically distort the image size when the height and length were described. The results of psychophysical studies of distance estimates are less clear than those of length estimation, however. Early studies by Gibson and Bergman (1954) and Gibson, Bergman, and Purdy (1955) found people remarkably accurate in estimating distances; they concluded that psychological distance does in fact vary linearly with actual distance. However, this conclusion was soon challenged: If distance is estimated using apparent size in the frontal plane, the exponent is greater than 1, predicting overestimation of distance with increasing extents. But if distance is estimated along a surface (as would occur, for example, if one were "looking at the animal's feet on the ground"), the exponent is *less* than 1—predicting underestimation of distance with increasing extents. Further, the size of the exponent often varies with the range of distances and other variables (see Baird, 1970; Galanter and Galanter, 1973; Teghtsoonian and Teghtsoonian, 1969). We have no way of knowing exactly how subjects made their internal distance estimates. Fortunately, the results with the small labeled drawings in the fourth experiment of the series undercut this worry: These images spanned the same size range as the stimuli used in the first experiment, and yet the angle remained constant for different-sized animals. Unless the distance-estimation procedure was different for the two kinds of stimuli, which seems unlikely, the results of the first experiment, in which animals were simply named and their sizes presented, cannot be due to the estimation procedure per se. Because the criterion for "overflow" seems to be adjustable, however, the lack of a constant angle is not inexplicable: Perhaps people simply know less about remembered large animals, and hence do not bother to image them as "close" as possible to see every possible detail (but, because the image is sketchy, still move them relatively close, accounting for the generally larger angles with these stimuli).

In a way, the variability in sizes of angles, and even the failure always to find constant angles subtended by different-sized stimuli, are saving graces: If subjects had somehow discerned the purposes and predictions of these experiments—which they denied when queried afterward—and tried to confirm the hypotheses, these aberrations should not have occurred. That is, if subjects had simply applied some formula to the longest axis (or somehow calculated the greatest extent), there should have been nice regularity in the results, especially those of the fourth experiment, in which the same people participated in more than one task.

These findings, then, support the claim that images depict spatial properties. To say that an image is constrained by the spatial properties of the medium in which it occurs makes no sense if images do not in fact *depict* information, as characterized in the first section of this chapter.

3.0 CONCLUSIONS

The four classes of experiments described in this chapter converge in demonstrating that images are functional, quasi-pictorial representations, the special properties of which can affect cognitive processes. We would not expect the results obtained here if people represented all information in abstract list-structures and if such structures were used in anything like a straightforward way. In order to provide accounts of these results without an appeal to processing of quasi-pictorial images one would have to formulate not only ad hoc and post hoc models, but rather different ones for each set of results. The more parsimonious interpretation of these findings is simply to accept the notion that people have quasi-pictorial image representations and can use these representations in cognitive processing.

4. The Origins of Images

We now have abundant evidence that the experience of "having" an image reflects the presence of a functional quasi-pictorial representation in active memory. The next issues to be addressed are concerned with how images are represented when we are not aware of them, and how images are derived from these long-term memory representations. We can schematize the present research program as constructing a tree, on which the nodes correspond to issues and the branches correspond to alternative positions on the issues. Figure 4.1 illustrates this decision tree thus far. The second node, at the bottom of the branch representing the hypothesis that images are not epiphenomenal, represents the most basic issue of how images arise. On the one hand, the long-term memory representation of an image may consist of encoded perceptual information that is simply retrieved much as a slide is projected onto a screen. Perhaps images are stored as a set of "cell assemblies" or neural networks, and the only difference between the long-term memory representation and the active memory one is whether the cells are firing. On the other hand, images may not be simply played back or projected, but may be actively composed. In this case, the representation in long-term memory may be quite different from the one in active memory that underlies our experience of an image (for example, involving different sets of cells, one set exciting another when fired). As popular as is this latter view (see, for example, Neisser, 1967; Paivio, 1971), there is very little evidence that images are constructed, and even less evidence detailing the nature of this process.

On the face of things, two sorts of data might help us discover whether images are retrieved or composed. First, it might be possible to make inferences on the basis of the content of images. One tack has been to focus on the nature of the errors in our images, both of omission of details and of addition of spurious ones. As Pylyshyn (1973) points out, the portions of images that people forget do not seem to be arbitrary: we tend to leave out whole objects or complete parts of an object. However, this introspection could simply reflect the fact that we do not necessarily encode all the information about an object or scene. That is, deletion of parts in an

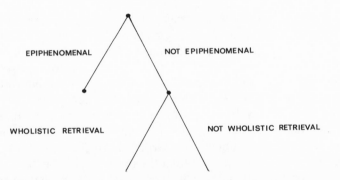

Figure 4.1. The decision tree illustrating the relationship between the new issue and that of chapter 3. Note that the new issue is not simply a refinement of the first, as would occur in "20 Questions." Rather, the second issue is predicated on a particular resolution of the first issue and builds on that position.

image could be due not to omission of a stored part during image construction but to an initial encoding failure; one simply may not have seen all the parts when initially viewing the imaged object or scene. This interpretation is weakened, though, by my observation that some people report being able to insert a forgotten portion of an image when reminded of its existence. This sort of argument rests on an uncritical acceptance of our ability to interpret and describe our introspections correctly, however, which is an oft-debated assumption (see, for example, Nisbett and Wilson, 1977). Furthermore, even if people can interpret their introspections reasonably well, the introspections about placing new material in an image do not rule out the possibility that one is simply *replacing* an impoverished image with a more detailed version—as opposed to actually integrating new parts into an existing image. Thus, simple reports about the contents of images do not seem sufficient to answer the kinds of questions about underlying mechanisms I am asking here.

The second kind of methodology one could use to study both the way in which images are formed in active memory and the nature of the representations in long-term memory involves measuring the time required to form different images. I have again found measuring reaction times to be an effective way of investigating the operation of the imagery representation system, and we have used this methodology extensively in the experiments described below.

1.0 ISSUE I

Are images stored in long-term memory in the same form as they occur in active memory, and simply retrieved when evoked? We began by trying to discover whether the imagery system is built such that images are stored intact and later simply retrieved from long-term memory. The first data that bear on this issue were originally used to provide a control in the experiments on detecting parts of images discussed in chapter 3, section 2.2. Recall that that experiment showed that subjectively larger images required more time to evoke than did smaller ones. One interpretation of these results is as follows: Because parts of larger images are easier to see, more details may be added to larger images because one can see where these parts belong. If so, then it makes sense that people require more time to construct subjectively larger, more detailed images—which then are inspected more quickly than the more easily constructed but impoverished subjectively smaller images. Alternatively, however, the effects of size on image-formation time might simply reflect how long it takes to decide that an image has been retrieved. That is, perhaps smaller images are denser, and hence they become sharper more quickly than larger ones or one sees their advent more easily than one detects larger, dimmer images. If so, then the smaller image will appear to be retrieved more quickly.

The next experiment was designed to allow us to contrast the two accounts of the time required to form images at different subjective sizes. If images are simply retrieved, and the denser the image the faster it reaches some "sharpness criterion," then people should report having formed images of more cluttered drawings more quickly than they report having formed images of more impoverished drawings. Alternatively, if images are composed by amalgamating information gleaned from multiple encodings, and if more "units" are encoded from—and later integrated into images of—more detailed drawings, then more detailed drawings should take more time to image.

In this experiment subjects first saw drawings of animals. Every animal appeared in two versions, one including many details and internal texture, and one relatively undetailed, as illustrated in figure 4.2. A subject saw a given drawing, it was removed, and the subject then was cued to image the drawing and push a button when the image was as sharp and clear as possible. Following this, the subject was to hold the image in mind and wait for a probe. The probe named a property that might or might not have been in the drawing (and hence in the image); the subject was to look for the probed property exactly as in the property-detection experiments discussed in chapter 3, section 2.2. After evaluating the image for the probed property, the subject was shown two drawings of the animal, one of which had in fact been imaged, and then asked to indicate which drawing he or she had seen previously. This last manipulation was included in an effort to ensure that the subjects closely attended to the details of the drawings, and also further served to obscure the fact that our real interest at this point was in the image-formation times. Incidentally, the subjects were never aware (when queried after the experiment) that the first

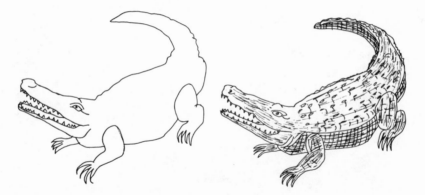

Figure 4.2.   Examples of undetailed and detailed versions of the drawings subjects were asked to image or recall.

button push, the image-formation time, was the measure of primary interest.

This experiment also included a control group, members of which were
never told anything about imagery but were simply asked to study the pictures and then were cued to push a button when they had "quickly reviewed the properties of the pictured animal, as if in preparation for a
test." This group was included to allow us to argue against demand characteristic explanations (such as that subjects deduced that more elaborate
drawings should require more time to recall simply because they are more
complex) and to counter possible propositionalist accounts of the results
from the imagery group (such as that more detailed drawings engendered
encoding of a lengthier list of properties which was subsequently activated).

The image-formation times (for the imagery group) and preparation
times (for the no-imagery group) are illustrated in figure 4.3. As is evident,
more detailed versions of the drawings required more time to image, but
not more time to "quickly review." The imagery results are exactly the
reverse of what one would predict if "density" were used to decide when
an image was completed: the denser drawings took more time—not less
—to image. These results allow us to argue that images are not simply
retrieved, simply played back in toto. The failure to find effects of complexity in the no-imagery control is important because it is inconsistent
with demand characteristic explanations of the imagery results. This result also allows us to argue against the notion that the imagery results
were really due to scanning through lists of properties, with more detailed
pictures having more entries on their lists. Presumably, just such a list
structure was formed in the control condition, but was scanned so quickly
as not to produce significant complexity effects; Atkinson and Juola
(1973) estimate that lists in long-term memory require only a few milli-

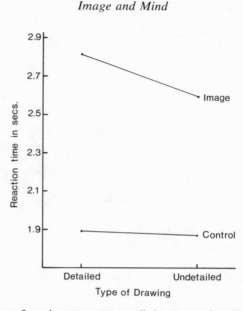

Figure 4.3.   Time to form images or to recall the properties of detailed and undetailed drawings.

seconds per item to scan, so the failure to find complexity effects here is not terribly surprising. Finally, none of these subjects reported deducing the hypothesis when queried after the experiment (although some in the imagery group reported noticing the effect when explicitly asked about it). I will defer discussing the results on time to inspect these images until chapter 7, which is exclusively concerned with this topic within the context of the model. (See Kosslyn, Reiser, Farah and Fliegel, in preparation, for details of the procedures and results for the experiments described in this chapter.)

After performing the foregoing experiment we realized that the results could be interpreted in an entirely different way: One could argue that people do in fact simply play back images, but that once the image is present they scan over it to see if all details are there. Thus, subjects take longer to respond after having retrieved larger images because more area must be scanned, and take longer to respond with images of more complex drawings because more details must be scanned across. If people do in fact insert missing parts when they discover a gap, then this counter interpretation is not consistent with the simple retrieval hypothesis being considered here. In this case, people would be using an initial image as a retrieval cue for inserting additional detail, for integrating multiple representations. But if people simply scan the image, and do not add any new parts as a consequence of their inspection, then the increases in times observed in the previous experiments say nothing at all about an image-construction process.

We next investigated the hypothesis that our previous findings really reflected time to scan images after retrieving them, rather than time to generate an image from representations of separate components. This experiment made use of two earlier findings: First, we knew that subjectively smaller images of simple drawings require less time to scan than do larger ones. This was demonstrated in the experiments with the schematic faces described in chapter 3. Second, other work had shown that parts of smaller versions of the line drawings used in the previous experiment do not require more time to see in an image than do parts of larger ones. (This was also true in the analogous perceptual experiment, where people actually looked at the pictures.)* We reasoned that if people simply scan more detailed images more thoroughly after retrieving them, not only should larger images require more time to evoke, but effects of detail should be greater with subjectively larger images (since more distance must be traversed between parts). New subjects were asked to image relatively large and small versions of the detailed and undetailed drawings illustrated in figure 4.2. Interestingly, detailed versions again required more time to image, but this difference was the same for both subjective sizes. In addition, there was no effect of size on image-formation times. This suggests that our subjects were not simply scanning the images after projecting them wholistically into active memory. The reader should note, however, that we now are faced with the task of explaining why there were no effects of subjective size here whereas we earlier found that it took more time to form subjectively larger images. As I will argue in chapter 6, much of the effect of image size is a consequence of how easily one can see where parts belong. Since parts were equally discriminable at the two sizes used here, there is no reason to believe that smaller images are less filled out than the larger ones. Further, since subjects were asked to verify properties of the image after evoking it, they were motivated to insert details into their images (as will be developed in chapter 6).

We are now in a position to reject the simplest class of models in which (*a*) images are stored in long-term memory in the same form as in active memory, and (*b*) images are always retrieved all of a piece when activated. The foregoing results, in conjunction with our earlier findings on effects of subjective size on image-formation time, are inconsistent with this view. We can dispatch this view so easily only because it is so simple

---

*It is interesting to note that other subjects rated the properties equally discriminable on the relatively large and small versions of these drawings—suggesting that our earlier effects of subjective size on ease of detecting properties were actually due to the discriminability of the properties, which decreased with smaller images of actual remembered animals.

and its implications so strong. More sophisticated (and hence less strong) alternative versions of this position are possible, but as far as I can tell all are subsumed by the following issue, which grows out of this one.

2.0 ISSUE II

Are images retrieved an arbitrary portion at a time or may they be generated from organized units? One interpretation of the finding that more complex pictures require more time to image is that images can be generated from separate components. However, one could argue with this inference: Perhaps images are stored integrally, but retrieving increasingly more detailed images somehow simply taxes the available processing capacity. If so, the foregoing results may not imply that one can construct an image from organized units; instead, they may simply reflect the fact that more material requires more time to retrieve. For example, images may be stored something like a set of points in a matrix, with more detailed images having more points. When retrieving images, one may retrieve arbitrarily selected points serially, or all points at once but with a larger distribution of times when more points are retrieved (because of limited processing capacity—see Townsend, 1972). In either case, images with more "points" will require more time to retrieve. This kind of "piecemeal retrieval" can be contrasted with a more generative scheme, wherein images may be stored as conglomerates of units which are individually retrieved and composed. This issue, then, defines another node in a decision tree, as illustrated in figure 4.4.

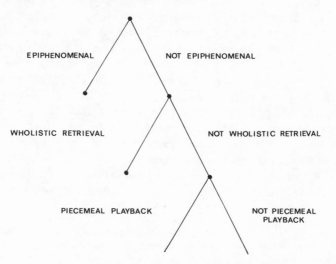

Figure 4.4. The decision tree illustrating another issue in relation to the previous ones.

If the "piecemeal retrieval" view is correct, then the simple amount of stored material will dictate how much time is required to form an image. Alternatively, if images may be composed from organized units, then the organization of a pattern, and not simply the amount of material present, should be critical in determining image-formation time. The following experiment was an attempt to demonstrate that the imagery system has the capacity to construct images from multiple underlying representations.* In this experiment we varied the number of underlying units in a pattern while holding constant the amount of material and the amount of area occluded. Rather than rely on differences in the actual stimuli to define relative numbers of units, as in the previous experiment, we used "conceptual" information to lead people to parse the exact same patterns into different numbers of units. Two groups of subjects were given the same set of geometric figures, but each group received different descriptions of the figures. The descriptions differed in terms of the number of units that were predicated. An important feature of this experiment is the fact that different people imaged patterns with different numbers of units. If the amount of time to form images of the figures increases when more units are predicated in the different descriptions, it is unlikely that this result is due to response to implicit task demands: Neither group was aware that other descriptions were used with another group to vary the number of units. (We also examined the ease of seeing different parts of the image when different descriptions were used, but these results are not relevant for present purposes.) If (*a*) conceptual information is used in defining units which are then encoded into memory and (*b*) these units are then composed together when an image of the pattern is formed, then the more units predicated, the more time ought to be required to generate the corresponding image.

We constructed ten geometric figures, which were composites of simple geometric shapes (triangles, squares, rectangles, parallelograms, and hexagons), as shown in figure 4.5. Each figure could be described in two alternative ways: Either in terms of a few large, overlapping shapes or in terms of a larger number of smaller, contiguous shapes. Two sets of these drawings were made, which differed only in which description was typed on the bottom of each page. Subjects were told to try to see the figures "in terms of" the parts named in the descriptions. Subjects were divided into two groups, each being told the general type of description which would accompany all of the figures in their notebook; for the group with many small, contiguous shapes named, we offered an analogy with tiles side-by-

---

*Although this experiment was designed to address this issue as here described (and hence is Phase I research), it was in fact conducted after we began to construct the model. This experiment replaced an earlier one that I discovered had severe methodological flaws; in the interests of the "converging evidence" approach, it seemed important to have a methodically sound experiment addressed to this question.

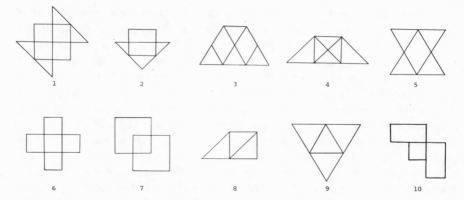

Figure 4.5. The ambiguous geometric forms that were imaged by subjects. Each pattern can be described in terms of either a set of contiguous forms or a set of overlapping forms.

side in a mosaic, and for the group with fewer, overlapping shapes, we made an analogy to clear plastic overlays. The subject was asked to turn to the page indicated by the first number of a trial, and to read the description on that page. This description was the same as that typed under the pattern, and prepared the subject to see the composition of the drawing on the next page. When the next number was presented, the subject was to turn to this drawing, and attempt to see it as it had been described. Following this, the subject was to cover the drawing with a piece of cardboard when the word "cover" occurred, and then to image the drawing when the word "image" occurred. As soon as the subject had a clear image of the drawing he or she was to push a button. (The subject was then to hold the image until the probe word appeared and to look for the probed part on the image; these results will be discussed in chapter 7).

In general, the group that received the descriptions predicating relatively many parts required more time to form images of the figures than the group receiving the descriptions predicating fewer parts. This result, however, might simply reflect some kind of unconscious demand characteristic or the like, especially if the experimenter somehow inadvertently urged the "few" group to respond faster in general. Thus, we used regression analysis to discover whether times increased systematically with the number of predicated units within and across each group. In order to perform this analysis we obtained a mean image formation time for each figure in each group and treated these means as the dependent variable. Not only did we enter the number of predicated units as an independent variable, but in order to investigate whether the complexity of the units themselves affected image-formation times, we entered a number of other measures of the complexity of the figure as a whole as independent variables. These measures included the subjects' ratings of the visual complexity of each figure (obtained after the experiment proper), the number of different lines in each figure, the number of different shapes, and the number of different stages that seemed to be required to form a figure from its described parts. Because several of these measures seemed likely to correlate highly with one another, we also performed partial correlations, controlling for all combinations of factors.

As illustrated in figure 4.6, the number of units predicated in the descriptions correlated very highly with the mean image-formation times, $r = .90$. Importantly, times increased linearly with increasing numbers of units even though different people contributed to the means for different numbers of units (as indicated by circles and triangles in the graph). This finding is inconsistent with a demand-characteristic interpretation of the results. Interestingly, none of the other variables correlated more than .39 with image-formation times.

The preferred interpretation of the foregoing results is that more units were encoded when more were predicated in the description, and hence more time was later taken to generate images composed of more units. Although it seems unlikely to me, however, there is a counter-interpretation of these results: It is possible that in this experiment images were

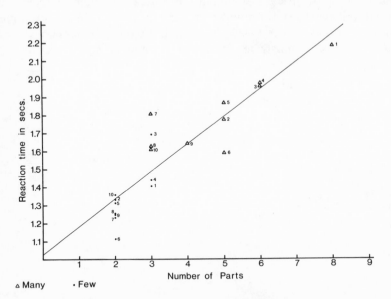

Figure 4.6. The time to form images of geometric patterns described in terms of different numbers of units. The numbers identify patterns illustrated in figure 4.5. Triangles indicate data from the group receiving descriptions in terms of many adjacent forms; circles indicate data from the group receiving descriptions in terms of few overlapping forms.

stored integrally but that units were imposed on them during the retrieval process. That is, in the previous experiment the description could have been stored along with an integral image of the pattern, and the description guided a kind of piecemeal retrieval at the time of image formation. If separately stored units cannot be amalgamated, then we will construct a very different model from the one we will construct if perceptual units can be stored separately and later integrated. In an effort to demonstrate that a valid model of imagery must be equipped to represent distinct units and later amalgamate them during image construction (recall the "capacities" approach), we performed another experiment. In this experiment we forced subjects to store units separately by presenting the units at different times. In addition, we now required subjects to remember the appearance of the stimuli for more than a few seconds. In the previous experiments it is possible that the nonactivated representation had some special properties because the subject knew it had to be retained only a brief while. We again varied the number of units underlying an imaged pattern while holding constant the amount of material and the area covered by the pattern. As in the previous experiment, ensuring that the exact same configuration of lines is produced by combining different numbers of units makes it unlikely that differences in image-formation times are due to differences in postretrieval scanning. In this experiment, subjects first learned to image a set of drawings of animals. The drawings were divided into three groups, defined as follows: In group one the animal was drawn on a single page, as illustrated at the top left of figure 4.7. In group two the

Figure 4.7. An illustration of the three presentation conditions. Animals could be presented drawn on a single page (upper left), on two pages (middle two drawings in the top row), or on five pages (upper right and bottom row).

animal was divided into two sections, each presented on a separate page. The first section always included the body, and the second contained appendages. Parts were presented in the correct relative portions of the pages, such that if the pages were aligned and held up to the light, the entire animal would be seen, as illustrated in the middle two drawings in the top row of figure 4.7. In the third group, the animal was divided into five sections, in a roughly hierarchical fashion working from the body outward, as illustrated in the rightmost drawing on the top line and the four drawings in the bottom line of figure 4.7. Again, if all five pages were aligned and held up to the light, the entire animal would be seen. There were twelve different drawings in all, and each subject received four in each presentation condition; as usual, using three groups of subjects allowed us to include each drawing in each presentation condition equally often.

In the first part of the experiment, the subject was to learn to form a vivid visual image of each animal upon being given its name. The subject would be able to see only one page at a time, and so would have to mentally "fuse" together animals drawn on more than one page. In the two- and five-part conditions, the experimenter first named the animal and told the subject how many pages were used in depicting it. The subject was then shown the body of the animal and was urged to take as much time as necessary to memorize exactly how that part looked. After the subject claimed to have encoded the material on the page, the experimenter removed that sheet and presented the next page in the series, asking the subject not only to memorize the material on this sheet but to fuse it mentally with the material pictured previously. Once the subject claimed to have memorized the two pages combined, this page was removed and the next presented (in the five-page condition) and so on until the subject claimed to have memorized the appearance of the composite animal.

After memorizing the drawings, the subjects participated in a reaction time task. They were asked to listen to a tape recording prepared for the set of drawings they had just memorized. Upon hearing an animal's name, they were to form a visual image of the drawing of that animal. This image was to be as vivid as possible, including the whole animal with all of its details and parts. We urged subjects to make all images equally vivid, no matter how they had learned them initially. As soon as the image was complete, the subject was to push a button. Following this, the subject was to maintain the image and wait for the next word to appear on the tape. This word would be the name of a property, which might or might not have been pictured in the drawing of the animal. The subject was to look at his or her image and decide as quickly as possible whether the property was present; the instructions used in this imagery-detection task were the same as those used in the experiments described in chapter 3.

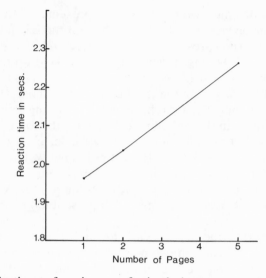

Figure 4.8.   The time to form images of animals drawn on one, two, or five pages.

The image-generation times are illustrated in figure 4.8. Surprisingly, times increased *linearly* with number of units. This result was not due to confusion about the appearance of the imaged object or difficulty in recognizing the individual parts: Not only did people claim to be able to integrate the parts into a whole image, but there were no differences in property-detection times among the three conditions. The finding of a linear increase with number of pages was so surprising that we repeated the experiment—and replicated the finding. Close examination revealed that individual subjects did *not* show linear increases in reaction times in the three conditions. This may have been because different people had different drawings in the different conditions (but all drawings appeared equally often in each presentation condition over subjects), because of sampling error (noise in the data), or because people spontaneously encoded different numbers of additional units in the different conditions, invalidating our estimate of how many units a given person had encoded. Presumably these idiosyncratic differences wash out when the data from different subjects are pooled and means are calculated. In any case, these results are difficult to explain if people cannot generate images from separate encodings: Not only does the sequential-presentation technique guarantee that separate units were encoded into memory, but since the same amount of material presumably was included in the image, and the same area was covered, we can conclude that the times really do reflect image-formation processes, and not just time to scan an image after retrieving it.

3.0 ISSUE III

Are images generated from only "depictive" information, or may they be generated using both "depictive" and "descriptive" information? The previous experiments seem to have eliminated a model of imagery that posits that images are stored only as single wholistic units that are later retrieved into active memory. The results reported above are most simply explained by positing that people can store separate units and amalgamate them into a single image, and that the more units there are, the more time it takes to form the image. Thus, at this point we have descended three levels in our decision tree, at each level adding another constraint to a theory of imagery. We have decided that the quasi-pictorial "surface image" is not epiphenomenal, that the system does not merely activate long-term memory representations whenever images are evoked, and that images can be formed from distinct units represented in long-term memory. The next issue, the next node in the decision tree, illustrated in figure 4.9, concerns the types of representations in long-term memory that can be used to form an image. The question now becomes: Should a model of imagery simply posit that images may be assembled from separate "de-

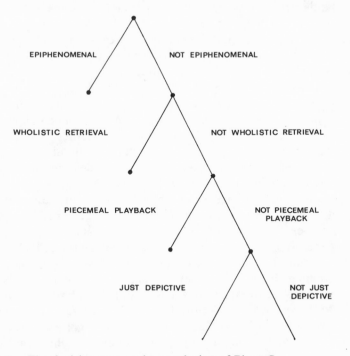

Figure 4.9. The decision tree at the conclusion of Phase I.

pictive" memories, or may construction involve an interplay between depictive and descriptive representations? That is, images could be composed only via a process like fitting together pieces of a puzzle, in which
the shape of the pieces alone dictates where they belong relative to each
other. Or, image generation may be able to proceed in a manner analogous
to placing photographs on a table in accordance with a description of the
configuration; here the relative positions are not dictated by the depictive
encodings alone, but also are indicated by more abstract descriptive
information.

In order to study this question, Louis Gomez and I began by conducting
a very simple experiment. Subjects were shown an array of capital X's
and told that they soon would read descriptions of similar stimuli and
would be asked to form mental images of these arrays. We asked our subjects to practice imaging the sample array (which was four rows by five
columns). Next, these subjects received two practice trials wherein they
were presented with a card that read "two rows of five," followed by one
reading "four columns of two." As soon as the subject read a card, he or
she was to form an image of X's like those in the sample, arranged as described; when the image was clearly in mind, the subject was to push a
button. We measured the time necessary to generate the image from the
moment the description was presented (in a tachistoscope). Descriptions
were written on the very bottom of a card, leaving plenty of room to
image the array. After the practice trials, we presented two test trials (the
order being counterbalanced over subjects). One trial required imaging an
array of X's as "three rows of six," and the other required "six columns of
three." Both descriptions produced the same image (although most subjects did not seem to realize this). Interestingly, more time (4.076 versus
3.800 seconds) was required when the array was described in terms of six
columns instead of three rows. We cannot say whether this was due to
having to generate more units, or to difficulty in generating columns instead of rows per se. In any case, the type of description clearly influenced how the image was generated.

This result is clear evidence that verbal/abstract information may work
in conjunction with depictive information in the image-generation process.
However, it does not demonstrate that *stored* verbal/abstract information
is used in generating images. In order to demonstrate this, Phil Greenbarg
and I used a variation of the task described above: The stimuli were
arrays containing three rows of letters, each row containing six items.
The letters were spaced equal distances from those above, below, to the
right, and to the left of them. We used two different arrays, one composed
of X's, and one of O's. The subjects were first shown one array and asked
to study it until they thought they could remember what was present.
Next the array was removed and the subject was told to think of that pattern as "three rows of six" or as "six columns of three" of the letter. At

the sound of a tone, the subject was to form a visual image of the array and to push a button when his or her image was complete. As before, a clock was started at the signal and stopped at the response, allowing us to measure image-formation time. All subjects received both arrays, one described each way; both arrays were presented in both serial orders and with both descriptions equally often over subjects, all conditions being completely counterbalanced.

We had a reason for asking the subjects to conceptualize an array only after it was removed. If the label had been given first, or along with the array, it might have affected how people encoded the perceptual information, and any later effects of description on time to generate an image might have been due simply to how many perceptual units had been encoded, more units (as would occur with the columns description) requiring more time. We were interested in demonstrating that both depictive and descriptive information are used at the time of generation itself. Thus, because we presented the description only after an array had been seen, any effects of the type of description can be ascribed to an interplay between depictive and descriptive memory representations per se. The results of this simple study were clear: More time was required to generate images of arrays conceptualized as six columns instead of three rows (3.422 versus 2.989 seconds). Thus, the way in which one conceptualizes an appearance seems to affect how one later regenerates that appearance in an image.

In the next experiment we attempted to discover whether people can use descriptive information to generate images of scenes in which objects are located at different distances. This seemed important because images seem specialized for depicting information about spatial extent, and an effective imagery system would provide for depicting the spatial relations noted in a description. We also wanted to distinguish the end-product of such image construction from the results of simply retrieving verbal information. This experiment not only allows us to examine how people image scenes containing multiple components arranged according to a description but also allows us to argue that a composite image was in fact generated. Subjects saw sets of two, three, or four different drawings with a description of how they were to be arranged, or they simply saw sets of descriptions. In both cases, interval distances among parts of the composite configuration were specified. Examples of the stimuli are shown in figure 4.10. The subjects first either learned to image the described array (in the imagery condition) or memorized the descriptions alone (in the verbalization condition). Following this, they participated in a reaction-time experiment in which they generated a given image or described a scene to themselves (depending on the condition). Again, time to perform the task was recorded. Next they were asked to verify a given spatial relation (such as whether one part was to the left of another). Half the time these

CUP SCENE
The rabbit is floating 5 feet above and 5 feet left of the cup.

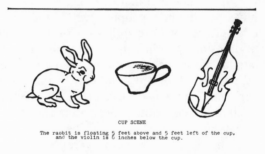

CUP SCENE
The rabbit is floating 5 feet above and 5 feet left of the cup,
and the violin is 6 inches below the cup.

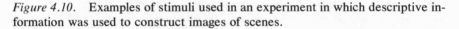

CUP SCENE
The rabbit is floating 5 feet above and 5 feet left of the cup.
The radio is 6 inches below the cup, and
the frying pan is 6 inches right of the cup.

Figure 4.10.   Examples of stimuli used in an experiment in which descriptive information was used to construct images of scenes.

probes were true and half the time they were false. Half of the true ones used the same relation used in the original descriptions and half used the converse relation and reversed the order of the nouns. The subjects in the imagery condition were told to be sure to see both objects clearly in their images, and to scan from one to the other in making the judgment. The subjects in the no-imagery condition were simply to evaluate the spatial relation as quickly as possible. We expected that more time would be required to assess things that were farther apart in the imagery condition but not in the no-imagery condition.

The results from the imagery group were straightforward: First, images containing more components took more time to generate. However, as is evident in figure 4.11, times did not increase linearly with increasing numbers of items. People reported grouping together closer items in the more

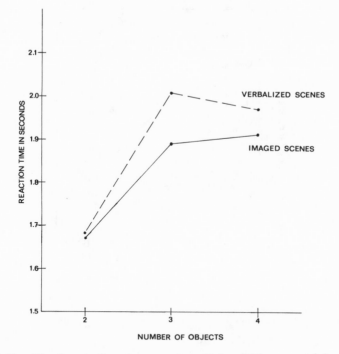

Figure 4.11. The time to form images or recall descriptions containing different numbers of objects.

complex images, which may have reduced the actual number of distinct units encoded. Second, as is illustrated in figure 4.12, evaluation times in the imagery group increased when the members of a queried pair were farther apart. Third, no less time was taken to verify a probe that used the same relation as appeared in the original description than to verify a probe that used the converse relation with the noun order reversed (for example, "*x* is six inches left of *y*" versus "*y* is six inches right of *x*"). Fourth, there were no differences in image-generation times in the two-item images where objects were described as being six inches versus five feet apart, although scanning times were longer in the latter case during the verification task. Thus, people apparently do not have to scan an image to place parts at different locations in it. This result again converges in demonstrating that subjects do not simply retrieve an image wholistically and scan it thereafter; if they did, we should have found distance effects in both the generation and the verification times.

The results for the verbal description group were as follows: First, verbal descriptions containing more items required more time to recall, not surprisingly. Also, retrieving such descriptions required more time in general than forming images, as is evident in figure 4.11. This result repli-

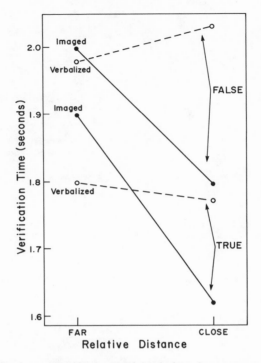

Figure 4.12. The time to verify the spatial relations between two objects imaged or described as relatively near or far apart.

cates a finding of the original experiment on scanning visual images, in which people who were asked to describe a picture took more time to retrieve descriptions of portions of it than people who simply scanned an image; presumably, verbal strings simply take more time to retrieve and process than do quasi-pictorial images (see also the results of Lea's 1975 experiment described in chapter 8). Interestingly, non-verbally encoded propositional information, which is not stored as sets of verbal statements, seems generally to require less time to retrieve than do images (as shown in the cat-claws versus cat-head experiment described in chapter 3, section 2.2.1, and in the first experiment of this series). Second, as is illustrated in figure 4.12, the distance between two objects did not effect evaluation times here, in contrast to the imagery results. This again replicates an earlier result (see chapter 3, section 2.1). Third, also in contrast to the imagery results, these subjects *did* respond faster if the probe contained the relation used in the original description. Finally, the time to recall a description did not depend on the stated distance among the objects. In summary, these results indicate that image generation is not to be confused with recalling a description; the two processes are distinct and have different consequences for subsequent processing of the activated information.

The results of these experiments, then, are good evidence that people can in fact use linguistic/descriptive information in generating images. This really does not seem surprising, given that most people claim to be able to image a novel scene described to them, like George Washington slapping Mr. Peanut on the back. Presumably, one constructs such an image by knowing what Messrs. Washington and Peanut look like and by knowing the meanings of the verb "slap" and the noun "back" and the relation "on" in this context. The problem was to gather data to verify this introspection and to constrain the form of an explicit model of image processing. The finding that one can image pairs of objects equally easily at different apparent distances (within the range studied here), for example, is not obvious and places real constraints on a theory of the mechanisms underlying image generation. In chapter 5 I will begin to develop a theory and model for how such processes may actually occur.

4.0 CONCLUSIONS

The experiments described here place certain constraints on a theory of how information underlying images is represented and processed. We must be able to account for how separate units are represented and then mapped, as units, into a composite surface image. In so doing, we must also explain how descriptive, "conceptual" information is used to amalgamate individual "depictive" perceptual memory encodings of appearance. We must also explain why generation time generally increases linearly with increasing numbers of units to be imaged. Further, our representation must be capable of producing images at different subjective sizes and at different "locations" in the display medium.

At this juncture the protomodel did not help me think of any additional fundamental issues, we had delimited a set of constraints on a theory of imagery, and the data collected thus far began to beg for a deeper and more thorough account than that offered heretofore. It was time to move on to Phase II of the project.

5. The Core Theory

The foregoing results of experiments place two sorts of constraints on theories of imagery. First, a theory should fall within the class delimited by the decisions made in descending the "decision tree." Second, a theory should provide straightforward accounts for the sum of the findings themselves. For example, the experiments on scanning images were conducted to demonstrate that images depict spatial extent, but in performing the experiments we also gathered data about scanning per se, data that must be explained in their own right. In addition, a theory should be precise enough to lead us to collect more data that will force further development of the theory. As I outline the structure of the theory and motivate the basic assumptions with data, I will take care to underline the essentials of the theory, and to distinguish this "core theory" from more tentative hypotheses.

1.0 FOUNDATIONS

Before presenting my theory, I wish to examine what I take to be its foundations and to explain some of the motivation behind why I did things as I did. This preliminary step seems especially important because of the almost haphazard, arbitrary approach to theorizing one sometimes sees in psychology, where a theory often seems more an expression of opinion than a work of science. The recent interest in the problem of formulating unique theories (that is, distinguishable in principle from alternative ones; see Anderson, 1978) has tended to support this inclination, which I find worrisome and counterproductive. Hence, I wish to begin at the beginning and develop the present theory on the basis of "first principles."

1.1 The Domain of the Theory

Before we can even begin to discuss data in the context of a theory, we must first be able to specify the class of data that is appropriately addressed by the theory. That is, we must identify the domain of the theory. This is not a trivial task. One way to look at this problem was recently suggested by George Smith: A theory can be regarded as a question-answering device; it is a set of principles that should specify (1) the class of appropriate questions, (2) the appropriate inputs necessary to obtain a correct answer to a question within that class, and (3) an algorithm for generating an answer, given the input. In this context, the initial problem becomes one of specifying "natural sets" of questions, questions that our theory ought to be able to answer.

The present theory is intended to provide answers to questions about how information is represented in and accessed from visual mental images. To remind the reader briefly, our paradigm case is the internal events that people often report when trying to answer a question like "What color is a bee's head?" People often claim to "mentally picture" the insect and then to "scan" to its head and "look" at the color. Our goal is to understand what it means to form such a "mental picture," how it is that one can inspect images, and what kinds of operations (like scanning, rotating, and so on) can be performed on such images. In addition, once I have cast the form of a theory of image representation and processing, I will extend this theory to the question of when people spontaneously use imagery to answer questions.

1.2 A Cognitive Explanation

In the foregoing chapters we have reviewed, if not a mountain, at least a hillock of data. We now are faced with the task of formulating explanations for these findings. But what *sort* of explanation is in order? We can distinguish three basic levels of explanations that might be appropriate, which I shall call "physical," "functional," and "intentional." Let me begin by illustrating the meanings of these terms, as used here, with an analogy to the news board in Times Square. This board is a giant matrix of light bulbs. Selectively turning on some of the bulbs makes it possible to spell out words, and selectively turning off some bulbs while turning on others makes words seem to move across the billboard. Consider a single case, a display of the letter *O*. This letter has an existence independent of the particular light bulbs that display it: The particular light bulbs displaying an *O* at any given time are the *physical realization* of the letter, but the letter can be displayed with a large number of different sets of bulbs, and it is defined not in terms of any particular bulbs, but in terms of a *functional relationship* among bulbs (namely, that they form an enclosed circular pattern). We cannot reduce O-hood to a simple set of statements about particular bulbs. The analogy here, of course, is to the mind and brain. I am taking Putnam's (1960) lead (see Block, in press; Fodor, 1968, for overviews) and treating "mental events" as events described at the level of functional states of the brain. These states arise from the brain but are not necessarily identical to particular configurations of neural activity. Perhaps a better analogy is the familiar computer metaphor: The operation of a given program cannot be identified completely with a particular set of physical states in the machine. When the same program is run twice in succession, it may use different parts of core, different disks, and so on. The program's existence even transcends the particular computer it runs on. Similarly, it may well be that the only thing the different neural states that correspond to a "functional brain state" have in common is their role in promoting a particular kind of computation, given the other events occurring in the brain at the same time (just as the only thing various sets of light bulbs in my example may have in common is the configuration they depict).

A computer program can be regarded as a description, at a particular level of analysis, of what the machine will do given specific inputs. In seeking an explanation of why a particular output is produced given a particular input, we do not want to know about the individual states in core; we want to know about the functional operations and how they are ordered. Similarly, in seeking an account of the sort of data decribed in the preceding chapters, we do not focus on the neurons, but on functional states of the brain. The important property of a functional explanation, for present purposes, is that it forces us to define the "capacities" underlying performance in some task and how they are interrelated.

Obviously, functional states and their physical realizations are not entirely independent: In the case of the Times Square news board, the possible shapes of an O (how circular? squarish?) are limited by the density of the grid; in a computer, certain programs cannot even run if enough core is not available. Furthermore, the optimal design of the "hardware," the physical medium, will differ depending on what sorts of functional states will be used: The matrix of lines used to display numbers in pocket calculators would be different if letters were to be displayed instead; computers specifically designed to run LISP programs have different hardware (have a different set of built-in basic machine operations) from less specialized machines. Thus, the structure of the brain will obviously bear on the kinds of functional states that are possible (and vice versa, I hasten to add). But we do not want our explanation of mental events to be couched in terms of brain events any more than a description of the architecture of a building should be couched in terms of locations of bricks and boards. A functional account can be offered quite independently of any specification of the physical device that has those functional capacities.

On my view, then, a "cognitive" theory will be a theory of the "functional capacities" of the brain and how they interact.

But what about the third level of explanation, the "intentional" account? Intentional explanation involves accounting for behavior using constructs like "intention," "desire," and "belief" (see Dennett, 1978). An intentional account draws inferences about a person's motives and so on directly from the person's behavior in a given context, and does not appeal to the functional states of the brain that underlie this behavior. The commonplace "psychological" explanation offered when one is gossiping about a friend's behavior is of this sort. It is important to realize that intentional accounts cannot be entirely reduced to functional accounts. Consider an anecdote told to me by Robert Matthews: He recognized an old friend walking by and ran out to greet the fellow, calling out his name. As it turned out, the person he "recognized" was not his old friend but the friend's identical twin brother. Bob was wrong, he had not recognized the person after all. Presumably the exact same functional states would have occurred if Bob had been right (just as the same pattern of bulbs could occur for the number zero or the letter O in our Times Square news board metaphor); the stimuli falling on his retina would have been processed the same way, the same information would have been retrieved from memory, and so on. But in one case these processes would have underlain his recognizing the person, while in another case they would not. Thus, one cannot equate the meanings of psychological terms like "recognize" or "know" with functional states, but must regard these terms as saying something about these states in context.

For present purposes, three points should be made about intentional explanations: First, it is important to note that English-word explanations of data that make use of intentional terms referring to a person's goals, beliefs, intentions, and so on are not sufficient: They are simply open to too many alternative interpretations at the level of information processing. Second, although there is no guarantee that there will be a simple mapping from intentional states to functional ones, it seems clear that intentional states cannot be entirely divorced from functional states either. One would not be likely to assign a given psychological term to a person's behavior unless a particular kind of functional state was extant; if a person's behavior was a consequence of a germ biting the spinal cord just right, we would not ascribe intentionality to that behavior. It seems likely to me that a particular functional state (or specifiable set of different states) is a necessary (but not sufficient) condition for a given intentional state. Eventually we would like to specify which functional states may underlie a given intentional state. True, it may turn out that the same functional state can correspond to "knowledge" or "belief," "recognition" or "false recognition," reference to H_2O or XYZ (see Schwartz, 1979), but this need not be the concern of the cognitive psychologist. Independent of whether Professor Matthews did or did not actually recognize his friend, a whole host of internal processes occurred, and understanding these processes and when they occur may constitute understanding the cognitive psychology (as opposed to the physical, metaphysical, and sociocultural aspects) of the matter (see Fodor, in press, for an interesting development of this viewpoint). Finally, it is sometimes convenient to use intentional terms to describe the operation of and relations among the functional capacities (see Dennett, 1978). For example, one may say that a procedure "recognizes" a particular data-structure. Because data-structures exist in the context of a closed processing system (in the sense that every possible symbol-type is specified) this kind of "recognition" does not depend on information outside the system, and can be identified with the way one formal entity stands in relation to others. Intentional terms are being used partly metaphorically in this way, however, and we should be careful not to import excess baggage from their conventional usage (for example, to say that a procedure is "trying" to accomplish some end does not imply anything about its behavior if prevented from operating in its usual mode).

Thus, one can be concerned with how images act as data-structures used in storing and processing information in human memory without worrying about all of the possible "meanings" of a given image. How images come to have particular content is partly a problem in perception, to be dealt with by a theory of how information is encoded, and is partly outside the realm of psychology, pertaining to the "true nature of things in the world." In this book we will sidestep questions about the precise operation of the perceptual "encoding system" by considering only highly structured situations (such as those occurring in my experiments) in which the relation between an image and object is greatly constrained (for example, because we have subjects learn to image drawings in the laboratory). In this case, we will assume that the constituent parts of an object and the relations among them are correctly encoded into memory; if this assumption is incorrect, it should prevent us from providing straightforward accounts of data (for example, scanning times will not correlate with the assumed distances between parts of an imaged object). In addition, we will completely ignore the aspects of intentional "meanings" that require a characterization of the actual—as opposed to perceived—state of the world; whether a person was originally shown an actual object or was fooled and shown a cardboard copy of it is of no consequence here (see Kosslyn, Pinker, Smith and Shwartz, in press, for further development of this point).

1.3 Theories and Models

Given the orientation outlined above, a cognitive theory ought to specify law-like relations among "functional capacities" of the brain. These

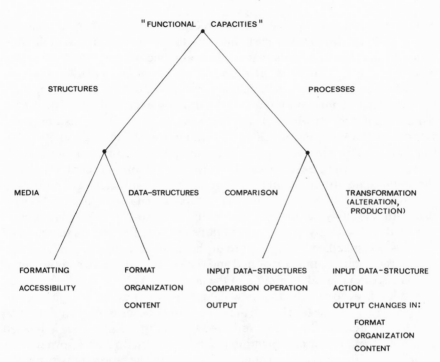

Figure 5.1. The components of a cognitive theory.

functional capacities will be of two kinds, structures and processes, as schematized in figure 5.1. On the structure side, one must specify the nature of the data-structures that can occur in memory and the nature of the internal media that support these data-structures. Data-structures are specified in terms of their format, their organization (for example, propositional representations may be organized hierarchically, as lists, and so on), and the kind of content that can be stored. Media are specified in terms of their "formatting" and accessibility. Formatting dictates which formats of data-structures can be supported within a medium (for example, a depictive format is required for a CRT-like spatial display medium). Accessibility specifies the ways in which the medium can be accessed and the relative availability of representations in different portions of the medium (for example, a medium consisting of a series of "slots" in which words are stored may be structured such that words can only be retrieved starting from one end). Note that all of the properties of the medium and the data-structures are by necessity defined in the context of a particular processing system; even though structures have an independent existence, and their nature imposes constraints on the kinds of processes that can be used, structures attain their functional properties only vis-à-vis the operation of particular processes (as was discussed in chapters 1 and 2).

On the process side, one must specify the nature of the operations that can access media and process data-structures. Some of these operations compare data-structures or parts thereof. These operations are defined in terms of the data-structures that can be compared, the nature of the actual comparison operation, and the output. The output can be a "match/mismatch" decision or a graded similarity measure, either of which may be accompanied by information about the process itself (such as where on a list a sought item was found). It will prove useful to distinguish between two additional kinds of processes. Alteration transformations alter an initial data-structure in some way, for example by deleting an item on a list or re-ordering the items. Production transformations, in contrast, leave the initial data-structure intact but treat it as a sufficient condition for creating or retrieving a new data-structure or data-structures. The new data-structure may be a copy of the initial one transformed in some way, but need not bear any structural relationship to it. Both types of transformations are specified by the nature of the input data-structure(s), the nature of the computation performed and the relationship between the initial data-structure(s) used as input and the new one(s) created after the transformation is accomplished. A new data-structure may differ from the initial one in its format (such as when a pattern is described), content (such as when an item is added to or removed from a list, or an object is imaged at a new size), and/or organization (such as when items are re-ordered on a list). It is difficult for me to conceive of how an alteration transformation can itself change the format of a data-structure, and this may prove to be a critical distinction between the two classes of transformations.*

Because the theory specifies the input conditions required by each operation (including availability of particular data-structures) and the results of executing a given operation, it also specifies "rules of combination" that constrain the order in which given operations can be executed in sequence. That is, when one operation has been executed, its output will serve as input for another, and so on; unless particular previous operations have been executed, any given operation will not be executed. A complete cognitive theory, then, would allow us to explain performance in all the tasks in the domain of the theory by specifying the ordered sequence in which operations process particular data-structures when people perform a given task. Knowing the number of such operations, their individual complexity, and so on would allow us to account for the amount of time necessary to perform the task, the probability of committing errors when performing the task, and so forth.

The reader should note that the actual expression of the theory may not

---

*Note that part of what a production transformation does when it produces a data-structure in a new format is to activate or make available the processors necessary to "read" the new format. Even if an alteration transformation moved the points depicting a cup to the shape "CUP," this would still be interpreted as a set of points depicting something, not as a word in the English language.

preserve the individual "functional capacities" as distinct terms. It may turn out that a more perspicuous statement of the theory can be made mathematically by grouping various capacities together at more abstract levels. I make no commitment as to the form of such an ultimate abstract expression, but only claim that it will express lawful relations among the kinds of cognitive entities described here. The job at this time, as I see it, is to isolate and develop the clearest possible characterization of the individual functional capacities and their interrelations.

One way to begin to formulate a cognitive theory is to develop a *model* of the presumed functional capacities. A model, as I use the term, is an entity that serves as a "range" into which the properties of a given "domain" (in this case, image processing in the brain) are being mapped. The *theory* picks out the relevant properties of the to-be-understood domain and maps them into selected aspects of the model. Thus, the relation between the model and the modeled domain is one of analogy. Under the correct description, the model captures the theory-relevant properties of the domain of study. A model airplane in a wind tunnel is a model insofar as the shape of the wings, fuselage, and so on accurately reflects that of the plane in question; the fact that the weight, type of material, color, and so on are not the same in the model and in the actual airplane is of no consequence. The decision of what aspects of the model are important and what aspects are unimportant is made on the basis of the theory, which tells us what is important about the plane itself. Thus, one way to test a theory is to construct a model, which will be a particular instantiation of (at least some of) the system of lawful relations expressed in the theory. Model building is especially useful when one does not have a complete theory, as it forces one to add properties to the model simply to obtain accounts of data; in a cognitive model, these properties will be new functional capacities or new characteristics of already posited functional capacities. Importantly, there may be equally viable ways of instantiating the model, and thus one may be led to perform experiments to eliminate possible alternatives. In so doing, data is collected that also leads to further development of the theory itself. In the airplane example, if the amount of sweep of the wings is not specified initially, one will reach an impasse when building the model, and will have to examine the domain itself, the plane, to discover what the actual shape is and how it should be modeled. In addition, a property of the model previously regarded as incidental (for example, in the model plane, the material) may turn out to be important, and hence place further constraints on the theory (see Hesse, 1963). Thus, both developing the model and studying its properties can provide motivation for further development of the theory itself.

It will prove useful to distinguish between two kinds of models, *specific* ones and *general* ones. Specific models are designed to account for performance in a particular task (see Clark and Chase, 1972; Sternberg, 1966, for example), whereas general ones embody the entire set of principles that should account for performance in all the tasks in a given domain (Anderson and Bower, 1973, and Newell and Simon, 1972, were developing general models; in physics, Bohr's atom was a general model). One problem with specific models is that it is difficult to be sure that any theoretical claims that emerge from developing them will be consistent with claims derived from other specific models. In a general model, since all the proposed functional capacities are available to be used in performing *any* task, one is forced to define precisely the input conditions and output characteristics of each process and is forced to be consistent across tasks. If the rules of combination are specified precisely enough, then a given particular input configuration will evoke only one sequence of operations—providing a specific model of how a particular task is accomplished. (Thus, I assume that although a given task logically *could* be accomplished in more than one way and in fact may be done differently on different occasions, such as when one is tired versus rested, on any given occasion the total input configuration and state of the system at the time will uniquely determine the way a task is performed.) Use of a general model seems to ensure that real accumulation of underlying regularities can occur, that putative functional capacities can come to supplement and complement each other.

Steven Shwartz and I have embodied a general model of imagery in a computer simulation, in which each process is represented by a distinct procedure and each structure has been implemented as well. The rules of combination are implicit in the conditions that call a procedure (including specifications of which data-structures must be accessed in a given situation) and the output of having executed each procedure (which serves as the input for subsequent procedures). The general model is in fact sufficient to generate specific models for many of the tasks falling in the present domain. But mere sufficiency is not enough to warrant accepting the model. In the next section we will consider other grounds for evaluating cognitive theories.

1.4 Evaluating Theories and Models

It is not entirely obvious how to evaluate theories and models of the sort being considered here, especially ones in which greater weight is placed on accounting for qualitative trends in data as opposed to quantitative goodness-of-fit (percentage of variance accounted for). Fortunately, this problem is not new and we can draw some inspiration from Chomsky's (1965, 1967) efforts to deal with the analogous problem in linguistics. Let us begin by distinguishing among three kinds of adequacy, which I shall call behavioral adequacy, process adequacy, and explanatory adequacy. (This taxonomy roughly parallels Chomsky's 1967 levels of observational, descriptive, and explanatory adequacy.) These three kinds of adequacy are assessed differently depending on whether one is evaluating specific models, theories, or general models. Table 5.1 summarizes the criteria for each type of adequacy for cognitive theories and models. First, let us consider "specific models," which are developed to account for performance in a particular task. The classic Sternberg (1966) model is a paradigmatic example of this type of model. Such a model is behaviorally adequate if it makes the correct predictions about stimulus-response relationships. These predictions can be either qualitative trends in data (verified by finding particular patterns of significantly different means), or actual quantitative fit (as measured by percentage of variance accounted for). The appropriateness of the weaker "trends" measure or stronger "variance accounted for" measure depends on the level of precision specified in the model. This metric is, of course, the old standby in cognitive psychology, the major dimension upon which we typically evaluate our models.

A specific model has process adequacy if it can account for the patterns in data by reference to how different variables affect different components of the underlying process. For example, Sternberg's (1966) model of high-speed scanning in short-term memory has something like process adequacy. This model is designed to account for performance in a task where subjects are given a set of stimuli, like digits, and then are asked to decide as quickly as possible whether a probe stimulus was in the initial set. Sternberg finds that decision times increase linearly as more items are included in the initial stimulus set, and that times are retarded overall if the probe stimulus is presented in a degraded form. Importantly, the effects of adding additional stimuli to the initial set are not affected by the quality of the probe stimulus. Sternberg accounts for these findings by referring to a description of the operations underlying task performance. In this case, separate processing stages are posited, one of which is an "encoding stage," which will be hampered if the probe is degraded; the subsequent stages are independent of this initial stage in that their operation depends only on the output of this stage, and not on how the encoding operation actually takes place on any given occasion. After a probe stimulus is encoded, its representation is compared serially to representations of each item in the initial stimulus set. Since each comparison requires an increment of time, decision times increase when larger stimulus sets are initially presented. Thus, a degraded stimulus will slow down times overall (by retarding the encoding operation), but does not affect the time to scan each item (which is determined by the operation of a subsequent, independent stage).

A specific model gains explanatory adequacy only by dint of a more general theory. The theory specifies why it is *those* particular operations, recruiting *those* particular data-structures, in *that* order. The theory pro-

Table 5.1. Three types of adequacy for specific models, theories, and general models.

	Behavioral adequacy	Process adequacy	Explanatory adequacy
Specific models	Correct predictions; variance accounted for.	The correct description of underlying processing in a task, accounting for patterns in data by reference to distinct processing components.	Theory specifies the processes, structures, and ordering.
Theories	Generates behaviorally adequate specific models for all tasks in a domain.	Assigns correct descriptions (models) of how people perform tasks in the domain, allowing description of the basis of relationships among different tasks.	The structure of the brain, computational requirements, experience.
General models	Generates behaviorally adequate specific models for all tasks in a domain.	Assigns correct descriptions (models) of how people perform tasks in the domain, allowing description of the basis of relationships among different tasks.	Theory specifies the processes, structures, and possible orderings among them necessary to generate process adequate models for all tasks in the domain.

vides the constraints that allow one to explain why it is *that* particular model and not some other one that will account for the numbers as well. Some of Anderson's (1976) specific models approach something like explanatory adequacy insofar as more general principles, like a limited-capacity activated memory and "spreading activation," constrain the structure of his accounts for specific results.

Now let us shift to the next row in table 5.1, and consider how one can evaluate cognitive *theories*. Unlike specific models, which deal only with some specific task, the theory is general across an entire domain, covering a very large number of tasks. A theory is behaviorally adequate if it can generate specific models for all the possible tasks within a domain, and if each of these models is itself behaviorally adequate as described above. The theory is process adequate if it specifies the correct set of functional capacities (data-structures, media, and processes, with the correct properties) for the specified domain. If the theory correctly describes cognitive processing in a given domain, it should allow one not only to generate specific models that themselves have process adequacy, but to predict which tasks will cluster in being relatively easy or difficult, and for what reasons, by virtue of shared components in the specific models underlying task performance.

A cognitive theory gains explanatory adequacy, on my view, from three possible sources: First, some components are necessary for purely computational reasons. It is difficult to imagine a processing system without some kind of comparison match/mismatch operation, for example. Second, and not independent of the first consideration, some properties of the cognitive system are as they are because of the brain itself. That is, the structure of the brain may be the underlying reason why some operations exist. This structure may be a consequence of two forces: (1) There may be inherent organizational principles dictating how neurons are interconnected. These may follow from the nature of the cells themselves. (2) The brain evolved in the service of performing sets of computations and presumably is partly "tailor made" to perform some kinds of computations more efficiently than others. However, the kinds of computations that the brain performs today need not be the same as those that shaped its evolution. The computations performed now may be forced to make use of neural structures originally evolved for quite different purposes. Thus, some of the constraints on cognitive processing may not be those that foster the most computationally efficient processing for the tasks at hand—giving us reason to take pause in stressing computational efficiency per se as the primary source of explanatory adequacy in a cognitive theory. Not surprisingly, then, even though we can formulate cognitive theories without regard to the underlying physiology, ultimately we must develop the interface between the functional level and the neural substrate. Returning to my analogy to the Times Square news board, at some point we will have to study the density of the grid in order to understand why the shapes of letters displayed by the bulbs are constrained as they are. However, we have a great deal of work to do before we will have to worry much about this depth of adequacy, and considerable progress can be made on a functional level before we will even know which detailed information about the brain will be helpful.*

The third source of explanatory adequacy in a theory may be the impact of the environment on the organism. One's personal history of interacting with the physical and social environment may shape the functional capacities in at least two ways: (1) The actual structure of the brain may itself be altered, either by diet or by direct experience. Hirsch and Spinelli (1970), for example, found that the nature of early visual experience alters the proportion of different kinds of cells in the visual cortex of the cat. (2) The functional capacities need not be equivalent to the operating instructions in a computer; they need not be the most reduced, primitive units of analysis (recall the discussion about the distinction between an "explanation" and a "parent of an explanation" in chapter 2). It is possible that some capacities are in fact composed from more elementary capacities, but come to function as single units at the level of analysis of a cognitive theory (Pylyshyn suggests that more elementary units may become "compiled" such that they are no longer distinct). If so, then it is possible that some functional capacities are developed as one has repeated cause to perform given functions.

In the bottom row of table 5.1 I have listed the properties of a general model. A general model is a particular embodiment of the theory. As such, it is behaviorally adequate insofar as it can generate models that are themselves behaviorally adequate for all the specific tasks that fall within the domain of the theory. It is process adequate in the same way as is the theory, by generating specific models that are themselves process adequate and that allow one to predict which tasks within the domain will cluster in being relatively easy or difficult, by virtue of which functional capacities are utilized in which ways. Finally, the general model gains explanatory adequacy from the theory itself, in the same way as does a specific model. The advantage of a general model is that it expresses all the lawful relationships among structures and processes specified by the theory, not just the subset required to explain performance in a particular task. Thus, by developing a general model one is forced to develop the theory itself, and one is likely to develop accounts for specific tasks that will complement each other, leading not only to behavioral, process and explanatory adequacy on the level of specific models, but to behavioral

*Note that this point cuts two ways: the explanatory adequacy of a theory of the brain per se will draw in part on computational considerations, which will presumably dictate some of the reasons why the brain does things the way it does. Thus, cognitive theories may well be of as much use to the brain theorist as brain theories are to the cognitivist.

and process adequacy on the level of the theory proper. In our program of research, we use these three forms of adequacy as guiding lights, continually working toward developing a theory that will satisfy these requirements.

1.5 Current Conceptions of Imagery

Before embarking on a discussion of the present theory and model, it will behoove us briefly to survey the theories and models already in the literature. This survey will have two purposes. First, it could be that a new theory is not really necessary, because some already exisiting theory will provide fully adequate accounts of the available data within the constraints derived during Phase I research. Second, during the course of considering the previous theories, we will explore the usefulness of our fledgling evaluation metric. In considering the conceptions of imagery that are current in the psychological literature, I will first describe a view, then attempt to classify it as primarily a specific model, a general model, or a theory, and finally assess its adequacy in terms of both model and theory. I will not provide a detailed treatment or critique of each view. In particular, Paivio (1971) presents a thorough discussion of the traditional percept-analogy theories of imagery, and I will not attempt to duplicate his efforts here. Since Paivio and others (for example, Richardson, 1969) do not provide as detailed a discussion of the more recent propositionalist views, I will spend more time on these positions.

1.5.1 Propositionalist Approaches

These theories posit that there is nothing special about the internal representation of mental images. Rather, the same kinds of discursive representations are used in all cognitive processing, and the experience of a quasi-pictorial image is an epiphenomenal concomitant of processing these kinds of representations. These discursive representations are formed by concatenating elementary propositions. Herbert Simon has over the years made some general claims of this sort that have had great impact on those who have attempted to embody theories of imagery in working computer simulations. Thus, although his specific comments on imagery have not had an enormous impact on the field, his general influence should not be underestimated. Simon (1972) proposed that a net structure of the sort employed in the simulation EPAM (''Elementary Perceiver and Memorizer,'' Simon and Feigenbaum, 1964) also can be used to model images. On this conception, nodes are descriptions of parts of an object, and these are related together via links in a graph. In such a representation of an image all of the information encoded about any component of an object or scene is directly accessible at the node for that part, and a node is related directly to every other node that "has been recognized as related to it in a specific way." Baylor and Simon (1966), Simon and Barenfeld (1969), Williams (1965), and others all utilize this sort of representation for visually perceived information (but not all make the claim that these representations necessarily correspond to mental images).

An important feature of Simon's claims, shared by all theorists who rely solely on propositional representations (for example, Anderson and Bower, 1973; Minsky and Papert, 1972; Rumelhart, Lindsay, and Norman, 1972), is that "all internal modalities employ basically the same kinds of structure for storage; their differences are differences in organization." That is, the same kind of propositional format, utilizing nodes (as representations of arguments) and links (as representations of relations), is hypothesized to be sufficient to represent in memory the functional component of images; further, the claim is that these representations can be processed in ways that allow one to account for the available data on human processing of mental images. Anderson and Bower (1973) in particular have claimed that such structures are sufficient to account for "image" representation and processing; they do not, however, develop this proposal in any depth, merely asserting that "image" structures make special use of spatial relations linking nodes of a graph. These spatial relations (like "left of" or "above") are expressed in the same format as other kinds of relations ("member of," "purer than"). This type of theory, of course, falls outside the class delineated by the results of Phase I research, summarized by the decision tree at the end of chapter 4. Nevertheless, it is of some interest to see just how far one can go with such an approach in terms of our adequacy criteria.

First, it is important to realize that Simon and Anderson and Bower have not proposed theories, and have offered only the barest bones of a model. Rather, their claims are primarily metatheoretical commitments to the form that a theory and model will ultimately take. As such, these claims are simply too abstract to be tested. Three detailed propositionalist models of imagery have been developed to date, all of which were embodied in computer programs. These programs were written at Carnegie-Mellon University, partly under the influence of Simon. Baylor's (1971) theory is of very limited scope, but makes explicit some general claims about the nature of imaginal representation. His computer simulation was designed to account for performance in certain kinds of "block visualization" tasks. For example, a person might be asked to make a visual image of a 1 x 4 x 4 inch block. The narrow sides are to be imaged as if they were painted red, and the top and bottom are to be mentally pictured blue. The person then is asked to slice the block into 16 one-inch cubes. Following this, the subject is asked to count how many cubes have both red and blue faces, how many have no painted faces, and so on. Baylor asked his subjects to describe aloud what they were doing mentally while performing this task and recorded these remarks; these verbal protocols later were used to guide the design of the computer simulation. The theory-relevant aspects of Baylor's specific model are as follows: Baylor posits two sorts of representation media, an I-space (for imaginal information), and an S-space (for symbolic, factual information). The representations in these media do not differ in quality (in format), but rather in specifics of organization and content. Information in the S-space is true about pieces of an object and their components in general; information in the I-space, in contrast, is true only for a particular piece and its components. The actual representation of a cube is in terms of elementary units and their relations; the units are faces, edges, and vertices. Each unit is classified as to its position, being tagged as left, right, front, back, top, or bottom.

An important feature of Baylor's image representation is that it is hierarchical; the structure mirrors the nesting relations implicit in part containment, as occurs with blocks having faces, faces having edges, and so on. The representation in the S-space is like a set of statements about blocks in general, without any information about particular edges or faces of the block. In fact, different vertices may be labeled the same in the S-space. The representation in the I-space (the "image" itself), in contrast, includes information about particular properties arising from a given three-dimensional orientation of a block. Each vertex now receives an individuating tag. Further, in addition to general relations (like "is a part of"), which are present in the S-space representation, particular spatial relations (like "is below"), which are relative to a given orientation of the cube, also are included in the I-space representation.

Although Baylor's model is clearly intended to embody some general theoretical claims, it is a specific model. It has behavioral adequacy for the cube-cutting task. Further, if verbal protocols are taken at face value as reflecting what subjects actually did, the model seems to have some process adequacy. That is, it assigns a description of underlying processing that at least in part captures the operation of functional capacities responsible for performance of the task. However, not only is Baylor's model not really an embodiment of a theory (it is a specific model—not a general one), it is only partly theory-specified. The distinction between I-space and S-space is an interesting one, and something like this distinction holds promise of allowing one to account for the fact that the image in active memory depicts information from a particular point of view, whereas the information in long-term memory may not. However, most of the explanatory adequacy of the model is drawn from Simon's methatheoretical commitments about the hegemony of propositional representation. And these assumptions do not lead to perspicuous accounts of the data discussed in chapter 3, which document the depictive properties of image representations. Thus, the theory on which the model is based is not even behaviorally adequate (it does not project to other tasks within the domain), nor does it have much in the way of process or explanatory adequacy. The explanatory power of the theoretical claims themselves seems based purely on considerations of computational efficiency. As I argued above, this is a tricky criterion to use, and in this case computational efficiency on a digital computer seems to fly in the face of what humans actually do—according to my interpretation of the findings reported in chapter 3.

Moran's (1973a, 1973b) theory also posits no qualitative differences between imagery and no-imagery representations. Moran goes one step further, rejecting even Baylor's sort of distinction between imagery and symbolic "spaces." Moran argues that the "most parsimonious hypothesis is that imagery is a symbolic process; that is, that there is no need for a distinct 'image space'" (Moran, 1973b). In addition, Moran claims that "there are no pure 'image operators'; but rather imagery depends strongly on structural (mostly hierarchic) information" (Moran, 1973b). A production system model (see Newell and Simon, 1972) is offered as sufficient to account for imagery phenomena. This kind of model is built around a collection of "productions," each of which has a "condition" and an "action." If the condition (for example, a given stimulus configuration encoded into short-term memory) is satisfied, the action is executed (for example, some fact or information is activated, which is equivalent to placing it in short-term memory). This model consists of a long-term store and a limited-capacity short-term store, the contents of which are continuously in flux as new information is activated from long-term memory or arrives from the senses, forcing out information already in the short-term store (see also Anderson, 1976).

Moran's model provides an account of how people perform a particular task. In this task a subject was asked to image a path described by a sequence of directions (such as, "north, north, west," and so on). For each direction, the subject imaged a line of unit length going in that direction. While performing the task, the subject "thought aloud," as in Baylor's task. After all directions were given, the subject attempted to "read off" the image and report the directions back to the experimenter. The actual simulation was developed to "satisfy not only the external constraints of the protocol, but also some of the known internal memory limitations of the human information processor" (as in most production system models, there were a priori constraints on how many chunks could be in short-term memory, based on findings in the experimental literature).

The image representation in Moran's model is a series of expressions in "short-term memory." A set of expressions makes up an "aggregate chunk," which is a linear list of symbols of any complexity. Lists may be hierarchically organized. The image, then, is a list in a propositional format residing in short-term memory; it contains not only spatial information but temporal information (relating parts of the path to each other) as well. This representation is modality-independent, and—as Moran himself notes—his model does not predict and cannot easily account for the well-known effects of modality-specific interference in imagery (where a visual image interferes with visual perception more than do auditory images but vice versa with auditory perception—as will be discussed in chapter 7).

Moran, then, also has proposed a specific model. This model seems to account for the protocols in the task Moran studied by appeal to underlying structures and processes. Hence, it has behavioral adequacy and some measure of process adequacy. Further, it includes a very deliberate attempt to introduce theory-based constraints into the model (for example, the limited short-term store), lending a degree of explanatory adequacy to the model. However, the model again falls far short of being a general model, and hence has difficulty in projecting beyond the particular task used to develop the model in the first place. As it now stands, the kind of theory that shaped the form of this model is not even behaviorally adequate, is not able to provide accounts for the data we have described in the preceding chapters. Critically, it is simply not clear how this class of models would provide accounts for the data described in chapter 3, except in the most ad hoc way. The theoretical claims that images have hierarchical structure and occur in a limited-capacity active memory store will prove to have some fairly general applications, however. But again, the theory itself is not strongly motivated by the sorts of considerations that would lead to explanatory adequacy. It should be noted that use of some general constraints discovered empirically (such as the size of the short-term buffer) does not lend explanatory adequacy to the *theory*— these data themselves are in need of explanation.

The most recent Carnegie-Mellon computer-based theory of imagery is that of Farley (1974), who posits that the image is a nonhierarchical structure of interrelated symbols. The major departures of this representation from Moran's concern the nonhierarchical organization, on the one hand, and the notion that the positions of the symbolized units are encoded in terms of an "imprecise ('fuzzy') absolute locational coordinate scale." Farley's program was designed to simulate behavior in a task in which subjects tried to identify a picture seen only through a small, movable hole. Farley's conception of imagery is very much related to the sorts of processes that underlie performance of this task: A visual image is defined as "visually related behavior," including that guiding visual search of the sort required in his task. His image representation is organized according to directly apparent spatial relations which mirror the relations extracted while performing his task. Farley claims that Baylor (1971), Moran (1973a), and Newell (1972) (who, incidentally, did not claim to be proposing a model of visual image representation) have not really modeled imag-

ery at all because they failed to devise representations that evinced these
sorts of nonhierarchical spatial relations. Instead, Farley relegates these
previous efforts to the domain of work on "short-term memory processes."

Thus, following in the tradition of his predecessors, Farley has also developed a specific model, once again highly tailored to provide an account
of behavior in a specific task. As before, it is not surprising that the model
apparently can provide an account of the findings in that task and does so
by appeal to underlying structural description of task performance. Also
as before, the model attains explanatory adequacy insofar as its features
are dictated by a theory, and a set of general notions do seem to have
shaped the form of this model. On the level of the theory proper, the theoretical notions that motivated the model themselves are not adequate in
any of the three ways discussed earlier—being unable to generate models
that will account for most of the results described in chapters 3 and 4 and
being relatively unmotivated. However, this model has the virtue of
allowing one to think about how images depict spatial extent, although it
would not lead one to predict effects of interval distance per se on processing time (items farther apart simply have more disparate values in the
coordinates stored with them).

An additional problem with all three of these propositional models is
that they may lack simple face validity. That is, they may not really model
imagery processing per se. All of these models are based on verbal (and
video, in Farley's case) protocols. Psychologists have long known the
dangers of relying exclusively on introspective reports, in part because
the process itself is notoriously unreliable, and in part because language
forces one to interpret one's introspections in terms of a particular conceptual vocabulary (which may not capture the actual experience itself).
The first problem is difficult to divorce from the nature of the beast—
images are private internal events, by definition. The basic technique of
relying on protocol analysis for studying and theorizing about these
events is, however, certainly not optimal; we simply may not be sensitive
to many of the properties of imagery (especially slight differences in time
to transform, inspect, and generate images) that will serve to distinguish
among competing models. (As was demonstrated in chapters 3 and 4, relatively small differences in time to use images under different conditions
provide the cutting edge for deciding among alternative conceptions of
imaging.) Further, the protocol analysis technique relies too heavily on
subjects' interpretations of their introspections; we have no guarantee
that theories based on the verbal behavior are in fact theories of the internal events so reported.

Finally, all these models are exceedingly limited due to the highly specialized nature of the kinds of performance they were designed to simulate. In fact, each model is so tailored for the specific tasks considered

that it is not clear it can deal even with the equally limited, but different, tasks used in motivating the other programs. And it is not clear to me how to extend these kinds of specific models in the natural way to allow even behavioral adequacy across the domain of imagery, let alone the stronger measures of adequacy. Thus, although there is something to be said in favor of each model, none of them seem a suitable starting place for development of a general theory of imagery.

1.5.2 Percept-Analogy Theories

The traditional view of imagery is that mental images in essence are percepts that arise from memory rather than from ongoing sensory stimulation. These theories have often been called "picture theories" (see for example, Hebb, 1968; Woodworth and Schlosberg, 1954), but, as discussed earlier, nobody claims that a physical picture is in the head. Rather, the claim is that images correspond to the internal events that produce the experience of seeing a picture. The sort of conception one has of imagery, then, depends on how one views perception.

The oldest and most primitive conception of imagery rests on the notions that (1) visual perception is a photography-like process and (2) mental "photographs" formed in the course of perception can be tucked away in memory and later retrieved for further perusal. Plato's famous "wax tablet" notion falls into this class. More recently, Bugelski (1970) seems to expound a similar idea. He claims that when imagery is used as a mnemonic, verbal materials are converted to mental pictures, stored, and later retrieved and described during recall of the words. As discussed in the previous chapters, this notion of imagery is clearly too simplistic. This view is based on an analogy and hence is probably best thought of as a model. Since it is not supposed to be specific to a particular task, we are forced to regard it as a very vague general model, failing severely on all three forms of adequacy.

Hebb's (1968) theory also falls into the class of percept-analogy theories. Hebb claims that an image is caused by activation from memory of the same neural structures that are activated when one is perceiving an object. That is, images are thought to be generated by activity of the cell-assemblies (see Hebb, 1949) that would be activated in processing the corresponding percept. In addition, eye movements similar to those that occur when actually viewing the imaged object serve to integrate outputs of lower-order cell-assemblies into coherent images. Further, images can be formed via activation of specific lower-order cell-assemblies, producing a sharp image of a particular exemplar, or via activation of higher-order cell-assemblies, producing a "fuzzy," generic image. According to Hebb, once an image is generated it acts as a spatial entity capable of being analyzed in many ways like the corresponding representation arising during perception. On his view the generated image is not like a photo, which can be scanned in any order (but see chapter 3, section 2.1), but is composed of parts that must be actively maintained, and these parts are organized in particular ways.

Hebb's notions seem best regarded as falling into the class of theories proper. But it is not clear what would constitute a test of the neurophysiological speculations he offers; does the fact that images *can* be scanned equally easily in different directions disprove this theory? On the face of things, the theory would not seem to have even behavioral adequacy. But the notion that images are actually constructed and maintained receives support in the data, and the eye-movement hypothesis may yet receive empirical support. However, the correspondence between psychological states and neurophysiological ones will probably not be as simple as here described, but—again—this remains to be tested.

Paivio (1971) also notes that imagery has much in common with like-modality perception, but he chooses to discuss imagery largely in contrast to verbal representation. This tack follows from Paivio's claim that only two codes, Image and Verbal, exist for representing information in memory; thus each is understood partly by reference to what it is not. A tenet of this approach, usually left implicit in the theoretical discussion, is that the long-term memory representations of images are qualitatively distinct from the representations underlying production and comprehension of language. It is left open whether the image, as occurs in active memory, is generated by some other representation in long-term memory; this presumably would be acceptable to Paivio as long as the long-term memory representations are distinct from those underlying verbal behavior. Questions of this level of detail are rarely addressed by dual-code theorists, who are more interested in the behavioral consequences of using imagery in cognition than in the structure of the image or the imagery system itself. Paivio, in fact, seems to define imagery almost entirely in terms of functional spatial processing (whereas verbal representations are most effectively used in sequential processing), and in terms of its usefulness for dealing with "concrete" tasks, which seem to be those most similar to tasks that could be performed on percepts (verbal representation, in contrast, is most effectively used in dealing with abstract tasks and materials).

Paivio's notions also rest heavily on an analogy to "mental pictures," but are not task-specific and hence may best be regarded as a general model. These views provide loose accounts for much data (see Paivio, 1971), and have led to the collection of massive amounts of interesting data. Thus, this approach to theorizing seems to hold promise of leading to specific models that are behaviorally adequate. But Paivio's approach will never provide process adequate accounts of data—simply because there are no precise descriptions of the underlying structures and processes that are recruited when one uses imagery.

Bower (1972) also presents a dual-code approach to understanding imagery. Bower's notion is that we can distinguish between *how* something appeared and *what* it looked like, and that this distinction parallels that between image and propositional representations (for Bower, the latter are the abstract representations of facts underlying verbal assertions). Memory images put us in "direct contact" with how a thing appeared in a given sensory modality, whereas propositions only tell us *about* a thing's appearance. The two sorts of information are represented in two distinct memory traces, which have different functional properties (of the sort discussed by Paivio). In regard to what an image actually is, Bower notes that "to say that a person is remembering in imagery is to say that some central mechanisms are generating a (probably sequential) pattern of information which corresponds more or less to the structural information in the original perception." In addition, he further asserts that there is some "structural isomorphism between the information presently available to us (in the image) and the information picked up from the stimulus event (while it was occurring) we are remembering." When actually discussing how images may be retrieved, Bower seems to modify his dual-code position slightly, now hypothesizing that a "common generative grammar" may underlie production of both verbal strings and images. (This leaning is developed in Anderson and Bower's (1973) theory to the point where images are no longer regarded as distinct representations, as was mentioned earlier.) Bower's ideas seem to be on the level of theory proper, not being bound to a particular task nor being embedded in a model. Insofar as the theory accounts for the advantage of using imagery in memory tasks, it has some measure of behavioral adequacy (although it does not approach general behavioral adequacy for the entire domain). But these ideas must be further elaborated in order to produce specific models, and until this is done the theory itself cannot be said to have either process or explanatory adequacy.

In rounding out this section, it is worth discussing the views of one more proponent of a percept-analogy theory, Ulrich Neisser (Neisser, 1967, 1972, 1976, 1978; Neisser and Kerr, 1973). In his earliest statement, Neisser emphasized that both imagery and perception are active, constructive processes, and that they utilize common processing mechanisms. As his early view evolved, he came to de-emphasize the notion that shared processing mechanisms wed imagery to perception. Instead, he adopted Gibson's (1966) characterization of perception as an "automatic," "direct" event. On this view, there is no processing of an internal picture-like array during perception; no "mental picture" acts as a mediator between input and interpretation. Rather, the claim is that one normally perceives *layouts*, which are shifting, textured, three-dimensional surfaces, not pictures. Thus, according to Neisser (1976), images in the visual modality are not mental pictures, but rather are "mental layouts." Neisser rejects Gibson's radical view that *no* processing is done in perception, and argues that the brain is in fact a processing device that operates without the benefit of distinct representations. Instead, the brain "picks up" information from the environment, partly in accordance with one's anticipations about one's surroundings. This kind of perceptual activity also may be evoked when one *anticipates* a stimulus in its absence, and this kind of "perceptual anticipation" corresponds to a mental image. Importantly, components of these "images" are perceived directly, and are not inferred or derived from some sort of pictorial display. Thus, relations among objects that are not "visible" in the image, according to Neisser, are still being imaged and are part of the information implicit in the image. (Neisser does not attempt to demonstrate, however, that these spatial relations he describes are in fact imaginal, as opposed to simply being semantic descriptions.)

My comments about Bower's theory apply to Neisser's as well: In general, the theory simply is too underspecified to produce specific models for many imagery tasks, and hence cannot be said to have process or explanatory adequacy. In addition, Kosslyn and Alper's (1977) finding that pictorial properties of images do affect memory for words (see chapter 3, section 2.3) would seem to violate a central claim of Neisser's position— precluding even behavioral adequacy.* Furthermore, there is some question in this case about the logical coherence of Neisser's views. For example, when an anticipated object fails to appear, aren't we usually surprised, disappointed, or otherwise aroused? But does this happen when we form an image and the object does not appear? See Hampson and Morris (1978) for an extended critique of Neisser's theory, and Neisser (1978) for a reply.

These brief summaries should make it clear that percept-analogy theories and models do not fill the present order. As they now stand, these notions really are not much better than the propositional ones at providing accounts for the data at hand. Whereas the propositional models are too particular and not general, the percept-analogy theories are too vague and unspecified. In fact, in most cases the theoretical buck is passed to workers in perception; when a successful theory of perception is developed, it will be extended to provide the details of image processing as well. Nevertheless, these theories do not necessarily violate the constraints derived in chapters 3 and 4, and I find elements of Bower's and Hebb's views par-

---

*See also Keenan and Moore (1979) for further data contradicting a prediction Neisser drew from his theory.

ticularly congenial. But as these theories now stand, they are simply too underdetermined to provide detailed accounts of data.

1.5.3 The State of the Art

None of the existing theories or models seems to provide even behaviorally adequate accounts of the data on imagery we have considered thus far. This is not surprising, however, as these theories and models predate the results reported here and hence were not designed with them in mind. Thus, the more interesting question is whether any of the current conceptions can be expanded to provide even behaviorally adequate accounts of the data. As noted earlier, propositional models will account for the data described in chapter 3 only with the most unnatural convolutions, and these accounts are unlikely to be the product of a process adequate theory, one able to assign descriptions of the underlying structures and processes used in performing tasks that will account for the interrelationships among performance in the different tasks.

The percept-analogy theories by and large do not fall clearly outside of the constraints inferred in Phase I, but this is mostly a consequence of the fact that they posit something like a quasi-pictorial image (except the later Neisser) and leave everything else open. The analogy to perception is not very helpful, given our ignorance about the computational mechanisms used in perception itself. As noted above, this analogy is often used as a substitute for specifying the nature of the image per se or the nature of the underlying representations in long-term memory. Thus, in principle one might be able to expand this class to account for the present results, but this would be difficult because these conceptions do not lead one to ask the right kinds of questions. That is (with the possible exception of Hebb's and Bower's notions), they do not help one to characterize the internal structures and processes that make up the image-processing system. Without specifying these kinds of underlying components, it will be impossible to achieve process adequacy either on the level of specific models (where patterns of data in a given task are explained by reference to a sequence of internal events that takes place when a person performs the task) or on the level of theories or general models (where the interrelationships among performance on different tasks are accounted for by appeal to similarities and differences in underlying processing).

Thus, we need to develop a new theory and general model, proceeding from the outset with an eye toward achieving the kinds of adequacy discussed above. The model developed here is an extension of the CRT protomodel. The protomodel is like the propositional models in specifying the functional capacities of a processing system, but does not violate any of the constraints delineated in the foregoing chapters. In addition, it is like most of the percept-analogy theories in positing a special imagery format. Thus, it shares the strengths of each of these general approaches. Specifically, the CRT protomodel has three virtues as a jumping-off place for developing an adequate theory of imagery: First, it is easy to develop the protomodel into an explicit general model that will fall within the class of acceptable models. Second, this kind of model is computational, and hence will tend to foster development of the right kind of theory (as here conceived), namely one that specifies the functional capacities used in imagery processing and the law-like relations among them. Finally, the general model developed from the protomodel seems likely to be able to serve the role the protomodel previously served in directing an empirical program of research. That is, often the theory will not dictate a unique specific model for a particular task. Conducting experiments to motivate construction of a specific model will result in further characterization of the functional capacities posited by the theory itself. Upon constraining the theory we will modify the general model accordingly, so that at any given time the model is an instantiation of the entire theory. Thus, in the ideal case the specific models that arise from our general one will be theory-governed and hence endowed with all three kinds of adequacy if the theory is correct. Note that although some modifications of specific models may be ad hoc for a particular task (even though motivated by data), the derived characterizations of the underlying functional capacities will not be ad hoc when used in explaining data from other tasks. This property of general models has promise of leading not only to behavioral adequacy on the level of the theory but to process adequacy as well— given that the same functional capacities are always potentially available for use in performing any task, and hence that different tasks will recruit varying numbers of the same underlying capacities.

2.0 THE THEORY AND THE GENERAL MODEL

The present theory is embodied in a running computer program. This program instantiates both the structures and the processes specified by the theory. The input conditions and output characteristics of the processes (each of which is represented by a separate subroutine) determine the sequence of events that takes place given an initial starting condition (which can consist in part of an instruction to image a particular thing in a particular way). Thus, the general model generates specific models to account for performance in specific tasks.

There are at least five reasons for constructing a computer model of a theory of mental functioning: First, it forces one to be explicit; hand-waving maketh not a program run. Second, it helps one to consider processes in terms of a system of interacting "functional capacities." Hence, it is likely to further formulation of a computational theory of the sort here envisaged. Third, it allows one to know whether one's ideas are sufficient to account for the data. If the program runs as expected, it is a kind of "sufficiency proof." This feature of simulation models promotes development of complex general theories by ensuring that explicit accounts of numerous results will remain consistent. In a way, the program serves the function of a note pad in arithmetic, saving one the effort of keeping too many things in mind at once. This is especially useful when numerous components are interacting in complex ways over the course of time (and this may be the main general advantage of simulation techniques over standard mathematical modeling). Fourth, the general approach outlined in chapter 1 emphasizes the importance of using the theory to produce new and interesting findings. The simulation medium has heuristic value in this regard, because it is a concrete realization of the theory itself. If one tries to remain honest, and motivate the operation of the simulation by the theory, then the act of constructing the simulation forces one to continue to elaborate the theory. In addition, we try not to take for granted accidental characteristics of the simulation (such as the square shape of the matrix within which images occur), but to use these characteristics to raise empirical questions (in this case pertaining to the actual shape of the image-display mechanism). This is the simulation's *directive* function. Finally, the simulation helps one realize that the theory makes certain predictions; this is its *deductive* function. If a mechanism originally posited to explain one sort of results *can* be easily used to explain performance in some other task, it *should* be so applied, leading to predictions about this behavior. Also, mechanisms originally posited to deal with particular sets of results do not exist independently, but affect one another's operation. Given a complex theory positing interactions among numerous components, it is not always obvious what are the predictions of the theory. Actually running the simulation sometimes produces unexpected results.

Along with its virtues, the simulation technique does have some problems. I claim that the simulation technique fosters the development of an explicit, general, self-consistent cognitive theory and then facilitates testing whether that theory is adequate to account for some results. The test for behavioral adequacy is straightforward: Given analogous input, the simulation should produce output analogous (in the relevant dimensions —for example, relative latency, not pressure of button-pushing) to that produced by human subjects. There is a major problem with this approach, however; the program will not actually run without numerous "kluges," numerous ad hoc manipulations required by the realities of working with a digital computer and a programming language like ALGOL or LISP.

The actual simulation, then, is a mixture of two kinds of structures and processes: those motivated by the theory and those of no theoretical interest but of crucial practical importance. The problem is to separate the kernels from the chaff. There are three reasons we need to do this. The first one concerns the problem of knowing what class of theories is embodied in a simulation. A given program could be taken as an instantiation of a very narrow, highly specified class, in which case all of the structures and processes would be treated as defining features of the class, or as an instantiation of a very broad, underdetermined class, in which case only a few structures and processes would have theoretical import. Without knowing what is important about a simulation we have no hope of knowing when two alternative models are in the same equivalence class. The second reason for specifying the theoretically important features of the program is a practical one: Without doing so, how can we test the theory? Only by claiming that certain features are sufficient to engender some consequence can we make predictions. The third reason is methodological, a way of turning the simulation technique into an even more powerful tool for use in theory building. If we can characterize the important aspects of programs, we then can compare programs that are alike in these regards but different in others. Should some of these programs prove to be better at simulating behavior than others, our attention will be directed to properties of the programs that we previously considered incidental. Simply by observing the workings of different instantiations of a class, then, we can gain information that will further constrain the class of acceptable theories.

In order for a computer program to serve as an embodiment of a theory, we must have a "metadescription" of the program. This description should state the important principles of the theory and describe the corresponding features of the program. If this is successfully accomplished, the program can be regarded as a "proof procedure," allowing one to see whether certain conclusions follow from one's premises (principles). The problem, of course, is in how to specify this metadescription. The ideal would be a precise, explicit language in which to specify the theory and how it maps into the program. I have only the faintest of glimmerings of how this could be done in the present case. Alternatively, as a stopgap we can (1) deliberately distinguish between the theory-relevant assumptions about structures and processes and the incidental properties of the model, and (2) choose our level of discourse about the program such that the theoretically important features are highlighted. It then becomes an empirical question, as far as I can see, whether all models that meet this description behave as claimed; finding that they do not would serve as a means for further defining the theory. Although this way of dealing with the "kernel/chaff problem" is clearly inadequate in the final analysis, it does not seem an unreasonable way to begin.

2.1 Structures

Images have two major components. The "surface representation" is the quasi-pictorial entity in active memory that is accompanied by the experience of "having an image." The "deep representation" is the information in long-term memory from which the surface image is derived. Although I will defer providing detailed accounts of the results presented earlier (and those in the literature) until later chapters, I will refer briefly to some of these findings in order to motivate aspects of the model.

2.1.1 The Surface Representation

The quasi-pictorial image that we experience is represented by a configuration of points in a matrix, which corresponds to a "visual buffer." An image is displayed by selectively filling in cells of this matrix. The surface image in the simulation derives its properties in part from properties of the medium in which it occurs, as described below.

2.1.1.1 The Medium

Formatting. 1. The visual buffer functions as if it were a coordinate space. Information is represented in this space by selectively filling in local regions to depict portions of the represented object or objects. The visual buffer is simulated in the model by an array, henceforth called the "surface matrix."

2. The visual buffer has only a limited spatial extent, as suggested by the experiments on measuring the visual angle of the mind's eye. Thus, images cannot be too large or they will not fit in the medium. This makes sense if this structure is also shared in vision, since the eyes subtend only a limited arc. This structure also has a specific shape. At least for the regions of highest resolution, this shape appears to be roughly circular (see chapter 3, section 2.4.1).

Accessibility. 1. The visual buffer has limited resolution, causing contours to become obscured if an object is pictured too small. This property is based on the finding that subjectively smaller images are more difficult to inspect. Importantly, in our model the surface matrix has a limited number of cells, and hence has a "grain." If images are too small (relative to the size of the matrix), a number of points will be mapped into the same cell, obscuring contour and texture information.* We expect that when

---

*This property of the model could have been built into the nature of the procedures that "inspect" the image. That is, the details could have been present in the matrix but, if too small, undetectable given the limited sensitivity of the interpretive routines. This is a good example of a "structure/process tradeoff" which seemed difficult to pursue empirically. We chose to place the bottleneck in the representation because it seemed a priori unlikely that a representational medium would have evolved to a precision in excess of the capacities of the interpretive procedures that operate on it.

more material is compressed into a smaller area, this region is "denser" or "sharper" than when such compression does not occur. We modeled this property by placing a capital letter in a cell when more than one point is mapped into that cell; when only a single point is mapped into a cell, a lower-case letter is used.

2. Images are most vivid and most sharply defined near the center of the medium in which they occur, and become more degraded toward the periphery. This property was suggested by the finding that estimates of the size of the angle of the mind's eye (measured in the experiments of chapter 3, section 2.4) were reduced when a stringent definition of "overflow" was provided in the instructions; this seems to indicate that resolution gradually fades off toward the periphery, that overflow is not all-or-none. This property may reflect either capacity limitations or structural variables. In the first case, the imagery system may have only a limited "processing capacity" (however defined, for present purposes) with which to display images. If so, some sort of distribution of activation may occur, and it makes sense that some region should be fully activated rather than the entire image being degraded. If the entire image were degraded, it would not be a very effective representational device. If some portion is more strongly activated than the others, it is reasonable to posit that the central region of the visual buffer is allocated full capacity; if not, the distribution of activation would be asymmetrical around the area of highest activation (if it were symmetrical, of course, the point of highest activation would be equivalent to the "center"). In this case, limited capacity could be modeled by simply having a lower proportion of squares filled near the edges of the surface matrix. The second reason resolution may decrease toward the periphery would lend genuine explanatory adequacy to the theory, if true: If the visual buffer also supports the representations underlying visual experience of a percept, then this structure needs to have high resolution only near the fovea. That is, the receptive fields on the retina become increasingly large and less sensitive with distance from the fovea. Hence, the central representational structure needs to be able to represent only relatively low-resolution material near the periphery. On this view, the squares of our matrix would become larger toward the periphery. Although the two alternative conceptions are potentially distinguishable empirically, considerations of potential explanatory adequacy and computational ease* led us to implement the current model the second way: the size of the "functional cells" increases toward the periphery, such that only one (randomly chosen) cell in a set of nine adjacent ones (forming a 3 x 3 square) is available to be filled in the outer

---

*It was extremely difficult to simulate scanning to overflowed regions (which requires filling in material at the leading edge, as will be discussed) using the first alternative, but very easy using the second one.

regions of the surface matrix. In the highly resolved central regions the grain is smaller and hence resolution is higher.*

3. Representations within the visual buffer are transient, requiring effort to maintain. That is, as soon as an image is generated, it begins to fade; if images are constructed by placing parts sequentially, only so much material can be placed before the initially activated portions fade away. Thus, the visual buffer has a limited "capacity" defined by the rate at which material in it fades and the rate at which new material can be inserted (or old material "refreshed"). Inclusion of this property was originally motivated by results reported earlier in chapter 3, section 2.2, which indicated that more time is required to see portions of more complex images; these results make sense if parts of images fade with time, and when an image has more parts it becomes increasingly less likely that the entire image can be maintained at once. In addition, numerous anecdotal reports indicate that images seem to fade in and out of awareness. In our model, relative sharpness (indicating recency of being "refreshed") is indicated by the letter used in depicting a part, letters nearer to the beginning of the alphabet indicating more recent generation.

2.1.1.2 Data-Structures

Format. The surface image depicts information about spatial extent; it also is capable of displaying information about texture, sharpness, contrast, and the like. As discussed earlier, for an image to depict a thing portions of it correspond to portions of the represented thing, the interpoint spatial relations among these portions are implicit in the image, and so on (see the characterization of the "privileged properties" of images in chapter 3, section 1.0). Inclusion of these properties was motivated by the results of the experiments demonstrating that imaged extent determines scanning time and that subjective size affects image-inspection time and later memory.

Organization. Individual images may be organized into a detailed rendition of a single object or into scenes by juxtaposing them spatially in the visual buffer. Because parts of composite images are posited to be constructed serially, and once constructed they immediately begin to fade, the individual parts of a composite image will be at different "fade phases." Fade phase imposes an organization on the surface image, because points at the same phase will be grouped together (according to the Gestalt law of "common fate"). Thus, the surface image itself may be parsed into component objects and parts thereof. (This property of sur-

---

*At one point we also posited an inactivated region of the visual buffer at the very periphery, where an image could "wait in the wings" (see Kosslyn and Shwartz, 1977.) This has proven unnecessary given the "inverse mapping function" discussed below, and we no longer posit such a region.

face images was not initially planned, but is a natural consequence of our claims about image generation and maintenance.)

Content. Images depict appearances. These appearances are "viewer centered" (to use Marr and Nishihara's, 1978, term), being depicted from a particular point of view. Images may be repositories of information about the depicted objects themselves, or images of objects may be used to represent other ideas. For example, an image of three people standing on a line may be used to represent their relative intelligence. Note that the content is determined not just by the image itself but also by the nature of the interpretive processes operating on the image. We are specifying the nature of a *system* in which the properties of data-structures are to be understood only in the context of the processes that operate on them. The range of the possible contents of images is at present an open empirical question, in part answered in the remaining chapters of this book.

In summary, the five properties of the visual buffer we modeled are as follows: (1) The visual buffer functions as a coordinate space. (2) The visual buffer has a limited spatial extent and a shape, as determined empirically. (3) The visual buffer has only a limited resolution; thus there are only a limited number of cells in the surface matrix in our model. (4) Resolution decreases from the center, as reflected in the model by the functional size of the cells in the surface matrix increasing toward the periphery. (5) Representations in the visual buffer are transient; this was implemented by using procedures that print parts of images with different letters, which index recency. The properties of the surface image data-structures are as follows: (1) Visual mental images are quasi-pictorial entities. As such they consist of patterns of activation in the visual buffer (surface matrix, in our model). These data-structures underlie the experience of seeing. (2) Individual images may be organized into a detailed image of a single object or into a scene. The individual components of a composite are preserved in the image, each being at a different relative "fade phase." (3) Images depict appearances of objects as seen from a particular point of view. The objects themselves can represent a wide, as yet unspecified, range of information.

2.2.2 The Underlying "Deep" Representations

Our earlier findings suggested that there are two sorts of representations underlying images, one "perceptual" (representing "literal" appearances, how something looked) and one discursive (describing a thing, a scene, or aspects thereof).*

---

*For want of a better term, I will use the word "literal" to refer to the long-term memory encodings of quasi-pictorial information, although these representations are not literally literal (as it were). That is, these representations are the products of a complex encoding process and are not photographically accurate.

2.2.2.1 The Literal Encodings

2.2.2.1.1 The Medium

Formatting. (1) The long-term memory medium does not function as a coordinate space. Rather, it stores encodings in nonspatial units, which are modeled by "files" on a disk storage device in the simulation. These units are structured to store the actual underlying literal encoding, be it a Fourier transform, shape primitives (like lines and angles), or something else. In the simulation, the files store lists of polar coordinates. (2) The units are identified by a name. The name indicates both the contents and the format of the encoding. In the model, the file name is followed by an IMG extension (for example, CHAIR.IMG) to identify it as containing a literal encoding.

Accessibility. (1) The units (files, in the model) are accessed by name. (2) Information about extent along a single dimension can be accessed directly, without the necessity of first generating a surface image. This property is required in order to adjust the size at which a part will be imaged so it will fit correctly on an imaged object (as will be discussed shortly).

2.2.2.1.2 The Data-Structures

Format. Because the surface representation in our model occurs in a matrix of filled or unfilled cells, the underlying representation of literal appearances consists of lists specifying where cells should be filled. We needed a format that would allow us to explain how people can preset the size of their images, since we had data indicating that people could readily image objects at different sizes. We also had data indicating that people could image two objects far apart as easily as close together. These concerns, plus considerations of parsimony, led us to adopt a polar coordinate format. That is, we specified the relative location of each point by an r, Θ pair, indicating distance and angular orientation relative to an origin in the surface matrix. This format makes it easy to vary size (by multiplying the r values), allows relatively easy shifting of location in the surface matrix by moving the origin, and is very economical (since blank cells need not be stored). It is obvious that a list of Cartesian coordinates would allow the same operations, but a little less easily. In the present version of the theory it is left open whether this format is in terms of Fourier transforms, "shape primitives" (like lines and angles), or something more abstract, or even whether the underlying literal representation is depictive in the sense defined in chapter 3. These are empirical questions. Note, however, that the claim that the content of these data-structures is information about the surface appearance of objects rules out a simple generalized cone or cylinder format (see Marr and Nishihara, 1978), which consists of only a description of the structure of a shape (represented by a set of axes), as the sole representational format in long-term memory.

Organization. (1) The results discussed in chapter 4 led us to assume that any given object may be represented in memory by more than just a single encoding. That is, those data seemed to indicate that people could encode multiple units and later amalgamate these into a single image. I hypothesize that all underlying image representations of objects have a "skeletal encoding," which represents a global shape (or the "central" shape). This encoding represents the literal information stored in memory upon an initial look. In addition, there may be subsidiary encodings of "second looks." (2) The individual encodings of literal information are linked together by propositional relations, according to the present theory. These propositions note where on the skeleton the part belongs and how it is attached (as will be discussed in more detail shortly).* These propositional relations result in image encodings being organized in a roughly hierarchical fashion. This structure was motivated by our finding that images of objects with more parts required more time to generate, even if the parts were created by simply cutting up the same object into more segments, and presenting the segments sequentially prior to imaging. Further, Rock, Halper, and Clayton (1972) provide data indicating that people first encode global shape information and only thereafter see particular details. In addition, Rock (1973) presents evidence that parts are recognized only in the context of the whole; if the orientation of a figure is mistakenly assigned, people misinterpret its parts. Presumably, one encodes the global information first and relates the parts to this—as we have modeled. Thus, we have a loosely hierarchical representation: Parts are encoded as being attached to other parts which ultimately must be attached to the "skeletal image."

Content. Literal encodings contain information that can evoke a surface image. As such, these encodings have the same content as the surface images themselves. In the model the origin of the polar coordinates is always set at the center of the object, but the precise contents of these encodings are dependent on the perceptual encoding processes, which fall outside the domain of an imagery theory.

2.2.2.2 The Propositional Encodings

The other component of the underlying representation of an image is a list of facts in a propositional format.

---

*The word "part" will be used to refer to any local region of an object. I assume that "bottom up" parsing procedures operate such that the perceived units—which may be encoded—usually correspond to parts of an object (such as the arms, legs and head of a person), but this need not be so. A subsidiary encoding can be of any arbitrary local region.

2.2.2.2.1 The Medium

Formatting. (1) The long-term memory medium is structured to contain sets of lists of propositions. These lists are stored in files in the model. (2) Lists are named, and the names indicate both the contents and format of the encodings. In the model, the names are followed by the extension PRP (for example, CAR.PRP) to indicate that the file contains propositional encodings.

Accessibility. (1) Lists are accessed by name. (2) Lists are searched serially, starting from the top. This assumption will allow us to explain why more highly associated parts of an object are affirmed more quickly than less associated ones when imagery is not used, if association strength reflects the way entries on the list are ordered.

2.2.2.2.2 The Data-Structures

Format. The entries on these lists are represented in a propositional format, as defined in chapter 3, section 1.0.

Organization. Lists may be organized hierarchically or in any graph structure. In the simulation this is accomplished by the structure of the "pointers" stored in the file; a pointer names another file that can be looked up in sequence. It is an empirical question how a given representation or class of representations is in fact organized.

Content. Lists contain the following information:

1. Parts of an object or scene, indexed in the model by the relation HASA followed by the part name (for example, HASA.ARM). If people have *any* propositional encodings, they surely have this sort. (See Anderson and Bower, 1973, and Anderson, 1976, for evidence that propositional representation does occur in human memory.)

2. The location of the imaged part on an object, or the location of an object in a scene. Locations are indicated by a relation and a "foundation part" (for "cushion," "LOCATION FLUSHON SEAT," FLUSHON being the relation, SEAT being the foundation part). We posit this kind of list-entry on the basis of our finding that memorized descriptions of relations among objects can be used in constructing images (chapter 4, section 3.0).

3. The rough size category to which the object or part belongs, which is ultimately relative to a single standard (such as human body size).* As will be discussed in chapter 9, we have data indicating that this sort of representation is in fact used in the course of cognition.

---

*It is an open question whether size tags are all relative to a single standard or are relative to different immediate standards, which themselves are measured relative to a single standard. For example, the size of parts could be relative to the objects to which they belong. The present claim is only that sizes of objects are ultimately relative to a single standard, allowing comparison of relative sizes of objects or parts thereof.

4. An abstract description of critical aspects of a part's or object's appearance. We obviously need some sort of description of things in order to recognize them. In the model this description is in terms of a set of procedures, which must be executed successfully in a specified sequence in order to identify and locate the object or part.

5. The name of the object's superordinate category (for example, "SUPERORD.FURNITURE" in the model). This is necessary if people can make deductions from superordinates, which seems clearly true (of adults —see Flavell, 1977).

6. The name(s) of encodings storing a literal representation of the part's or object's appearance. Since one usually sees numerous examples of parts and objects, one may have many names of these encodings (represented by r, Θ "image files" in the model) associated with a concept. The names may index the time and place of having seen the object as well as or instead of its English-word name.

7. Finally, we assume that people have representations of the meanings of various relations (like "left of," "flush on," "under," and so on). In the simulation we represent such information in separate files that are named by the relation. In these files are abstract encodings (numbers, in the model) that can used to determine which procedures should be executed to place the contents of two IMG files in the specified relation to each other. The specification of a relation may be very particular; that is, there may be many distinguishable sorts of "under," depending on what sorts of objects are involved. Many of these distinctions can be expressed in English with phrases ("tucked slightly in and under"), but some may not. We have simply used single words as names of relations in the model, but realize that something more abstract may in fact be required in order to provide an accurate model of human representation and processing of relations. "FLUSHON," for example, means that an added part (such as a cushion of a chair) should fit on another part (the seat) such that it neither overlaps nor fails to cover.

In summary, we assign the following characteristics to the long-term memory representations underlying images: The medium is not structured spatially, but stores units of information corresponding to files on a disk in a computer. These encodings are accessed by name. The names indicate the contents and the format of the encodings. The units are specialized to represent either literal encodings of appearance or lists of facts. Lists of facts are searched serially from the top. The actual data-structures have the following properties: (1) They have both "propositional" and "literal memory" components. (2) The literal memory component contains representations that underlie the quasi-pictorial experience of imaging; they produce an internal depiction of the appearance of an object or scene. A skeletal shape is always encoded, and representations of local regions may also be encoded. The literal representations may be easily adjusted

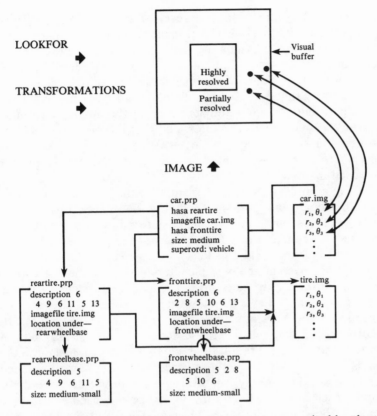

Figure 5.2. A schematic representation of the structures posited by the theory. The words in large type indicate the major processes and the locus of their action.

prior to producing a surface image to alter the subjective size of images, and to alter the relative locations of imaged parts or objects. (3) The "propositional" component consists of list-like structures. These lists contain the various types of information described above. (4) The underlying structure is loosely hierarchical, propositions indicating how images of parts ultimately are related to positions on a "skeletal" shape. Lists of propositions may also be organized into hierarchies and other graph structures. Figure 5.2 schematizes the way we have modeled the structures posited by the present theory.

2.3 Image Processes

The data-structures described above are processed in various ways, depending on the task being performed. Our theory posits three basic sorts of processes, all of which work together: procedures for mapping deep representations into surface representations, for generating images; procedures for evaluating a surface image, for finding a pattern representing some part or for evaluating the level of resolution of the image; and procedures for transforming an image, for adjusting size, for scanning, and for rotation. Some of the image transformations make use of an "inverse mapping function," which allows one to recover which underlying deep representations (coordinate pairs, in the model) were mapped into a given region of the visual buffer—allowing one to keep track of portions of the image when they are moved. We will consider each of these processes in turn. In subsequent chapters we will also consider when imagery is used in answering questions.

Describing a process model is difficult. On the one hand, it is easy to present a flowchart and then simply follow the arrows, discussing each box in turn. This is very concrete and easy to follow. On the other hand, this tack fails to convey the actual flavor of the operating simulation. It makes things look too rigid and lockstep. In reality, the very fact of a given transition, given all the possible alternatives, can be interesting and impressive. Further, flowcharts do not convey the theory dictating the processing sequence; they do not reveal the actual claims about processing, but only a description of how it proceeds in specific situations. On the other hand, simply listing the various posited processes in terms of their input conditions, operation (that is, what they do), and output characteristics fails to convey how these processes actually work in concert. Thus, I have decided to play it both ways. I will first describe the main procedures used in the program, the "functional capacities" posited by the theory. These procedures are all available all of the time, but are called up in a particular sequence depending on the particular circumstances (including task requirements) at hand. I claim that people have the functional capacities (that is, are capable of performing the functionally equivalent operations) that correspond to each of these procedures. Following the description of the main procedures used in a given task-domain, I will present a flowchart and trace through some examples of specific models derived from the general model. The theory-relevant procedures of the model are summarized in table 5.2.

2.3.1 Image Generation

The basic procedures used in generating images are called PICTURE, FIND, and PUT, all of which are coordinated by IMAGE. PICTURE converts a literal representation in long-term memory into the corresponding surface image. In the program, a file of r, Θ coordinates (representing the long-term memory of a literal visual appearance of an object) is converted into a set of points in the surface matrix; in so doing, a mapping function is used. This function adjusts the size of the image by multiplying or dividing the *r* values by some factor. The location may be set by shifting the placement of the origin (to which all *r*, Θ values are relative) in the Cartesian space of the matrix (which involves adding or subtracting values to those specified in the IMG file), and the orientation may be altered by adjusting the Θ values. (We did not initially plan on this last property of images, but it is clearly implied by our representation, as will be discussed in chapter 8).

FIND is used to locate the "foundation part" where a new part will be placed. FIND is an interface between a propositional representation of a category (such as a car's rear tire) and a spatial pattern corresponding to an exemplar of that category. In the simulation, FIND operates on the surface matrix. Upon locating a pattern of points that corresponds to a part or object, FIND passes back the location in the surface matrix (specified in Cartesian coordinates). In order to "look" for the location where a part should be placed, FIND first accesses the description of the foundation part, which is stored in a propositional file associated with the object's name, and then looks up and executes in an ordered sequence the tests corresponding to each component of the description. I make no claims that the specific procedures used by FIND actually reflect those used by people; to solve this problem would be to solve much of the problem of how people recognize patterns. Instead, I simply make the very weak claim (which can hardly be wrong) that *some* kinds of procedures are used in order to classify spatial patterns; the particulars of our procedures were constructed simply for convenience, and none of the explanatory power of the model rides on the details of these procedures.

PUT is a procedure that integrates a stored encoding of the appearance of a part into a pattern already in the surface image. For example, in the simulation PUT places a tire at the correct location on an image of a car's body. In order to integrate a part, PUT must first look up the location where the part should be placed and then locate that "foundation part" via FIND. FIND provides the information necessary for PUT to calculate the appropriate size of the to-be-integrated part. PUT also looks up a description of the relation (UNDER, here), and uses the size and relative offset specifications to specify what mapping function should be used when the points depicting the part are printed out (that is, how much should be added or subtracted or multiplied or divided to the *r*, Θ values when they are printed out). PUT then calls PICTURE, which actually generates the image of the part using the mapping function computed by PUT.

These three procedures are coordinated by a procedure called IMAGE, which in theory interfaces with the rest of the hypothesized cognitive system (that is, a language comprehender, problem-solving apparatus, and so on). In the actual model, IMAGE interfaces primarily with the user, who specifies which images to generate and may indicate the size orientation,

Table 5.2. Outline of the theory-relevant processes in the model.

Name	Type[1]	Input[2]	Operation	Output
PICTURE	P	r, θ file [size, location, orientation]	Maps points into surface matrix; mapping function may be adjusted to vary size, location, and/or orientation.	Configuration of points depicting contents of an IMG file (produces new format; if mapping function adjusted also produces new content).
FIND	C	Name of sought part	Looks up description; looks up procedures specified in description; executes procedures on surface matrix.	Passes back Locate/Not Locate; if Locate, passes back Cartesian coordinates of part.
PUT	P	Name of to-be-placed part	Looks up name of image file, location relation, and foundation part; looks up description of foundation part and relation; calls FIND to locate foundation part; adjusts mapping function; calls PICTURE.	Part integrated into image (produces new content).
IMAGE	P	Name of to-be-imaged object(s) [size, location, orientation, level of detail]	Locates IMG file; calls PICTURE [if size, location, or orientation specified, adjusts mapping function; if detail required, searches for HASA entries, calls PUT].	Detailed or skeletal image at specified or default size, location, and/or orientation (produces new content with different format, organization).
RESOLUTION	P	Surface image	Computes density of points in image.	A number indicating dot density of image (produces new format).
REGENERATE	A	Surface image	Works over surface matrix, refreshing most-faded parts first until all parts are refreshed.	Image reactivated, with sharpness relations among parts altered (alters content).

Command	Type	Input	Description	Effect
LOOKFOR	P	Command to find a named part or property on an image	Calls REGENERATE; looks up description and size of part; calls RESOLUTION; if density not optimal, calls ZOOM or PAN; checks whether image overflows in direction of part, if so calls SCAN; calls FIND; if part not located searches for relevant HASA entries, calls PUT to insert regions, calls FIND.	Found/Not Found response.
SCAN	A	Image, direction of required shift [rate]	Moves all points in surface matrix along vector; fills in new material at leading edge via inverse mapping function.	Image repositioned (alters content).
ZOOM	A	Surface image, target resolution [rate]	Moves all points in surface matrix out from the center; fills in new material via inverse mapping function; calls RESOLUTION; calls PUT to insert new parts as resolution allows.	Scale change in image, higher resolution, and new parts (alters content).
PAN	A	Surface image, target resolution [rate]	Moves all points in surface matrix in from the center.	Scale change in image, lower resolution (alters content).
ROTATE	A	Image, angle, and direction [rate]	Moves all points in bounded region in specified direction around a pivot.	Reorients image (alters content).

1. A indicates alteration transformations, which alter the initial data-structure; P indicates production transformations that do not alter the initial data-structure but produce a new one from it; C indicates comparison operations that compare two data-structures or parts thereof.

2. Optional input is indicated in brackets.

location, and level of detail desired. IMAGE looks up the to-be-imaged object's PRP file and looks to see if an IMG file is listed; it ceases searching as soon as one IMG file is found or as soon as the list is exhausted and no such listing is located. IMAGE calls PICTURE to actually form an image of the named object. If a particular size, location, or orientation is specified, IMAGE adjusts the mapping function used by PICTURE. If a detailed image is required, IMAGE searches for HASA entries in the object's PRP file, and if it finds one it calls PUT to integrate that part into the image. It does this until five or so HASA's have been found or until no more can be located in the object's PRP file. IMAGE also currently interfaces with question-answering procedures, allowing us to make some predictions about when imagery will be spontaneously used (as will be developed in chapter 9).

Probably the best way to illustrate how the structures and procedures described above work together during image generation is to trace through some examples. Thus, let us now consider a detailed flowchart.

2.3.1.1 Generating Images in the Process Model

Generating a skeletal image. The flowchart outlining how surface images are generated from deep representations is presented in figure 5.3. Figure 5.4 shows two simulated images of a car that were produced by our program, a "skeletal image" without added details (top), and an elaborated image (bottom). (All the images illustrated here are printouts of the surface matrix, depicting configurations of points available to the FIND procedures.) In order to generate the skeletal image, we first entered a command to image a car. The program immediately looked up a file listing facts about that object; if it could not find such a file, the named thing was novel and the program obviously could not proceed further.* Note that the underlying representations of names are in a propositional format, and hence are presumably accessed by different but synonymous words in natural language. The file located in generating this skeletal image was labeled CAR.PRP; the program assumes that files with a "PRP" extension contain statements in a propositional format. One of the statements listed in the file may be the name of another file, with an indication that this file contains information about the literal appearance of the object or part. In this case, only IMAGEFILE CAR.IMG was listed in the CAR.PRP file (see figure 5.2). Upon locating this, the IMAGE procedure then looked up this file, which contains a list of r, Θ coordinates. The next step is to call the PICTURE procedures, to print the stored points in the surface matrix.

---

*In a more detailed flowchart there would be a test for the presence of a sought representation after every attempt to look one up; if a sought representation is not found, the program sends an error message, unless explicit provisions (noted above) are provided. In the service of clarity, I have not included each of these tests in the flowcharts presented here.

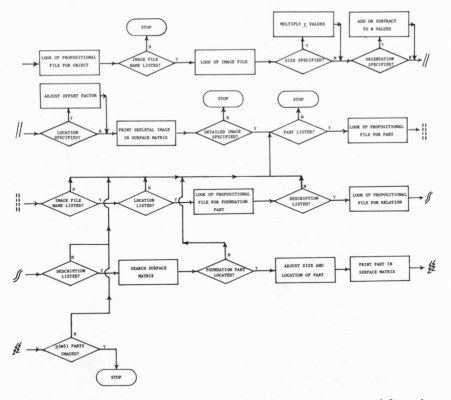

Figure 5.3. A flowchart outlining how surface images are generated from deep representations.

Before doing so, however, one can specify the size (by altering r values), orientation (by altering Θ values), and/or location (by altering the origin) of the object in the image. In the examples in figure 5.4, the image was centered in the surface matrix, since no explicit location specifications were provided, and printed so it fell just into the most activated portion of the surface matrix, which is the default size used when no explicit size requirement is entered. (The motivation for these default values will be discussed in chapter 6.) One can specify a command like "IMAGE CAR LARGE AT 10, 20," which will cause the r values to be adjusted and the origin (which is always the center of the imaged object) to be moved to the specified place.

We have yet to perform research indicating whether the "skeletal file" ought to contain a low-resolution global representation or a representation of just the most structurally central part (the body, in this case). Either option can be incorporated without changes in the formal structure of the model. We have chosen to store only the body of the car in the skele-

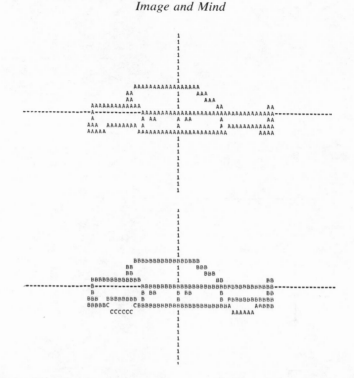

Figure 5.4. Two simulated images of a car: a "skeletal image" without added details (top) and an elaborated image (bottom).

tal file for expository purposes; this allows us to illustrate more clearly how "second looks," additional details, are integrated into the image. In chapter 6 I will discuss some of the conditions that govern how much detail is inserted into an image; in some cases people may generate a skeletal image and cease construction with that (perhaps waiting for additional task requirements before filling in further information). In any event, we have demonstrated that people *can* generate elaborated images, and that generation time increases linearly with number of underlying units (see chapter 4). Thus, let us now consider how our model composes an image from multiple underlying parts.

Generating an elaborated image. Although the default is to generate only the skeleton, one can specify generation of a fully elaborated image, as is illustrated at the bottom of figure 5.4. In this case, the skeletal image first is constructed as discussed above. Next the IMAGE procedure checks to see whether the object has parts explicitly noted in the object's propositional file. Here, HASA.REARTIRE was found. At this point, PUT is called and looks up the propositional file associated with this object (REARTIRE.PRP) and tries to find a statement that an image of this part is stored in memory (we are now in the third row of figure 5.3). If, as here, it finds a notation that an image file exists—IMAGEFILE TIRE.IMG—the program goes on to try to integrate this part into the image. If it does not find an image file associated with the part, it returns control to IMAGE, which returns to the object's propositional file and looks for another part listing. This is clearly a first approximation to human imagery; people probably have all sorts of inference procedures that will allow them to construct *some* image of an object, if only by imaging components listed in a description. This much more highly constructive imagery will not—I claim—differ in kind from that described here, and seems not worth developing in detail until we understand the simpler cases studied here. In general, at this point we frequently have the simulation simply terminate processing in cases where a human would adopt a more complex strategy; we assume that these strategies will not contradict any principled claims of the core theory, but will simply be more intricate applications of our principles or—at worst—will require new assumptions that will supplement, not contradict, the existing ones.

Having found that the object has a part, and that there is a literal representation of the part's appearance, the program will next attempt to add the image of the part into the already generated skeletal image. PUT now looks up the location of the part, the rear tire in this case. Locations consist of two parts, a relation (UNDER, in this case) and a foundation part (REARWHEELBASE). If either of these specifications is missing, PUT will not be able to adjust the part's location correctly, and hence IMAGE will give up with this part and check to see whether another part is listed in the object's PRP file (and then will repeat the above procedure with this part). (It often seems, however, that we can know what some part or thing looks like without knowing where it belongs; for example, one may know what a friend's ring looks like, but never notice which finger—or which hand, for that matter—it is worn on. An improved version of the program might have "best guess" inference procedures for integrating parts when locations are not fully specified; this is easier said than done, however.)

If PUT successfully looks up the location proposition in the part's PRP file, it then must locate the foundation part in the image (on the skeleton, in this case; in theory, however, parts can sometimes be attached to other parts). In order to do this, it needs a description of the appearance of the foundation part. Thus, the propositional file associated with the foundation part, REARWHEELBASE.PRP in this example, is looked up. A part's description is specified simply as an ordered list of numbers that index procedures. (In the model the procedures are things like "find the lowest and left-most point," "proceed right along a straight line until reaching an intersection with another line," and so on.) If the part is present, these procedures should be able to be executed in sequence successfully. We currently have a "library" of search procedures, each of which is numbered; a series of these numbers constitutes the description. We could have stored descriptions as a list of names corresponding to what the procedures actually do; our suspicion was, however, that natural language is too weak to easily draw the distinctions necessary to specify the different procedures humans actually use, and that such descriptions are probably stored in some kind of abstract format.

If PUT locates the description of the foundation part, it next looks up the PRP file named by the relation and looks for its description. This description corresponds to a set of spatial relations, each of which also corresponds to an entry in a "library" of procedures; these procedures indicate how to adjust parts so they are in the correct spatial locations.

If descriptions of both the foundation part and the relation are found, PUT begins to integrate the tire into the image. FIND is called to locate the foundation part on the image. If all the description procedures are satisfied, FIND has located the part, and the location is passed back to PUT. If the part is not found, IMAGE takes over and attempts to look up another HASA entry in the object's PRP file and integrate this part into the image. (Thus, if fewer foundation parts can be found on smaller images, fewer parts will be processed to the point of actually placing them in the image, and less time spent in generation.) If the foundation part is located in the surface image, its size is assessed. This information is used in conjunction with the description of the relation to adjust the mapping function used by PICTURE when the part is printed out. PUT first adjusts the size scale of the part relative to the skeleton. That is, the skeleton may have been generated at any number of sizes, and the part must be matched to scale. This is done by assessing the size of the foundation part (the wheelbase in this case) and then adjusting to scale the factor by which the r values in the deep representation of the part (the tire) should be multiplied or divided when printed out. That is, the extent of the foundation part along a single dimension (horizontally) is assessed in the image, and then the mapping function for r values (used by PICTURE) is adjusted until the sum of the maximum horizontal (within a tolerance) r values will be the same size. Once the size is adjusted, the origin of the image of the part is adjusted in accordance with the specifications associated with the relation (UNDER, here). These specifications indicate an "offset factor" that should be added or subtracted to the coordinates to place the part in correct relation to the foundation part. Once the values of the mapping function are set, the part is printed out in the image via PICTURE.

This entire procedure may be repeated for up to five or so parts (this value was specified empirically, as will be discussed). On the bottom of figure 5.4, a front tire was also imaged. In this case, the same tire was simply placed in the front. We wanted the model to have this capability because we suspected that people often assume that all tires look alike (or all trees!), and are quite happy to save effort by encoding only a single exemplar, and using it in multiple contexts.

Once an image is constructed, it does not remain transfixed, etched forever before one's mind's eye. The ephemeral, transitory nature of images is well known. In our model, a part begins to fade as soon as it is generated, and work is required to maintain it. In the program, there is a procedure called REGENERATE that "reactivates" parts of the surface image. The theory here is that regenerating parts occurs directly at the surface, that regions in the visual buffer can be kept activated without having to generate the image anew repeatedly. Regenerating from the surface saves one the effort of repeatedly looking up the propositional encodings, relations, and so on. REGENERATE operates by scanning through the surface matrix. When the image is initially generated, each part is printed out with a different letter, the first being printed with an *a*, the next with a *b*, and so on. REGENERATE refreshes the oldest parts first, and the letters are reassigned such that more recently refreshed parts are printed with letters nearer to the beginning of the alphabet. The different letters in the car at the bottom of figure 5.4 reflect recency of being refreshed. In our current implementation, we refresh the surface image only when the program is asked to hold an image or before it looks for a given part (as will be discussed). Unless fading rates vary capriciously, the theory commits us to defining one limit on "image processing capacity" in terms of the rate at which construction and fading proceed: If there are so many parts to be placed that the initially placed ones fade away by the time the last is generated, all parts will not be displayed simultaneously—and "processing capacity" will have been exceeded.*

Generating images at different subjective sizes. We found that people generate subjectively smaller images more quickly than larger ones (but

---

*The original model reported in Kosslyn and Shwartz (1977, 1978) refreshed the image whenever FIND was called. However, when implementing the model this way, we had not considered the fact that FIND was called by IMAGE as well as LOOKFOR. This had an unexpected consequence in that the number of parts refreshed increased nonlinearly with the number of parts added during image generation, since all previously placed parts were refreshed every time prior to placing a new part. Thus, for images with 1, 2, 3, 4, and 5 parts the total number of times REGENERATE updated letters was 1, 3, 6, 10, and 15, respectively. At first blush, it appeared that the model had been disconfirmed before we really got started, given that image-generation times increase linearly with the number of parts added. Upon closer inspection, however, it turned out that the second derivative of the function relating number of times parts are refreshed to number of parts is 1. That is, the increase in the increase of the number of parts refreshed was only 1 for every extra part placed on the image. Given that 15 REGENERATE cycles were executed when 5 parts were placed, the effects of 1 additional part being refreshed were proportionately small. Further, it is possible that smaller parts are refreshed faster than larger ones; if this is so and if parts generally tend to be smaller as more are included in the image, this will further lessen the departure from linearity in increased times. Given the level of precision of measurement in the kind of experiments reported here, the available data do not distinguish between this theory and the simpler one described in this chapter, and thus I chose the simpler one. Which theory is correct, however, is still an open question.

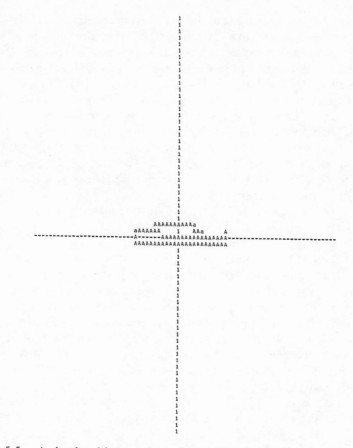

Figure 5.5.   A simulated image of a car at a subjectively small size.

that larger ones are inspected more easily). We hypothesized that this result was due to (*a*) people placing fewer parts on smaller images, and (*b*)
larger parts themselves requiring more time to be evident in an image. In
generating a subjectively small image, a skeletal image is first generated as
before, but now with a smaller size factor. As is evident in figure 5.5, the
resolution is too poor for the wheelbase to be clearly delineated; hence,
the procedure checking for a gap is not satisfied, the foundation part is not
located, and PUT is not provided with the information necessary to place
the tire. Thus, a smaller image will be constructed faster than a larger
elaborated one, since fewer parts will be placed. In addition since less material (fewer dots in the model) must be placed, each part of a smaller
image reaches a given dot density (corresponding to level of sharpness, in
theory) more quickly than will the corresponding parts of a larger image.

Images may also be constructed so large that they overflow the visual buffer, as is illustrated in figure 5.6. As is evident, overflow at the periphery is not all-or-none, but occurs gradually—as mandated by the data described earlier (chapter 3, section 2.4). As the image becomes larger, parts become more sharply delineated (as is evinced by the door handles, which are barely discernible even in figure 5.4 but are clearly evident in figure 5.6).

2.3.2 Inspecting Images

Consider again the kind of phenomenon we are discussing: Try to determine from memory the shape of a beagle's ears. Faced with this request, most people report mentally picturing the animal and then looking at the ears, seeing that they are rounded. We have so far been concerned with what it means to "mentally picture" something, and will now turn to what it means to "look" at an image.

One of the hobbyhorses of the anti-imagery camp is the purported ab-

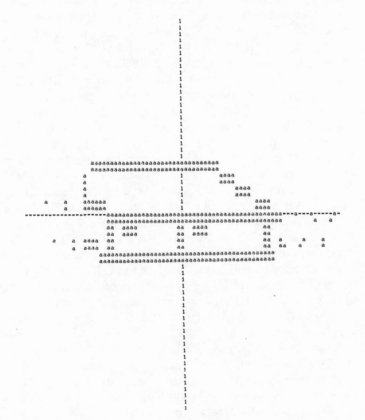

Figure 5.6. A simulated image of a car that has overflowed the surface matrix.

surdity of a "mind's eye." I reviewed most of the arguments in the second chapter of this book, many of which were drawn from Pylyshyn's (1973) paper entitled "What the Mind's Eye Tells the Mind's Brain: A Critique of Mental Imagery." Critics of this idea commonly harp on the observations that there is no eyeball in the brain, and that if there were, there would have to be another brain for the eyeball to report to, which would require yet another eyeball to see the report, and so on in infinite regress. Pomerantz and I argued that these problems are fallacious (Kosslyn and Pomerantz, 1977), and they are in fact nowhere apparent in the simulation model. In the model described here, the "mind's eye" is equated with a set of procedures that operate to categorize spatial patterns; it is an interface between propositional representations and depictive representations. In this section I will describe the way the simulation "inspects" images. Again, I will first describe the procedures, the functional capacities, used in inspecting images, and then use a flowchart to trace through some examples.

I claim that people use the following procedures in inspecting images: FIND classifies parts in terms of semantic categories and their relations, as was described above. RESOLUTION assesses the resolution of the image; in the model, RESOLUTION computes the density of points within an envelope around the image. REGENERATE refreshes the image, as described above. ZOOM, PAN, SCAN and ROTATE transform images to reveal previously obscured parts. These procedures operate in the simulation by selectively moving points in the surface matrix; their operation will be described in more detail in the next section. The image generation procedures PUT and PICTURE are also used sometimes in image inspection. In this case, they are called to elaborate the region of the image where a sought part should be located. Finally, the foregoing procedures are coordinated by another procedure, called LOOKFOR in our program. LOOKFOR accepts commands to locate some part. In so doing, LOOKFOR calls REGENERATE, so the image is as sharp as possible. LOOKFOR also calls RESOLUTION to check to see whether the resolution of the imaged object is in the appropriate range such that the sought part will be visible. LOOKFOR also looks up the size specification of the part and converts it into an optimal density specification, and then compares this to the computed resolution of the image. If need be, LOOKFOR can then call ZOOM or PAN. These procedures adjust the scale of the image to a given "target resolution," as will be described shortly. LOOKFOR also looks up the description of the part and its direction (which is implicit in its description), and then checks to see whether the image has overflowed in that direction. If so, SCAN is called, and the relevant part is centered (and hence most sharply in focus). In addition, LOOKFOR calls FIND, which searches for the sought part. If FIND is unsuccessful, LOOKFOR enters the object's PRP file and searches for HASA entries in the appropriate region. Upon finding a relevant HASA, LOOKFOR calls PUT, which causes the appropriate regions of the image to be filled out by calling PICTURE to print out additional encodings of the appropriate region. So, for example, if the rear tire is not found, all parts near the rear wheelbase will be printed out, in hopes that the tire is an incidental portion depicted in one of these encodings (for example an encoding of the fender region may be imaged, in case the file also contains an encoding of the tire). After the region is elaborated by PUT, FIND is called again. In this case, if FIND locates the part, an affirmative response is given, otherwise a negative response is made. Figure 5.7 schematizes the inspection process; let us now trace through this sequence with a couple of examples.

Locating a part of a centered, medium-sized image. In this example, the program is asked to find the rear tire of a car that is imaged centered and at a medium size (illustrated at the bottom of figure 5.4). First, LOOKFOR calls REGENERATE. Next it attempts to locate a propositional file addressed by the name of the queried property; if no such file can be found, the property is novel and the program will not continue. In this example, the file labeled REARTIRE.PRP is found. The program then looks for a description of the part. We reasoned that if one does not know what a capacitor, for example, looks like, one will not bother exam-

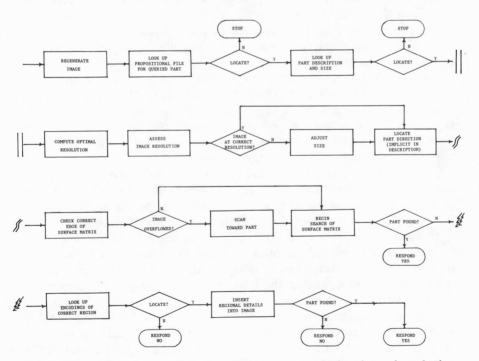

Figure 5.7. A flowchart outlining how images are searched to determine whether the object has a named part.

ining an image of a radio for it, even if one knows—vaguely—what a capacitor is. Given that one knows what the sought part looks like, we posit that one does not immediately begin to search for it. We conjecture that people probably do not bother to examine an image that is clearly too small or too large, but first check the level of resolution of the image and adjust the apparent size if necessary. Our program simulates this by first attempting to look up the size of the part. We now assume two things: (1) that every part that one knows about has a size category associated with it, and (2) that the categories are relative to a common standard (such as the human body). Either of these assumptions could be wrong: One may often infer or guess the size, perhaps by considering the size of the foundation part to which the sought part is attached; and as noted earlier, one may encode part size relative to the object, which in turn is categorized relative to a common standard. We could deal with either possibility without doing any violence to the theory.

As the program now stands, each size category is associated with an "optimal level of resolution" necessary to see the part clearly. Resolution of an image is indexed in our model by dot density; denser images are less resolved, as points run into one another and details are obscured (in our model this is indicated in part by number of capital letters, which indicate overprinting). Ideally, the optimal resolution should take into account information about the material of which an object is composed: If dots represent places where light is deflected by local perturbations on the surface, then mirrors will have fewer dots than cardboard; hence, knowledge of both size and material will be necessary to calculate how dense dots ought to be in order to be able to optimally see some part. In any case, once LOOKFOR computes the optimal dot density, the current level of density is assessed and compared with the optimal; if the current density is not within some specified range, the program "zooms in" or "pans out" as appropriate (via ZOOM or PAN, as will be described shortly) until the dots are at the correct level of density.

Once it has been determined that the image is within the range of resolution necessary to see the sought part, LOOKFOR looks up the direction of the sought part and determines whether the image has begun to overflow the most highly resolved part of the surface matrix in that direction. In this example it has not, so FIND is called directly. FIND is used as it is in generating fully elaborated images: Again, the description of the part is retrieved, and the surface matrix is searched. Given that the whole image is "visible" at once, and at the correct size, the sought part should be evident and the program able to respond in the affirmative, *if* the part is present on the image. That is, we have hypothesized that some relatively small number of parts (outputs from IMG files in the model) can be maintained in the visual buffer at any one time. Thus, there is some probability that a part will not in fact be on the image when it is sought. The ordering of the name of the part (or the region of which it is a portion) in the object's propositional file will determine the likelihood that the part is on the image. We assume that the association strength between a part and an object reflects the relative ordering in this propositional list, as will be discussed in chapters 6 and 7.

If a part is not on the image at the time of query, then, it is placed on the image when needed. LOOKFOR now searches the object's PRP file for the name of the region where the part should be found. It would make sense to look up a HASA entry for the part itself and then to image that part if one were asked to categorize its shape (as with a dog's ears) or relative position (as with the relative height of a horse's knees and the tip of its tail). Usually, however, one probably uses an image to search for the presence of a part only if the part is not directly listed in the object's propositional file (as will be discussed in chapter 9). After the appropriate HASA entries are found (assuming such are encoded), PUT is called, and it tries to insert the relevant parts into the image (as described in the preceding section). FIND is now called again and inspects the elaborated region for the sought part. If the sought part is successfully inserted and then seen, an affirmative response is made. If the foundation part is clearly in focus, we assume the auxiliary encodings of the region can be integrated, so if the sought part is not found at this point the program responds in the negative.

Locating an overflowed part. How does one know the direction in which to scan when searching for a part? If an image either is too large subjectively (occupies too great an area in the visual buffer) or is not centered correctly, a sought part may not be visually interpretable (because it partially or fully overflows the visual buffer). Consider a case, illustrated in figure 5.8, where the front end of a car has overflowed, and one is asked to find the front tire in the image. In this case, in the simulation LOOK-FOR will first scan to the relevant region of the imaged object. LOOK-FOR assesses the direction of the part by sifting through the description of the part and finding an instruction to use a procedure that indicates a particular spatial direction or location of the part; this information is used to direct SCAN to scan in that direction. In our program, SCAN moves the image such that the material previously at the appropriate edge of the surface matrix is shifted into the center, filling in new material at the "leading edge" and deleting material that overflows at the other edge (how this "filling in" process operates will be discussed shortly). Thus, since the front tire is defined as being at the front—which here is equated with "right"—the rightmost portion of the image is shifted to the center.*

---

*The reader will note that parts (such as the rear tire) currently are defined in terms of left and right; this clearly is inadequate, as the car could face either direction. Ideally, we should probably correct this deficit by having the program locate a "landmark" (such as the shape of the front end or the hood ornament) that establishes the direction of the front, and the FIND procedures should be written in terms of orientation-invariant relations like "front" and "back."

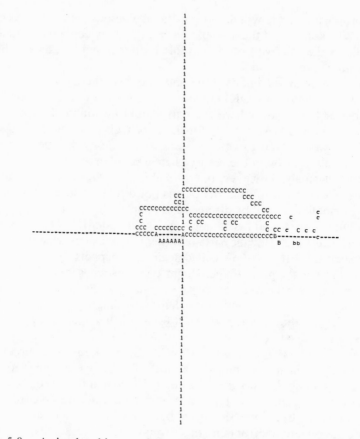

Figure 5.8. A simulated image of a car that has overflowed at one end of the surface matrix.

In theory, FIND inspects the image all the while it is being scanned, but this was difficult to program. In the simulation, once the correct portions of the image are shifted far enough to be sharply in focus, FIND should be able to locate the part on the image after it has been filled in, if the part in fact belongs on the imaged object.*

At present we execute SCAN only after ZOOM or PAN, but it may be that these operations should be called in the opposite order or perhaps simultaneously. In chapter 8, I will discuss research bearing on these hypotheses.

---

*It may be of some interest that the entire problem of how to scan to overflowed regions was neglected until the program was faced with the situation described here. At one point, it could not find the tire, and it seemed as if it had a bug until the image was printed out and the problem realized.

2.3.3 Transforming Images

I have claimed that images may be transformed in the course of inspecting them. For example, if asked whether a frog has a short tail, some people report imaging the animal, and then "rotating" the image and "zooming in" to see whether there is a tail, and if so, whether it is short. As will be discussed, the general finding in investigations of image transformation is that transformations seem to pass through intermediate states. Whether the image is transformed "continuously" or in very small discrete steps is not to the point; the problem is to explain why one passes through the intermediate states in the first place, rather than transforming the image directly from one orientation to another, from one apparent size to another, and so on. At first glance, it may appear that there is no problem here: Images simply rotate, expand, bend, and so on. However, an image is not a picture, is not a rigid physical object that can actually be moved in space and that obeys the laws of physics. As is apparent when one examines our model, the spatial qualities of image representations per se do not necessarily entail continuous or even stepwise transformations; this is a real problem to be explained that is not accounted for simply by appeal to the existence of spatial images (see Pylyshyn, in press).

There are any number of ways of accounting for the fact that images are commonly transformed incrementally. Unfortunately, the spadework necessary to delimit the appropriate class of models has not been done. Thus, I am not in a position to offer seriously a theory of mental transformations. Instead, I will try to use the framework of the model to formulate questions that one would want resolved before committing oneself to a theory. In essense, then, we want guidance in growing a new "decision tree" for this component of the general model. One easy way to raise empirical questions is to consider a number of ways the model can be developed and then to examine the ways in which these accounts differ.

First, there are accounts of image transformations that do not explain the empirical results by appeal to formal properties of the structure of images per se. For example, images could be transformed gradually to allow one to check continuously whether the necessary orientation, resolution, point of focus, and so on had been reached. This would be desirable because an "all-at-once" transformation, in which the transformation is accomplished in one operation regardless of its size, would require one to calculate *exactly* how much to transform the image. If the image overshot or fell short of the mark, additional steps would be required. And the "control structure" required for this kind of convergence procedure is more complicated than one that simply iteratively shifts an image a given number of equal-sized steps until it is correctly adjusted.* Another example of an account that does not rest on properties of images per se

*This account is due to Steven Shwartz.

(such as their being composed of parts that can become scrambled, as will be discussed below) is that offered in chapter 2: Images could be manipulated iteratively because the system evolved to provide simulations of the analogous physical transformations. The problem with these accounts, for present purposes, is that they do not help us to structure a set of issues that can guide an empirical research program. Thus, we have focused on the following classes of accounts, which I hoped would have the virtue of leading to fruitful experiments.

In this theory, transformations involve shifting portions of the image through the visual buffer. Two different sorts of accounts were considered in some detail, each of which had several variants (as will be discussed at length in chapter 8). Both of these classes of accounts rest primarily on the assumption that images are represented not as integral wholes but as configurations of parts. In one model, the points that delineate an imaged object are shifted sequentially through the surface matrix. We could have transformed the points serially and waited until all were transformed before printing them out, but this would have required an additional buffer to hold the transformed points until all were processed—which seemed less than parsimonious. Thus, we decided to move points sequentially and print them as soon as they were transformed. This procedure presents a problem: If a given portion (set of points) is moved too far in one increment, the image becomes fragmented and scrambled. Thus, we posited that there was a limit on how far individual points could be shifted at any one time; this limit depends on the distance a given portion can be moved before a noticeable gap or deformation occurs in the image (and hence depends on the size of the image, among other factors). Thus, only relatively small changes can be made at a time, requiring a series of relatively small transformations. This sort of notion, then, results in increasingly more incremental transformations being made when increasingly larger alterations are made in the size, orientation, or position of an image in the surface display, and hence conforms to the qualitative results in the literature.

The second kind of model of the transformation results we explored involves simulating a mechanism that does not depend on points being shifted sequentially.* On this second view, there are four premises:

Premise 1. Images are transformed a portion at a time (either in parallel or serially).

Premise 2. The system is inherently "noisy" (like all physical systems).

Premise 3. There is a variance around and proportional to the distance a portion is moved in an image (partly because of Premise 2).

---

*Due to the serial nature of the computer, of course, points are never actually shifted in parallel. This fact is irrelevant for purposes of the simulation itself.

Therefore: Portions of images become increasingly scrambled in proportion to the step size.

Premise 4. Procedures that realign portions are effective only with relatively minor amounts of deformation.

Therefore: Portions will be moved only relatively small amounts at any given increment, and transformations will be accomplished by a series of relatively small steps. Hence, more increments will be required for larger transformations.

It is important to realize that the premises outline a class of theories; they delineate the form of an account. They do not define a particular theory or account. The main purpose of this kind of exercise, at this point in the model-building process, is to structure a program of empirical research. In order to develop a detailed account within this framework we must first refine the terms of the premises. As it now stands many of the terms in the premises are "place holders," awaiting further specification, which will arise from a combination of empirical and theoretical work. In particular, we must fix the reference of terms like "portion." (For example, does this term refer to an organized part of the imaged object? an arbitrary portion of the visual buffer in which images occur? or what?). This is largely an empirical exercise. Obviously, it will be very difficult to develop the above framework into a complete model, but we will at least embark on this effort in chapter 8. We must also test the validity of the premises themselves, or—more properly—of the classes of premises specified by each premise in the above framework.*

Upon running our simulation we realized that there was in fact a way of distinguishing between the two broad kinds of account: the piece-at-a-time model (where step size is limited in theory by how far a part may be moved before the image seems to fragment) and the scramble-and-realign model just outlined. In the former model, the step sizes used in a transformation depend on the initial size of the image. The amount a portion can be "moved" without fragmenting the image is larger for larger images than for smaller ones (since the critical variable here would seem to be something like a just-noticeable-difference measure, which depends not on the absolute distance a portion is moved but on the distance relative to the size of the image itself. If this model were correct, then, we would expect (*a*) scanning rates to be generally faster when people scan larger images and (*b*) the rate of size change to increase as an image is expanded, because portions can be moved farther as the size of the image increases (thus, there should be "acceleration" as one "zooms in" on an image). The scramble-and-realign model makes no such predictions. As the Fates

*We have not attempted to distinguish between the serial and parallel versions of Premise 1, however, because nothing else of current theoretical import depends on this distinction.

would have it, the more easily implemented piece-at-a-time model does not fare well at the hands of the reaction-time clock. In addition, the scramble-and-realign model seems more consonant with many people's introspections, especially of what seems to happen when one mentally rotates alphanumeric figures. I, for one, find that even with something as simple as an image of a block-letter R, the front leg bends as I rotate it clockwise, and must be realigned. With something as complicated as a face, the eyes become hopelessly scrambled when I rotate past about 90 degrees; in this case, I seem to lack the necessary "clean-up procedures," and cannot realign the face correctly. Interestingly enough, people are almost unbelievably terrible at recognizing inverted faces (Yin, 1970; Carey, 1978).

We have implemented variants of both sorts of transformation schemes. It should be noted, however, that it is quite difficult to implement the "clean-up" routines necessary for the second scheme to operate, and thus, this scheme works only for a limited (and impoverished) set of images. The specific schemes we have implemented are described below. The most important theoretical aspect of these implementations is that the surface image per se is manipulated. That is, we could have had the transformations operate by altering the mapping function from the deep representation up (for example, by multiplying or dividing the r values when changing size). This was a real possibility that we considered and rejected on empirical grounds (as will be discussed in chapter 8), and is an example of the "directive" function of the model.

In the present theory we distinguish between two types of transformations: *field-general* and *region-bounded*. Field-general transformations necessarily operate over the entire visual buffer, whereas region-bounded ones operate only within a local region of the visual buffer. Scanning and "zooming in" (and its inverse, "panning back") are members of the first class. These operations cannot be limited to selected parts of the visual buffer. Transposition (as in imaging a salt shaker moving across a table top) and relative size changing (such as imaging a salt shaker suddenly growing on a table) are the region-bounded analogues of scanning and zooming. In addition to these transformations, rotation and "special transforms" operate on bounded regions. The latter transforms consist of moving a bounded region of points to produce a given end-configuration (to simulate sheer, stretching, bending, melting, and so on). The transformations we have actually implemented in the general model are described below; these transformations were implemented because they were necessary to provide accounts in our problem-domain (notably scanning and zooming) or have been intensively studied (rotations).

An important feature of the theory at hand is the claim that there is an *inverse mapping function* which allows one to compute which encodings in the deep image representation were mapped into a given portion of the visual buffer. This is necessary for scanning (where new material must be filled in at the leading edge), and scale transformations (which also require filling in, or deletion, of material). In our implementation, there are four parameters that are updated as the image is transformed. One of these is a multiplicative factor for r values, one an additive factor for Θ values, one an additive factor for X coordinates (in the surface matrix), and one an additive factor for Y coordinates. These four parameters specify the size scale, orientation, and offset of the location relative to that encoded in the underlying IMG file. These parameters are set initially to the values used by PICTURE when the image was first printed out, and are updated as points are moved. We can use these values to calculate the range of the underlying r and Θ values mapped into a given coordinate in the surface matrix (as occurs when the image is very small and more than one point is placed in each cell). This "roundoff range" allows us to use the inverse mapping function to recover which underlying r, Θ pairs were overprinted into a single cell. A separate set of parameters must be stored for each part inserted into the image. (This was discovered empirically, by running the program. We initially began by storing only a single set of parameters which applied to all material in the surface matrix; when the image was rotated, however, the parts did not move together around the center of the image, but instead each one rotated around its own origin!)

Scale adjustment. Two transformations alter the apparent scale of imaged objects (not relative size), "zooming in" (ZOOM) or "panning out" (PAN). In the model, these transformations work by first defining a sequence of "rings" around the center of the surface matrix. For zooming in, the outer ring is moved outward and then each ring toward the center is moved outward in succession. For panning out, the rings are pulled in toward the center, again one step at a time starting at the innermost ring. In the first class of models (where fragmentation is the main constraint on step size), the maximal step size of each cycle is set by the starting size of the image; thus, rates of dilation, for example, may increase as the size increases; this prediction was not borne out in the data. Both size alteration schemes result in larger transformations requiring more time, which is consonant with the data to be discussed in chapter 8.

In the course of dilation, points previously mapped into a single cell can be mapped into separate cells, but vice versa if the apparent size scale is reduced. The inverse mapping function allows the program to update the location of every point in the underlying representation so that no points are "forgotten" even when overprinting (placing multiple points per cell) occurs. Further, the inverse mapping function allows the program to keep track of the precise locations of points, even when rounding off of coordinates results in overprinting. The problem here is to explain how images become better delineated as one "zooms in." In order to account for the sharpening of contour as one zooms in, we "move" points in the surface matrix unless the point has been overprinted (as indexed by a capital letter, indicating higher density). In this case, the inverse mapping function is used to recover the underlying coordinates and move the points the proper distance—which may result in two points becoming distinct after having been initially printed into the same cell (because of the roundoff necessary given the grain of the surface matrix). (The reader should keep in mind that these implementation details are intended to model functional capacities of the brain, not copy them.) The foregoing operations are thought of as akin to overcoming spatial summation that occurs when portions are too close together. In addition to this factor, new parts are automatically added as the resolution allows. In the model, the ZOOM procedure repeatedly calls RESOLUTION, which indicates when parts of a given size can be inserted. PUT is called whenever the resolution will allow insertion of one of the five HASA entries listed highest on the object's PRP list. Thus, zooming in not only sharpens contours, but results in additional detail being inserted into the image.

Scanning. In this theory scanning is treated as simply another kind of image transformation. Instead of moving an activated region across the image, in the model we march the points delineating an image across the surface matrix until the sought configuration (part) is in the center of the region of highest resolution. As with the other transformations, the theory posits that portions are moved individually through the visual buffer in a series of small increments. One reason for positing this scanning mechanism is as follows: The data indicated that image acuity gradually drops off toward the periphery. Recall that this finding led us to posit that the center of the visual buffer has the highest resolution; whatever part is centered in the image, then, will be most sharply in focus. Thus, one would accomplish much the same thing by shifting the image such that different portions fall in the center of the visual buffer as by shifting the point of focus itself over the image. In addition, if surface images and the central representations of percepts (those underlying the experience of seeing during perception) do in fact occur in the same neural medium, then the above sort of notion makes sense for the following reason: Many people claim to be able to scan 360 degrees around them in a mental image of a room, but the visual structures need to support only the limited visual arc subtended by the eyes. Thus, one should "bump into edges" if scanning images consists of moving an activated region through the representational structure. If one moves the image through the medium, in contrast, then it is perfectly natural that one can seem to scan indefinitely in a given direction, as long as new portions of the image are continually being constructed at the leading edge. The inverse mapping function is used to selectively print out the underlying portions of the image that will fall in the region exposed at the "leading edge" of the visual buffer. That is, in the model this function picks out the r, Θ pairs that would have been represented by points falling just outside (that is, the distance of an increment outside) the boundaries of the surface matrix, and allows these points to be placed in the gap created by shifting the contents of the matrix in a specified direction.

The basic scanning scheme accounts for the fact that longer distances require more time to traverse. Further, it accounts for the fact that we found no difference in the effects of distance when subjects scanned to overflowed regions versus visible parts of the image. If both kinds of scanning make use of this same shift mechanism, these results make perfect sense. This scheme also makes several predictions, some of which will be tested later. Finally, it leads us to look for similarities between scanning and other imagery transformations, as will be discussed in chapter 8.

Rotation. Image rotation is accomplished by (1) defining a bounded region of the visual buffer (around the to-be-rotated imaged object) and (2) sequentially shifting portions of the image within this region in a given direction. In our model, a wedge of points first is moved in the desired direction, leaving a gap that is filled in by another wedge, and so on until the image has inched all the way around to the first part. The serial nature of the computer left us with an implementation problem: Namely, the initially moved portion overlaps an unmoved portion, and this unmoved portion must be shifted. We distinguish among points delineating the moved portion by making them "brighter" (as indexed by a different symbol). Furthermore, when a point falls into a cell that is already occupied, the brightness is increased even more (represented by yet another symbol). Thus, the program knows that bright dots are not to be moved, but that very bright dots consist of one dot to be moved and one to be left alone. This detail may or may not reflect something of interest about human imagery; if parts are moved in parallel, it does not, but if parts are in fact rotated sequentially a similar problem may arise in humans. This remains an open question.

The foregoing descriptions are obviously quite sketchy and will be elaborated in the subsequent chapters. In particular, we will consider how the various schemes had to be elaborated to account for special conditions.

Special transformations. In addition to the most frequently studied transforms noted above, any local region of points can be shifted in arbitrary directions. We have not implemented these transformations because they are not necessary in the present problem-domain. If one wants to study the role of imagery in problem-solving, however (as we eventually will want to do), these kinds of special transforms seem mandated.

3.0 CONCLUDING REMARKS

Our model allows us to consider the ontological status of the image in a more concrete context than before. First, however, one might ask whether we really have an "image" in this system. After all, the computer doesn't have anything vaguely like a "picture in its head." This is the wrong way to look at things. The correct interpretive device for the image is not a human eye, but the internal "mind's eye," the procedures that access the internal representations. The properties of this interpretive function result in the representation evincing spatial attributes like adjacency, distance, and all of the other characteristic properties of quasi-pictorial images (see chapter 3, section 1.0). This structure/process pair, then, produces an image that has the spatial properties of a picture, even though it isn't one.

In response to this argument, one could agree that our image representation is spatial, but still challenge the idea that it is an "image." That is, one could claim that the representation is really a list of points and their coordinates. This attack rests on a basic confusion. It is like confusing an explanation with a "parent of an explanation." Using Putnam's (1973) example cited earlier, one would not want to explain why a square peg will not fit in a round hole by reference to molecules, electrons, and so on. Rather, the proper level of analysis involves constructs like shape and rigidity—which are not necessarily uniquely derivable from a knowledge of the constituent elements considered in isolation. Similarly, when points are juxtaposed in a matrix, patterns (like "roundness") emerge that were not explicitly noted or easily derivable from a list of points.

Examination of our model suggests some reasons why a quasi-pictorial image representation makes some sense: First, a medium for spatial representation allows one to compose numerous perceptual memories into a common framework. It is not clear how information in the CAR.IMG and TIRE.IMG files in our model could be integrated into a single representation (given differences in distance at the time of encoding and so on) without translation into a common framework. And it is not clear how conversion to a common size standard, a prerequisite for integration, could occur without a spatial array.

Second, one reason one would have trouble integrating separate encodings of appearance involves semantic interpretation: The *tire* must be adjusted to fit the *wheelbase*. How does one know which pairs of r, Θ coordinates delineate a wheelbase? This is especially difficult if information about the wheelbase's appearance is stored in more than one file (representing "multiple looks"). Even if interpretive procedures could be written to accomplish this task by processing deep representations directly, these procedures surely would be less efficient than ours, given that descriptions of parts would refer to spatial patterns. For example, in our model it is trivial to determine whether a straight line, an arc, or another spatial configuration is present in a surface representation. However, if one attempts to discover whether a line is delineated somewhere within a list of unordered coordinates (like our r, Θ pairs) without constructing something like our surface representation, one must pass through the entire list numerous times. No list-ordering will solve this problem, as no unidimensional ordering can capture all of the information about spatial proximities inherent in a two-dimensional space (let alone a three-dimensional one). The same problems would exist, of course, if we simply listed Cartesian coordinates.

Third, it makes sense to compose spatial information in a visual short-term buffer from the point of view of storage efficiency: Storage of this information in an unreduced form in long-term memory would take up much more room (see Funt, 1976). In our model, the coordinate pairs underlying an image are stored in relatively small space compared to the amount required to store an entire matrix, including empty cells. Thus, not only is a visual short-term store probably efficient for integrating appearances remembered from separate occasions and for classifying such information, but the ability to construct such quasi-pictorial images may be the most economical option over the long run, when many memories must be stored in long-term memory.

Finally, as Funt (1976) and others have noted, many sorts of inferences (for example, about relative spatial positions of parts) are easily derived from the image representation. That is, it is useful as a computational aid.

In this chapter, then, I have outlined the core theory and described the general model in which it is embodied. It seems clear that there is nothing mystical or unscientific about the concept of a "mental image," given that we can model image processing on a computer. We now will take the measure of the theory and model by discovering how well they explain and predict data as well as how effectively they lead us to ask fruitful questions. In the course of providing accounts for the research findings in the present domain we will be forced to expand and refine the theory. How successfully this can be done without doing violence to the core assumptions is yet another measure of the worth of the present theory.

6. Generating Visual Images

Given that the model was motivated primarily by our earlier findings, it would be surprising if it did not provide accounts for them. In addition, however, the model should also provide accounts for data we did not explicitly consider when we constructed it. This chapter and the following ones are divided into two parts. In the first section I show how the model is consistent with the results that motivated us to construct it as we did in the first place. Perhaps not surprisingly, the initial model was *not* capable of providing precise accounts of the data that were collected during Phase I, and some unanticipated new issues were raised almost from the start. In the second section, I report new experiments that test or further constrain the theory, and I use the principles of the theory to provide accounts of data that the model was not tailor-made to explain.* In a way, then, the second section provides a "validity test," a way of checking the model by seeing if it is consistent with results in the domain in general. If the model has behavioral adequacy, it should be capable of being extended beyond the initial data-base.

Even if the model does prove capable of generalizing to the results in the literature, this may be neither impressive nor important: Many of these results may often be so similar to those obtained earlier that a *failure* to produce plausible accounts would be surprising. Thus, the primary purpose of Phase II was not simply to use the model to explain data, but to help us generate new issues, to help us collect more data that would ultimately force us to articulate further the model and theory. As the theory becomes more precise and constrained, so do its predictions. Only when we have non-obvious or very specific predictions does it make sense to try to confirm a theory, and this usually seems to occur only dur-

*In point of fact I had read only the Weber and Bach (1969), Weber and Harnish (1974) and Weber, Kelley and Little (1972) papers at the time the theory was formulated, and did not tailor the theory with an eye toward explaining the specific results reported in these papers.

ing the later stages of theory-development. At this juncture it is of interest to examine the available data with an eye toward raising new questions within the context of the model. It is useful to discriminate among five kinds of findings that we shall turn to shortly:

Class 1: Confirmation. These results are easily and precisely accounted for by the core theory. This class can be divided into two subclasses: Class 1a, strong confirmation, results are not related to those that the theory was originally intended to explain. These are the truly impressive findings. Class 1b, weak confirmation, results are those so similar to the ones collected initially that it is unimpressive that we can account for them. In practice, however, it is quite difficult to distinguish reliably between these two subclasses, and thus this class is not very interesting— given the possibility that we can explain some result simply because we *constructed* the model to explain that kind of result in the first place.

Class 2: Multiple Interpretation. These results can be easily accounted for in more than one way by the model and lead us to seek ways of further constraining the theory.

Class 3: Theory Supplementation. These results cannot be explained without introducing additional assumptions, about either the structure or process components. These assumptions supplement those already incorporated in the theory and do not require any modification of the core theory itself.

Class 4: Domain Contamination. These results suffer from some methodological flaw which makes them difficult to interpret. Essentially, they fall outside the "natural class" of phenomena addressed by the theory, since they hinge on cognitive processes other than those of current interest. These may often seem like Class 3 findings, but would require elaboration of the theory outside the present domain.

Class 5: Disconfirmation. These results contradict the core theory. There are two subclasses here: Class 5a, weak disconfirmations, can be dealt with by backtracking and revising some aspect of the theory. Class 5b, strong disconfirmations, contradict the theory so fundamentally that we have no idea how to repair it to account for the sum of the available findings.*

On my view, only results in the fifth class are damaging to this enterprise. Given the difficulty of discriminating between Classes 1a and 1b (strong and weak confirmation), results that are neatly predicted by our model may not be of great import. Results in Classes 2 and 3 (multiple interpretation and theory supplementation) are of most interest, since they force us to develop the theory further. In the second case, it is as if we have too many degrees of freedom, and should decrease them, while

---

*I am indebted to George Smith for his help in developing this taxonomy, which was initially his idea.

in the third case it is as if we must increase our degrees of freedom. There is a tension between these two cases: We do not want to have such an impoverished theory that we cannot account for interesting patterns in the data. And yet we also do not want to expand the theory too far or leave too many degrees of freedom; if we do this, we begin to lose explanatory power. This tension between "descriptive power" (which increases as broader ranges of data can be explained) and "explanatory power" (which increases as fewer principles are invoked) seems to be present in all sciences; eventually we must have some formal way of evaluating the trade-offs between the two, but other sciences have progressed without such a metric and I see no reason why we cannot also do so in psychology.

Each of the following sections begins with a description of the results to be explained or a reminder of the relevant findings (if they were discussed earlier). I will try to specify what I take to be the relevant aspects of the data in need of an account from the theory. At this juncture I often will not propose a detailed account of the precise size of the observed effects, but will deal with the relative orderings of reaction times and quantitative relationships that bear on the internal consistency of the model. Often the task will be to explain why a given pattern of results was obtained—in contrast to other possible patterns we could have found. The accounts offered in this chapter primarily rely on the following assumptions of the core theory:

1. Images are quasi-pictorial representations that occur in a limited-resolution spatial medium.

2. Literal perceptual memories are represented in long-term memory by an encoding of the global shape or central shape (a skeletal encoding) and supplementary encodings of local regions. I assume that supplemental encodings usually will contain organized units, not just arbitrary portions (this assumption is based on observed principles of perceptual organization—see Kaufman, 1974). Thus, I will refer to the contents of secondary files in the model, the encodings of local regions, as "parts," although strictly speaking this may not always be correct.

3. The literal encodings in long-term memory (r, Θ pairs in our model) are individually placed in the visual buffer during image generation.

4. The separate literal memory encodings are joined into a single image via application of propositional relations that describe how parts fit together. These representations have two parts, a relation and a "foundation part."

5. The foundation part is defined as a spatial pattern in the visual buffer itself; hence, images are composed via inspection of material already included in the surface image. That is, separate encodings are joined by first locating the relevant foundation part on an available image and then placing the new part at the correct location.

1.0 CONSISTENCY TESTS

In this first section we return to the findings described in chapter 4. Now, however, we are not interested merely in whether a general "functional capacity" seems implicated by a finding. In chapter 4 we were satisfied to note that a result was better explained by one class of theories over others; now we will attempt to formulate detailed models of task performance.

1.1 Effects of Number of Units

Let us begin with the results of the experiment that most clearly ensured that people did in fact encode separate units. In this experiment, subjects saw different parts at different times. Number of units was varied by the number of pages used to present a given drawing: A drawing was presented intact on a single page, was divided up so that parts appeared (in the correct relative locations) on two pages, or was divided up so that parts appeared on five separate pages (see chapter 4, section 2.0). Recall that these subjects were asked to glue the separate parts together mentally, and claimed to have thoroughly memorized the drawings prior to the experiment proper. They were asked to evoke an image of a given animal and to push a button when it was clearly in mind. Surprisingly, generation time increased linearly with the number of pages used in presenting the drawing. We repeated this experiment and replicated the original findings. The individual subjects did not all show linear increases in time with increases in the number of pages, however. This could show that our measurements were noisy or that somewhat idiosyncratic "natural" parsing procedures sometimes supplemented our imposed parse. In fact, our finding was unexpected because we thought that natural parsing would operate to produce additional parses per page (and not necessarily constant numbers, across subjects).

If the page-dividing system generally overrode natural parsing procedures, organized the naturally parsed parts into higher-order units, or simply added new units to the natural ones, the present results can be assigned to Class 1 (confirmation).* If each page is encoded as a separate unit (or simply results in the addition of one new unit, on the average, to those spontaneously encoded), the linear increase makes perfect sense: An additional increment of time (around 50 milliseconds) is required to integrate each additional unit into the image, even if the resultant output is

---

*Note that the fact that there are alternative possible parsing and encoding processes does not make this a Class 2 (multiple interpretation) result. The specification of these operations falls outside the domain of a theory of imagery proper.

the same in the final image that results. This is due to the additional operations of looking up the relational information and finding the foundation
part and so on for each additional part. Table 6.1 presents a trace of the
operation of the simulation when generating an image of a car with details.
The reader should note the importance of findings like linear increases: if
we can explain these by reference to some kind of incremental process we
have some evidence that we have chosen the correct functional components in our theory.

In another experiment the number of units in a stimulus was varied by
"top down" parsing procedures. (How such procedures actually operate
would be specified by a theory of perception, and is outside the domain of
the present project.) Subjects viewed line drawings of geometric shapes
(illustrated in figure 4.5), each of which was described in one of two ways
for a given subject. The alternative descriptions differed in the number of
parts that were predicated (either a relatively few overlapping forms or
relatively many adjacent shapes; for example, two overlapping rectangles
versus five squares). The group receiving descriptions in terms of fewer
numbers of overlapping shapes required less time in general to generate
images of the patterns than did the group receiving descriptions predicating more units. In addition, pooling data from both groups, we found that
times increased approximately linearly with increased numbers of units in
the description (see figure 4.6).

These results are explained in a straightforward way from our theory,
but this is not surprising since the theory was tailored to explain just this
sort of result: As is evident in table 6.1, a set of processes are simply
repeated for each additional part, and hence when more parts are integrated individually into an image, more time is required to generate it. The
fact that around 150 additional milliseconds were required to generate patterns for each additional unit is slightly discomforting, however, compared with our earlier estimate of 50 milliseconds per part.* The actual
magnitude of the effect, then, is a Class 3 (theory supplementation)
finding. The disparity in time per unit could be due to the ease of "seeing"
where a part belongs and/or differences in the difficulties of imaging the
individual parts themselves. We will examine these hypotheses in the second half of this chapter (see section 2.1).

According to the theory as now cast, supplementary encodings of literal
appearances are integrated in sequence. This need not be so, however.
The model could easily mimic a system in which some parts are placed in
parallel. If more units require more time to place in parallel because of

---

*It is difficult to do appropriate statistical tests for differences in slopes across different
experiments. In my experience with experiments of this sort differences of around 100
milliseconds usually are significant, however, and thus I will use this as a rule of thumb in
deciding which disparities to take seriously.

processing capacity limits (see Kahneman, 1973), the present findings are consistent with both a parallel-whenever-possible model and a sequential model.* We decided to compare the adequacy of these two theories by examining whether "structural dependencies" affected the generation times. A structural dependency occurs when one part requires the presence of another part before it can be placed. If parts are always placed sequentially, this variable should not affect generation times. But if parts are placed simultaneously whenever possible, this variable—which prevents parallel integration of parts—should prove important. For many of our stimuli, there is no a priori reason why one could not at the same time place several pieces on the skeletal pattern of the lower left figure illustrated in figure 4.5; there are no "structural dependencies" preventing all of the four outer squares from being imaged at once. In the animal drawings illustrated in figure 4.7 (where pieces are presented on one, two, or five separate pages), in contrast, structural dependencies would seem to prevent parallel generation of all parts. In this example, one would probably need to image the forelegs before the paws, the thighs before the forelegs, and so on. We examined the notion that "structural dependencies" of this sort affect the generation process by reanalyzing the data from the experiment described above. As it turned out, the descriptions predicated relationships with either one or two structural dependencies. We entered this variable into a regression equation along with number of parts, number of lines, and several other factors as independent variables, and used generation time as the dependent variable. Somewhat to my surprise, there were no observable effects of number of structural dependencies. It is of course dangerous to draw strong conclusions from negative results, but we will find further evidence (in section 2.1) that parts are in fact placed sequentially. Parts of the geometric forms may have been placed sequentially in images because not all the units were in fact encoded, but only the nonredundant ones. That is, subjects may have generated the images on the basis of a description, as will be discussed in detail shortly. In this case, only one literal encoding of each separate geometrical shape was stored, along with a set of instructions specifying the order and position in which to place a limited set of forms in the visual buffer.

1.2 Effects of Detail on a Picture

Subjects required more time to evoke images of more detailed drawings of animals (see chapter 4, section 1.0). Simple relative ordering of these times can be explained by positing that more parts were encoded for the detailed drawings (or more properly, that more encodings were stored—

---

*If parts are placed in parallel, a linear increase is expected only if a number of other assumptions are met; see Taylor, 1976; Townsend, 1971, 1972, 1974.

Table 6.1. Trace of the simulation generating an elaborated image of a car at the default size and location.

---

*IMAGE FULL CAR

IMAGE BEGINS
LOOKING FOR PROPOSITIONAL FILE FOR CAR
CAR.PRP OPENED

CHECKING PROPOSITIONAL FILE FOR NAME OF IMAGE FILE
NAME OF IMAGE FOUND: CAR.IMG

LOOKING FOR IMAGE FILE CAR.IMG
CAR.IMG OPENED

PICTURE BEGINS
TURNING ON POINTS IN SURFACE MATRIX WITH SIZE
  FACTOR = 1.0
PICTURE ENDS

CHECKING PROPOSITIONAL FILE FOR NAMES OF PARTS
PART FOUND: HASA REARTIRE

PUT BEGINS
LOOKING FOR PROPOSITIONAL FILE FOR REARTIRE
REARTIRE.PRP OPENED

CHECKING PROPOSITIONAL FILE FOR NAME OF IMAGE FILE
NAME OF IMAGE FILE STORED: TIRE.IMG

CHECKING PROPOSITIONAL FILE FOR LOCATION OF REARTIRE
LOCATION FOUND: UNDER REARWHEELBASE

LOOKING FOR PROPOSITIONAL FILE FOR REARWHEELBASE
REARWHEELBASE.PRP OPENED

CHECKING PROPOSITIONAL FILE FOR DESCRIPTION OF
  REARWHEELBASE
DESCRIPTION FOUND

LOOKING FOR PROPOSITIONAL FILE FOR UNDER
UNDER.PRP OPENED

CHECKING PROPOSITIONAL FILE FOR DESCRIPTION OF UNDER
DESCRIPTION FOUND

FIND BEGINS
BEGIN SEARCHING SURFACE MATRIX FOR REARWHEELBASE

SEARCHING FOR LOWEST POINT LEFT
FOUND AT -23 -3

FOLLOWING HORIZONTAL RIGHT TO END
FOUND AT -19 -3

SEARCHING FOR NEXT HORIZONTAL POINT RIGHT
FOUND AT -10 -3
FIND ENDS

BEGIN TO PUT ON PART: REARTIRE

PICTURE BEGINS
TURNING ON POINTS IN SURFACE MATRIX WITH SIZE
  FACTOR = 0.9
PICTURE ENDS
PUT ENDS

CHECKING PROPOSITIONAL FILE FOR NAMES OF PARTS
PART FOUND: HASA FRONTTIRE

PUT BEGINS
LOOKING FOR PROPOSITIONAL FILE FOR FRONTTIRE
FRONTTIRE.PRP OPENED

CHECKING PROPOSITIONAL FILE FOR NAME OF IMAGE FILE
NAME OF IMAGE FILE STORED: TIRE.IMG

CHECKING PROPOSITIONAL FILE FOR LOCATION OF FRONTTIRE
LOCATION FOUND: UNDER FRONTWHEELBASE

LOOKING FOR PROPOSITIONAL FILE FOR FRONTWHEELBASE
FRONTWHEELBASE.PRP OPENED

CHECKING PROPOSITIONAL FILE FOR DESCRIPTION OF
  FRONTWHEELBASE
DESCRIPTION FOUND

LOOKING FOR PROPOSITIONAL FILE FOR UNDER
UNDER.PRP OPENED

CHECKING PROPOSITIONAL FILE FOR DESCRIPTION OF UNDER
DESCRIPTION FOUND

FIND BEGINS
BEGIN SEARCHING SURFACE MATRIX FOR FRONTWHEELBASE

SEARCHING FOR LOWEST POINT RIGHT
FOUND AT   24   −3

FOLLOWING HORIZONTAL LEFT TO END
FOUND AT   21   −3

SEARCHING FOR NEXT HORIZONTAL POINT LEFT
FOUND AT   12   −3
FIND ENDS

BEGIN TO PUT ON PART: FRONTTIRE

PICTURE BEGINS
TURNING ON POINTS IN SURFACE MATRIX WITH SIZE
  FACTOR = 0.9
PICTURE ENDS
PUT ENDS

CHECKING PROPOSITIONAL FILE FOR NAMES OF PARTS
CAN'T FIND AND MORE PARTS
IMAGE ENDS

IMAGE COMPLETED

as each encoding could be of the same part but with particular portions attended to more acutely) and later integrated into the image. The magnitude of the difference between time to generate images of detailed versus undetailed pictures was 200 milliseconds. This suggests that only about four more units, at most, were included in an image of a detailed drawing than in an image of an undetailed one. This result, then, falls in Class 1 of our taxonomy (confirmation).

1.3 Using Descriptions to Generate Images

Consider the results from two small studies described earlier, in which subjects were shown three-by-six arrays of letters. In both studies, the arrays were labeled either "three rows of six" or "six columns of three," but these labels were given either at the time of study or only after the array had been removed. In both cases, more time was later required to image the array if it had been described in terms of six columns rather than three rows. The results of the first experiment, in which labels were presented along with the array, fall in Class 2 of our taxonomy (multiple interpretation). These results can be explained equally easily in two ways: (1) The labels could have resulted in people parsing the patterns into different numbers of units (rows or columns), which were stored as separate literal encodings. The generation data can henceforth be treated in the same way as were the data from the experiments discussed in section 1.1. (2) Alternatively, the subjects may not have actually encoded every letter in the array. Rather, the letters may have been stored in memory by a propositional representation of the description (indicating how many letters should be printed in each line and how many lines should be printed at what intervals) and an image of a single letter. In the model, a single IMG file can be printed out repeatedly in accordance with a description. In this case, the previously placed letter would serve as the foundation part for the next one, within a unit, and previously placed units would provide a reference for location of the next unit (row or column). Note that this account leads us to expect that more time should be required to image rows or columns containing more letters. Alternatively, one row or column could be encoded as a unit, and then placed the requisite number of times in relation to the preceding unit imaged. If the same amount of time was required to image an encoding (file, in the model) regardless of the amount of material it contained, this would explain our results. The results of the second experiment, in which subjects received labels only after the array was removed, can be explained in the same way: When viewing the array, they needed only to note which letter was used, and then to encode the subsequent description. This account would lead one to expect that the number of elements per unit would also influence generation times, however, which was not tested in this experiment but was tested in a subsequent experiment described in the second half of this chapter.

In addition to studying how parts are amalgamated to form single objects or how objects are composed into an array, we performed an experiment in which people constructed images of described scenes. The same principles of our model invoked to explain the foregoing results will also help us explain these. To briefly review (see chapter 4, section 3.0), people were given descriptions of scenes containing from two to four separate objects. The descriptions specified relative spatial relations and distances among the objects (for example "the rabbit is floating five feet above and five feet left of the cup, and the violin is six inches below the cup"). Each scene was labeled by one of the component objects included in it. One group of subjects was shown pictures of each object and asked to construct a mental image of the described scene, whereas another group was asked merely to memorize the statements. As expected, the more objects, the more time the first group required to generate an image of the scene when later given its name. Further, although more time was later required to scan among objects that should have been imaged at longer distances, no more time was required to generate images of pairs of objects separated by longer distances. Generation time did not increase linearly with increased numbers of objects, especially when two objects were described as being very close together.

First, the finding that times tended to increase with number of imaged objects is neatly explained by our theory. The written descriptions are stored as propositional encodings in a list addressed by the name of the scene. These propositions dictate how literal image encodings (of the pictures) should be printed out in relation to one another. Thus, images of the objects are generated at the correct relative locations via application of propositional relations. Presumably, the object used to label a scene is first imaged, and then serves as the foundation part for the next object, and so on. Hence, as discussed above, more time will be required as more units are placed in the visual buffer. Second, since the origins (to which the r, Θ pairs are related in the model) of the imagery encodings can be set from the deep level, we expect that two objects can be imaged at relatively long distances as easily as at shorter distances (as long as both objects are in the most resolved part of the visual buffer; if parts begin to overflow, the subjects' motivation to form detailed images will affect the results—as will be discussed in section 2.2). Finally, the fact that images of two near objects sometimes were generated as easily as images of one object is explained if the near objects were grouped into a single unit via the Gestalt Law of Proximity. If the two objects were grouped into a single "perceptual unit," they would be stored in a single IMG file in our model, not requiring separate generation and integration; this would explain the nonlinearity in the increase in generation time with additional objects.

1.4 Effects of Subjective Size

In earlier work (Kosslyn, 1975), I found that subjectively larger images (those subtending larger "visual angles") of named animals require more time to generate than do subjectively smaller ones when the subject attempts to construct all images at the same level of vividness. This result was independent of the actual size of the imaged object (although the size range was rather narrow; see chapter 3, section 2.2).

This relative increase in time falls in Class 2 of our taxonomy (multiple interpretation), and can be easily explained in two (nonexclusive) ways within the context of our model. First, fewer of the r, Θ pairs must be activated before a certain sharpness level (dot density, in our model) is reached if an image is generated at a subjectively small size than if it is generated at a larger size. This account, then, ascribes the effects of size to a sharpness criterion used by the subjects to decide when an image is complete: Smaller images reach a given level of sharpness sooner than do larger images. Note, however, that in the present model there is no provision for halting PICTURE once a given dot density is reached. In fact, in order for the ZOOM procedure to produce more resolved images we had to assume that the same amount of the underlying literal encodings is eventually activated in both cases, but that one sometimes judges an image complete before one finishes imaging the full encoding. (In the model, the same number of r, Θ pairs is activated regardless of the value of the r mapping parameter used by PICTURE.) Second, when an image is small, portions of the skeleton are obscured due to the fixed resolution of the surface matrix, as is evident in figure 5.5. Thus, the foundation part (such as the wheelbase) will be more likely to be obscured, and hence additional parts (such as wheels) will not be added. When the image is larger, in contrast, foundation parts will be discernible and details may be added—requiring more time than when the image is subjectively smaller. In our model, the grain of the surface matrix prevents foundation parts from being "visible" to the FIND procedures if the image is too small. Thus, fewer parts will be placed when the image is small than when it is larger, resulting in faster generation times. The trace from the simulation when a small image is generated is like that in table 6.1 except that the foundation part is not found and hence the part is not adjusted to size and printed out.

2.0 VALIDATION AND GENERALIZATION TESTS

It is important to test the theory against data that were not considered when it was initially formulated: If we can provide accounts for these data, and can see how to develop the theory without backtracking (without altering an already existing part of the theory) to account for data we cannot currently explain, we will be doing well indeed. But we should not lose sight of the fact that merely providing accounts of data is not the primary purpose of the following exercise. Given our uncertainty about how to measure the "similarity" of results, we cannot be sure that a novel finding is not explained simply because it is an old finding in new clothes —and the theory was formulated from the onset with an eye toward explaining the earlier finding. Thus, in the following review we are most interested in (*a*) potential disconfirmation of the theory by results that are not easily explained and (*b*) results that will force us either to constrain the theory further by eliminating alternative accounts now possible within .it or to expand the theory further by adding additional properties to the putative representation and processing system.

2.1 Variations in Part-Generation Times

Before beginning to provide accounts for data in the literature, we decided to investigate directly some of the assumptions that play a major role in our accounts of image generation. We hypothesized that one reason smaller images are generated more quickly than larger ones is because one cannot place as many parts on the smaller images. On this view, the grain of the visual buffer obscures the foundation parts of small images, and hence one cannot "see" where to put the parts. Similarly, in other experiments we observed substantial variations in the time required to add each additional part to an image (ranging from 50 to 150 milliseconds), and hypothesized that these differences may have been due in part to differences in the ease of seeing where a part belonged. Both accounts rest on the assumption that individual units are amalgamated into an image by examining the material already in the image and finding the location where a new unit should be placed. We conducted an experiment to test this claim. In this experiment, subjects were shown arrays of letters organized according to the Gestalt Law of Similarity. The arrays were composed of twelve letters arranged in two rows six letters across. Each array was composed of two different letters, which were either very visually similar and relatively hard to discriminate (such as *M* and *N*) or dissimilar and easily discriminable (such as *M* and *G*). The letters were either grouped together (for example, the left half of the array containing only *M* and the right half only *G*), resulting in two parts, or placed in alternating columns (such as rows of *MGMGMG*), resulting in six parts. After studying an array, a subject formed an image of it at either twice or half the size at which it was presented. The subject was cued to form the image by presentation of a rectangle, and was asked to "project" his or her image so it just filled the rectangle (and not at some medium size that then was adjusted). The time to form the image was the measure of primary interest here. After forming an image, the subject used it as a template in a matching task with a second array, which was displayed at either twice or half the initial size.

If images are constructed by amalgamating individual units, and if the Gestalt Law of Similarity dictates unitization, then we expect that more time should be required to image the six-unit arrays than the two-unit ones—even though the same number of letters appears in both types of arrays. Further, if people do construct images by examining the material already in the image, then we expect that more time should be taken to construct images composed of similar letters; the similarity will make it more difficult to ascertain whether one is placing a new unit in juxtaposition to the correct existing unit(s). In addition, if units are in fact placed by examining an existing image, then the effects of discriminability of the letters ought to be exacerbated when more units are placed, because each one will be more difficult to insert into the image. Finally, if larger images require more time to form because more parts are added, and if number of parts is kept constant here, we have no reason to expect effects of image size on image-formation times.

More time was required to form images of arrays composed of more units (2.958 versus 2.440 seconds). This is, of course, as one would expect if our theory is correct, and images are formed by amalgamating units that were encoded separately. In this case, around 130 additional milliseconds were required for each additional unit.* In addition, more time was required to form images composed of relatively indiscriminable letters than to form images of highly discriminable letters (2.814 versus 2.584 seconds). Interestingly, whereas an additional 374 milliseconds were required to image the six-unit arrays composed of less discriminable letters, only an additional 87 milliseconds were required for less discriminable arrays when only two units were incorporated. This result makes sense if people form images by imaging separate units in sequence, inspecting the already available units in the act of placing the additional ones. In this case, the discriminability of the letters presumably affected the ease with which each unit was placed. And when more units were to be amalgamated, each one apparently required more time when the component

*It is dangerous to make estimates of time per unit when only two different numbers of units are used. However, given the linear increases in time with increasing numbers of units found in chapter 4 (figures 4.6 and 4.8) this did not seem an unreasonable procedure here.

letters were less discriminable. These findings lead us not to expect a constant amount of time per unit placed in an image. We found that an additional 94 milliseconds were required per unit when the letters were discriminable, whereas an additional 165 milliseconds were required when the units were similar and presumably more difficult to place. Hence, differences in time per unit should arise insofar as there are differences in the ease of locating the foundation parts where additional material should be imaged. Finally, although there was a trend for larger images to require more time to generate, this difference was not significant.

On first blush, this last result would seem to contradict my earlier one (Kosslyn, 1975), that subjectively larger images required more time to form. But I previously asked people to form images from long-term memory of common animals, not specifying the number of parts that should be included on the image. In the present experiment the stimuli had a specified number of units. Further, the fact that letter discriminability, which would constrain the ease of seeing where units go, had the same effects when images were formed at the two sizes suggests that subjects could fill in equivalent amounts of detail at both sizes. And the fact that number of units had the same effects at both sizes suggests that subjects did in fact fill in images at both sizes to equivalent amounts of detail. In contrast, in my earlier experiment subjects may have inserted fewer units into the smaller images because at least some of the foundation parts simply were not discernible in the image.

Another reason we have found differences in the time to image each additional unit in different experiments may be that more elaborate parts require more time to image. In terms of the model, IMG files containing greater numbers of r, Θ pairs may require more time to map into the surface matrix. This possibility led us to vary how many letters were used to compose each "unit" in an experiment investigating two additional Gestalt Laws of Organization, the Law of Good Continuation and the Law of Proximity. For each law there were four basic patterns in which we varied the number of units and the number of elements (letters) per unit. For arrays organized according to the Law of Proximity, a two-unit array was formed by arranging the spacing between the letters such that half the letters were in a group on the left side of the array and the rest were in a group on the right side. A four-unit array was constructed such that four columns were equally spaced across the same area occupied by the two-unit arrays. For arrays organized according to the Law of Continuity, the letters either were arranged into two columns six elements deep or were composed by breaking each of these columns into two columns by moving the lower three elements two spaces to the left. For each array the columns were either one or two letters wide. All arrays were the same overall length and height on the CRT screen.

The subjects in this experiment first viewed an array composed of the letter X. When the subject felt able to form an accurate image of that pattern, he or she was to press a button. A few seconds later, a single letter appeared on the screen (never the letter X). The subject was to form an image of the pattern just presented, but now composed of this new letter, and to press a button when the image was formed. On one-quarter of the trials a second array would appear and the subject was to decide as quickly as possible whether it was the same as or different from the array being imaged. These trials were included to increase the subjects' motivation to form accurate images of the arrays. The only statistically significant results of this experiment were as follows: Arrays composed of more units required more time to form (an average of 204 milliseconds per unit), and arrays composed of more letters required more to form (an average of 66 milliseconds per additional letter).

Why did the amount of material contained in a unit matter here, but not in the animal-pieces experiment described in the first section of this chapter? The big difference between the two experiments was that the letter arrays could be easily described in terms of a configuration of discrete elements. Thus, it makes sense that subjects would describe the initial array, and generate the image using this description (some subjects in fact reported being aware of doing this). In the model, each array would be stored as a propositional description of how many units there were and how they were juxtaposed. If the units were identical, as they are here, a single additional PRP file would store a description of the number and arrangement of the letters in a unit. Also stored would be an IMG file of a single letter plus, perhaps, a global skeleton to help in placing the individual letters. Thus, there are two relevant parameters here: An additional increment of time will be required to locate the position of each unit in the visual buffer and an additional increment will be required to print out each letter specified in the PRP file. That is, in the model, the same IMG file will be printed out repeatedly in imaging each unit. The reader will notice that the same TIRE.IMG file was used to put both the front and rear tires in the detailed car illustration in figure 5.4 (see table 6.1 and the schematic of the data structures of this image in figure 5.2), and the same process will operate here. This account, then, rests on the assumptions that (*a*) images can be generated in part by making use of stored descriptions, and (*b*) a single literal encoding can be imaged repeatedly at different locations in the visual buffer.

2.2 Effects of Subjective Size

One account of the effects of subjective size rests on the claim that subjectively larger images are generated with more details than are smaller ones. This claim leads us to an interesting prediction: If more complex images require more time to generate than do simpler ones because people integrate more parts together, as claimed earlier, then we should find a greater difference in the time to image a complex object at large versus small sizes than in the time to image simple objects at different sizes. That is, if larger images take more time to construct than smaller ones because more parts are added, this should be especially noticeable when many more parts are available to be placed on a relatively large image. Martha Farah and I tested this idea (see Kosslyn, Reiser, Farah, and Fliegel, in preparation) by showing people objects that looked either complex (such as a typewriter, a Swiss Army knife with all blades extended) or simple (a featureless box, an eraser). These people were asked to memorize the appearance of the objects so that they could form accurate visual images of them. Next, the subjects sat in front of two squares drawn on a wall, one subtending 1.5 degrees and the other 7 degrees of visual arc. Upon hearing the name of a square and then an object, the subject was to "project" an image of the object into the appropriate frame and push a button when the image was completed. Next the subject heard a probe word and decided whether he or she could find the named property on the image (as in the imagery-detection experiments described in chapter 3). The results from the generation-time task are illustrated in figure 6.1.

As is apparent, the findings were exactly backward from what was expected! *More* time was taken to generate images of complex objects at

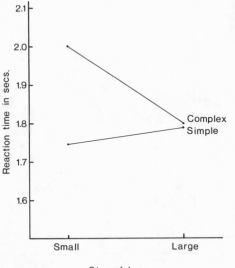

Figure 6.1. The time to generate images of simple and complex objects at small and large sizes. In this experiment subjects received a property-probe after indicating that their images had been generated.

smaller sizes, not less. Is this a Class 5 (disconfirmation) result, inexplicable within the context of the present model? We had reason to suspect
not: Many of these subjects claimed after the experiment that it was
harder to place the details on the small complex objects, but since they
knew they would soon be asked about details they tried (without necessarily succeeding) to put them there anyway. Our simulation, unlike the
flesh-and-blood subject, is not much motivated by impending fates, and if
at first it fails, it gives up and simply doesn't put the part there. Further,
subjects may have been so absorbed in their difficulties with the small size
that they did not bother to elaborate the larger, easily-seen images. Thus,
this result may not fall into Class 5; it requires not backtracking but perhaps an additional assumption: We could implement a "motivation parameter" in our model such that it would try repeatedly to place parts in
certain circumstances but not in others, but this would be terribly ad hoc,
post hoc, and unprincipled. To buttress this interpretation, and to demonstrate that this motivation factor can simply be added to the present
model, we conducted a second experiment.

In the second experiment we decided to remove the source of the subjects' motivation to try harder to elaborate the smaller images. Thus, we
simply deleted the probes asking about the properties of the object. Now
subjects were asked merely to "project" their images into the appropriate
box and to push a button when an image was clear and vivid. The results
of this task are represented in figure 6.2. As is illustrated, our predictions

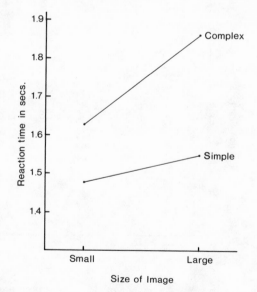

Figure 6.2. The time to generate images of simple and complex objects at small
and large sizes. In this experiment subjects were not queried about properties of
the imaged objects after indicating that their images had been generated.

now came to fruition: More time was taken to generate complex objects at relatively large sizes, and this effect was more pronounced than when subjects imaged relatively simple objects at the two sizes.

The foregoing finding supports the claim that larger images require more time to form because more parts are added, but this does not rule out the other possible factor, that larger images per se, independent of number of parts, require more time to reach a given level of sharpness. One source of evidence that size per se also affects response time comes from an experiment conducted by Steve Shwartz and me. We collected some data on time to image letters at different sizes. In this task, a subject saw a letter (on a computer-controlled CRT) at a large or small size, then the letter was removed and a large or small box presented. The subject formed an image of the letter in this box. Next he or she transformed the letter to a new size, as will be discussed in chapter 8. For present purposes, it is important to note that regardless of how large the actual stimulus was, more time was required for subjects to report having generated larger images of the letter. In addition, less time was required if the image did not have to be generated at an unseen size; this result is consistent with the idea that an extra operation, like multiplying r values in the course of printing them into the matrix in our model, occurred when an unseen size was used.

However, recall that in our model size per se does not affect time to image the entire contents of a literal encoding; PICTURE requires the same number of operations if any nonstandard size is used (requiring multiplying or dividing the r values). Thus, the effects of size per se are ascribed to larger images getting sharper less quickly than smaller ones (because points are distributed over a larger area in the visual buffer). It is possible, however, that smaller images are actually constructed faster because less material is accessed from long-term memory. I have reason to suspect that size per se in fact does not affect actual generation time, however. In an experiment (described in chapter 4, section 1.0) we asked people to image simple line drawings, which were presented at two different sizes, and then to image the drawing at the size presented. Here we did not find effects of size per se. In this case the subjects may have waited for the image to be completed because of the motivation factor noted above—which is especially plausible given that subjects in this experiment verified properties of the pictures after imaging them.

2.3 Effects of Number of Units

The studies of image generation in the literature all involve imaging distinct objects as if they were placed together in a single scene. The stimuli used in these experiments were either common objects or letters of the alphabet. The first of these experiments in recent times were reported by

Pear and Cohen (1971). In their first experiment, a word or pair of words appeared naming common animals, and the subject formed an image of the creature(s). As soon as the image was formed, the subject rated its clarity on a 100-point scale. Time to rate was recorded surreptitiously. If the subjects saw pairs of words, they were to image both animals simultaneously and then to rate the clarity of the pair as a whole. More time was required to image and rate the pairs of words than the single ones, and pairs were rated as less vivid than single words. The first result falls into Class 1 (confirmation) if we assume that time to make the rating itself was relatively constant for the different conditions, and that differences in time are due to the generation process per se. In this case, the following account for the effects of number of imaged items would follow from our model: The PRP and IMG files for each word are looked up sequentially and the items are imaged next to each other. Additional increments of time are required for each of the operations required to generate images of the referents of each word. Unfortunately, we could argue as easily that this is a Class 4 (domain contamination) result: Perhaps the results reflect the fact that two words take more time to read than does a single word, or perhaps images of two items are simply more difficult to rate. The fact that the more complex images were rated as less vivid is also consonant with our model, as will be discussed in the following chapter; in this case, more time elapses between successive regeneration of each item in a pair, and hence items in pairs are more faded on the average than images of single objects.

Pear and Cohen's second experiment was like the first, but the pairs of words were presented first, demonstrating that the previous effects were not a consequence of the order of the conditions. The third experiment was also like the first, but the single words and pairs of words were not presented in distinct blocks of trials but were alternated. Again, the objects named by single words were imaged and rated more quickly than those named in pairs of words, and pairs of images were rated as less vivid than solitary images. The accounts offered for the foregoing results generalize not only to these results but to those from the follow-up experiments described below.

McGlynn and Gordon (1973) worried that Pear and Cohen had tested too few subjects (only three, two, and one subjects were used in their first, second, and third experiments, respectively), and wondered if the earlier results would extend across greater ranges of image complexity. Thus, McGlynn and Gordon used Pear and Cohen's basic task but asked people to image and rate scenes including one, two, or three animals. These experimenters measured the time subjects required to turn a card, read the name(s), make the rating, and turn to a new card. Subjects were never told anything about speed, nor were the effects of reading time and rating time controlled. And thus these results too may fall in Class 4, domain contamination. The interstimulus intervals were measured manually from another room by an experimenter who did not know what was on the card the subject was processing at any given time. Not surprisingly, more time was taken to process three words than two, and two words required more time than a single word. In addition, according to subjects' ratings, the more words there were, the less clear, on the average, were the images. Presumably, one component of the time to process a given trial is image-generation time, and this component is explained exactly as I explained the same component of the Pear and Cohen experiment (assuming that the other uncontrolled factors did not wash away the image-generation effects).

McGlynn, Hofius, and Watulak (1974), recognizing that the earlier experiments had in fact measured more than just the image-generation times, attempted to obtain more direct measures of generation time per se. In their first experiment, bogus physiological recordings were taken to confuse the subjects. Again, one, two, or three names appeared, but now the subject was simply asked to push a button when the image was complete. The experimenter manually started a clock when the stimulus words were presented, and the subject's response stopped the clock. For one, two, and three words, response times averaged 4.91, 8.07, and 9.95 seconds, respectively. The monotonic increase in times here is a Class 1 finding, but what about the actual size of the effects? We earlier estimated much less time per additional item; is this a Class 5 (disconfirmation) finding, challenging a basic assumption of the model? No. These times reflect the operations required to image an entire object, not just additional parts. Presumably each item has parts of its own, and thus times reflect more than the time to retrieve and generate the contents of a single literal encoding (IMG file in the model). In addition, it is possible (this is an open question) that more time may be required to image the skeletal encoding than to image individual ancillary literal encodings. At worst this is a Class 2 (multiple interpretation) finding, where the model can explain these results in too many different ways—calling for further refinement via empirical work. Alternatively, this finding may fall in Class 4 (domain contamination): The longer times may be attributable to the fact that they include reading time and subjects were not asked to perform the task as quickly as possible.

These findings also present us with another problem: Although times did increase as more objects were included in the image, they did not increase linearly with number of objects. This is a Class 3 (theory supplementation) finding, at worst, perhaps requiring additional elaboration of the model. Perhaps single images were filled out to greater levels of detail than were the images in the multiple-object scenes (perhaps due to capacity limits or the like). Alternatively, this result may fall in Class 4 (domain contamination), indicating that reading times did not increase linearly with each additional item or that subjects dawdled with a single image (speed was not required) or that subjects simply terminated processing at around 10 seconds (that is, that there was a ceiling effect) and so on. Given these methodological concerns it seems inappropriate to alter the model at this juncture.

McGlynn, Hofius, and Watulak's second experiment examined the clarity ratings when the visualization time was controlled. Subjects were told to continue to hold the image until a tone had occurred, and the tone was presented 7.64 seconds after the words were shown (7.64 seconds was the mean of the generation times in the first experiment). Subjects rated image clarity only after the tone had occurred. Clarity ratings systematically decreased with more items. McGlynn, Hofius, and Watulak hypothesize that subjects in the earlier experiment put a disproportionate amount of additional work into generating the three-object images, bringing these images up to a more comparable level of clarity than occurred in this experiment. In any event, these findings are easily explained by our model, as will be clear in the following chapter.

Paivio (1975a) also describes an experiment on image-generation time. In this experiment, subjects again received different numbers of words (two, three, or four in this case) and were asked to generate images of the named objects in a single scene. Again, times increased fairly linearly with each additional item, but it appears (from the graph) as if about three seconds more were required for each additional concrete word. Thus, the pattern of the means is a Class 1 (confirmation) finding (explained as described above), but the magnitude of the effect is again askew. This finding is, at worst, in Class 2 (multiple interpretation) or Class 4 (domain contamination): In addition to differences in reading time and the like, subjects in this experiment were asked to draw the image, and the time required to begin drawing after receiving the words was measured. Thus, an additional component due to setting up and executing the "motor programs" necessary to make the drawings was also measured here. Given the recent findings by Sternberg, Monsell, Knoll, and Wright (1978), that time to begin responding increases with number of units in the response set, the drawing task may well have introduced another component that also increased systematically with number of imaged words—and hence inflated the size of the increase in time per additional word.

Paivio, Yuille, and Madigan (1968) had demonstrated that subjects required more time to generate images when given abstract words than when given concrete ones, and that result was replicated by Paivio (1975a). In addition, more time was required to generate images when a larger number of abstract words were presented, but the increases were much less per additional item than was found for concrete words. In the context of our model, it is sensible that abstract words require more time to image if it is more difficult to locate the name of an IMG file either in the appropriate PRP file or in one associated with it for abstract words than for concrete words. For example, "liberty" or "justice" may call to mind an image of scales, but this is not an image of *justice*, merely an image associated with the word. Time to look up the file containing this associate and then an appropriate IMG file would be longer than time to find an IMG file listed directly in a PRP file for a concrete word. In any case, this is another example of a Class 3 (theory supplementation) finding, requiring a rather straightforward extension of the model. The fact that there were smaller increments in additional time per additional item with abstract words, however, is a Class 4 (domain contamination), or at worst, a Class 3 (theory supplementation) finding: The very long reaction times (with means of up to 15 seconds) suggest that a ceiling effect may be present here; perhaps subjects felt they were taking too long to respond and hence sometimes responded before they were actually finished (for example, as soon as they had located an appropriate set of literal encodings but before they had imaged all of them). Again, when basic methodological concerns arise I am hesitant to add additional assumptions to the model.

Morris and Reid (1973) also report an experiment in which the time to image the referents of words was measured. This experiment had two parts. In one part, subjects received a set of high-imagery words and a set of low-imagery words (as defined by Paivio, Yuille and Madigan, 1968), and pushed a button after an image for each word had been formed. Following this, the original words and an equal number of new words were presented in a random order. The subjects now generated images for these words and indicated whether the word was an old one or a new one. If a word had been in the original set, the subject also indicated whether the image he or she formed was the same as the one formed originally. The results of this task were as follows:

1. Subjects generated images of the referents of high-imagery words more quickly than they generated images for the low-imagery words. The account of this result is the same as that offered above for Paivio's (1975a) finding, given that most high-imagery words are concrete.

2. For high-imagery words, there was no difference in the amount of time to generate an image the first time or the second time. This result may fall in Class 4 (domain contamination), since subjects were also deciding whether a word was old or new when it was presented the second time, which might have slowed down the responses. The fact that low-imagery words did show improvement on the second occurrence does not eliminate this problem, because they may have shown even greater improvement if the decision task were not required. Nevertheless, the difference between the two types of words in the degree of improvement on the second trial is interesting, and is also a Class 3 (theory supplementation) result. In the model, after looking up the PRP file of an associate and finding a listing of an IMG file there, one could then store the name of the

IMG encoding directly in the low-imagery word's PRP file. This would reduce the time to locate an appropriate image on subsequent trials. The generation times for low-imagery words on the second trial were still slower than the times for high-imagery words on the first trial, however, which suggests that subjects did not always store the name of an appropriate image encoding in a low-imagery word's propositional file after the first trial. The decrease in time for low-imagery words on the second trial was not due to gross practice effects, as witnessed by no significant difference between the time to generate an image for the initially presented words and for the new words presented during the recognition task.

3. Subjects reported that on 91.5 percent of the trials the same image was generated both times a high-imagery word was presented, and on 73.4 percent of the trials the same image was generated both times a low-imagery word was presented. The fact that the same image was generated so consistently on both presentations of high-imagery words is a Class 1 (confirmation) finding, given that we claim in the model that the first IMG listing one encounters will determine which IMG file is looked up and imaged. If the order of entries in the object's PRP file remains constant during the task, which seems reasonable to suppose for high-imagery words in this experiment, then the same IMG file name will be encountered first on both trials. Given that the model was not intended to account for this result or any like it, this result in fact falls in Class 1a (strong confirmation). The difference in the percentage of times the same image was generated for high-imagery and low-imagery words is consistent with the view that subjects initially must compute which image or images would be appropriate for an abstract concept. If the name of the image used on the first trial is not always stored in the word's PRP file, there is some probability that a different image will be selected on the second trial. This account is consistent with the finding that the time to generate a new image on the second presentation of a low-imagery word was not significantly different from the time to generate the initial image. Further, it is also consistent with the fact that when subjects claimed to have generated the same image on both presentations of a word, they were faster than when the second image was reportedly novel. This last result was also found for high-imagery words, and makes sense here if the image generated initially is the one listed highest in a PRP list, and thus other images require more time to look up. If the IMG entry in a low-imagery word's PRP file is relatively lower than in a high-imagery word's file (which makes sense if the list entries are ordered in terms of the usefulness of the information or the like), this explains one more finding: Even when the same image was generated on both trials, subjects still required more time to form an image when given a low-imagery word on the second trial than to image the referent of a high-imagery word.

4. Finally, there were very few errors. This is at least in part a Class 4

(domain contamination) finding: the nature and frequency of errors in recognition tasks depends in large part on the nature of the distractors, and the present theory says nothing about how target items are discriminated from foils. This finding draws at least in part on a theory of decision making, and this kind of decision-making falls beyond the bounds of the present theory.

In addition to the task described above, Morris and Reid also presented subjects with pairs of words and asked them to generate an image of the two objects interacting in some way. These items were presented in a separate set from the first, with half the subjects receiving each set first. Only high-imagery words were used here, and after the initial set of pairs was presented subjects were presented with a second set of items, half of which had been included in the first set. In this case, however, half of the items were pairs and half were single words (either taken from a pair or novel). Time to image the named object or objects was again measured on all trials. The results were as follows:

1. Less time was required to image a pair on the second occasion it was presented. This result again falls in Class 3 (theory supplementation). Now, one presumably has to generate a description of the interaction before imaging the items. If this description is stored, this will save time on the second occasion the image is generated. Alternatively, it is possible that the first image was itself encoded from the visual buffer, and stored in a single representation. Imaging this encoding would be faster than forming an image containing two separately encoded units.

2. On trials in which a pair or single word was presented for the first time, the pair required 420 additional milliseconds to image than did the single word. The fact that more time was taken when two objects were imaged falls in Class 1 (confirmation), but the actual magnitude of the difference either falls in Class 2 (multiple interpretation) or Class 4 (domain contamination). That is, each object could be imaged with parts, and thus more time is required for an additional object than was required for each additional part in our experiments described earlier. Further, even if only a skeletal encoding of each object was imaged, it may require more time to image the skeleton than to image parts (for which less material may be stored in the literal encodings). Alternatively, these increased times may not be due to imagery processing per se. They could reflect partly the additional time to read more words, which may have been exacerbated here because one of the two words was in lower case and one in upper case. The case differences could have impeded reading the pairs, which resulted in the large difference in response times. In addition, subjects knew that sometimes the word in capitals would be presented alone in a later recognition test, which may have prompted them to try to encode separately both the pair and the word, and this too could have added to the response times.

3. Subjects reported generating the same image on both presentations of a pair on 93.9 percent of the trials. This makes sense if the same description was used on both occasions or if the initial image itself was encoded. There is some support for this second interpretation in the fact that no more time was required to image a pair on the second trial than to image a single item for the first time.

In short, then, the results of the Morris and Reid experiment are easily explained within the context of the model, and lead to several testable hypotheses. In particular, it seems worth testing the notions that images can become associated directly with abstract words and that the first image name located in the object's propositional file will be used. This last hypothesis seems likely to be wrong as a general claim, to my mind; I would be surprised if the particular image one generates of an object does not usually depend on the particular requirements of the task at hand. If this conjecture is true, however, an account would require a theory of decision-making as well as a theory of imagery proper.

Robert Weber and his colleagues have conducted a number of ingenious experiments on image generation. In a series of papers, these researchers have examined how people image letters of the alphabet under various circumstances. Weber and Bach (1969) began by having their subjects recite the alphabet aloud, two times in succession as rapidly as possible. The subjects were then divided into three groups. In one group, subjects were again asked to recite the alphabet aloud; in another, they were to go through the alphabet silently, "talking to themselves"; and in the final group, they were to close their eyes and image each letter passing before them, as if each was a black character on a white screen (it was emphasized that each letter should appear distinctly and in succession). The time to go through the entire alphabet in each condition twice was measured over a series of ten trials. Interestingly, spoken and silent speech rates were practically identical, averaging around 6.5 letters per second, but time to image each letter was markedly slower—averaging only about 2.5 letters per second. There were much greater individual differences in the imagery group, however, producing a relatively large variance; further, there was a practice effect in the visual imagery condition only for some of the subjects (and no practice effects for the other groups after the first trial). Weber and Bach also asked people to try to localize where in their heads the process was taking place; subjects in the imagery group most often located the subjective sensation of imaging in the front and middle, "almost as if visual imagery were achieved by using the interior forehead as a projective screen," in Weber and Bach's words. In the final chapter I will have something to say about the phenomenology of imaging and the noncoincidental relationship between my characterization of the underlying functional state (the surface representation) and the actual experience, the *quale*, of imaging.

Weber and Castleman (1970) began by replicating Weber and Bach's experiment, but used the same subjects in all conditions and asked them to pass through the alphabet only once per trial. In addition, only subjects who claimed that they could project, with their eyes open, an image of a letter onto a blank screen were tested (51 percent of 81 people claimed they could do this, whereas 91 percent claimed they could visualize with their eyes closed). Weber and Castleman also included an additional imagery task, requiring subjects to project each letter onto a blank sheet of white typing paper. At the end of the tasks, the subjects were asked to rank the tasks in the order of difficulty and then to rate their difficulty on a five-point scale. The Weber and Bach results were replicated: As before, about six letters per second could be processed in both the silent and spoken speech conditions, and about two letters per second in the two imagery conditions. Subjects were fairly good at knowing which tasks were more difficult, and again there was a slight practice effect for imagery but not in the highly overlearned speech conditions.

In Weber and Castleman's second experiment, a more "objective" task was used to address the same questions. A new condition was introduced wherein subjects were asked to image and classify aloud each letter of the alphabet, in order, as being relatively vertically large (that is, tall, for example *t* and *l*) or small (for example, *i* and *a*). Thus, subjects now said "small," "large," "small" (for *a*, *b*, *c*) in working through the alphabet. (As we shall see in chapter 9, this is exactly the sort of task in which we would expect imagery to be used, because this information is probably not propositionally encoded with the letters but is implicit in their images.) Each letter was shown and classified for the subject before the experiment actually began. Subjects also performed the spoken-aloud and eyes-closed imagery tasks used in the first experiment. The spoken-aloud task was easiest (with a rate of about 5 letters per second), followed by the visual imagery task (1.76 letters per second), and the classification task was most difficult (.95 letters per second). Not surprisingly, the largest practice effect was in the letter-classification condition, in which subjects were performing a relatively novel task.

The final experiment reported by Weber and Castleman was conducted to allow the authors to argue that subjects did not learn the large/small assignment when they were shown how to classify each letter at the onset of the experiment. A new group of subjects was asked to learn whether the digit "1" or "2" went with each letter, and this was compared to learning whether the word "large" or "small" belonged with each letter. Not surprisingly, it was much more difficult to learn the arbitrary digit pairings. This does not show that subjects did not memorize the classifications in the prior experiment, however, as the size class is not an arbitrary pairing, and was in fact learned relatively quickly. As will be developed in chapter 10, we would expect increases in speed with practice, as were found in the foregoing experiments, if the subjects gradually recoded the information implicit in an image into propositional form during the course of the experiment, and there is no reason to suspect that they did not begin such recoding during the initial training sessions. This would also affect the processing rates, of course.

At first blush the reader might worry about the disparity in the image times obtained here and in our earlier experiments. In fact, this is a case where the model has too many possible options in explaining these results. The basic account of the imagery findings reported by Weber and his collaborators is straightforward: In performing this task, people presumably generate images of the letters in sequence. In our model, each letter would be represented in a file containing the name of the PRP file for the next letter in the alphabet (or perhaps a group of letters, organized as a single "phrase" or "chunk"). A series of images over a span of time could be constructed just as additional parts are added to an image in sequence, but now the prior image must be allowed to fade before the subsequent one is generated at the same origin in the visual buffer. Thus, the two-plus letter-per-second rate reflects not only the time to generate the images but the time necessary for a prior letter to fade before a new one can be placed. Recall that I claim the visual buffer is a short-term store in which items will decay if not actively maintained; we assume here only that fading requires some finite amount of time. This additional parameter is one reason these generation times are slower than those observed earlier. In one regard, the increased times per item are actually a Class 1a (strong confirmation) finding, then, in that they are expected due to a feature of the model not originally built in expressly to explain these or like data. In fact, in pilot experiments we have demonstrated that more time is required to replace a large image with a subsequent one than to replace a small image. This finding lends support to the inclusion of the fade-before-replacement parameter; with small initial images, construction of the new image could commence prior to fading of the previous one, but not so when the first images were larger.

In addition to the fade-time factor, the relatively long times per item reported by Weber and his collaborators could be due to the factors mentioned when we discussed McGlynn, Hofius and Watulak's (1974) findings: each image of a letter may be constructed from parts, and thus these times may reflect more than that to activate and image a single file. Further, even if letters are stored as a simple skeletal file, it could be that time to retrieve and activate a skeletal file is simply longer than time to integrate additional parts to a skeleton (which was presumably estimated in our experiments). Finally, the fact that speech rates are faster than imagery rates is interesting, and Weber, Kelley, and Little (1972) present some data suggesting that images are actually prompted by implicit speech (auditory images of the names of the letters, in this case) as will be described in a subsequent section. If so, then the additional time required to image in this experiment makes sense, since the visual imagery components are added to the speech imagery ones. Any or all of these factors could underlie the disparities in the values of the generation-time parameter observed here, and this is but one example of a set of questions raised by our modeling enterprise.

The final result from the experiments described above that we must explain is the slower image rates when the classification task is used. This is clearly a Class 1 (confirmation) result: Presumably, the difference between the rates in the classification task and those in the simple sequential imagery task reflects the additional component of making the classification itself (via application of something like our FIND procedures) and is not due to differences in looking up and generating each letter in succession.

Weber and Harnish (1974) used the image-classification task to investigate how many letters can be generated in an imaged word simultaneously with no additional effort. In their second experiment (the first is not relevant here), subjects first were given a digit, indicating which letter of a word should be classified as soon as the word was presented. The words were either three or five letters long (the five-letter ones were sometimes generated by pluralizing four-letter words, however, in order to control for relative frequency and the like). In this task, subjects either imaged a word upon hearing its name or looked directly at a perceptual display of it. More time was required to classify letters in longer words, and more time was required to image a word and process it than to process a perceptual display. Further, as is illustrated in figure 6.3, there were different effects of serial position in the two presentation mode conditions. It appears that for three-letter words, about 65 additional milliseconds were required to classify each letter from the left in the imagery condition. The fact that there are no differences for different serial positions in the perceptual condition may suggest that the imagery effect is not due to scanning times; however, this argument assumes that image and perceptual scanning have similar characteristics (which receives some support from a number of experiments reported by Pinker, in press). If in fact this increase reflects time to generate an image of each letter in succession, these rates are much faster than those estimated in the earlier experiments. One possible reason for this will become clear when we discuss the Weber, Kelley, and Little results. Unlike letters of the alphabet, letters of very familiar words do not seem to require "verbal prompting." If so, then it is not surprising that this estimate of time to place additional parts is very much in the same ball park as those obtained in our animal-pieces experiment—which presumably also did not involve verbal prompting. Thus, the results for imaging three-letter words are in Class 1 (confirmation). But what about the five-letter words? For the first three

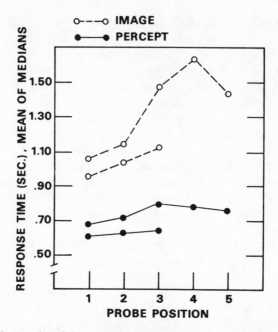

Figure 6.3. The results of the second experiment reported by Weber and Harnish (1974). This graph illustrates the time to classify letters in different positions of words that were imaged or seen at the time of probe.

letters or so, the slope is roughly like that for the shorter words, but the fourth letter requires more time than we might expect, with a 65-milli-second slope, and the fifth letter requires *less* time, as is evident in figure 6.3. The perturbations found here may in fact fall in Class 4 (domain contamination): The effects for the fourth letter may reflect random variation (there is no way of telling if the point is significantly off the expected linear slope). The dip in time to classify the fifth letters of imaged words could reflect the fact that the final letter sometimes was *s*, which subjects would quickly learn to classify without using imagery. In the worst case, this result is not in Class 5 (disconfirmation), requiring revision of a principle of the model—it only requires additional assumptions about the order in which parts may be generated (and thus may be a Class 3 finding). I admit that the methodological accounts for the aberrations in the five-letter imagery data are not very interesting, but again I hesitate to add additional properties to the processing capabilities of the model without good motivation.

Another experiment on image generation was reported by Crovitz, Rosof, and Shiffman in 1971. They examined how rapidly a light could be imaged blinking before the individual flashes could no longer be distinguished. A flickering light was presented to the right eye. It initially was set to turn on and off at a .5 Hz rate, and the rate was increased .5 Hz on every trial. A trial consisted of watching a light for 7 seconds, then trying to "visualize or recall in your mind's eye the exact rate of flicker previously seen." Subjects were asked to "try to match in your mind's eye what you just saw." A run ended when the subject reported a failure to image the preceding sensory stimulus. Not only the rate of flicker but also the luminance of the light varied. For most subjects, approximately 4 Hz was the maximum flicker imaged.*

The authors made the analogous comparison in the perceptual condition, when subjects noted when they could no longer see the light flicker, and found much higher frequencies before fusion occurred. In addition, higher frequencies of flicker could be discerned prior to fusion with higher luminance than with lower luminance in the perceptual condition—but luminance did not affect the frequency at which fusion occurred in the imagery condition. Thus, it would appear that intensity information is not depicted very well in images, which is consistent with some data reported by Kerst and Howard (1978). For present purposes, it is of most interest that a simple pulse of light could be imaged over twice as fast as letters of the alphabet can be imaged in sequence. This result can be explained in numerous ways by our model, and hence falls in Class 2 (multiple interpretation). In the case of letters, each additional letter requires that one look up (perhaps with the aid of verbal prompts) at least one encoding (perhaps more, if the image itself contains parts). In contrast, the same simple uniform change in intensity in a given region need only be repeatedly imaged in the blinking-light experiment. Alternatively (or in addition), the fusion task may in fact tell us more about how long it takes an image to fade than about how quickly images can be generated in succession. As noted earlier, this additional factor affects all of Weber's experiments in which letters are imaged in sequence, and could in part be responsible for the fact that more time is required to image a series of letters than to add a sequence of parts into a single image.

2.4 Using Descriptions to Generate Visual Images

If the present theory is correct, we can expect the encoding of new descriptive information per se to alter the way one forms an image of a previously seen object. This prediction rests on the claim that propositional "instructions" can be used to coordinate encodings of literal appearances when one forms an image. Louis Gomez and I decided to investigate this prediction.

---

*I calculated this number from the data for individual subjects, which the authors supplied in a table.

We showed subjects an array of letters (X's and Y's) and then removed the array and gave them a description of it. This description required the subjects to mentally substitute letters to form new patterns in the array. We were interested in the effects on later image-generation time of the number of groups of letters supposed to have been substituted into the array. Six different arrays were constructed, the number of letters in the rows and columns being 2,4; 2,5; 2,6; 3,5; 3,6; and 4,6, respectively. Three conditions were defined by the descriptions of the arrangement of letters: (1) "homogeneous" arrays were described as being composed of only a single letter; (2) "alternating" arrays were described as being composed of alternate rows or columns of X's and Y's; (3) binary-split arrays were described as being made of X's grouped on one side of the major axis and Y's grouped on the other. For even numbers of rows or columns, half of the figure was composed of one letter, half the other. When an odd number of rows or columns was used, we divided the figure in half as closely as possible and counterbalanced such that each letter appeared equally often considered over the set of patterns. The number of words used in the descriptions of homogeneous, alternating, and binary-split arrays were two, three, and seven, respectively.

Subjects were presented with one array at a time. After it had been studied, it was removed and the subject was given a description of the way it should be altered mentally. This description included a row-by-column specification (such as "two rows of four letters each," abbreviated, "2 row 4") and instructions on how to image its internal structure (such as alternating rows). Each of the three types of descriptions occurred equally often. The subject was asked to press a button when he or she had read and understood the description. Shortly after the button was pressed, one of two squares, which differed in size, was presented, and the subject was to "project" an image of the array, in the modified form specified in the description, into the frame. When this image was complete, the subject was to push the button again. This time required to respond was measured from the moment the frame was presented. After responding the subjects saw another array and were asked to decide, as quickly as possible, whether that one matched the array they were imaging. Half the time the second array was presented at the same size as the frame, and half the time at the size of the other frame. Further, half the time in each size condition the test array did meet the description, and half the time it did not. Subjects were asked to respond on the basis of constituent structure, irrespective of size. This task was included in an effort to encourage subjects to generate an image of the array as described. The "different" matrices were composed either by using a different row/column composition or by using a different internal distribution of letters (each type was used equally often). We hoped that if subjects were in fact generating an image, they would take longer to make this match if the matrix was at the other size than if it was congruent with the image (see Larsen and Bundeson, 1978).

The results of this experiment were straightforward: First, more time was required to generate images when they were described in terms of the more numerous dimension, replicating our earlier finding. Second, as expected, the most time was taken when an array was described as having alternating rows or columns of *X*'s and *Y*'s and the least time was taken when the array was described as homogeneous, with time to construct the binary-split patterns falling in between. This result is a Class 1 (confirmation) finding: In our model, the description would be used in coordinating the contents of IMG files into a single image, with more units again requiring more time. Interestingly, the additional time required for each additional predicated row or column added onto (was independent of) the additional time due to the number of higher-order units in the description. This makes sense if people store a hierarchical description of each array. In the model, each higher-order unit (a half of the array in the binary-split condition, for example) would have its own PRP file; within these files would be a description of the number and positions of the elements (in terms of rows or columns) and the name of the IMG file storing the appearance of the letter. Thus, an increment of time would be required to look up each PRP file, and each line of letters represented within would require time to print out.

In addition to measuring the time to generate the images, we measured the time required to read the descriptions. Interestingly, although there were reliable differences in time to read the descriptions of the different constituent structures, the ordering of the conditions did not mirror the ordering of the respective generation times. The most time was required in the binary-split condition and the least time in the homogenous condition, with the alternating condition falling in between; these times mirror the ordering of the length of the descriptions, and demonstrate further that our generation times are distinct from simple comprehension times or the like. In short, then, the results of this experiment are just as we would expect, given the present theory and model. These results provide genuine support for the claims made here, especially since the reorganization paradigm differs considerably from those used in Phase 1 research.

In an exceptionally clever experiment Weber, Kelley and Little (1972) present some evidence that not only is abstract propositional information used in amalgamating parts into a single image but that "verbal" information can serve to prompt one to look up and place particular parts. They made use of Brooks's (1967) finding that imaging and responding in the same modality (for example, visual imagery and visually guided responding) interfere with each other more than do imaging and responding in different modalities (visual imagery and verbal responding). The logic of the experiment was based on Brooks's finding coupled with the Weber and

Castleman result that implicit and explicit speech rates are similar. There were four conditions, each including different people as subjects. All subjects first learned to classify the relative heights of lower-case letters, as in the earlier experiments, but upper-case letters were also included; these letters were to be classified in terms of whether they contained a long vertical line. The case of the letters was alternated over blocks of trials in all conditions. In two of the conditions, subjects scanned through the alphabet by speaking aloud; one group of subjects classified each letter by saying aloud the word "yes" or "no" whereas another wrote "/" for yes, and "." for no. In the remaining two groups, the subjects scanned through the alphabet in an unspecified, silent way (they were not told to speak the name of each letter silently to themselves); one of these groups again made classification responses aloud and the other wrote them down. Subjects kept their eyes closed in all conditions (preventing interference between watching one's own writing and imaging). Speed-with-accuracy instructions were given. There were six major findings: (1) Mean times were almost identical for spoken and silent scanning, as would be expected if subjects were speaking silently to themselves. (2) Writing the responses was faster than saying them aloud, as would be expected if saying something aloud interfered with simultaneously saying something silently to oneself. (3) The same results were obtained with both alphabetic cases, showing that the classification technique has some generality beyond just classifying relative heights of letters. (4) People improved with practice. (5) There was no convergence in response times with practice, so the results are probably not due to some kind of difference in familiarity with the different tasks or the like. (6) Subjects had strong subjective impressions of having to say the letters, even in the silent condition.

The second experiment in this series was essentially a control. If writing in general requires less time than speaking, then the results of the first experiment may say nothing about like-modality interference. The subjects in the second experiment were shown two kinds of stimuli, the letters of the alphabet or twenty-six word sequences of "yes" and "no" written on a page. Subjects either made a written response (writing the letter if the alphabet was shown, or writing a slash or a dot when a sequence of yeses and nos was shown) or made a verbal response (saying aloud the name of the letter or the word yes or no, depending on the stimulus sequence). Writing actually required more time than speaking for both kinds of strings. Since in both cases subjects read the same stimuli, reading and comprehension time presumably is not relevant here and the results of the first experiment can be inferred to be due to something other than simple response times.

The final experiment reported in the Weber, Kelley, and Little paper was concerned with whether parts of images must be represented sequentially. Paivio (1971, 1975a) emphasizes that parts of images can be represented simultaneously, as does our model (if different portions of the skeleton are considered to be different "parts"). In our model, however, only a very few distinct parts (from separate IMG files) can be maintained at the same time in an image, but this number is certainly greater than one. Weber, Kelley, and Little report the introspection that all of the letters of a word like "cat" seem to pop into an image in parallel, without each letter being prompted verbally, in contrast to the way letters seem to come in sequence in the tasks described in the earlier papers. This introspection was examined in an experiment in which the relative rate of classifying visual properties of the letters of the alphabet was compared to the rate of classifying properties of letters in words. As in the preceding experiment, different response and scanning conditions were used; subjects either were asked to speak each letter aloud or were given silent (without explicit instructions to say the words or letters themselves) scan instructions, and letters were classified either aloud or by writing the two symbols used earlier. If forming an image of a word is the same as successively retrieving the letters of the alphabet, and both are verbally prompted, then (1) there should be the same scan times for spoken and nonspoken scanning, and this should be true with both words and letters of the alphabet, and (2) written responses should be faster in both conditions, since speaking would impair saying the letters to oneself. If the letters of the words are not named, however, there should be less of a difference between the two response modes with words than with letters of the alphabet, and there should be an effect of scan mode for words (since subjects would be doing something different in the silent condition than in the spoken one) but not for letters of the alphabet. The basic letter-classification task was used with eighteen very familiar four-letter one-syllable words used as stimuli, in addition to the letters of the alphabet. The results supported the notion that words need not be spelled out in the course of imaging them: Critically, the difference between spoken and silent scanning was greater with words, and the difference between spoken and written response was greater with the alphabet. In addition, subjects were generally faster with words, and there were no practice effects over trials with words, but scanning the alphabet did improve over trials (but again there were no differences in the degree of improvement in the different conditions). So, it would appear that verbal control over individual letters is not needed for short, very familiar words. Instead, they may be imaged very rapidly, with only small increments in time per additional letters (around 65 milliseconds, in the Weber and Harnish experiment described in the previous section). When an implicit verbal response must be generated as the stimulus to produce the next image, however, much larger increments in time are required to produce each additional image (on the order of 450 milliseconds per letter).

Detailed accounts of the foregoing results depend on a model of how percepts are encoded and how they interfere with images, which extends beyond the range of the present theory. Thus, for our purposes the main results to be explained are (1) the apparent evidence that *verbal* prompts (not propositional ones) are used in imaging sequences of letters in the alphabet and (2) the evidence that such verbal prompting does not occur with words. The first finding is a clear Class 3 (theory supplementation) result. From the point of view of our model, the critical question about the Weber alphabet-classification task is why one would ever use actual verbal responses as prompts. We could build in a "verbal loop," but it seems horribly inefficient, on the face of things. One reason for the apparent existence of such an internal self-prompt system may be that the alphabet is stored as an auditory image (with distinct pauses and rhythm), and not as chains of propositions. As children, we learn the alphabet as a chant, which also parses the letters into four- or five-letter "chunks." It would be interesting to note whether processing takes more time when it crosses chunk boundaries (for example, between *g* and *h*) than within a chunk, and whether simultaneous imagery of music or the like disrupts recalling the alphabet. My suspicion is that both factors would prove important, which would be consistent with the foregoing intuitions about how we store the alphabet. This book does not address the question of how auditory imagery works, but my bet is that it is quite similar structurally to visual imagery, except that the nature of the surface display medium is different (it is nonspatial, being an auditory short-term-memory buffer), and the contents of the deep literal encodings must of course also be different (since they do not activate spatial displays but instead replay auditory percepts). In any event, the present model does not provide a detailed account for how this kind of auditory/verbal prompting would operate—but this finding falls in the third class: The core theory needs to be supplemented, not altered.

The result that verbal prompting is not required in order to image a word is a Class 1 (confirmation) finding. In the model, the name of a letter would address an IMG file storing an encoding of the literal appearance of the letter, and an encoding of the phonological shape of the word would name a PRP file specifying the letter-sequence of the word. This information would allow IMAGE to look up IMG files of each letter in turn and have them imaged in the correct locations in the surface matrix. The image of the first letter would serve as a foundation part for the second one and so on. The 65-millisecond increase per additional letter is consistent with our earlier estimates of time to place an additional part on an image.*

---

*Note that although Weber and his collaborators showed subjects the type fonts and thus gave them an opportunity to store the necessary encodings, subjects probably could have done the task without being shown a particular font. If so, the question arises how a given image of a letter is selected to be imaged. Presumably "canonical" letters are imaged, but how this is done remains an open question.

Finally, the finding that more time was required in the alphabet condition falls in Class 2 (multiple interpretation). It may reflect not only the verbal-loop process but also the facts that (1) letters were imaged in the same location in the alphabet condition (and thus the prior letter had to fade first) whereas letters were placed side by side in the word condition, and hence (2) the imaged letters were probably subjectively larger in the alphabet condition than in the word one (where multiple letters had to be visible at once), and larger letters required more time to image than did smaller ones.

Beech and Allport (1978) performed a number of experiments examining how people form images from descriptions. They examined a number of "conceptual" factors in an effort to explore the role of this kind of information in image generation. In their first experiment, subjects listened to descriptions of spatial arrangements of objects and visualized the described scenes. The time to generate the image was measured from the end of the description. The descriptions were selected with a number of criteria in mind. A group of undergraduates was first asked to generate sentences describing a simple spatial relationship between two familiar objects; they were given a noun (such as "boy") to be used as the subject of the statement. The object ("tree," if the statement offered had been "The boy is standing under a tree") was then given to someone else as the subject of a new sentence, and so on, until a sequence of the desired length was produced. This chaining technique produced what Beech and Allport call "first-order contextual association" items. Second-order contextual items were produced by giving subjects a description of two preceding objects in a spatial relation and asking for a continuation sentence; third-order sequences were produced by giving subjects three objects (in two complete preceding sentences) and asking them to produce yet another relation to a new object. Finally, for "text" statements, the subjects were asked to compose a complete passage relating a set of items. In all conditions, no two successive sentences could contain the same spatial connectives. In addition, two kinds of spatial arrays were constructed, one- and three-dimensional. In one-dimensional arrays, only "left of" and "right of" were used as spatial connectives. Two, four, six, eight, or ten objects were in both kinds of arrays in first-order, second-order, third-order, or text contexts. The sentences were recorded so that the last word caused a clock to start, which was stopped when the subject pushed a button. There were two different instruction conditions: A "comprehension" group pushed the button after understanding the sentence; a "visualization" group pushed the button after forming an image of the composite array. All sentences of a given length (array size) were presented together in a block to reduce uncertainty over when the sentence would end.

The results of Beech and Allport's first experiment (which were obtained independently from ours) are illustrated in figure 6.4. First, there was a linear increase in response time with the number of objects in the

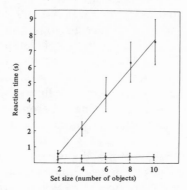

Figure 6.4. The results of the first experiment reported by Beech and Allport (1978). This graph illustrates the time to image scenes containing different numbers of items or to comprehend descriptions of these scenes.

array for the visualization group; this is exactly as expected by our model, of course. Second, there was only a slight increase in response time with the number of items for the comprehension group. Further, as Moore (1915) found, more time was required to image a scene than to comprehend a description of it. Strictly speaking, this result falls outside the domain of the present imagery theory, but the relatively smaller increases in time per additional item and the overall decrease in time found here are easily explained in the context of our model: If one decides one has "comprehended" a scene when one has located the PRP files of the objects and relations (and perhaps not even all of them), then of course this will be faster than locating the files, searching for the name of an IMG file, looking up this file, generating the image, and so on. Third, in this experiment, an additional 902 milliseconds were required to generate images for each additional item, compared to only 24 milliseconds per item for the comprehension group. The increase in generation time per item is appreciably longer than found in our earlier experiments, but this result is at worst a Class 3 (theory supplementation) finding. On first glance, it might appear that we could simply chalk up this disparity to the fact that these people were asked to image entire objects (which may themselves be initially generated with parts). However, in the previous experiments in which entire objects were imaged, times increased only about a third of what they did here. Thus, to be internally consistent we cannot invoke this account both here and in the earlier cases. However, we can explain the results by positing that subjects had less available "processing capacity" with which to generate images of individual items in this experiment because of the large amount of material that had to be held in memory. "Processing-capacity limits" can be implemented in numerous ways (for example, an executive program with limited switching speed which, in this case, must maintain memory for the words and form images at the same time).* Alternatively, it is possible that because of differences in the populations sampled, these subjects were simply slower than others; these subjects were housewives whereas all of the others were your standard "undergraduate volunteers." Given this possible account I am loath to complicate the theory at this stage (although eventually we should be able to account for individual differences—as will be discussed later). Fourth, in the visualization condition, one-dimensional scenes required more time than did three-dimensional ones; there were no effects of number of dimensions on comprehension time. The imagery findings fall in Class 2 (multiple interpretation): Beech and Allport note that the three-dimensional scenes were "more compact"; if so, then the one-dimensional scenes may have either (*a*) been larger than the three-dimensional ones or (*b*) partially overflowed the most resolved region of the visual buffer, requiring shifting the image and readjusting its size during the course of completing the scene. In either case, our model has no trouble in providing an account for this finding. If the overall size of the image were controlled and the use of only two relations in the one-dimensional case did not make these arrays more confusing and difficult to understand than the three-dimensional ones, then our model would lead us not to expect differences in generation time (all else being equal—like the familiarity of the imaged items, relations, and so on). Fifth, decreasing contextual association resulted in more time to generate the images. This finding falls into Class 4 (domain contamination). Following Beech and Allport, the best way to explain the effects of context is by reference to the ease of encoding the "meaning" of the words: Presumably one can look up the correct lists of propositions and appropriate relational procedures more quickly when the words occur in a more coherent context. This conjecture is consistent with Nappe and Wollen's (1973) finding that subjects took longer to visualize two objects in a bizarre relation than in a more normal one. Presumably, additional time is required to look up the appropriate relational procedures, to find the best approximation to the foundation part, and so on for unusual relations than for more familiar ones. Unfortunately, if this interpretation is correct, context also should have affected times for the comprehension group, and this was not found. However, the

---

*Note that the second interpretation *could* have been introduced earlier to explain the relatively large increments per item. It seems possible that whenever we can think of multiple interpretations the result could be considered in Class 2 or 3 (multiple interpretation or theory supplementation). The distinction between the first class and the others is that if only one simple account of the results is available, it is in Class 1 vis- à-vis our model; if more than one account is plausible within the model, the result falls in Class 2; only if new assumptions must be incorporated into the model in order to explain a result is that result placed in Class 3. Thus, in the interests of parsimony we reject a competing Class 3 account if a Class 1 or 2 account is available.

results of Beech and Allport's second experiment challenge the claim that
the findings from the comprehension group truly reflect the time necessary to understand the stated relations.

Their second experiment used the same materials as the first one, but
now subjects rated the ease of understanding, ease of imaging, and the
bizarreness of each array (using standard seven-point scales). The size of
the array, number of dimensions, and contextual constraint all affected
the ratings on all three scales, except that one versus three dimensions did
not affect rated ease of imaging. The important result for present purposes
is that subjects did rate passages with less contextual constraint as less
comprehensible (and more bizarre, and more difficult to image). Beech
and Allport suggest that "comprehension latencies, obtained in the first
experiment, may reflect little more than the comprehension of the individual words or phrases in the description." Thus, the effects of contextual constraint may well reflect ease of comprehension, and not image-
specific processing per se.

The final experiment reported by Beech and Allport was designed to
test two hypotheses about why more time was taken to generate images
when more items were included in an array. On one view, these effects
reflect "cumulative lag." That is, the image-generation time may have
been outdistanced by the presentation rate of the material (a sentence,
mentioning two objects, occurred every 2.5 seconds). Thus, subjects may
have been trying to catch up after the sentence had been fully presented,
and this may have been what was being measured here. Alternatively,
image generation may not have begun until the description was over. In
this case, the subject would first comprehend the description and then
image the entire scene in one fell swoop. If the cumulative lag hypotheses
were correct, Beech and Allport reasoned, then the presentation rate of
the sentences ought to be crucial: Larger effects of array size ought to be
obtained when increasingly less time is allowed per item, because more
items will now lag behind the ones being presented. This idea was tested
by asking subjects to image an array of pigeon-holes and then to image
named items (like a crab, a phone, a book) in the holes in a specified order
(starting from the center, and then moving up, down, right, or left, as described). Arrays contained from one to five items, and six groups of subjects were tested, each hearing the stimulus words at a different presentation rate (from .75 to 5 seconds per item). A tone signaled the end of the
stimulus sequence of words, and response times were measured from this
tone. The results are illustrated in figure 6.5. As is evident, time to image
the array increased monotonically, but not linearly, with array size at all
presentation rates; there was no systematic effect of presentation rate on
image-generation time.

The finding that times increased monotonically with increasing numbers of items in this experiment is easily explained by our model: An

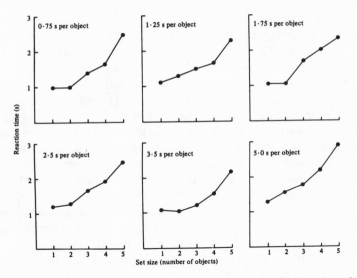

Figure 6.5. The results of the second experiment reported by Beech and Allport (1978). These graphs illustrate the time to generate images of scenes when items were named at different presentation rates.

image of a pigeonhole array would serve as a skeletal image, and the designated boxes as foundation parts specified by the location relations (up, right, and so on). Images of the named objects would be adjusted to fit into the holes exactly as an image of a tire is adjusted by our simulation to fit into a wheelbase of a car imaged at some size and position in the visual buffer. The only potentially troublesome result of this experiment is the fact that times did not increase linearly with increasing numbers of items. This result, however, falls in Class 2 (multiple interpretation) of our taxomony. One account rests on the following claims of the theory: (1) Images are refreshed by scanning the visual buffer and reactivating fading regions directly, saving the extra effort of finding the foundation parts, looking up propositional relations, and so on that would be required if images were simply generated anew when they faded. (2) Only a limited number of items can be held in an image at once, as determined by the rate at which items are imaged and the rate at which they fade. If the initially generated images have faded by the time the last item is imaged, the "image capacity" has been exceeded. In the present case, subjects may have imaged each object as it was named, even when the fastest presentation rate was used. This is not implausible given that at least 750 milliseconds were allotted between words, which is far more time than has been observed to be necessary to image an object in any experiment in which college undergraduates were used as subjects and no more than five items were imaged in an array (for example, the difference between imaging two and three items in a scene in one of our experiments was 220 milliseconds—see figure 4.11). In this case, however, the additional requirement of holding an image of a pigeonhole array may have proven too taxing, resulting in it being increasingly unlikely that all of the items would be maintained in larger arrays at the time the tone was sounded. If so, then with larger array sizes it would become increasingly likely that one would have to generate an image of at least one item from the deep level, which would require more time than refreshing an item at the surface. The greater difficulty of generating an image from the deep level, then, would result in nonlinear increases in image-generation time with increasing numbers of items. Note, however, that for this account to be consistent with our account of the results of Beech and Allport's first experiment we must assume that only two or possibly three items were maintained and directly regenerated. If people can hold more than this number of items, we would not expect linear increases in the first experiment either.

The account offered above is not the only possible one for the nonlinear increases. The relatively small differences in time to image arrays with two items instead of just one could be due to the objects in the one-item arrays being filled out in more detail than were the objects in the two-item arrays (so that the number of parts actually placed in the visual buffer may often have been roughly equivalent in the two conditions). The relative increases for times for the larger arrays could be due to increased difficulty in comprehending the relationships among the arrays; the relations were similar, and not very—if at all—constrained by the context. (Beech and Allport do report that in their first experiment some especially long latencies occurred for the lowest order of context for the large arrays.) An account that treats the deviations from linearity for the smaller arrays differently from the deviations for the larger arrays is obviously less parsimonious than an account that explains both by appeal to the same mechanism. Further, the first account offered above also allows us to explain the failure of presentation rate to alter the effects of array size on generation time: In all cases subjects were able to generate an image of each named object in the time allotted, and the probability that an object was not in the image at the time the tone was sounded depended on the number of items (in addition to the pigeonhole array itself). Thus, in all cases subjects would refresh the items in the image after the tone sounded, and then generate images of any missing items.

The finding that presentation rate did not systematically affect generation times is, however, also a Class 2 (multiple interpretation) finding. In addition to the account offered above, we could hypothesize that subjects merely comprehended the stimulus sequences at the time they were presented and formed their images only after hearing the tone. Presumably part of comprehending, in this situation, is locating the relevant propositional encodings. I find this account unlikely, however, especially given the unstructured spatial configurations used here. I personally would al-most have to try to project images upon hearing the names, or at least note the locations of the objects in an image of the pigeonholes, in order to keep track of the different locations (especially with the longer descrip-tions). As in most cases where a Class 2 (multiple interpretation) result is found, an interesting experiment is in the making. In this case, it might be worthwhile to use a word-by-word visual presentation technique in this task, to try to discourage on-line image formation during the presentation stage; my suspicion is that this would make the task noticeably more diffi-cult, suggesting that subjects do not usually wait until the end before beginning to construct any image at all. This kind of experiment is worth considering because it may tell us something about the possible advan-tages of employing mental imagery; it may be that building up and main-taining an imagistic representation as one comprehends a description is much more efficient than trying to encode the description by rote.

Finally, consider the magnitude of the effect observed here: An average of 330 milliseconds were required for each additional item in this experi-ment, versus around 900 before. As before, the fact that these times are longer than those observed for each additional part added to an image in our experiments is not troublesome. Perhaps each object had more than a single part, which would explain the longer times, or perhaps skeletal images require more time to activate than additional parts. In addition, it may have been more difficult to locate the foundation parts in this experi-ment (given the similarity of the possible alternatives).

2.5 Default Values Used in Generating Images

In constructing our model, we often had to specify a "default value" in some process. For example, if the size was not specified, at which size should an image be generated? Similarly, what about location and orienta-tion? The first of these questions is the only one that I have decent data on, both from our laboratory and from Robert Weber's. My experiments (reported in detail in Kosslyn, 1978a) were attempts to estimate not the largest subjective size, but the default one. People may usually image ob-jects at the maximal subjective size, or they may commonly image them smaller, or larger (such that parts overflow). Alternatively, people may selectively image large objects at one size and smaller ones at another to optimize the depiction of various details or because certain objects are usually seen at far distances. In one experiment people were asked to image animals and estimate how far away the animal seemed in the image. These estimates and the sizes of the animals were used to calculate the angle subtended by these images. This experiment included two sets of materials, the names of animals used in the first experiment measuring the visual angle of the mind's eye (chapter 3, section 2.4) and the pictures

used in the second experiment of that series. Since there was some disagreement about the sizes specified for the animals in the first experiment,
I decided to obtain normative estimates of heights and lengths of the various animals for this experiment. These estimates were obtained from a
new group of undergraduates, who were given a randomized list of the
animals and asked simply to write down the average height and length of
each beast. Although the mean estimates of the longest axis did not differ
significantly from the values used before, the greatest disagreements
tended to be with the largest animals. Thus, I decided to use the rated
sizes in the present experiment and to replicate the earlier experiment
(with point-of-overflow instructions) using the mean estimated sizes in
order to compare the two conditions.

For the animal names (without drawings), one group was given point-
of-overflow instructions exactly like those used previously (see chapter 3,
section 2.4). The procedure and materials were identical to those used
before, except that the new sizes were listed next to animal names. The
other group received the same response sheets but was asked simply to
image each animal as if it were the size listed to its right. After imaging it,
the subject was asked to estimate how far away the animal would be if it
were actually being seen at that subjective size (visual angle subtended).
Distance estimates were written down in a space next to the animal's
name.

A third group of people was shown the pictures used in the second experiment of the previous series, one at a time in a random order. After a
picture was presented and studied until the subject thought he or she
could image it, it was removed and the subject mentally imaged it. After
imaging a picture, the subject was asked to stand away from a blank white
wall the distance that the picture seemed in this image; distances from the
wall again were measured.

As is evident in figure 6.6 (top panel), when the point-of-overflow instructions were used, the angles calculated along the best-fitting function
again did not remain constant when the largest animals were included;
when the two largest animals were excluded, the angle was constant
around 50 degrees, which did not differ significantly from the angle calculated in the previous experiment. Thus, even though slightly different
sizes were used, these results are remarkably similar to those obtained
earlier (see figure 3.20).

With the new (default size) instructions, larger animals again tended to
be imaged at longer distances, as is evident in the bottom panel of figure
6.6. There was a high correlation between longest axis and estimated distance. The angle calculated along the best-fitting function did not,
however, remain constant; larger animals seem to have been imaged at
subjectively larger sizes, even if the largest animals are excluded from the
analysis (this is not graphed in figure 6.6 since it made absolutely no dif-

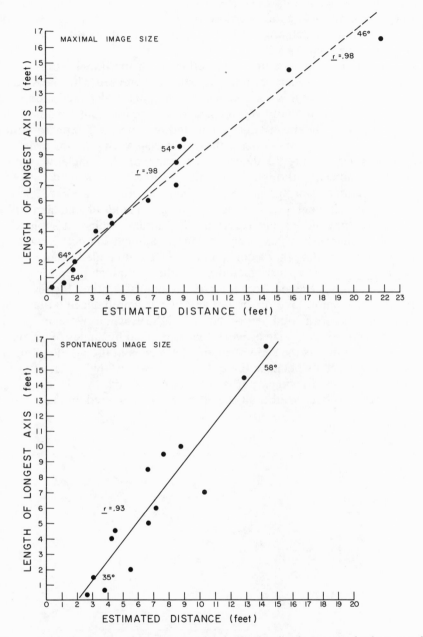

Figure 6.6. The mean distance at which imaged animals appeared when people imaged them at the point of overflow (top) or at spontaneous sizes (bottom). The stimuli in these experiments were names and sizes of animals, which subjects imaged from long-term memory.

ference in the calculations). The mean angle calculated here did not differ from that obtained using the overflow instructions, and this angle was not different from that calculated in the first experiment of the series reported in chapter 3, section 2.4.

The results of using the new instructions with the drawings are illustrated in figure 6.7. Again, estimated distance increased with the size of the imaged object. In this case, however, the angle calculated along the best-fitting function did not vary much as size increased, but remained relatively constant. The mean angle calculated here was different from that calculated in the experiment using these materials with point-of-overflow instructions (35 versus 20 degrees); the size of this angle was not, however, significantly different from that (43 degrees) obtained with the same instructions using the names of animals as stimuli.

To sum up, although people tended to image smaller objects as if they were closer, they did not always seem to maintain a constant subjective size in their images; even excluding the larger animals did not allow us to fit a function indicating that a constant angle was subtended when images were evoked from long-term memory. Further, although people seemed to image animals retrieved from long-term memory at about the maximal subjective size before overflowing, the drawings were imaged larger than the maximal size estimated before; however, the drawings were imaged at about the same average size as were images evoked by names of animals. Perhaps the drawings overflowed at smaller angles in the previous maximal-size experiments because the criterion for "overflow" was set more stringently for the drawings, perhaps because the edges of the drawings were more sharply defined than the edges of remembered animals.

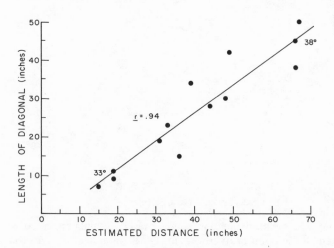

Figure 6.7. The mean distance at which images of line drawings appeared when people imaged them at a spontaneous size.

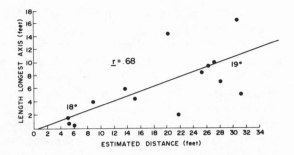

Figure 6.8.   The average rated viewing distance for the animals imaged from long-term memory.

Why were long-term memory images (those evoked by name) of larger animals imaged at larger subjective sizes? Perhaps people's images do preserve some information about the relative sizes of animals, although only slightly (note that the larger animals subtended less than twice the angle of the smaller ones, and yet the actual sizes were over an order of magnitude larger). Alternatively, perhaps the small animals were imaged too far away. That is, perhaps because we rarely see small animals at extremely close distances, we do not gain anything by moving these any closer. The relatively constant angle obtained with the drawings, which were all viewed at the same distance, indicates that people do not always simply image things as they are used to seeing them. Nonetheless, there may be some effect of the distance at which we are used to seeing things; when asked to image some object, we may often image a typical exemplar at a typical distance. This could also be a factor in explaining our consistent finding that images of large animals constructed from long-term memory seem to overflow at a longer distance than we would expect if a constant angle is subtended at the point of overflow (see figures 3.20 and 3.23). The following experiment was conducted in order to investigate this possibility.

A new group of students was given the same list of animal names and sizes used in the first two conditions of the preceding experiment. These people were simply asked to write down the average distance at which they had viewed each animal. The results are illustrated in figure 6.8. As is evident, larger animals are reportedly seen at greater distances than smaller ones, although the relationship between size and distance is not as strong as those observed previously. The fact that people tend to see smaller objects at shorter distances is in itself a trivial finding; small objects simply cannot be seen if they are too far away. In fact, if the smallest five animals are excluded from the analysis, the correlation between longest extent and distance drops to $r = .32$. In any case, the constant angle observed in this experiment, evident in figure 6.8, makes it difficult to argue that average viewing distance influenced the lack of a constant angle evident in either panel of figure 6.6. Further, the difference in size between the angle obtained here and those obtained with the other instructions underscores the fact that subjects were not simply recalling average viewing distance when performing the other tasks.*

Weber and Malmstrom (1979) also attempted to measure how large mental images are spontaneously constructed, using very different techniques from those I used. In their first experiment, they tested three groups of subjects. In one group, words were presented at a small size, in another they were presented at a large size, and in the third they were spelled out a letter at a time. The words were three, five, or seven letters long. The subject imaged a given word against a blank screen and adjusted two pointers indicating the boundaries of the image. Large words subtended between 17 and 38 degrees, small words around 2 to 4 degrees. Although the relative sizes of the words were preserved, there was considerable "regression to the mean": Large words were imaged smaller than they had appeared, but small words were imaged larger. This result converges with my findings when only animal names were given. The angles of the images ranged from about 3 to 13 degrees. There were no effects of the meaning of the words here; names of larger objects were not imaged larger (nor should they be, under most straightforward accounts I can think of). The angles measured here were all noticeably smaller than those I estimated. The angles obtained here are most similar to those obtained in the experiments reported in chapter 3, section 2.4, in which a very strict criterion of "overflow" was used. This is a Class 3 (theory supplementation) finding, requiring further elaboration of the model. My suspicion is that a relatively high degree of resolution is necessary in an image to see letters in the course of performing the Weber and Malmstrom task, and thus the images were smaller than in my task (and did not extend to less resolved regions of the visual buffer).

In Weber and Malmstrom's second experiment a very different technique was used to estimate the size at which images are spontaneously constructed. Subjects viewed a large grid or a small one (subtending the same angles as the large and the small words in the first experiment). Each grid consisted of four boxes aligned end to end. Following this, four consonants were presented and the subjects were to image one per box and then to focus on a given position. Next they heard the name of a letter and were asked to decide whether it was a relatively tall letter or a short one. The distance between the focused upon letter and the probed one was systematically varied. There was also a default condition, where no grid was

---

*George Smith conjectures that objects are imaged just large enough to insert the characteristics that distinguish them from similar entities. This principle is clearly able to be incorporated into our model and is empirically testable.

presented. Extrapolating from the size of the eye movements and response time per degree in the grid conditions made it possible to estimate the size of the image in the no-grid condition. The results indicated that default images are generated at about 8 degrees, which is not far from the approximate maximal size of 13 degees (with seven letters and a large picture) observed in Weber and Malmstrom's first experiment—or from my estimates of the size of an image when a very strict criterion for overflow is used (around 12 to 19 degrees; see figure 3.23). Oddly enough, there was no difference in response times when different-sized grids (which should have required different amounts of image scanning) were used, although times did increase with longer distances between letters. But this is at worst a Class 2 (multiple interpretation) finding: It could be due to subjects slowing down their scanning rates with smaller images, which is especially plausible if a high degree of resolution is necessary to perform the task; in addition, subjects could be more cautious when using smaller images, not wishing to "overshoot" the target. Finally, the differences in the size of the maximal angle observed in these experiments and mine are also a Class 2 result, explainable in many ways. For example, this disparity could be due to having to project an image versus forming one with one's eyes closed. Weber and Castleman found that a much higher proportion of people could form images with their eyes closed than with them open—perhaps because of interference from visual input. Perhaps the images in the second experiment reported by Weber and Malmstrom were smaller because it takes extra effort to maintain larger images with one's eyes open. In any case, we know that the size at which an image can be generated is subject to strategic adjustment: We have demonstrated that people can generate images at different sizes at will. Thus, it is not a surprise that there is not an absolute default size at which images are generated, but that the size at which an image is formed depends in part on task requirements. In our model, images are generated to just fill the most resolved region of the visual buffer, all else being equal. This does not seem an unreasonable assumption, given the data taken as a whole.

3.0 CONCLUDING REMARKS

In attempting to provide detailed accounts of data, both those collected during Phase I and those in the literature, we were led to develop the research strategy, general model, and theory in some interesting ways. First, we found it useful to consider data with respect to a five-class taxonomy. The interesting thing about this taxonomy is that it leads one not to place too much importance on cases in which the model provides precise accounts of data. The problem here is that the theory and the model were constructed with an eye toward providing accounts for certain data in the first place, and one cannot be sure that "new" data are in fact unrelated to the data which motivated us to formulate the theory and the model as we did initially. The most interesting classes were Class 2 (multiple interpretation), 3 (theory supplementation), and 5 (disconfirmation). When data fell in Class 2 or 3 we were faced with a situation that begged for more experimentation to constrain the theory further or to motivate the way it should be expanded. If any data had clearly belonged in Class 5, we would have been faced with the challenge of revising the theory with as little violence as possible.

The data supported the validity of a number of central claims of the theory: (1) Images can be generated from separate literal encodings. (2) Individual parts are placed serially in the visual buffer. (3) Propositional information can be used to coordinate juxtaposition of individual parts in the visual buffer. (4) Propositional encodings associated with the name of a word are accessed prior to accessing the literal image encoding (see the account of the Beech and Allport findings, for example). (5) Images are constructed by examining material already in the visual buffer. (6) The underlying deep representation of an image may be hierarchically structured, and this structuring is a consequence of stored propositional relations (among higher-order units and rows and columns of letters, in our experiment). (7) One searches an ordered list for the name of an image encoding, and images the contents of the encoding named highest on the list. (8) An extra operation is required to image objects at a previously unseen size. (9) Only a very limited number of parts can be maintained in an image at one time.

We also discovered support for three accounts of the differences in generation time per part observed in the different experiments: (1) Some foundation parts are more difficult to see than others; (2) parts (defined by the Gestalt Laws of Organization, in our experiments) containing more material require more time to image, at least if the part is composed of discrete elements; and (3) in experiments in which the parts were imaged in the same location in the visual buffer, the time required for the first image to fade may have affected the time necessary to place the second image. In addition, we discovered that the default size of images is not constant, but depends on (1) the size of the object being imaged (larger objects being imaged slightly larger), (2) the nature of the materials (ones with sharper edges being imaged smaller), and (3) the nature of the task (tasks requiring higher resolution appearing to engender formation of smaller images).

Finally, we were led to hypothesize on the basis of the data that: (1) skeletal images require more time to generate than do parts; (2) judgments of image completion may be based on assessment of "sharpness level," and smaller images may become sharper more quickly than larger ones;

(3) a subject's motivation affects how hard he or she will try to fill in all the details on an image; (4) actual verbal encodings (not just propositional ones) can be used to prompt a sequence of images; (5) parts do not appear to be ordered in terms of level of "structural dependency"; (6) one forms images for abstract words by looking up encodings of associated words and searching for image encodings of these objects. The name of this image encoding may then be stored directly with the abstract word, but will initially not be very strongly associated with the word (as reflected by the ordering of the entry in the word's PRP list in the model).

7. Inspecting Visual Images

Visual mental images, I have claimed, serve as repositories of information in human memory. Before we can truly understand how information is represented in a system, we must specify how interpretive processes operate on the data-structures. In the present case, we must specify how surface images are "inspected." Our computer simulation is capable of inspecting its images, and I claim that the principles that describe its operation also describe how human beings perform the analogous activity. In this chapter I will consider the data on "inspecting" visual mental images, to see whether straightforward accounts of these findings emerge from the theory. Of course, the theory was initially formulated with some of these findings in mind, so some reasonable accounts should be forthcoming. As in the previous chapter, we are most interested here in (1) accounts of new data, not similar to data that initially motivated us to formulate the theory as we did; (2) the options left unspecified that become apparent when we consider more detailed accounts of the data; (3) cases where we must consider how to supplement the theory; and (4) data that directly contradict the model (the fifth class of our taxonomy). In addition, as the need to account for increasingly more data begins to narrow our options, we become increasingly interested in (1) the internal constraints that emerge when we account for the sum of the findings taken together and (2) predictions that follow from our accounts. As in the previous chapter, I will begin by considering the data collected during Phase I, and then will turn to other results in the literature.

1.0 CONSISTENCY TESTS

1.1 The Effects of Size

The accounts offered in this section generally hinge on the following claims of the theory: (1) the visual buffer has only a limited resolution; (2) the visual buffer is spatially bounded; (3) images begin to fade as soon as they are generated, and must be actively refreshed to be maintained; (4) parts of images may be inserted into the image as needed if the size scale

224

is appropriate (that is, the foundation parts are visible); and (5) "zooming in" dilates the image in increments, resulting in increasing amounts of detail becoming visible. Additional claims of the theory will be invoked in special cases, as appropriate.

1.1.1 Indirect Manipulation of Size

In several of our experiments the size of a "target" image was varied indirectly by varying the size relative to a context image. In these experiments, subjects imaged a scene containing a target animal (such as a goose) next to either (*a*) a context animal (an elephant or a fly), (*b*) a matrix (of four versus sixteen cells), or (*c*) a set of digits (two or four—see Kosslyn, 1975). When subjects imaged a target next to an appropriately scaled elephant they required more time to see properties of the target (for example, a collie's feet) than when it was next to an appropriately scaled fly. This finding was reversed when elephants were imaged tiny and flies huge. Similarly, more time was required to see properties of animals imaged relatively small next to a complex or simple matrix or next to two or four imaginary digits; the effects of relative size were the same regardless of the complexity of the adjacent matrix or the number of digits included in the image. In these experiments subjects were told to place the property on the animal and then to see whether it "looked right" prior to making a response. That is, even if a property was clearly false (horns for a goose), the subjects were to image it on the appropriate part of the animal before making their judgments. More time was required to evaluate both true and false queries when target animals were mentally pictured at subjectively small sizes in all three experiments.

The longer times to inspect images of relatively small target objects are explained if (1) there is only a limited display area, most of which is taken up by the relatively large context image (such as an elephant), leaving little room for the smaller target animal (such as a rabbit), and (2) when the target animal is smaller, the limited resolution of the display obscures most of its parts (and prevents many parts from being inserted into the image when it is generated—as argued in the preceding chapter). Hence, one "zooms in" before looking for the part, as occurs in our model. The simulated image of a car illustrated in figure 5.5 illustrates the effects of resolution: The wheelbases are obscured, which prevented adding the wheels themselves when the image was generated, and thus the wheels are not evident in the image. As soon as the resolution permits, the appropriate regions of the image are elaborated and inspected, as described in chapter 5. Subjectively large images do not require zooming in, and—as long as they do not overflow the most highly resolved region of the visual buffer—do not require scanning to identify a part in our model (we will consider data bearing on this claim shortly). Further, since foundation parts are more often discernible, it is more likely that the sought part will be visible on the larger image in the first place. Thus, more time will be required to inspect subjectively smaller images. (Note: I assume that in the experiments in which size was manipulated indirectly the subjects knew which image of a pair was a target object and hence which to inspect.)

Thus, on the face of things this is an example of a Class 1 (confirmation) finding, but uninterestingly so because we formulated the model with an eye toward explaining these data from the outset. Somewhat to my surprise, after the model was constructed I realized this was in fact a Class 2 (multiple interpretation) finding, since another account for the results was available within the context of the model. Since this account will not generalize to data discussed in the next section, where size is manipulated directly, I will first present the preferred account. The alternative account will be introduced in section 1.1.3, where it will be rejected in the face of additional data.

It is important to note that we currently claim that the wheels were not on the small image—no amount of "squinting" or the like could allow one to see them: The size effect is not a "criterion" effect. That is, we could have posited that all parts are present on subjectively tiny images, even if they are not "visible." If so, then simply trying harder to see a part would render it perceptible, but would also require more time than when "squinting" was not required. I rejected this account, however, for three reasons: (1) The image-generation scheme is inconsistent with this view because we claim that parts are added via inspection of the surface image itself and that the limited resolution of the visual buffer prevents (or at least seriously impairs) adding parts if the image is too small. If this is not true, then there is no reason why parts would not be present on smaller images. Yet our data suggest that people prefer to omit parts on smaller images and have difficulty putting them there even when they try. (2) Given the claim that parts fade as soon as they are placed, it is unlikely that one can always construct an image of an object that depicts all that one knows about it, and hence later insertion of details will be required sometimes. (3) We would have expected significantly more errors with small images if criterion changes ("squinting") had been occurring, because people would settle for less information as depicting a part. For example, a glint on the door of an imaged car could be interpreted as its handle, if one's criterion were set low enough. But in my experiments there almost never is a significant difference between error rates for subjectively small images and large images.

If we were trying to explain the actual magnitude of the size effect, rather than simply the existence of it, our findings would be in Class 2 (multiple interpretation) vis-à-vis the model. At issue here is how much detail commonly occurs even in normal-sized images. Perhaps filling in is almost always required here as well. If so, then the increased time to inspect subjectively smaller images is due to "zoom time," and not to "zoom-plus-fill-in time." This question has been raised by our attempt to explain the foregoing findings in the most internally consistent way possible, and represents an example of the "directive function" of the model. An additional example of this function is the question of why zooming in occurs, rather than simple regeneration of the image at a more perspicuous size. The answer to this question rests at the heart of why existing images are easier to alter than to replace, which is one of the central questions of chapter 8.

1.1.2 Direct Manipulation of Subjective Size

When subjects were asked to image animals at different relative sizes, as indicated by the sizes of boxes studied before the experiment, more time was taken to see "true" properties if animals were imaged subjectively small, but there were no effects of size for "false" properties. In the preceding experiments, subjects were asked always to place properties on the image before making a truth evaluation; in this experiment, however, subjects were merely told to "look at the appropriate area" and "look for" the queried property (if the animal had the property, the subjects were told, they should be able to find it). When data from one subject with extremely long times were eliminated, there was no difference in times for the two medium sizes, although there was a size difference between these times and those for true properties of the largest and smallest images (1827, 1695, 1691, and 1590 milliseconds for smallest to largest images, respectively).*

The effects of subjective size of an image on the ease of detecting parts

---

*For subjects who reported using imagery less than 80 percent of the time (when queried after the experiment), I actually found a trend toward a *reverse* size effect: More time tended to be required for the larger images. This trend was not significant, however (but perhaps only because there were not enough data available). In any case, if this result is real it may simply indicate that subjects selectively tended to fail to follow instructions: The smaller the image is, the more difficult it is to use, and hence the more likely it is that subjects will answer on the basis of propositional encodings. As we shall see, in this type of task subjects generally are faster if propositional processing is used. Given the lack of statistical significance of this result, however, the finding is rather banal: It simply demonstrates again (as was found in the experiments on map-scanning in chapter 3) that nonimaginal processing does not evince the hallmarks of imagery processing. It is somewhat curious, however, that this is the only experiment in which we had more than simply two size variations, and the only one where the results seemed to depend on high levels of imagery use. Perhaps the added difficulty of keeping the four sizes distinct was especially extreme with the smaller sizes, which may also have encouraged delinquent responding. Although this kind of account is ad hoc, it is not entirely worthless in that it would lead us to make certain predictions in the future.

are explained exactly the same way we explained the results described in the previous section. The lack of a distinguishable effect for the two intermediate sizes is a Class 2 (multiple interpretation) finding, amenable to many accounts: Perhaps people simply have trouble keeping these sizes distinct, as indicated by postsession self-reports. Alternatively, the difference in resolution may not have been large enough to affect times, given the grain of the visual buffer and the sensitivity of the interpretive procedures. In order to study this, however, we need some measure of the "visual acuity of the mind's eye." (This is another example of the "directive function" of our model.)

Finally, the failure to find effects with false probes here is easily explained. In this experiment, subjects were not told to place the property on the animal before responding. Instead, they were simply asked to look at the appropriate place and to be sure that they could see that the property did not belong there. If a property is unusual and inappropriate, this fact will be evident quickly via propositional processing, as will be discussed in chapter 9. If this sort of propositional evaluation occurs in parallel with image generation and inspection (as I will argue in chapter 9), it is not surprising that subjects can make a decision without using imagery more quickly than a decision based on generating and inspecting an image (see chapter 3, sections 2.1 and 2.2). The problem becomes one of setting a criterion for responding. How long should one look before deciding that a property is not present? There is no reason why this "wait time" should vary systematically with the subjective size of an image. It is of some interest that the mean times for false probes corresponded to the mean time for "true" statements in the experiment described above, suggesting that subjects waited an "average time" before responding. In fact, there was no significant difference between mean times for true and false probes in any of the experiments using these sorts of instructions. We have not implemented this "wait time" strategy in our model, but it would be trivial to do so. This finding, then, falls into Class 3 (theory supplementation), but we did not develop the core theory to account for it, for two reasons: (1) It is not clear that it falls into the domain of a theory of imagery. Given that subjects never in fact accessed the sought information, these data probably do not tell much about how images do in fact represent information. (2) This clearly is a task-specific result of little relevance to nonlaboratory, real-world processing.

1.1.3 Identification of Objects Imaged at Different Sizes

People required more time to see digits imaged small next to an animal than to see digits imaged at subjectively larger sizes. This difference was of the same magnitude whether two or four digits were included in the image. This result was obtained for both true and false trials. The explanation for the findings in the true trials is identical to that for the results described above: When digits were small, one "zoomed in" and simultaneously filled in missing portions, requiring more time than when no size adjustment was necessary. In this case there was a clear way to use the image to decide that a given digit was not in the set: by inspecting each of the digits that were in fact in the image. As one would expect if this occurred, more time was in fact required for "false" digit probes when the set was imaged at a subjectively small size instead of a larger size (where each digit could be checked without zooming in being required). However, because the effects of set size were the same for true and false trials, we must assume that the set was exhaustively examined in both cases (as would follow from the findings of Sternberg, 1966). The fact that in general more time was required for false probes than for true ones is itself a Class 3 (theory supplementation) or Class 4 (domain contamination) finding, requiring either further specification of the decision procedures used by FIND in the model, or specification of a theory of response processes.

The effects of inspecting different-sized digits allow us to rule out a plausible counterinterpretation of some of the results discussed in section 1.1.1. On this alternative account, the size effect in the set of experiments using context images (animals, matrices, or digits) could have been due to *scanning* effects: The small target image was less likely to be focused upon at the time the query was delivered than was the large context image, and hence more time was required to see parts of smaller target animals not because of resolution limits, but because of increased distance usually scanned (from the context image instead of from another part of the target animal itself). If this account is correct, however, then the inclusion of four digits (or the more complex matrix) should have resulted in relatively more time being spent focusing on the digits or matrix (instead of the adjacent animal) relative to the two-digit (or less complex matrix) case. If so, then we would expect a smaller effect of the relative size of a digit on time to detect one of four digits instead of one of two digits because in general less scanning would be required. But this was not true: Equal effects of the size of imaged digits were obtained for the two- and four-digit images. Furthermore, if this counterinterpretation were true, we should not have found additive effects of size and complexity on time to see parts of imaged animals, which were in fact found. Rather, the two factors should have interacted, with smaller effects of the size of an imaged animal being observed when fewer digits or a less complex matrix was imaged next to it.

1.1.4 Delay Effects

The effects of size persisted when subjects were asked to hold an image for varying amounts of time before receiving the name of a possible property. There were equal and appreciable effects of size when "true" prop-

erties were presented between six and ten seconds after the name of the
to-be-imaged animal was presented (see figure 3.18). Although the size effects with "false" properties were not as dramatic, there was no statistical difference among the effects of size when these properties were presented at different delays after an image had been evoked. Similarly, in
the experiments to be described in the next section, we found that the
same amount of time was required to see a property on an image generated at the same time the property was presented as on one generated
six seconds in advance.

The lack of effects of how long an image is held prior to inspection do
not make sense if images are constructed with many details and slowly
fade over time. If this were true, we would expect more extreme effects of
size at relatively short delays after an image had been constructed (if
small images are so difficult to see from the onset that fading only alters
the ease of seeing large images) or more extreme effects at longer delays
(if fading differentially obscures smaller images), neither of which occurred. In fact, we did not even find that more time in general was required
when images were maintained for longer intervals. The finding that the
length of the retention interval did not alter the size effect is a clear case
of a Class 1 (confirmation) result. On the present account, these results
reflect the facts that (1) images are "refreshed" before being inspected,
and (2) most parts are placed on an image only when they are required. In
this case, the queried part usually would have to be generated on the
image at any size, but the small skeletal image itself would need to be
refreshed and then expanded prior to elaboration. The present account
is not simply an empty ad hoc exercise, because it turns on our earlier
claim—made for entirely different reasons—that only a few details are
usually maintained in images. Further, it is internally consistent with our
account of the basic size effect. Finally, it suggests some new predictions,
as will be discussed in the second part of this chapter.

1.1.5 Detecting Properties of Different Sizes

In addition to studying the effects of the subjective size of an imaged
object, we examined the ease of detecting different-sized parts on the
same image. The effects of property size were investigated in two separate sets of experiments. The first set included three very similar experiments, each of which required people to detect properties that were small
and highly associated (such as "claws" for a cat) or large and not highly
associated (such as "head" for a cat). In one experiment, subjects were
given six seconds to form an image of the animal before being queried
about a part; in another, subjects received the animal and part names in
rapid sequence and were asked to look for the part on an image of the

whole animal; in the third variation, subjects were again given the animal and part names in rapid sequence but were asked simply to see the part in isolation (or the area where it ought to be, if the property was false). As was noted in chapter 3, these same subjects also evaluated the same kind of properties without using imagery, which served to distinguish between imaginal and nonimaginal processing. For present purposes, however, we are interested only in the imagery results. In chapter 9, we will consider the results obtained with no imagery instructions in the context of the role of imagery in question-answering processes.

The results for the first two experiments were virtually identical; when imagery was required, less time was required to see the larger properties than the smaller ones. These results are accounted for in the same way as those of the prior experiments: In this case, zooming in is required to obtain the resolution necessary to see the locations at which smaller parts should be inserted. The grain of the display medium results in only relatively large foundation parts being clearly visible, which is necessary before the requisite part can be generated. For example, if asked to image a dog and then asked to see its claws, one will place the claws only when they are queried, and will have to zoom in on the paw in order to do so; in contrast, zooming in will not be necessary and part-insertion may not be necessary for a large property (like the head)—even if it is not very highly associated with the object in question. Whether or not filling in is necessary for a large property depends on whether (*a*) it is an intrinsic part of the skeleton (as the roof is on our car) or (*b*) it has a high probability of having been generated on the image initially. In section 2.1.1 we will investigate some of the factors that dictate whether a part will be inserted into an image when it is initially generated.

At first glance, this finding may seem to fall into Class 2 (multiple interpretation). Again one could argue that the effects of property size were due not to resolution but to scanning. That is, finding smaller properties may have required more scanning, on the average, than did locating larger ones. The lack of a difference in the effects of size in the first two imagery conditions seems to belie this, however: In the second experiment the subjects had no images upon which to focus before placing the part, and thus were not likely to have to scan to see small parts. Rather, they knew which part of the image to attend to from the outset, but were required to generate an image of the whole animal and then to see the part on it. Thus, it seems unlikely that the same amount of scanning would be required in the two conditions, and more likely that the similar effects of property size (see figure 3.19) reflect effects of limited resolution.

The third variation, in which only the local region appropriate to the part was imaged, did not differ significantly from the first two in any respect in an analysis of variance. In this case, subjects presumably generated images of the parts in isolation, not on the skeleton or other foundation part. A post hoc test, however, revealed no effects of size in the imagery condition of this experiment. This was not surprising because different-sized animals did not require different amounts of time to image at the same subjective size (in experiments described in chapter 6, section 1.1). Finally, as noted earlier, the mean inspection times were the same in all three variations, which is consistent with the idea that images are refreshed prior to inspection and parts are often placed only as they are needed.* The only fly in the ointment here is the lack of effects of association strength, which would be expected if PRP lists are searched before parts are inserted. We will turn to this apparent problem shortly.

I also addressed the same issue in a slightly different way. Instead of selecting the items ahead of time for particular variations in size and association strength, I dug into my files and found a set of statements (such as "A lion has a mane") for which Keith Nelson and I (unpublished, ca. 1971) had collected verification-time data. In the original experiment, different subjects evaluated the statements either via imagery or simply as quickly as possible. In 1975 I obtained ratings of the size and the association strength of each property relative to the appropriate animal for the stimuli used in our reaction-time experiment, and then used these ratings as the independent variables in a regression analysis of the original verification latencies. Sure enough, when subjects were asked to use images of the whole animal, more time was required for smaller properties than for larger ones and association strength was of no consequence. When imagery was not required, in contrast, more strongly associated properties were affirmed more quickly, and size was of no consequence. The accounts of these results parallel those offered above. In another condition of the original experiment, subjects were not given time to image the whole animal before query and received instructions like those used in the third variation of the experiment described above. In this case, association strength now affected both imagery and no-imagery decisions. An account of these findings will be forthcoming from a new experiment which will be described shortly.

1.1.6 The Effects of Image Size on Later Memory

Kosslyn and Alper (1977) conducted a number of experiments (described in chapter 3, section 2.3) in which subjects were asked to image pairs of objects. On half the trials, one of the objects in a pair was to be mentally pictured at a tiny size relative to the other; on the other half of

---

*It is tempting to argue that if subjects were scanning in the first two variations, this should have introduced an additional component into these reaction times, relative to the third variation (where isolated parts were imaged). However, it may be that different propositional lists and image encodings (of the parts themselves), which were less readily accessible, were accessed in this last experiment.

the trials, both objects were imaged at normal sizes. In all of our experiments we found that later memory for the pair was worse if one of the objects had been imaged at a relatively tiny size. These findings fall in Class 3 (theory supplementation), requiring further development of the theory and general model, but such development will not require backtracking of any sort. The results are easily explained by the model if the surface image itself can be encoded into a new IMG file, labeled such that it is identified as an encoding of some stimulus object or objects presented during the experiment (although not necessarily labeled with the name or names of the contents). One file might contain both imaged objects, or they might be contained in separate files that are associated together in a PRP list. Later, when asked to recall the stimuli, this file or files would be printed out and FIND (probably in conjunction with other sorts of pattern-recognition procedures, as yet unspecified) would attempt to identify the objects. If the encoding were of a relatively small image, the grain of the visual buffer would obscure parts of the object—making it more difficult to identify when later imaged again. Since the original encoding of a small image is impoverished, "zooming in" would not help matters because there would not be any additional information available to be filled in. In order to develop an explicit model of processing in this task, then, we must take the following steps: (1) Develop the encoding scheme, wherein surface images are parsed into underlying IMG files. We currently have a primitive scheme that converts patterns of points in the surface matrix into a set of polar coordinates, but no actual parsing occurs. (Kosslyn, Heldmeyer, and Glass, 1980, report preliminary experiments examining how such a parsing scheme should operate.) (2) Develop the tagging scheme, which results in the files being labeled appropriately. (3) Develop retrieval procedures that would be used in this sort of task. (4) Develop the recognition procedures that would allow identification of a pattern in the visual buffer. Obviously, this is no small order, in part requiring building most of a pattern-recognition device, such as would be used in actually identifying patterns encoded on-line from the eyes.

1.2 Effects of Complexity

Parts of more complex imaged scenes required more time to see than did parts of less complex scenes. Our account for this difference in time will rest on the following principles of the theory: (1) the contents of separate encodings can be amalgamated into a single image; (2) because parts require time to image, and they fade with time, there is a limit on how many parts can be maintained in an image at once; (3) parts are imaged individually, and an increment of time is required to place each part; and (4) scanning is an iterative process, resulting in more time being required to scan longer distances across an image.

1.2.1 Inspecting Images in More or Less Complex Contexts

In an experiment reported in Kosslyn (1975) people imaged animals next to an imaginary matrix containing either four or sixteen cells (see figure 3.12). These subjects were asked to look for a given animal part, and if it was not present, to place it at the correct location on the imaged animal, and then to evaluate its appropriateness for the beast. For both true and false probes, more time was required to see parts of animals next to the sixteen-cell matrix. In another experiment, the sixteen-cell matrix was replaced by four digits imaged on an imaginary wall, and the four-cell matrix was replaced by two digits. Now, more time was required in the four-digit condition either to verify a true or false digit or to verify a property of the adjacent animal. In both of these experiments the relative size of the animal and matrix or digits was also varied, and the effects of complexity were the same regardless of relative size. This result, somewhat to my surprise, falls in Class 2 (multiple interpretation). Further, neither of these interpretations is the one I had in mind when originally formulating the theory and model.

At first glance, the most straightforward account of these results is as follows: As more parts must be refreshed, more time passes between repeated activations of any given part. Hence, each part is likely to be more faded, on the average—and thus more time will usually be required to see parts of more complex images. This is the view suggested in Kosslyn (1975), which followed from an analogy to "flicker" on a CRT, and which was the original motivation for positing that "image capacity" was limited by part generation and fade rates. Unfortunately, this account is inconsistent with the account of the effects of subjective size and with the accounts of data on image generation and maintenance: On the view developed earlier, many—perhaps most—parts of images are not maintained in the image, but are filled in only as they are needed. Thus one will often have to fill in a queried part, regardless of whether an imaged object occurs in a simple or a complex scene. The account for the complexity effect just described may be true for the small number of parts of an image that are actively being retained in a given display, but is unsatisfactory as an account of the general effect. Many more than even ten separate parts were queried (on different animals), during the course of these experiments, and it is unlikely that all of these were in the image at the time of probe.

Although the simple analogy to flicker will not provide an account of these results, a slightly more sophisticated version of the same idea will. This account, like many for Class 2 (multiple interpretation) results, is interesting because the model was not constructed intentionally to provide this explanation for these data. Now there are two critical variables: the likelihood that the queried part will be activated and, in the event that it is not, the likelihood that its foundation part will be present in the image at the time of query. As one spends more time constructing and maintaining more complex context images, it is less likely that one will be regenerating the foundation parts, or will have recently regenerated them, at the time of query. Hence, the additional time to see parts of images constructed next to more complex context matrices or next to more digits is due in part to the time required to elaborate the foundation part itself. Interestingly enough, in the experiments on image generation about 50 to 150 milliseconds usually were required to add a new part, and an additional 115 to 170 milliseconds or so were required to see parts of animals in more complex scenes in the two experiments. This makes sense if people generate the foundation part before placing the queried part on (or elaborating the appropriate region of) a target animal when it is imaged in a more complex context but often need only place the queried part when the animal occurs in a less complex context. This account also provides a neat explanation for the fact that including two additional digits in the image increased time to detect a digit by the same amount as it increased time to see an animal part: With two digits it is more likely that the queried digit is in the image at the time of probe, whereas with four it becomes more likely that the queried digit must be regenerated prior to detection. Thus, the fact that digit and animal-property probes increased by about the same amount (see figure 3.14) when two more digits were added makes sense: In both cases, this increase reflects an increased probability of having to generate a part, either a digit or foundation part. Note also in figure 3.14 that the increase in time to see a part when four digits were included in the image is about the same as the overall increase in time to see a part instead of a digit. This makes perfect sense if no digits and one animal part are inserted in two-digit scenes whereas one digit and two animal parts are inserted (on the average) in four digit scenes. This account, then, gains plausibility because a single mechanism explains not just the directions of the observed differences but also the relative magnitudes of these differences.

A second kind of account hinges on the claim that images are refreshed by scanning across the surface image. As long as a part (a set of points) is not entirely faded, it can be refreshed directly (without the necessity of repeatedly searching memory for the relevant files, using propositional relations, and so on). On this view, scanning time is at the root of the effects of complexity. The more material in an image, the more "fixations" are required when scanning it to regenerate parts. Thus, more time is spent focused on the sixteen-cell matrix or on the four digits, and less time is spent fixating on the adjacent animal, than when a more simple matrix or fewer digits are included in the image. On this account, then, when the animal is queried, it is more likely that one will have to scan to it (and then fill in the part) if a sixteen-cell matrix or four digits are imaged next to it than if only a four-cell matrix or two digits are being imaged. And when four digits are present, it is more likely that the queried one has faded altogether and needs to be regenerated. If so, then the 200-millisecond difference in time to see one of four digits instead of one of two is due to time to generate an image of at least one digit and then to search through more digits. On this account, it is merely a coincidence that adding two digits to the scene increased the time to evaluate digit probes the same amount as it increased time to evaluate animal-property probes. We need only assume that digits require more time to generate (perhaps because they are verbally prompted) than do animal parts (which could well be true, given the data reported in chapter 6), and this additional time compensates for the lesser probability of having to scan to the digits when four are present.

The critical issue here, then, is whether one in fact fixates on different parts of an image while maintaining it and whether one then must scan to the region of the queried part (which may overflow as one scans about the image while maintaining it). We will consider this issue in the second half of this chapter.

1.2.2 Inspecting Images of Drawings of Single Objects

Kosslyn, Reiser, Farah, and Fliegel (in preparation) found that more time was required to image more detailed drawings than to image less detailed ones, and yet no more time was required to detect parts on images of more detailed drawings. This was also true of images formed from different numbers of parts in the experiment in which people mentally assembled a composite image, even though much more time was required to generate images of drawings presented in multiple pieces. Why did we not find longer times to inspect the more complex (as indexed by increased generation times) images? I initially thought this was a Class 2 (multiple interpretation) result. However, it turned out to be difficult to formulate even one viable account while remaining consistent with previous commitments. For purposes of illustration, let us begin by discussing one account I initially considered.

On this view, one scans over an image in the act of retaining it. When the probe is delivered, one often must scan to the relevant region. While scanning, one can fill in any missing material. Thus, even if a part is missing, it can be filled in en route, and there is no difference in time to see parts on images of detailed versus undetailed drawings. However, it is not clear why one would have to scan to see a part if the image does not overflow (and these subjects were told to be sure their images did not overflow). According to our theory, inspection is not like viewing an object through a peephole in a piece of cardboard being moved over it; in theory multiple portions of an image can be seen simultaneously—as was assessed in the experiments measuring the visual angle of the mind's eye (chapter 3, section 2.4). But perhaps subjects did image the drawings a little too large, such that portions fell in the less resolved regions of the visual buffer. We performed a number of experiments which demonstrated that people do often seem to image objects at larger than optimal sizes (see chapter 6, section 2.5). Or, perhaps parts partially overflow as one scans from region to region on the image in the course of refreshing it. The critical assumption, then, is that the filling in can be accomplished in the time required to scan to the target. On this view, the same amount of scanning—on the average—will be required for detailed and undetailed images (since the area is the same). The question here, however, is, why are scanning rates not slower with more complex images, given the finding that more time is required to scan over each additional item in an array (chapter 3, section 2.1)? Possible answers: (1) Rates are variable, and since people know where they are scanning to they can compensate for increased detail by speeding up the rate. This is ad hoc and post hoc, and thus is to be avoided. (2) The effects of number of intervening items observed earlier were due to "inspection time," and people do not bother to inspect parts of an image that they know are obviously inappropriate, and hence actual scanning time is the same. The problem here is, how do people know the parts are irrelevant before they inspect them? If the relative locations of parts are specified in enough detail, a ballistic scan is possible (that is, without feedback from monitoring the material being scanned over)—and in fact, this is how we have implemented scanning when our simulation is searching for a part. The final question is why is it not more likely that one will be focused on the wrong detail on an image of a more detailed drawing, and hence more likely that one will have to scan to the queried part? If true, more time should be required to inspect images of more detailed drawings. An ad hoc account could be provided, but our previous commitments seem to be painting us into a corner at a rapid rate.

Another way to explain the lack of effects of image complexity on image-inspection times hinges on the fact that the stimuli were drawings of familiar animals. Perhaps people did image the drawings but always filled in queried parts from long-term memory representations of parts of actual animals themselves—not from representations of parts on the particular drawings. Serendipitously, we discovered that we had collected some data in support of this idea. One of the drawings was inadvertently altered such that the probed part (eyelids) was not included on the undetailed version—but *every* subject mistakenly responded "true" to this probe for this drawing. If the long-term memory encodings for the actual animal were in fact being accessed and used to direct insertion of parts in the image, then it is not surprising that amount of detail on the drawing did not affect detection time. This interpretation is buttressed by our finding (to be discussed in the next section) that when drawings of novel geomet-

rical forms were imaged, and only data from subjects who reported actually inspecting their images at least 65 percent of the time were analyzed, significantly more time was now required to see a part of a figure
when the figure had been described in terms of more units. Since these
forms were novel, people had to use information encoded about the particular pattern studied when they evaluated a probe.

1.2.3 Effects of Conceptual Organization

We earlier found that more time was required to evoke an image of a
pattern if it had been described in terms of relatively many parts than if it
had been described as having fewer parts (for example, five squares versus two overlapping rectangles—see chapter 4, section 3.0). There were
two primary findings pertaining to inspection time in these experiments:
(1) When only data from subjects who claimed to have actually used the
image at least 65 percent the time were examined, images of more complexly described drawings required more time to inspect; and (2) parts included in the initial description were "easier to see" than parts not mentioned. The first result can be explained in two ways, paralleling the
"flicker" and scanning alternative accounts offered in section 1.2.1. First,
the present results are easily explained by the capacity-limit notion originally based on an analogy to "flicker" on a CRT (that initial portions are
faded when latter ones are placed), because the figures had so few parts
(one to four different subpatterns were used—see figure 4.5). If there
were few enough different parts in the more simply described figures, at
least one of the parts of the queried shape usually would be present in the
image. But with the more complex figures a queried shape was not as
likely to be in the image, and hence was likely to require additional time to
generate. Thus, the fact that the "flicker" account is appropriate here is
somewhat interesting, if only because the most complex figures had only
four differently shaped units—which is consistent with the position that
only a few parts can be maintained in an image, as developed in chapter 6.

The second account of the complexity effect is that with more differently shaped subpatterns in an image the subject was more likely to be
focusing on the wrong part at the time of query, and hence to have to scan
to the correct part, perhaps filling it in while scanning. This account
hinges on the claim that images are maintained via scanning through the
visual buffer, a claim that will be investigated directly shortly. Note also
that this explanation is in dead opposition to the first one offered to explain the *lack* of complexity effects in the previous section, although it
seems adequate to account for this particular finding. The requirement of
constructing a general model obviously forces us to reject contradictory
specific models, given that the same functional capacities presumably are
recruited (as needed) in all these image-inspection tasks.

The second result, that it was easier to see parts if they were congruent with the presumed parts of the image, has two obvious accounts, one trivial and one interesting. First, since the part was mentioned in the label, the subject was "primed for it" (for example, had a lower response "criterion" or "detection threshold" in the terminology used by Morton, 1969). There seems to be no easy way of eliminating this mundane account. Alternatively, it could be that the parts themselves had been "conceptually parsed" via the description and separately encoded into memory (as separate files, in our model). Later, these parts would be generated individually when the person constructed an image of the pattern. As noted in chapter 4, the number of parts predicated in the description was very highly correlated with the time to form an image of the pattern, supporting the notion that the pattern was in fact parsed in accordance with the description. If each part, as defined in the description, was imaged as a single unit, then the segments that composed a part should have faded together and thus cohered in the image (because of the Gestalt law of "common fate"). In our simulation all the portions of a part are printed with the same letter, and different parts with different letters. Thus, parts (for example, a square) maintain their identities in the surface image. If the individual segments cohere, it should be easy to see the pattern they form. By the same token, segments belonging to different parts—and hence at different levels of "fade phase"—should be more difficult to organize. Thus, patterns that draw upon segments belonging to different parts should be difficult to see—making it difficult to perceive rectangles when squares were imaged and vice versa. The reader should note that there would be even more problems if one constructed images of only some of the squares and then tried to find a rectangle. As before, one would have to fill in parts prior to detection. One interesting question here is what are the constraints on our ability to reorganize images. This will depend on the number of segments that can be maintained at once and the speed of the reassignment processes. It should, however, be easier to reorganize fewer units into more units than vice versa, as fewer initial boundaries need to be maintained simultaneously (as with the rectangle description of the lower left pattern in figure 4.5).

2.0 VALIDATION AND GENERALIZATION TESTS

The foregoing treatments of our earlier results lead us to make a number of predictions. If these predictions turn out to be entirely off base, this will be an indication that the theory has gone astray. Thus, we will begin by considering some predictions that arise from the model taken as a whole, predictions that were overlooked when the topics were studied separately. In addition, the underspecification of the model forced us to put many of the findings just described in Class 2 (multiple interpretation). In particular, the role of scanning in image maintenance must be further specified before we can offer more precise accounts, and thus we will consider this topic before reviewing the relevant literature.

2.1 Testing Predictions

2.1.1 Property Size and Association Strength

In the course of formulating an explanation for the effects of different types of properties, I realized I had a problem. As is illustrated in the trace presented in Table 7.1, in the model parts of imaged objects are often filled in only when needed. Time to fill in parts is partially dependent on the ordering of HASA entries in the PRP lists; HASA entries nearer the top of the list are located more quickly than those farther down or not in the list at all (and hence must be deduced via accessing a superordinate file—as will be discussed in chapter 9). These orderings, I will later claim, reflect (or, rather, underlie) association strength. Thus association strength *should* affect image-inspection time. The fact that it did not appear to do so in our experiments, I hoped, merely demonstrated that effects of association strength can be overshadowed by a size effect when the surface image must be consulted. In order to test the internal consistency of the model, which clearly predicts that association strength should be relevant in image inspection, we conducted the following experiment.

Table 7.1.   Trace of the simulation inspecting an impoverished image of a car, which requires filling in a region.

---

*LOOKFOR REARTIRE

LOOKFOR BEGINS
REGENERATE BEGINS
REGENERATING IMAGE
REGENERATE ENDS

LOOKING FOR PROPOSITIONAL FILE FOR REARTIRE
REARTIRE.PRP OPENED

CHECKING PROPOSITIONAL FILE FOR DESCRIPTION OF REARTIRE
DESCRIPTION FOUND

CHECKING PROPOSITIONAL FILE FOR SIZE TAG
SIZE TAG FOUND: MEDIUM   OPTIMAL RESOLUTION = 85.0

RESOLUTION BEGINS
CHECKING CURRENT RESOLUTION OF IMAGE
CURRENT RESOLUTION = 89.4
RESOLUTION ENDS

IMAGE AT CORRECT RESOLUTION—NO NEED TO ZOOM OR PAN

CHECKING PROPOSITIONAL FILE FOR DIRECTION OF PART
DIRECTION FOUND: LEFT

IMAGE NOT OVERFLOWED IN THAT DIRECTION—NO NEED TO
  SCAN

FIND BEGINS
BEGIN SEARCHING SURFACE MATRIX FOR REARTIRE

SEARCHING FOR LOWEST POINT LEFT
FOUND AT   −23   −3

FOLLOWING HORIZONTAL RIGHT TO END
FOUND AT   −19   −3

SEARCHING NEXT HORIZONTAL POINT RIGHT
FOUND AT   −10   −3

LOOKING FOR PART BELOW
PROCEDURE FAILED
FIND ENDS

CAN'T FIND REARTIRE

LOOKING FOR PROPOSITIONAL FILE FOR CAR
CAR.PRP OPENED

CHECKING PROPOSITIONAL FILE FOR REGIONAL DETAILS
REGION FOUND: HASA.REARREGION

PUT BEGINS
LOOKING FOR PROPOSITIONAL FILE FOR REARREGION
REARREGION.PRP OPENED

CHECKING PROPOSITIONAL FILE FOR NAME OF IMAGE FILE
NAME OF IMAGE FILE STORED: REARREGION.IMG

CHECKING PROPOSITIONAL FILE FOR LOCATION OF
  REARREGION
LOCATION FOUND: UNDER REARWHEELBASE

LOOKING FOR PROPOSITIONAL FILE FOR REARWHEELBASE
REARWHEELBASE.PRP OPENED

CHECKING PROPOSITIONAL FILE FOR DESCRIPTION OF
  REARWHEELBASE
DESCRIPTION FOUND

LOOKING FOR PROPOSITIONAL FILE FOR UNDER
UNDER.PRP OPENED

```
CHECKING PROPOSITIONAL FILE FOR DESCRIPTION OF UNDER
DESCRIPTION FOUND

***FIND BEGINS***
BEGIN SEARCHING SURFACE MATRIX FOR REARWHEELBASE

SEARCHING FOR LOWEST POINT LEFT
FOUND AT              -23              -3

FOLLOWING HORIZONTAL RIGHT TO END
FOUND AT              -19              -3

SEARCHING FOR NEXT HORIZONTAL POINT RIGHT
FOUND AT              -10              -3
***FIND ENDS***

BEGIN TO PUT ON PART: REARREGION

***PICTURE BEGINS***
TURNING ON POINTS IN SURFACE MATRIX WITH SIZE
   FACTOR = 1.0
***PICTURE ENDS***

***PUT ENDS***

***FIND BEGINS***
BEGIN SEARCHING SURFACE MATRIX FOR REARTIRE

SEARCHING FOR LOWEST POINT LEFT
FOUND AT              -23              -3

FOLLOWING HORIZONTAL RIGHT TO END
FOUND AT              -17              -3

SEARCHING FOR NEXT HORIZONTAL POINT RIGHT
FOUND AT              -11              -3

LOOKING FOR PART BELOW
***FIND ENDS***

REARTIRE FOUND
***LOOKFOR ENDS***
```

We began by obtaining ratings of the association strength between a set of nouns and properties and of the relative sizes of the properties. We were able to select four types of "true" properties: large and highly associated, small and highly associated, large and not highly associated, and small and not highly associated. The mean rated size of the large high-association properties was the same as the mean size of the large low-association properties, and the mean size of the small high-association properties was the same as the mean size of the small low-association properties (both of which were rated significantly smaller than the large properties). Similarly, the mean association ratings for the two high conditions were the same, as were the means for the two low conditions, even though the sizes varied (but again the ratings for the high-association items were significantly different from the ratings for the low-association ones). These items are listed in table 7.2. Sharon Fliegel, Bill Shebar, and I then used these items in an experiment like the one described earlier in which we used small and highly associated properties and large and not highly associated properties (see chapter 3, section 2.2.1). As before, subjects received a no-imagery block, in which they were asked simply to decide as quickly as possible whether the property was a bona fide characteristic of the named animal. Subjects also received a block of trials in which they were asked to form an image of the animal during the five seconds before the property word was presented, and were given our standard image-inspection instructions. Unlike the earlier experiment, however, half the subjects received the no-imagery block before the imagery one and half received the blocks in the reverse order. This counterbalancing was used because we worried that the rates of scanning the PRP files would increase with practice, thus diminishing the magnitude of the effects of association strength. As usual, counterbalancing groups were created such that each item occurred equally often in each condition.

The results of this experiment are presented in figure 7.1. As is evident, subjects were faster at seeing larger properties and more highly associated properties. In the earlier experiment, in which only two types of "true" properties were used, we essentially compared the lower point on the top

Table 7.2. Animal properties that vary in size and association strength.

Animal	Small, high association	Large, high association	Small, low association	Large, low association
Alligator	teeth	jaws	eyes	belly
Bear	claws	fur	shin	shoulders
Bee	stinger	wings	head	abdomen
Elephant	tusks	back	knees	flanks
Frog	tongue	legs	cheeks	back
Horse	hoofs	head	eyelid	belly
Leopard	spots	haunches	feet	sides
Rat	eyes	tail	ears	back
Lobster	antennae	claws	legs	abdomen
Owl	eyes	wings	feet	chest
Turtle	head	shell	legs	stomach
Lion	whiskers	mane	nostrils	sides

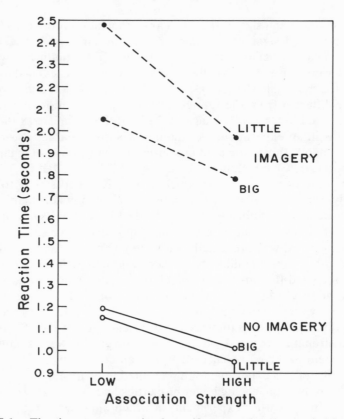

Figure 7.1. The time to see or simply verify properties that varied in size and association strength.

function to the upper point on the bottom function. Note that the direction—and size—of the difference between these two points depend on two things: (1) The difference between time to see large parts and time to see small ones, reflected in the spread between the two imagery functions in figure 7.1. If the functions are spread far apart, small, highly associated properties will require more time to see than large, not highly associated properties, as was found earlier. (2) The difference between time to see highly associated parts and time to see not highly associated ones, reflected by the steepness of the functions. If the low-association times were a little longer and the high-association times a little shorter, the earlier result again would be reversed. But note that in any event when imagery is not used the effects of association strength will not be mitigated by those of size. Importantly, the present results continue to distinguish between imaginal and nonimaginal processing: Only in the imagery condition did the size of a property affect detection times (if anything, there is a slight trend in the wrong direction in the nonimagery data). These findings, then, fall in Class 1 of our taxonomy (confirmation).

If the effects of association strength reflect time to find a propositional representation of the probed part, we reasoned, then degree of association strength should have similar-sized effects both when imagery is used (and parts are filled in) and when imagery is not used (and lists are simply scanned). This was not the case here, however. The effects of association strength were more pronounced in the imagery condition, especially so for the small properties (there was a 527-millisecond difference between high- and low-association items here, versus a 204-millisecond difference in the no-imagery condition); for the large properties, the data were more in line with our expectations (a 270-millisecond difference between high- and low-association items in the imagery condition, versus a 172-millisecond difference in the no-imagery condition). This result falls in Class 3 (theory supplementation). We suspected that other components of the part-insertion procedures might also be affected by the association strength of the part. For example, locating the correct IMG file in our model might be more difficult for low-association parts, perhaps because the parts may not be stored in separate files labeled by the part name, but instead may be implicitly represented in an encoding of the region in which the part belongs. If so, then the inference procedures that deduce the name of the correct IMG file will consume extra time for low-association parts. In addition, we hypothesized that when subjects placed parts on an image they had to find the foundation part first, and we speculated that the foundation parts of less associated, smaller parts themselves may have been harder to locate. In order to examine these possibilities, we tested two additional groups of subjects in a simple task. These people were asked to generate images of the parts. The stimuli were the animal and property names read in rapid succession; upon hearing the pair the subject was to form an image of the named part and push a button when the image was complete. One group was asked to image the parts in isolation, and the other to image the parts on an image of the entire animal. In the latter case, but not in the former, factors like the difficulty of locating the foundation part should affect times.

The results of the part-generation experiment are illustrated in figure 7.2. As is evident, the effects of association strength were more pronounced when subjects were asked to image only parts of the animals, and the difference in times is similar to those observed in the part-detection experiment (270 versus 299 milliseconds for the large parts, and 527 versus 399 milliseconds for the small ones). Importantly, association strength had the same effects in both of these conditions and in the part-detection experiments; the apparent differences did not even approach statistical significance. Although there was a trend for larger parts to be imaged more quickly, this effect was not statistically significant, nor was the

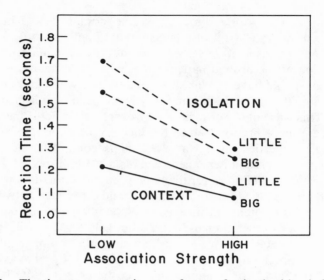

Figure 7.2. The time to generate images of parts of animals either in isolation or on the animal. The parts varied in size and association strength.

overall difference in times between the two groups of subjects. It appears that the difficulty of locating the foundation parts was not a factor in producing the large effects of association strength.* The failure to find effects of the size of a part is not surprising if the main reason size affects generation time is that larger images can be further elaborated. Further, this result dovetails with our earlier failure to find an effect of "structural contingencies" on generation time, given that large parts will serve as foundation parts more often than will smaller parts. Highly associated parts may be given high priority because they are distinctive properties, and hence distinguish an object from other similar objects. The effects of size on part-detection time, then, reflect inspecting the image after the part or relevant region has been inserted, and not the insertion process itself. Thus, all told, the data are consistent with the claim that parts are sometimes inserted into images at the time of probe, and apparent contradictions to the earlier findings on ease of detecting parts have been resolved.

*The fact that different people were in the different conditions contributed a large amount of variability, however. It would be of interest to discover whether the difference in overall times between the conditions is observed when the same people participate in both conditions—if imaging isolated parts takes longer than imaging parts in context, this will be difficult to explain without expanding the present theory because more operations would seem to be required to place a part in context than to image it in isolation. It is possible, however, that in the isolation condition subjects sometimes generated parts embedded in an image of a region, and then deleted extra material (this was sometimes reported after the experiment). If so, further work would be required to provide a model of this deletion transformation.

2.1.2 Scanning and Image Maintenance

We have repeatedly been able to formulate accounts of data that hinge on the assumption that images are refreshed by scanning through the visual buffer, fixating on different parts of the imaged object. According to our theory, images fade unless they are actively maintained. We have posited that images are regenerated directly from the surface. In our model, the procedure REGENERATE works over the surface matrix and updates the recency of points, less recently placed points being updated first. In the model, however, the REGENERATE procedure does not fixate at different locations, it does not "scan" as we have defined scanning. But this was not intended to be a theory-relevant part of the model. The question here is whether we should alter this property of the model or promote it to the level of theory. Martha Farah, Roger Wallach, and I reasoned that if images were refreshed by scanning through the visual buffer, then inhibiting subjects from scanning should impair maintaining the image. We tested two groups of subjects, asking one to "mentally focus" at the center of each image while holding it and giving the other no instructions about what to do while holding an image. Subjects in both groups first heard the name of an animal and pressed a button when a visual image had been formed. Images were to be as large as possible while not overflowing. Either zero, three, or six seconds thereafter (the different delays being presented in a random order) a property word was presented and subjects were to look for it on their images in the usual way. The major results of this experiment are presented in figure 7.3. Note that the time to see a part increased with the amount of time after the image was formed *only* for the group told to focus at the center of the image. For the group not asked to fixate, we actually found that times *decreased* with increasing delay. This was unexpected, but is very interpretable given the fine-grained analysis to be discussed below. Interestingly, when queried after the experiment subjects in the nonfocus group almost invariably reported having scanned over their images in the act of maintaining them.

In this experiment we used the four types of "true" properties listed in table 7.2. This manipulation was performed to examine an implication of the assumption that only a few parts are maintained in an image at any one time. We assumed that if only a few parts are in fact maintained, then when subjects are asked to find a part they often may have to insert it (or the region in which it belongs) at the time of probe. If parts are generated when needed, we reasoned, then the speed with which the part can be generated should affect the speed with which one can see the part. In our theory, the order of the names of parts or relevant regions in an object's propositional file will affect the ease of locating that representation; in the model, HASA entries higher on the list are reached sooner than those lower down, and we found earlier that association strength indexes the relative accessibility of an object's properties.

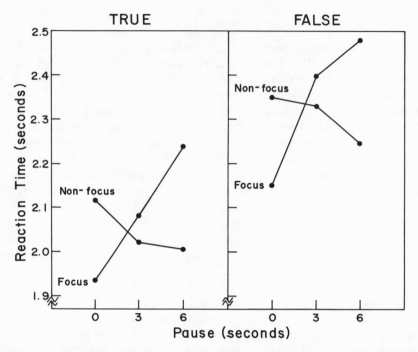

Figure 7.3. The time to see parts of images that were maintained for three different periods of time when subjects were or were not asked to focus on the center of
the imaged animal while holding the image. Data in the left panel are from "true"
trials, and data in the right panel are from "false" trials.

Figure 7.4 contains the same data illustrated in the left panel of figure
7.3, but broken down by property type. The most important thing to notice in both conditions is that the relative time to see parts is ordered just
as are the means in figure 7.2. The fact that size now had appreciable effects is probably due to the fact that subjects had to look for a part on the
image after generating the region. Interestingly, the effects of increased
lag were the same for all types of properties in the focus condition, but not
in the nonfocus condition. In the nonfocus condition subjects became increasingly slower for the large high-association properties, and faster for
the others. It is as if they initially began by placing large, highly associated
properties in the image (and fixated upon them, in the nonfocus group),
and over time scanned around the image and placed other sorts of properties—to the partial detriment of the large, highly asociated ones. These
results, then, not only support the view that scanning is a functional component of image maintenance but provide further support for the claim
that people maintain an image with only very few elaborated regions or
parts, and elaborate or add parts only when needed. Presumably, in the
fixation group the skeletal image itself faded altogether and hence needed
to be generated anew.

The foregoing results, then, implicate at least some scanning in the image-maintenance process but do not tell us either how much scanning is used or *why* scanning is used. Scanning may be used to provide "visual prompts," helping one recall what to insert into the image (this would require considerable extension of our model). Or, if scanning consists of moving the image through the visual buffer, it might function as do saccades in vision: In either case a "stabilized image" may fatigue the cells that receive stimulation (from light, in the case of the retina, and from long-term memory, in the case of the visual buffer), resulting in the image fading (see Neisser, 1967, for a brief description of some work on stabilized images on the retina).

At first glance, one might think that one aspect of the foregoing results falls in Class 5 (disconfirmation): If our model is correct, images are always refreshed prior to inspection. If so, why should more time be required when the image is more faded if it will always be regenerated anyway? This finding is in fact in Class 2 (multiple interpretation). First, if the visual buffer itself becomes fatigued when one fixates on an image, it may simply be more difficult to generate an image in the fatigued region—thus explaining the effects of delay in the fixation condition. Second, if the image is faded altogether, as may have happened with the longer delays in

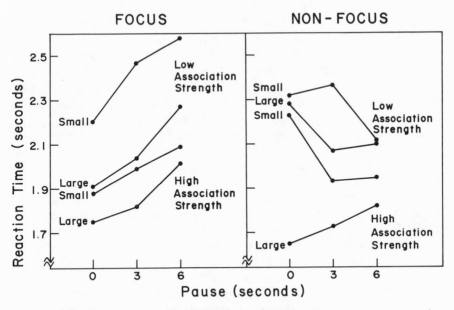

Figure 7.4. The time to see four types of properties on images that were maintained for different periods of time. These data are a fine-grade analysis of those presented in the left panel of figure 7.3, obtained from one group asked to focus on the center of an animal while holding the image and another group not asked to focus.

the focus condition, it may have to be generated anew from the deep representation—which may require more time than "holding" the image
from the surface. The first hypothesis is especially interesting because it
directly implicates a spatial medium. If it turned out that local regions of
the visual buffer can become fatigued, making it selectively difficult to
place an image at those locations, this would be very difficult to explain
without appeal to a spatial medium of the sort posited here. Once again,
then, the model leads us to ask questions that, once answered, will further
elaborate the theory proper.

The results of the previous experiment are consistent with a model in
which images are actually scanned, with parts being fixated upon individually, and a model in which the image is not thoroughly scanned, but
merely "jiggled" through the visual buffer so that it does not fade. On this
second view, fixation might occur in general regions not very far removed
from the center. In the following experiment we tested the hypothesis that
one actually fixates on each item while maintaining it, which was a linch-
pin in several alternative explanations offered when we tried to explain
the effects of image complexity on part-detection time. This experiment
used the same paradigm used in one of the experiments on image detection described in chapter 3, section 2.2. In that experiment, subjects
imaged an animal against an imaginary wall, and either two or four digits
were to be imaged on the wall to the animal's left. Subjects were asked to
"find" either a named digit or a part of the animal, and detection times
were measured. Jim Wheaton and I repeated this procedure, but now also
varied the distance between the animal and the digits. Subjects were
shown templates illustrating a wall with positions on it indicating different
arrangements of animals and digits. The templates were constructed to
ensure that the subject did not vary the size of the digits or animals in the
different arrangements. In addition to this, we also used the "true" properties previously rated to be large or small and highly or not highly associated with the animal in question. The subject first was given a set of either two or four digits and an animal name, and then imaged these stimuli
in a particular configuration. The subject was told to image the entire wall,
seeing the animal and digits in the specified locations. On half the trials
the digits were nestled around the animal, and on half they were imaged
some distance to its left. We reasoned that if subjects spontaneously
scanned the image during the six-second interval in which they were required to hold it, then it would be more likely that scanning would be required to see a target digit or property probe when the imaged digits were
separated from the animal. When the digits were right next to the animal,
however, little scanning should be required no matter where the probed
item was located. Further, when four digits were present, subjects would
be more likely to be fixated on the digits at the time of probe. Thus, the
effects of distance on time to see animal properties should be more pronounced when four digits were in the image rather than two.

The results were as follows: When digit and property probes were ana-lyzed together, more time was required to see parts of imaged scenes when more digits were included and when the distance separating the digits and animal was longer. Critically, we did *not* find more pronounced effects of distance on time to see animal parts when four digits were in-cluded in the image rather than just two. If subjects tended to linger more on the digits when more were present, they should have had to scan more often to the animal than when fewer digits were included. We again found subjects generally to be faster to see larger or more highly associated parts, but we found no differences in the effects of distance on time to see different properties. We had included the different types of properties with an eye toward discovering whether one could see (or fill in) larger, more associated ones without scanning, although one would have to scan to fill in the smaller, harder-to-see parts. There was no support for this hypothesis.

In the previous experiment subjects were asked to maintain an image of the entire wall against which the digits and animal were to be imaged. We reasoned that perhaps subjects scanned over this entire area, which did not vary in the different conditions, and this is why we did not find exacer-bated effects of distance when four digits were included in the image. Thus, we repeated the previous experiment with a new group of subjects but asked these people to ignore the blank part of the wall and simply to hold an image of the animal and digits—at their correct sizes and loca-tions—for six seconds prior to probe. Considering all of the data, we again found that more time generally was required when the image in-cluded four digits or a longer distance between digits and animal. Criti-cally, the effects of distance did not become more pronounced when four digits were being imaged instead of just two, and this was again true for all types of "true" properties.

All told, then, it would seem that some scanning does in fact take place when one maintains an image, but this does not seem to be a key factor in accounting for our earlier results. The data are explained if either (*a*) people do not fixate on individual parts of an image, but merely general regions (and hence need not spend more time fixating on the digits when there are more of them) or (*b*) people do in fact fixate on individual items, but do not need to scan to see a part that is still in the region of highest resolution in the visual buffer. The precise role of scanning in maintaining images is still an open question, and it seems likely that the answer will not be simple.

2.2 Detecting Parts of Composite Images

Seamon (1972) investigated the ease with which subjects could retrieve information from imaged scenes that contained different numbers of elements. In his experiment, subjects were asked to remember sets of one, two, or three concrete nouns. Three groups of subjects were tested, differing only in how they memorized the words in the sets: one group simply rehearsed the words; another group imaged the named objects separately, not touching or interacting, and was to think of each image in succession until the probe word occurred; the third group imaged the named objects in an interactive scene. Subjects in the last two groups were to tell the experimenter if they could not form an appropriate image (but very few ever did). Subjects were given five additional seconds to encode each additional word in a set. After the memory set was encoded, an auditory warning occurred and then a probe word was presented. On half the trials the probe word was a member of the memory set, and on half the trials it was not. Subjects were to decide as quickly as possible whether or not the probe word was a member of the memorized set.

An analysis of variance indicated that reaction times increased with set size in the rehearsal group but not in the imagery groups. The means did increase for larger set sizes in the separate-imagery group, however, and a linear trend analysis was significant in these data. For the interactive-imagery group, however, there were absolutely no effects of set size. These results are illustrated in figure 7.5.

On the face of things, these results fall in Class 5 (disconfirmation). Our theory leads us to expect increased inspection times with more material in the image for a number of reasons: First, each item presumably is represented by a separate skeletal image (if not an elaborated skeleton), and

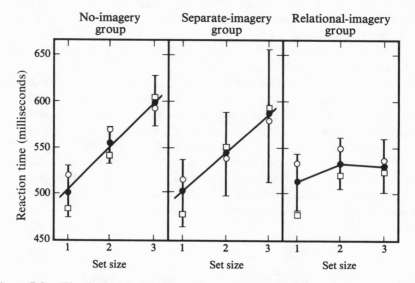

Figure 7.5.   The time to decide if a probe word was a member of a memory set in Seamon's (1972) experiment.

hence the image should be fuzzier overall with more items—regardless of how they are juxtaposed. If the images are at all detailed, the larger arrays should suffer due to "flicker" effects more than should the smaller ones, if we are to remain consistent with our earlier accounts. Second, the probability that an item will need to be regenerated from the deep level will increase with the number of items (recall my account of the Beech and Allport findings in chapter 6, section 2.4). Third, if items are sometimes imaged only when needed, then even time to look up a given item should increase with larger set sizes, if objects are listed in a single file. That is, in the model a PRP file for each list would presumably be encoded, and each object would be listed as a HASA. The relations among the objects would be represented in the same way as are relations among the parts of a single object (see chapter 5, section 2.0). Fourth, with increasing numbers of items it becomes increasingly likely that at least one will fall into the less resolved regions of the visual buffer, requiring the subject to scan in order to see it clearly. Or, if all items are packed into the limited area of greatest resolution, the size of each one will decrease as more items are imaged—and hence each one will be harder to identify. It is relatively difficult, then, to reconcile the present theory with Seamon's results.

Before shrugging our shoulders and thinking about revising the theory, however, it will behoove us to take a closer look at Seamon's data and some results of follow-up experiments. First, Seamon's subjects required a mean of less than 600 milliseconds in every condition—far less than the times usually observed in our experiments. Given the facts that only six subjects participated in each group, that there was very large variability in reaction times, and that the interaction between instructions and set size was not statistically significant in a standard analysis of variance—let alone one which also used item variability in the error term (see Clark, 1973)—it is clear that we should take Seamon's reported findings with a grain of salt. Further, the results of several follow-up experiments give us some comfort, suggesting that Seamon's findings most properly belong in Class 4 (domain contamination).

Rothstein and Atkinson (1975) attempted to replicate Seamon's (1972) results, using rehearsal and interactive-imagery groups, with four times the number of subjects and one-third more trials per subject. Subjects were asked to hold the same image or same set of rehearsed words over a block of eight trials. Probe words were presented visually, in a tachistoscope. The subjects were asked to refresh their images before each trial and to tell the experimenter afterward if they had lost the image on that trial. Although subjects in the imagery condition were encouraged to form an image by being asked to describe the image to the experimenter, they were not actually told to *use* the image in making their decisions. Thus, the results found here may not in fact tell us much about image use. Given the design of the experiment, it is extremely unlikely that subjects would

in fact use the image if allowed another option (after all, the same set—
sometimes consisting of only one word—was probed on eight consecutive trials). Thus, however these results come out they probably belong in
Class 4 (domain contamination) because of these methodological points.
Given the usual results obtained with Sternberg tasks, then, it is not surprising that Rothstein and Atkinson found increased verification times
when more words were included in a memory set for both groups. It is
worth noting that the increased time per additional item was the same in
the imagery and rehearsal groups. And, again, reaction times were generally under 650 milliseconds, much faster than I have ever found in an
imagery-inspection task.

Rothstein and Atkinson learned of my objections and performed another experiment. Eight new subjects were explicitly asked to look for the
presence of an object named by a probe word in an imaged scene. The
results of this experiment were very much like those described above:
When more objects were imaged, more time was taken to inspect the
image. Thus, these results fall in Class 1 (confirmation), and lead us to be
chary of making too much of Seamon's earlier findings. Rothstein and Atkinson's subjects were also asked to rate "how easy the scene was to
keep in mind" on a five-point scale. For each subject reaction times were
split into two groups, those above the median rating and those below, for
each set size. The median was used because the mean "image goodness"
decreased with increased numbers of words to be held in the image, just
as our model would lead one to expect (because time between successive
regenerations of each image increases with the number of units included
in a scene). There was a small but significant advantage (23 milliseconds)
for inspection of "high image goodness" scenes, and the size of this advantage was the same for different set sizes. This result lends some credence to the claim that images were in fact inspected, and also makes
sense if less good images require regeneration prior to inspection more
often than do better images. Alternatively, these results may be due to
some possible methodological flaws: (1) It is not clear from the description of the experiment when the ratings were actually made (see Rothstein
and Atkinson, 1975, p. 543); if they were made right after responses, it
could be that subjects based their ratings in part on how difficult it was to
make the response, which is not of any interest for present purposes; (2)
"image goodness" may be confounded with some other variable (such as
word frequency) that is really responsible for the effect. There seems no
way of choosing between these explanations given only these data, but in
any case the results do not challenge any of the principles of the core theory.*

---

*Although I was aware of the Seamon and Rothstein and Atkinson work before the theory
was formulated, the theory was not intentionally tailored to provide accounts of these data.

Kerst (1976) conducted the most elaborate experiments of this type. In his first experiment he included a rehearsal group, a group asked to generate successive images of the items, a group asked to generate sentences connecting the items, an interactive-imagery group, and a group asked to merge all the objects into a tightly knit scene (emphasizing touching). Five additional seconds of study time were allowed for each additional word in a set, and four seconds were allowed after the last study interval before the probe word was presented (visually). Given the Rothstein and Atkinson findings, it is not surprising that times generally increased with larger set sizes in all groups in this experiment. Again, reaction times were very fast (generally in the 450- to 650-millisecond range). Only in the "true" responses for the tightly knit interactive-imagery condition were there no effects of set size, but this result did not replicate.

In Kerst's second experiment, subjects were shown pictures and asked to image an interactive scene or to hold separate images, or were shown a picture of an interactive scene and asked to image it. The probes used were pictures taken from the scene, but they were not necessarily presented in the same part of the picture frame as they had been located in initially. In addition, the probe picture apparently was not the same as the one initially studied when two pictures were presented; for example, if a knife was pictured cutting an apple, the probe would be the whole knife— even though part of it had been concealed initially. The differences in position and shape would act to impair actual "template matching" with an image. Thus, findings from this study will fall into Class 4 (domain contamination), for present purposes, regardless of the actual outcome. All things considered, it is not surprising that more time was generally taken when two items were included in the scene. A later memory test revealed that both image-interaction groups remembered the items better than did the noninteractive group, but that there was no difference between the subject-generated-interaction group and the experimenter-provided-interaction group. The memory results were taken as evidence that subjects really did use imagery, but of course they need not be so interpreted: Even if these results did demonstrate that the items had been encoded into images (but see section 2.5 of this chapter), this would not indicate that these images were used in the verification task. Perhaps the most striking thing about Kerst's results is how similar they are to standard results using the Sternberg memory-scanning task with no imagery instructions. Kerst even found about the same rate of increase in time per additional item as did Sternberg, who simply asked people to verify probes as quickly as possible. This finding could simply reflect time to look up the items in a list.

Having said this much, it seems appropriate to mention that there is one other paper (Just and Brownell, 1974) that reports results like those of Seamon (1972). Given the results of the follow-up experiments described above, however, we have some reason to be chary of these findings. This experiment did not use imagery instructions, and thus may not even be relevant. However, Just and Brownell did vary the concreteness of words in a context that makes it plausible that imagery was in fact used. They asked subjects to memorize short paragraphs that described concrete or abstract attributes of some object (the examples all refer to properties of a person). This is one of their paragraphs:

> At last I could clearly remember who Jack was. First of all, his very straight teeth amazed people. When I think about it, his thin lips come to mind. I remember too that his cleft chin never seemed attractive to me personally. Again, his thick eyebrows reinforced this feeling. The aspect of him that really was attractive was his very silky hair.

An abstract version of this paragraph was created by substituting phrases like "strange opinions" and "quiet manner" for "straight teeth" and "thin lips." Thus, the same frame was used, which ensured the same degree of organization in both concrete and abstract versions. Two different paragraph frames were created at four different lengths, ranging from two to five sentences. Each subject saw half of the paragraphs with concrete phrases and half with abstract phrases. Subjects first studied a paragraph and then saw sentences in a tachistoscope, half of which were drawn from the paragraph and half of which substituted antonymous adjectives; subjects judged the statements as true or false of the paragraph as quickly as possible.

The results were as follows: (1) Concrete statements were easier to verify than were abstract ones. (2) More time was required for longer paragraphs, but this effect was more pronounced with false statements. (3) Although the effects of paragraph length did not differ for concrete and abstract statements in an analysis of variance, separate analyses revealed that time to evaluate abstract statements did increase with longer paragraphs (62 milliseconds for each additional sentence for true statements, 206 for false ones); for concrete statements, however, there was no significant increase in times with longer paragraphs (average increases of 28 and 56 milliseconds per additional item for true and false probes, respectively). (4) False statements generally required more time to evaluate than true ones, but this effect may just reflect the fact that very similar distractors were used.

There is a major problem in interpreting the results of this experiment: The amount of learning of the individual statements was not controlled. Thus, longer paragraphs may simply have been less well learned than shorter ones. Further, it is known that concrete material is more quickly learned (see Postman, 1974), and this factor may account for the overall greater ease in evaluating concrete statements. The failure to find a significant increase in time to evaluate statements for longer concrete paragraphs may also be explained by appeal to this variable. There was in fact a 106-millisecond increase for the true responses taken from paragraphs including five versus two content statements. This difference was not significant, however, perhaps because of the increased variance due to different amounts of overlearning for the different statements. That is, in the longer paragraphs some statements may have been learned much better than others, which would produce considerable noise. In similar experiments, a difference of 100 milliseconds is often significant given overall means in the range of 1350 milliseconds, as were these (see, for example, some of the experiments described in chapter 3). The increased effects of paragraph length for false statements (which were very similar to true ones) could also reflect increased uncertainty about the longer paragraphs due to poorer learning. Taking a different tack, it is also interesting to note that most of the errors with the concrete sentences were "false alarms" (errors of commission). It would be interesting to know if these errors tended to be to the more common possibility; thin eyebrows, for example, may be more likely to be included in a prototypical image of a face than thick ones. If prototypical images are simply modified for the occasion, one is led to ask, why should one assume that the subjects leave off usual parts? For example, the fact that a nose was not mentioned in the paragraph does not guarantee that subjects will omit noses from their images (in fact, I would be surprised if they did). And if undescribed parts are inserted, why should one necessarily expect effects of the length of the list of described parts? Thus, for present purposes the Just and Brownell findings fall in Class 4 (domain contamination) and do not present a challenge to our model.

Given the multiple reasons for my initial discomfort with Seamon's results, it should not be surprising that the results of the experiments using a set-member-verification task fall in Class 2 of our taxonomy (multiple interpretation). One account is as follows: The subject first looks up the propositional list containing the to-be-remembered items and finds a listing of the probed item (if it is true) prior to inspecting the image. (The details of this kind of processing will be described further in chapter 9.) If the image is in fact processed at all, it may be generated after the probe word is found in the list, much as a part is inserted when queried.* The subject responds after either seeing the item (via application of FIND) or realizing that the item is not in the list and cannot be imaged. Thus, equal effects of set size are expected for true and false probes if the propositional list is exhaustively scanned, as Sternberg (1966) argues. But in the

---

*I say "much as" instead of "just as" because a part may be inserted as a portion of another part; for example, claws may be included in an image of a paw, which may be printed out in the course of looking for claws.

"true" case subjects may wait to see the queried item become sharper as it is regenerated into the image. Since "false" decisions generally require more time in this kind of task (perhaps because of response processes, as Clark and Chase, 1972, suggest), we cannot expect "trues" to necessarily be faster than "falses," but there should be only a minimal difference, if any at all. In fact, in 8 of the 15 conditions in Kerst's experiments "falses" were faster than "trues," but this difference does not appear to be significant. In Rothstein and Atkinson's (1975) experiments, however, "falses" did require more time than "trues." This is a Class 4 (domain contamination) finding, which we will ascribe to another domain (response processes); we will not try to explain the inconsistency with the Kerst results. Since our account rests on searching propositional lists, it is not surprising that the magnitude of the set-size effects is the same as that obtained when no imagery instructions are given.

Alternatively, one could explain the foregoing results by arguing that the subject encodes the words in a list and images the objects. If few enough objects are in the imaged scene, the subject is likely to see the probed one at the time of query (or to see that it is not a member of the set). If the list is too large, the images may be fuzzy and hard to identify, perhaps inducing the subject to regenerate the entire set from the deep level. In either case, the subject already has the description of each object stored in memory in a list addressed by its name. In the model, this description would be looked up as soon as the probe was presented, and then used by FIND to locate the object in the image. If the image were too decayed to be refreshed from the surface, FIND would be applied again after the image was regenerated. On this view, the equivalent increases in times with increasing set size in these imagery experiments and in the analogous nonimagery ones would be mere coincidence, which seems implausible to me.

Other explanations for the effects of set size are possible, hinging on the possibility that with larger set sizes items sometimes overflow or are made smaller and hence are harder to identify. But again, the similarity in results with imagery and no-imagery instructions is ascribed to mere coincidence. On my view, it probably is very difficult for subjects actually to use imagery in this kind of simple verification task, for reasons suggested by the "parallel race" model of how propositional and image information are retrieved, which will be developed in chapter 9.

Weber and Harnish (1974) also report finding that more complex images are more difficult to examine. They asked subjects to image words using lower-case letters and then to decide whether the nth letter was vertically large or small. In the first experiment (which is the only one relevant here) three- and five-letter words were used, with tall and short letters appearing equally often in each serial position. Prior to the experiment proper, subjects spelled and classified the letters of all stimulus words, to ensure that they could perform the task. In addition to an imagery condition, where words were named and the subjects imaged them, there was a condition where words were presented and left displayed in front of the subject at the time of query. Four seconds after a word was presented, the name of a digit was read aloud, indicating which position was being probed. A clock started when the digit was presented and stopped when the subject made his or her response. Half of the subjects received only three-letter words and half received only five-letter words. All subjects received both imagery and perceptual conditions.

The results were as follows: (1) As one would expect, given the previous discussion, longer words required more time to inspect. (2) There was no difference in time to inspect images versus perceptual displays, nor were any other effects or interactions significant. (3) Although there did appear to be a slight deficit in time to investigate the last three letters of the five-letter words in the imagery condition, the relevant interaction was not significant (but post hoc comparisons did reveal a tendency for longer reaction times in trials probing these positions in this condition). These findings are illustrated in figure 7.6.

These results are difficult to interpret partly because subjects were never told to use imagery when making their judgments from memory,

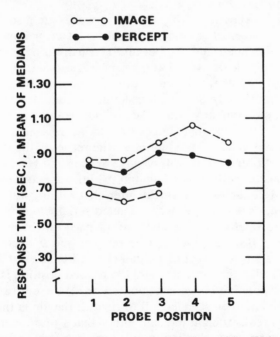

Figure 7.6. The results of the first experiment reported by Weber and Harnish (1974). This graph illustrates time to classify letters in different positions in images or percepts of words.

and in fact made all judgments (of the sixty test words) prior to the experiment proper. The main problem here, however, is that subjects must have been doing *something* during the four-second interstimulus interval, perhaps forming a list of the classifications of each letter indexed by position. If subjects were able to classify and propositionally encode the classifications for all letters of the shorter words but only for some letters of the longer words, this would explain the fact that letters of longer words required more time to classify (given that scanning a propositional list is generally faster than inspecting an image—as the data reported in chapter 3 suggest). If a list was formed, however, it was not serially scanned, or if it was, letters were encoded in random order, because times did not increase for letters closer to the end of the word. The lack of a serial position effect for the three-letter words suggests that each letter in each location was equally accessible, on the average, which would be expected if all the letters could be imaged at once in the most resolved region of the visual buffer. Alternatively, subjects could be cycling through a list of letter-classification pairs and the probe could occur equally often while they were at different positions in the list. Thus, we cannot reject the possibility that the effects of word length fall into Class 4 (domain contamination), reflecting primarily the operation of propositional encoding, storage, and retrieval processes.

The serial-position effects with five-letter words are also difficult to interpret, for a number of reasons. First, it is not clear how many of the five-letter words ended in *s*; Weber and Harnish do note in the method section of their article that four-letter words were sometimes pluralized. If many of the five-letter words were formed this way, then the task may have been easier as only the first four letters needed to be maintained in the image and subsequently consulted. In fact, leaving out the fifth position, one might conclude that images (or lists) were scanned left to right, because there is a trend toward monotonic increases in the imagery condition for the first four positions. If we give Weber and Harnish their claim that a serial position effect was found in the imagery condition but not in the perceptual condition, we might infer that letters were regenerated only as needed, or that images were scanned serially (whereas perceptual displays were "randomly accessed" or all parts of them were in view simultaneously). If imaged words were regenerated as needed, our simulation would lead us to expect that either (1) the PRP files of the individual letters are looked up in sequence until the probed position is reached and then the corresponding image is generated or (2) the entire word is generated as a unit and then scanned left to right. If the dip at the end of five-letter words is real, it might indicate either that *s* often is a special case or that the letters can be looked up or scanned partly from the ends in. Unfortunately, Weber and Harnish do not present an item analysis (see Clark, 1973), so we have no way of knowing for sure whether even the post hoc marginally significant serial-position effects in the imagery condition should be taken seriously.

2.3 Effects of Perceptual Organization

There have been two kinds of experiments investigating the effects of perceptual organization (usually dictated by Gestalt laws) on image inspection. The first sort involves seeing some specified part in an image, and the second involves discovering whether some parts, once assembled into a whole, will correspond to a given pattern. We shall treat this second kind of experiment, which really involves image comparison, as a special kind of image inspection; in this case, one is not searching for a particular part of an image, but is considering the global, overall structure of the image.

2.3.1 Detecting Parts of Images

Reed (1974) describes two experiments in which subjects were asked to decide from memory whether a given configuration was part of a geometrical figure. In his first experiment, a pattern was presented (for example, a Star of David) for one second, followed by a blank field, and then a possible embedded part was presented (for example, a triangle or a hexagon). Subjects were to make a true or false judgment as quickly as possible upon seeing the part. Parts were presented at the same size they had appeared in the original figure, but not necessarily in the same positions (which may have impaired performing a direct template match with an image of the figure). Subjects also gave confidence ratings after each judgment. Two groups of subjects were tested, differing only in whether the blank field was interposed between the pattern and the part for 1.5 or 5.5 seconds.

Reed found that subjects were quite accurate in verifying the presence of some parts but quite poor in recognizing others. For example, a triangle was much more easily verified as a part of a Star of David than was a hexagon. There was no effect of the duration of the interstimulus interval (67.3 percent correct for the shorter interval, 68.6 percent for the longer). Subjects had no difficulty in identifying the entire pattern, a finding that led Reed to argue that they had not simply forgotten selected portions. (This argument is flawed, however, as subjects could recognize the pattern on the basis of partial cues, and the nature of the distractors in the recognition task obviously is critical in determining how easily the patterns will be recognized—if the "new" items had been only subtly different from the "old" ones, Reed might have found that subjects did not remember the figures very well after all.) As expected, more time was also required to detect "harder" parts (the reaction-time results will be discussed in detail below).

Reed's second experiment was like the first except that (1) only one second intervened between termination of the pattern and presentation of a possible part; (2) the test part remained on the screen for five seconds before the subject was asked to respond; and (3) reaction times were not recorded. The point of this experiment was to ensure that subjects fully encoded the part. No overall improvement or other significant difference in accuracy was found between these results and those of the first experiment. As before, some parts were reliably more difficult to verify than others.

Reed reports that in his first experiment 68 percent of the subjects reported using imagery in performing the task, 12 percent reported using both imagery and verbal descriptions, and 20 percent reported relying exclusively on verbal descriptions. Thus, one could reasonably expect that a theory of imagery should speak to these results. On Reed's view, these findings demonstrate that images are best considered as "structural descriptions," as defined by Narasimhan (1969). These descriptions utilize a pictorial language which includes a set of primitives, attributes, relations, composition rules, and transformations. This approach is an instantiation of the kind of propositional models described earlier in this book.

Additional experiments in this series were reported by Reed and Johnsen (1975). Their first experiment replicated the first experiment of Reed (1974) using the 1.5-second interstimulus interval. As before, half of the probed parts were in fact present in the pattern and half were not. In this case, however, the part was presented first, and then the pattern. Thus, this task was in some ways the perceptual analogue of the earlier imagery task, requiring detecting the (presumably) imaged part in the physically present pattern. For "true" probes, where the part was in fact in the pattern, 1.58 seconds were required in general to respond versus 1.64 in the earlier imagery experiment. Parts that were intuitively judged "hard" (difficult to detect) required more time than "easy" parts. For example, 1.11 seconds were required to verify that a triangular part was embedded in the Star of David, compared to 1.82 seconds for the hexagon. The correlation between verification times in this experiment and in the imagery analogue was $r = .64$.

In the second experiment of this series, Reed and Johnsen varied the order in which the pattern and part were presented. One group received the pattern before the part (with a one-second interstimulus interval) and the other group the part before the pattern. Subjects in both conditions were now forced to wait ten seconds after seeing the second stimulus before responding. Following a positive response, subjects were to say "perception" if they had previously seen the part and encoded it at the time, or "memory" if they had not explicitly noticed it earlier. The results were as follows: (1) Errors occurred on 14 percent of the trials when the pattern was presented second versus 48 percent of the trials when it came first. (2) Of the 272 correct responses in the pattern-part condition, 94 were reportedly based on perception. When responses reportedly based on the subject's having explicitly noticed the part when encoding the stimulus are eliminated, the error probability for the positive pairs rose from 48 to 72 percent. It is important to note that *none* of the 32 false alarms (mistaken "true" responses) in this condition was reportedly based on "perception," lending some validity to the evaluations. (3) Subjects in the pattern-part condition did about as well as those in the part-pattern condition in detecting "easy" parts, but did worse in detecting "hard" parts. (4) Finally, the ten-second wait time before responding did lower error rates relative to the first experiment of this paper and the corresponding experiment in Reed (1974).

The final experiment in this series was intended to investigate the accuracy of visual images. Subjects saw a pattern, then saw a part, and then drew the pattern. Subjects were virtually perfect in drawing the pattern. However, we should note that this does not guarantee that their *images* were perfect, only that they had encoded enough information to reconstruct the figure when drawing it. If a figure were complex enough, for example, an image of it certainly would not be perfect—even though one might be able to draw it perfectly.

Our account of these results rests on the assumptions underlying the accounts offered in section 1.2.3 (for our findings on the ease of detecting parts of conceptually parsed geometric figures). In this case, however, subjects' spontaneously supplied descriptions of the figures (for example, "two triangles") plus Gestalt principles presumably dictate how the figures were parsed and stored. As before, when images are later generated, the parts maintain distinct identities due to relative fading phase. Hence, it will be relatively difficult to detect patterns composed of segments belonging to different imaged parts. In addition, it seems reasonable to assume that the "mind's eye" interpretive devices also incorporate Gestalt principles. Our FIND procedures implicitly utilize the Gestalt principle of good continuity, for example, in imposing lines on series of dots that can be fitted by a simple function (by "looking for" dots falling along a given vector). These sorts of principles dictate ease of seeing parts embedded in physically present figures (see, for example, Bower and Glass, 1976). Thus, detecting parts of remembered (and presumably imaged) patterns was especially difficult for "hard" parts because (1) the elements of the part did not cohere in the image and (2) the part itself violated principles of pattern interpretation. Only the second factor is operative in the part-pattern condition, a fact that accounts for both the lower error rates for "hard" parts in this condition and the high but not perfect correlation between times in the two conditions. The results of having subjects classify their detection strategies (memory versus perception) in Reed and Johnsen's second experiment support our claim that an image is especially difficult to inspect for patterns not corresponding to parts used to construct it initially. These findings are in Class 1 (confirmation) insofar as they depend on the structure of the image; but to the extent that the nature of the FIND procedures determines these results, these results are in Class 3 (theory supplementation), requiring further refinement of the theory and general model.

2.3.2 Effects of Part Composition on Image-Percept Comparison

The final experiment to be considered in this section was reported by Nielson and Smith (1973).* Half of these subjects were initially shown and asked to image schematic faces that were constructed with five parts: ears, eyebrows, eyes, nose, and mouth. Each of these attributes could be depicted at one of three sizes. One group of these subjects was asked to remember a face for one second and then to decide as quickly as possible whether another face was the same or different. Another group imaged the faces for ten seconds before seeing the test stimulus. The faces differed with respect to how many dimensions (features) were declared relevant to the decision, either three, four, or five. Separate blocks of trials were used for each of these three conditions and subjects were told in advance which features were relevant. The other half of the subjects initially saw a description of a face (which provided size specifications only for the relevant features), and then saw a test face. All subjects were asked to decide, as quickly as possible, whether the test face was identical (with respect to the relevant features) to the first face or description. The logic of the experiment was as follows: If the group receiving a description initially showed increases with number of relevant features and the image-retention group did not, this would provide some evidence that subjects can use an image as a wholistic template.

Let us begin by considering the results from "same" decisions, when the test stimulus matched the initial face or description: First, subjects who held an image of the study face were unaffected by the number of relevant dimensions at both intervals, but subjects who received a list of feature names required more time as more features were listed. The imagery result falls in Class 3 (theory supplementation) and is explained if an image of the study face was used as a template over the incoming test stimulus. In our simulation, one set of letters could be used to depict an imaged object in the surface matrix, and another set used to depict a percept (recall that letters indicate relative activation of a region). The per-

---

*This experiment grew out of the Smith and Nielson (1970) experiment, in which subjects were hypothesized to have used imagery spontaneously. However, since imagery instructions were not used, and Smith and Nielson themselves explain much of their findings by appeal to nonimaginal processing, it seems inappropriate to offer accounts of these data here.

centage of overlapping points could be computed and inversely weighted by the number and extent of the nonoverlapping points (a few very deviant points would be more important than a larger number of not very deviant ones). If this "overlap index" was greater than a criterion, a successful match would have been made. If a successful match was not accomplished, a variety of normalization procedures (to be discussed in chapter 8) would occur and/or other procedures would be used (such as sequential comparison of parts). A second result was that less time was required to make a "same" judgment when imagery was used than when descriptions were given. This result makes sense if each feature in a description had to be checked sequentially, and each inspection operation was not much faster than an image-template comparison. (Note that this also is a Class 3 (theory supplementation) finding, requiring specification of the comparison operation.) This result also was obtained at both interstimulus intervals. Third, in this experiment, delay did have some effects on verification time. More time in general was required when the delay was longer in the imagery condition. This finding is explained if the elements of the image fade over time and hence longer delays mean that either a more laborious comparison process must take place or parts must be added prior to comparison. In contrast to the imagery group, relatively *less* time was required with longer interstimulus intervals when a list of features was initially presented. Further, for the group initially receiving descriptions, the effects of increased numbers of features were diminished when the longer interval was used. This is either a Class 3 (theory supplementation) or a Class 4 (domain contamination) result from the point of view of our model. That is, we could view it as requiring some additional assumptions, or as out of court. Nielson and Smith suggest that these subjects may have spontaneously converted the descriptions into images when given enough time, which would explain the lessening of effects of number of relevant features and the overall speeding up of these times relative to those obtained with shorter delays in the same condition. This kind of process would be easy to simulate with our model, given that a skeletal image of a featureless face was encoded and that images of each feature were also in memory. In this case, generation of the composite face would be precisely like the generation of any elaborated image (see chapter 6). Our task here is, however, to predict when this sort of recoding will take place. Until we have a principled way of doing so, the foregoing remains merely one of many possible ad hoc explanations.

Half of the test faces were not the same as the initial face or did not meet the initial description. These "different" test stimuli were constructed by altering various numbers of the relevant features of the initial stimulus. The results from "different" trials were as follows:

1. Times decreased as test faces differed from the study ones on more features. This result is easily explained if a threshold percentage of non-

overlap is reached faster with more disparate stimuli, both when images are used as templates and when feature lists are searched. Nielson and Smith explain these results by positing that wholistic images were matched template-like against the test stimulus; the more features that differed, the less was the overall similarity, and hence the faster were the evaluation times. This effect of similarity on evaluation time is well known in the literature, and is obtained even when a single, integral dimension is varied (see Nickerson, 1972).

2. This decline in times was much more extreme when the initial stimulus was a list of features than when it was a face. This again is a Class 3 (theory supplementation) or a Class 4 (domain contamination) finding: The account for this result depends on the details of the template-matching process and the list-search procedures, which are not central to the present theory (if a natural part of it at all) and hence are left unspecified here.

3. Overall "different" judgment times were faster when a face instead of a feature list was given initially. Again, this account rests on here-unspecified details of the comparison process.

4. There again was no overall effect of amount of delay on response times for "different" stimuli. We have a problem here because the "same" times did increase with delay. It is not hard to conceive of comparison mechanisms that would produce this result, depending on how much resolution is necessary to see enough to reach a criterion of dissimilarity versus to see enough to reach a criterion of similarity. If the image must be more highly resolved for one to see enough to make a "same" decision, it may have to be regenerated with longer delays only when "same" (or very difficult-to-discern "different") responses are made. Again, more work needs to be done to motivate this sort of account, and it probably tells us more about the operation of the comparison procedures than about imagery per se.

5. For both types of initial stimuli, when the number of features that differed between study and test stimuli was held constant, more time was required when there were more relevant dimensions to inspect. The effects of number of relevant dimensions would make some sense if subjects selectively attended to the relevant features, and only compared these against the test stimulus. Now, the more features to be maintained in an image, the fuzzier it will be and the worse it will serve as a template. Unfortunately, we cannot have our cake and eat it too. We earlier wanted to explain the *lack* of effects of number of relevant features on "same" times by asserting that all relevant features could be held in the image well enough to serve as templates. This led us to expect no effects of number of relevant dimensions on decision times if images are in fact used as templates, and Smith and Nielson found no such effects. There is a way to explain the difference between the two results, however, which rests on

the fact that trials were ordered such that all the stimuli with a specific number of relevant dimensions occurred together. This would allow subjects to vary their criteria of what constitutes "similar" and "dissimilar" stimuli from one set of trials to another. This account also hinges on the observation that *only* when the "different" face had three different features did the number of relevant dimensions matter in the Nielson and Smith experiment. Nielson and Smith constructed their stimuli so that there were one, two, or three different features when there were three relevant dimensions; two, three, or four when there were four relevant dimensions; and three, four, or five when there were five relevant dimensions. Thus, merely considering the effects of number of relevant dimensions when the number of different features is held constant at three overlooks an important confounding (as Nielson and Smith themselves note): The increase in number of relevant dimensions is here systematically related to the ordinal similarity of the "different" faces to the initial stimuli. When fewer dimensions were relevant, the face with three different features was relatively less similar to the initial face—and thus one would expect it to be rejected more quickly. The problem now becomes (*a*) specifying the similarity metric whereby one attends to and compares only the relevant dimensions (presumably all in parallel) and (*b*) specifying how one adjusts one's criterion for "dissimilar" to account for the range of possible variation. The reader should note that we tend to have increasing trouble as more nonimagery components are introduced. This reflects the fact that our theory does not speak to these components, and thus leaves us only with some requirements for an interface with other components of the cognitive system.

It is important to realize that the foregoing account of the data depends on an assumption about the difference between performing a template match and locating and classifying a part via FIND. The template-match procedure described above does not depend on semantically interpreting the parts and can be performed purely on the basis of physical shape. The categorization of a part, in contrast, requires the FIND procedures to *classify* a given spatial configuration. The degree of resolution desirable for making such classifications results in the image being regenerated or shifted so that the target area is centered in the visual buffer—in the region of highest resolution—prior to inspection. A template match does not require this since the corresponding portions of the image and perceptual representations are degraded to the same extent, and hence matching need only proceed on what is in fact present in the visual buffer. Thus, set-size effects are obtained in feature categorization because parts must be regenerated (and perhaps sometimes scanned to) prior to classification. But because lower resolution is posited to be adequate for template matches, no set-size effects are expected for "same" matches at short intervals. The interest here is that a new prediction is forthcoming: We would not expect set-size effects in the categorization task if a *drawing* of a part was presented—at the correct size and location—on the test slide. If the entire image can be used as a template in this kind of task (given that only a few units are involved and the image has not been held too long), a single part of the image should also be able to be used as a template— leading us to predict that there will be no effects of number of relevant dimensions if imagery is used.

2.4 Inspecting Imaged and Perceived Objects

In chapter 3, we reviewed a number of experiments that were taken to support the notion that imagery is a distinct representational format in human memory. The results from the experiments on the visual angle of the mind's eye (chapter 3, section 2.4) are explained by reference to the properties of the surface representation display medium itself. It seems plausible on the face of things that the visual buffer and the "mind's eye" interpretive procedures would be recruited in perceptual processing as well as in imagery, if only on grounds of parsimony. In this section we will first consider some data that bear directly on this claim, and then turn to more general results bearing on the interface between imagery and perception.

2.4.1 The Role of the Visual Buffer in Perception

The visual buffer is here treated as a hard-wired, special-purpose, short-term memory buffer that also is used in supporting the representations underlying the experience of seeing during perception proper. I argued earlier on this basis that it makes sense that this structure has only a limited spatial extent; after all, the central structures presumably evolved to process information from the sense organs, and thus only need depict the limited arc subtended by the eyes. If this notion is correct, I reasoned, the same spatial constraints should affect how large an angle an imaged object can seem to subtend while remaining entirely visible and how large an angle an actual object can subtend while being perceived in its entirety at a single glance. In order to begin to investigate this idea, the mental-walk/distance-estimation task (see chapter 3, section 2.4) was repeated, but this time with rectangles actually mounted on a wall in front of the subject. The instructions were to "move as close as possible while still being able to see the edges of the figure sharply as you stare at the center." The results of this experiment are illustrated in figure 7.7, and are virtually identical to the results from the analogous imagery experiment using the same stimuli (see figure 3.22).

When providing a motivation for the way we structured the surface matrix in our model, I interpreted the effects of criterion on the size of the estimated angle to indicate that resolution becomes poorer toward the pe-

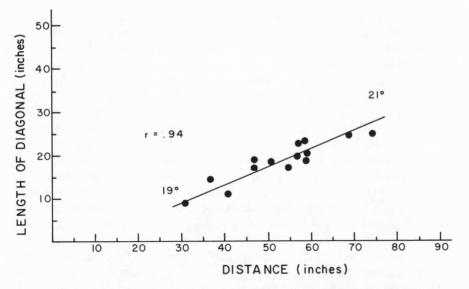

Figure 7.7. The mean distance at which subjects claimed that rectangles just began to overflow their fields of highest visual acuity.

riphery. I could have interpreted this result without making this inference, simply by positing that subjects distribute "attention" over a smaller region when told to be more sensitive to sharp detail. "Attention" could correspond to the number of cells that are activated or to the loci where interpretive procedures are operating. Ronald Finke and I (1980) performed an experiment designed to support the notion that the display medium itself is limited in spatial extent and that resolution within it decreases gradually toward the periphery. We also investigated the idea that attention can be shifted about in this medium, altering the relative distance toward the periphery at which images are visible.

In our first experiment, we varied the distance between two dots, and asked subjects to image the pair moving toward the periphery until the dots were no longer distinctly separated. Each subject performed this task by imaging three pairs of dots (separated different amounts), and also performed the perceptual analogue of this task, where the dots were physically present. Subjects imaged the dots equally often as if they were moving along a horizontal line and as if they were moving along a vertical line. Not only did acuity drop off further toward the periphery with more separated dots, but the amount of dropoff was the same in both the imagery and perception conditions. Furthermore, the shape of the field became more elliptical with lower acuity, and this change in shape was the same in both imagery and perception. The actual magnitude of the angles found here was larger than those observed before, and now was in the range of the angles reported in the literature (see Aulhorn and Harms, 1972). We hypothesized that this disparity occurred because subjects in this experiment could allocate all of their processing resources to a very particular region of the visual or imagery field, and hence were more sensitive here than when they had to attend to a large region of the field in the earlier experiments. This was demonstrated in a second experiment, in which subjects imaged two pairs of dots, both moving away from the center. Now we again obtained angles in the range of those observed using the mental-walk/distance-estimation task. This last finding falls in Class 3 (theory supplementation), requiring us to elaborate the FIND procedures further in order to provide a mechanism for "distributing attention" in the visual buffer (see also Pinker, in press, for more data motivating such development). If in fact the visual buffer is shared in imagery and perception, this sort of attention allocation could underlie subjects' abilities to read selectively from different spatial locations in iconic images (see Sperling, 1960).

But how do we actually explain performance in our mental-walk/distance-estimation task? There are three distinct components to this task: (1) generating an image that preserves the correct size; (2) "zooming in" on this image until it starts to overflow; and (3) estimating the apparent distance. The first process was explained in the last chapter, if we assume that the contents of the deep literal encodings preserve "size constancy," and the second will be explained in the next chapter. The third component is wedded to a theory of how distance is estimated in perception proper. Given that the object is farther away than ten feet or so, the various binocularity mechanisms are no longer relevant, and the same stimulus properties of an object of perception that guide inference of distance in the world can also guide the analogous process in the image. There are many possible ways of judging distance, and I will not try to enumerate or evaluate them here. A procedure that would be very easy to implement in our model depends on one knowing the size of an object, which would allow one to use the "visual angle" subtended by the imaged object (its size in the visual buffer) to compute distance. This is somewhat plausible for the experiments in which the sizes of the objects were explicitly given. Note, however, that the lack of a constant angle for remembered animals (see chapter 3, section 2.4) argues that subjects were not intentionally calculating a constant angle in response to implicit demand characteristics. It would be of interest to see whether people can estimate how far away an object would have to be to appear at various pictured sizes. If people were good at this, the present account would gain plausibility.

2.4.2 The Image as a Surrogate Percept

The second-oldest tradition in the scientific study of mental imagery involves studying the similarities between images and percepts. Recall that the British Empiricists, notably Hume, claimed that images were like percepts except for their weaker "force and liveliness." This suggests that images and percepts are represented in the same way and may be processed by the same mechanisms. In fact, much of the early work took this as practically axiomatic and was concerned with how people could distinguish images from percepts (see Segal, 1971, for a review).

2.4.2.1 Confusing Images and Percepts

The earliest work on the potential confusion of images and percepts had near-fatal methodological flaws: Kulpe (1909) and Rieffert (1912) had subjects sit in a dark room and try to tell when very faint visual stimuli were projected on the wall. On some of the trials, nothing really happened after the "ready" signal. But subjects often reported seeing stimuli when none were present. This was interpreted to indicate that subjects mistook their images for percepts. Presumably, subjects sometimes imaged a stimulus and then had to decide whether the experience was due to the image or an actual projected stimulus. Today, however, we would refer to these errors as "false alarms"—using the jargon of signal-detection theory (see Green and Swets, 1966)—which may simply reflect a "lowered criterion." That is, any source of noise (such as random firings of neurons in the lateral-geniculate body or the like) could be interpreted as a visual signal if one's threshold is set low enough. Further, the situation was structured such that demand characteristics could have led subjects to feel they ought to report visual stimuli, even when they were not really sure.

More interesting experiments were done by Scripture (1896) and Perky (1910) wherein subjects were led to mistake percepts for images. Perky's experiment was carefully thought out and conducted, and is deservedly a classic: Subjects were seated before a one-way mirror in a well-lit room and asked to project on this "screen" a visual image of a common object, like a banana. Unbeknownst to the subject, on the other side of the mirror was a projector displaying a picture of the object on the screen. As soon as the subject projected an image, the level of illumination of the projector was slowly turned up until it was above threshold. Interestingly, the subjects were so concerned with maintaining a good image that *none* (of 24, all students) noticed that an actual picture was before them. This finding was interpreted to show that percepts could be mistaken for images. Unfortunately, this result could have been due to simple demand characteristics. Perky remarks that all observers "noted that the banana was on end, and not as they had been supposing they thought of it; yet the circumstance aroused no suspicion." The introspections the subjects offered make it clear that they tried hard to cooperate and to please, and of course had no reason to suspect that an actual picture was being displayed in front of them.

As far as I can tell, no work was done on this topic between 1912 and 1964. By the middle 1960s, however, cognitive psychology was coming into its own and the problem again received serious attention, with improved methodology and more rigorous experimental design (see Denis, 1979, for a more thorough review than that offered here). The earliest modern incarnation of this tradition seems to have been the Antrobus and Singer (1964) experiment. Subjects in this study were encouraged to engage in daydreaming-like behavior (free-associative speech), or to count backward. Concurrent performance in a visual signal-detection task was inferior when subjects generated free associations instead of counting backward. This result in no way demonstrates that imagery and perception compete for the same specific "channel space," however, since free association simply could be more effortful or generally (not modality-specifically) distracting than counting backward.

The best experiment in this tradition, in my opinion, was performed by Segal and Fusella (1970). They asked people to evoke either visual or auditory mental images while simultaneously performing one of two signal-detection tasks. In one case, they were to report when a very faint blue dot appeared on a screen in front of them; in another case, they were to report the occurrence of a faint tone embedded in noise. Interestingly, maintaining a visual mental image impaired visual detection more than auditory detection, and maintaining an auditory image impaired auditory detection more. Segal and Fusella used standard signal-detection techniques in analyzing their data and were able to show that these findings were due to actual decrements in sensitivity, and not to response biases.

The foregoing findings all fall in Class 3 (theory supplementation), requiring further development of the theory and model. Without a "perceptual parser" that determines how stimuli will be mapped into the visual buffer, we can only provide a fragment of an explanation for the disrupting effects of imagery on visual perception. Presumably, the visual buffer is used in both imagery and perception, and the same interpretive procedures are used in both cases. The major differences between a percept and an image in this kind of task may be that percepts are more stable (less subject to decay over time) and vivid. In this case, then, it is likely that there will be a range of relative stability and vividness for both images and perceptual material represented in the visual buffer, and the variability may be such that some images are actually more vivid and stable than some percepts. The problem then becomes the classic one of signal-detection theory, of deciding from which distribution an apparent stimulus is drawn. In some cases errors will be made: Visual stimuli will be mistaken for images, and hence a signal will not be detected, and images will be mistaken for visual signals, producing "false alarms." Since our model is solely concerned with visual processing, we cannot provide an account of the modality-specific effects found in these experiments. Presumably, however, there will be an analogue to the visual buffer in the auditory system, which itself supports information both from the ears and from memory. Confusions will occur in this structure as well, but because images are represented in the same medium as are the representations of like-modality perceptual input, and are interpreted by some of the same procedures, confusions will be more likely to occur between images and percepts in the same modality than between images and percepts in different modalities (the representations of which occur in different media and are interpreted by different processors).

The model and theory ultimately must be expanded to account for the interface between imagery and perception. Not only should we be able to explain performance in tasks like those described above, but we should be able to specify how perceptual parsing produces the long-term memory file structure underlying images. It seems unwise to begin on the basis of the foregoing results, however, because they are susceptible to another class of explanations that have yet to be ruled out. On this view, when asked to image an object, the subject in fact activates a set of propositions that incorporate various spatial relations (such as "left of" or "above"). These same relations appear in the descriptions generated by the perceptual apparatus. Since the propositions describing visual "images" are similar in form to those describing visual percepts, they are difficult to distinguish from each other. A person might mistakenly interpret a percept to be an image, and thus fail to perceive the stimulus as such. If propositions representing material encoded in different modalities use different relations (as seems necessary), then it will be easier to distinguish these propositions from each other than it will be to distinguish among propositions encoding material in the same modality (using similar relations and structure). Even given the experience of an image, then, we cannot be sure that the surface image itself plays a functional role in this task, given only these data. If the propositional model is correct, however, one might be able to establish perception-like representations verbally, perhaps by describing a scene and asking a person to remember the content of the description. In this case, selective decreases in visual perceptual sensitivity ought to occur without imagery instructions. An imagery account of these data, of course, would be unlikely to lead to this prediction.

2.4.2.2 Studies of "Second-Order Isomorphism"

Roger Shepard and his colleagues have developed a technique that allows comparison of memory representations with representations arising during perception. Shepard wants to demonstrate that internal representations preserve the structure of an object in a way isomorphic to the perceptual representation of the object. Shepard rejects the notion that we have literal "pictures" in our heads (the position of "first-order isomorphism'') in favor of a more abstract isomorphism: "the proposed equivalence between perception and imagination implies a more abstract or 'second order' isomorphism in which the functional relations among objects as imagined must to some degree mirror the functional relations among objects actually perceived.'' (Shepard, 1978, p. 17). Shepard has developed two experimental paradigms for studying second-order isomorphism, one utilizing multidimensional scaling techniques and one using an imagery-projection technique.

Multidimensional scaling studies. A typical example of the multidimensional scaling approach was reported by Shepard and Chipman (1970). People made similarity judgments of pairs of states of the United States in two conditions, either with drawings of the shapes actually in front of them or with only the names physically present. The similarity judgments were then submitted to a multidimensional scaling analysis, which constructs a geometric representation in which (1) stimulus objects are represented as points in a "space" and (2) the order of interpoint distances, from shortest to longest, preserves the ordering of similarities in the data. So, in this case, states judged more similar would be located closer together in the space than states judged less similar. The similarity judgments constrain the locations of the points such that reasonably unique solutions may be obtained (given a number of conditions, like the number of stimuli relative to the number of dimensions in the space). There were two interesting results of scaling the judgments performed in the Shepard and Chipman experiment. First, the solutions obtained in the two presentation conditions were very similar; this was taken to indicate that the names evoked an internal representation that preserved the shape information about the states. Second, the space seemed to be organized in terms of shape; squarish-shaped states clustered in one portion, states with a panhandle in another, and so on. This finding buttresses the argument that people evoked some spatial representations upon receiving the names, which then were compared just as were the actual shapes.

The conclusion that memory representations are structured and processed analogously to the corresponding perceptual representations has been supported by additional experiments using colors, single-digit numbers (which were presented as patterns of dots, written words, or the Arabic numbers as well as auditorily), faces, odors, and sounds of musical instruments (see Shepard, 1975). Generally speaking, the results converge in demonstrating that people judge similarities in the same way when stimuli are evoked from memory and when they are physically present.

These results would make perfect sense if (*a*) images evoked by the names produced the same configuration in the visual buffer as did actually encoding the stimuli perceptually, (*b*) the same interpretive procedures were used in the comparison process in both cases, and (*c*) the comparison operator used the same similarity metric in comparing configurations in the visual buffer, regardless of their origin. To provide an explicit account of these results, then, we would need to specify how the perceptual stimuli were parsed and encoded and the nature of the comparison process underlying the similarity judgments. Both developments of the theory would merely supplement our present model.

Before proceeding, however, it is worth noting that, again, we must first independently motivate the assumed format of the perceptual encodings (by appeal to data like those described in chapter 3) before we can rule out the following kinds of accounts: On one view, people simply describe the stimuli (forming propositional representations) when they see them. Hence, our memory of the stimuli (encoded during an earlier encounter) is in terms of propositions and the representations encoded when seeing them also are in terms of propositions. These encodings consist of lists of properties of the object and how the properties are interrelated. When judging the similarity between two objects, one calculates the number of features in common (perhaps in a way like that described by Tversky, 1977); the more features in common, the more similar the items are judged to be. At first glance, this propositional account seems somewhat strained for the results using color, odor, and sounds. In this case, however, one could argue that although these stimuli per se may not be decomposable into features, they have more or less common associations (to events, affective states, objects, and so on) that may serve as "features" in the assessment process. This notion might be testable using novel stimuli, but even the computer-generated blobs used by Shepard and Cermak (1973) seemed capable of evoking various semantic interpretations and associations (also recall the sad history of work with so-called nonsense syllables—which turned out to be not so nonsensical after all; see Adams, 1967).

Alternatively, in both cases judgments are made on the basis of similarities among representations already encoded in memory, which are lists of propositions: In the perceptual case one "recognizes" the by-and-large familiar stimuli and then makes judgments on the basis of the information already in memory—which is, of course, also used when only the names of the stimuli are presented.

Projecting imagery. Recognizing the possibility of nonimagery counterinterpretations of the sort of data reported above, Shepard has designed another technique to circumvent them (see Shepard, 1978). In this paradigm, subjects are shown a blank grid and are asked to "project" an image of a block letter or the like into the grid by "blacking out" the appropriate cells. Following this, the subject is to decide whether a dot or dots actually placed in the grid would fall on the letter if it were actually present. This condition is compared to one in which the pattern is presented by physically blacking out cells of the matrix. So, for example, the subjects might be imaging or seeing an F superimposed on a 5×5 matrix of squares, and then receive a dot falling in a square occluded by the bottom of the letter. In this case, they would push one button as quickly as possible; if the dot fell off the figure, they would push another (see Podgorny and Shepard, 1978). Although times were usually a bit quicker overall in the perceptual condition, the effects of various manipulations were the same in both conditions (there was a main effect but no interactions). That is, in both conditions when a probe was off the figure, response times decreased with distance from the figure in the grid; when the probe was on the figure, responses were faster to probes when multiple dots fell on the figure, especially when they were on different bars, on intersections, or on more compact figures with a smaller total number of bars. People could do the imagery task with considerable accuracy, and times did not vary systematically with the actual position of the probe within the grid. In other words, it looked as though those people did not perform some sort of systematic left-right (or the like) search.

Again, our model would have to be supplemented to provide an account of these results. We would posit that the grid is encoded in the visual buffer, which is also used in displaying images. The perceptual input so represented is supplemented by material from memory in the imagery condition. Thus, the composite representation is part image (the filled-in squares) and part percept (the grid). This representation is very like that evoked when the squares in the stimulus grid are actually filled, and is processed in the same way when a dot is encoded into the display. The actual pattern of reaction times depends primarily on how the interpretive procedures work, the details of which are left unspecified at present in our model. Podgorny and Shepard interpret their results as being consistent with the notion that a limited-resource parallel-search processor is "tuned" to the figural portion of the grid, and that this processor works exactly the same way regardless of whether the pattern is imaged on the grid or is physically present. Since the same processor is operating in both cases, and the representations are similar, the relative ease of detecting dots in various conditions (whether more or fewer dots are present, whether the figure is more compact, and so on) is the same in the imagery and perceptual situations. But because images are weaker than percepts (due to capacity limits), it is more difficult in general to detect a dot falling on an image. Although the Podgorny and Shepard notions seem plausible, considerably more work needs to be done to motivate implementation of the interpretive procedures that will actually simulate the observed results.

2.5 Re-encoding Mental Images: Imagery as a Mnemonic

It has long been believed that mental images, once formed, can themselves be "inspected" and re-encoded into long-term memory. Once encoded, information purportedly can later be used to regenerate the previous mental image, which then can be inspected and recognized. Thus, imagery has been thought to serve as a memory aid, a supplement to verbal or other forms of encoding. Probably the oldest prescientific tradition in the study of imagery focuses on its role as a mnemonic. The Ancient Greek Simonodies, the story goes, was performing his role as bard and orator at a banquet when he was called outside to receive a message. At just that time, the ceiling collapsed, mangling all the dinner guests beyond recognition. When asked to recount who the hapless victims were, Simonodies discovered that he could mentally picture the table and "walk around it," seeing all those seated with his mind's eye. Simonodies reportedly found it quite easy to name all those in attendance by employing this technique, and went on to develop it as a general way of improving one's memory. The product of Simonodies' and his methodological descendants' efforts is usually called "the method of loci." The method of loci involves first selecting a series of familiar places, among which one can imagine walking in sequence. Then, when one is trying to memorize a list, one imagines walking from place to place and "leaving" an image of each item in the list at each successive location. When later recalling the list, one then again walks by the loci, and "sees" what is present at each one (see Yates, 1966; Paivio, 1971).

Simonodies' insights have inspired much empirical work since 1960 or so. As Allan Paivio deserves much of the credit for reawakening interest in this topic, and personally providing much rich data about the relationship between imagery variables and memory, it is fitting that his book is the most complete review of the area—and I will not attempt a similar review here (see also Denis, 1979). Instead, let me simply mention the three basic approaches to studying the role of imagery in encoding material into memory. All three tacks rest on the following assumptions: (*a*) one can form a mental image, "inspect" it, and re-encode it into memory; and (*b*) later, the image can be recalled—perhaps in addition to the name of the object—and this image can then be "recognized," allowing one to recall the original stimulus object.

2.5.1 Varying Stimulus Materials

Paivio has demonstrated that concrete words (which name picturable objects, such as "rock") are recalled better than abstract words (naming nonpicturable things, such as "truth"). In addition, objects are remembered better than pictures, and pictures better than concrete words. These results are not due to a confounding between level of concreteness and frequency or "meaningfulness" (as measured by Nobel's m—the number of associations to the word in a fixed amount of time). Paivio (1971), Postman and Burns (1973), and others have found that pairs of concrete words are learned more quickly than pairs of abstract words. Further, Postman (1974) presents evidence that if the initial amount of learning is equated, there are no differences in later long-term memory for concrete versus abstract words. As I see it, then, the major (although perhaps not entire) task of an account of the memory differences seems to be an account of why there are differences in ease of learning.

These findings fall in Class 3 (theory supplementation), requiring that our theory and model be supplemented in order to provide an account. Briefly, the model could provide an account for these results if we assume that when a concrete word is presented, an image of the named object is formed and re-encoded into a new IMG file, labeled by the fact that the word was on the list. This image-encoding process may occur at the same time the word itself is encoded in a PRP file. When one is later asked to recall the words on the list, then, concrete words will have two underlying encodings, one consisting of an IMG file and one of the word itself, encoded in a PRP file listing the words presented during the experiment. Abstract words, in contrast, are encoded only in a PRP list. It seems reasonable to assume that there is a finite probability that one will fail to retrieve any given representation (for example, for reasons like those hypothesized by Anderson and Bower, 1973). Thus, since concrete words are encoded two ways, if one encoding is lost another is still available, whereas this is not true for abstract words. Hence concrete words tend to be learned better than abstract ones. The effect of having multiple encoding modalities is most important in determining how much information can be encoded initially and quickly. When required to learn abstract and concrete words equally well, one may equate the number of encodings by forming multiple PRP encodings of abstract words, so that there will be no later differences in memory for concrete and abstract words. At present we do have a procedure that re-encodes a surface image into a new IMG file, but the model would require considerable work before it could actually simulate the above processes.

The fact that pictures are remembered even better than concrete words can be explained in multiple ways within the framework of our model. It may be that one looks at numerous different portions of a picture, and hence encodes multiple IMG representations of it. Or, a percept of a picture may be more detailed than an image evoked by a word, so that the image encoded from seeing a picture is more vivid than the image encoded from internally seeing the image evoked by a concrete word. And the more vivid the encoded image, the easier it is later to recognize the represented object (Bower, 1972, reports some findings supporting this view). Similarly, with objects, one can see around corners and thus encode even more information. In addition, one can build up an image with rich information about the three-dimensional characteristics of the object, resulting in still more information that can be used as later recognition cues.

I am uncomfortable in actually developing the model to account for the foregoing data, however, as there is some uncertainty that the data really do reflect image processing. Consider the following account: The effects of materials may be due to "semantic elaboration" (see Anderson and Reder, 1974). If one posits that memorability is partly a consequence of the number of separate "pathways" to a node in memory, as follows from many propositional models of memory (such as Anderson and Bower, 1973), then an important variable is the number of separate entry points to a node. The richer the stimulus, the more associations and/or separate encodings one can easily generate to it, resulting in more cues that will later improve retrieval. Learning is easier, then, when more information can be readily encoded. This account produces the object, picture, concrete word ordering in the following way: These classes of stimuli are ordered in terms of the number of potential separate, auxiliary encodings; objects can be seen from more than one viewpoint, and hence offer more potentially distinct encodings than do pictures, which are more multidimensional than are concrete words. Any one of the multiple encodings can be used to access the stimulus, and hence memory is improved with increasing numbers of encodings. The problem now is in explaining why concrete words are learned more easily than are abstract ones. These results may be due to "depth of processing" (see Craik, 1973). Because concrete words have palpable properties associated with them, one may activate more information when receiving a concrete word, and thus may have more opportunity for encoding "retrieval tags"—which will later facilitate recall. This account at first glance seems refuted by the fact that Paivio has controlled m, which measures number of associated words, and still finds concreteness effects. There are at least three loopholes in this procedure: (1) Perhaps the initial rate of associating, not total number of associates in 30 seconds (see Paivio, Yuille, and Madigan, 1968) is the critical variable. If more associations come to mind quickly with concrete words, this will be critical if one customarily only tags connecting links for the first few seconds after receiving a stimulus. (2) Paivio has not controlled m for the words associated with the word in question. That is, although a given abstract word and concrete word might evoke the same number of associations within a given time (which is how Nobel measures m), each of these words in turn may not evoke the same number of associations. Thus, there may be many more potential pathways leading to concrete words, and thus a higher probability of later stumbling upon a tag. (3) Associates of abstract words may be less symmetrically associated with the words than associates of concrete words, and hence may serve as poor retrieval cues. For example, "truth" may call to mind "scroll," "scales," "blindfolds," and so on, but these words may not call up "truth" very reliably. For concrete words, in contrast, the associations may be more symmetrical. For example, "cup" may evoke "milk," "coffee," "saucer"—each of which could easily cue the original stimulus word. This possible disparity in symmetry could result either from directional links between nodes or from the way in which inference procedures operate on the nodes (see Anderson, 1976).*

On this account, then, the effects of equating the amount of initial learning on later memory of concrete versus abstract words are straightforward: An equal number of pathways are tagged (although it is more difficult and takes longer to find the ones leading to abstract word-concepts), and hence later recall is equated.

The two kinds of accounts do not really differ appreciably in their explanations of the relative memorability of objects, pictures, and concrete words. Although the difference between concrete and abstract words seems slightly more difficult to explain with a propositional account, it is likely that some sort of explanation will be forthcoming simply because one can never isolate a given variable (like concreteness) from all others. That is, new variables are invented every day, and some of them, like the one-step-removed m described above, will always be confounded with the variable of interest. Thus, there is some question in my mind whether this sort of data, based on simple comparisons of memorability of different materials, in principle could ever be an identifiable result of using imagery per se.

2.5.2 Varying Instructions

One way of studying the role of imagery in memory encoding relies on *instructing* subjects to use or not to use imagery. Kirkpatrick (1894) seems to have been the first to conduct experiments using this paradigm. He asked people to try to remember lists of concrete nouns, and asked some of his subjects to form mental pictures of each named object. Interestingly, imagery instructions improved memory—even though the words were concrete and should have evoked imagery spontaneously if Paivio's Dual Code notion is correct (but perhaps the spontaneously evoked images were less vivid—and hence less efficacious—than the intentionally formed ones). In any case, Rogers (reported in Paivio, 1971) attempted to replicate this early result, and failed to do so.

Probably the best experiments in this genre have been conducted by Gordon H. Bower and his associates (see Bower, 1972). In a typical experiment, Bower asked people to memorize pairs of concrete words using one of three methods: simply rehearsing the association; constructing images of the two named objects such that they were separated and not touching; or constructing images of the named objects interacting in some way. Interestingly, although imaging in any way was superior to simple

---

*This idea was developed in discussions with James Varanese.

rote rehearsal, constructing an image of objects interacting was by far the most effective strategy. It should be noted, however, that when Bower later asked people to relate pairs of words by making up sentences describing the two objects interacting in some way, memory for the words was almost as good as memory in the interactive imagery condition. One could argue, however, that subjects used images in making up the sentences (or vice versa).

These results also are not accounted for by our current model, but also can be explained by simply supplementing the existing theory. Such an account would rest on two general principles, "redundancy" and "double jeopardy": the more representations that encode the same thing, the better, but the more that *must* be retrieved, the worse. Thus, the superior memory for imaging the referents of two words, instead of just rehearsing the words, is due to "dual coding," to encoding an image of an object and its name (as discussed above) in the first case, but not in the second. Both encodings would have links "pointing" to the other word of the pair, indicating that the representations are of words that appeared together. If one has two encodings, the probability of later being able to retrieve at least one of them is presumably higher than the probability of being able to retrieve only a single verbal encoding. Second, the superior recall that follows generating integrated images instead of separate ones can be ascribed to the fact that in the separate case each image is encoded individually, which results in double jeopardy, since both must be retrieved. In the interactive case, only a single image must be retrieved.

Again, however, I hesitate to elaborate the model to provide accounts of these data, as there is reasonable doubt that the results reflect image processing per se. Consider the following possible story: Memory can be improved in two ways: First, the individual words can be made more memorable (can be more associated with the experimental context). Second, the particular connections between pairs can be strengthened. In either case, memory is improved when more connections are formed between the stimulus item (be it the experimental context or the other member of a pair) and the to-be-remembered word. Rote rehearsal results in relatively few encoded retrieval tags and few interword connections; hence, memory is relatively poor. When one is asked to encode separate images, one encodes not only the name of the object but a description of its appearance. These cues later facilitate recall of individual words, but do not ensure correct pairing of words. Thus, these instructions result in better performance than is found in the rehearsal condition, but performance is still not optimal. When one is asked to form an interactive image, not only are encodings about appearance of individual objects produced, but one can now also connect elements of these descriptions, providing more pathways for later retrieving one member of a pair when given the other. Thus, instructions to form interactive images both facilitate recall of individual words and enhance the degree of interword association. (See Anderson and Bower, 1973, for a slightly different propositionalist account of these data.)

It is difficult to distinguish between the two classes of explanations because it seems almost impossible to perform experiments in which one can ensure that semantic processing occurs without imagery or vice versa. One technique that has been tried involves testing blind subjects. But even the fact that imagery instructions improve blind people's memory does not settle the issue. For example, Jonides, Kahn and Rozin (1975) described a possible relation among to-be-recalled items (such as a dishtowel wrapped around a locomotive). A blind person may take this as a cue to describe relations among pairs of items. And the fact that recall improved about the same amount with imagery instructions in blind and sighted subjects could merely demonstrate that two different strategies, imagery and description, are about equally effective. Bower found that subjects show almost equal memory when pairs are learned by forming interactive images or by generating connecting sentences. However, he also found that people cannot later recall the method by which a pair was learned (in an incidental learning situation, in which they would not intentionally encode modality information). This result could indicate that Bower's subjects did not really use imagery, or that they used imagery in all cases, or that in this situation images are in fact only epiphenomenal concomitants of more abstract encodings. We have no way of eliminating any of these possibilities given only the present data.

2.5.3. Interference Studies

What seems needed here is some independent evidence that imagery per se is important in the learning process. One way this could be demonstrated, it was thought, was by showing that visual processing disrupts learning of concrete material more than does auditory/verbal processing, but vice versa for learning of abstract material. Atwood (1971) attempted to demonstrate this by asking two groups of subjects to learn phrases, which were either concrete (such as "nudist devouring a bird") or abstract "the theory of Freud is nonsense"; let us ignore the fact that phrases were used as concrete stimuli, but sentences were actually used as abstract stimuli). Concrete phrases were to be learned by visualization, abstract ones by "contemplating the meaning" of the phrases. Subjects were later given the first noun of each phrase and asked to recall the second. However, after receiving each phrase, one of three things could happen: The subject might hear the number "one" or "two," and then say aloud the one not received; the subject might see a "1" or a "2," and say the name of the other digit; or no interfering task might be presented. As hoped, later memory for the concrete phrases was more disrupted by the visual presentation of digits whereas memory for the abstract phrases was more disrupted when digits were presented auditorially. It is a puzzle to me why auditory presentation should interfere more with retention of an abstract representation. Presumably, in order to say the correct number, a person would have to access "conceptual" representations in either case, and the original modality of input should not be of critical importance. In this light, it should not be surprising that Atwood's experiment has failed to replicate (Bower, Munoz, and Arnold, unpublished; Brooks, personal communication; see Anderson and Bower, 1973). Further, Keith Holyoak and I tried numerous variations of this task over a period of months, all to no avail. In two experiments, done in collaboration with Catherine Huffman (Kosslyn, Holyoak and Huffman, 1976), we asked people to memorize a series of words by either imaging the named things interacting in some way, imaging the things separately, or rehearsing the names. People were asked to scan a list of letters before recalling the words; these subjects searched for either visual targets (letters of particular shapes) or auditory targets (letters that rhymed with a given sound or sounds). As expected, memory for rehearsed words was disrupted more when auditory targets were sought—but visually imaged items were *not* differentially affected by the two search tasks. We had hoped that visual images would be more disrupted by the visual search task, as implied by Atwood's results.

We performed two additional experiments using a slightly different interference paradigm. We had people learn lists either by encoding all of the words as images, by rehearsing all of the words, or by encoding half of the words by using imagery and the other half by rehearsing. We reasoned that words encoded in the same modality should be more mutually interfering than words encoded in different modalities, and hence that memory should be best in the mixed case. This prediction was grounded in the idea that imagery in different modalities recruits different processing mechanisms. The data were consistent with this expectation (but see Kosslyn, Holyoak, and Huffman, 1976, for the details). We also expected clustering during output according to the encoded modality—even if modality cut across semantic categories. That is, half the words in each list were in one category (such as animals or articles of clothing) and half were in another, but half the words in each category were learned via imagery and the other half were learned by rehearsing. This expectation was based on the idea that all of the representations within a given medium would tend to be "read out" together, simply because it was easier to do this than to switch back and forth between separate buffers. Clustering by modality did in fact occur. Further, we found that the rehearsed words tended to be recalled first, and then the imaged words.

At this point it should not be surprising that we have not developed the model to provide an explicit account of these results. Again, there is no strong assurance that these results are not consequences of nonimagery processing. If a visual perception task had interfered more with memory for visually imaged words than for rehearsed words, we would explain this result in the same kind of way we explained Segal and Fusella's (1970) results discussed earlier. As it now stands, however, I do not see any convincing evidence that imagery per se is involved in intentional learning of words, except perhaps as a device forcing one to organize material. (Recall, however, that image size did affect later memory when subjects received a surprise memory test and hence did not intentionally try to encode the words—see chapter 3, section 2.3.) The Kosslyn, Holyoak, and Huffman findings may be taken to indicate that one engages in "deeper levels of processing" for the "visual images" than occurs in rehearsing words. That is, in rehearsing words, a proposition describing the word's sound may be held in active (short-term) memory. In generating a visual image, a list of properties may be looked up in long-term memory, and a richer set of information is held in active memory. However, the visual properties and relations used in the descriptions that correspond to visual images interfere with each other more than they do with the representations underlying auditory images of the names and vice versa, explaining the interference effects. The clustering effect again is due to the order of output: Since only the sound of the word is encoded during rehearsal, and thus memory is more fragile (because fewer pathways need to be lost before the word is entirely inaccessible), it behooves one to recall this first. In the case of visual images, the underlying representations are much richer. Thus, numerous components can be lost before one is totally unable to identify the imaged object (by using the properties as retrieval cues or by making inferences on the basis of the properties) and recall the name.

In short, then, before our theory can be extended to deal with the role of imagery in learning we need reliable data that speak directly to this issue. In order to place constraints on a theory of how imagery serves as a mnemonic device, we need to know whether particular findings do in fact tell us about properties of the imagery system per se, as opposed to properties of a more abstract, language-like system. Essentially, we need to repeat the procedure of Phase I but cast the issues within the context of the present model. Only in recent years has the technology developed to allow one to study imagery per se, and this technology must be applied to this problem before we will have a data-base that will provide the motivation for further developing our theory in this direction.

3.0 CONCLUDING REMARKS

The theory and model have again fared well in the face of new data. The findings considered in this chapter lent support to a number of major assumptions of the theory: (1) New parts are often inserted into images only when needed. (2) Images are regenerated before being inspected. (3) Only a limited amount of material can be maintained in an image at any given time. (4) Lists of propositions are scanned when one is looking for the relevant part or region to fill into an image. (5) The visual buffer has only a limited resolution, and resolution decreases toward the periphery. (6) One adjusts the size scale of the image before inspecting it. (7) Parts cohere as units once generated, perhaps due to "fade phase." (8) The visual buffer has a limited spatial extent. (9) The visual buffer is used to support both surface images and visual percepts.

In addition, the following new results were obtained in the course of accounting for the data: (1) The fact that images of more complex scenes require more time to inspect is not due to one having more locations upon which to fixate while maintaining the image, making it more probable that one will have to scan to the relevant region. (2) Relative association strength reflects the ordering (relative accessibility) of parts of an object, which determines (at least in part) how easily a part can be inserted into an image. Time to see parts on an image is statistically identical to time to image the part (either in isolation or on an image of the entire object), but is not identical to time to evaluate parts without using imagery. (3) The size of a property does not seem to index its accessibility in long-term memory. This result dovetails with one of chapter 6, where we discovered that "structural contingencies" do not seem to underlie the ordering of parts (if in fact it is more likely that large parts will be foundation parts). (4) Resolution decreases toward the periphery in the visual buffer to the same degree in both imagery and perception. (5) The region of highest resolution in the visual buffer is circular, but the lower-resolution regions are elliptical. (6) One can allocate attention to different parts of the visual buffer, increasing acuity toward the periphery. (7) Some parts fade as an image is retained whereas others appear to be inserted into the image over time. (8) Some scanning seems necessary to maintain an image.

The following general hypotheses were offered in the course of trying to account for data: (1) Images fade in part because the regions of the visual buffer become fatigued; scanning an image is equivalent to moving it around the visual buffer, preventing the image from becoming "stabilized." (2) Capacity limits can influence inspection time by affecting the probability that a given foundation part will be present in the image at the time of inspection. (3) More highly associated parts may be inserted into an image first because these parts distinguish the object from other, similar ones. Over time, however, new parts may be inserted in accordance with perceived usefulness for performing a task. (4) Images may be able to be used as wholistic templates, matched to a percept; if so, the resolution adequate for this template match may be lower than the resolution necessary to categorize most parts of images (as is done by FIND in the model). (5) The contents of the underlying literal encodings may preserve size constancy. (6) Surface images can be re-encoded into memory and later generated anew.

A couple of new ideas follow from the foregoing claims, findings, and hypotheses: When initially generated, images may contain many more parts and more detail than can be maintained. This is both because the visual buffer itself fatigues and because more parts may be able to be placed initially than can be maintained at the surface. If so, this would account for my introspection that when I form an image it seems almost photographically clear for an instant, but rapidly fades—appearing much like a flash of a picture in a tachistoscope. The image I maintain is much fuzzier than the original one, perhaps being not much more than the global skeletal image itself. In addition, if the notion that the visual buffer itself fatigues is correct, then one should be able to maintain a moving image longer than a stabilized one. And in fact, I find (for what it's worth) that I can hold up an image of a book sliding around on a tabletop much longer than I can maintain a static image of a book.

8. Transforming Images

Probably the most frequently cited paper I encountered in all my reading for this book was published by Lynn Cooper and Roger Shepard in 1973. It reported two experiments that seemed to show that more time is required to rotate an image through greater arcs. Why did this paper have such an impact? For three reasons, I believe: First, the data were strikingly clean and systematic. It seemed clear that Cooper and Shepard's task had tapped a basic functional capacity of the cognitive system. Second, on the face of things the best account for their data was that people have pictures in their heads, which can be cranked around to any desired orientation. But we know people do not literally have pictures in their heads, let alone ones that physically rotate, are rigid, and obey the laws of physics (think of how uncomfortable this would be!). So these findings (and the analogous results in other domains to be discussed shortly) present something of a paradox. The third reason these results were received with such interest served to heighten the sense of apparent paradox. Toward the end of the 1960s, the apparent successes of artificial intelligence computer programs led many cognitive psychologists to draw strong analogies between human processing and that of the then-current A.I. programs (for example, see Minsky and Papert, 1972, for an overview of the M.I.T. work of that period). In these programs, information was always represented in lists or networks of propositional information (and, in some cases, "procedural knowledge" in the form of subroutines), and it was attractive to assume that humans also rely on only this type of discursive representation. It is of some interest that Pylyshyn's propositionalist attack on imagery and Anderson and Bower's propositionalist theory of human associative memory also were published in 1973. At this time, then, there was a growing enchantment with computational theories in cognitive psychology, and in particular with propositional schemes for representing information. This kind of model, however, does not offer compelling or obvious explanations for the mental-rotation findings. For example, consider Anderson's (1978) model, in which parts are related to some central axis and the spatial relations between the parts and the axis are updated as the represented orientation is changed. The problem here

287

is that there is no reason why orientation should be altered in small increments; it is just as easy to effect large changes in the orientation represented as to make small ones. In this kind of model, there is no reason why images should be transformed in small increments—or any increments at all. Palmer (1975) offers a similar account, but notes that if parts are represented relative to an origin, their relative orientations can be updated gradually. Again, there is no reason offered *why* rotations should occur in small increments. In other words, these specific models lack explanatory adequacy.

Obviously, many different accounts can be formulated for the mental-rotation results. What we need to do here is first to repeat the procedure of Phase I, to narrow down the class of acceptable models. That is, the mechanisms employed by the transformation procedures are relatively independent of the rest of the imagery system, and we need further constraints on the acceptable class of models before we can offer detailed accounts of data. Thus, this chapter is organized differently from the preceding ones. We first will attempt to motivate principled accounts for the findings on image transformations. Only after this will we turn to the detailed explanations of the findings on mental transformations and other kinds of image transformations. It is important to note that the basic finding to be explained is *not* that images are transformed continuously; a discrete sequence can be formulated to approximate a continuous variation to any desired degree of precision, as anyone who has taken calculus knows. The task at hand is to explain why images seem to pass through intermediate points along a trajectory when they are transformed. My preferred type of account of this phenomenon was outlined in chapter 5. This class of accounts rests primarily on the notion that images are not processed as integral wholes but are manipulated a portion at a time. Before we can begin to define a "portion," however, we must know whether images are transformed at the surface level or the underlying level. If the latter, we have far fewer options than if surface images are transformed directly. Thus, this issue is the first node of a new decision tree.

1.0 DISCRIMINATING AMONG ALTERNATIVE MODELS

1.1 Issue I: The Locus of Image Transformations

There are two different ways the transformation procedures can be easily implemented in our simulation, and Shwartz and I have programmed both. In our most primitive simulation (which, as it turned out, was a better approximation to human processing in this respect), we transformed images by moving the points themselves through the surface matrix. At the stage of Kosslyn and Shwartz (1977a), we had not yet implemented the "inverse mapping function" (which allows one to recover the deep literal file representation(s) underlying any point in the surface matrix), and so we were faced with a major problem in trying to move the points in the surface image directly: namely, making sure that all points in an image were moved even when overprinting had occurred. That is, if the image was relatively small, some points did not have a distinct identity in the surface representation, and so were not transformed. Thus, how could points be separated during "zooming in" to produce a more highly resolved image? We initially tried to circumvent this problem by using two matrices to simulate the visual buffer. One of these was very fine-grained and contained all the details of an image; this matrix was the one actually operated on by the transformational procedures. We mapped blocks of four adjacent cells in this matrix into a single cell of another matrix, which was the one accessible to the mind's-eye interpretive functions. This model was designed to simulate "spatial summation," and was a way of having our cake and eating it too. That is, we needed all the points to be in the matrix, so all would be transformed, but we also needed a "grain" to account for the effects of subjective size. This move to having two matrices, one that would be transformed but not seen, never sat too well with us (it was hardly the paragon of elegance!), and we were stuck with the fact that no matter how fine we made the new underlying matrix, parts would still be lost due to overprinting if we generated images at small enough sizes. In addition to these problems, it was enormously time-consuming and expensive to work iteratively through the surface matrix numerous times in inching the image around. Thus, we decided to explore the properties of a second implementation.

In our second generation of simulations (see Kosslyn and Shwartz, 1978), we implemented an inverse mapping function. This function was quite different from that used in our current model (which, at this writing, is fifth-generation). In the earlier version, each cell in the surface matrix had two parts, one containing information about relative level of activation and one containing a pointer to the underlying coordinates. If overprinting occurred, the coordinates of the underlying pointers were linked into a list. This linked list served as a mapping function back to the long-term memory representations. That is, when an image was generated, a copy of each underlying coordinate was linked to the cell where that point was placed. When a point was moved, the underlying coordinate was updated (note that the actual long-term memory representation was not changed, only the temporary mapping to it). Thus, when a file was printed out, all the information in that file became potentially available to the mind's eye, even if overprinting occurred initially. Given this kind of system, it was easy to effect transformations by adding a constant to the Θ values (if rotation was required), multiplying the r values (if size change was required), or moving the origin (in order to accomplish changes in position in the surface matrix). Thus, in this model transformations were accomplished from the deep level, not by moving the points themselves in the surface matrix. The advantage of doing this was that overprinted points would become distinct as the image was expanded. Because these operations affect the surface representation, we were still in theory forced to make a series of relatively small adjustments if the image was not to be scrambled. We speculated that cleanup operations can be performed only on the surface image, where numerous files are amalgamated into patterns that the FIND procedures can interpret. If these cleanup procedures require recognizing the relationships among parts, then it makes sense that they operate on the surface representation (where FIND can be implemented). If so, then when parts became too scrambled—as will occur with large step sizes—"landmarks" may become either unrecognizable or so misaligned that they cannot be used as aids in readjusting other parts (for example, if the eyes of a face are aligned vis-à-vis the nose, and the nose becomes distorted, it may become impossible to realign the eyes when they become distorted as an imaged face is mentally rotated).

The two transformational schemes we implemented make different predictions regarding how the subjective size of an image will affect rotation rate. In the first model, larger images occlude more area in the visual buffer, and hence more cells must be processed. When objects are rotated, a region surrounding the object is defined and all cells within are processed. Thus, more time is required to rotate larger images in this model. This prediction follows from the assumptions that (1) the surface representation itself is manipulated, and (2) the available "processing capacity" is increasingly taxed as more area must be processed (so, for example, the rate of working through the cells in the surface matrix cannot increase arbitrarily as more cells must be processed). In the second model, in contrast, the size of an image does not affect rotation rates; size is represented simply as a factor multiplying or dividing the r values when the IMG file is mapped into the surface matrix by PICTURE.

Shwartz (1979) conducted an experiment to discover whether the size of an image affects rotation rates. In addition to varying size, he varied the complexity of the stimuli (for reasons to be discussed in section 1.3 below). Subjects in this experiment first saw and studied an Attneave random polygon. Shortly thereafter, the stimulus was removed and an orientation cue was presented. The subject's task was to rotate an image of the figure until it was at the indicated orientation, and to push a button when it was correctly reoriented. Following this, a second polygon was presented and the subject judged whether it was the same as or different from the imaged pattern. The results of present interest are the rotation times, which are illustrated in figure 8.1. Not only did larger images require more time in general to rotate, but increasingly more time was required to ro-

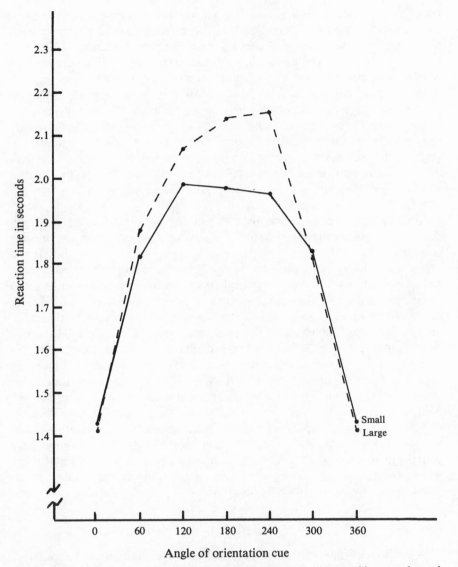

Figure 8.1. The time to rotate subjectively large and small mental images through varying degrees of arc (from Shwartz, 1979).

tate larger images farther. The peaked functions are just as one would pre-dict if subjects rotated the image the shortest direction, clockwise or counterclockwise, to bring the pattern to the indicated orientation. Shwartz has since replicated this finding, using a slightly different paradigm. This result is exactly as expected if a bounded region in the visual buffer is pro-cessed such that for larger images more material has to be processed at every iteration of the image transformation. Thus, our second version of the simulation was rejected. Further, these results are also inconsistent with propositional models of the sort proposed by Anderson, 1978. The idea that a bounded region in a spatial display is processed neatly accommodates the results, whereas the other scheme, or Anderson's model, requires ad hoc and implausible modification to explain these data (that is, the rate at which coordinates are altered would have to be sensitive to the magnitude of a size parameter). Thus, although the foregoing result really only speaks to how that one transformation, rotation, procedes, it also implicates the functional capacity to transform images from the surface. Not all transformations need be accomplished in this way, but the fact that at least one is allows us to reject one broad class of models and accept another.

Although it is computationally more taxing to transform images from the surface using a digital computer (which is irrelevant, given the present concerns), it is satisfying that the results turned out as they did. If the image were always transformed from the deep level up, one would wonder why such a system had evolved (because the image would be, in a sense, just along for the ride). Further, it is not clear why a new image could not be generated in the final transformed state as easily as the existing image could be moved a relatively small amount through the matrix. That is, in this case exactly the same procedures would be used regardless of the size of the value added to or subtracted from the Θ values. Thus, it is not clear what advantage is accrued by modifying an existing image, instead of simply forming a new image in the desired position. If the image is in fact generally moved from the surface, however, we can posit that different functional capacities—with different operating principles—are at work from when a new image is constructed. Hence, it is internally consistent to claim that, even though it is more work in our digital computer, in humans it is easier to modify an existing surface image than to generate a new image from the deep level.

1.2 Issue II: The Transformation Process

Regardless of how we define the "portion" operated on by the transformation procedures, two kinds of accounts for the incremental nature of image transformations are easily formulated within the context of our model: On the first account, a given portion can be moved only a relatively small amount before the image seems to fragment and become disrupted. To prevent this fragmentation, portions are moved in relatively small increments. On the second account, we make the assumption that the distance a given part is moved is not precise, that there is a variance around the size of the increments. That is, when one attempts to move portions of an image a given amount, one does not in fact move all portions exactly the same distance—unlike a digital computer. Thus, if the variance increases with the mean "step size," then when large positional translations are used the image becomes very scrambled. Small increments, on the other hand, allow easier "cleanup" operations, and there will be some tendency for random perturbations to cancel each other out if enough small shifts are used.

As was noted in chapter 5, the model hinging on sequential shifting without fragmenting leads one to expect faster scanning rates with larger images, since portions can be moved farther than at smaller sizes while maintaining the same proportional distance. This expectation was not borne out when subjects scanned images of very simple schematic faces (see chapter 3, section 2.1). (Note that the schematic nature of these stimuli removed a host of other factors, like the ease of seeing the target, that could have resulted in slower rates—but for reasons irrelevant to the present concern.) Further, this model also leads one to expect "acceleration" as images are expanded increasing amounts, for the same reason. Neither Bundesen and Larsen (1975), Larsen and Bundesen (1978), Sekuler and Nash (1972), nor Shwartz and I have reliably found this pattern. Thus, the second account, which hinges on increased scrambling with larger step sizes, is to be preferred; this mechanism predicts no rate or acceleration effects that depend on image size.

1.3 Issue III: The Nature of a "Portion"

Our account for the foregoing results rests on the claim that the surface image is manipulated a portion at a time. Before we can formulate explicit accounts for data on mental transformations, however, we need to define the "portions" that are operated on when images are transformed. The next node of this decision tree, then, has two branches extending from it, one representing the notion that higher-order parts of some kind are manipulated, and one representing the alternative view that arbitrarily defined portions or "molecular" elements are manipulated. In our model, the portions can be defined in terms of one or more of the following: (a) the primitive underlying substratum of images, which corresponds to the states of cells of the visual buffer (which may be thought of as representing primitive neural states or the like); (b) arbitrarily defined portions of the visual buffer; (c) higher-order units of the images (corresponding to parsed parts of the object), indicated by different letters in the model; or (d) units imposed on the image by the transformation procedures only at the time of transformation. In our first model (Kosslyn and Shwartz, 1977a), rotation began by arbitrarily dividing the region of the surface matrix bounded by the to-be-rotated pattern into wedges, and all the material in a given wedge was shifted at a time. This procedure was adopted largely for convenience, however, and we should scrutinize it carefully before taking it seriously.

There are a number of experiments in the literature that bear on the present issue. These experiments explore the effects of the complexity of the to-be-imaged stimuli on the ease of mental rotation. If more "complex" images, defined in terms of the number and arrangement of parts of the imaged stimuli, are more difficult to transform mentally, this will help us define the level of "unit" operated on by the transformation procedures. The first of these experiments was reported by Cooper (1975). In the first experiment described in this paper subjects first learned Attneave random polygons at five different levels of rated complexity—incorporating 6, 8, 12, 16, and 24 points. The orientation chosen to be the "standard" was systematically varied over the subjects. After learning to discriminate between normal and mirror-reversed versions of the stimuli, subjects were shown the stimuli at different degrees of angular disparity from the original orientation and were asked to judge, as quickly as possible, whether each stimulus was normal or reversed. Subjects were tested for five days, receiving 32 retraining trials (to review the standard orientation and normal/reversed discrimination) followed by 128 test trials (in addition, any trials on which there were errors were retested at the end of the session). The results of this experiment, along with the Attneave polygons, are illustrated in figure 8.2. As is evident, times increased linearly with the angular departure of the test stimulus from the trained standard upright. Further, there were no differences among times to evaluate forms of different complexity. This was somewhat surprising to Cooper, given the generally longer times for these figures than those obtained when letters and digits were used in the Cooper and Shepard (1973) experiment (which were, of course, also much more familiar).

In her second experiment Cooper (1975) examined not only the time to evaluate the direction of a test stimulus but the time required to "prepare" for a particular orientation of the stimulus. Cooper and Shepard had demonstrated that if subjects were given both identity and orientation information before the stimulus was presented, and were allowed sufficient time to prepare, the absolute orientation of the test stimulus did not affect evaluation times. Presumably, with enough time, subjects rotated an image into the expected orientation of the stimulus, and then used the image to perform a template match to the stimulus. Thus, in this experiment Cooper expected that more time would be required to accomplish longer rotations in preparation for the stimulus, but that once an image was rotated into position, the absolute orientation of the test stimulus would be irrelevant. Subjects first saw an outline drawing of the form, followed by a black arrow indicating the orientation at which the test stimulus would be presented. The subjects began to prepare as soon as the arrow was presented and indicated when they were ready; these subjects

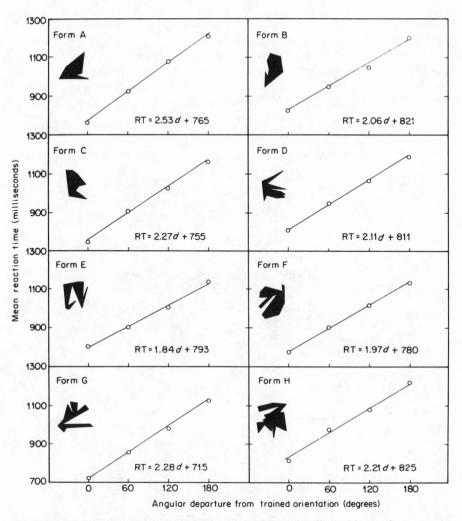

Figure 8.2. Mean evaluation times for each of the stimuli used in the first experiment reported by Cooper (1975) when the stimuli were presented at different angular disparities from the trained upright.

were explicitly asked to generate and rotate a mental image of the stimulus in preparation for making the discrimination, and to rotate the image in a single direction. The test stimulus appeared immediately after the subject indicated that the image had been rotated into position. On half of the blocks of trials, images were rotated clockwise, and on half they were rotated counterclockwise; 576 reaction times (half preparatory, half evaluation) were collected for each subject, in addition to retaking error trials. In order to shorten the task, Cooper used only four different forms per subject, which precludes a systematic examination of effects of complexity in this experiment.

The results of this experiment are presented in figure 8.3. As expected, more time was required to prepare when an image had to be rotated through greater arcs. Further, once rotated, the orientation of the test stimulus was not an important determinant of evaluation time. Finally, the increases in times for additional amounts of rotation in this experi-

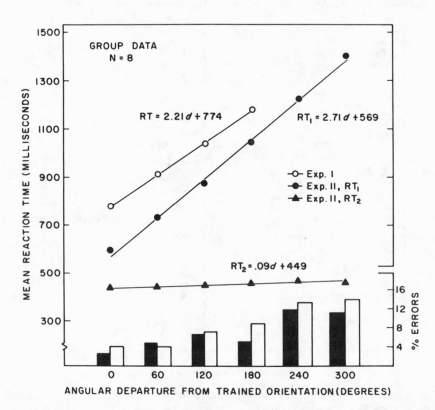

Figure 8.3. The results of the second experiment reported by Cooper (1975). This graph illustrates the mean reaction time to process stimuli at varying angular departures from the trained orientation. The uppermost function includes data from Cooper's first experiment, in which subjects were presented with stimuli at different orientations and asked to decide whether the stimulus was normal or mirror-reversed. The middle function illustrates the amount of time subjects required to prepare for a to-be-presented stimulus when cued that the stimulus would be presented at different amounts of angular disparity from the trained orientation. The bottom function illustrates time to evaluate the test stimulus after subjects received a cue indicating its orientation and were allowed to prepare for it. The solid bars represent errors when the figure faced the original way and the open bars represent errors when the figures were mirror-reversed.

ment were equivalent to those found in Cooper's first experiment, supporting the claim that the same kind of mental-rotation operation occurred in both. Interestingly, however, there were no hints of effects of stimulus complexity in these data. If this is a genuine result, it would seem to narrow our options regarding the level of unit moved in mental rotation. Before we accept a null finding, however, we had best be sure it is not some kind of artifact or methodological quirk. Cooper felt the same way, and thus further pursued the issue.

Cooper and Podgorny (1976) extended the third experiment of Cooper's earlier paper in order to examine further the effects of stimulus complexity on rotation time. They conjectured that Cooper's failure to find that complexity affected the rate of rotation may have been due to the required discrimination being too easy. Perhaps, they worried, subjects could make the discrimination without having to rotate the entire form. Thus, Cooper and Podgorny selected seven Attneave forms, incorporating 6, 8, 12, 16, and 24 points. They then generated a number of versions of each form by randomly perturbing points, and asked eight subjects to rate the similarity of each variant to the original. Six of these variants plus the mirror reversal of the original were selected as distractors for a same/different task. These forms were used in the preparation-time paradigm described above; subjects were told to mentally rotate a "memory representation" of the standard form in preparation for the test stimulus, and to indicate when they were ready. All rotations were to be performed in a clockwise direction. Prior to the experimental sessions, subjects participated in two kinds of practice trials: They learned to discriminate the standard form from the distractors and then received 30 practice trials in the task itself. Five one-hour test sessions followed this, involving 420 test trials. Half of the test stimuli were standard forms and half were distractors; each distractor appeared equally often. Thus, it was hoped that use of similar distractors would force the subjects to encode and rotate the stimulus in full detail.

As before, preparation time increased linearly with the angular departure of the orientation cue from the upright. This was true even though people rotated the figures past the 180-degree orientation (because they rotated only in a clockwise direction). Further, there again were no effects of complexity of the stimuli on preparation times. Again replicating the previous results, once an image was rotated into position, the absolute orientation of the test stimulus did not affect time to evaluate it. In addition, time to classify a distractor as "different" decreased for distractors rated to be decreasingly similar to the standard form, replicating a common finding in the literature on stimulus discrimination (see Nickerson, 1972; note that this is a Class 4 (domain contamination) finding vis-à-vis the present theory).

Cooper and Podgorny's findings, on the face of things, disconfirm the

entire class of models in which parts are defined as they were in their experiments (recall that portions of the image are moved individually, and
this leads us to expect images with more parts to require more time to
rotate—providing the range of complexity is great enough so that neither
floor nor ceiling effects occur in how much processing capacity is taxed;
see Kahneman, 1973 and Shwartz, 1979). However, there are reasons to
be cautious in taking Cooper and Podgorny's results at face value: First,
their subjects were highly practiced and their results may reflect a floor
effect in the rotation operation (that is, these people may have become so
practiced that they reached the physical limits of the system for all stimuli). This conjecture is supported by the fact that error rates did not vary
for different levels of stimulus complexity; if the stimuli were in fact of
different complexity the more complex ones surely would have been more
difficult to remember, all else being equal. Cooper and Podgorny argue
against the possibility of a floor effect by pointing out that there was no
difference in rotation slopes in their experiment and Cooper's (1975) earlier study, but this could imply that the floor effect was evident in both
studies (which seems not unlikely given that large numbers of trials over
multiple sessions were used in both experiments). Second, Cooper and
Podgorny used only six different stimuli. It is possible that due to sampling error they did not in fact manipulate psychological complexity
within their stimulus set. In fact, if they *had* found effects of complexity,
this could have been due to peculiarities of the particular stimuli representing different degrees of complexity. Third, Anderson (1978) has argued that Cooper and Podgorny's subjects may have been using a "reduced" image for the complex polygons. He points out that since more
complex polygons had more points perturbed when "different" stimuli
were generated, subjects had to remember a smaller proportion of points
in a complex image than in a simple image to achieve the same probability
of detecting a "different" test stimulus. In order to demonstrate that mental rotation is not affected by image complexity, the task must force the
subject to maintain in the image all of the information present in the original stimulus. Anderson suggests that the appropriate modification of the
Cooper and Podgorny task would be to perturb the same number of points
by the same amount for all levels of stimulus complexity. Shwartz (1979)
did just this in his experiment.

    The Shwartz (1979) experiment discussed earlier also was designed to
study the effects of stimulus complexity on rotation time. Recall that
Shwartz's experiment made use of the task devised by Cooper and Podgorny and used Attneave forms as stimuli. These polygons had either 6 or
10 points, and the "different" test stimuli had a single point perturbed by
the same amount in every case. Polygons of each level of complexity appeared equally often at each size. Subjects were naive and each subject
received different stimuli in each of the conditions, in order to minimize

any stimulus-specific strategies that subjects might try to adopt. In addition, to encourage subjects to process the stimuli carefully and to fully prepare for a test stimulus before responding that they were ready, subjects were paid for each correct judgment made within a time limit.

The results of the complexity manipulation in this experiment are illustrated in figure 8.4. As is evident, more time was required to rotate the image farther and to rotate more complex images. These results were the same for both sizes of stimuli (the two factors were statistically independent). As noted earlier, increasingly more time was required to rotate larger images farther than was required to rotate smaller images farther. This result is as expected if material in the surface image is in fact being iteratively shifted. However, the increased time to rotate more complex images farther amounts, relative to the increases for simpler images, was not significant—in violation of our expectations if the complex images had more higher-order units and these units were being shifted: If the complex images had more parts, each of which was individually shifted, they should have required increasingly more time to rotate farther, because increasing numbers of iterations (each taking more time than with simple images) should have occurred. The fact that images of complex objects required more time in general could indicate that subjects had more difficulty in defining the bounded region prior to beginning the rotation, that fading reduced the effective difference in complexity as images were rotated farther, or any number of other things. One particularly disturbing possibility was that the complex forms were simply too difficult to remember with the three-second encoding interval used. Thus, Shwartz performed another experiment increasing the exposure time, and again failed to find effects of complexity on rotation rate, even though the error rates decreased.

The problem with the foregoing experiments is that we cannot be sure that "complexity" is correctly defined by reference to the number of points on a random polygon. Perhaps some other way of estimating the number of units in an imaged stimulus would produce different results. And in fact Pylyshyn (1979a) reports two experiments in which complexity of a stimulus was defined differently, and claims to have found support for the view that images are rotated in terms of higher-order units. Because these results purportedly speak directly to the present issue it seems worthwhile to discuss them briefly, even though the methodology used excludes the results from necessarily being included in the domain of the present theory (as will become apparent shortly). Pylyshyn's subjects saw two stimuli stimultaneously, one a geometric figure (containing internal lines dividing it into subpatterns) and the other a possible part of the figure. The part was presented at different angular disparities from the orientation of the figure. The subject was asked to decide whether the part was a component of the figure, rotating the figure into congruence with

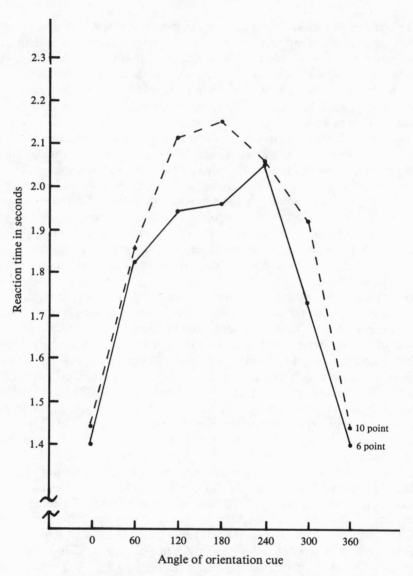

Figure 8.4. The results of an experiment reported by Shwartz (1979) in which Attneave random polygons varied in complexity. This graph indicates the time to rotate a mental image of six- and ten-point figures in preparation for a test stimulus.

the part if necessary. The main result of interest here was that the amount of time required with greater amounts of rotation increased more sharply when the part was not a "good" (in the Gestalt sense) subpattern. Unfortunately, these results may not bear on the present issue. For one thing, they may reflect, as Pylyshyn suggests, a "piecemeal rotate and compare" process. Perhaps the subjects did not encode the entire figure into a mental image, but encoded only parts that they hoped would help in performing the task. If they guessed wrong, they returned to the figure and encoded a new "parse" of it. In this case, the worse the part (the more it violated natural parsing procedures), the more difficult it would be to locate it when the figure was at increasingly disparate orientations. If this account is correct, then this result says nothing about how entire figures are rotated, but merely speaks to specific strategies subjects adopt when performing this particular task. Another possibility is that these results are due to a visual comparison process, where subjects never encode or rotate a mental image—even of a part. On this account, the results simply indicate that the "embedded figures test" becomes increasingly difficult for "bad" parts when the subpattern is rotated farther. A third possibility is that even if subjects did encode the entire figure and then mentally rotate it into congruence with the part, the results simply show that the image becomes increasingly degraded with more rotation, and that "good" parts are still relatively easily detectable at amounts of degradation that make it difficult to detect "bad" parts (see my discussion of Reed's findings in chapter 7).

In addition to these results, Pylyshyn found that figures with more internal detail seemed to be rotated *more* easily into congruence with a drawing of the outline of the figure. In this case, however, it should be noted that the two less articulated stimuli had only three outer sides, making them more symmetrical than the more articulated stimuli, which were irregular four-sided polygons. Thus, the increased time could simply reflect the fact that the distractors (the "false" subpatterns) were mirror-reversals of the targets: Because the triangles were more symmetrical it was more difficult to decide whether they were normal or reversed, and this discrimination became increasingly more difficult as the figures were rotated from the upright because it became more difficult to locate the top of the outline when carrying out a visual comparison process. In short, although it is tempting to take the Pylyshyn results as support for the claim that images are rotated by shifting higher-order units, these findings in fact fall in Class 4 of our taxonomy (domain contamination). The problems here are general to all methodologies in which two stimuli are presented simultaneously for comparison; in all such cases, we have no guarantee that mental images were ever encoded and operated upon, and thus no compelling reason to expect the data to bear on our theory. Considerations like this led me to omit discussion of the earlier Shepard and Metzler (1971) experiment, which showed that more time is required to decide that two figures are identical when they are presented at larger angular disparities, and the Hochberg and Gellman (1977) experiment, which showed that figures are more easily compared when highly evident "landmarks" are present. I would have no trouble proposing an explanation for these kinds of results within the context of our model, but I have some doubts as to the appropriateness of such a purely mental account (that is, not dependent on on-line perceptual processing, as in making successive visual comparisons of corresponding parts) when the task could easily have been performed by making sequential perceptual comparisons (see also Just and Carpenter, 1976).

Beth Adelson and I conducted another experiment on this issue. We wanted to ensure that subjects were rotating images and to discover once and for all whether images of figures containing more units require progressively more time to mentally rotate increasingly far. In this experiment we used the ambiguous geometric forms illustrated in figure 4.5. Recall that these forms could be described in terms of either a few overlapping forms or relatively many adjacent forms. Further, different figures were described in terms of different numbers of parts. There were two groups of subjects, differing only in which set of descriptions (overlapping or adjacent forms) they received. A subject read a description and then was presented with a form and asked to "see it" as it was described. Next the subject was asked to form an image of the figure and press a button when the image was complete. These image-generation times were recorded and are illustrated in figure 8.5. As is evident, we replicated the earlier results, again showing that more complexly described patterns required more time to image (the correlation between generation time and number of units was $r = .96$). These findings gave us some confidence that the subjects' images really did contain different numbers of units. After a subject had indicated that an image was formed, he or she was cued to rotate that image either 60 or 120 degrees (practice with actual physical rotation was given prior to the task, so subjects knew the correct amounts of rotation), and then to push a button. As expected, more time was required to rotate the images farther. In addition, the group receiving the descriptions predicating many adjacent units generally required more time to rotate their images than did the other group. Further, as is evident in figure 8.5, more time in general was required to rotate the more complex forms (the correlation between rotation times, pooling over the amount of rotation, the number of units was $r = .95$). Importantly, however, images of the more complexly described figures required the same amount of time to rotate an additional 60 degrees as did images of the more simply described patterns. This result runs counter to the prediction of models positing that higher-order units (as defined by the descriptions) are moved individually.

We hypothesized that the general increase in time to rotate more complex images could be explained by positing that subjects require more time to regenerate these figures before commencing rotation. But once underway, it is just as easy to rotate figures of different complexity. Thus, we simply subtracted the mean generation times from the rotation times and correlated the residual times with the number of units in a figure. This correlation was $r = .61$. Thus, the effects of additional units were more

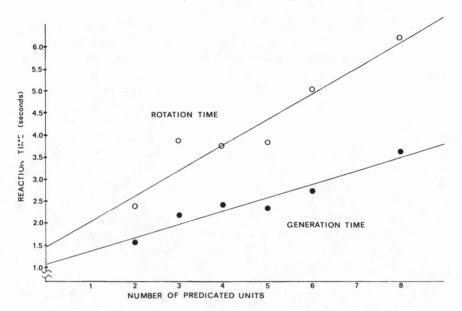

Figure 8.5. The bottom function represents the time to generate images of patterns that were described in terms of different numbers of units (the patterns illustrated in figure 4.5.); the means illustrated here were averaged over all patterns containing a given number of units. The top function represents time to rotate images of the patterns, averaging both over data from different patterns having the same number of units in their descriptions and over times from 50 to 120 degree rotations.

severe in the rotation times than in the generation times, as it appears in figure 8.5. An average of 301 milliseconds were required to image each additional unit, and 581 additional milliseconds were required to rotate images for each additional unit. If the effect of complexity on overall rotation speed is just a consequence of regenerating the image at the outset, then we must posit that it becomes increasingly difficult to refresh images of increasingly more complex patterns (perhaps because of increased fatigue in the visual buffer). Another alternative is that people check each unit at the end of the transformation, and hence require more time with more units. Finally, it is of some interest that the increase in time to generate an image of each additional part was about twice that found before. This could be another piece of evidence that generation time is affected by the purpose of generating the image, by the task to follow. Or, it could simply reflect individual differences among the subjects.

1.4 Inferences about Models

The foregoing exercise was not as useful as it could have been, had we been led to select different alternatives on the basis of the data. That is, as luck would have it the results of our experiments on the second two issues led us to reject viable options, leaving vast classes of alternatives open. At the present juncture, then, we have motivation for positing that at least some transformations operate directly on the surface representation, and that transformations do not seem to operate by moving portions sequentially, if the distance moved is proportional to the size of the image. We also have evidence that people do not transform images by moving organized units individually—if the system has only limited "processing capacity." Thus, at this stage, we do not have very much in the way of motivation for selecting among any number of viable theories of why image transformation proceeds incrementally. Among the viable options are the following: (1) Transformations operate at a "noncognitive level," being analogue processes in the brain itself; in our model this would be equivalent to moving the dots incrementally by fiat. (2) Transformations operate on arbitrarily small portions of an imaged object, like the dots in our model. (3) Transformations operate on arbitrary portions of the visual buffer, like the wedges that the first version of our simulation defined and shifted (and the time taken to move a wedge is independent of the material represented in a wedge). (4) Transformations operate on organized units that are imposed on the object only at the time of transformation; these units would not necessarily correspond to units of the object itself. (5) Transformations operate on individual units, but there is sufficient "processing capacity" that it is just as easy to move many units in parallel as few units.

When I first began to think about this problem I was drawn to the first two accounts noted above because it seemed to me that I mentally rotated an image of even a single line, which presumably had only one part, in increments. Upon further introspection, however, I noticed that my single line would bend near the pivot point if I rotated it too quickly. The line did not seem to be a rigid, primitive entity. Taken at face value, and considered with the results reported above, this introspection could indicate either that the transformations operate on arbitrary portions of the visual buffer, or that organized units are imposed on the object in the course of performing a transformation (that is, that the line may be treated as two parts, even if it is presented and imaged as one). This introspection should not be given much weight, of course, but true to the "quantification of introspection" approach mentioned in chapter 1, it does suggest hypotheses that can be tested empirically.

At this point, then, we do not have any motivation for selecting among some handful of viable theories. All of these theories are nested within the general class of theories instantiated in our model, however, and all are consistent with the theoretical claims that form the core of the present theory of image representation and processing. Thus, this is one more example of the directive function of our model-construction enterprise. The model can help us formulate questions that have promise of leading to answers that will further articulate the theory.

We have not yet tried to distinguish among the foregoing alternatives, or to formulate further hypotheses, for two main reasons. First, we have adopted a "breadth first" approach to model building. That is, we have tried to maintain about the same depth of analysis of each topic relative to the rest. We have avoided becoming sidetracked into studying one narrow topic, losing sight of the theory as a whole. Only after the broad foundations are firm will it make sense to flesh out all the details. Second, we now know enough to formulate reasonably detailed accounts of the data in the literature—and these accounts will remain largely unchanged if it turns out that the preferred approach, resting on formal properties of the structure of images per se (stated in chapter 5), is incorrect. In a way, the actual mechanism of transformation is an autonomous component of the theory, with little else depending on the precise details. In fact, it is of some interest to note that the difficulties we experience in providing precise accounts in the following sections of this chapter have nothing to do with the details of the operation of the transformation mechanism itself.

2.0 CONSISTENCY AND GENERALIZATION TESTS

Let us now take our model at its present stage of development and try to provide accounts for the empirical findings on image transformations. The three kinds of transformations that have received the most attention are rotation, size change, and scanning. Thus, I will devote a section below to each of these topics. In addition, I will briefly mention some work on miscellaneous image transformations in the fourth section. Let us begin with a review of work on mental rotation, given that (partly for historical reasons) the bulk of work in the field is on this topic.

2.1 Mental Rotation

The first experiment on mental rotation that required people to use a memory representation (as opposed to having them compare two physically present stimuli, as in Shepard and Metzler, 1971) was performed by Shepard and Klun (described in Cooper and Shepard, 1973). In this experiment, subjects were given single letters or digits at different orientations. The alphanumeric characters were asymmetric (for example, F, G, J, R, 2, 5), and could appear at various tilted orientations about the circle. Half the time the character was presented facing the normal direction, and half the time it was presented mirror-reversed; the subject's task was to decide, as quickly as possible, whether it was normal or reversed. Two results of interest emerged from this experiment: (1) Verification time increased, although not linearly, with the degree of angular departure of the character from the standard upright; and (2) subjects took less time to respond "normal" than to respond "backward." Subjects reported mentally rotating the character into the standard upright and then classifying the direction it faced. Shepard and Klun performed a second experiment wherein subjects again were asked to decide whether characters were normal or backward, and the orientation at which the characters were presented was again varied. In this experiment, however, before the stimulus was presented, subjects were told its identity and/or orientation. The advance information was presented auditorially: letters were named and positions on the clock (such as, "the six o'clock position") were used to indicate orientation. The following results were obtained: (1) With no advance information, evaluation times increased with the angular departure from the standard upright of the figure. (2) When either identity or orientation information was presented alone, verification times again increased with angular departure. (3) But when both kinds of advance information were given, verification times varied much less for different degrees of tilt, and, for some subjects, were the same regardless of the orientation of the figure. Because the subjects in this experiment who did show differences for different degrees of orientation claimed to have difficulty in forming an image when receiving the identity and orientation information aurally, Cooper and Shepard conducted an additional experiment to rectify this possible problem.

Cooper and Shepard (1973) used the same task as had Shepard and Klun but modified it in several ways. They presented the advance information visually: the identity of a test stimulus was provided by showing the subject an outline drawing of the normal, upright version of the stimulus, and orientation was indicated by a drawing of an arrow pointing in the direction at which the top of the character would appear. The experiment now included five conditions: (1) no advance information at all (this replicated Shepard and Klun's first experiment); (2) identity information only; (3) orientation information only; (4) both identity and orientation information, presented in a single display of an outline of the test stimulus which was displayed at the correct orientation (this display was presented for two seconds, followed by a blank field for one second before the stimulus was presented); and (5) both identity and orientation information, presented separately (an outline of the upcoming stimulus at the standard orientation would appear, followed two seconds later by an arrow).

The fifth condition was in turn divided into four conditions by varying the time that the orientation cue was made available from 100 to 1000 milliseconds. The notion was that if subjects are rotating an image of the test stimulus, then they may not successfully complete this transformation before the test stimulus is presented if they are given only a brief time to prepare. And if they are not prepared, then the orientation of the test stimulus should affect verification times. But to the degree that an image was readied at the appropriate orientation, the orientation of the test stimulus would not affect verification times. The major results of this experiment are presented in figure 8.6. As is apparent, only when both identity and orientation information were presented was the orientation of the test stimulus irrelevant (note that only one of the four subconditions of condition 5 is presented in figure 8.6, the one in which the orientation cue was left on a full second). When only orientation or only identity information was given, or no advance information was given at all, Cooper and Shepard replicated the earlier results from Shepard and Klun's first experi-

3. ROTATION OF MENTAL IMAGES

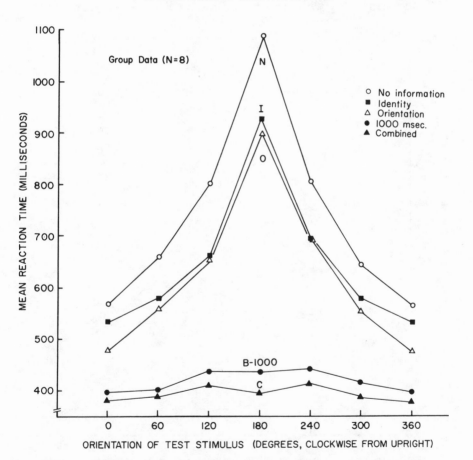

Figure 8.6. Results of the first experiment reported by Cooper and Shepard (1973). This graph illustrates the mean time to evaluate stimuli presented at different orientations in the five different conditions.

ment. Again, times increased with angular departure from the standard upright to l80 degrees, but the increase was not linear. Figure 8.7 presents the results from all four of the conditions in which identity information and orientation information were presented sequentially. The important result here is that when more time was allowed for subjects to mentally rotate the image to the indicated orientation, the actual orientation of the test stimulus had a diminished effect on verification times. When a full second was allowed, the results were virtually the same as when the identity and orientation information were presented in a single figure. The fact that more time was required for further amounts of rotation is a Class 1 (confirmation) result, but uninterestingly so. Of primary importance here is the Class 3 (theory supplementation) finding that time apparently did not increase linearly with amount of rotation. Because this result is very

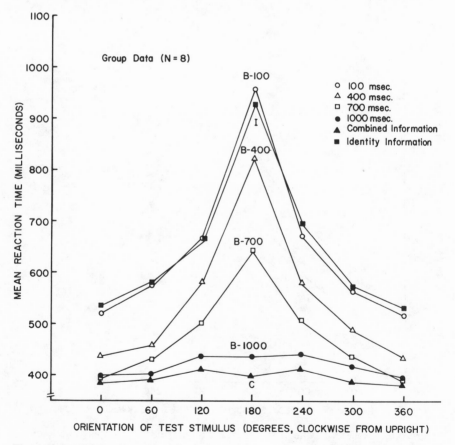

Figure 8.7. Time to evaluate figures in the first experiment reported by Cooper and Shepard (1973) when identity information was presented ahead of time.

sensitive to the paradigm used, I will defer providing an account until we have considered more data.

Cooper and Shepard (1973) conducted a second experiment with an eye toward explaining the nonlinearity in their rotation effects (which was unexpected if a constant rotation rate is assumed) and examining the sense in which images were "rotated." The logic underlying this experiment hinges on the notion that if images are actually rotated they should pass through intermediate points along the trajectory to the final orientation. Subjects imaged an alphanumeric character rotating 60 degrees clockwise every time a cue was given. At a random point, a normal or backward version of the character was presented; half the time this test stimulus was in the orientation that the subjects should have been imaging at the time, and half the time it was not. If subjects really possess a template-image that is moving through each of the 60-degree steps, then the absolute orientation of a test stimulus should not affect time to make a normal/backward discrimination when the stimulus and the image are in the same orientation. If the image and test stimulus are in different orientations, however, then more time should be required as more rotation is necessary to bring them into congruence.

On a given trial, a subject was shown an outline of the character and then received the command "up," which cued him or her to generate an image and begin rotating it from the standard upright orientation. This image was "projected" into a blank circle that had six small tick marks staggered at 60-degree intervals along the border. Every time the subjects heard the cue "tip," they were to rotate their image clockwise to the next mark (the cues occurred every half-second). The words "up" and "down" were used as cues for the 0-degree and 180-degree orientations, respectively, to help the subject keep track of the cues. The probe stimulus appeared at one of the six orientations, and the subject classified the direction the figure faced. The results when the probe was in the expected position are illustrated in figure 8.8. In this case, the average increase from 0 degrees to 180 degrees is now around 80 to 90 milliseconds, as compared to 400 to 500 milliseconds in the previous experiment when no advance information was given. In addition, subjects were faster when the stimulus was in the normal direction—which presumably matched their images; when the figure was reversed, additional time may have been required to decide if it required further rotation (or, "negative" responses may simply require an extra response operation, as suggested by Clark and Chase, 1972). Figure 8.9 illustrates times when the test stimulus appeared at an unexpected orientation. Here, times increased dramatically and linearly as the orientation of the test stimulus increasingly diverged from that of the image. In fact, the overall increase from 0 degrees to 180 degrees was around 400 milliseconds, suggesting that people reoriented their images into congruence with the stimulus (as will be dis-

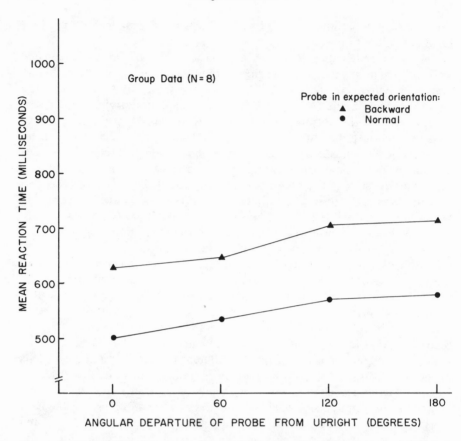

Figure 8.8. Results of the second experiment reported by Cooper and Shepard (1973). These data are from trials in which the image of the stimulus was rotated different amounts from the standard upright and the test stimulus was presented at the same orientation as that of the image.

cussed shortly). Finally, figure 8.10 presents the time necessary to evaluate the direction of a character when the image was at one particular absolute orientation and the character at another; note that the farther the image is from the standard upright, the less well it serves as a template, if we evaluate only the 0-degree departure condition. Further, there is again a nonlinear relation between departure from the upright and reaction time.

Some aspects of Cooper and Shepard's data fall in Class 3 (theory supplementation) vis-à-vis our theory and model, requiring the introduction of additional principles (some of which are uninteresting because they are so task-specific). We can account for Cooper and Shepard's results if we make the following assumptions: (1) Subjects can identify which of a small set of alphanumeric characters is present relatively easily even when the character is in nonstandard orientations (as Cooper and Shepard also assume). In our model, this identification would involve using the FIND procedures to identify criterial attributes. (2) Subjects can identify the top of the figure regardless of orientation. Again, the top may be identified by executing a series of tests like those used by FIND. For example, presumably people know that the top of a letter *R* is the rounded part bordering on an enclosed region at the opposite end of the opening formed by the legs. (3) Once the top is identified, the figure may be rotated the shortest way around to the standard upright. (4) An image may serve as a template which is compared to a test stimulus. In our model, the match would be performed as discussed in chapter 7, section 2.3.2. (5) The image is ro-

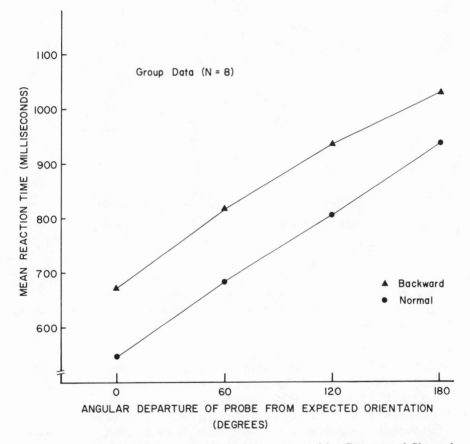

Figure 8.9. Results of the second experiment reported by Cooper and Shepard (1973). These data are from trials in which the image of the stimulus was rotated different amounts relative to the orientation of the test stimulus.

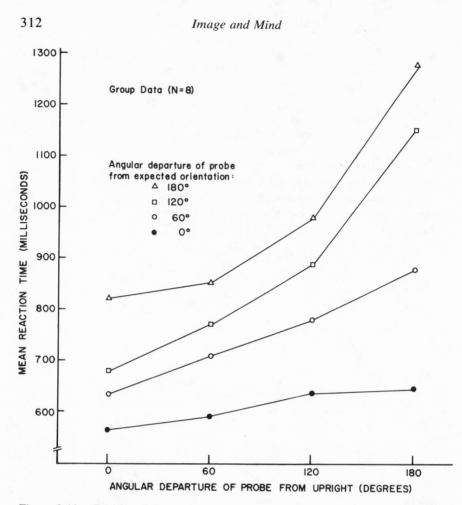

Figure 8.10. Results of the second experiment reported by Cooper and Shepard (1973). This graph illustrates the mean evaluation times as a function of angular departure of the test stimulus from the standard upright orientation. These data are plotted separately for each of the four angular departures of the test stimulus from the orientation of the image. (Times to evaluate normal and backward test stimuli are averaged together here.)

tated only as far as necessary in order to make the requisite discrimination. (6) When the image has been rotated beforehand, portions have faded and it is less sharp than when it is in its original orientation. And when the image is more degraded, it is a less effective template.

Given these assumptions, we can explain the major findings of Cooper and Shepard's (1973) experiments as follows:

1. Time to evaluate a stimulus increased monotonically with the deviation in its orientation from the standard upright when no advance informa-

tion was given. This result makes sense if people identify the figure, identify its top, and then rotate it to the standard upright. This will be necessary only if the procedures that perform the normal/backward discrimination are effective only when the figure is relatively upright, which places another constraint on the operation of the FIND procedures in our model. It is of some interest to note that it was equally easy to rotate in either direction, which is exactly as expected given the rotation routines in our model.

2. When the subject was not given advance information about the identity and orientation of the test stimulus, the increase in evaluation times itself increased with further deviations from the standard upright. This nonlinearity in increasing time may be due to the fact that the normal/backward evaluation procedure (which is used on a single letter) does not require that a figure be rotated all the way to the upright; thus, for small angular deviations, little if any rotation is necessary to assess the direction in which a figure faces, resulting in the bow-shaped curves evident in figures 8.6 and 8.7. We will develop this idea further and consider an experiment investigating it shortly.

3. When the subject was given advance information about the orientation and identity of a figure, times increased linearly with the angular disparity between the expected and presented orientation of the test stimulus. In this case, the subject rotated an image to the expected orientation (in accordance with the tilt of an arrow or of the study stimulus in the first experiment, or in a sequence of 60-degree steps, one per cue, in the second); when the test stimulus was presented it was mapped into the visual buffer, the top of it was identified, and the initial image was rotated into congruence with it. In this case, a template match was performed in making the discrimination. This is unlike the case in which a single letter is presented, imaged, and rotated to the point where the evaluation procedures can assess the direction in which it faces. When these procedures are used, the image has to be rotated only far enough for the discrimination to be made, as we shall see shortly. When a prior image is available, however, a template match may be more efficient (if the image has not been held too long). In this case, the image is rotated fully into congruence, resulting in linear increases in times with amount of angular disparity between the orientation of the image and test stimulus. Note that on this account the linear effects observed in figure 8.9 are due to rotating an available image so it can be used as a template, whereas the nonlinear findings occur when there is no prior image to be used as a template, and hence an image of the test stimulus is formed and rotated and then evaluated by searching for direction-specifying features. I must admit that I find it somewhat odd that even when a normal stimulus was presented upright, more time was taken to respond when the image was formed at greater departures from the stimulus orientation. But the times obtained

when stimuli were presented upright and FIND-like interpretive procedures were purportedly used (see figure 8.6) are much faster than when
the test stimulus was upright but the image was upside down in the second
experiment (see figure 8.10). Although the model can in fact explain these
results, the account seems flawed to me. It simply is not clear why mental
image comparison was necessary in this condition. It is hared to believe
that subjects really found it easier to rotate the image and perform a
template match when test stimuli were presented at the standard upright
in the second experiment. According to this account, then, there is a
strategic variable here, and the subjects may have used rotation and template matching even when this was not an optimal strategy in this one
condition, perhaps because this procedure was most efficient in the other
conditions and a kind of "habit-set" was formed. This is not satisfying,
and I would hope that a more principled account could be motivated by
collection of new data.

4. When the image was rotated prior to presentation of the test stimulus, slightly, but only slightly, more time was required for test stimuli at
orientations farther from the standard upright when the image was in the
same orientation as the test stimulus. Presumably, the farther one had to
rotate the image, the more faded it became and the poorer it was as a template. (The slight increases in time here mirror those found in the experiment Shwartz performed, as will be discussed below, but are less extreme; this makes sense if Cooper and Shepard's subjects were able to
form better images in general of the highly familiar alphanumeric
characters than Shwartz's subjects were able to form of the novel Attneave forms.) This supposition is further supported by the fact that even
more extreme effects of deviation from the standard upright were found
when the test stimulus was not at the expected orientation (see figure
8.10). The family of curves in figure 8.10 is easily explained by a model in
which the image fades with time, so that as more time passes while it is
being rotated (both initially and after the probe is presented) it becomes a
less effective template. In fact, it is possible that the initial image (formed
from advance information) is so degraded by the time it is rotated 180 degrees that the subjects cannot use it at all. In this case, they revert to the
strategy of rotating an image of the test stimulus to the standard upright
and look for direction-specifying features, just as they do when no advance information is given (this strategy will produce the bow shape in the
top curve of figure 8.10 if the image of the test stimulus does not need to
be rotated fully to the upright position).

5. When identity and orientation information were given sequentially,
the effects of angular departure from the upright were increasingly
evident as less time was given to study the orientation information. Presumably rotation takes time, and if the test stimulus is presented before an
initial image is fully rotated into position, time is required to complete the
rotation. The greater the angular departure from the upright, the longer it

takes to rotate the image, and hence the less likely it is that the image will be fully rotated into position when the test stimulus is presented. Also, the farther the test probe is from the standard upright, the more additional rotation will be necessary to bring the image into proper position after the probe is presented. On this account, if preparation time of 400 milliseconds or less is allowed, subjects will not generate a useful image before seeing the test stimulus. In this case, they will revert to imaging the test probe itself and rotating and evaluating this image. Thus, the nonlinearity in times for different angular disparities evident in figure 8.7 for 100 and 400 milliseconds of preparation time resembles those found when identity and orientation information were not given (this nonlinearity, I claim, is caused by the way the FIND-like classification procedures operate). When 700 milliseconds or more are allowed before seeing the test stimulus, a reasonably good image can be generated and used as a template. Although this image may not be fully rotated at the time of probe, it still can serve as a template, resulting in fairly linear increases in time with larger angular disparities (see figure 8.7). Although we can provide an account of the data, we are still left with a nagging question: Why did subjects image the figure at the upright position and then rotate it? We address this question in the next paragraph, in confronting the lack of effects of orientation-only advance information.

6. When the subject was given advance information about *only* the identity or the orientation, times increased with angular departure from the standard upright orientation. This makes sense in the context of our model. With only one of these kinds of information, an image cannot be generated and rotated into the proper orientation to be used as an effective template; thus, an image of the test stimulus itself must be formed, rotated, and examined (producing nonlinear increases with angular disparity). It is especially important that advance information of the orientation alone was not enough to eliminate the rotation effects: If subjects found it easy to update the orientation of a represented stimulus simply by altering the spatial relations in the deep representation (by inserting a constant to be added to or subtracted from the Θ values, in our model), knowing the upcoming orientation would allow them to set the orientation parameter so that the image could be transformed in a single step to the upright. In our model, however, the FIND procedures are orientation-specific; they cannot locate the foundation parts upon which to image details of an object if the skeleton is at a nonstandard orientation. Thus, we are led to predict that only skeletal images will be able to be generated at arbitrary orientations. Note that if propositional models of the sort described by Anderson (1978) were correct, advance information about orientation should be able to be used to update the appropriate relations in a single operation, regardless of the size of the value of the parameter, and the present results would not have been obtained.

7. When the subject was given advance information about only the ori-

entation or identity of a figure, times were reduced overall (but more time was still required when the test stimulus was presented at greater tilts). This is a Class 3 (theory supplementation) or Class 4 (domain contamination) finding. We could explain it by assuming that subjects "save" an encoding operation when they know either the location of the top or which figure will be presented. Since we have not modeled perceptual encoding mechanisms, we cannot explain how these kinds of "set" effects operate.

8. Finally, evaluation times were faster when stimuli faced their normal direction than when they were reversed. As usual, we are weak on explaining the effects of response type. This result is in Class 4 (domain contamination), falling outside the domain of the present theory: It could be due to a response-set effect, as suggested by Clark and Chase (1972); they propose that people are set to respond "true," and have to alter an output command if a "false" response is appropriate. Alternatively, since we are more familiar with the normal orientations, we may recognize them and respond quickly, whereas we may be hesitant to respond "backward" if we do not recognize the normal direction because the figures may simply be at a nonstandard tilt. (We have no way of sorting among these possibilities given the present data.)

The one seemingly awkward result of Cooper and Shepard's experiments, from the point of view of our model, is that verification times did not increase linearly with angular disparity from the standard upright when no advance information was given. I have appealed to this result above in arguing that in some conditions subjects used images as templates and in some they imaged and rotated the test stimulus itself. The problem now is how to account for this nonlinearity when a single image is rotated and inspected. Two possible explanations of this result come to mind: First, one could claim that the image "accelerates" as it overcomes "inertia" in its rotation. This account is unappealing in that (a) it takes the picture metaphor too literally, and (b) it does not explain why time to evaluate a test stimulus increased linearly with the disparity between its orientation and that of an image that was generated beforehand (in the conditions where both orientation and identity information were provided beforehand). Second, the evaluation procedures that establish the direction in which a figure is facing may be effective only when the figure is oriented more or less vertically. This account assumes that when no advance information is given a template match is not performed. I see two viable versions of this hypothesis: On one view, the evaluation procedures simply cannot operate correctly until the figure is correctly aligned in the visual buffer, but this need not be the full standard upright; thus, the image does not need to be rotated much for small tilts, but must be rotated an increasing proportion of the distance to the upright for greater tilts. On the other view, the discrimination becomes more difficult as the image is rotated farther because the image fades, and hence increasingly more time is required when the stimulus is presented at further tilts.

An ingenious experiment performed by Hock and Tromley (1978) provides some support for the first version of this last hypothesis. Hock and Tromley hypothesized that a figure must be rotated so that the top of the figure is the uppermost point in the picture plane; only then can the direction in which the figure is facing be assessed. In the context of our model, this is a claim about how the FIND procedures operate. This notion was motivated by findings (by, for example, Rock and Heimer, 1957; Attneave and Olson, 1967) that memory representations for familiar stimuli are coded in terms of an assignment for the "top." Hock and Tromley tested this idea by selecting stimuli that would need to be rotated different amounts before the top of the figure would be in the topmost part of the picture plane. *L* and *J* need to be rotated relatively little from a horizontal orientation before the tops are the highest part of the display, whereas a very circular *G* and *e* need to be rotated fully before the top is the highest part of the picture, and *R* and *F* are intermediate cases. Thus, Hock and Tromley expected greater departures from nonlinearity when *L* and *J* were used as stimuli than when *G* and *e* were used. The most basic Shepard and Klun paradigm was used to test this idea, with no advance information being presented before the test stimulus. The letters or their mirror-reversals were presented at one of nine different orientations, staggered at 36-degree intervals about the circle. Subjects were simply asked to classify the figures as normal or backward.

The results of Hock and Tromley's experiment are presented in figure 8.11. As in the analogous condition in Cooper and Shepard's (1973) first experiment, times were longest when figures were presented at 180 degrees, suggesting that people rotated an image of the figure the shortest way to the upright. The important result was that there were significant nonlinear trends in the data for *L*, *J*, *F* and *R*—but not for *G* and *e*. Only for these very round figures did times increase linearly with increased angular disparity from the standard upright. It did in fact appear as if the other figures had to be rotated only to the point where the top of the figure was the highest point in the picture plane. Times increased linearly with rotations past 108 degrees for all figures, but the linear trends were not aligned with the 0-degree orientation for *L*, *J*, *F*, and *R* (as would be expected if the figures were in fact rotated to the full upright). In addition to these general findings, there was a particular prediction that I find especially convincing. A normal *F* has a broader range in which the top of the figure is at the top of the picture plane when it is rotated counterclockwise than when it is rotated clockwise, but vice versa for a mirror-reversed *F*. Thus, if the figure is rotated only until its top is at the top of the picture plane, we should find more extreme deviations from linear increases with degree of tilt when a normal *F* is rotated counterclockwise instead of clockwise, and when a mirror-reversed *F* is rotated clockwise instead of counterclockwise. This was in fact true. Not only does this finding provide support for Hock and Tromley's hypothesis, but it is at variance with

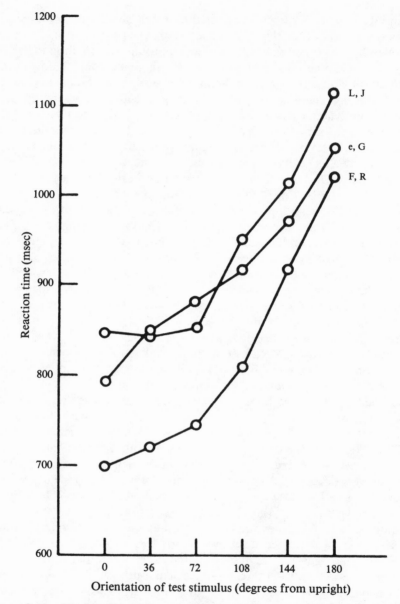

Figure 8.11. The results of the experiment performed by Hock and Tromley (1978). This graph illustrates the time to evaluate the direction of letters presented at different angular departures from the standard upright.

the view that the nonlinearities observed earlier are simply due to increased fading of images as they are rotated further.

The foregoing account rests on subjects being very familiar with the stimuli, familiar enough that evaluations can be made before the stimulus is at its full standard upright. Presumably, over the course of time one sees letters and digits at numerous orientations and learns enough about them to be able to classify the direction they face under a variety of circumstances. With relatively unfamiliar stimuli, however, people may not have this skill. Cooper's (1975) first experiment is relevant here. Cooper's subjects participated in the task used in the first experiment reported by Cooper and Shepard (1973). Instead of alphanumeric characters, however, these people first learned the six Attneave forms illustrated in figure 8.2. These forms were arbitrarily assigned a standard upright, and subjects learned to discriminate between a standard and a mirror-image version of each before the experiment proper. The forms Cooper used were found by Vanderplas and Garvin (1959) to have relatively little tendency to elicit verbal associations. The results of using these stimuli in the Shepard and Klun task, with no advance information, are illusrated in figure 8.12. There are three results of interest: (1) Cooper and Shepard's findings were replicated insofar as more time was required to evaluate figures rotated farther from the standard upright; (2) these results, unlike those of the Cooper and Shepard experiment, show no nonlinearity; and (3) overall times were greater than with the alphanumeric characters used before (a mean reaction time of around 875 milliseconds, versus 575 in the previous experiment); the rotation rates, however, are very similar in the two experiments (369 degrees per second here versus 360 before). These data make sense if subjects rotated the figures to the full upright, which was necessary because the evaluation procedures used to decide which direction a figure faced can only operate when the figure is fully upright. This restriction would follow from the fact that subjects initially learned this discrimination with only upright figures. The mean difference again could reflect time to delimit the region around the figure and/or to regenerate it prior to beginning rotation. This makes sense if the Attneave forms on the average have more complex contours than do the letters and digits Cooper and Shepard used.

Cooper (1976) reports a further extension of the second experiment conducted by Cooper and Shepard (1973). In this experiment the same subjects tested in the Cooper (1975) experiments were again tested, using the same set of Attneave random polygons as stimuli. Subjects saw a stimulus at the standard upright orientation, it was removed, and then a blank circle was presented. As soon as the circle appeared the subjects were to image the form and begin to rotate it within the circle at their "normal" rate. Shortly thereafter, a test stimulus was presented at some orientation about the circle, and the subject was to decide if it faced nor-

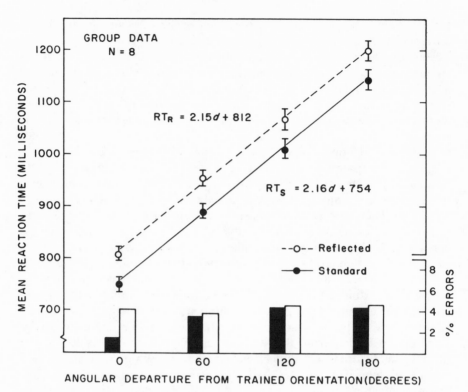

Figure 8.12. The mean evaluation times when test forms were presented at different angular disparities from the trained orientation in Cooper's (1975) first experiment. Solid bars represent errors when figures were in the trained orientation, and open bars when they were mirror-reversed.

mally or was mirror-reversed. The trick here is that Cooper used the rotation rates calculated in her earlier experiments to predict how a given person's image would be oriented after a given amount of time had elapsed following presentation of the circle. Cooper presented the test stimuli either at the orientation at which a given person's image should be, or at a 60, 120 or 180 degree angular disparity from this orientation. Further, on the trials where the stimulus was presented at the predicted orientation in the image, the orientation was either a familiar one (one of the six positions about the circle—staggered at 60 degree intervals—used in the previous experiments) or an unfamiliar one falling between the positions used previously. The results were exactly as one would expect on the basis of the Cooper and Shepard (1973) results: When the test stimulus was presented at the predicted orientation of the image, there were no differences in the times to make matches to test stimuli presented at different orientations. This was true both for the familiar orientations and the unfamiliar ones; further, no more time was required to make matches at the novel positions. This is especially impressive because these novel positions were used on only 36 of the total of 252 trials. These results, then, support the notion that people really do rotate images along a trajectory, passing through intermediate positions. The results when test stimuli were presented at orientations disparate from the predicted orientation of the image were also as expected: now, times increased linearly with the angular disparity between the orientation of the test stimulus and the predicted orientation of the image. Further, the increase in time with greater angular disparities was the same as that observed in Cooper's earlier experiments. The result from these "unexpected orientation" trials are critical: without this finding, it could be argued that the stimuli were simply categorized equally easily at all orientations, without ever being rotated at all. These findings, then, mirror those of Cooper and Shepard and can be explained in exactly the same way. However, these results force us to posit that if images are transformed in increments, in rotation these increments are less than or equal to 30 degrees.

Recall that Shwartz (1979) used the Cooper and Podgorny paradigm to study the effects of size and complexity on rotation rate. Although this experiment was conducted primarily to collect the rotation times described above, the subjects also matched their images to test stimuli. The results from the same/different task were less straightforward than those from the rotation task that preceded it. The only findings that were exactly as expected were those for "same" responses when the test stimulus was at the orientation specified by the cue or ±30 degrees from this orientation. In this case, subjects were faster when the test stimulus was at the expected orientation. This result makes sense if subjects could perform a template match with their image as discussed in chapter 7; when the stimulus was not at the expected orientation, times may have increased because the image had to be rotated prior to comparison. This account, however, does not lead one to expect that the absolute orientation of the test stimulus would matter, but Shwartz found that it did. That is, for "same" judgments, comparisons required more time when the image had to be rotated farther in preparation for the test stimulus. There are a number of possible accounts for this result. First, perhaps the subjects did not fully rotate their images prior to preparation. This possibility raises worries that the less complex and smaller images were not rotated as far, on the average, as the more complex and larger ones—and this is why there were effects of complexity and size on rotation time. If so, then we would expect that *more* time should be required to match less complex and smaller stimuli, since at the time of comparison these images would require more adjustment than larger and more complex images. This was not found; in fact, less time was required to match the less complex and smaller stimuli. A second possible account is that more complex images faded more by the time they were rotated into position, and hence were more difficult to use as templates. This would make some sense because more complex and larger images required longer to rotate, and hence had more opportunity to degrade. This account does not help us to understand why angle mattered only for "same" judgments, however. A third account places this result in Class 4 (domain contamination) by focusing on the very high error rates found in this experiment, which were a consequence of Shwartz's desire to force the subjects to prepare fully for the discrimination task by rotating the complete image into position. Perhaps subjects simply had a higher criterion for responding "same" when images had been rotated farther. A raised criterion might reflect subjects' awareness of how much images faded or became distorted when they were rotated greater amounts. The fact that there were slightly fewer errors for the 180-degree condition (which also had longer times) than for the other conditions is consistent with this hypothesis. This criterion notion would also explain why only the "same" comparison times varied systematically with angular disparity from the initial upright: Subjects may simply have been more conservative before making a "same" judgment, resulting in more careful comparison before responding. This conjecture is consistent with both the longer times for "same" responses than for "different" ones and the higher error rates for "different" judgments. Perhaps the best hypothesis for how subjects decided whether something was "different" is that they made some kind of initial rough similarity assessment and responded "different" if the test stimulus was sufficiently unlike the study stimulus. If the test stimulus was not sufficiently unlike the study stimulus, however, a more careful comparison would be completed. In any event, it is interesting to note in passing that data from unpracticed subjects sometimes is very different—and noisier, of course—from data obtained from highly motivated, practiced subjects.

Another experiment of this sort was conducted by Shepard and Feng (reported in Shepard, 1975), who demonstrated that when images are rotated information that was not previously apparent becomes available to the subject. Shepard and Feng's subjects were asked to report what they saw when a particular operation or sequence of operations was performed on a letter; the letter was not actually shown, but merely named. For example, a subject might be asked "What results when you rotate 90 degrees to the left the following capital letter: N." The time between presentation of the test letter, N in this case, and the subject's response, Z here, was measured. Subjects were asked at various times to use rotations of 90 degrees counterclockwise, rotations of 180 degrees, reflections about the vertical axis or horizontal axis, and the double reflection about the vertical axis followed by a reflection around the horizontal axis. The letters M, N, W, Z, P, b, and d were used as stimuli. The subject either reported the new letter it became, reported that it remained the same letter, or re-

ported that it became a nameless form after the specified transforma-
tion(s). Ninety-degree rotations were the fastest transformation, and the
double reflection required the most time of all. Interestingly, although 180-
degree rotations and double reflections result in identical images, there
was a 900-millisecond difference between the two. This demonstrates that
subjects were in fact doing something different internally in performing
the task upon being given the two instructions. Most important, perhaps,
is the fact that subjects were able to perform this task at all, were able to
see new patterns emerge as a consequence of performing the requisite
transformations. This is expected, of course, given the way the image-inspection processes operate in our model. We have not implemented
letter-identification procedures, but—given the limited number of alternatives—it is clear how one could implement an ad hoc set of FIND procedures to do the job. We have not bothered with this exercise, having no
theory of the correct FIND procedures to simulate human pattern recognition. But again, this result places constraints on how we should further
expand the model into the more general domain of pattern recognition.

2.1.1 Mental Rotation: A Visual Process?

I want to conclude this section with a discussion of an experiment purportedly demonstrating mental rotation in the blind. This experiment is of
interest here for two reasons: First, if it is correct, it opens an entire bag
of worms, suggesting that the foregoing results may have nothing to do
with the processing of visual mental images. Second, in discussing this
work I will again justify my criteria for choosing which data the theory
should explain. Marmor and Zaback (1976) studied mental rotation in the
blind by using a tactile analogue to the Shepard and Metzler (1971) task,
which involves comparing two stimuli presented side by side but in different orientations. Three groups of people served as subjects in this experiment: early blind subjects, who had lost their sight before five years of
age; late blind subjects, who had been sighted until the age of 15 or so; and
sighted adults wearing blindfolds. Late blind subjects were of special interest because of Jastrow's (1888) interview study, wherein he reported
that adults blinded after the age of seven claim to dream in visual imagery
but that adults blinded before age five make no such claim. Subjects
received pairs of teardrop-shaped wedges with rounded edges. A curved
"bite" was taken out of either the right or the left side of a wedge, and all
four possible combinations of bite positions were presented. Further, the
stimuli were presented at different relative orientations. The subject's
task was to use touch alone to determine, as quickly as possible, whether
both forms had bites taken out of the same sides. A clock started as soon
as the subject touched a form and stopped when he or she pushed either of
two foot pedals. The left stimulus was always aligned at the full upright,

and the right was rotated 0, 30, 60, 120, or 150 degrees clockwise. In addition to measuring decision times proper, Marmor and Zaback conducted separate trials requiring subjects simply to push the pedal as soon as they could locate the rounded top of the right stimulus. This time increased with increasing rotation, and was used as a correction factor for the decision times. That is, this identification time was subtracted from the time to make the bite-location comparison. Even after making this correction, decision times still increased linearly with the disparity in orientation between the two figures. The rotation rates were 59, 114, and 233 degrees per second for early blind, late blind, and sighted subjects, respectively; the rates for the two blind groups were not significantly different, nor were the rates for the late blind and sighted subjects. Times did not increase linearly with angular disparity for the early blind and sighted; Marmor and Zaback suggest that this may reflect use of a verbal strategy, which allowed easy assessment of 150- and 120-degree disparities by searching for the tip and using it as an anchor point for the "bite": If the bite was on the same side for both stimuli and the points were in the same direction, the stimuli were the same, otherwise they were different. The sighted and late blind were faster overall than the early blind in performing this task, and made fewer errors. Finally, 63 percent, 94 percent, and 69 percent of the early blind, late blind, and sighted, respectively, reported after the experiment using some form of mental rotation.

Although I find Marmor and Zaback's results interesting, they probably belong in Class 4 (domain contamination) vis-à-vis our model; I am not sure that they bear on the issue of what is being mentally rotated in the experiments discussed in the previous parts of this chapter. Unlike the foregoing experiments, this one does not depend on manipulating some internal representation per se. That is, one presumably can perform this task by touching the figures in corresponding places. If so, then the relevant variable is how much time is required to locate the corresponding regions. Although Marmor and Zaback tried to control for this by measuring the time to find the top, this was the wrong control. Surely it is more difficult to locate a bite than the top, and there is no guarantee that this difficulty does not increase with tilt as sharply as did the comparison times. Thus, the identification-time correction used here does not preclude the possibility that comparison times are determined by the time to locate the bite on the rightmost figure. This kind of comparison process is prevented in the imagery tasks discussed above, simply because two stimuli are never physically present at the same time.

2.2 Adjusting the Apparent Size of Mental Images

Sekuler and Nash (1972) reported the first experiment on size transformation of mental representations. On a given trial, subjects saw two rectangles presented in rapid succession. The task was to decide, as quickly as possible, whether the height-to-width ratios of the two rectangles were the same. The centers of the rectangles were aligned, so that they would have appeared concentric if they had been presented simultaneously. The second rectangle was either the same size as the first, one of three larger sizes, or one of three smaller sizes. Further, the first rectangle itself was one of three sizes. The relative orientations of the two rectangles were also varied: On half the trials, the two rectangles had different height-width ratios; on one-quarter of the trials, they were the same form but rotated 90 degrees; and on the remaining quarter of the trials, they were identical in height-width ratio and orientation. Each combination of sizes occurred equally often in each of these conditions. The results of this experiment are presented in figure 8.13. As is evident, times increased roughly linearly both as the relative size disparity increased and when the

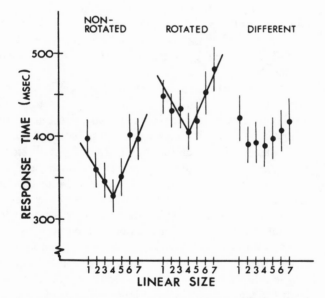

Figure 8.13. Results of the experiment reported by Sekuler and Nash (1972) in which subjects decided whether two consecutive rectangles had the same proportions. The graph illustrates mean response time as a function of the size of the second of two rectangles in a pair. The "nonrotated" rectangles had the same form and orientation, the "rotated" rectangles had the same form but differed by 90 degrees in their orientations in the frontal plane, and the "different" rectangles differed in their forms. In each case, the value 4 corresponds to the condition in which the two rectangles were the same size; smaller numbers indicate that the second rectangle was smaller than the first, and larger numbers indicate that it was larger.

angular orientation was different. The two effects, of size and orientation, were statistically independent in this experiment. The relative increases in time were roughly the same to expand or contract an image (presumably) the same amount; about 70 milliseconds were required to alter the size by 50 percent in either case. This result is inconsistent, the reader will recall, with the model positing that transformations occur by sequentially shifting portions and that small step sizes are used to prevent image fragmentation. If this model is valid, expansion should have sped up as the process progressed. Interestingly, it also took only around 70 milliseconds to rotate the image (if subjects did rotate it) 90 degrees, which is much faster than the times observed with the more complex stimuli of Cooper and Shepard (1973), Cooper (1975), and Cooper and Podgorny (1976); this finding could indicate, however, that the initial start-up time was faster or that these figures did not need to be rotated a full 90 degrees for the comparison to be performed. It is also worth noting that Shwartz and I found that around 300 milliseconds were required to shift the size of images of letters by 50 percent, which again may indicate that the rectangles did not have to be brought into congruence in order for the requisite comparison to be made. The finding that rotation and size alteration are additive is somewhat surprising, as no inherent constraints in the model lead one to expect this.

Hayes (1973) also reports an experiment that is relevant here. The single subject tested (Hayes himself) first saw a row of four dots, each separated from the next by half a degree. He visualized one of eight capital letters in an upright orientation either just fitting between the outer two dots (at a "large" size) or between the inner two dots (at a "small" size). As soon as the image was generated, he pressed a button and one of the letters appeared. Half the time it was at the size of the image, and half the time at the other size; further, for each size, half the time the letter was the same as that being imaged, and half the time it was not. The subject was to decide whether the letter was the same as the one he was imaging, irrespective of size. When the test stimulus was the same letter that was being imaged, verification times were an average of more than 60 milliseconds faster when the size of the presented letter matched the size of the image than when the sizes were incongruent; when a different letter appeared, there were no effects of image size. This result demonstrates that images can preserve subjective size, which is of course a Class 1 (confirmation) finding. Presumably, if the similarity between an image and the test stimulus is high enough, the image is scaled down to the same size as the stimulus and a template match performed. In this case, our model leads us to expect that the greater the disparity in sizes, the longer should be the difference in time. When the test probe and the image are not very similar, however, a relatively fast "different" response presumably can be generated without rescaling the image. (This basic sort of notion is also evident in the Smith, Shoben, and Rips (1974) model of semantic memory, where subtler decisions require more fine-grade processing than do grosser discriminations.) The fact that overall time to respond "different" was 77 milliseconds slower than time to respond "same" may simply indicate that the subject is predisposed to answer "same" and additional time is required to alter the response mechanism (see Clark and Chase, 1972). In addition, subjects may double check stimuli before responding "different," realizing that "same" stimuli may not initially look the same if they are at different sizes. Thus, the results with "different" stimuli fall in Class 3 (theory supplementation); our account rests on assumptions about the nature of the comparison process, which are not specified here. For present purposes, it is enough to see that plausible assumptions about these processes allow us easily to explain the relevant results. These results do not challenge the model; in fact they help to motivate its further development.

The only other experiments on size scaling of internal representations that meet our criteria of relevance were reported by Larsen and Bundesen (1978). In their first experiment, subjects viewed an Attneave form for one second, saw a blank field for two seconds, and then saw a second shape. The second shape was one of five sizes, and was the same as the initial shape or rotated upside down. The subject decided whether the shape was the same orientation as the original or not, regardless of size, as quickly as possible. Evaluation times increased linearly with the size ratio of the two figures, and "same" responses were faster than "different" ones. Interestingly, the increase in time for larger disparities in size was less severe when the second stimulus was larger than when the first stimulus was larger. The reader may recall that this result is predicted by the scheme in which portions are moved sequentially. Given the other results in the literature, however, it is not too surprising that Larsen and Bundesen did not replicate this difference in slopes in their other experiments. (In fact, in one experiment Shwartz and I found the reverse trend, with shallower effects for shrinking than for expansion; this finding also was not replicated —these experiments are tricky because so many strategic variables are present, like the possibility of rate adjustment and "blink transforms," as will be discussed.) Finally, Larsen and Bundesen interviewed their subjects about how they performed the task; all subjects (including Larsen and Bundesen themselves) claimed to have held the first figure in a "visual form." Several claimed that the image was highly schematic, however, and introspections were less clear about how the actual decision was reached.

Subjects in Larsen and Bundesen's second experiment received letters as stimuli, at one of four sizes. As before, "different" stimuli were simple 180-degree rotations of the test stimuli. In this experiment, there was a .75 probability that a stimulus would appear at the same size as the one on the prior test trial. Subjects were informed about this probability, and again were asked simply to decide whether each letter presented was normal or upside down. Two and a half seconds after each response, a new letter was presented. Subjects reported "setting themselves" for different sizes. Interestingly, evaluation times were faster when a stimulus appeared at the size cued by the previous stimulus. When the new stimulus was a different size from the cue, times increased with size, but not linearly. Instead, times increased with the log of the difference in sizes. It is of interest to note that these findings contradict the analogous results from Cooper and Shepard's (1973) first experiment in which presentation of orientation information only did not obviate rotation effects. Here, however, it would appear as if the size of a "frame of attention" in the visual field can be calibrated, independently of the particular stimulus about to be judged. If so, then it is possible that the data discussed above are a consequence of this factor—and not of mental adjustment time (with the exception of our own findings, which measured time to prepare for stimuli at different sizes). This possibility seems a little remote, however, given the consistent findings in the previous experiments that times increase linearly with size disparity and the findings here that times increase with the log of the size difference.

Larsen and Bundesen conducted another experiment to further examine the increases in time with the log of the disparity in the sizes of two stimuli. Subjects were again shown a series of slides, each of which displayed a single capital letter. Letters appeared at one of three sizes with linear size ratios. A "positive set" was defined as the letters A, B, and C or a subset thereof; negative letters were those falling between D and Z in the alphabet. As before, there was a .75 transitional probability that the same size would occur on the $n+1$ trial. A given positive set was used in a block of around 75 items. Because the positive set was so small, there were runs in which a given positive probe was repeated. The notion was that if an image of the probe lingers and is used in identifying the next probe, then a linear effect of size disparity between successive stimuli ought to occur when a given stimulus appears again. When a new probe appears, however, effects of the scale calibration of the sampling field, and not image-adjustment time, ought to be evident—producing the log effects with size disparity. The problem here is how the subjects know which kind of transformation to accomplish—altering the size of the image or altering the field from which they sample. Larsen and Bundesen claim that people attempt both operations in parallel, and whichever runs to completion first determines the characteristics of the data. And in fact, times that presumably reflect the image-matching process are generally faster than times purportedly produced by the scale-changing operation. Thus, if the image is altered and it does not match the stimulus, this process stops and the subject continues to recalibrate his or her "attentional field'' until the letter can be encoded and matched to the memory representations of items in the positive set. The results of this experiment were as expected: If the same letter was repeated in succession, times increased linearly with the difference in size. As one would expect if an image were in fact being matched, when stimulus repetitions appeared, there was only a slight effect of the number of items in the positive set; the small effect they did observe could simply reflect the fact that a given target appeared more often with smaller set sizes. When a stimulus was not a repetition of the previous one, however, times increased with the log of the size difference, presumably reflecting time to adjust the scope of one's field of attention. In addition, there now was a substantial effect of set size. This makes sense if the subject has to enter memory and search a list of the positive set items, as discussed in chapter 7. Peculiarly enough, in the stimulus repetition trials (where an image match supposedly occurred) there was a slight advantage for larger letters per se. This is a Class 2 (multiple interpretation) result, which might indicate that smaller images were less resolved and more difficult to compare; this effect was so tiny, however, averaging only 7 milliseconds, that I am loath to make much of it.

The results of this last experiment, then, suggest that there were two different factors operating in Larsen and Bundesen's second two experiments. First, images were being adjusted as in the foregoing experiments, in accordance with the transformation schemes in our model. In addition, however, subjects were able to set the range of the spatial field from which they would encode information. This latter process is outside the bounds of our theory, although we will have some speculations about similar imagery processes in the following chapter.

2.3 Scanning Visual Images

In our computer simulation, it was most parsimonious to treat scanning as another kind of image transformation. That is, instead of a region of activation moving across an image, the image itself moves across the structure in which it occurs, such that different portions of the imaged object fall under the central, most highly resolved region. This account was appealing because it explained why one seems to scan across intermediate points in the course of reaching some target area of an image. Just as rotations proceed in increments to prevent disruption of the image, so too the position of the image shifts gradually across the visual buffer. Let us first consider some of the work discussed in chapter 3 and then turn to work in the literature.

The first experiment in which the time to scan mental images was measured was reported by me in 1973. In this experiment, I found that the farther people had to scan from some initial focus point to a target, the more time was taken. Further, it was equally easy to scan in any direction. These results are in Class 1 (confirmation), and are explained in our model because when longer distances were scanned the image would have to be shifted farther through the visual buffer before the target region was centered (and hence most sharply in focus). Since positional shifts occur in increments, more increments are required for longer distances. Further, the time per increment is independent of the direction in which points are shifted.

The original scanning experiment was flawed, however, because more parts of the image had to be scanned over when one scanned longer distances. Thus, Lea (1975) argued that subjects may encode lists of propositions describing parts of objects and scenes, and that ordering in this list mirrors ordering on the object or in the scene. My results were reinterpreted as showing that subjects had to scan farther down a list of properties when the target was farther away. Lea performed three experiments, the results of which seemed more consistent with his view than mine. In his first experiment, subjects received a list of 12 buildings on the Carnegie-Mellon campus (where the work was done); these buildings are arranged in a circular pattern on campus. After the subjects had memorized these locations, they were given 12 concrete words and asked to associate each word with a separate location. Following this, the subjects participated in a reaction-time task. There were two kinds of trials in this task. In the locus condition, the experimenter named a starting location and the subject responded as quickly as possible by naming a building n locations from that (in a given direction). Subjects received blocks of trials in which n was 1, 2, or 3. In the item condition, subjects performed the same task but named the word associated with the specified location rather than the location itself. Half the subjects named locations or items in a clockwise direction from the starting location, and half named them in a counterclockwise direction. Lea found that 643 milliseconds were required to name a location for each additional step from the starting point, and an additional 373 milliseconds were added onto this time to name the item associated with a location. There were no effects of distance per se here in a post hoc analysis, nor did it take different amounts of time to scan different directions. There were some effects of which particular location served as the starting place, but the details of the form of these interactions are not given. (They may simply reflect differences in familiarity or the like with the different locations.)

Lea's second experiment was like the first but made use of a drawing of a park scene with 12 objects arranged in a circle for stimuli, as illustrated in figure 8.14. This circle was constructed so that the distance between two adjacent points was one, two, three, or four units, which allowed Lea to examine the effects of distance per se in a systematic way. The subjects were first asked to learn a picture so they could "visualize it." Subjects

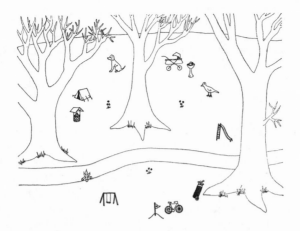

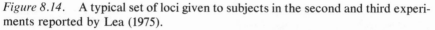

Figure 8.14. A typical set of loci given to subjects in the second and third experiments reported by Lea (1975).

again associated items with locations, and again participated in the reaction-time naming task used earlier. In this experiment, 960 milliseconds were required to scan each additional item, and an additional 284 milliseconds were required to name an associated word instead of just the location. Oddly, the additional time to retrieve an associated word was only marginally significant; Lea speculates that some subjects may have scanned the items and retrieved the locations from these encodings (if so, this should be evident in individual subject data, which was not reported). The physical distance between locations again did not affect retrieval time, and subjects again could scan equally easily in either direction.

The final experiment in Lea's paper utilized the same task, but subjects were asked to report locations and items up to five away from the initial starting point. The qualitative results were again the same, more time being required to scan over additional locations, but now fully 1139 milliseconds were required for each additional location scanned over, and 972 additional milliseconds were required to report an associated word instead of the location itself. As before, there was no difference in time to scan different distances per se.

As discussed in chapter 3, Kosslyn, Ball, and Reiser (1978) conducted a series of experiments to discover whether distance in itself affects scanning time. Our conclusion was a rousing "yes!" How do we reconcile our findings with Lea's failure to discover that distance affects scanning time? First, Lea never actually told his subjects to scan an image of the array; he told them only to learn it via visualization and to begin at a set location. Thus, it may be that subjects used a propositional list in his task. The metered search task itself certainly is well suited to processing ordered lists, and I suspect that the amount of material in the stimulus arrays exceeds the amount one can image easily or clearly. The problem with this account, however, is why the scan times were so slow; we have earlier claimed that scanning through lists of propositions is a relatively fast operation, and will develop this claim in the following chapter. Second, as is evident in figure 8.14, several features of the picture (the tree, stream) cut across the scan path between close items; this presumably would contaminate the effects of distance per se, being equivalent to introducing more items to scan over. Finally, Lea found larger increases in time to scan over each additional item than I found to scan across an entire image of a line drawing (Kosslyn, 1973); often these line drawings had more than a single property falling between the two ends (see figure 3.2). The huge increase in time per item in Lea's experiment suggests that subjects were doing very different things in his task and in my task. The nonscanning components of Lea's search task may simply have drowned out any effects of distance. But we have no real reason to expect effects of distance: Perhaps scanning an image simply never occurred in this task. Given the learning procedure it seems likely that subjects had labeled images of each item in the arrays, as well as information stringing them together. In our model, each item would have its own PRP and IMG file, and the PRP file could contain an entry indicating the next item in either direction. If the PRP file also contained the name of a word associated with the location there would be no need ever to use imagery in performing this task: One would simply have to look up each successive entry in each item's PRP file until the correct number of steps was counted. This process presumably would take more time than scanning an existent image or searching through a single PRP file. When a given item was looked up, its IMG file could be accessed and printed out—resulting in a disconnected series of images as one progressed around the circle. (According to one of Lea's subjects I happened to meet, something like a series of images does occur in performing this task.) Perhaps the image itself serves as a retrieval cue for the next PRP file, analogous to Weber, Kelley, and Little's "verbal prompts" discussed in chapter 6, section 2.4. If so, there would be no effects of distance per se.

Our model, then, can explain all of the findings on time to scan visual mental images—when a given image is in fact retained and scanned—if the image is iteratively shifted across the visual buffer (so different parts fall under the central, most sharply focused portion). When more items are scanned over, presumably the FIND procedures are executed more often in an attempt to locate the target—and hence more time is required. If so, then when parts of an image are less discriminable, people may scan more slowly. And in fact although more time overall was required to see a target on an image of the map illustrated in figure 3.6 when it was imaged at half size instead of full size, the scanning rates were the same. Subjects claimed that they had more difficulty seeing locations on their small images of the map, and also had to slow down their scan rate to avoid overshooting the target. Only after considerable pilot work were the faces illustrated in figure 3.9 hit upon; these stimuli are so barren of internal detail that extraneous factors did not affect the scanning rates for images of different subjective sizes—resulting in faster times to scan across subjectively smaller images. The rate parameter is adjustable in our model, however; people can always slow down—and this makes it tricky to compare scanning in different experiments with different subjects, experimenters, and materials.

The finding that people can scan to overflowed parts of their images (see chapter 3, sections 2.1 and 2.4) is also in Class 1 (confirmation), being explained by reference to the inverse-mapping function. In the model, the contents of each cell of the surface matrix (if any) are translated to a nearby location and the values of the parameters of PICTURE (which maps the underlying deep representation to the surface representation at some size, location, and orientation) are updated appropriately. As coordinates are systematically shifted, some of the portions that had originally overflowed (and hence whose points were not placed in the surface matrix) now are assigned coordinates that do exist in the matrix. Thus, the underlying deep representations can be accessed and the appropriate points printed out. During scanning, then, new material is continually being constructed at the "leading edge" of the visual buffer (and previously imaged material disappears at the other edge as portions run over). This account also allows us to explain why people find it as easy to scan a given distance to a location within the visual buffer as to a location that has overflowed (see figure 3.24): The imaged stimulus is shifted the same amount across the visual buffer in both cases.

It is important to note that we posit that scanning, like zooming and panning, is a "field general" transformation, always operating over the whole visual buffer. Expanding or shrinking the size of an imaged object, rotations, and the "special transformations" all can be directed from the surface to operate only within a bounded region, only on a given subset of points. Thus, a single object in an imaged scene can be expanded, shrunk, or rotated. In the case of rotation, we showed that larger images—which occupy a larger part of the visual buffer—require more time to rotate than do smaller ones; this would not be true if the rotation routines could not circumscribe a portion of the visual buffer (that occupied by an object) and operate directly on it. We will consider some implications of the distinction between field-general and region-bounded transformations in the last part of this chapter.

2.4 Special Purpose Transformations

In addition to the three kinds of transformations just discussed, I propose that arbitrary portions of a surface image can be moved in arbitrary ways (but portions that include material from the same unit ought to be easier to move than portions cutting across units, because the relevant points are all "marked" by a common level of activation). The results of the Pinker and Kosslyn (1978) experiment support this claim. We found that subjects could in fact alter the relative positions of individual objects in the image: Time to scan between pairs of imaged objects was determined by the distances that should have existed if objects were actually moved in the specified way, not by the original distances. Although our model is silent about the details, it requires rules of some kind governing how portions will be moved to accomplish some end. Further, we would expect these rules often to incorporate the laws of physics and to result in imagery manipulations "simulating" the analogous physical manipulations. We have not implemented any of these special-purpose rules for governing how regions of points ought to be shifted to attain some end; it seems obvious that *some* set of such rules can be implemented to achieve any desired end, and I see nothing to be gained at present from trying to understand in detail how any of the particular tasks described below are performed. Nevertheless, it will be useful to consider briefly a couple of the kinds of transformations for which a complete theory of image representation and processing ought to provide accounts.

Roger Shepard and his colleagues have reported the most interesting experiments using special-purpose image transformations. Shepard and Feng (1972) showed people unfolded cubes (series of squares connected to each other); within two of the squares was an arrow, which pointed at one side of the square. The subject's job was to decide, as quickly as possible, whether the arrows would meet when the sides were folded into a cube. A shaded square was designated the base, allowing Shepard and Feng to specify how the image was to be manipulated. Decision time did not increase linearly with number of bends but did increase linearly with the number of squares that had to be moved to form the cube. This is just as one would expect if time is determined by how many parts must be moved. The interesting thing about the Shepard and Feng task, from the point of view of our model, is that most of the transformations are in the third dimension. We could easily model this in two ways: either by introducing a third axis in the surface matrix or by introducing special translation rules that produce the two-dimensional projection of a three-dimensional transformation. The interesting feature of this last notion is that we should find systematic distortions in how images are transformed and represented in the third dimension. For example, people are used to seeing a drawing of a cube with no foreshortening (the frontmost face is drawn as a square, even though it is tilted slightly so one can see the top and one of the sides). It would be interesting if when one mentally rotated a cube, one produced this kind of conventional representation—and not the optically correct configuration. This could be tested by using a template-matching technique, wherein one asked subjects to transform a given image and then examine "true" trials where the to-be-matched test stimulus was systematically distorted in accordance with convention or was optically correct. Subjects presumably would be faster at evaluating a stimulus that just matched their image than at evaluating a slightly different one. If this result is obtained, it will be difficult to explain unless some kind of translation rules (which are shaped in part by convention) are used in executing the transformation. At present, however, it remains an open question how to extend the model to account for the representation of three-dimensional space in mental images.

In another experiment, Cooper and Shepard (1975) examined the role of image transformations in how people recognize whether a hand is a right or left one. This work was based on the introspection that when one is presented with a picture of a hand in some arbitrary position, one may image one's own hand in that position and then check to see whether the thumbs of one's own hand and the drawn one are correctly aligned. This notion was examined by presenting subjects with schematic hands. The orientation of the upcoming stimulus could be indicated by a thumbless hand used as a cue. The results indicated that people did seem to mentally rotate and flip images of hands. The rotation component presumably operates as in the experiments described earlier. The "flip" operation again requires some provisions for transforming images in the third dimension, which have not been implemented in our model. In some cases, subjects apparently attempted to match an image of one hand and, if that failed, generated an image of another hand which was "readied" and waiting; if this too failed to match, the first hand was again imaged and transformed. This sort of operation is easily modeled in the context of our theory, using the procedures described in chapter 6 (for generation) and 7 (for matching). We have not implemented a detailed model for this task because the task itself was not so fundamental that other interesting tasks would incorporate it as a subtask.

Shepard (1975) describes a number of additional experiments that may bear on the kinds of mental transformations people can perform. However, since these experiments involve making comparisons of simultaneously present stimuli, the results may reflect "nonmental transformation components" as well—which are not explained within the context of our theory. Thus, although the results are consistent with the general line of the theory (more time is usually taken when stimuli are more disparate in orientation), it seems inappropriate to describe them in detail here.

3.0 VALIDATION TESTS

According to the present theory, transformations can be distinguished not only in terms of their input-output characteristics but in terms of how the computations are performed.

3.1 Two Ways of Transforming Images

In developing our computer simulation, we came to realize that the simulated images did not have to be transformed iteratively. Alternatively, an image could be allowed to fade and a new, transformed image could be generated. That is, the underlying image representation could be mapped into the surface matrix using different parameters for size, orientation, and/or position. Because the transition from the first image to the revised one is discontinuous in this case, we call this kind of a transformation a "blink" transform. The reason blink transforms do not usually occur, we hypothesized, is that this process requires more effort than simply maintaining and transforming an existent image. But need this always be so? The farther one shifts the points in the image, the more time is required; there may be a point where it becomes cheaper to abandon the image and start again from scratch. Shwartz and I performed a number of experiments testing this notion. In each experiment, one group of subjects was asked to transform an image from one size, position (point of focus), or orientation to another, whereas another group was told to erase the first image and form another image of the object correctly transformed. Not only did we expect that blink transforms would require more time than shift transforms, but we did not necessarily expect more time to be required to effect larger transforms. In fact, in our first experiment we were able to use the model to predict that in one condition time to perform a blink transformation would actually *decrease* when larger transformations were required, as will be described in the following section.

3.1.1 Size Adjustment

In the first two experiments of this series we investigated how people can alter the subjective size of an image. For present purposes we are not distinguishing between size changes and scale changes, which differ in that the former is region-bounded and the latter is field-general; this distinction is irrelevant here because the stimuli in these experiments are isolated objects. Alteration of subjective size of an image is an especially good dimension for testing our notions about the two kinds of transformations because it leads to clearly distinct predictions: If one begins with a subjectively large image, more time should be required to shrink it greater amounts if a shift transform is used. In contrast, if one begins with a large image and uses a blink transformation, *less* time should be required to transform it to smaller and smaller sizes. This prediction follows from our finding (see chapter 6) that smaller images usually require less time to generate than do larger ones, in part because fewer details or parts are placed on them. Thus, the critical variable for blink size transformations (starting from a given size) is not the extent of the transformation, but the size of the final image. When one starts with a subjectively small image, larger increases in size should require more time when either method is used. Finally, if subjects in the previous experiments did not spontaneously perform blink transforms because they are more effortful than shift transforms, then we also expect blink transforms to require more time in general than shift transforms.

Thus, subjects saw a letter (composed of dots on a CRT) at either a large or small size, followed by a box at one of five sizes. The subjects adjusted the size of an image of the letter, by using either a shift transform or a blink transform, until it just fit inside the box, at which point they pushed a button (allowing adjustment time to be measured). Following this, the letter or a slight variation of it appeared at the size of the image or a different size, and the subject decided whether the letter matched the imaged one irrespective of size.

As expected, more time was generally required to transform images greater amounts in the shift condition. Further, the increase in time for each increment of area changed was the same when images were expanded or contracted, although there was a tendency for it to be easier to expand an image than to shrink one. These findings are illustrated in figure 8.15.

The results in the blink condition were quite different from those in the shift condition. Here, the amount of change had different consequences depending on whether the initial size was large or small, as expected, but the precise form of the interaction was not quite as predicted. The pattern of the smallest three amounts of size change was precisely as hoped, greater amounts of change requiring more time when the initial image was small but increasingly less time when the initial image was larger. The time required to alter the initial image the two greatest amounts did not systematically change as expected, however, and was especially peculiar when the image was initially large. One account of these findings is that it became hard to "fit all the dots" delineating a large stimulus into the smallest boxes. Thus, this additional effort resulted in more, not less, time being required to generate the smallest images. This result is reminiscent of that illustrated in figure 6.1, where the subjects' motivation apparently resulted in small images of complex forms being harder to form than larger images.

Two other findings also served to distinguish the two kinds of transformations from each other. First, as expected, blink transforms required more time in general than did shift transforms. Second, initially large letters required more time to transform than did small ones in the shift condition, but vice versa in the blink condition.

We also analyzed the times to judge the letters as "same" or "different." In the shift-transformation group, "different" responses were faster than "same" responses, and less time tended to be required when the image size matched the size of the probe (but this effect was not statisti-

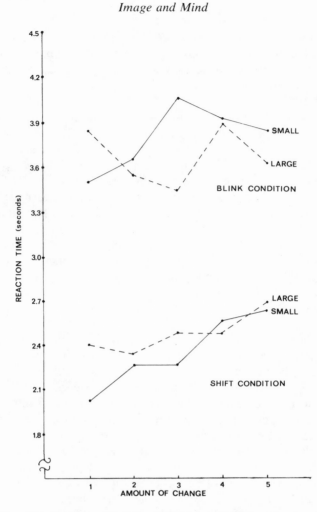

Figure 8.15. The time to adjust the size of a mental image when the original image was retained and altered (the shift condition), and when the original image was replaced by a subsequent image at the target size (the blink condition).

cally significant). The decision times in the blink-transform group followed much the same pattern: Again, "different" responses were faster than "same" responses, but now there was no hint of an effect of congruence between image size and stimulus size. Finally, unlike the transformation task, this task showed no overall difference in times between the two groups.

The results of the comparison task were disappointing. Even for the shift-transformation group, where we had unambiguous evidence that subjects adjusted their images to the requisite sizes, we found no effects of whether or not an image was at the size of the test stimulus. These results contradict those of Hayes (1973) and Larsen and Bundesen (1978). It may be that images of letters composed of numerous dots are simply more difficult to maintain or use. This result, then, may best be placed in Class 3 (theory supplementation) or Class 4 (domain contamination).

3.1.2 Scanning

If image scanning really is another kind of image transformation, then it makes sense to ask whether blink-scans are possible. If so, we have no reason to expect the amount of distance between an initial point of focus and a target region to affect time to erase and regenerate an image at a new position.

We examined the two kinds of scans using the schematic faces illustrated in figure 3.9. Our subjects imaged one of three schematic faces at one of three subjective sizes. The faces had either light or dark eyes, and the eyes were one of three distances from the mouth. These people were asked to focus their attention on the mouth of a face that was imaged as large as possible without overflowing, half this size, or so large that only the mouth remained visible in the image. On hearing the word "light" or "dark," subjects were to "erase" their image and regenerate a new image of the face, positioned so that the eyes were clearly in focus. If the probe word correctly described the color of the eyes, the subject was to push one button; if not, he or she was to push the other. In all respects other than the use of "blink" instructions, this experiment was identical to the fourth experiment reported in the Kosslyn, Ball, and Reiser (1978) paper, described in chapter 3, section 2.1, in which subjects were simply told to "glance up" at the eyes in their image upon hearing the probe word. Thus, we can compare the results obtained here with those from the earlier experiment.

The results of this experiment were clear-cut: Unlike the earlier experiment, times did not increase with decreasing distance between the mouth and eyes of an imaged face. Times did increase when faces were imaged progressively larger, however. Although there was a slight tendency for times to be longest for the medium distances for the half-sized and overflowed faces, but not for the full-sized ones, this interaction failed to reach significance. As is evident in figure 8.16, although "true" responses were generally faster than "false" ones, there were no systematic differences in the effects of distance or size for the different responses.

The fact that distance had no effects when blink-scans were used is a Class 1a (strong confirmation) result; the model was not initially constructed to explain the consequences of performing a blink-scan. In the model, images are represented in long-term memory in part by lists of polar coordinates; an offset parameter allows one to alter the location at which points will be placed in the surface matrix, and this operation does

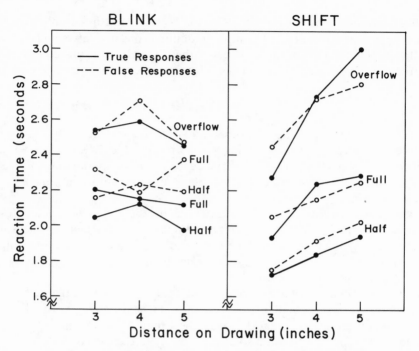

Figure 8.16. Time to shift attention three distances from the mouth to the eyes of schematic faces imaged at three sizes. The subjects in the shift condition scanned the image, whereas the subjects in the blink condition replaced an initial image in which they were focusing on the mouth by one in which they were focusing on the eyes.

not take any more time when greater changes are required. We also found that larger images required more time to generate anew, which is a Class 2 (multiple interpretation) result. This result could in part reflect error in the size of the new parameters used when generating the image (that is, precision of the "aim" may have been poorer), requiring some shift-scanning to make adjustments, or could be due to smaller images becoming sharper more quickly (as discussed in chapter 6). An unexpected finding of this experiment was that blink-scans did not always require more time in general than shift-scans. It is interesting to note that, in all cases but one, whenever the amount of time for a shift-scan exceeded that for a blink-scan there is a bend in the function plotted in the right panel of figure 8.16, which is reproduced from Kosslyn, Ball, and Reiser (1978). That is, less time tended to be required to perform a shift scan over a given distance than would be expected from the effects of scanning shorter distances. It is as if these subjects spontaneously performed a blink-scan when it was easier. This is, of course, consistent with the claim that images are usually transformed gradually because it is easier to maintain and transform an existent image than to generate a new one; if it becomes easier to replace an existing image, we would expect exactly the sorts of deviations from linearity that are visible in the right panel of figure 8.16. Although this finding is merely suggestive, it clearly is worth investigating which factors will make which strategy more efficient, and whether qualitatively different results emerge when the different kinds of transformations are spontaneously performed.

3.2 Two Classes of Image Transformations

I have drawn a distinction between two kinds of transformations. A field-general (FG) transformation consists of moving the entire contents of the visual buffer in a specified way, independent of the identity of the imaged patterns (a shift FG transform in our model consists of translating the cells in the surface matrix stepwise along a vector). A region-bounded (RB) transformation, in contrast, consists of first defining a local region of the visual buffer and then altering only the material within it. Virtually every FG transformation has an RB analogue. For example, zooming in is field-general, but imaging an object growing larger is region-bounded; scanning is FG (where the image is shifted such that different portions fall under the center of the visual buffer, which is most sharply in focus), whereas position translation (for example, imaging an object sliding along a tabletop) is RB. In general, we expect effects of complexity of an imaged object on image transformation time only with RB transformations. In this case, the more difficult it is to define the bounded region, the more time should be taken. Thus, objects with more complex contours should generally require more time to begin transforming. And as more objects in a scene are RB transformed, more time should be required. Further, the more objects that must be held in an image while one object is being manipulated, the more difficult it should be to manipulate the object (assuming that the same procedures that monitor the visual buffer during image maintenance also guide the transformation procedures). For FG transformations, the actual content of the image is irrelevant, if our model is correct, and we expect effects of neither the complexity of the imaged objects nor the number of objects in an imaged scene.

Thus, if one images zooming in on a scene, the complexity and/or number of items in the scene should not affect time; but if one images the items actually growing, more time should be required with more complex objects and/or with a greater number of objects. This prediction has yet to be tested, but an analogous one has been: On the present theory, no more time should be required to scan a scene with more items (providing that the same number of items is scanned over in the course of traversing the image). Pinker and Kosslyn (1978) in fact found that people could scan between pairs of objects just as easily when a scene contained a total of six objects as when it contained only four. In contrast, our theory predicts that time to move a single object in a scene in relation to the others should increase with more complex objects or a greater number of objects in the scene. Although we did not have the FG/RB distinction at the time (and hence floundered around trying to explain our data) the results of the Pinker and Kosslyn experiment are consistent with this prediction. In this case, subjects required more time to mentally move a single object in an imaged scene when the scene contained six objects than when it contained only four (but we did not examine whether there was an increased *rate* with more items, as would be expected if the foregoing ideas are correct). Given that the FG/RB distinction was originally formulated purely on grounds of computational efficiency (explaining how the inverse-mapping function works), this is a genuine Class 1a (strong confirmation) finding, one not initially used in motivating the theory or similar to a finding so used. Thus, there is some preliminary data supporting the present distinction, and it clearly suggests additional experiments that should be conducted.

3.3 Combining Image Transformations

It seems clear that in some of the tasks described earlier, subjects were using more than a single transformation; they may have had to scan and zoom in, for example, while possibly also rotating an image slightly in order to see some part clearly. It becomes important to discover the order, if there is an order, in which the different image transformations are performed. For one thing, we showed that more time was taken to scan longer distances—and yet *less* time is generally taken to see parts on subjectively larger (nonoverflowing) images. On the face of things, there seems to be a paradox here: Why don't the two effects, those of distance and resolution, cancel each other out? According to our theory, there is no paradox because people do not have to scan in order to see a part on a large (but not overflowing) image, but do have to zoom in to see parts on small images. But what if people do tend to scan to the region at which a part is located? This will occur if images are often generated at sizes that begin to overflow the most resolved portions of the visual buffer, as the data reported in chapter 6, section 2.5, led us to suspect. Even if so, one still should not be able to scan across most small images and see a part, because the resolution should be too poor (the schematic faces illustrated in figure 3.9 should be an exception to this generalization, having been designed so that the critical feature—the eyes—would be visible even with poor resolution). If so, then people may first zoom and then scan, in which case an extra operation is required if the image is initially too small to be able to see a part. Alternatively, zooming and scanning may occur in parallel, in which case the time required by each of the two processes will be critical in determining whether there is a size effect. Bill Shebar and I investigated these notions. We conducted one of our standard imagery-detection experiments, asking subjects to focus on various parts of images that were generated at a very small subjective size or as "large as possible without overflowing." In addition, we systematically varied the location of the focus point and queried properties such that a "true" probed property was located where the subject was focusing, at the opposite side of the image, or at a location halfway across the image. Each focus condition was used equally often with each size, allowing us to discover whether the effects of distance scanned and the effects of size are additive. If they are, this will indicate that the scanning and zooming processes occur sequentially. If one factor mitigates the effects of the other, however, this may suggest (depending on the form of the interaction) that the two processes go on in parallel. The results of this experiment are illustrated in figure 8.17. As is apparent, when the image was full-sized, we found our usual effects of scanning, with scanning time increasing linearly with increased distance to be scanned. (This effect was much more pronounced than usual, however, for unknown reasons.) For subjectively small images, in contrast, times did not increase linearly with distance scanned. (In fact, it seems as if the subjects either did not need to zoom all the way to the large

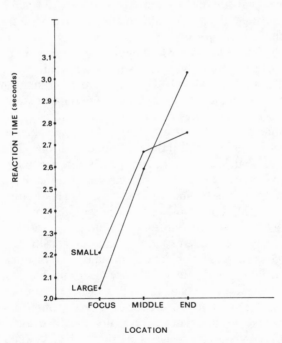

Figure 8.17. Time to scan three different distances across images that initially were very small and across images that were as large as possible without overflowing.

size in order to see the parts or could finish scanning either halfway or all the way across the image before zooming was complete.) Note the center two points: We find here that even having to scan more distance to traverse halfway across a larger image did not cancel out the advantage of beginning with a more resolved, larger image. Thus, although the difference in time for the two sizes was not as large as when no scanning was required, we still found effects of size when an "average" amount of scanning occurred, assuming that on the average one scans at most halfway across an image to reach any given location.

In short, there is no paradox in our findings on effects of size and distance, even if subjects sometimes do scan to the region of the probed part: One simply needs a certain level of resolution before one can see a part, eliminating any advantage of having to scan less distance on smaller images.

4.0 CONCLUDING REMARKS

In this chapter the theory has been developed to an unusual degree in the course of considering data. This is true largely because we made so few commitments at the outset, and the claims we did make for the core theory were informed by the results of the new decision tree developed here. The following claims are now part of core theory: (1) Image transformations may be accomplished by operating directly on material in the visual buffer, which generally requires less computation than transforming an image from the deep level. (2) Images are not transformed generally by shifting portions sequentially. (3) Images are not transformed generally by moving higher-order parts of the imaged object. (4) Some transformations operate over the entire visual buffer, irrespective of content, and some operate only within bounded regions in the visual buffer. (5) The procedures that locate foundation parts operate only within a relatively narrow range of orientations, making it difficult to generate an elaborated image at a nonstandard orientation. (This notion, then, leads us to predict that blink-rotations should be possible only with the most simple stimuli). (6) The procedures that categorize subtle or unfamiliar properties of imaged objects also are orientation-sensitive, requiring that the orientation of an imaged object be normalized prior to categorization. However, procedures that categorize very discriminable or familiar properties (such as those that locate the top of a letter) are not as sensitive to orientation and do not require prior orientation-normalization. (7) Images may serve as templates which are matched against percepts. (This was offered as an hypothesis at the end of chapter 7, but was so central to our accounts here that is should be promoted to the level of theory proper.) Finally, it should be noted that we have yet to support the view that images are transformed incrementally because they would become scrambled or fragmented if they were not so transformed, as posited by the core theory. At present, the actual mechanism underlying the transformations is left open.

The following new findings were reported in the course of further developing our theory and model: (1) Larger images require more time to rotate. (2) The complexity of an imaged pattern sometimes affects the overall mean time, but does not alter rotation rate. (3) Images may be transformed by replacing an initial image with an altered one (a procedure I have dubbed a "blink" transformation), but this generally requires more time than modifying an existing image incrementally (a "shift" transform). (4) The additional time to zoom in on a small image is not cancelled out by the time to scan an "average distance" when inspecting a larger image (if in fact images are often scanned when inspected). This finding removes a potential paradox, our having found that smaller images require more time to inspect (chapter 7) but larger ones require more time to scan.

A host of new hypotheses follow from our investigation of image transformations. The following ones are among the most important: (1) Literal encodings in long-term memory are themselves never altered, although the mapping function used to generate a surface image can be adjusted. (2) Images often may be regenerated immediately before being transformed, but if so, increasingly more complex images are increasingly more difficult to refresh. (3) Although one may be able to maintain a moving image longer (as hypothesized in chapter 7), it fades very quickly to a level of activation that impairs its use as a template. (4) Transformation rates are variable and are determined by various task requirements, such as the ease of seeing parts of an imaged object.

An important feature of the accounts offered in this chapter is the idea that images fade rapidly. But we earlier hypothesized that images fade at the surface level, perhaps because of fatigue of regions of the visual buffer itself. If this is true, why does not rotating an image preserve it at a higher level of activation? We are forced to hypothesize that the mechanism that refreshes surface images directly cannot reactivate an image very much. It seems increasingly likely to me that only the vaguest image can be retained by most people for more than a second or two.

The newest version of the simulation provides another reason why sharp images may be maintained only by regeneration from the deep level. Our original motivation for regeneration from the surface was to save the effort of having to look up the relevant propositional files, relations, and so on. But after implementing the inverse mapping function, we had to store the values of the parameters used to map each underlying IMG representation into the surface matrix. Once these values are available, one need not go through the rigamarole required when initially generating an image (recall that the main purpose of PUT is to compute the correct mapping function for the different parts). The time to generate an image from the deep level may still be long enough to make a surface re-generation scheme profitable, but this remains an empirical question at present. We see, then, how accounting for increasingly more data begins to put real constraints on a general model.

9. *Using Visual Images to Answer Questions*

So far I have been developing a theory of the way images serve as repositories of information in human memory; I have only barely discussed when and why these representations are accessed during the course of cognition. The question of when people use images to help them answer simple questions about objects has been considered by those studying "semantic memory," which has been defined as the part of long-term memory where word-meaning and other linguistically based information is represented (see Tulving, 1972). Smith (1978) provides a fine review of the fundamental findings and theories in the literature on semantic memory, and I will not duplicate his efforts here. Briefly, there are two basic sorts of models, those which liken semantic memory to a network of propositions wherein concepts are nodes in a graph, and those which focus on the representation of unorganized concepts, each of which corresponds to a conglomerate of features. The distinction between the two classes of models breaks down rather quickly when one begins to speak of "property lists" associated with nodes in a graph (which can serve as collections of features) in the first case, and rewrite rules to allow inferences (which function as links) in the second case; the interested reader is referred to Hollan (1975) and to Glass and Holyoak (1975) for discussions of the usefulness and coherence of the distinction between the two classes. The classes of models do differ in their relative emphasis on properties of the representation versus properties of the processes that work on them (see Smith, 1978), with the network theorists being more concerned about the nature of the internal representations themselves. Thus, it is not surprising that the role of imagery in answering questions has been considered at any length only by those subscribing to the network view.

The basic network model was first proposed by Collins and Quillian in 1969. They proposed that semantic memory is best characterized in terms of a system of "nodes" that are interconnected hierarchically. A given node corresponds to a "word concept," and has associated with it information about the properties of exemplars of the concept. In retrieving property information about an object, one must traverse a path connecting the representation of the concept with the representation of the property in this net. Time to verify that a stated noun-property relationship (such as "A lion has a mane") is true depends on how far apart in the network the representations of the noun and property are. Distance in the net was originally hypothesized to be based on the generality of the property: Storage was made as efficient as possible by representing properties only with the most general appropriate superordinate concept. So, for example, one would not store the property "can eat" directly with "collie," "ape," "octopus" and so on, but would store it with "animal." The more particular the property is to an object, the closer it will be stored to the representation of the object in memory. For example, the property "mane" might be stored directly with "lion," the property "fur" with "mammal" (a distance of one link from "lion" in the hypothetical net), and the property "skin" with "animal" (two links from "lion"). Collins and Quillian (1969) reported that the inferred distance between a concept and a property predicted time to verify statements: The farther apart they were, the more time was required. In some early work, Keith Nelson and I (Kosslyn and Nelson, 1973) found that this effect was due to a confounding between "node distance" (the putative distance in the net between the concept and property representations) and simple association-strength between the noun and property. In fact, when association strength was factored out, times actually seemed to decrease with increasingly general properties—they did not increase, as was initially reported (see Kosslyn, 1976b; Nelson and Kosslyn, 1975). Numerous other experiments (for example, Conrad, 1972; Kosslyn, 1976a) have shown that the strength of association between a noun and property, the frequency with which the two are paired, or the like does predict verification times. We can use these measures, then, as an index of "distance" in some hypothetical graph structure.

Collins and Quillian (1972) hypothesized that imagery is a "secondary check" process used only after a path has been established through the semantic net or after search through the net has failed to establish a pathway between the representations of a noun and a property. They reported that subjects often claimed to use imagery when evaluating statements like "An almond cookie has a fortune," but they did not present any data relevant to this claim. In contrast, Jorgensen and Kintsch (1972) claimed that imaginal information can be accessed independently of propositional information. They tested this idea by having people assess the truth of statements that differed in concreteness, and found that sentences that are easy to image ("A cat has fur") can be verified more quickly than difficult-to-image sentences ("Hickory cures bacon"). The problem here stems from the fact that different sentences, with different nouns and verbs, were necessarily used in the two conditions. Thus, any number of other variables merely associated with imagery could be responsible for the effect. In fact, Holyoak (1974) reports just such a confounding.

Thus, we must again begin by attempting to delimit the acceptable class of models. The two classes just considered are but a subset of the possibilities suggested by the structure of our general model. Given that there are two sorts of internal representations (corresponding to the contents of PRP and IMG files in the general model), one could (1) access only propositional information in answering questions, as Anderson and Bower (1973), Pylyshyn (1973), and others suggest; (2) access only imagery, as Tichner seemed to suggest; (3) access propositional information and then imagery, if need be (as Collins and Quillian suggest); (4) access imagery first and then propositional representations; or (5) access propositional information and imagery independently, as Jorgensen and Kintsch (1972) suggest. In the fifth case, we can imagine all sorts of variations: The two representations could be accessed in parallel, or accessed in some kind of serial time-sharing sequence, or accessed one at a time, but with some probability of each being accessed first, and so on. We investigated these five classes of models using a size-comparison task, which requires the subject to decide which of two named objects is larger. We will begin this chapter, then, by recapitulating again the strategy of Phase I, but again (as in the previous chapter) working within the context of the present general model and theory. The results of a set of experiments will allow us to eliminate four of the classes of models (as much as one can ever really "eliminate" a class of models). Following discussion of this research, we will apply the results to the study of how people decide whether an object has a given property.

1.0 MAKING COMPARISONS OF SIZE FROM MEMORY

How do you, the reader, decide which is larger, a mouse or a hamster? Many people report that when asked to make such a decision they seem to generate and inspect mental images of the two creatures standing side by side. Now consider which is larger, a rat or an elephant. In this case, most people report that they do not need to consult imagery, that they "just know" an elephant is larger. These sorts of introspections suggest that two kinds of formats are included in our internal representations of categories like "mouse." The first example is consistent with the claim that we have encodings that depict information about size, in this case in the form of mental images. In our model, information that allows one to reconstruct a depiction of size in a surface image also is present in the underlying literal perceptual memories (implemented as pairs of r, Θ coordinates). The second example is consistent with the notion that some of our internal representations are in a propositional format. In this case the descriptions of mice and elephants may include the information that the former are small and the latter large, and this descriptive information may be used in mentally comparing the animals' sizes. In our model, various sorts of information are listed in the PRP files, including a tag that indexes a rough size category (small, medium, large) of an object or a part. I theorized that these categories are relative to a common standard (such as human body size) and that these tags are used in the procedure that adjusts the resolution of the image (see chapter 5).

Is there any evidence that people do use depictive and descriptive encodings in performing size comparisons from memory? And if so, do any of these data help us cull out any of the five classes of models of when image representations are used? The research on mental comparison of size can be divided into two groups. By far the bulk of the work has been concerned with explicitly ordered series; either a set of stimuli is presumed to be ordered in long-term memory before the subjects arrive to participate in the experiment (for example, using digits as stimuli, see Banks, 1977; Banks, Fujii, and Kayra-Stuart, 1976; Buckley and Gillman, 1974; Fairbank and Capehart, 1969; Moyer and Landauer, 1967, 1973; Parkman, 1971), or the subjects are taught some ordering of the stimuli (see, for example, Potts, 1972, 1974; Trabasso and Riley, 1975; Woocher, Glass, and Holyoak, 1978). A minority of the studies, in contrast, has been concerned with comparison of objects that were not stored in memory as an ordered sequence. In this sort of experiment, people knew the absolute sizes of objects and compared them on this basis, not on the basis of relative position in a sequence. Because we are interested in generalizing to other kinds of question-answering, we will consider only the latter situation, wherein people access the categories named by stimuli and then compare retrieved information along some dimension (rather than locate the relative positions of the stimuli in an ordered sequence).

Moyer (1973) and Jamieson and Petrusic (1975) asked people to decide which of two animals was larger, and Paivio (1975b) asked subjects to evaluate the relative sizes of named objects. In these experiments, the time necessary to judge which of two named objects was larger decreased as the difference in size between the named objects increased. This effect of "size disparity" was independent of the absolute size of the objects and of whether the named objects were in the same category or in different categories. In fact, the data bear a striking resemblance to data from similar perceptual tasks, both sorts of results seeming to evince the effects of simple "discriminability." Noting this correspondence in data from mental and perceptual comparisons, it seemed reasonable to some researchers to hypothesize that people perform the mental comparison by judging representations that depict the stimuli, capturing the variations in size evident in percepts. Proponents of this view (such as Paivio, 1975b) claim that some of the same sorts of processes may be brought to bear when analyzing and comparing percepts and when analyzing and comparing depictive representations in memory. These representations need not be surface images, but may be underlying image encodings as well. Thus, to leave open the question of whether surface or deep imagery representations are used, I will use the term "imagistic" to refer to both sorts of imagery representations.

The inference that imagistic representations are used in mental comparisons is not based wholly on correlational evidence of the sort described above. Moyer and Bayer (1976) attempted to test experimentally the notion that mental representation preserves absolute differences in size, not merely ordinal differences. They had subjects learn to associate three-letter nonsense-syllables (CVC's) with different-sized circles; half of the subjects worked with four circles ranging in size from 11 to 17 millimeters in diameter, and half worked with circles ranging from 11 to 23 millimeters. After learning the associations, subjects were presented with pairs of the nonsense syllables, and were asked to decide which of the two named the larger circle. The task was in fact easier with the larger circles, which were perceptually more discriminable. Further, the results from another condition, where subjects actually judged the pairs perceptually, were similar to those obtained in the memory condition. This correspondence was not complete, however, as there was evidence that pairs involving larger circles were processed more quickly than other pairs in the memory condition, but not in the perceptual condition. Thus, it appeared that although people participating in Moyer and Bayer's task may have compared imagistic representations, this was not all they did; Moyer and Bayer hypothesized that people first retrieve and consult discrete representations, and then turn to comparison of depictive representations.

1.1 Models of Mental Size-Comparison Processes

Although most of the research on mental comparisons has been with explicitly ordered stimuli, some of the specific models developed to account for these data also may be generalized to account for evaluations of pairs not explicitly ordered into a sequence prior to testing. We can sort the rather simple, straightforward models into the five basic classes offered below. These models differ in the role they posit for processing of imagistic and propositional representations.

1. *Pure imagistic models.* These models posit that imagistic memory representations—surface images and/or the contents of underlying literal encodings—are compared much as percepts are compared. This kind of model has been suggested by Moyer and Landauer (1967), Moyer (1973), and Paivio (1975b). Moyer and Bayer's (1976) results do not support a pure imagistic model.

2. *Pure propositional models.* These models posit that people retrieve some sort of propositional statements or tags and use only these sorts of representations in the comparison task. According to one version, the

representation of every object in memory includes a representation of its rough size-category and a representation of its detailed size. The effect of disparity in size is accounted for by differences in the probability that retrieval of both representations will be required for a decision; the closer the two stimuli are in size, the greater the probability that both operations —rather than just one—will be required to reach a decision (see for example, Banks, Yu, and Lippincott, 1978).

Figure 9.1 illustrates the major components of such a model. In this case, one would receive a pair of names of objects as stimuli. Upon comprehending the names (which for present purposes is equivalent to accessing the long-term memory encodings of information about the named objects), one retrieves tags indicating the rough size of the object. For example, an elephant may be thought of as "large" and a mouse as "small." Presumably, only about five to seven different categories of size are represented, and the sizes are relative to a common standard (such as the human body; Paivio's (1975b) findings make it unlikely that sizes are indicated by tags that specify size only relative to the object's "basic" category, given that the size-disparity effect was independent of whether the stimuli were in the same or different categories). After the tags are retrieved, they are compared; if they do not match, as with elephant and mouse, the object associated with the larger tag is selected as being larger and a response is generated. If the tags match, as might occur with mouse and hamster, both of which are "small," further operations are required. In this case, more detailed information on size, represented perhaps in inches or the like, is retrieved and compared prior to generating a response. In a pure propositional model, each stage requires a constant amount of time, but as objects become closer in size, the probability that tags will match (necessitating second-stage processing) increases.

This sort of model does not require that the stages be executed serially. Alternatively, one could begin looking for gross and detailed information simultaneously. In order to account for the size-disparity effect, however, search and comparison of detailed information must require more time than the gross comparison. That is, pairs of objects more disparate in size should be processed more quickly, solely on the basis of gross informa-

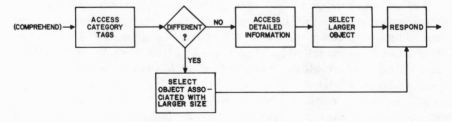

Figure 9.1.   An outline of the general serial processing model.

tion, whereas pairs closer in size will be more likely to require more time-consuming detailed comparisons. If both sorts of retrieval processes require about the same amount of time, the fact that more subtle discriminations require more time will not be explained. Thus, a pure propositional model positing parallel processing of gross and detailed information must include the constraint that the detailed comparison process requires more time than the gross comparison. Hence, the detailed process always will follow, in a functional (but not necessarily a structural) sense, the gross process.

3. *Mixed models: (a) propositional-imagistic serial processing*. According to this sort of notion, one first retrieves propositional representations and then, if need be, retrieves imagistic representations. Figure 9.1 can be taken to illustrate such a model if in the second stage one accesses not a propositional representation but an imagistic representation.

4. *Mixed models: (b) imagistic-propositional serial processing*. Two basic sorts of models fall into this class. First, some models posit that imagistic representations are first accessed very cursorily. If the size disparity between two objects is large enough, the larger object can be distinguished in this initial comparison. If the difference in sizes is not large enough to allow this imagistic comparison to be successful, then some sort of propositional representations of detailed size must be accessed and compared. Thus, as the difference in size between the stimuli in a pair increases, the probability of having to access the propositional representations decreases (and overall time decreases). Second, some imagistic-propositional models posit that category tags are initially generated from imagistic representations; following this, these category tags are compared and processed as in pure propositional models. If the gross tags are not sufficient to allow selection of the larger object, then more detailed propositional representations are retrieved and compared (see Banks, Fujii, and Kayra-Stewart, 1978).

5. *Mixed models: (c) imagistic-propositional parallel processing*. According to this sort of model, illustrated in figure 9.2, one retrieves and processes propositional and imagistic representations at the same time. The process that runs to completion first determines the pattern of the response times, as will be discussed in the next section.

These five classes are not presented as an exhaustive taxonomy of all possible models. For example, we can imagine models in which stochastic processes determine what sorts of tags, gross or detailed, are initially retrieved and consulted; models in which tags may be in different formats, requiring various sorts of conversion operations before they can be compared; models in which tags require more or less time to retrieve depending on how much processing capacity is consumed in accessing the tags for the other stimulus of the pair, and so on. (See Banks, 1977; Potts et al., 1978; and Trabasso and Riley, 1975, for consideration of a variety

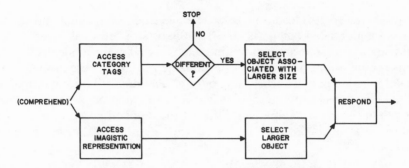

Figure 9.2.   An outline of the general parallel processing model.

of models.) I consider only these five classes of models for two reasons: First, it is not clear how general more subtle and complex explanations are; if these specific models only account for mental comparison of size (and perhaps only within a certain stimulus domain) and have only the most minimal implications for how one retrieves and uses other sorts of information, they seem unlikely to have implications for a general model of the sort being developed here. Second, the data to be gleaned from the forthcoming experiments will render many of the more complex models implausible. Knowing this, it seems senseless to dwell on models that lack parsimony, elegance, and intuitive appeal (to me!) at this stage. It would seem that practically an infinite number of models can be designed to deal with any data or task; we are not interested in playing out this exercise, but rather in attempting to gain insight into some general principles about information representation and processing by examining a few broad classes of plausible models.

1.2 Discriminating among the Models

Consider the following experiment: Subjects learn to draw six simple line drawings of stick men; each figure is a different size and a different color. When given a color, the subjects are asked to draw the corresponding figure; this procedure is repeated until the subjects become very good at producing the figure at the correct size. Following this, the figures are categorized: The smallest three are considered "small" and the largest three "large." The subjects learn to categorize each figure such that they can both name from memory the category to which a figure belongs when given the color of the figure and name which figures belong to a category (large or small) when given the category name. The critical variable of interest in this experiment is how well overlearned the category labels are. For half of the subjects, the category associations are tested until a criterion of 200 percent overlearning is reached; for the other half, testing is continued until categories are overlearned by 500 percent (that is, until subjects have recalled all the correct associations perfectly five times in a row). The subjects then are given pairs of color names, and are asked to judge as quickly as possible which name labels the larger figure. The results of primary interest concern pairs which contain stimuli that are (1) of similar or dissimilar sizes and (2) in the same or different categories. The various models lead us to expect different effects of the amount of over-learning of categories on how the degree of size disparity and category membership influence decision times. Let us consider the predictions of each sort of model (taken in their most general form for now).

1. The pure imagistic model predicts that times should decrease as the difference in size increases. No effects of category membership are predicted, and amount of overlearning should not alter the size-disparity effect. Overlearning may have the effect of speeding decisions overall, however, as people will presumably become more practiced in retrieving the representations in the course of overlearning category labels.

2. In order to derive predictions from pure propositional models, we must make several assumptions. Retrieving the size category tags (large or small, in this case) may reasonably be considered to be part of the first-stage comparison process. If so, then the 500 percent overlearning group ought to be faster overall than the 200 percent group, since overlearning should make the tags more readily retrieved. No effects of size disparity ought to occur in either group, however. Size-disparity effects, according to this sort of model, are a consequence of whether judgments require retrieving and comparing one or two representations. By controlling category membership, we presumably also control whether or not both of the retrieval and comparison operations are necessary. When the stimuli are in the same category the general and detailed representations always should be accessed; when different-category pairs are used, only general category information must be accessed. Thus, if this model is correct no size-disparity effects should be found when people perform this task. This prediction is based on the simplest version of a pure propositional model; by hypothesizing that the category tags require more or less time to retrieve depending on the relative size of a figure, one can generate numerous other sorts of predictions. Discussion of more convoluted versions of this model will be deferred until later, however.

The variation of the pure propositional model in which gross and detailed processes occur in parallel makes similar predictions. In this case, however, overlearning should differentially speed up decisions that can be made on the basis of gross information (category names). Thus, the model leads us to expect different-category decisions (when a pair is composed of stimuli from different size-categories) to be faster for the 500 percent group; time to perform same-category decisions, however, ought to be the same for both groups. As in the pure propositional serial model, we expect no effects of size disparity per se if this model is correct (because we presumably have removed the probabilistic element in the comparison process, and thus have controlled whether a judgment can be made solely on the basis of gross information or requires detailed information as well).

3. Propositional-imagistic serial models make predictions similar to those of the serial two-stage pure propositional model. The major difference between the two conceptualizations is that the propositional-imagistic serial model leads us to expect size disparity effects when both members of a stimulus pair are in the same category. In this case, the first comparison (of tags) fails to provide information upon which to base a decision, necessitating recourse to imagistic comparison processes. Thus, by analogy to perceptual comparison processes, we expect effects of size disparity when imagistic representations are retrieved (when members are in the same category, preventing tag comparison from being helpful).

4. Imagistic-propositional serial models lead us to expect no effects of category learning on the size-disparity effect. In the first sort of model, an initial quick imagistic comparison is made. If this process is successful, a fast decision can be executed; if not, detailed propositional information must be retrieved. Category learning does not affect this process, and we have no reason to expect any differences in processing of same-category and different-category pairs if this sort of model is correct. In the second sort of model, the category tags are not stored with the representation of the named object in memory. Instead, tags are generated from imagistic representations and then compared. Thus, we again have no reason to expect any effects of category or amount of overlearning in the task described above if this sort of model is correct.

5. Finally, the imagistic-propositional parallel process model predicts different effects of category membership on time to compare items of similar and dissimilar sizes for the 200 percent and 500 percent overlearning groups. According to this sort of model, the more quickly the category tags can be accessed and processed, the more likely it is that propositional processing will run to completion if the tags mismatch (if they are the same, no decision can be based on tag comparison, as is evident in figure 9.2). We expect that the 500 percent group will be able to access the category tags more quickly than the 200 percent group. Thus, if the people in the 500 percent overlearning condition can retrieve and compare size tags before imagistic comparisons are completed, we expect no effects of size disparity when pairs contain members from different categories (in this case, the category tags mismatch, and thus imagistic processing is not required). This prediction assumes, of course, that tags for the different figures are retrieved in about the same amount of time (as will be discussed shortly). With the 200 percent group, in contrast, the tags will be retrieved more slowly, giving the imagistic processes more of a chance to "outrace" the propositional process operations. And when imagistic processing underlies a given decision, we expect that the amount of disparity

between the sizes of members of a pair will affect decision time; that is, larger disparities will be evaluted more quickly. The effects of size disparity, then, are likely to be evident in data from the 200 percent group both when members of a pair are drawn from the same category and when they are drawn from different categories; in contrast, for the 500 percent group, we expect effects of size disparity only when members of pairs are in the same category, when category tags cannot be used to select the larger figure.

The experiment described above was conducted in an effort to begin to evaluate the various models (see Kosslyn et al., 1977, for more details). The predictions outlined above are rather simple-minded, and can be altered by introducing more assumptions about how given processes would work. The predictions offered thus far, however, are basic enough that a model will become relatively unparsimonious if altered so that it no longer generates them.

Six drawings of simple stick men were used. These figures ranged in height from .75 inches to 4.50 inches, progressing from small to large in .75-inch increments. Each figure was drawn in a different color: blue, green, red, black, orange, or brown. The subjects first learned to draw the figures when given the corresponding color. Following this, we proceeded to the categorization task. Subjects now were handed a new version of the drawings of the figures. These drawings were different from the originals only in the kind of border drawn around the card, the three "small" drawings having one kind (dashed or solid) and three "large" drawings having the other. The subjects were told that the borders served to tell which category the figure belonged to, the large or small one. Subjects inspected the cards one at a time, learning to categorize the figures. When the subjects claimed to know which figures belonged to which category (after about two to five minutes of study), they were tested in two ways: The experimenter named a color, and the subject responded with the correct category (large or small), or the experimenter named a category and the subject named the colors of the members of that category. The two sorts of trials were intermingled. Subjects were divided into two groups: Subjects in the 200 percent group were tested until they answered each sort of query correctly twice in a row; those in the 500 percent group were tested until they responded correctly to each type of question five times in a row.

After finishing with the learning phase, the subjects were told that they would hear the names of two colors read in succession. If the first color labeled the larger figure, they were to press one button; if it labeled the smaller figure they were to press the other. The subjects were told to respond as quickly as possible, keeping errors to a minimum, but were told to wait for both names before responding because sometimes both words would be the same (and in fact six of the trials contained duplicate names); in this case, they were not to respond at all. This sort of catch-

trial was included to discourage the subjects from making judgments on
the basis of hearing only one member of a pair, notably a name that labeled either the largest or smallest of the six figures.

The finding of primary interest is clearly evident in figure 9.3. Times
decreased with size disparity in all cases but the one in which members of
pairs were drawn from different categories for the 500 percent group. This
result was documented by a significant interaction among overlearning
group, size difference, and category composition. In addition, pairs containing larger disparities of size were generally evaluated more quickly,
and pairs containing figures in the same category were evaluated more
quickly than pairs with members from different categories. Finally, the
overall difference in time between the two overlearning groups was not
significant, nor were any other interactions significant.

We also examined all pairs composed of items from different categories. In this analysis, the effects of size disparity were very apparent and

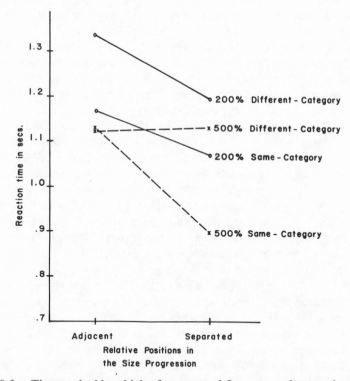

Figure 9.3.   Time to decide which of two named figures was larger when the figures were more or less disparate in size and belonged to the same categories or
different categories. The effects of these variables depend on whether the size tags
were overlearned 500 percent or only 200 percent.

were roughly the same for both overlearning groups. The means for adjacent, separated by one, two, three, and four figures in the progession were 1.338, 1.194, 1.126, 1.062, and .951 seconds for the 200 percent group and 1.125, 1.134, 1.018, .956, and .798 seconds for the 500 percent group. Thus, although the effects of size disparity were eliminated for the adjacent and separated-by-one pairs for the 500 percent group, they were not eliminated for larger size disparities. The imagistic-propositional parallel model would predict that as size disparity increases the imagistic comparison process becomes increasingly likely to "outrace" the category-tag comparison process; and when decisions are based upon imagistic comparison, size disparity ought to affect comparison time (for the same reasons it affects perceptual comparison times; we will consider a possible stimulus-sampling mechanism in the next experiment). In this experiment, however, pairs with greater size disparity also include the endpoints more often than pairs with less disparity; thus, the effects of size disparity for pairs separated by more than one in the progression may be artifactual. However, in the third experiment of this series, we will encounter evidence that this result is not simply an artifact of inclusion of endpoints.

Category retrieval-time control group. The findings just presented seem to run counter to those predicted by all but the imagistic-propositional parallel model. A critic might point out, however, that the models as outlined earlier include the unreasonable assumption that category representations (tags) are retrieved equally easily for all figures. If in fact tags are retrieved more quickly for figures as they become nearer to the extreme sizes (largest and smallest), then effects of size disparity may be caused by differences in ease of accessing tags. That is, pairs containing members with greater disparity in size may be judged more quickly not because they are evaluated via imagistic processing but because the propositional representations stored with the individual members become more easily accessed in pairs in which members are nearer to the extremes. As size disparity increases, at least one member of a pair must become close to the endpoint size, whereas this need not occur in pairs in which the members are close in size.

In order to examine this possibility, we tested a new group of subjects in a reaction-time task. After learning to draw the figures exactly as had the previous subjects, half of these people overlearned the category labels to a criterion of 200 percent and half to 500 percent, as before. Next, these people participated in a simple task. Each color name was presented in a random order, and the subject pressed one button if the color named a figure belonging to the "large" category and another button if it named a figure belonging to the "small" category. As usual, classifications were to be performed as quickly as possible without error.

The results are presented in figure 9.4. The first finding of interest is the

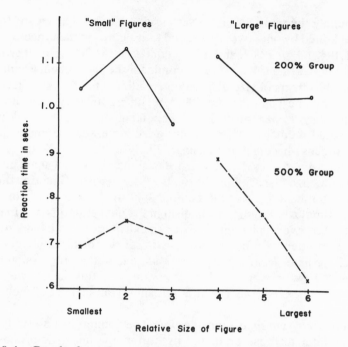

Figure 9.4. Results from the category retrieval-time control group.

mean times to categorize figures that were compared in the earlier task. We will begin by calculating the mean amount of time to classify members of pairs containing figures drawn from different categories. For the 200 percent group, figures that were combined to form pairs close in size (adjacent in the size progression) in the size-comparison experiment were categorized in a mean of 1.036 seconds, compared to 1.067 seconds for pairs containing members more disparate in size (separated by one). This difference is very small and is in the wrong direction to support the argument outlined above; categorization times increased as size disparity increased, although comparison times decreased with size disparity in the experiment for the 200 percent group. For the 500 percent group, pairs containing members close in size (adjacent) were categorized in an average of .814 seconds, compared to .783 seconds for pairs containing figures more disparate in size (separated by one). Again, this difference is small and does not reflect the data from the mental-comparison task. These data allow us to argue forcibly that the difference in time to retrieve category tags could not have produced the size-disparity effects in the 200 percent different-category condition.

There were two other important results from this experiment: First, although some of the figures were classified more quickly than others, the pattern of these differences was the same for both overlearning groups.

Thus, differences in category-retrieval times for different figures cannot be appealed to as an explanation of the differences between the overlearning groups in the mental-comparison task. Second, people in the 500 percent group generally were faster than those in the 200 percent group. This finding is important because the predictions derived from the imagistic-propositional parallel model rest on the notion that overlearning will increase the probability that category retrieval and comparison processes will be quicker than imagistic processing. It was this claim that led us to expect diminished effects of size disparity for different-category pairs for the 500 percent group, but to expect size disparity effects for all pairs for the 200 percent group.

1.2.1 Evaluating the Models

The results of the experiment and the control seem inconsistent with all but the imagistic-propositional parallel model. Only with relatively large amounts of overlearning of categories was the size-disparity effect eliminated (for adjacent and separated-by-one pairs) when people mentally compared stimuli belonging to different categories. Because the category tags were retrieved more quickly with more overlearning, the parallel model would lead us to expect that the category-comparison process often would run to completion before an imagistic comparison process. Hence, when stimuli in adjacent and separated-by-one pairs were in different categories, and the categories were well overlearned, no imagistic comparison—and accompanying effects of size disparity—occurred. When category tags were the same, however, imagistic processes had to be completed, engendering a size-disparity effect. The only hitch in this interpretation of the results is in the fact that the comparisons involving same-category pairs were generally faster than those involving different-category pairs (see figure 9.3). At first blush, we should have expected the reverse. However, the same-category pairs all included the "endpoints," whereas the different-category pairs did not. Imagistic representations of the endpoints may have been retrieved more quickly because they were better learned than the other stimuli (as would be expected due to standard serial-position effects). Alternatively, there may simply be a special algorithm for responding one way whenever the name of an endpoint is encoded, circumventing all true comparison processes.*

The failings of the other sorts of models are worth a brief look. First, the fact that categories mattered at all runs counter to the predictions of the pure imagistic model. Second, pure propositional models that incorporate two types of processing cannot deal with the observed effects of amount of overlearning of size categories on the size-disparity effect; ac-

---

*Christine Riley has advanced this last view for some of her recent results (personal communication).

cording to these models no effects of size-disparity are expected for different-category pairs, regardless of amount of overlearning. Further,
these models must strain to account for the size-disparity effects observed
with same-category pairs, since with these pairs detailed information
should always be retrieved and compared. Third, the propositional imagistic serial model also is inadequate in the face of the effects of category
overlearning on the effects of size disparity; again, according to these
models no effects of size disparity should occur when objects are in different categories. The subjects in the 200 percent group definitely knew the
correct category of each figure, and these models state that such information always is retrieved and checked initially. This failure to observe effects of categories was recently observed by Woocher, Glass, and Holyoak (1978) in a task wherein stimuli were explicitly ordered, and seems
the rule rather than the exception when large amounts of overlearning are
not used (George Potts also reports failing to find effects of categories,
without using large amounts of overlearning). Finally, the imagistic propositional serial models also are faced with difficulties; if they were correct the amount of overlearning should not have influenced the size-disparity effect.

The partisan reader whose favorite model has just been dismissed will
undoubtedly raise many objections at this point. With a few added assumptions, he or she might declare, any of the models could be salvaged.
Trabasso and Riley (1975), for example, point out that something like our
"imagistic" representations could be "warped" internally, such that the
endpoints could be accentuated in terms of size disparity. One could
argue that overlearning served merely to modify the sizes represented by
the surface or deep imagery representations; some possible configuration
of sizes would allow a pure imagistic model to produce the observed effects. We asked people to draw the figures after the comparison task, and
found them to be remarkably accurate, even on the endpoints—a finding
that seems to run counter to such a claim in the present case; however,
one could always argue that drawings do not really reflect the nature of
the imagistic representations in memory. And so on. Such a running defense probably can be made for any of the models. However, doing so
makes the models become not only lamentably post hoc but ad hoc as
well.

The question of post hoc and ad hoc modifications brings up a basic
issue concerning the purpose of modeling of the sort under discussion. Do
we really care about the time it takes to compare internally the sizes of
two stick men? About the time to perform mental comparisons in general?
Why should we construct elaborate models of such processes in the first
place? Obviously, we are striving for something more than just an account
of performance in one task. Presumably, we study this sort of narrow,
constrained task not simply because it is tractable but also because we

have hopes of discovering some general principles of cognition. Thus, we are not so much interested in explaining every bit of the data (which has little intrinsic interest in its own right, it seems to me) as in using the data to make inferences about the functional capacities of the human mind. Some researchers seem to have strayed from this goal and take it upon themselves to produce models of such limited generality as to be useless for anything except explaining performance in some particular laboratory task. As stated earlier, our goal is to formulate a general theory, embodied in a general model. The main purposes of developing specific models (ones for particular tasks) are to evaluate the adequacy of the theory (as was done in chapters 6 and 7) and to help develop the theory by discovering new properties of the "functional capacities." This consideration motivated us to stay at the level of generality we have worked at thus far, and not to quantify the models by filling in values of possible parameters (as now seems to be the vogue in this area).

The data seem to be most comfortably subsumed within the class of models incorporating parallel processing of imagistic and propositional information, and this is why our experiment is of some interest. In psychology, however, one experiment obviously is not "crucial," is not capable of doing away with alternative conceptions at a single blow. But the weight of accumulated evidence begins to lean one way or another, especially if the data are collected judiciously, with an eye toward distinguishing among theoretical positions. In this project, the general model as a whole provides a framework for casting more detailed specific models and for delineating the issues that distinguish among the classes of such models. That is, we essentially repeat the procedure used in Phase I, but now for submodels embedded within the whole. Given that the results of the first experiment seem to favor the parallel model, we now will consider further predictions derived from that kind of model that are not easily derived from others; if data on a variety of phenomena are consistent with this conception of mental comparison, we will become more confident in this type of model and more inclined to take it seriously when considering related tasks.

1.2.2 Convergent Evidence for the "Race Model"

The "congruity effect" in size comparison occurs when one can decide which of two relatively large things is the larger more quickly than one can decide which is the smaller, but vice versa for two relatively small things (see also Banks, 1977; Banks, Clark and Lucy, 1975; Jamieson and Petrusic, 1975; Potts et al., 1978). The second experiment in this series was concerned with the congruity effect. The congruity effect has been cited as a major source of evidence for use of propositional, "symbolic" internal representations in mental size comparison. We can distinguish three basic sorts of explanations for this effect: the "stochastic," "match/mismatch," and "recalibration" notions. These conceptions are affiliated with particular models of mental-comparison processes considered above.

The stochastic explanation rests on the assertion that a representation is sampled for the presence of different properties. This conception is best understood by analogy to the congruity effects observed in perception by Audley and Wallis (1964), who formulated the stochastic explanation. They asked people which of two lights was dimmer or brighter, and found that dim lights were evaluated more quickly in terms of dimness but bright lights were evaluated more quickly in terms of brightness. They hypothesized that the stimuli evoked "implicit responses" in terms of how much brightness and dimness was present. Brighter lights evoked more "bright" responses than "dim" responses whereas the reverse was true of dim lights. If one was asked to determine which of two bright lights was brighter, then, enough "bright" responses were evoked that one of the lights reached criterion for "brighter" rather quickly; since few "dim" responses were evoked by bright lights, however, it took appreciably longer for a criterial number of "dim" responses to be accumulated for making the assessment. The reverse situation, of course, occurred in the case where both lights were relatively dim.

A similar explanation can be offered for the congruity effect in mental comparisons. In this case, the mental representation is sampled and various implicit responses are evoked until a criterial number are accrued and the required comparison is accomplished. This sort of explanation is aligned with pure imagistic models of mental-comparison processes, and it does not lead us to expect any change in the magnitude of the congruity effect when the items being compared are members of categories that are more or less well overlearned. It should be mentioned, however, that imagistic models of mental comparison are also compatible with "dispersion theories" (see Marks, 1972) of the congruity effect. This sort of theory has already been demonstrated to be problematical, however (see Banks, Clark and Lucy, 1975; Jamieson and Petrusic, 1976), and thus will not be discussed in detail here. Suffice it to say that this sort of explanation also does not predict that the amount of overlearning of categories will affect the congruity effect.

The match/mismatch account of the congruity effect hinges on the claim that a category tag is stored with, or generated for, a mental representation of an object. The form of this tag may or may not match that of a question, and therein lies the rub. For example, two large objects might be tagged L and $L+$ ($L+$ indicating the larger of the two), and two small objects might be tagged S and $S+$ ($S+$ indicating the smaller). If asked about the relative sizes of two objects, one presumably encodes the question into a representation in the same format as the memory tags, and then compares this representation to the tags. Thus, if asked which of two objects is larger, one translates this request into an internal representation in terms of L, and compares this representation to the memory representations. If the memory representations are also in terms of L, comparison is easy; if they are in terms of S, however, the representation of the query must be converted into the L form before comparison is possible. Thus, when the form of the question mismatches that of the memory representations, more time is required. This sort of model is closely aligned to the pure propositional models of memory comparison (see Banks, Fujii, and Kayra-Stuart, 1976; Clark, 1972; Clark, Carpenter, and Just, 1973), but is also compatible with the propositional-imagistic serial model. In either model, the category tags will be compared to the representation of the question at the outset, at the first stage of processing, and will or will not match its form. The pure propositional and propositional-imagistic serial models differ only in what occurs after the first comparison stage. Thus, in either case the amount of overlearning in the task used previously should not affect the magnitude of the congruity effect: The time necessary to convert the tags from one form to the other should not be affected by the amount of of overlearning of categories. These same expectations also hold for response-competition explanations (Wallis and Audley, 1964), which Banks, Clark, and Lucy (1975) class as variants of the match/mismatch notion.

The third explanation of the congruity effect to be considered here rests on the notion that an evaluative procedure is "set" differently when one expects to compare large things from when one expects small things; this procedure needs to be "recalibrated" if the initial setting is inappropriate (for example, is too sensitive or not sensitive enough) for the actual sizes of the stimuli to be compared. Thus, more time will be required to evaluate which of two small things is "larger" than which is "smaller," for example, if the comparative term results in one calibrating the evaluative procedure inappropriately in the first case, but appropriately in the second. This explanation is associated with the imagistic-propositional parallel model for reasons that will become apparent shortly.

Although all sorts of processes could be specialized for evaluating specific sizes or magnitudes of stimuli, it seemed most profitable to develop just one example of how the recalibration notion might work in the context of our simulation. We know that the congruity effect is most pronounced for objects that are close in size (or along whatever dimension is being compared—see Banks, 1977), which suggests that tag comparison does not produce the evaluation. That is, the closer two objects are, the more likely it is that they are categorized the same way, so that the imagistic comparison process must perform the judgment. So, let us conjecture for now that the congruity effect arises from processing imagistic (surface or deep imagery) representations. In our model the sizes of objects can be represented in a nondiscursive way by r, Θ pairs, which preserve a direct mapping point-for-point to the object (as seen from a particular point of view, in the current model), as opposed to a description of the appearance. We assumed earlier that the range of r values reflects the actual size of the object. That is, when one views an object, one encodes not the visual angle it subtends but its actual size: One maintains "size constancy." (Whether this is in fact true seems to be an open question.) When comparing the sizes of two objects, one will try to find size tags in the corresponding propositional files and see whether these mismatch. At the same time, one will begin sampling the underlying literal representations of the objects' appearance. Recall that we posit that the procedure PUT has access to the size ranges of the r values, and in fact PUT must have such access in order to adjust the size of parts so they will be correctly related to foundation parts. Thus, it makes sense that this sort of information can be available for other purposes as well. Now, one could compare every coordinate pair, but this would be very time-consuming and inefficient. It is as if one were trying to decide in which of two lakes the biggest fish lived (not which had bigger fish on the average); one could throw back fish below a certain size, and not bother to measure them or compare them with fish from the other lake. Similarly, one can set one's sampling mechanisms to select only pairs with r values over some cutoff. If one is expecting the objects to be large, this cutoff will be high, whereas if one is expecting small objects, it will be lower. The congruity effect arises when one is set for large objects but receives small ones, and discovers that one has inspected some proportion of the pairs without finding any over the cutoff—requiring resetting the cutoff and starting over again; similarly, if one is set for small objects and is sampling from representations of large objects, too many pairs will be sampled, again requiring recalibration. After we have collected more data, we will describe how we actually implemented the question-answering processes, including those requiring mental comparison, in our computer model.

The recalibration idea leads us to expect congruity effects in mental comparison when imagistic representations are processed. We claim that imagistic representations must be utilized whenever category tags are the same for two memory representations. According to the imagistic-propositional parallel model, however, propositional information and imagistic representations can be retrieved simultaneously. There is no reason why "cross-talk" between the two processes should not occur. If so, perhaps propositional information once retrieved can be used to recalibrate the evaluation procedures evoked by the comparative adjective presented to the subject. That is, in mental comparisons, the sampling range can be reset by difficulties in comparing the imagistic representations, as described above (and as would presumably occur in perception); in addition, if size-category information is available, this too may be brought to bear in calibrating the comparison mechanisms for effective evaluation of a pair. If the category information is available long enough before the imagistic information is retrieved (or constructed, if surface images must be used—as will be discussed), it may cause the size of the to-be-sampled range to be reset before the imagistic representations are compared. To the extent that recalibration can occur prior to imagistic processing, we expect the congruity effect to be attenuated.

In order to test this prediction we again asked people to participate in the task of the first experiment in this series, again using two groups of subjects differing in how well category tags were overlearned for a set of stimuli. After learning the figures and the categories associated with them, people received pairs of color names and, as quickly as possible, compared the relative sizes of the figures from memory. In this experiment, each pair was presented twice, once to be evaluated in terms of which member was smaller, and once in terms of which member was larger. We were primarily interested in pairs composed of stimuli drawn from the same category, so that the category-membership information could not be used successfully to make the comparison.

The primary results are illustrated in figure 9.5. Pairs composed of

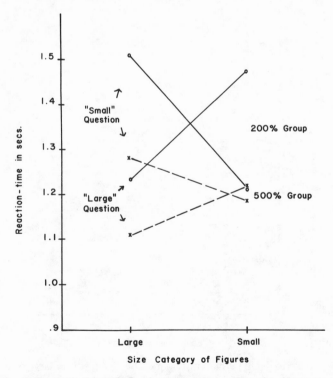

Figure 9.5. Time to decide which of two members of a pair of large or small stimuli was the larger or smaller. These data include times from pairs containing endpoints.

names of figures from the "large" category were generally evaluated more quickly in terms of which member was larger than in terms of which was smaller, but the reverse was true for pairs of "small" stimuli. This is, of course, simply the basic "congruity effect." As is evident in figure 9.5, this effect was slightly less apparent in the 500 percent group, but this trend was not borne out when we performed the appropriate statistical comparison. However, this analysis included pairs that contain endpoints (the smallest or largest figure). We reasoned that these stimuli might be especially well learned (because of serial position effects) and thus that for these stimuli the imagistic information might be retrieved or generated especially quickly. The category-retrieval times collected earlier indicated that the tags were not accessed especially quickly for the endpoints. Thus, perhaps the tag-information comparison process more frequently was "outraced" by the imagistic comparison process, not allowing the evaluation processor to be recalibrated prior to retrieval of the imagistic representations.

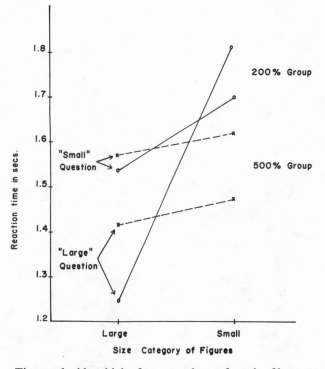

Figure 9.6. Time to decide which of two members of a pair of large or small stimuli was the larger or smaller. These data do not include times from pairs containing endpoints.

This reasoning led us to repeat our analysis excluding the data on all pairs containing an endpoint. We again found a congruity effect, but only for the 200 percent group. These results, illustrated in figure 9.6, are consistent with the recalibration notion as embodied in an imagistic-propositional parallel model.* The remaining models seem hard pressed to account for this finding in a relatively straightforward manner.

1.3 The Role of the Surface Image

Thus far I have not made a strong commitment about when—if ever—surface images are generated and consulted. Yet, this chapter began with a discussion of the role of imagery—surface, quasi-pictorial images—in answering questions. In making a judgment in terms of a single dimension, like height, one should be able to extract this information from the underlying long-term memory representations, if our simulation model is correct. But we have not hypothesized that PUT can compute area by integrating information about extent along several dimensions. This sort of information becomes manifest, however, when a surface image is constructed (in fact integration becomes trivially simple—just counting the number of filled cells allows computation of the area within the two-dimensional envelope, no matter how convoluted). Thus, when one is asked which of two things is bigger (that is, occludes more area in a photo), surface images should be required if the size-tags are the same; images make explicit properties like overall size, which emerge from a number of separate components. We will develop this idea further after considering the results of the following series of experiments.

The only research other than ours on the role of imagery in mental size comparison was reported by Keith Holyoak in 1977. In one experiment, Holyoak asked people to image an object at one of three subjective sizes: very large, normal, or very small. Following this, the name of a second object was presented (in a tachistoscope), and the subject was to decide as quickly as possible whether that object was larger or smaller (in actual —not imaged—size) than the first object. When people were asked to use the initial image and to compare it to an image of the second object when performing this task, more time was required if the initial image was too small or too large than if it was at the normal size. This result falls in Class 1 (confirmation), making perfect sense if people have to adjust an off-sized image before using it to perform a comparison, but can use the normal-sized image without adjustment. In a control group, subjects were asked to image the first object at one of three sizes, but were not asked to

---

*As is evident, the interaction found for the 200 percent group is not a true "crossover effect"; the large figures were always judged more quickly than the small ones. I have no ready explanation for this finding.

use this image in the comparison task. Rather, these people were asked simply to evaluate the relative sizes of the two named objects as quickly as possible, and were told that image consultation was not necessary. The decision times were not generally slower when subjects in the control group began with a subjectively smaller image, even for pairs composed of items relatively close in size (although reaction time was generally longer if the initial size of the first object was incongruent with the decision, as would occur if the larger object was initially imaged small). If people spontaneously consult images when items are close in size, as seems likely if the objects fall into the same size category (as is increasingly likely as the size difference between two objects decreases), an effect of initial size of image per se should have occurred for close pairs even for this control group.

In a second experiment, Holyoak found some evidence that imagery is in fact used spontaneously when people compare items relatively close in size. He asked subjects first either to image a set of digits or to rehearse them; following this, a pair of names was presented and the sizes of the named objects were evaluated. The results on modality-specific interference (see Chapter 7, section 2.4.2) led Holyoak to expect that imaging the digits would interfere with size comparison more than would rehearsing the digits, if people evaluated size via imagery. Two groups of subjects were used: One group was explicitly told to image the objects and consult the images; the other group was simply asked to make the size decision as quickly as possible, and no mention was made of any specific method. As expected, imaging the digits interfered more with decision times for the imagery group. Interestingly, this trend was also observed for the control group when the pairs included items relatively close in size, but not for pairs wherein the items were more disparate in size. Taken with the results of Holyoak's first experiment, then, we are left uncertain about whether imagery is spontaneously used when people mentally compare objects close in size. The earlier failure to find results consistent with this hypothesis may have been in part a consequence of Holyoak's presenting his stimuli visually, which could possibly have interfered with imaging the items (see Brooks, 1967, 1968).

Our next experiments used a technique like that of Holyoak's first experiment. We asked people to image one object at a very small subjective size or at a normal subjective size. Following this, another object was named and the subjects compared the actual sizes of the two objects. We reasoned that if images of the two objects were compared, more time should be required if an initial image was subjectively small instead of normal-sized, because zooming in would be required. In this experiment the main variables of interest were the closeness in size of the objects in a pair and whether the objects in a pair fell in the same or different size-categories. As in the first experiment in this series, one group of subjects learned beforehand to categorize the stimuli into "large" and "small" classes, but now another group did not learn to categorize the objects at all. We expected that if the categories were very well overlearned, the effects of initial size of an image would be eliminated when pairs contained items drawn from different categories (because imagery would not be used), but would be evident for pairs composed of items from the same category (because imagery would be used). Further, we expected that if categories were well overlearned, the effects of size disparity would be attenuated for different-category pairs, as before. These predictions follow from the notion that when category tags mismatch, size comparison may be successfully accomplished by comparing the tags prior to completion of imagistic processing. When tags match, in contrast, decisions must be based upon imagistic processing, in the form of comparison of surface images, and size-disparity effects should be evident. For the group not receiving category training, we expected image use when items were close in size but not when items were of more disparate sizes. In this case, less disparate items were expected to fall often into the same "natural" (already in long-term memory when the subject arrived for the experiment) category; more disparate items, in contrast, were expected to fall usually in different natural categories.

In our next experiment, we used auditory presentation of stimuli and used items selected from Paivio's (1975b) norms to ensure that they were close in size (and thus likely to belong to the same natural category at the outset). Five of the items were relatively small (ant, eye, tomato, hand, and teapot), and five were relatively large (dog, dishwasher, donkey, elephant, iceberg). The remaining ten items used were of intermediate size (football, blender, coffeepot, rooster, arm, lamp, watermelon, goose, beaver, and eagle). The medium items were selected to be as close to each other in size as possible while still being discriminable; the large and small items, in contrast, were selected to be easily distinguishable by size. These words then were combined to form pairs in the following way: Ten pairs were selected from the set of possible combinations of the smallest five items such that no two words were paired together twice and no pair contained the same word repeated twice. This same procedure was employed to form ten pairs from the smallest five of the medium-sized items, ten pairs from the largest of the medium-sized items, and ten pairs from the largest five items. Because each of these pairs includes items drawn only from the same half of the total size range (above or below the median), we shall refer to them as *within-half* pairs. In addition to these 40 pairs, 40 more were generated by combining items that fell below the median size with items from above the median. Of these pairs, 20 were formed by combining items from the smallest five and the largest five items, and 20 by combining names from the smallest five medium items and the largest five medium items. Because each of these pairs contains items from different halves of the size range, we shall refer to them as *across-half* pairs. Every name appeared equally often in the stimulus pairs.

Because the smallest five and the largest five objects were selected to be more discrepant in size than were the medium items, there are relatively large differences between the sizes of objects included in pairs containing the largest and/or smallest five items; hence, we shall refer to these pairs as *far* pairs. In comparison, there are only minimal differences between the sizes of objects named in pairs containing only the medium-sized objects; hence, we shall refer to these pairs as *near* pairs.

The inclusion of within-half and across-half pairs was critical for our experiment, since we wanted to examine the effects of having people learn to categorize the ten medium, near, objects into "large" and "small" classes; prior to such training, we expected little—if any—effects of whether a pair included items from only one half of the size progression or from both halves. We expected that after subjects learned to categorize these items down the middle, however, ease of judging the relative sizes of items in a pair would depend very much on whether the pair included within-half or across-half items.

The subjects were divided into two groups. One group received extensive training in classifying the ten largest items into a "large" category and the ten smallest items into a "small" category. Subjects in this group overlearned the categories at least 1000 percent. The other group did not receive training in size classification. In all other respects, the two groups were treated identically, both receiving the same instructions and the same mental-comparison task.

The subjects were told that they soon would hear pairs of words on a tape, and were to decide which word named the larger object. Prior to hearing each pair, however, the subject would be directed to image the first named object either at its normal size, or "as subjectively small as possible, while still being able to identify the imaged object." As usual, every item appeared in both size conditions equally often over subjects. Subjects were asked to maintain the image of the first object at the specified size until they heard the second word of the pair. The subjects were to decide as quickly as possible, keeping errors to a minimum, which word named the larger (in terms of actual, real-life size) object; importantly, subjects were told that they did not have to use imagery in performing the comparisons, but should simply try to decide as quickly as possible by any available means.

The first finding of interest is that more time was required to evaluate pairs when the first-named object was imaged at a tiny size instead of at a normal size. This effect was slightly more pronounced when the first item was the larger compared to when it was the smaller of the pair (in actual size). Holyoak also found the latter result and speculated that it may have been due to a "congruity effect" similar to that obtained by Paivio (1975b) in a picture-comparison task. Another explanation would posit that a tiny image of a small object needs to be expanded a relatively small amount in order to be compared to an image of a larger object; a tiny image of a large object, in contrast, requires more expansion prior to imaginal comparisons.

To our surprise, the effects of size of the initial image were the same for near and far pairs. Further, category learning did not influence the effects of initial size, nor did the effects of size of initial image differ for near and far pairs more in one group than in the other. In addition, in a separate analysis of only the data from the category-learning group, across-half pairs evinced the same effects of initial image size as did within-half pairs. These results, illustrated in figure 9.7, obviously ran counter to our hopes and expectations. If anything, the findings presented thus far are most consistent with a pure imagistic model of mental-comparison processes.

There were only two unambiguous effects of category learning on the results: First, although across-half pairs were evaluated more quickly than within-half pairs, this was more the case for the category-learning group than for the other group. The second effect resembles that obtained

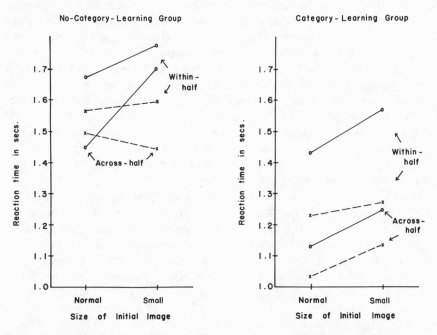

Figure 9.7. Results of the first experiment in which subjects imaged one object at a tiny or normal size and then decided whether that object was in fact larger than a second named object. Solid lines indicate that the first object was larger; dotted lines indicate that the second object was larger.

in the first experiment of this series, in which category learning eliminated size-disparity effects only for relatively near pairs (adjacent or separated by one in the size progression), but with larger disparities decision times decreased even with relatively large amounts of overlearning. Our conception of an imagistic-propositional "race" led us to expect this: Pairs incorporating more size disparity between items should be processed faster by imagistic means than pairs incorporating less size disparity; hence, the imagistic process should be more likely to finish before the propositional comparison process. This reasoning led us to examine only the pairs formed by combining the ten medium-sized items in this experiment; all of these pairs had relatively small disparities in the sizes of the component items. We examined the across- and within-half pairs. Further, we divided each of these sets of ten pairs into two groups, those with the smallest size disparities and those with the largest size disparities. Next, we obtained one mean for each of these four groups of pairs (pooling over whether the first item was imaged relatively small or normally, which was completely counterbalanced) for the no-category-learning and the category-learning groups. These means are presented in figure 9.8. As is evident in the figure, the size-disparity effect was eliminated only for across-half pairs for the category-learning group. In fact, figure 9.8 resembles figure 9.3, except that now same-category (within-half) pairs are evaluated more slowly than different-category (across-half) pairs, as we would expect if tag matching outraced imagistic processing; this is probably because the present data exclude pairs containing endpoints. It is worth noting, however, that even for the near items presented in figure 9.8, more time was required to respond when the initial image was subjectively tiny than when it was at a normal size; the advantage of beginning with a normal-sized image was 164 milleseconds for across-half pairs and 190 milliseconds for within-half pairs in the category-learning group, and 287 milliseconds for across-half pairs and 97 milliseconds for within-half pairs in the no-category-learning group.

The results of this experiment contrast with those reported by Holyoak (1977). Holyoak found results like ours only when his subjects were explicitly instructed to make their mental comparisons by comparing images of the named objects. When his subjects were given instructions like those used in our experiment, he found no effects of initial image size. But we always found that more time was required to evaluate a pair when the initial image was subjectively very small instead of normal-sized. This effect occurred whether the size disparity between the items in a pair was small or large, and whether the items in a pair belonged to the same category or different categories. Further, the magnitude of the effects of initial image size was about the same across all of the conditions of the experiment (except for a tendency for a slightly diminished effect when the larger object was presented second). The most straightforward interpreta-

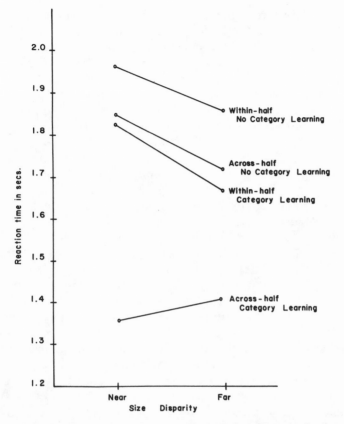

Figure 9.8. Fine-grained analysis of the size-disparity effects in the data from the first experiment in which the size of the initial image was varied. The ratios of the mean ratings of sizes for objects in near pairs were 1.027 and 1.090 for the within-half and across-half pairs, respectively; for the far pairs, the ratios were 1.108 and 1.227 for within-half and across-half pairs, respectively.

tion of these results is that subjects used imagery all of the time, even though they were told that they could make their judgments in any way they preferred.

We do have some evidence, however, that a purely imagistic comparison process was not used here. First, the across-half pairs were evaluated more quickly than within-half pairs in general, but especially so by the category-learning group. This result would be expected if category-tag comparisons could be used in evaluation and occasionally were completed before imagistic comparison processes were finished. Second, we essentially replicated the results of the first experiment for relatively near pairs: There were no size-disparity effects for across-half pairs for the category-learning group (for whom the members of these pairs fell in differ-

ent categories), whereas there were such effects for the no-category-
learning group. Further, both groups were faster with far (more disparate)
within-half pairs than with near pairs (wherein the items were in the same
category for the category-learning group, preventing tag comparison from
aiding evaluation).

Given this evidence that category information was in fact used, how do
we explain the ubiquitous effects of subjective size of the initial image?
Two explanations present themselves. First, asking people to image the
first item beforehand may give the imagery process a "head start" over
the propositional process in a parallel race. This head start would have
increased the probability that imagery comparison would run to completion prior to comparison of category tags. The effects of category learning
would be attributed here to consequences of practice in generating images
of the items while learning to categorize them; although post hoc and slippery, such an account probably could be formulated for the present results (albeit with difficulty for the finding that size-disparity effects are
partly eliminated by category learning).

A second explanation might be that our use of pairs of items of very
similar sizes forced the subjects to rely on imagery for those trials, and
thereafter they simply got into the habit of using this strategy. Thus, even
after reaching a judgment via category-tag comparison, subjects may have
performed a cursory imagery comparison before responding. This explanation is consistent with the subjects' own interpretations of their behavior, as explained when queried after the task. In our next experiment, we
will attempt to discover whether this last explanation is useful; if not, we
then will examine others. We hoped that one of the two foregoing
accounts would be supported so that we would not have to abandon the
imagistic-propositional parallel model as a general conception of how
such memory tasks are performed.

In the previous experiment, near and far (in terms of size disparity)
pairs were intermingled in the presentation sequence. Thus, we
conjectured, people may have come to use imaginal comparisons as a
matter of course as they discovered that this procedure often was required to reach a decision. In our next experiment, we repeated the instructions and the procedure of the previous one with two changes: First,
the far pairs were eliminated altogether; second, the near pairs (now consisting of only the ten intermediate-sized items used previously) were presented in two blocks, with the within-half pairs in one block and the
across-half pairs in the other. We again included a no-category-learning
group and a category-learning group. The category-learning group overlearned the categories to a criterion of 1200 percent in this experiment.
Categories, if used, divided the items into a "large" class (the largest five
medium items) and a "small" class (the smallest five medium items).
Thus, for the category-learning group, the across-half pairs were com-

posed of items in different categories whereas within-half pairs contained items in the same category.

When the across-half block is evaluated, the imagistic-propositional parallel model leads us to expect effects of initial image size for the no-category-learning group, but not to expect such effects for the category-learning group (assuming that all of the items fall into the same rough "natural" category, as seems reasonable, given the similarity in sizes of the named objects). Effects of initial image size should, however, be evident in both groups when within-half pairs are evaluated. If using the blocked design of this experiment eliminates the effects of initial image size for across-half pairs evaluated by the category-learning group, we can surmise that something about intermixing the various sorts of pairs in the presentation sequence engendered unnecessary use of imagery in the previous experiment.

The results of this experiment were encouraging; the most interesting findings are presented in figure 9.9. We obtained significant effects of initial image size for both within-half and across-half pairs in the no-category-learning group, but found no effects of initial image size for across-half

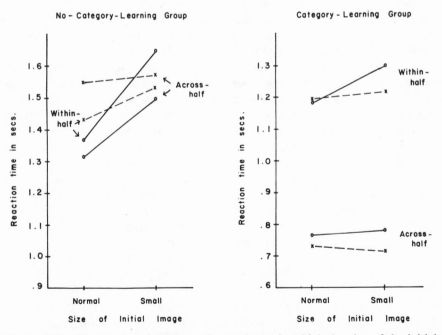

Figure 9.9. The results of the second experiment in which the size of the initial image was varied. In this experiment subjects received the within-half and across-half items in separate sets. Solid lines indicate that the first object was larger; dotted lines indicate that the second object was larger.

pairs in the category-learning group, as hoped. We did, however, find some effects of initial image size in the within-half pairs of the category-learning group (see Kosslyn et al., 1977, for details). As before, across-half pairs were evaluated more quickly than within-half pairs in general, but this was especially the case for the category-learning group. In addition, the category-learning group was faster overall than the other group. Initial image size again especially affected verification time when the first object was the larger, presumably because more image adjustment was required if a small image of a large object was initially formed than if a small image of a small object was used.

After the foregoing experiment was conducted we decided to test yet another category-learning group, now varying how well people over-learned the category assignments. The method and procedure used with this additional group were identical to those used with the previous category-learning group, except that this group was tested to a criterion of 200 percent overlearning, whereas the previous one was tested to a criterion of 1200 percent overlearning. Using the same logic underlying the very first experiment of this series (which used stick men as stimuli), we now expected that the categories would not attenuate the effects of imagistic processing on decision times. Thus, we tested this group to provide more converging evidence for the imagistic-propositional parallel model. Kosslyn and Jolicoeur (in press) present additional details and statistics for the results obtained from this group, which are illustrated in figure 9.10. First, significantly more time was generally required to compare the two named objects if the initial image was small (the interactions between pair-type and initial image size and between response and initial image size were not significant, although in figure 9.10 there appears to be a lessened effect of initial image size for the across-half pairs when the first object was actually smaller—mirroring the results obtained previously). Importantly, the effects of initial image size were the same for the within-half and across-half pairs. This is just expected as if the decreased amount of over-learning resulted in decreased availability of the size tags—which resulted in imagery processing outracing propositional processing. Analyzing the results from the 200 percent overlearning group with those from the 1200 percent overlearning group provided direct support for the imagistic-propositional model: First, the effects of initial image size were different for the across-half pairs in the two groups; smaller initial images retarded times only for the 200 percent group, as expected if imagery is used when the category tags are not very well overlearned. Second, the effects of initial image size were the same for the within-half pairs for the two groups; smaller images always retarded times, as expected if imagery must be used when the tags are the same. Also as expected, the 1200 percent group was generally faster.

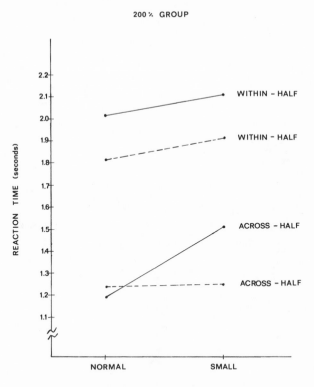

Figure 9.10. The results of a 200 percent overlearning group in which the size of the initial image was varied. Solid lines indicate that the first object was larger; dotted lines that the second object was larger.

We also examined the effects of disparity in the sizes of objects in pairs (not the image size). As in the previous experiment, we tested for the effects of size disparity in the across- and within-half pairs in the different groups; the results for all three groups are illustrated in figure 9.11. As is evident, for the 1200 percent overlearning group, relatively near across-half pairs (containing items from different categories) were evaluated in the same amount of time as were relatively far (more disparate) pairs; when members of a pair were within-half (and from the same category), size disparity effects were obtained as before, with more time being required for relatively near pairs. For the 200 percent group and the no-category-learning group, in contrast, pairs containing objects of similar sizes required more time to evaluate than pairs made up of objects differing more widely in size, for both across-half and within-half pairs. Importantly, when the data from the two category-learning groups were ana-

Image and Mind

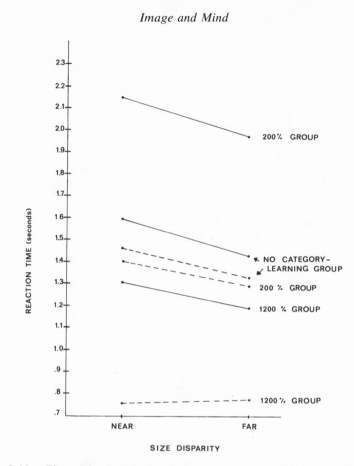

Figure 9.11. Fine-grained analysis of the size-disparity effects in the data from the second experiment in which the size of the initial image was varied.

lyzed together, the results nicely replicated those of the first experiment of the series—with the three-way interaction among size disparity, category membership, and overlearning group again attaining statistical significance.

As encouraging as the foregoing results are, all is not sweetness and light: As the model is currently formulated, there is no reason to expect that the times for within-half pairs should differ for the different groups. In all cases, these decisions are putatively based on imagistic processing. And yet, as is clearly evident in figure 9.11, the within-half pairs for the 200 percent group were evaluated more slowly than the others, and the within-half pairs for the 1200 percent group were evaluated more quickly. My first suspicion was that this may have been due to cases where the within-half block followed the across-half block, resulting in subjects intentionally trying to use the tags even when this was not profitable. But there were absolutely no significant effects of (or interactions with) presentation order in the analysis of variance. Another account is suggested by the post-session reports of some of the subjects in the 1200 percent group; these people claimed that they began to form sub-categories within the "large" and "small" categories (including ordering the stimuli by size) during the initial learning procedure. If so, then some of the within-half pairs may in fact have been evaluated using propositional processing, which would explain not only the faster times but the slightly less robust effects of initial image size in this condition (see Kosslyn et al. for details). The minimal amount of category learning for the 200 percent group may have had the opposite effect: instead of allowing subjects to further differentiate the sizes of the items within the two categories, it may have encouraged them to equate the sizes of the items. If so, this would also account for the very high error rates observed for the within-half pairs for the 200 percent overlearning group. Thus, this result might best be regarded as falling in Class 4 (domain contamination), pertaining to stimulus encoding processes. Even if this result were in Class 3 (theory supplementation) it would be rather uninteresting, however, given that an account would be very much tied to the specifics of performing this particular task.

In closing this section I should mention that we also tested one last group of subjects, using only the far pairs used in the first experiment in which image size was varied. These subjects received instructions and a procedure exactly like those given to the no-category-learning group in the previous experiment. This small experiment was conducted to see whether "natural" categories—which probably differed for the largest and smallest items used to compose the far pairs—would be used instead of imagery comparisons when near pairs (which seem to require imagery) were eliminated. The results were clear-cut: There were no effects of the size of the initial image whatsoever.

In short, presenting the across-half and the within-half items in separate blocks of trials had the desired consequences: Now imagery seemed to be used spontaneously when to-be-judged items were close in size, unless the items fell in different categories and the category associations were highly overlearned. Our results are entirely consistent with the notion that category tags were used to reach decisions before imagery comparisons were completed only when the tags were highly overlearned, and hence very easily accessed. However, when no differentiating category tags were available or tags were not highly overlearned, the subjects compared pairs of images and based decisions upon this comparison. Since the near pairs were composed of objects that probably do fall into the same "natural" category, and hence the available category tags could not be used to compare sizes, it is gratifying that imagery does seem to be used habitually in evaluating these pairs. The results from the no-category-learning group with the far pairs support the notion that our model can be generalized to real-world situations, where categories are not explicitly taught for use in size-comparison tasks. If our model accounted only for tasks in which categories were explicitly taught, it would be of little value, some might say of "academic interest" only.

All of these results taken together seem to support the claim that both propositional representations, like entries in the PRP files in our model, and imagistic representations, like entries in the IMG files and surface images themselves, are used in performing mental comparisons. Further, people seem to access and begin to use both sorts of information simultaneously. Models that assume that only one type of representation is used seem hard-pressed to account for all of our data. Although any given finding probably can be explained by a number of theoretical conceptions, different specific models will be required to account for different aspects of our results. Only the imagistic-propositional parallel model seems to account for the sum of these findings in a relatively straightforward manner.

Before examining the implications of this model for other sorts of tasks, like fact retrieval, it will be useful to develop an explicit statement of this part of our general theory. Considering how our computer simulation deals with the task of mental comparison will be a useful exercise, if only because it illustrates how the structure of the general model constrains the sort of account we can offer here.

1.4 A Computer Model for Mental Comparison

The theory of mental comparison adds a new functional capacity to our theory of imagery. Marc Johnson and I implemented this new COMPARE process in the general model. We decided to work out the details of how mental comparison processes may occur for a number of reasons. First, it is a paradigmatic case of a form of question-answering in which imagery is actually used spontaneously. Second, it involves some complex interactions among different components of the system, and promised to be a reasonable check of the internal consistency of the theory as a whole. And third, it is a nice exercise showing how the general model can be used to promote development of reasonably detailed specific models, should the need arise.

The structures and processes of our model constrain how we can implement a model for a specific task, like mental comparison. For example, we include the assumption that images are usually printed out at about the size that just fills the most resolved region of the visual buffer. Thus, a pair of large objects will seem farther away in an image than a pair of small objects, if both are normalized to subtend the same visual angle. This property precludes using differences in size scale in the image to explain the congruity effect, as was mistakenly implied by Kosslyn et al. (1977). The model suggests three loci for the effects observed in the experiments discussed above: comparison of propositional tags, comparison of surface images, and comparison of the underlying literal encodings (files of r, Θ coordinates in the model). That is, because we have allowed the program to adjust the r values of a part before integrating it into an image, we should also allow the program to look up this sort of information in performing this task. Recall that in order to put a tire on an image of a car at the correct subjective size, for example, we had to assume that the program could look up the r values of the part; if so, then it should be able to look up directly imagistic information about the size of an object for use in performing the present task. This assumption is consistent with our finding that although processing of surface images tends to require more time than does processing of propositional representations in question-answering, imagistic processing can often "outrace" propositional processing in the size-comparison task. In this case, the underlying literal encodings may be accessed directly, without need of actually generating images and inspecting them (given that the comparison is along a single dimension, which is accessible directly in the underlying encoding).

The data collected thus far seem to implicate a parallel search, with a propositional retrieval and comparison process proceeding at the same time as an imagistic search. We do not claim that these processes are actually going on simultaneously in a formal sense (see Townsend, 1972), but only in a functional, practical sense. That is, it could be that the two processes are "time sharing" the same pool of general "capacity," and hence are really alternating serial processes. But since the execution of one does not necessarily depend on prior results from the other, and the two processes can be executed during the same period of time, we can treat them as if they were truly occurring in parallel. It is clear how to implement one arm of this search, the propositional tag retrieval and comparison. In our model, we simply look up and retrieve the SIZE tags. These same category names are used in deciding whether to zoom in or pan back from an image when searching for a given part (see chapter 5). If two objects are categorized differently, the program will select the one that has the size tag with the largest value (recall that tags have a semantics that allows translation into a size range and an optimal resolution based on this range). Speed of retrieving size tags depends on how high in the PRP list these tags are stored; this is the only free parameter affecting this process in our model, since we assume that the comparison and decision processes require a constant amount of time. The more strongly one overlearns a size tag, the higher on the list this tag will be stored and hence the more quickly it may be retrieved. If the tags found in the two objects' PRP files are the same, the propositional comparison process grinds to a halt and gives the imagistic processes free rein to finish.

The putative imagistic process is more complicated. According to the model, there are two kinds of imagistic processes, one involving sampling from long-term memory representations directly and one involving using those representations to generate surface images, which are then compared. In our current simulation, we posit that people use surface images only after sampling the underlying literal encodings directly. Let us trace through the imagistic processes. First, we assume that literal perceptual memories are stored in something like our r, Θ files. That is, whatever the memories are like, they can be sampled a portion at a time. At this juncture, we had to make a critical decision: Size could be represented directly in the underlying literal representation, or could be accessed only via some sort of inference procedures. That is, we can assume that the encoding processes preserve size constancy, so that an object is encoded in terms of its actual size—and not the visual angle subtended. Alternatively, we can assume that the visual angle subtended by the object is encoded. If we do this, then we must assume either that distance at the time of encoding is also encoded or that some information is represented that will allow calculation of distance at the time of encoding. The geometry of the situation demands information about distance and visual angle if actual size is to be inferred; if either sort of information is not directly represented or able to be inferred, the size of an object will not be available for use in performing mental comparisons. There were two straightforward ways in which we could have implemented a system that inferred actual size. First, we could have allowed the visual angle at the time of encoding to be represented directly. That is, the range of r values could have reflected apparent size at the time of perception. In this case, distance either could have been represented explicitly or could have been implicit in the distribution of spatial frequencies in the representation. That is, as an object moves farther away, fewer low spatial frequencies are evident. This information is potentially available in the density of dots, if we assume that the farther apart dots are, the greater is the proportion of lower spatial frequencies depicted. In this case, then, distance could have been inferred from the dot density and a knowledge of the material of which an object was made (given that different materials will have different spatial frequency components; in our model, for example, cardboard would be represented by more dots than would glass). Whether distance is encoded or inferred, this general conception rests on the assumption that people are very good at remembering the visual angle subtended by an object at the time of encoding, even if the object appears with contextual cues. My suspicion was that people are not built this way, but I could find little support for either position in the literature (see Baird, 1970).

The second way we easily could have implemented a system that infers actual size involved assuming that all visual knowledge is represented in a "canonical form." That is, perhaps all information is normalized to the same internal "size," which presumably will aid recognition when objects appear at different distances. In this case, a constant range of *r* values will be used, no matter how large is the actual represented object. The task here is to somehow infer not just the distance, but also the visual angle at the time of encoding. This can be done if one knows about the surface texture of the objects. In this case, in the model the density of dots at the time of encoding would be preserved when the object is normalized, so a given density will (relative to a standard associated with the material of which the object is made) index distance. If there is a propositional encoding of the actual number of dots at the time of encoding, this will allow computation of the visual angle subtended by the object (fewer dots reflecting a smaller visual angle; this computation requires that one already knows how many dots appear in the material at a given distance, however). Thus, number of dots and dot density will index visual angle and distance. This notion assumes that we are very good at remembering information about texture. I find this assumption dubious; the fuzziness of an object just does not seem to be a very salient characteristic, nor does it seem subjectively to change much within a great range of relatively short distances. Again, however, I could not locate any definitive data showing that people are or are not good at estimating absolute distance solely on the basis of textural cues.

In the absence of compelling data on the issue, we stuck with our earlier hypothesis (see chapter 7) that size is reflected directly in the underlying representation. Thus, in our model the range of *r* values in an IMG file reflects the actual size of an object. If this were an important decision, one that would be further built upon, we would not make such a choice without evidence. Instead, we would take this as an instance of the "directive function" of the model, and conduct the relevant research. But, since this exercise is primarily a demonstration that our model can be made sufficiently explicit to account for the obtained data, we have not performed the needed experiments. Before this particular implementation is to be taken seriously, however, the background assumptions must be examined empirically.

In our model, then, we wanted to efficiently sample the *r*, Θ pairs in the IMG files for two objects, looking to see which represented the larger object. Consider the analogy offered before: Imagine that we are interested in which of two lakes contains the largest fish (not simply larger on the average). In this case, we will only bother to record the sizes of relatively large fish, and will simply throw back the minnows. Thus, we will first set a criterion, *C*, which will determine which fish we will reject; in our model, we will consider only *r* values above some cutoff. This value will depend in part on the range and distribution of sizes one expects. If we were sampling from inland seas instead of lakes, the sizes that would correspond to "large" would be different. In our model, different *r* values will be rejected depending on the general size ranges under consideration. The way the question is presented should also affect where the cutoff point is set: If asked "which is larger," one may expect both objects to be large (relative to the sample space); whereas the question "which is smaller" may make one expect both objects to be small, and adjust C accordingly. If one expected fish the size of tuna and sharks in two inland seas, it would be silly to weigh and record perch. But if one were expecting fish only as large as perch, it would be silly to set one's criterion for rejection to exclude all but fish the size of tuna and sharks.

Consider what would happen if C were set incorrectly: If the objects to be compared were small, but the question was "which object is larger," C might be set so high that the r values sampled would never reach it, in which case we would never record anything later to be compared. If the objects were large but the question was "which is smaller," C might be set so low that we would record and consider every r value, which would be very inefficient. In either case, we would want to recalibrate the criterion so that only a few cases would have to be considered. But how far should the setting be changed? If the objects being considered were of medium size, it would not help to replace a criterion appropriate for large objects with one suitable for small ones. This would be just trading in one problem for another. In our model C is altered in small increments. If it is set too high, such that too great a proportion of r values are rejected, it is reduced in steps until the correct proportion of r values is sampled; if it is set too low, so too many r values are compared, it is moved up in increments. Thus, the greater the disparity between the C established by the form of the question and the actual size of the objects, the larger should be the congruity effect. And this is true, as Banks (1977) has shown (although Banks does not interpret his findings in this way).

The decision of which IMG file contains significantly larger r values is accomplished by a simple statistical test. This test reaches significance more quickly when objects more disparate in size are compared, accounting for the size-disparity effect; this account is entirely consonant with our claims about the characteristics of comparing imagistic representations in the foregoing experiments. If sampling has proceeded for a long enough time (or if enough pairs have been sampled) and there is no significant difference, the program assumes that the size difference is subtle and prints out an image of both objects. Since size is preserved in long-term memory, the sizes of the images automatically represent the actual sizes if the same r mapping value is used by PICTURE when printing out both files. The adjacent images are then compared simply by calculating how many "squares" of the surface matrix are covered by each. If one image is available at the outset, it is adjusted to fill half the surface matrix and the other image is then printed out next to it. The new image probably should be printed while the first is adjusted (to explain the effects of actual size of the first imaged object), however, but all things considered the model sketches out a plausible account of our data.

This model makes two predictions: First, the congruity effect should not be present if images are generated first and subjects base their decisions by inspecting the images, but should occur if imagery follows direct sampling from the underlying long-term memory representations. Second, if we allow subjects to assume that a given size range is being sampled from, and then present items outside of that range, a "congruity effect" should result—even if the question is appropriate. For example, if people are answering questions about vegetables, and then are asked which is larger, an elephant or a truck, we should find longer reaction times than if they were asked about a watermelon and a pumpkin—even though the elephant and truck are both "large." This "reverse" congruity effect is a consequence of recalibration of the criterion, C.

This kind of modeling exercise, then, is useful in the same way the original CRT metaphor was useful. First, it raises questions that one would like answered before developing an explicit particular theory; and second, it produces interesting predictions. In addition, it is useful to have a demonstration that the kinds of structures and processes incorporated in our general model can be extended in a straightforward way to deal with particular tasks that are different from the ones that motivated us to construct it as we did in the first place.

2.0 IMAGERY IN FACT RETRIEVAL

The findings described in the previous section led us to suppose that propositional representations are processed at the same time as imagery representations, and that the relative speed of processing the two sorts of information determines which representation is in fact used in answering a question. This basic line of attack can be extended into the more general domain of fact retrieval. In this section, we will consider when imagery is used in deciding that an object has some property; only concrete, potentially imageable properties will be considered here, since it seems clear that if one cannot image a property, imagery will not be used (at least in a simple way) in retrieving the information.

We began by positing a new functional capacity, one that coordinates the different ways in which a fact may be ascertained in memory. Figure 9.12 outlines the sequence of events involved when our program is given an ANSWERIF command. The ANSWERIF procedures answer questions of the form "Does an x have a y?" The first step the program takes when given an ANSWERIF command is to determine whether the query is reasonable. For example, if one were asked "Does a fish have leaves?" one could respond with a very fast "no." We included this property for

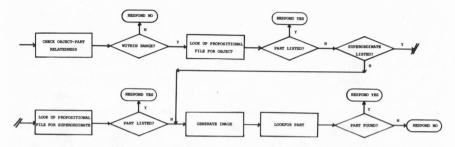

Figure 9.12. A flowchart outlining the processing accomplished by the AN-SWERIF procedure in the model.

the same reasons Smith, Shoben, and Rips (1974) posit a first stage of fast processing, and for the intuitively satisfying reasons discussed by Lindsay and Norman (1977). It seems clear that we do not search all of memory when asked whether Ben Franklin drove a Cadillac, and some mechanism must be posited to account for this sort of shortcut. In our model, we assume that the semantic memory system makes a global "property comparison" or the like (for example, searching for representations in memory that relate the two concepts together) resulting in a measure of how related are an object and a part. If this value is lower than a set criterion value, a fast "no" response is made, and no actual searching occurs. We have not actually simulated the operation of this global comparison process, however. Instead, the program simply calls up a "dummy" subroutine that looks up the "relatedness value" of the object and part, which is listed in a table. This is an unabashed kluge, but nothing to be ashamed of: We are not in the business of constructing a model of semantic memory, but only of how imagery interfaces with it. Thus, as long as we specify the main input and output features of compatible models of the remaining parts of memory and perception, we have fulfilled our obligation. We leave specification of the actual details of this fast global comparison process to others specifically interested in this question. We are noncommittal in regard to the question of whether this initial check precedes both imagery and propositional search or is just the initial part of propositional search; in either case, if the property and object are very unrelated, this process will terminate processing before much processing of either variety is very far under way.

If the queried part is related to the object over the criterial amount, two sorts of processing in theory begin in parallel: propositional search and image generation and inspection. In the model, the propositional search begins first by looking directly in the part's file for an entry that the object has the part. For example, if the program is asked if a car has a rear tire, it will search in the CAR.PRP file for HASA.REARTIRE. If this representation is found, the program exits with an affirmative response. When people are asked to evaluate an object's properties, more associated, more frequently co-occurring, or more typical properties are affirmed more quickly than less associated, less frequently co-occurring, or less typical properties (see chapter 3, section 2.2.1). For convenience, since these variables are highly correlated, we will refer to this factor as simple "association strength." In our model, the more highly associated a part is with an object, the more likely it is that it will be noted directly in the object's PRP list; further, if we assume that the list is serially scanned, more associated properties will be stored higher up, and thus will be encountered more quickly in the search. Second, some properties will not be stored directly with a property, but must be inferred from the superordinate. That is, if asked about a part that is not noted in the propositional file, the program will look up the name of the superordinate category most associated with the object and will search for a representation of the part in that superordinate's PRP file. This notion is very similar to that proposed by Collins and Quillian (1969).

If the program cannot find an explicit representation of the part stored in the object's or its superordinate's file, the propositional search terminates. At this point, any decision will be based on inspection of the image. The imagery inspection procedures are exactly like those described earlier (chapters 5 and 7). An image of the object is generated and the description of the part is looked up and the surface image is inspected; if the person knows what the part looks like, we posit that such a description is stored in memory.

The current simulation is an inadequate model of this process in a very obvious way: It is not a true parallel device. In fact, we now have imagery processes occurring only if the sought information is not located in the object's file and the superordinate inference procedures fail. We justify this by reference to the fact (chapter 3, sections 2.1 and 2.2) that inspection of surface images usually requires more time than propositional search (in contrast to direct sampling of the literal encodings; recall that we posit that one cannot interpret the category of a shape unless the underlying r, Θ files are printed into the visual buffer). Hence, image use will usually follow propositional search in practice if not by necessity. In addition to this major problem, we have simply sidestepped most of the issues about propositional search. For example, it would make sense that the property's PRP file would also be searched for the name of the object at the same time that the object's file was searched for the name of the property (see Meyer, 1970). In any case, in addition to raising a number of interesting empirical questions, our current implementation allows us to generate a host of predictions—some of which will be considered in the remainder of this chapter and in the following chapter.

3.0 VALIDATION AND GENERALIZATION TESTS

The ANSWERIF procedure in our model leads us to make several predictions and provides ready accounts for data in the literature.

3.1 Testing Predictions

The most basic implication of our model is that the faster of the two processes—propositional or imagery—will be the one that generates a decision. Thus, if propositional search is impeded, it becomes more likely that imagery processes will succeed in running to completion. Presumably, easy judgments will be ones where the requisite information is stored in a very accessible form, requiring no deduction or image generation and inspection. If the difficulty of evaluating the truth of an assertion is determined in part by the difficulty of locating the necessary propositional information, then the more difficult it is to decide whether an object has a visible property, the more likely it should be that imagery is used in reaching a decision. We tested this notion with a very simple preliminary experiment. People were asked to read a set of sentences and to indicate whether each sentence was a true or false assertion, and to rate, on a seven-pont scale, how much they thought they had to use imagery in order to make the decision, how difficult they thought it was to make the decision, and how frequently they thought they had considered the asserted fact in the past. There were three types of sentences, all asserting facts about the properties of concrete objects: One-third had no adjectives ("Lions have fur"); one-third had one adjective ("Trucks have big wheels"); and one-third had two adjectives ("Donkeys have long furry ears"). Half of each type of statement were true and half were false.

We expected that the more qualified properties probably would not be stored explicitly, either with an object-concept or its superordinate concept. Thus, we expected these statements to be more difficult to verify, and to be more likely to require imagery. We also expected subjects to report considering the more qualified statements less frequently in the past. And we expected that the less often one had thought of an object as having some property, the less likely the property was to be explicitly encoded in the object's PRP file, and hence the more likely it was that imagery would be used verify it.

The results were as follows: For "true" statements, for which subjects presumably found a representation of the stated fact in memory, statements rated to be more difficult to evaluate also reportedly tended to evoke imagery use, as evinced by a high correlation between the two ratings, $r = .84$. Rated frequency-of-consideration and imagery use were also systematically related, $r = -.64$. Thus, as expected, more difficult and less frequent assertions tended to evoke imagery use in verification.

This result falls in Class 1 of our taxonomy (confirmation). The mean imagery ratings, with higher numbers indicating more use, for statements with zero, one, and two adjectives were 2.56 (SD = .772), 3.38 (SD = .909), and 3.08 (SD = .586), respectively. Thus, although statements with one adjective engendered imagery use more than those with no adjectives, statements with two adjectives engendered less imagery than expected. This is a Class 2 (multiple interpretation) finding, perhaps simply indicating that one adjective was enough to engender the maximal amount of imagery use. Alternatively, perhaps sometimes the pair of adjectives together were distinctive enough that they were stored as a unit in the object's PRP file, and hence imagery sometimes is not required with two adjectives.

The results for "false" statements also revealed that the more difficult to assess statements required more imagery, $r = .84$ again. Interestingly, we found here that reported imagery use increased—not decreased, as it did with "true" statements—for evaluations of more frequently considered assertions, $r = .60$. This is a Class 3 (theory supplementation) result: Perhaps the more one had encountered some association, the more plausible it seemed, and since more plausible false properties require more time to evaluate in semantic memory tasks (which usually are presumably performed via processing of propositional representations—see Collins and Quillian, 1972; Smith, Shoben, and Rips, 1974), the image procedures may have had time simply to "outrace" the propositional ones. The mean ratings for the zero, one, and two-adjective "false" statements were 2.15 (SD = .565), 3.29 (SD = .807), and 3.23 (SD = .688), respectively. Again, imagery did not increase as much as expected with two adjectives. In addition to the first interpretation offered for the corresponding finding with "true" statements, in this case the increased specification may sometimes have rendered the two-adjective pair itself less probable for any object, allowing easy rejection.

Thus, we have some support for the claim that the speed with which propositional encodings of properties are located should in part determine whether an image will be consulted when one is answering a question. This is a fundamental characteristic of the image-proposition "race" discussed in the previous section. One key variable here was the degree to which the noun and the property were associated; for example, "A zebra has stripes" includes a noun and a property that are highly associated, according to normative ratings, whereas "A zebra has knees" contains a noun and a property that are not very highly associated. Our parallel race model posits that if the search for the property in the object's propositional file should fail, then one will attempt to deduce the answer via looking up the superordinate category. In this case, the speed with which one retrieves the superordinate file for the object and then finds the property in the superordinate's propositional file should also influence whether or not imagery is used. The relative speeds of this sort of processing and

image generation and inspection should determine the outcome of the
race between the imagery processes and the propositional search and deduction processes. Thus, this model accounts for our earlier result that
more difficult statements more often were evaluated with imagery in the
following way: "Less difficult" statements are those requiring relatively
few propositional operations which run relatively quickly; increasingly
"more difficult" statements tap relatively poorly overlearned propositional information, require deduction, or cannot be answered via propositional search and deduction because the requisite encodings are not available. Each of these factors operate to slow down propositional
processing, and hence increase the likelihood that imagery will be used.

In an additional experiment Pierre Jolicoeur and I tried to capture three
characteristics of the deductive aspect of the propositional search procedures by varying (1) the association strength between a part or property of
an object and the object itself, (2) the association strength between an object and its most frequently co-occuring superordinate, and (3) the association strength between the property and the superordinate category. We
hypothesized that low association strength between an object and a property of that object implies that the property is very low in the list of propositions associated with the object, or that this list is unlikely to contain a
proposition stating the relationship between the object and part. In either
case, the propositional representation should require more time to locate
than when an object and part are highly associated, and thus the imagery
system will become more likely to "outrace" the propositional processes.
Similarly, if the part is not listed in the object's file, then the association
strength between the object and the most frequently co-occuring superordinate should reflect the ease of looking up the superordinate's name (in
the object's list), and thus should influence the time to look up the list associated with the superordinate. Thereafter, the association strength
between the part and the superordinate should reflect ease of looking up
the proper entry. Thus, low association in both cases should lead to
longer processing times and should increase the probability that the imagery system will produce the information faster than will propositional
search and deduction.

We began to explore these predictions with the same simple rating task
used earlier: We asked our subjects whether a declarative statement was
true or false. Each statement had the form "An x has y" or "An x has a
y." A list of 152 object-property pairs was composed to be used in the
construction of statements for the verification task. Each property consisted of an adjective followed by a noun (for example, "A canary has
yellow feathers"). We first wanted to obtain the most appropriate superordinates for each object in our pairs. Thus, we asked a group of undergraduates to write down up to three superordinates for each of the objects. We asked our subjects to write these names in the order in which

they thought of them. For each subject, the first response to each object was later assigned a score of 3; the second, a score of 2; and the third, a score of 1. The superordinate with the largest mean score was taken as the "best" superordinate for the object in question and was used in categorizing our test items for later analysis of the data.

We now had a list of object-property-superordinate triplets. For each triplet we obtained association ratings between each pair of items (words) from a new group of undergraduates. These people were asked to rate, on a standard seven-point scale, how highly associated with each other the members of each pair of items were, how easy it was to form a mental image of the object, and how easy it was to see the part or property on the image of the object. The imagery ratings were obtained in an effort to estimate the ease of performing the imagery processes. Perhaps fortunately, the ratings of ease of forming an image of the object showed very little variance. Thus, we postulated that for the items used here imagery processes should be relatively constant for items differing in association strength. Differences in imagery use, then, ought to be determined by differences in the speed of the propositional system.

After obtaining these ratings, we realized that the familiarity of an object could have an effect on the processes under investigation, if familiarity dictates how many encodings are likely to be entered in an object's propositional list. That is, more familiar objects could have more properties explicitly encoded, and hence would less often require deductive processes. Thus, we obtained ratings of familiarity with the objects from a new group of undergraduates. At the same time we collected an additional set of object-part association ratings for each of the 152 triplets. The new association ratings were collected to be compared with the first ratings to establish their reliability. (And in fact the correlation between two sets of object-part association ratings was quite high, $r = .90$.) The second set of association ratings was used in all subsequent analyses because we had slightly more confidence in it, given that the overall rating task was easier (because fewer ratings were required) for these subjects; in addition, because we used the familiarity ratings, it seemed a good idea to use the association ratings from the same people.

In addition to the 152 "true" statements, composed from the rated stimuli, an equal number of false statements were constructed to be used as distractors. The false statements ranged from being quite subtle and nonobvious to being relatively easy, according to our intuitions. A new group of undergraduates decided whether each of the 304 statements was true or false. Immediately after each true/false evaluation, the subjects were asked to rate how much they had consulted an image in arriving at their decision, again using a seven-point scale.

For purposes of analysis, the "true" object-part-superordinate triplets were divided into eight association-strength patterns. The association between the object and the property could be either high or low; the association between the part and the superordinate could be high or low; and the association between the object and the superordinate could be high or low. Thus, we constructed a $2 \times 2 \times 2$ cube to represent every possible combination of association ratings.

Within each cell, ten triplets were retained for analysis. For four of these cells, we kept the ten triplets with the highest mean object-part association ratings. These four cells are the top two cells in each of the 2×2 tables shown in table 9.1. Similarly, the remaining four cells were filled with ten triplets with the lowest mean object-part association ratings. Within each of these groups of four cells, items were further sorted according to whether the mean ratings were above or below the overall mean for the object-superordinate and superordinate-part judgments. Thus, each statement was assigned to one of the eight cells in table 9.1. In selecting the items to be rated, we tried to ensure a spread along the three dimensions, and that all combinations of values would be likely; fortunately, our intuitions proved reasonably sound and allowed us to assign 10 items to each cell, resulting in 80 statements being used in the analyses (see Kosslyn and Jolicoeur, in press, for details of the method and procedure).

The mean imagery-use ratings obtained for each cell are shown in table 9.1. Our major hypotheses received support: The cells with high association between all pairs of variables and the cells with low association between all pairs of variables contain the lowest and highest imagery-use ratings. Furthermore, a comparison of cells in which we predicted relatively high imagery use with those in which we did not expect imagery use was highly significant. These results fall in Class 1 (confirmation). A regression analysis revealed that familiarity per se was unrelated to rated imagery use in this experiment, which is a Class 2 (multiple interpretation) finding, perhaps indicating that one does not necessarily propositionally

Table 9.1. Mean imagery ratings in the eight conditions of the experiment on spontaneous use of imagery ("high" and "low" refer to relative association strength along the relevant dimensions).

| | Object-superordinate | | | |
| | High Part-superordinate | | Low Part-superordinate | |
Object-part	High	Low	High	Low
High	2.775	3.355	3.215	3.390
Low	4.085	3.960	3.490	4.315

encode more information about more familiar objects. Alternatively, image processing speed may increase for more familiar objects, partly compensating for effects of increased numbers of propositional encodings.*

Thus, our hypotheses received good support from the data; although the magnitude of the differences observed was not overwhelming, the differences were in the directions predicted and were statistically significant.

3.1.1 Validating the Ratings Technique

The ratings data were interesting enough to motivate us to attempt to validate them with a reaction-time task. We took a representative sample of the rated items, such that there was an even spread of difficulty and frequency and such that each noun occurred twice, once paired with a true property and once paired with a false one. Further, we selected these items so that all properties were on one end or the other (right, left, top, or bottom—depending on the orientation of the object). Half of the "true" properties had been rated as tending to require imagery use to evaluate and half had been rated as not tending to require imagery. A new group of subjects heard a tape recording which cued them to image a particular object and then to mentally focus on one end. Following this, a possible property was named, and the subject was to answer as quickly as possible whether that property belonged to the object. We specifically told these people that they did not have to use imagery once the property word was presented, but only needed to respond correctly as quickly as possible. A given subject focused on the end closest to the named property on half of the "true" trials and on the other end on the other half of the "true" trials. Two groups of subjects were tested, such that each end of each object was the point of focus equally often. We expected that if imagery was in fact used, then responses should be affected by how far the subject had to scan to see the probe or the relevant area. In contrast, if imagery was not actually used, there should be no effects of where on an initial image a subject was focusing. The items were presented in a random order, so a subject could not deduce whether a particular object would be paired with a high-imagery property (and in fact these subjects did not even know that two sorts of properties were being presented).

The results of this experiment are presented in figure 9.13. As

---

*In another study Jolicoeur and I found the effects of the degree of association between a noun and property on rated imagery use to depend on the familiarity of the noun: Only with more familiar objects did more highly associated properties evoke less reported image use than less associated properties. Presumably, only with more familiar objects do we have an appreciable number of properties entered in the objects' lists of propositions, and even then only the most associated properties are explicitly stored. If so, then only with these items will propositional processing be able to outrace imagery processing.

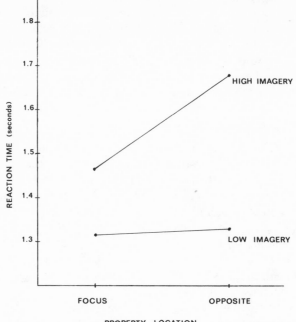

Figure 9.13.   Time to verify an object's properties when the subject began by focusing on one end and the property was on that end or the opposite one. Two kinds
of properties were used, those previously rated to require imagery to verify and
those previously rated not to require imagery. Subjects in this experiment were
not told to use the image in verifying the properties, but only to form an image of
the to-be-queried object and to focus on one end.

expected, we obtained effects of the focus location only for the high-imagery items. In addition, we again found that these items required generally
more time to evaluate than did low-imagery items (which presumably
were evaluated via more efficient propositional processing). These
findings, then, not only validate the imagery rating procedure, but fall in
Class 1 of our taxonomy (confirmation). In addition, these results strongly
counter "demand characteristic" interpretations of our earlier scanning
results: Not only were these subjects not told to scan (or to use the image
at all), but they were not told that scanning was expected only for a subset
of the items. I cannot think of an even marginally plausible account of
these results that hinges on implicit task demands.

3.2 Accounts of Results in the Literature

The theory is fleshed out enough at this point to allow us to attempt to
explain results reported in the literature. In addition, it provides a frame-

work for asking questions about how to extend the theory to address the nature of individual differences in imagery use. Let us consider each of these topics in turn.

3.2.1 Retrieval of Remembered Spatial Relations

The present theory makes predictions about when imagery should be used in a number of other tasks. Whenever some previously unconsidered spatial relation (which hence is unlikely to be encoded propositionally) is queried, and this relation is implicit in an encoded image, then the subject should spontaneously use imagery in answering a question about the relation. For example, many people report using imagery when asked "Which is higher off the ground, a horse's knees or the tip of its tail?" This prediction is borne out in a study reported by Brooks (1968). Brooks asked people to participate in two different tasks. In one task, subjects were to image a block drawing of a letter of the alphabet and then to classify the corners of the letter. One of the classification tasks, for example, involved responding yes or no regarding whether each successive corner of the letter was at the extreme top or bottom of the figure, starting in a specified corner and proceeding clockwise. Responding was done in one of three ways: by saying yes or no, by pointing to the appropriate letter, Y (yes) or N (no) on a response sheet (which required working down columns of Y and N that were staggered on the page, requiring close visual guidance), or by tapping with one hand for yes and the other hand for no. The logic of these studies assumes that imagery and like-modality perception share common specialized processing resources that are not utilized by verbal processes. Hence, if imagery is used the task should be most difficult when visually guided responding is required. Of primary interest is the finding that having to point to the correct letter on a response sheet did indeed most severely disrupt the rate of responding in this task. In Brook's other task, in contrast, subjects received a sentence and had to categorize each word according to whether or not it was a noun, again using one of the three modes of responding. In this case, saying the responses was slower than pointing. These results are consistent with the idea that visual imagery was used in the letter-classification task (assuming that visual imagery selectively shares some resources with visual perception), and auditory images were used in the word-classification task, assuming that auditory imagery selectively shares some resources with hearing (so that auditory images are disrupted when hearing one's own voice). These assumptions remain to be conclusively demonstrated, however (see chapter 7, section 2.4.2), but the Brooks findings are in Class 1 (confirmation) if his dependent measure is indeed valid.

Byrne (1974) used the Brooks paradigm in an effort to discover whether the interference effects really reflect use of visual imagery per se or are a consequence of using a more general "spatial system." Byrne gave some people arrays containing pictures of objects, which they were to scan and classify (as living or nonliving), and other people simply learned lists or sequences of pictures. Subjects responded by saying yes or no or by pointing to the word yes or no written in an array on a page, progressing farther through the array with each response. Byrne found that classification from memory of the stimulus items was selectively impaired when pointing responses were required only if the objects were presented in an array. When people merely classified remembered pictures that had initially been presented sequentially, responding by pointing did not selectively disrupt task performance. Thus, Byrne conjectured that scanning an image, and not merely possessing an image, was required to obtain interference with the visual response task. Further, even when the objects were learned in an array, Byrne found less interference when a subject progressed through the response array in the same pattern that one passed through while scanning the imaged array. When direction of image scanning and response scanning conflicted, interference was most marked. Byrne's findings fall in Class 2 (multiple interpretation). One may simply remember the names in a list when words or pictures are presented in sequence, so that no imagery is required to classify the objects. When an array is presented, however, numerous orderings of items are implicit in the array, depending on the scan instructions. Thus, subjects may encode it as an image, given that imagery—by its spatial nature—effectively encodes spatial relations in two and three dimensions (according to the findings reported by Pinker, in press). Although we do not expect imagery use in the sequential presentation condition—since there is no reason why simple propositional descriptions of the stimuli will not allow one to perform the task—Byrne's failure to find interference when pictures were learned sequentially (instead of in an array) does not necessarily rule out the possibility that imagery was used even here: It may have been easier to use imagery in this condition (perhaps because one could generate isolated sequences of images instead of the entire array), and hence less vivid images may have been used, or images may have been maintained for shorter durations. In either case, imagery might not have interfered as much with perception. Further, it may simply be that Byrne's dependent measure is not sensitive to imagery use per se, but rather is a reflection of how one is *scanning* an image. This interpretation is supported by Byrne's finding that compatibility of direction of image and response selection greatly affected ease of performing the task.

It is worth noting in passing that the task used by Weber and his colleagues, requiring classification from memory of whether letters are relatively tall or short (see chapter 7, section 2.2), is just the kind of task in which people should use imagery spontaneously, if our theory is correct. In this case, it seems unlikely that subjects had ever explicitly encoded the relative size of individual letters. Thus, since a propositional encoding of the relative height was not stored in a list associated with each letter's name, and this information could not be deduced from a list storing information about letters in general, subjects would have no other recourse than to use imagery. And Weber's data consistently suggest that people do in fact use imagery in this task—even when they are not explicitly told to do so (see, for example, Weber, Kelley, and Little, 1972).

3.2.2 Research on Individual Differences

An enormous amount of effort has been expended in studying individual differences in imagery. Much of this effort has been directed toward discovering which kinds of imagery (for example, visual or auditory) are superior in given individuals, and our theory does not speak to these data. But some of the studies do bear on the relative efficacy of visual imagery in different individuals and how these differences affect one's abilities to use imagery.

3.2.2.1 Self-Report Techniques

Self-report techniques are the oldest method of studying imagery. Because different people say different things, this technique became closely intertwined with the study of individual differences. The observation that people differ in their ability to call up sensory experiences from memory was made in the literature as early as 1860 by Fechner, and later—in more detail, with more data—by Galton in 1883. Fechner asked people to evoke an image of some named object, and discovered that some people were able to get only momentary glimpses whereas others claimed to have more detailed percept-like experiences. Galton's study made use of the now-famous "breakfast table" questionnaire. This technique involved asking one to image one's breakfast table as it had looked that morning. Subjects were then asked a number of things about the image, such as the brightness (relative to the actual scene), color, and amount of detail. Interestingly, slightly over 10 percent of his subjects claimed not to have any images—and in fact doubted the very existence of mental images! Because the nonimagers tended to be successful scholars and scientists, Galton surmised that imagery was the characteristic mode of thought of those with lesser mental abilities.

The examination of individual differences in imagery was carried on by others, some of whom studied the predominance of different types of imagery (Stricker, 1880) or imagery in famous individuals (Toulouse, 1897). In addition, Galton's work was refined by Betts (1909), who developed a questionnaire that not only required people to assign a numerical value for vividness of their images, but tested multiple sensory modalities as well (such as auditory and olfactory, in addition to visual). In Betts's initial studies, auditory and visual images were reported to be more vivid than the others, but only slightly more so. In more recent work (see McKellar, 1965, 1977; White, Sheehan, and Ashton, 1977) people report vast dispari- ties in the frequency and quality of nonvisual and nonauditory imagery. Interestingly, McKellar (1965) recently studied 500 adult members of Mensa, an organization requiring a high score on an IQ test for admission. Niney-seven percent of these people claimed to experience visual mental imagery, and over half reported having imagery in at least seven different modalities. The disparity in the early findings and the contemporary ones could indicate either that the early or more recent methodology was flawed or that the distribution of image abilities has in fact changed over time. We cannot assess the validity of the second conjecture, but the truth of the first is clear: Not only does rated vividness often vary depending on incidental details (such as the identity of the experimenter—see Sheehan and Neisser, 1969), but it often fails to predict anything once the effects of other factors have been controlled out (see, for example, Kosslyn and Alper, 1977). As far as I can tell, only Marks (for example, 1973, 1977) and Finke (for example, Finke and Schmidt, 1977) are having much luck with subjective assessments of image vividness. For instance, Marks's VVIQ test (an expanded version of the visual scales of Betts's test) seems to predict who will evince certain kinds of eye movements while remem- bering parts of pictures: People who form vivid images show *fewer* eye movements than do people who form less vivid images (presumably to re- duce competing visual input), and people whose images are more vivid remember more details of pictures.

In our theory, vividness could correspond either to the amount of detail or to the quality (level of activation of points, in the model) of the image. In either case, a long-term memory encoding of a less vivid image (in the model, a new IMG file encoded from the surface matrix) will be more dif- ficult to "recognize" when later imaged than will an encoding of a more vivid image. Presumably, individual differences in vividness could be due to (a) differences in the grain quality of the visual buffer, (b) differences in the maximal amount of "activation" (brightness) in the visual buffer, (c) differences in the degree of precision of the interpretive procedures, (d) differences in the amount of time the visual buffer can "retain a charge" (hold the image) before needing to be refreshed, and/or (e) differences in the speed with which portions of the image can be refreshed. It is an em- pirical question which, if any, of these factors underlies differences in vi- vidness of visual images. These alternatives are not likely to be distin- guished using self-report techniques, however: There is no way to be sure that everyone knows the referent of the word "image" or that everyone sets his or her criterion to the same level in assessing images. Further, as Sheehan and Neisser (1969) have demonstrated, this technique seems especially susceptible to demand characteristics, response biases, and the like.

3.2.2.2 "Objective" Tests

Woodworth (1938) describes a number of tests of individual differences developed in the first decade or so of the twentieth century (see also Angell, 1910; Fernald, 1912). Because Woodworth's book is not readily available, it seems worthwhile not only to describe each technique but to note Woodworth's analyses of them in addition to my own. Virtually all of the following findings fall in Class 4 of our taxonomy (domain contamination). As will become apparent, each set of results is open to multiple interpretations, many having nothing to do with imagery. In such cases we are loath to modify the model, if such would be required to provide an imagery account.

Association method. A person is given five minutes to recall objects having some characteristic colors and five minutes to remember things having given sounds. People are judged "visualizers" if color is a better cue, and "audiles" if sound is a better cue. Woodworth objects to this method because one "may recall a violin as being a sounding object without any image of the sound." Another objection is that one's experience with different sorts of objects will determine how strongly associated given properties are with particular objects—regardless of how one actually uses given modalities in thought. In any event, our theory is limited to visual imagery, and hence cannot speak to actual differences in preferred types of imagery, should they exist.

Word-type frequency in prose. In this case, the relative frequency of sight-words, sound-words, and so on, is tabulated in a person's prose. The relative frequencies again are used in diagnosis. The objections raised above also apply here. Further, Woodworth reports, "Instances are on record in which an author remarkable for his vivid descriptions of scenes reports himself *not* a visualist. There is nothing to prevent the non-visualist from seeing what is worth seeing and remembering it so as later to incorporate it in his writing." Yes, indeed.

Learning by eye or ear. These studies examined optimal presentation modality in list-learning. People were categorized according to relative memory for visually presented versus auditorily presented lists. Woodworth points out that there is nothing to prevent one from translating modalities internally immediately after a stimulus is presented (almost everyone can read a written word either aloud or silently). Thus, presentation modality is not an index of how the material was actually represented internally. Further, one can imagine cases where an audile becomes deaf but this does not disrupt his or her thinking style. Finally, Woodworth reports that adults, regardless of whether they are visualists or audiles, learn visually presented words more quickly (but I suspect this depends on presentation rates and the like). Woodworth's criticisms of this technique are very important and have yet to be grasped by numerous contemporary researchers: Simply showing people a picture does not guarantee that they remember it via imagery. Glanzer and Clark (1964) even argue that one remembers visual material by describing it, and support this claim by demonstrating that people are better able to remember more easily described pictures (unfortunately, however, more difficult-to-describe pictures often may also be more visually complicated, so the fact that intricacy of description predicts recall is not surprising, for any number of reasons).

Method of distraction. The logic of this method rests on the idea that internal processing will be disrupted more if one has to process multiple stimuli in the same modality than if one can process multiple stimuli in different modalities. Thus, people were asked to learn lists of words while being subjected to auditory, visual, or kinesthetic distractions. As Woodworth points out, however, dealing with the different stimuli may simply have been more or less effortful—and thus a stimulus may have been more or less distracting for reasons other than the mode of internal representation. The fact that different modalities are differentially distracting for different people could simply reflect relative practice with, or familiarity with, stimuli of that sort.

Spelling. This task has since been named the Hebb test (see Hebb, 1968; Weber and Harnish, 1974). Basically, words are read to a subject, and he or she is asked to spell them backward. The logic is that if one has a photographic image, one can read the letters off as easily in reverse as in the normal order. According to our theory, however, images are not static, but rather fade in and out (in accordance with the speed of refreshing an image and the speed with which images fade). Thus, it is not surprising that Fernald (1912) found that nobody could in fact read images equally easily in arbitrary orders (although, as noted in chapter 7, section 2.2, Weber and Harnish present evidence that is consistent with the claim that each letter of an imaged three-letter word is equally accessible). Interestingly, subjects in these experiments reported that letters (or syllables) seemed to fade in and out—exactly as predicted by our theory. In fact, the assumption that images were photograph-like had already been undercut by 1912 with Koffka's descriptions of subjects' imagery, which seemed to show that one could image a coin of no particular denomination, an animal of no given species, and so on. That is, Koffka's subjects reported decidedly nonphotographic images which were vague with missing details and indeterminate parts. These sorts of images sound suspiciously like the skeletal images posited in our theory. Woodworth reports that "on the whole, those reporting visual imagery do somewhat better than other subjects in this form of test." But in any case, this test rests on dubious assumptions about the nature of images, and has questionable validity as a measure of imagery ability per se (for example, it could simply reflect ability to "chunk" words into letter-groups, or greater memory capacity).

The letter square. In this technique, one is read a series of letters or numbers, and asked to arrange them mentally into a matrix of n rows by k columns. One is then asked to read up or down the rows, across the columns, along the diagonals, and so on. The logic is the same as that underlying the spelling task: A photographic image should be able to be read in any direction. Thus, those able to read off arbitrary portions were classified as visualists. This logic was found flawed in two ways, according to Woodworth: (1) Even the most visual of the subjects reported being unable to maintain a rigid, static, photograph-like image. Muller (1917) found that his "most competent visual learner" required four times longer to read the columns from top to bottom than to read the rows from left to right, and over seven times longer to read obliques than rows. (2) The assumption that the auditory learner would be inordinately affected by the encoding order, and virtually unable to retrieve in different orders, was faulty. People can impose groupings and other structures on the input, allowing them to repeat the items in other orders later.

Description and memory. Introspective reports of imagery were obtained when a subject described a picture. People who reported more visualization gave more complex descriptions, but verbalizers were less likely to falsely elaborate the picture (and hence were more accurate). Davis (1932) repeated some of Fernald's earlier work and found that those who reported auditory images recalled tones more accurately than those who did not, whereas those who reported visual imagery recalled nonsense forms better than those who did not. The problem here is attention. Perhaps the preferred imagery mode per se has nothing to do with performance, but people reporting predominant auditory imagery "listen better" and people reporting visual imagery "look better," and hence initially encode more in the relevant modality.

In addition to the kind of work described above, there also is a long tradition of attempting to distill imagery or spatial factors that underlie performance across a variety of tasks. Although it has long been claimed in the psychometric literature that visual and spatial abilities are distinct from verbal abilities (see Smith, 1964; Spearman, 1927; Thurstone, 1938), this inference is based on somewhat subjective interpretations of correlational and factor-analytic studies. Typically, performance on a set of tests and/or tasks is correlated and these correlations themselves are analyzed for underlying patterns. The experimenter must interpret the "meaning" of a dimension or factor by abstracting what seem to be the common elements showed by the tasks that load highly on that dimension or factor (and intuiting what seems missing from those tasks that do not load on the dimension or factor). This approach seems to compound the problems in interpreting the results of a given individual test or task. Now, one must worry about multiple interpretations (including some having nothing to do with imagery, as illustrated above) of a dimension or factor, based on multiple interpretations of the results of particular tasks. This approach would be useful if one had some prior reason for believing that given tasks do in fact require imagery, but this is not the case. Given a lack of a priori justification for this assumption, it is difficult to draw inferences about individual differences in imagery per se from the factor-analytic studies.

In short, then, although a plausible theory of individual differences in imagery is possible within the present framework, the available data do not warrant development of such a theory. Presumably, people can differ in the efficacy and/or the properties of each of the functional capacities— which will selectively affect performance in different imagery tasks. It would be easy to design tasks to tap the individual functional capacities; for example, a battery of tasks like those described in the foregoing chapters could be used to measure the acuity and extent of a person's visual buffer, the speed with which one places parts on images, the number of parts that tend to be placed on an image by default, and so on. An imagery-strength "profile" could be composed for individual people, which could then be used to study performance in tasks drawing on multiple components of the imagery system. Not only would this approach lead to a deeper understanding of individual differences in imagery and how they affect task performance, but it would help establish the process adequacy of the theory itself: If we have correctly characterized the functional capacities, we should be able to predict which imagery tasks a given person will find relatively easy or difficult on the basis of that person's "profile" of relative strengths. This seems like a promising approach to the study of individual differences in imagery, and further illustrates the ways in which our approach to theorizing is fruitful in guiding a program of empirical research.

4.0 CONCLUDING REMARKS

In this chapter we explored the properties of two functional capacities not considered previously. One of these, called COMPARE in the model, coordinates the way information is accessed and compared when one is trying to decide which of two named objects is larger. The other, called ANSWERIF in the model, coordinates the way information is looked up and processed when one is asked to decide whether a statement is true or false. Both of these procedures incorporate the principle that, in theory, imagery and propositional processing are carried out at the same time, and whichever process finishes first will supply the information used in reaching a judgment. These functional capacities draw on other components of the theory and model, and hence provide indirect support for them by the very fact that a coherent extension could be performed without altering any of the earlier claims.

The particular assumptions of the theory that proved most important in explaining the data in this chapter were as follows: (1) Propositional and literal encodings are stored for objects. (2) Literal encodings may be accessed directly, without a surface image being generated. (3) Propositional information may be organized hierarchically. (4) Lists of propositions are scanned serially. (5) Size tags are associated with objects. (6) The size of images can be adjusted at the surface or by altering the mapping function at the deep level. (7) Scanning is required to bring a portion of the image into high resolution, and scanning requires time.

The following new results were obtained in the course of investigating the issues discussed in this chapter: (1) The size-disparity effect can be partially eliminated if the compared objects fall in different categories and size tags are highly overlearned. (2) The congruity effect can be attenuated (and possibly eliminated) if the compared objects fall in different categories and size tags are highly overlearned. (3) Imagery is usually used to compare the sizes of two objects if the difference in size is subtle. (4) Even if two objects are very similar in size, however, imagery will not be used if they fall in different categories and the category-associations are highly overlearned. (5) Imagery is not used when people compare the sizes of objects that are very disparate in size. (6) Properties that are less associated with an object or less frequently encountered are more likely to require imagery to verify. (7) The association strength of the most common superordinate of an object in part affects whether imagery will be used in evaluating properties of the object shared by all members of the superordinate category. (8) Subjects reported having to use imagery more often to assess harder-to-evaluate statements about concrete properties of objects than to assess easier-to-evaluate statements. (9) Subjects spontaneously scanned to properties rated (by other subjects) to require imagery to evaluate, and did not scan to properties rated not to require imagery.

The following hypotheses evolved from the process of explaining the data described in this chapter: (1) The more overlearned a fact is, the higher it is stored in a list of propositions associated with an object. (2) A "congruity effect" may occur whenever a sampling criterion needs to be reset, even if the size of the to-be-compared objects is appropriate for the comparison word, but is outside the range of the items being evaluated. (3) The congruity effect is due to the way literal encodings are sampled. Hence, no congruity effect should occur if two images of items are formed side by side and subjects evaluate size by inspecting the image (note, to test this hypothesis many different dimensions would have to be queried, otherwise the subject would make the size comparison before the images were completed and prior to query). (4) More highly asociated properties have a greater probability of having been entered as items in the list of propositions associated with an object. (5) Imagery is often used spontaneously when people think about spatial relations among parts of objects or scenes. This is a consequence of the large number of possible relations, and the correspondingly small probability that any given relation is encoded propositionally. (6) Individual differences may profitably be studied by composing "imagery-strength profiles" for people, formulated by measuring their perfomance on tasks that tap each of the functional capacities posited by our theory.

10. Imagery and Cognitive Development

Many theories of development rely implicitly upon a "backward extrapolation strategy," where the theorist's knowledge of the mature end-state directs his or her conception of the developmental process. Most developmentalists fail to characterize the end-state in a rigorous manner, however, relying instead upon intuitions and introspections. This has serious consequences, for if one's notions about the end products of development are awry, they can misdirect one's conceptions of the developmental process as well.

This chapter has two main thrusts. First, it is an initial attempt to outline a methodology for studying memory and perceptual development. This methodology is rooted in a "teleological" conception of development: Not only is the child father to the man, but the man is son of the child. That is, the child's development can be seen in hindsight to have been drawn forward to the achievement of adulthood.* I will take the "backward extrapolation" technique seriously, and attempt to use our model of imaginal processing to guide developmental work. Any rich characterization of adult processing should reveal junctures where development could have taken place, and thus should help one to formulate interesting developmental hypotheses. Second, I will develop these ideas within the context of a particular issue, what I call the "representational-development hypothesis." According to this hypothesis, young children rely predominantly upon imagery when accessing information stored in memory, whereas older people tend to use more abstract propositional or verbal representations.

*This use of the word "teleological" does not imply that children know that they will eventually become adults and are striving toward achieving that goal. Rather the assumption is that since reproduction occurs after puberty, many of the properties of young children have been propagated because they led to adaptive properties in adults. Further, quite aside from such tenuous arguments, the present claim is that it is *useful* to view development as being goal-directed, as being "designed" to produce the adult.

407

1.0 THE REPRESENTATIONAL-DEVELOPMENT HYPOTHESIS

The representational-development hypothesis has three parts: (1) The type of internal representation that is predominantly utilized changes over age; (2) the ontogenetically later forms of representation are more powerful than the earlier ones; and (3) thus, although early forms of representation are not eradicated but rather are supplemented by later forms, later forms tend to overshadow the previously preferred modes.

It is important to realize that these are claims about changes in representational *format* over age, not changes in the *content* of representations. The format dictates the way information is represented, the type of code used (see chapter 3). Recall that any given piece of information (content) can be represented in a variety of formats (a word can be spoken, written, tapped out in Morse Code, and so on). Although some formats may be more efficient for representing particular sorts of information, there is no guarantee that people do things in the optimal way (even if we can be sure that a given sort of representation *is* optimal for a given purpose). Thus, it is important to note that the fact that children may tend to remember "appearances" has no necessary direct bearing on the issue of representational development.

This chapter is concerned with only one possible case of representational development, the purported transition from a predominantly imagery-based representational mode to increasing reliance upon propositional/verbal representations; further, we shall be concerned only with visual imagery. This particular representational shift is of interest for three reasons: First, numerous theorists have made the claim that young children rely upon imaginal representations, whereas older people are usually thought to rely upon more "abstract" representations of one sort or another (for example, Bruner, Olver, and Greenfield, 1966; Church, 1961; Kosslyn and Bower, 1974; Piaget and Inhelder, 1971). Second, the concept of an "image" has received much attention in the psychological and philosophical literature, and—as the foregoing chapters have expressed—I believe we now have some understanding of imagery; thus, we have some hope of being able to think clearly about what it would mean to have evidence of reliance upon imaginal representation. Third, the purported shift from imagery to "abstract" representation has received the most attention from researchers in the field of cognitive development, providing us with a reasonably large data-base to consider.

1.1 Previous Formulations

The two most important formulations of the representational-development hypothesis to date have been advanced by Bruner, Olver, and

Greenfield (1966) and by Piaget and Inhelder (1971). Bruner, Olver, and Greenfield claim that the child starts off with "enactive" representations. This format is specialized for representing actions one may perform on an object. Until about the end of the first year of life, the child is thought of as being able to represent information solely in an enactive format. A second stage in representation is said to emerge when a child comes to be able to represent the world via imagery, which is relatively independent of action. This "ikonic" representation is likened to a "picture in one's head" (the vagueness of this sort of definition raises numerous problems, as we shall see). This form of representation is hypothesized to dominate the child's thought for a period of years thereafter (although never explicitly specified, it seems implied that the child relies primarily on ikonic representation until around age seven or so). Ikonic representation is thought to be the root of the child's "inflexibility" of thought, "dependence upon small details embedded in diffuseness," "self-centeredness" and so on (p. 21ff). Images are conceived of as static and relatively integral; the child cannot relate to parts independently from the whole because of these properties. Further, true "abstract thought" cannot take place if only these sorts of representations are available. Language is used in abstract reasoning only after the "symbolic" stage is reached. In this stage, the child acquires a "symbolic system" which has characteristics of "categorality, hierarchy, prediction, causation and modification" (p. 47). According to Bruner and his colleagues, development of new sorts of representations is a consequence of "disequilibration," of attempting to resolve conflicts between systems of representation.

It is difficult to critique Bruner's notions because the nature and consequences of each form of representation are left vague and not well specified. For example, although Bruner usually speaks of the ikonic representation as though it were an internal picture (and its use as an explanatory construct rests solely upon this metaphor), he notes in passing that ikonic representations are partly "symbolic." This doesn't help us much, however, as he never is very clear about how symbols are represented internally. Further, Bruner's account of the mechanisms responsible for representational development is weak. The concept of "disequilibration" as an explanatory construct has not been well worked out by Piaget himself, who has expended considerably more effort in its exposition, and cannot easily be invoked to help explain representational development. Consider an example offered by Bruner: "there may be a conflict between 'appearance' and 'reality,' the one being ikonic and the other symbolic" (pp. 11-12). The claim is that in order to resolve this conflict, the child must develop a new form of representation to supplement the ikonic one. First, it makes no sense to speak of reality as being "symbolic." People discern symbols; reality is not inherently symbolic or nonsymbolic. Second, in order to have such a conflict between forms of representation, it would seem that both forms must be present. This "mechanism," however, was advanced as a way of accounting for the development of new, not yet possessed, forms. Third, as with Piaget, the "mechanism" at hand is not well enough defined to be used as an explanation. Simply positing that equilibration (resulting in reduction in conflict) is accomplished is not enough; we need to know how this operation is supposed to occur. Without such specification, the notion becomes very difficult to disprove. As the theory now stands, Bruner, Olver, and Greenfield probably can account for any finding or its converse with nearly equal ease. Fodor (1975) offers additional criticisms of Bruner's claims, which focus on whether images can serve as "meanings"; we will consider this line of argument in the next chapter in the context of the history of theorizing about imagery.

Piaget and Inhelder (1971) advance a formulation of the representational-development hypothesis that is embedded in the larger frame of Piaget's theory as a whole, and thus is difficult to consider in isolation. The following discussion will touch on the main ideas Piaget and Inhelder offer regarding representational development, but this should not be considered an exhaustive description of their ideas (nor of the problems with these notions). Piaget and Inhelder claim that the young infant in the "sensorimotor period" represents objects in terms of the actions that can be performed on them. Images are not used as internal representations until the child is around one and a half years of age; prior to the advent of imagery, the child is thought of as being "presentational," of dealing with things only in their immediate presence. Only after imagery representation comes to be possible is the child thought of as being "representational," capable of thinking about things in their absence. According to Piaget and Inhelder, images are not derived from perception, but rather arise from "an interiorization of imitation." Further, in contrast to Bruner's conception, Piaget and Inhelder emphasize that imagery itself changes over age, and that the way in which images represent information changes in the course of development: After about seven or eight years of age, the "concrete operations" purportedly are used in conjunction with imagery, allowing images to become "anticipatory," able to be transformed in accordance with expectation; before this age images are merely "reproductive" and static.

The roots of my problems in understanding Piaget and Inhelder lie in their insistence that images are "interiorized imitations." It never is clear exactly what is imitated, or how such imitation occurs. Piaget and Inhelder seem to rule out the notion that images are derived from perception; but even if they allowed this possibility, what would it mean to "imitate" a perception? The explanation for how image representation arises rests on the observation that at around this age the child can perform "deferred imitation," can imitate things in their absence. By analogy, they conjecture that children can imitate a stimulus to themselves in the absence of that stimulus. The concept of "imitation" is stretched rather thin by this usage. Even if it were clear what was meant, this sort of treatment would seem closer to describing what is taking place than to explaining it. I do not want to deny the value of describing a phenomenon; rich descriptions facilitate theorizing, and there is no more astute observer than Piaget. But on my view explanations of cognitive phenomena should specify the ways in which functional capacities operate. Piaget and Inhelder's account is more on the level of intentionality (see chapter 5), and hence is open to multiple interpretations on the level of the function of the brain. They do not specify how interiorized imitation operates, nor have they specified the format or content of the image. This level of discourse will never produce process adequacy, and hence seems of limited value.

1.2 The Present Formulation

In what ways does our model address this representational-development hypothesis? If a fact is not explicitly noted in an object's propositional file, it can be retrieved in two ways: It can be looked up in a superordinate file, or it can be found implicitly represented in an image. For example, consider how you answer the following queries. "Do Volkswagen Beetles have ventwings (little triangular windows near the front of the door)?" and "Do Chevrolet Novas have wheels?" In the first case, most people report having to image the car to answer the question. It is unlikely that this information is stored directly with the concept of Beetle, and since it is not common to all cars, it cannot be deduced from information stored with the general "car" concept. For the second question, most people report being able to answer without consulting an image (although one may be present incidentally). Again, it seems unlikely that this information was stored directly with the "Nova" concept; rather, it was deducible from the knowledge that the Nova is a car and that cars have wheels (see Collins and Quillian, 1972).

Thus, according to our model imagery will necessarily be used if one is asked a question about a concrete object and neither has the necessary information stored explicitly in the object's propositional file nor can deduce it from information stored in another propositional file. Further, if propositional processing is relatively slow, imagery will be used because image processing "outraces" propositional processing. Therefore, if few facts are encoded explicitly, or if deduction is difficult, imagery will be increasingly likely to be used. As development proceeds, then, learning (as reflected in increased propositional knowledge) and maturation (providing more "processing capacity," resulting in deduction becoming easier) may result in reduced use of imagery.

1.2.1 Learning with Experience

As the child grows older he or she will have more occasions to access facts. With increasing use of a particular fact, it becomes increasingly likely that that fact is encoded into the appropriate propositional file. For example, consider again whether VW Beetles have ventwings (please answer). And again. By the third time it should no longer be necessary to consult an image. Instead, the fact that the car has ventwings should now be stored explicitly—assuming, of course, that you had the information in your image initially. This example illustrates one form of memory development, where the child may recode information into propositional form as he or she accesses that information repeatedly. This recoding idea leads us to expect that frequently accessed facts will be represented in an explicit format, and will not require imagery. Some support for this claim was reported in chapter 9.

In addition to internal recoding of the sort described above, people often learn by being taught. Certain facts are communicated linguistically and presumably memorized in a propositional format, especially facts that are important for identifying objects and/or getting around in the world. Retrieval of these sorts of facts, then, should not require consultation of an image.

A disheartening fact of human psychology is that we sometimes are unable to learn some rule or strategy (see, for example, Smedslund, 1961); sometimes information simply doesn't "stick." This is especially true of young children. Thus, even if a child is explicitly taught a fact, or has accessed that information repeatedly, the child still may not use propositional processing on subsequent occasions. Let us now consider why children may use imagery even when they do not have to.

1.2.2 Effects of Maturation

A major change over age may be quantitative in nature: The maximal speed of information processing may increase as the child matures. That is, myelinization or the like may be responsible for the quicker reaction times commonly observed with increasing age (see, for example, Kosslyn, 1976b; Nelson and Kosslyn, 1975). If activation starts to fade as soon as a representation is accessed, then the speed of decay and the speed of reactivation will determine how many representations can be held in mind at once. It is like juggling: The faster one can move one's hands, the more balls one can keep aloft. How much material can be kept in an image at once may affect how easily the child can make deductions. Consider what would happen in our model if it were asked, "ANSWERIF A NOVA HAS WHEELS," and if this fact were stored in the superordinate CAR propositional file but not in the NOVA propositional file. To deduce this fact about Novas, the program would have to: (1) know how to infer it, that is, which procedure to use; (2) store the name of the sought property; (3) store the name of the superordinate, once found in the NOVA propositional file; and (4) store the name of the object, NOVA, after going to the superordinate file, if it needs to know to which object the fact was relevant. If any one of the first three pieces of information were not available, the deduction would not go through. Thus, if children have only a limited "activated memory" capacity and tend to forget some of this information, they will be unable to deduce the sought fact. Hence, although the child may seem to know all the individual pieces of information (including the deduction algorithm) necessary to make the inference, in practice he or she may often use imagery instead. That is, even when verifying something like "Dogs have four legs," young children may consult an image (which may be a skeletal image—corresponding to one "cognitive chunk" which is easily maintained by the child), rather than deducing the answer from propositionally encoded information about animals, because of constraints imposed by activation/decay rates on propositional processing. Although it may be more efficient to perform deductions using propositional encodings if they can be performed, deduction may require more (or different) resources than those tapped by the imagery system.

In short, then, the basic claim of the representational-development hypothesis is about reliance upon imaginal representations. Obviously, if the child has few representations in other formats there is not much choice about which sort to use. But even if other sorts of representations are available for use, the child may tend to use imagery anyway. In the context of our model, the image-retrieval processes may simply "outrace" the propositional ones. The representational-development hypothesis as currently formulated, then, does not claim that children *always* use imagery; it would be surprising if they did not occasionally memorize linguistic input (especially when something is described to them). Rather, the claim is that young children rely predominantly upon imagery in accessing and using information in memory.

The fact that a theoretical conception is potentially programmable gives one hope that it is reasonably explicit, self-consistent, and not inherently flawed. The present conception is easily simulated by our model, requiring only a new procedure for entering new HASA's in an object's PRP file and an additional parameter constraining how many propositions can be held in a temporary store simultaneously.

2.0 CONCEPTUAL DIFFICULTIES

There are two major problems that plague research on representational development. I have discussed these issues elsewhere in this book, but they merit another brief mention here.

2.1 Images, Words, and Propositions

Many writers have assumed that there are two kinds of mental representations, verbal and imaginal (see Paivio, 1971). This assumption simplifies things considerably; if one possibility is eliminated, only one other candidate remains. Recently, however, many theorists have claimed that a third sort of representation occurs in memory (see, for example, Anderson and Bower, 1973; Norman and Rumelhart, 1975; Simon, 1972), namely "abstract propositions." Recall that propositions are posited to be amodal, allowing them to represent with equal facility the relations expressed in linguistic and sensory representations. As discussed in chapter 2, many of those who argue that propositional representation occurs in memory also tend to argue that it is the *only* form of representation that actually occurs in memory; all other forms are considered to be derived from propositions somehow (see Pylyshyn, 1973).

It may be important to realize, however, that if the claims about the internal hegemony of propositional representations are correct, then the representational-development hypothesis as currently formulated is totally misguided. If only one form of internal representation exists in humans, then it makes no sense to talk of changes in representational format over age. In this case, only the content (what is encoded) and organization of the propositions in memory may change with age. Thus, we are faced with no mean task in attempting to provide support for the representational-development hypothesis; not only must we find age differences suggestive of imagery reliance, but we must be certain that these differences cannot be accounted for by positing representations consisting of various concatenations of propositions.

2.2 Structure and Process

In our critical review of the literature, we occasionally will want to consider the possibility that some effect is due to process variables, not structural properties of accessed representations. It may help first to review the distinction between structure and process. In an important way, structure and process are inseparable: If a structure does not affect *any* sort of processing, it not only will be impossible to study but will be nonexistent for all intents and purposes. The functional properties of representations depend in part on the nature of the processes that operate on them. For example, two values in adjacent cells of a matrix stored in a computer are "adjacent" only because the cells are accessed in a paticular order. Given that order of accessing, it does not matter whether the values are stored physically next to each other—they could just as easily be in separate memory banks in different rooms. Piaget (1970) goes so far as to define a structure in terms of an "ordered system of transformations." But the structural properties of representations also derive in part from the way data is stored. Different ways of storing data in a given system are compatible with only particular processes (for example, a list of words cannot be interpreted by our FIND procedures). Asking about the functional properties of a structure without regard to both the nature of the encoding and the nature of the interpretive processes is a little like asking whether there is a sound if a tree falls but no one is there to hear it, but now the question is: If someone *is* present, which is more important for hearing the sound, the falling tree or the person's ears?

It is important to realize, however, that the structural properties of a representation need not affect all processing in which that representation is involved. For example, consider possible processing of a matrix of numbers stored in a computer. If the matrix is scanned row by row, column by column, it will be easier to "move" from a given cell to an adjacent one than to a cell more distant in the matrix. Once the values stored in the cells are retrieved, however, the properties of the original representation may be irrelevant. The values may be entered into a list in order of magnitude (not original location), and further processing may only access this list. Or retrieved values may be translated into a new representation (such as the sum), which then might be processed. And so on. Thus, it is critical that one's measures tap the phase of task performance that does in fact reflect properties of the representation of interest.

In addition to the foregoing considerations, in the case of children, we must be certain that our subjects can perform critical processes. That is, children may have a representational structure, but not yet have learned (or otherwise developed) given strategies for using it; if our assessment procedures depend upon use of these strategies, we may be led astray (see the discussion of imagery and learning strategies in section 3.1 below). Further, a child's processing capacity may be so limited that only under ideal conditions can given processes successfully operate upon a representation (making experimental design especially important). Only converging experiments using different operations seem to provide hope of eliminating these possible sources of obfuscating contamination.

3.0 EVIDENCE FOR REPRESENTATIONAL DEVELOPMENT

Given the long-standing popularity of the idea, there is surprisingly little evidence that young children really do utilize mental imagery more than do adults. Let us consider the five approaches that have previously been taken in investigating the representational-development hypothesis. As we shall see, most of the conceptual pitfalls encountered in this research stem from a failure to consider how information might be represented in memory in general, and from a failure to consider how images might serve as internal representations in particular. Since these sorts of issues have only recently been broached in the psychological literature, researchers cannot be criticized harshly for their oversights. However, now that these issues have been exposed, we should take heed. The final approach discussed below is offered as a way of avoiding the conceptual difficulties encountered by the preceding four approaches.

3.1 Pictures versus Words

The basic notion underlying the interpretation of these data is that there are only two ways of representing information internally, images and words; thus, if children are demonstrably not using one means, it follows that they must be using the other. This reasoning is sometimes applied to data on the child's use, or lack of use, of "verbal mediation," which have been taken to support the representational-development hypothesis, and to data on the child's learning of pictures, which have been taken to contradict the hypothesis.

"Verbal mediation" involves naming and (typically) rehearsing the names of some stimuli a person is trying to remember. Children over the age of seven years or so typically employ verbal mediation spontaneously when asked to remember some stimulus set. Younger children, in contrast, do not seem predisposed to label or verbalize spontaneously (R. Conrad, 1971; Flavell, 1970; Hagan, 1972). And yet, even though they don't seem to encode verbal information, young children still recall at better than chance levels. This finding has led some researchers to conclude that young children encode into memory images of the stimuli. This inference is based on the assumption that memory can be either in a verbal-linguistic format or an imagery format; if one isn't used, in this case the verbal mode, then the other is implicated by default. However, as noted above, this reasoning contains a major flaw: The fact that no other form of representation may be conveniently externalizable does not preclude the possibility that more "abstract" ways of representing information exist. Thus, the fact that verbal encoding may not be used spontaneously by young children gives us no firm grounds for concluding that imagery is used. (This same reasoning also precludes concluding that children who score poorly on imagery tests are therefore highly verbal, as Hollenberg, 1970, seems to assume.)

Next, let us consider some findings on children's memory for pictures versus words that possibly constitute evidence against the representational-development hypothesis as currently conceived. Rohwer (1970, p. 401) argues that "The ability to use a linguistic or verbal means for storing and preserving information emerges earlier developmentally than the ability to use visual or imagery processes for accomplishing the same ends." This conclusion is based on the finding that young children, unlike adults, perform better in a paired-associates task if the stimulus member of the pair is a word rather than a picture (Ducharme and Fraisse, 1965; Milgram, 1967; Paivio, 1970). Presumably, since pictures are not encoded as words, they must be encoded as images. It is worth noting that Jones (1973) has pointed out that at least four characteristics of these experiments prevent us from confidently drawing conclusions from them. Most notably, these experiments all rely on verbal responses—which require an additional step in output if material is in fact stored visually rather than verbally. When Jones corrected these flaws (for example, by allowing the subject to select the response picture from a set of three alternatives instead of naming it), children now too were better when pictures served as stimulus members and, in fact, were better able to remember visual-visual pairs than verbal-verbal pairs. These results suggest caution in readily accepting Rohwer's conclusions.

The actual results aside, it is not even clear that such experiments on children's learning are relevant to our present concerns: The representational-development hypothesis makes no claims about children's abilities to use imagery strategies such as those required in paired-associates learning experiments (see Reese, 1970). Rather, the claim is that young children rely predominantly upon imagery in accessing information in memory; the images encoded need not be those that most effectively encode the information at hand. For example, the child might encode two images separately, not interacting in a single scene; this variation has a large effect on how well the imaged items will later be recalled (Bower, 1972). Further, the child's ability to retrieve images may depend in part upon the particular linguistic or propositional "tags" used to label the image; if these are not appropriate to the task, later retrieval may be hampered—even if the images themselves are in memory.

In short, results from experiments on memory for pictures may have nothing to do with imagery; pictures need not be encoded solely in an imagery format, but may be encoded linguistically or propositionally as well. Thus, we cannot infer that young children's relatively superior retention of visually presented material implicates imagery use, as some have suggested (for example, Corsini, 1969a, 1969b, 1970). By the same token, findings on preferred encoding modality have no necessary relevance to the present issue.

3.2 Questionnaires and Tests

This approach grows out of the psychometric tradition, wherein imagery characteristics are treated as if they were traits. The two most widely used questionnaires are the Betts Vividness of Imagery Questionnaire (and its descendent, Marks's VVIQ, which is an extended version of the visual imagery scales) and the Gordon Control of Imagery Questionnaire (see the appendix to Richardson, 1969). In the Betts test, people are asked to rate, on a seven-point scale, the clarity of various images in various modalities. In the Gordon test, a person is asked whether or not he or she can image a car in various situations; the transformations included in the image become increasingly difficult with each item.

Forisha (1975) appears to be the only person to have used these tests in investigating the representational-development hypothesis; she used, however, a three-point rating scale with the Betts test to make it easier to administer to children. Although Forisha tested children in the first through fifth grades, she does not report the actual imagery vividness and control scores obtained over age. She does report that these scores did not correlate with other imagery tests (which will be discussed shortly), and concludes that these questionnaires measure a "subjective imagery" factor (as revealed by factor analysis of the scores) that is important for younger children but not for older children. This finding could be taken as support for the representational-development hypothesis. In addition, there were small but significant positive correlations (.31 or lower) between verbal ability and imagery vividness and control for the younger children.

It is worth pausing here briefly to note that a positive correlation between measured imaginal qualities and verbal ability does not constitute evidence against the representational-development hypothesis, for two reasons: First, this hypothesis states that new representational formats *supplement* old ones; it does not state that imagery representation is *replaced* by subsequently developed forms. If it did make the latter claim, then negative correlations might be expected. But since it does not make this claim, we have no reason to expect that people who excel at verbal/linguistic representation will not also excel at imaginal representation. Second, "verbal ability" and preponderance of verbal representations are not the same thing. We do not know the relationship between how much a child relies upon verbal encodings and how much verbal ability he or she possesses; plausible arguments could be made that verbal ability precedes reliance upon verbal representations in memory, or vice versa. Thus, the obtained correlation between measured verbal ability and imagery qualities may not have direct bearing upon the representational-development hypothesis.

There are some general problems with using the questionnaire approach in studying the representational-development hypothesis: First, the ratings technique forces one to assume that people of different ages all have equal introspective access to their internal processes. This assumption seems unwarranted, as a reasonable argument could be made that either children or adults have better introspective ability, depending upon whether experience clouds or hones introspection skills. Second, even if people of different ages have the same ability to access their images, we still have no guarantee that they will externalize their assessments in the same way; children and adults may not use rating scales in terms of the same baselines and criteria. Unfortunately, we have no way at present of separating "criterion" from "sensitivity," to draw an analogy to signal detection theory (see Green and Swets, 1966). Thus, we cannot know whether ratings or scores reflect the nature of underlying structures, or whether they simply reflect various sorts of biases in how ratings or evaluation scales are to be used. Third, this sort of technique seems especially susceptible to the influence of "demand characteristics," which, although not insurmountable, may constitute special problems in working with children. As noted earlier, the results of imagery ratings of the sort discussed above are often difficult to interpret, and often seem to be influenced by all sorts of extraneous variables (such as the identity of the experimenter; see Sheehan and Neisser, 1969). Fourth, the processes required in ratings tasks may be substantially different from those that operate when children and/or adults actually use imagery in thinking, and hence performance on questionnaires may not tell us anything relevant to the issues at hand. In short, ratings data on the prevalence or qualities of imagery at different ages might be most profitably relegated to a supplementary role, used in conjunction with other types of measures.

The testing approach is like the questionnaire approach in that it also makes use of paper-and-pencil measures, but it requires the subject to do more than simply introspect. These tests require the subject to perform some mental transformations on a standard and then to select which of a set of alternatives corresponds to the product of applying these transformations. The Primary Mental Abilities: Spatial Relations test, for example, requires subjects to complete a square pattern by selecting the correct part from a set of alternatives. The Kuhlman-Finch Rotations subtest requires people to perform matches between standards and rotated alternatives. The Minnesota Paper Form Board requires the subject to select a figure corresponding to the correct assembly of a set of parts. These tests are mentioned because they were also used in the Forisha (1975) study, but numerous other spatial abilities tests also are available.

Kuhlman (1960; see Hollenberg, 1970) performed a now-classic study using testing methodology that has been taken to bear on the representational-development hypothesis. She found that young children who scored high on her imagery tests were better at a picture memory task than at a concept learning task, but vice versa for low-imagery young children (who were presumed to be high-verbal). This reliable individual difference became attenuated with age, and was not found at all with older children. For some reason, Bruner (in Bruner, Olver, and Greenfield, 1966) seems to think that this finding supports his version of the representational-development hypothesis. It is not clear, however, why the finding that stable individual differences disappear with age constitutes support;

if anything, it is something of an embarrassment: Ideally, the young children should be homogeneous in their reliance upon imagery. The fact of individual differences in the youngest age group can, however, be explained away by positing that some children are more precocious than others, and only some children have begun to rely on verbal/linguistic representations.

Forisha (1975) improved on the Kuhlman approach, not only including explicit tests of verbal ability but comparing questionnaire measures with imagery test scores. Forisha found that measured imagery and verbal abilities increased at the same rate over age, both increasing rapidly in the early years and then tapering off somewhat. She also performed a factor analysis of these scores; a separate "spatial" and "verbal" dimension were found to emerge with age. These results were taken to be most consistent with Piaget and Inhelder's version of the representational-development hypothesis.

This approach to investigating the representational-development hypothesis is fraught with difficulties. First, one cannot be certain that the tests really measure imagery processes per se; they never have been validated in a sufficiently rigorous manner. Second, even if the tests do measure imagery processes in one age-group, there is no guarantee that a given test necessarily taps the same processes at different ages; for example, with increasing age, more nonimaginal strategies could be brought to bear to increase performance, or at early ages attentional deficits could selectively operate to reduce a child's scores for certain types of items (such as where details must be systematically compared). Third, factor analysis of test scores only compounds these problems: We are now faced with the additional uncertainties surrounding interpretation of the derived dimensions; we cannot know with conviction what elements of similarity and dissimilarity in the tests are responsible for the obtained configuration. Finally, the basic testing approach is inherently ill-suited for examining competing hypotheses or interpretations. It is difficult to conceive of how one could use this approach to distinguish between imagery and propositional interpretations of the data. This problem of ruling out propositional explanations is difficult to deal with, as will become increasingly apparent as we proceed.

3.3 Children's Drawings

Some researchers have been tempted to treat children's drawings as data about their imagery. Piaget and Inhelder (1971), for example, asked children to draw a falling stick, and noted that they failed to represent continuity or a proper trajectory. This property was taken to indicate that the child's imagery also fails to preserve these qualities (see also Dean, 1976). Unfortunately, this might simply say something about the child's conventions in drawing, about how the child externalizes internal events onto two-dimensional surfaces. The child's imagery could be perfect but his or her drawing skills limited. Similarly, if a child is able to draw something but is not able to describe it, this does not necessarily show that his or her internal representations are in terms of images, but may only indicate that one response mode is more advanced than another. (We can design computer systems in which a given propositional representation may be more easily externalized via one output device than another, depending on how many conversion operations and the like are required.)

The main interest of late in children's drawings is not as evidence for imagery use, but exactly the opposite: as evidence against imagery. Minsky and Papert (1972), for example, report that their young subject depicted a cube by drawing a central square with an equal-sized square attached to each side. When asked why he drew a cube that way, the child purportedly indicated that it represented the parts and their relations in a clear, straightforward manner. Minsky and Papert, Moran (1973), Pylyshyn (in press), and others treat the "diagrammatic" quality of children's drawings as evidence that children represent information internally in terms of "symbolic" descriptions of parts and how these parts are put together. Kosslyn, Heldmeyer, and Locklear (1977) showed that although young children sometimes do draw diagrammatically, they do not *prefer* these renditions as a rule. In this experiment, we used a paired-comparison paradigm, where children were asked to select which of a pair of drawings more accurately depicted the object in question. A series of pairs were presented, the members differing along some particular dimension, allowing us to zero in on the bases for the children's preferences. Importantly, the few children who did prefer diagrammatic drawings to perspective ones seemed to base this preference on repetition of the front face, not on the way the parts were connected. It was especially interesting to note that although most children preferred drawings with perspective, most could not draw them (see also Hayes, 1978). And these children often expressed dissatisfaction with their drawings, realizing that they were unable to depict all of the characteristics they knew about the appearance of the object.

Although it was interesting to demonstrate that children's drawings did not depict all they knew about an object's appearance, these data are really superfluous in the present context. No matter what the children's drawings look like, we probably can posit an interpretive process that will convert practically any internal representation into that drawing. That is, a perfectly photographic image could be processed such that key features are identified and then drawn, with little attention to how these features are related. This procedure could produce a diagrammatic drawing. Or, a description of an object plus rules for portrayal of perspective could be used to generate a standard perspective drawing. Clearly, the child's (or

adult's) conventions about drawing per se will have important consequences on what is drawn. In short, children's drawings do not provide
support for the view that the child's representations in memory are like
descriptions of an object's parts and their interrelations, nor do drawings
support the view that the child's memory representations are pictorial
images.

3.4 Interference Paradigms

This research tack rests on the notion that imagery and like-modality
perception utilize more common processing mechanisms than do imagery
and perception in other modalities. If so, then one might argue that when
some sort of mental activity selectively interferes with visual perception
(relative to perception in other modalities), visual imagery is involved in
the mental activity (see Segal and Fusella, 1970). The same logic could
lead us to examine whether the mode of presentation of interfering information had effects upon later memory of a set of stimuli; if we found that
visual input disrupted memory more than did auditory/verbal input, this
might constitute support for the claim that imagery was used as a representational device. If this diagnostic technique were found to be valid, it
could be used to study the representational-development hypothesis. This
logic has proved problematical in the study of imagery in adults, however,
for reasons discussed in chapter 7, and is of dubious use to us in our present task. The problems with this approach are evident when we consider
one possible example.

Lippman and Grote (1974) described a very interesting study that could
be taken to have bearing on the representational-development hypothesis,
although the authors themselves do not conceptualize it in these terms.
They asked children to remember a sequence of three differently colored
chips that were contained within a matrix of nine. The three chips were
either shown to the child, (pointed out in the matrix) or named verbally,
and the child was then shown or told the names of three more chips. Children were carefully instructed to try to remember the first set of three and
to ignore the last set of three. Interestingly, verbal interference resulted in
marked disruption of fifth-grade children's memories for the first set,
somewhat less disruption for second graders, and no disruption for pre-
schoolers. In contrast, when the children were *shown* the to-be-ignored
chips, the preschool children exhibited the most memory disruption and
the fifth graders the least, with the second graders falling in between.
(These effects were the same for both sorts of initial input, which might
reflect the sort of modality recoding demonstrated by Tversky, 1973).

Although Lippman and Grote did not make this inference, these data
could be taken to support the notion that young children rely upon imagery whereas older children rely upon verbal representations. We should

be dissuaded from making such inferences about results like these for two reasons: First, we cannot with certainty localize these effects in memory as opposed to the encoding stage; in order for these data to bear directly upon the representational-development hypothesis, it must be demonstrated that effects are due to interference among like-modality memory representations per se. Young children may simply find visual input more engrossing than verbal input—and thus encode more information when it is presented in that modality—but vice versa for older children. In this case, simple quantity of interfering input that is encoded, not similarities in mode of internal representation, could account for "selective interference" effects.

A second reason to take care in interpreting selective interference effects is that even if we were able to localize interference to differences in memory representations, we would still have no evidence that qualitative differences in type of *format* were involved. To recapitulate: It is possible that both verbal and visual inputs might be stored in a propositional format, but in lists with different sorts of organizations. That is, visual input during perception might be encoded as a list-structure composed of propositions such as "*x* is left of *y*." Propositions encoding visual information stored in memory may utilize the same types of relations and be similarly structured. In contrast, propositions encoding verbal information often may (unless consciously transformed) incorporate different sorts of relations and be differently structured from those underlying visual representations. Thus, simple principles of similarity of the sort exposited in the verbal-learning literature (for example, Adams, 1967) could allow us to explain "selective interference" results; the more similar propositional representations are (as assessed by number of common relations and structures), the more mutually disruptive they will be. In part, subjects may simply confuse portions of one representation with portions of the other.

Selective interference paradigms, then, seem inappropriate for studying the representational-development hypothesis as presently formulated. However, we can posit a weaker version of this hypothesis that can be appropriately addressed by such techniques. Unlike the stronger formulation, this version does not posit changes over age in the *format* of predominantly accessed memory structures; instead, the claim is only that the basis of list-organization develops with age. That is, we could hypothesize that young children tend to rely upon spatial representations, even if they are simply representations composed of propositions incorporating spatial relations ("left of," "above"). This sort of representation incorporates a different organizational structure from verbal/linguistic representations. This claim makes no reference to actual qualitative differences in formats over age, but only posits changes in organization and content (and hence is less interesting, to my mind, than the stronger version of the hypothesis). In order to take evidence of selective interference as evidence for this weaker hypothesis, however, we must rule out the possibility of differential encoding of different modalities by younger and older children.

3.5 The Picture-Metaphor Approach

By far the bulk of research on the representational-development hypothesis rests on the assumption that images are "pictures in the head." The predictions of these studies are based upon the notions (1) that mentally photographing a set of stimuli should aid memory by capturing difficult-to-describe details or, the other side of the coin, (2) that mental photographing should hinder memory for nonpicturable aspects of stimuli. The first sort of strategy is illustrated by London and Robinson's (1968, 1971) experiments. Their paradigm involved having subjects of differing ages view drawings of easily named things or difficult-to-describe blobs. If imagery is used, they reasoned, nameability should not affect memory. Unfortunately, the easily named stimuli also often were symmetrical and more regular than the more amorphous difficult-to-describe drawings (and probably were more familiar as well). Thus, their finding that "nameability" increases memory even for young children may not be evidence for or against the representational-development hypothesis, but may only be evidence for the inadequacy of simple picture-metaphor conceptualizations of imagery. The data reviewed earlier suggest that images are not like static, integral internal photographs, but are the products of a constructive process that has only limited resources. If so, then more "complex" (by practically any measure of complexity) drawings, which also happen to be less easily named, may be more poorly remembered even if subjects represent them in the form of images, because more complex drawings are more difficult to image than simple ones.

The second type of research based on the picture metaphor, which rests on the notion that image use will impair memory for nonpicturable information, also has its pitfalls. Consider an experiment by Kosslyn and Bower (1974), which explored the notion that young children encode evoked images when asked to remember sentences (rather than encode some sort of abstract "gist" information). We reasoned that if children heard a sentence like "The lion killed the buffalo because it was hungry" and encoded an image, they would be no more likely to recognize this sentence subsequently than to mistakenly recognize a sentence like "The lion killed the buffalo, so it must have been hungry." This prediction follows from the fact that both sentences evoke the same visual image (as assessed by ratings data). Adults, in contrast, were expected to be less likely to fall prey to pictorial similarity, and thus more often to distinguish the genuine original from an image-similar distractor. Unfortunately, the fact that this finding was obtained may not really tell us anything about imagery use. Perhaps difficult-to-picture distinctions are difficult to encode and recall because they are more complex, or subtler in regard to other sorts of dimensions, not because of the difficulty of imaging them per se.

The most frequent use of the simple picture-metaphor is less precise than those described above. Usually, the picture metaphor is invoked simply to justify the supposition that an image is "static," as is a photograph. This assumption is rarely explicitly noted and rarely defended. If the claim that imagery is static is addressed at all, it usually is addressed in a circular way: Once a behavior is assumed to indicate imagery use (by virtue of the static nature of the behavior), inferences about the nature of imagery are made (namely, that it is static). As a case in point, consider the evidence offered by Bruner, Olver, and Greenfield (1966) that imagery is the predominant form of mental representation during early childhood. In one experiment, the fact that children in this age range had difficulty rearranging from memory a seriated matrix of jars (ordered in terms of height and width) is taken as evidence for reliance upon static imagery. Older children, who are successful at this task, are assumed not to rely on imagery but instead to work out "verbal rules" that guide them in producing the required transposition. The finding that young children have trouble systematically investigating which pattern is prewired into an array of lights is also taken to support Bruner's version of the representational-development hypothesis. The rationale for inferring that imagery is the culprit, is the root of the child's troubles, rests upon the supposition that imagery is "static," much like a mental photograph in which parts are inextricably bound to the whole; this last inference is, however, derived from the very data being explained. There would seem to be no a priori reason to expect that imagery necessarily has static properties at any given age; it is an empirical question whether images are static, dynamic, in flux, existent, nonexistent, or whatever at different ages.

Consider the other side of the coin: Would one set out to discover properties of imagery at different ages by simply *assuming* that imagery is in fact responsible for some behavior, and hence evinces certain qualities? Probably not (although this seems to be exactly what Piaget and Inhelder did). One would want to be confident that the behavior under scrutiny derived from imagery use before making inferences about imagery from that behavior. By the same token, one should not begin by assuming that images are "static," and then take indications of "static" mental representation to be evidence of imagery use. Further, "static" behavior may not even tell us that the underlying memory *structures* are static. The representations may have nothing to do with the seemingly static properties of a child's thought or behavior; these qualities may reflect purely *process* limitations, such as constraints upon the amount of information that can be operated upon at any one time.

Some of these objections can also be levied against Piaget and Inhelder (1971). They claim that imagery is static until children have "concrete operations" with which to transform their images. Much of the young children's difficulties in conceptualizing transformations are attributed to their reliance upon the static imagery representations that occur prior to the advent of the "operations." For example, one of their findings is that young children are unable to anticipate how high a column of water will be when the contents of a short wide container are poured into a tall thin one. Similarly, young children are unable to show how a toy "pilot" will be oriented when a toy plane is doing loop-the-loops, being upside down at the top of each loop. These sorts of findings are taken as evidence that the children cannot form "anticipatory" images, but rather are constrained by the "static" imagery that is solely available to them.

As was the case with Bruner, Olver, and Greenfield, Piaget and Inhelder have little basis for inferring that imagery had anything to do with their results. For example, the young child's problems may arise from faulty verbal rules that do not involve imagery at all; later successes may not reflect more flexible imagery, but simply better systems of rules for predicting the consequences of various transformations. Piaget and Inhelder assume too much about the properties of imagery and the consequences of imagery use. These same sorts of criticisms can be applied to virtually all of the imagery work in the Piagetian tradition.

4.0 AN EXPERIMENT

The fundamental problem with the previous efforts at investigating the representational-development hypothesis is that the predictions of the studies do not hinge on the "privileged properties" of imagery. If one is trying to discover the role of imagery in some task or context, I have argued, one should seek evidence that these properties—not shared by other forms of internal representation—affect processing. Thus, for present purposes the important thing about the notion of images as surface representations is that it narrows down the sense in which an image is a "pictorial" representation. Many of the consequences of using imagery that are implied by a simple picture-metaphor are not implied by my conception; notably, there is no reason to believe that people take mental snapshots and tuck away in memory static, integral mental photographs. We cannot be sure that children's imagery necessarily suffers the "capacity limitations" observed on adult imagery, of course (see chapters 3 and 4). In fact, there is a long history (see, for example, Jaensch, 1930) that children's imagery is "eidetic," is photographically clear and accurate. The last word in this debate, though, seems to be that no higher percentage of young children than of older children or adults possess eidetic imagery (see Leask, Haber, and Haber, 1969). In any case, given that adult imagery is limited in certain ways, we are probably safest in assuming that children's imagery is also limited, and we should not rely on properties like integrality and the like in assessing whether children use imagery. Our approach does lead us to expect imagery to have some special properties, however, including those stemming from the way in which images depict spatial extent. Thus, size and distance ought to influence processing times if images are used.

How might we attempt to use our earlier findings to study the claim that young children use imagery in memory retrieval more than do adults? I investigated this claim by exploiting the finding that image size affects the time to see a property. Recall my experiment that used items where the association strength and size of a property were pitted against each other (chapter 3, section 2.2.1). For example, for a cat the properties used were "claws" and "head," where the smaller property also was rated as being more strongly associated with the animal in question. In this experiment the range of sizes and association strengths was selected so that the larger properties were faster when imagery was used, but the smaller, more strongly associated properties were faster when imagery was not used. I used these same items in another experiment, now testing children of different ages (see Kosslyn, 1976b). It also seemed that data from properties inappropriately paired with an animal might help to distinguish imagery use from other ways of accessing information. In this case, larger properties might be more quickly "seen to be missing." In order to contrast imaginal and nonimaginal processing, however, I selected the larger false property also to be *more* associated with the animal in question (for example, "cat-mane" versus "cat-thumb"). This decision was motivated by the finding that when imagery is not used, highly associated false properties require more time to assess than do less associated ones (see Smith, Shoben, and Rips, 1974). Thus, when imagery is used to evaluate a fact about an animal, the larger false property ought to be rejected more quickly; but when imagery is not used, the smaller—but less associated —property ought to be assessed with greater ease.

When people are asked to decide whether an object has some property, we have found repeatedly that information is retrieved from abstract, nonimaginal representations more quickly than from surface images. I have hypothesized that this added efficiency arises because propositional representations are organized into easily accessed lists and the like, and because images are not retrieved directly but need to be generated prior to being inspected. If children rely predominantly on imagery when representing information in memory, but increasingly develop abstract representations as they grow older, we might form several hypotheses: First, if adults are not asked to use any particular means of retrieving information, they presumably will utilize the most efficient accessing strategy they have available, which may involve retrieving information stored in a propositional format. Young children, in contrast, may not have much of their knowledge represented propositionally, and may rely predominantly on accessing images whether or not they are explicitly instructed to do so. Thus, overall times should be roughly the same whether or not imagery instructions are given to the children; when adults are asked to use imagery, however, this may prove a less efficient, more time-consuming procedure than that usually employed when imagery is not required. A second hypothesis concerns the effects of size and association strength of properties: If young children really do utilize imagery spontaneously, size should affect how easily an object's properties can be evaluated. Association strength will have some effects, however, if properties are sometimes filled in when needed. But we know from the earlier experiment described in chapter 3, section 2.2.1, that the effects of size overshadow those of association strength if adults use imagery with the set of items used here. This prediction rests on the expectation, of course, that children will in fact evaluate larger properties more quickly when explicitly instructed to use imagery, replicating our previous findings with adults. Adults and older children, in contrast, should be faster to evaluate highly associated, although smaller, properties when imagery instructions are not given.

If the different types of properties have different effects for first graders than for older people when imagery instructions are not given, it could be argued that this simply indicates a difference in what is "highly associated" for them. Thus, rankings of association strength for the "true" items were obtained from first graders, fourth graders, and college students. None of these subjects participated in the reaction-time tasks, but all were drawn from a population as similar as possible to that used in the reaction-time experiment. Subjects in this rating task were asked, "What goes more with an X: Y or Z?" X was an animal name, and Y and Z were property names. They were told to choose the first one they thought of, or the one they thought of more, when they thought of the animal.

A second ranking condition was also included, in which subjects were asked to look at a line drawing of the animal in question, and then asked "which do you think of more" when looking at the picture, X or Y. Both properties were clearly evident in the drawing; special care was taken not to emphasize the smaller properties (in fact, these properties were noticeably less perceptually salient than the larger properties according to the experimenters' intuitions). This condition was included to discover whether size per se would influence association rankings even when people were asked to consult a picture. If not, I thought, there is no reason to expect property size to dictate association rankings if mental images of the animals were consulted in the no-picture ranking condition.

The mean rankings obtained in the no-picture condition agreed remarkably well with the original adult ratings. Similar results were obtained in the picture condition. Thus, we might argue that even if children have an image before their "mind's eye" when making association ratings from memory, their ratings will not be determined by the predominance of the property on this picture.

The reaction-time experiment proceeded as follows: First graders, fourth graders, and college students received two blocks of trials. The first block was not preceded by imagery instructions, while the second was. Since interactions, not main effects, were of primary interest, this seemed an acceptable procedure; it also seemed likely that if the imagery block preceded the uninstructed block, some subjects would adopt an imagery strategy during that block as well. The instructions preceding the no-imagery block directed the subject to consider whether the animal had the property; each subject was asked to try not to anticipate the type of response but actually to evaluate the part before deciding on the appropriate response. The instructions in the no-imagery block directed the subject to "think about the properties of the whole animal, not just part of it" as soon as the name of the animal was presented. In this block, the subject never was told explicitly to avoid imagery, but simply was not instructed to use it. The instructions emphasized responding as quickly as possible (while keeping errors to a minimum), by pressing one button if the property was appropriate and the other if it was inappropriate.

At the conclusion of the first block of trials, the subject was asked (in appropriate phrasing, of course) about how he or she had evaluated the properties: by first finding the property on a visual image of the animal, and responding *only* after consulting the image; by "just knowing" the answer intuitively or through verbal knowledge, even though an image may have occurred incidentally; or by some combination of these two strategies (subjects who were not sure of their strategy were also assigned to this category).

The second block of trials (using the remaining set of items) was preceded by my usual image-detection instructions. This session occurred about one week after the first for the children, but on the same day as the first for the adults. The instructions emphasized making a visual image of the entire animal upon hearing its name, and evaluating a property by examining the image. As soon as the property was found, the subjects were to push the button for "true." If they looked at the appropriate area or part and did not find the property (for example, looked at the head of a collie and did not discover horns), or found a contradiction (spots instead of stripes on a tiger), the subjects were to respond "false" by pushing the appropriate button. The subjects were informed that all properties were potentially visible without recourse to "x-ray vision" or the like. It was underscored that the subjects should be sure to base all responses in this block on inspection of the image, even if they intuitively "knew" the answer more quickly than they could see the property. The subjects were asked repeatedly during the 10 practice trials (which preceded the test trials and used different animals) about their mental processes; all subjects seemed to understand how to use images in this situation. After responding to the 44 test trials, the subjects were asked whether they had been able to use imagery most of the time and were asked to try to deduce the hypothesis being investigated. Fortunately, all the subjects included in the study claimed to have used imagery the bulk of the time and none of the subjects consciously inferred the purposes of the experiment.

Figure 10.1 presents the major findings with "true" properties. Although imaged items required more time to evaluate than nonimaged

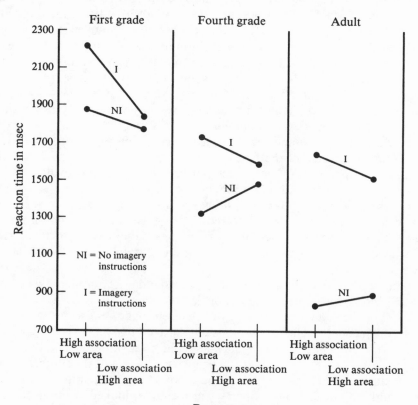

Figure 10.1. Time to verify two types of "true" properties when imagery instructions were given and when no imagery instructions were given.

items, the effect was not consistent over age: Imagery instructions made relatively little difference in the youngest children's overall times, but a virtual temporal chasm separated the two instructional conditions in the adult data. While overall times did decrease with age, it is clear from figure 10.1 that this effect was primarily a consequence of evaluations made when no imagery instructions were given. Older people were slightly faster than the children when imagery was required, but had a huge advantage when imagery was not required. The imagery items, of course, always followed the no-imagery items, but the usual finding in studies of reaction time (for example, Conrad, 1972) is an effect of practice—with decreasing response times over trials—not an effect of fatigue.*

Probably the most intriguing effects illustrated in figure 10.1 concern the time to evaluate the two sorts of properties in the two instructional conditions. In general, when imagery instructions were not given, high-association, low-area properties were verified more quickly than less highly associated but larger properties. In contrast, when subjects explicitly were asked to use imagery, low-association, high-area properties were assessed more quickly. As is apparent in figure 10.1, however, the first graders' no-imagery data do not show the same effects of property type as do the data from the other two age-groups. Rather, area seems to be the important determinant of verification time, independent of instructions. Some caution must be exercised in interpreting this result, however, as the relevant statistical tests were only marginally significant (see Kosslyn, 1976b). Finally, when the imagery items are considered in isolation, the effects of property type are notably more pronounced for younger children.

Figure 10.1 shows apparent differences in the effects of property type in the no-imagery condition for the first graders compared with older subjects. The statistic testing this interaction failed to attain the desired level of significance, however. This failure can be localized, in part, to high variability among subjects: Not all subjects showed the no-imagery effects of property type that characterized their particular age-group as a whole. With this in mind, the no-imagery data were reanalyzed in terms of the postsession self-reports of verification strategy. The results of this analysis are presented in figure 10.2. Although this analysis is admittedly post hoc and inconclusive, it is certainly suggestive. Two points might be made about the outcome of this analysis: First, the number of people reporting imagery use varies systematically at the different ages. Only one person in the fourth grade and one in college claimed to use imagery predominantly, while almost half of the first graders did so. Furthermore, the

---

*This experiment was in fact performed at the same time as the one with only adults, described in chapter 3, section 2.2.1. The data from adults plotted here are from the first 14 subjects in the Pause/Whole Group illustrated in figure 3.19.

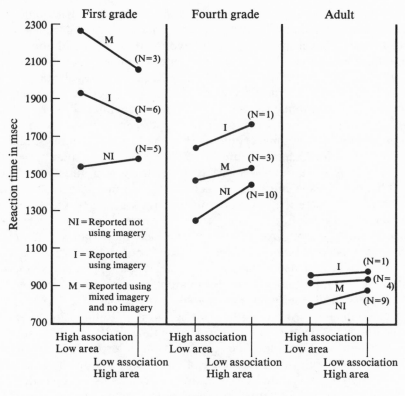

Figure 10.2.   Time to verify two types of "true" properties for three self-reported verification strategies when subjects were not told to use imagery.

data give us some reason to suspect that the three "mixed strategy" first graders actually relied predominantly on imagery (the assessment procedure was such that equivocation and doubt were relegated to the "mixed" category). It is worth noting, however, that by far the majority of subjects, even the youngest, had no difficulty in classifying their mental strategy. Second, for the first-grade children who reported not using imagery the effects of property type look like those of the adults, whereas for those who claimed to use imagery the means resemble those obtained from first graders who received imagery instructions. Of course, only in the first grade are there enough people in the three groups to make comparisons of reaction times meaningful, and even here the number of observations involved is dangerously low. Nonetheless, the differences in the size of the effects of property type for the first graders in the two instructional conditions illustrated in figure 10.1 may in part be due to the subjects who did not use imagery spontaneously but showed effects like those which characterized the adults and older children.

One final point ought to be made about figure 10.2. In contrast to the slight improvements with age in evaluation times observed when imagery instructions were given, times decreased markedly with age when imagery was reportedly used spontaneously. In fact, the adults who reported using some imagery in the uninstructed condition were, on the average, more than one second faster than the first graders who claimed to use some imagery spontaneously.

I also analyzed the responses from the trials with "false" properties. In most respects, the "false" data mirror the data from "true" items: Imaged items took longer to assess than items in the no-imagery condition, but this effect was more pronounced for the adults. Older subjects were faster than younger subjects, mostly due to the contribution of the no-imagery items. For all three ages, when no imagery instructions were given, low-association, low-area properties were responded to more quickly than high-association, high-area properties. When imagery instructions were given, in contrast, high-association, high-area properties were evaluated more quickly than low-association, low-area ones. Unlike the "true" data, the effects of property type for the "false" items were essentially the same for the different age-groups, as is evident in figure 10.3. Unfortunately, however, the pattern of errors in the imagery condition presents a classic case of a "speed-accuracy trade-off," making these results impossible to interpret. That is, in contrast to the errors for "true" properties, the errors for imaged items in the "false" data do not tend to increase with increasing verification times. Instead, subjects generally made more errors with high-association, high-area properties while also evaluating these properties more quickly. Thus, the reaction times may reflect nothing other than the willingness to make fast guesses, and we cannot make reliable inferences from the imagery times for "false" items.

The results of this experiment, then, are largely consistent with expectations derived from a straightforward extension of our model. First, the fact that times decreased with age when imagery was not required is easily explained by positing that the number of entries in the propositional lists generally tends to increase over the age range considered here, and such entries can in fact be "looked up" much more easily than images can be generated and inspected. Second, there was at least some evidence that young children rely more on imagery than do adults, as would be expected if they have fewer entries on their propositional lists and are less adept at performing deductions than are adults.

Some unexpected findings of this experiment may have interesting implications. I found larger effects of property size in the imagery condition for the youngest children than for the other groups. Several possible explanations of this finding come to mind: (1) Perhaps children have less

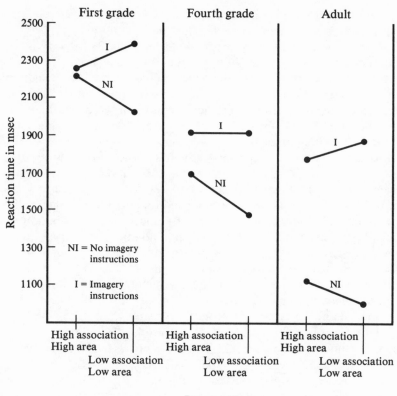

Figure 10.3. Time to evaluate two types of "false" properties when imagery instructions were given and when no imagery instructions were given.

"processing capacity" than do older people, and hence zooming in on an image requires more time for them than for adults. (2) Perhaps because young children are generally slower processors they can maintain only a very few units in an image at any one time. Thus, it is more likely that smaller parts will not be included on their images, requiring filling in from long-term memory. This account is not to be preferred, however, because I posit that even adults maintain very few units on an image and usually fill in parts only as needed. (3) We know that people become better with age in locating and attending to a part of a picture (see Gibson, 1969); perhaps something similar occurs with imagery. That is, larger properties may be more easily "stumbled upon" than smaller ones if the FIND-like search strategies are haphazard or inefficient. This notion might also help explain the suggestive finding that adults are much faster than children in their spontaneous imagery; when adults use imagery spontaneously, perhaps they tend to wait for the property word to be presented and then image only the portion of the animal where the property is likely to be found. Further, being able to focus immediately on the relevant location may allow adults to recognize a part before the image is completely constructed. This procedure would certainly be faster than that advocated in the imagery instructions used here, requiring searching a well-constructed image of the whole animal. Young children, in contrast, may not access images so efficiently and may search across a complete image of an object whenever they use imagery. If so, then it is not surprising that young children take about the same time to evaluate induced and spontaneous imagery.

Does this experiment finally provide unambiguous support for the representational-development hypothesis? It is one piece of convergent evidence, but does not provide conclusive evidence on its own. In particular, one could argue that subjects are in fact processing a list of propositions representing an animal's properties, and that these propositions are ordered in terms of size. Thus, if the child searches from the top to the bottom of the list, the representations of larger properties will be reached sooner. This ordering might be a consequence of the order in which the properties tend to be seen when one is actually looking at the animal; all else being equal, larger properties are more likely than smaller properties to be fixated upon initially. Or the list could be ordered in accordance with when the child learned the names of the properties, which might be highly correlated with size. And so on. I puzzle over why these factors did not also dictate the association-strength rankings, but I am sure some kind of a story can be concocted.

The inference that the effects of property size implicate imagery use would be supported if we had convergent evidence from other experiments. For example, in one experiment we might ask people of different ages to remember arrays composed of familiar objects drawn at different sizes; use of counterbalancing over subjects would allow us to eliminate any possible confoundings between a particular object and its pictured size. In addition, arrays could be built up piecemeal, controlling for encoding order. This technique could be used in building composite objects as well as composite arrays. For example, a "mythical animal" might be constructed one part at a time in any desired order. A given part, like the horns, could vary from being pictured at a very large size for some children to a very small size for others. By asking the child to name the color (or the like) of each object or part as it was presented, we would be sure the child noticed the components as they were presented. After the child saw a stimulus, it would be removed, and then the child would decide, as quickly as possible, whether or not various objects or parts were present in the array. As in the earlier experiment, names of large and small items would be presented for evaluation, and times would be recorded. If subjects were explicitly instructed to use imagery, or if they used imagery spontaneously, the evaluation times would be expected to increase as the size of the object or part decreased. An important feature of this general approach is the inclusion of a condition where imagery instructions are administered, allowing us to verify that imagery use does produce the expected effects.

Numerous other sorts of experiments could be conducted using size or —more generally—discriminability as the independent variable. In addition, distance could be used here, as in our reaction-time studies in which subjects focused on different parts of an image before being asked about a property of the object. Again, however, we would have to take care to ensure that explanations based on propositional lists could not account for the results.

We did not do these additional experiments because they did not really seem to lead anywhere. The experiment just described was conducted early in this research program, during what I now call Phase I. In retrospect, it seems clear that the simplest version of the representational-development hypothesis, claiming that children use imagery more than do adults, is too simple-minded and not very interesting. The theory as presently developed leads one to expect that children tend to use imagery in some situations but not in others. According to our theory, the probability that imagery is used in a given task depends partly on one's familiarity with a content area and on how one has used information in the past (such as talking about it). Thus, given the differences in the kinds of situations encountered by children and adults, we do not necessarily expect children to use imagery more than do adults in all contexts. Further, it is likely that other sorts of factors, like the *affect* associated with particular information, influence the way in which information tends to be accessed. In this case, the content that evokes particular affective reactions probably changes over age, and hence people of different ages may use imagery to recall different kinds of information. For example, an adult may use imagery when thinking about attractive people of the opposite sex—even if there are adequate propositional encodings to process the information without using imagery. Young children, in contrast, may not be much inclined to use imagery in such contexts, but may use imagery when thinking about toys, chocolate cakes, or birthdays. In general, I suspect that affect will prove an important component in generating specific models (as will motivation—see chapter 6), but will supplement the kinds of functional capacities investigated here, and will not force wholesale revision of the present theory. This is clearly a direction for future research (see Abelson, 1963).

In short, we now have the two necessary ingredients to mount a research program on the representational-development hypothesis: a rich theoretical framework and some powerful methodological tools. Our model leads us to make a number of predictions about when children use imagery, and for what reasons. And now that we know some of the hallmarks of imagery use (see chapter 3), we can test these ideas.

5.0 CONCLUDING REMARKS

In this chapter we considered the hypothesis that young children tend to use imagery in their thinking more than do adults. We were able to formulate a version of this hypothesis within the context of the present theory, drawing primarily on our claims about the nature of the data-structures in human memory. In addition, we extended the notions developed in the previous chapter to consider constraints on how deductions may be carried out.

The following results were obtained in the course of considering the "representational-development hypothesis": (1) When instructed to use imagery, young children and adults require similar amounts of time to see properties; but when left to their own devices, adults are very much faster than young children in verifying properties. (2) Even when young children are not explicitly instructed to use imagery, the size of a property has some effects on the time they require to verify the property. (3) Young children require more time to see small properties on images, relative to the time they require to see larger ones, than do adults. (4) The size of a property does not affect ratings of association strength, even when pictures are consulted. (5) There was a decrease over age in the time required to verify properties when imagery was reportedly used spontaneously.

The following hypotheses were offered in this chapter: (1) Information in images is spontaneously described and entered into a propositional list if one has increasing occasion to use the information. (2) When images are used depends not only on formal properties of the system but on the affect associated with a piece of information. (3) Adults can image only as much material as is needed to perform some task, whereas children are much less efficient. (4) Young children require more time to zoom in than do adults or are unable to search images as effectively as are adults.

11. Imagery in Perspective

What is the proper place of imagery in a theory of mind? I shall address this question by placing the present issues in historical context: There is more than a little precedent for being preoccupied with mental images and their role in mental processes. I can think of no area in cognitive psychology that stands to gain more by considering the errors of the past. Thus, it will be useful to consider in some depth why imagery was traditionally so popular in academic psychology, why it fell out of favor, and why it is undergoing a revival in the field today.

1.0 IMAGERY IN PSYCHOLOGY: THE FIRST CYCLE

So important has imagery been in the history of psychology that a thorough review of the history of imagery would in fact be a history of most of psychology. Rather than attempt a superficial summary of such an account here (see Boring, 1950; Humphrey, 1951; and Woodworth, 1938, for excellent discussions), let me just remind the reader of the high and low points of the early history. Wilhelm Wundt, the founder of scientific psychology, defined psychology as the "science of immediate experience." His goal was to construct a periodic table of the mind, to specify the elementary sensations of which all experience is composed and to specify the rules of composition. The main methodology used in Wundt's laboratory was introspection, and the main subject matter was imagery. Researchers tried to fathom the structure of their images. Images were like percepts, but without the immediate source of sensory stimulation. But let Wundt speak for himself:

> The whole task of psychology can therefore be summed up in these two problems: (1) What are the elements of consciousness? (2) What combinations do these elements undergo and what laws govern these combinations? (Wundt, 1912, p. 44)

> An idea, in the general sense in which we are here using the word, is always something composite. A visual image is made up of spatially distinguishable parts; a sound is constituted of clangs,

438

while it is also conceived of as coming to us in a certain direction,—*i.e.,* is associated with spatial ideas. Our first problem in analysing ideas, therefore, consists in the determination of their simplest constituent elements, and in the investigation of the psychological properties of these. (Wundt, 1894, p. 14-15)

There is no question that Wundt's meaning of the term "image" was similar to mine. In fact, Wundt made an even stronger equation between on-line perceptual representation and mental images than I have urged:

> The terminology adopted in many Psychologies, according to which the images of memory and fancy are alone designated "ideas," while the direct effects of sense-impressions are termed exclusively "perceptions," we must judge to be unjustifiable and misleading. It lends colour to the view that there is some essential psychological difference between these two kinds of mental process, whereas such a difference is nowhere discoverable. (Wundt, 1894, p.14)

By 1913 the "imageless thought controversy" began to shake the very foundations of Wundt's enterprise. Oswaldo Kulpe and other researchers of the Würzburg school inadvertently discovered that some thoughts were not accompanied by mental images. In the first, and typical, experiment of this genre, a subject was asked to lift two weights and to judge which was heavier. What was surprising was that the subject had no notion of how the judgment was made. To be sure, there were plenty of experiences of images and sensations, but the judgment itself was not heralded by a syllogistic sequence of coherent steps. Rather, the judgment just seemed to pop into mind full-blown and unguided by conscious processing. In other experiments, it was found that one could understand the meaning of a word more quickly than one could image the named object, demonstrating that imagery and meaning were not one and the same thing (see Moore, 1915). Although Kulpe was relatively moderate in interpreting these findings, others took them to indicate that the Wundtian approach was inherently flawed.

With the appearance in 1913 of "Psychology as the Behaviorist Sees It," by John B. Watson, psychology was on a new course (the spirit of which was later amplified and developed by the Logical Positivists). Instead of simply rejecting the claim that all mental phenomena were reflected by or accessible via our imagery, Watson attacked the whole idea of trying to study the mind. On Watson's view, imagery did not belong to the domain of the mind, but was subsumed by "subvocal thinking." Subvocal thinking was thought to consist of tiny laryngeal movements that could be measured directly if proper equipment were available. The arguments against imagery hinged on the purported "nonobjectivity" of mental events, and on metaphysical commitments about how the nervous system supposedly operates. Note that Watson offered no data to support what he took to be the critical points in his following remarks (italics are his):

> But the behaviorist, having made a clean sweep of all the rubbish called consciousness, comes back at you: "Prove to me," he says, "that you have auditory images, visual images, or any other kinds of disembodied processes. So far I have only your unverified and unsupported word that you have them." Science must have objective evidence to base its theories upon. The behaviorist, on the contrary, founds his systems upon the belief supported at every point by known facts of physiology that *the brain is stimulated always and only from the outside by a sense organ process*. The nervous system works only in arcs—first the sense organ is stimulated by an *object* from the *outside* or through the *movement* of our muscles and glands on the *inside*. The impulse travels to the brain and from the brain to the muscles or glands. Always when there is activity on the part of the organism one or several of these complete arcs are functioning. In other words, there is always an object stimulating us— if not a chair or table, then some organic or muscular process such as the muscular process in the throat that we use in whispering to ourselves (thought). (1928, pp. 75–76)

Interestingly, Watson's treatment of imagery foreshadowed Ryle's (1949) and Dennet's (1969) attempts to consign images to the status of "intentional objects," just a way of talking about internal events. I cannot help wondering what Watson would make of the kinds of results I have described in the foregoing chapters. The following quote reveals a strong metatheoretical bias that runs somewhat counter to the conclusions drawn in this book:

> What then becomes of images? Why, they remain unproven— mythological, the figment of the psychologist's terminology. If our everyday vocabulary and the whole of literature had not become so enmeshed in this terminology we should hear nothing of imagery. What have we in their place? What does a person mean when he closes his eyes or ears (figuratively speaking) and says, "I see the house where I was born, the trundle bed in my mother's room where I used to sleep—I can even see my mother as she comes to tuck me in and I can even hear her voice as she softly says good-night"? Touching, of course, but sheer bunk. We are merely dramatizing. The behaviorist finds no proof of imagery in all this. *We have put all these things in words long, long ago* and we constantly rehearse those scenes verbally whenever the occasion arises. . . What we mean by being conscious of events which happened in our past is that we can carry on a conversation about them either to ourselves (thought) or with some one else (talk). (Watson, 1928, pp. 76-77)

Probably the most important consequence of the introduction of the behaviorist paradigm was that the structure of the "important problems" came to be altered. Now imagery was largely ignored in favor of more easily observed stimulus-response relations. It is instructive to note that in Woodworth's 1938 classic text *Experimental Psychology* fully 8 of the 45 pages of the first substantive chapter, on memory, are concerned with imagery. In the 1954 edition, revised with Schlosberg, fewer than 2 pages out of a chapter of 37 pages are concerned with imagery. Given that the second edition was considerably longer (in a two-column-per-page format instead of the earlier single-column one, taking up some 50 additional pages), this tells us something about the drift of the field.

2.0 IMAGERY IN PHILOSOPHY

So imagery began by being enormously important in psychology, but soon was reduced to a negligible—if not nonexistent—role. What went on here? Why was imagery so popular initially, and why was so much emphasis placed on imagery that efforts to study the mind were largely abandoned when the study of imagery proved problematical? Further, what bearing does this history have on contemporary approaches to imagery and mind? It seems clear that imagery was given too central a role in Wundt's psychology, but why? And what *should* be the proper role of imagery in a theory of mind? Before we can place imagery in perspective, before we can formulate the boundaries of a theory of imagery, we must understand why imagery was so appealing in the first place. An interesting analysis of this appeal follows from an examination of the philosophical foundations from which psychology emerged. Imagery played a major role in the writings of many philosophers before psychology was considered a separate discipline, and it would not be a surprising to find that some of the basic assumptions that elevated imagery to this role had continued to exert an influence on the first true psychologists.

2.1 Documentation

What evidence is there that imagery did in fact have an important role in early conceptions of mind? Consider the importance Aristotle seems to have placed on mental imagery:

> Now we have already discussed imagination in the treatise *On the Soul* and we concluded there that thought is impossible without an image. (*On Memory and Recollection,* 450a 5)

> Memory, even the memory of concepts, does not take place without an image. (450a 7)

The nature of memory and its process has now been explained
as the persistent possession of an image, in the sense of a copy
of the thing to which the image refers, and it has been further
explained to what faculty in us this belongs, viz. to the primary
power of sensation . . . (451a 19)

An emphasis on imagery as a form of internal representation became
almost standard practice in ensuing generations. The importance ascribed
to imagery cut across numerous other differences, as is evident in the following brief sampling of relevant quotes. Most of these conceptions of imagery are direct ancestors of my own, as should be evident by the emphasis on the quasi-pictorial properties of images.

In the *Third Meditation*, Descartes seems to have subscribed to the notion that images could serve as internal representations in memory:
"Some of my thoughts are as it were pictures of objects, and these alone
are properly called ideas." Further, his imagery notion likened images to
percepts arising from information stored in memory (the province of the
soul), which are much like those arising from the senses (of the body; see
p. 340, in the edition listed in the references). There is some confusion
about Descartes's precise use of the terms "image" and "idea." In fact,
in reacting to Hobbes and Gassendi, Descartes asserted that ideas are not
images. Kenny (1968) proposes that in this controversy Descartes was
using the term "image" more literally, and was denying that there are *actual* pictures in the brain, not that there are mental images. The following
passage is consistent with this view:

> . . . it is not only images pictured in the fancy that I call ideas;
> nay, to such images I here decidedly refuse the title of ideas, in
> so far as they are pictures in the corporeal fancy, i.e., in some
> part of the brain. They are ideas only in so far as they inhere in
> the mind itself when it is directed towards that part of the brain.
> (*Arguments Demonstrating the Existence of God and the Dis-
> tinction Between Soul and Body,* Haldane and Ross, trans.,
> vol. II, p. 52)

Hobbes seemed to have conceived of images as being identified with
physical events in the brain, as is suggested by the physical analogy offered here:

> When a Body is once in motion, it moveth (unless something els
> hinder it) eternally; and whatsoever hindreth it, cannot in an in-
> stant, but in time, and by degrees quite extinguish it: And as wee
> see in the water, though the wind cease, the waves give not over
> rowling for a long time after; so also it happeneth in that motion,
> which is made in the internall parts of a man, then, when he
> Sees, Dreams, &c. For after the object is removed, or the eye
> shut, wee still retain an image of the thing seen, though more ob-

scure than when we see it. And this is it, the Latines call *Imagi-nation*, from the image made in seeing; and apply the same, though improperly, to all the other senses. But the Greeks call it *Fancy;* which signifies *appearance,* and is as proper to one sense, as to another. *Imagination* therefore is nothing but *decaying sense;* and is found in men, and many other living Creatures, as well sleeping, as waking. (*Leviathan,* Part I, chapter II, p. 5)

The extent of Hobbes's reliance on imagery as a form of internal representation is evident in the following quote, wherein a virtual equation between memory representation and images is offered. The choice between the terms "memory" and "imagination" seems, on Hobbes's view, entirely a matter of whether one wishes to emphasize the decay process or the representation itself. Hobbes continues,

. . . so also after a great distance of time, our imagination of the Past is weak; and wee lose (for example) of Cities wee have seen, many particular Streets; and of Actions, many particular Circumstances. This *decaying sense* when wee would express the thing it self, (I mean *Fancy* it selfe,) wee call *imagination,* as I said before: But when wee would express the *decay,* and signifie that the Sense is fading, old, and past, it is called *Memory.* So that *Imagination* and *Memory,* are but one thing, which for divers considerations hath divers names. (p. 5)

Interestingly, Hobbes seems to have appreciated the generative nature of imagery, and the fact that images may be constructed from separate encodings. The final part of this passage, however, admits to a much broader melding of descriptive and depictive information than currently exists in our model.

Much memory, or memory of many things, is called *Experience.* Againe, Imagination being only of those things which have been formerly perceived by Sense, either all at once, or by parts at severall times; the former, (which is the imagining the whole object, as it was presented to the sense) is *simple Imagination,* as when one imagineth a man, or horse, which he hath seen before. The other is *Compounded,* as when from the sight of a man at one time, and of a horse at another, we conceive in our mind a Centaure. So when a man compoundeth the image of his own person, with the image of the actions of an other man; as when a man imagins himselfe a *Hercules,* or an *Alexander,* (which happeneth often to them that are much taken with reading of Romants) it is a compound imagination, and properly but a Fiction of the mind. (pp. 5-6)

Spinoza, in the *Ethics*, also maintained that images could act as surrogate percepts, evoking many of the same responses as do the actual objects (interestingly, this idea is the pivot point of most image-desensitiza-
tion forms of psychotherapy; see, for example, Wolpe, 1958): "Prop.
XVIII. A man is affected with the same emotion of pleasure or pain from
the image of a thing past or future as from the image of a thing present."

Perhaps more than any other school, the British Empiricists are re-
nowned for their emphasis on the role of imagery in thinking. Locke did
make use of something like our current conception of imagery, but he did
not, as far as I can tell, identify the term "idea" with an image in the present sense. In what follows note that the idea is not equated with the
image, but rather the image is the vehicle for an idea. This will turn out to
be an important distinction:

> For the narrow mind of man, not being capable of having many
> ideas under view and consideration at once, it was necessary to
> have a repository to lay up those ideas, which at another time it
> might have use of. (But our ideas being nothing but actual per-
> ceptions in the mind, which cease to be anything when there is
> no perception of them, this laying up of our ideas in the reposi-
> tory of the memory signifies no more but this—that the mind has
> a power, in many cases, to revive perceptions which it has once
> had, with this additional perception annexed to them, that it has
> had them before. And in this sense it is that our ideas are said to
> be in our memories, when indeed they are actually no where, but
> only there is an ability in the mind when it will to revive them
> again, and, as it were, paint them anew on itself, though some
> with more, some with less, difficulty; some more lively, and
> others, more obscurely.) And thus it is by the assistance of this
> faculty that we are said to have all those ideas in our understand-
> ings, which though we do not actually contemplate, yet we can
> bring in sight, and make appear again and be the objects of our
> thoughts, without the help of those sensible qualities which first
> imprinted them there. (*An Essay Concerning Human
> Understanding*, pp. 64-65)

The fact that Locke had in mind something like a visual image, which
could be inspected by a "mind's eye" seems evident in the following passage:

> In this secondary perception, as I may so call it, or viewing again
> the ideas that are lodged in the memory, the mind is oftentimes
> more than barely passive; the appearance of those dormant pic-
> tures depending sometimes on the will. The mind very often sets
> itself on work in search of some hidden idea, and turns as it were
> the eye of the soul upon it . . . This further is to be observed,
> concerning ideas lodged in the memory, and upon occasion re-
> vived by the mind, that they are not only (as the word "revive"

imports) none of them new ones, but also that the mind takes notice of them as of a former impression, and renews its acquaint-
ance with them as with ideas it had known before. (pp. 67-68)

Probably the classic Associationist treatment of imagery is to be found
in the writings of Hume. *A Treatise of Human Nature* begins:

All the perceptions of the human mind resolve themselves into
two distinct kinds, which I shall call *Impressions* and *Ideas*.
The difference betwixt these consists in the degrees of force and
liveliness with which they strike upon the mind, and make their
way into our thought or consciousness. Those perceptions,
which enter with most force and violence, we may name *impressions,* and under this name I comprehend all our sensations,
passions and emotions, as they make their first appearance in
the soul. By *ideas* I mean the faint images of these in thinking
and reasoning; such as, for instance, are all the perceptions ex-
cited by the present discourse, excepting only, those which arise
from the sight and touch, and excepting the immediate pleasure
or uneasiness it may occasion.

The notion that images are like rather weak percepts has survived to this
day.

James Mill also saw fit to emphasize the role of images in representing
ideas. The first part of the following passage leaves no doubt that Mill was
talking about the same kind of image as has been discussed in this book.

. . . by shutting my eyes see him no longer, I can still think of
him. I have still a feeling, the consequence of the sensation,
which, though I can distinguish it from the sensation, and treat it
as not the sensation, but something different from the sensation,
is yet more like the sensation, than anything else can be; so like,
that I call it a copy, an image, of the sensation; sometimes, a representation, or a trace, of the sensation.

Another name, by which we denote this trace, this copy, of
the sensation, which remains after the sensation ceases, is IDEA.
This is a very convenient name, and it is that by which the copies
of the sensation thus described will be commonly denominated
in the present work. The word IDEA, in this sense, will express
no theory whatsoever; nothing but the bare fact, which is indis-
putable. We have two classes of feelings; one, that which exists
when the object of sense is present; another, that which exists
after the object of sense has ceased to be present. The one class
of feelings I call SENSATIONS; the other class of feelings I call
IDEAS. (*Analysis of the Phenomena of the Human Mind,* p. 52)

The foregoing passages demonstrate the importance of imagery in historical treatments of the nature of the mind and mental events; this is not
to say that there were not many philosophers who ignored imagery, but

by the same token, there is no shortage of additional writers who made points like those noted here. The question now is why has this been so, and what—if anything—is the difference between the way imagery is treated in this book and the way it was treated by the early philosophical and psychological community?

2.2 The Appeal of Imagery

Can we ascribe the prominant role of imagery simply to bad introspection or the insidious influence of Aristotle? This seems to be Boring's suggestion. Jerry Fodor has argued, in contrast, that there were overriding concerns that virtually dictated the treatment of imagery illustrated above. Fodor's argument goes something like this: There are only two basic ways in which people have tried to understand the nature of "mental" states such as thinking, believing, hoping, liking, and so on. The behaviorists equated "thinking" and the like with particular behavioral predispositions. Formally, we can represent this with a single relation, standing for the behavioral state, which takes one argument, standing for the organism to which that relation applies (for example, if John liked dogs, this would be represented by S_j). This approach is very different from the traditional interpretation of "mental" states, which is shared by modern cognitive psychology. The traditional way of regarding these kinds of states is in terms of a relation between a person and some mental representation and a relation between the mental representation and an object in (or state of) the world. Thus, the basic scheme requires two relations, each of which takes two arguments. The first relation ascribes to a particular person a particular mental representation, and the second relation maps the mental representation to the actual thing being represented. For example, if John liked dogs, this would be represented by $jLx, xRd,$ where $j, x,$ and d represent John, a mental representation, and dogs, respectively, and L and R are the relations of liking and representing, respectively. As far as I can tell, all philosophers who draw or imply a distinction between "intension" and "extension" would seem to subscribe to something like this basic view.

In the language of contemporary cognitive psychology, we would assume that if John "likes" something, this says something about the kind of information represented in John's head and the kinds of processing in which this information may take part (in a given context—see chapter 5). Given this approach, the fundamental psychological issue is how to characterize the internal representations. Fodor sketches three traditional requirements for an internal representation, and argues that these requirements were primarily responsible for the appeal of imagery.

1. The representation must be a mental entity, but it must be able to be used as an argument by both mental relations and nonmental ones. In our

earlier example, we represented John's liking dogs by jLx, xRd, where x was a mental representation that could take part in internal processing and also could be related to objects in the world. In the jargon of contemporary psychology, information must be represented as part of an internal processing system, and that system must be constructed such that the data-structures can represent information about the world.

2. The relation between objects and the most basic mental representations cannot be *conventional*. If it were, it would have to be learned. But learning itself requires prior representations, and these cannot be conventional; if they were, they would have to be learned, which would require prior representations, and so on, in infinite regress. The Empiricists traditionally assumed some nonarbitrary relation between internal representations and referenced objects such that all that must be learned are associations among these internal representations. In other words, at the bottom line we need an invariant encoding process that transforms a given pattern of sensory input into a particular internal representation.*

3. Finally, on the traditional view, the nature of the internal representation should determine the objects to which the encoded information applies (that is, "intension" should determine "extension"). This requires a decoding process that allows the nature of an internal representation to be mapped back into the world. In short, one must be able to tell what a representation is a representation *of*. An idea cannot simply be an idea of whatever caused that idea; if it were, one could not tell what an idea was an idea of unless one recalled its etiology, but how could the etiology be represented? However the etiology was represented, we would need somehow to be able to "read" that representation, which would only push the problem back a step.

These three requirements, according to Fodor, historically seemed satisfied only by an image. The basic idea goes something like this: (*a*) A percept arises when light stimulates the retina, resulting in physical energy being transduced to neural impulses; thus, physical causes result in brain states. (*b*) These states can be "recorded" and later reinstated in the form of an image, which is just like a percept but lacking in "force and liveliness" (for now we will adopt a materialist view of mind and identify mental states with brain states). (*c*) Because images *resemble* the percept of

---

*Occasionally ambiguous stimuli can produce patterns of stimulation which can be encoded into one of a number of different internal representations, and occasionally two or more different objects (for example, a square and a rectangular box viewed from particular angles) may invoke the same internal representation; further, one's knowledge and experience will affect what one sees. I assume that the reading of an ambiguous figure and effects of prior knowledge are consequences of differences in what one attends to and hence encodes. Thus, the internal representation encoded is a consequence of the information attended to and extracted, and there is a direct mapping from this information (that is, the stimulus properties) and the consequent internal representation.

the represented object or scene, they serve as surrogate percepts, allowing one to reason about the represented object in its absence.

The logic outlined above is nowhere more evident than in the writings of David Hume.

> An impression first strikes upon the senses, and makes us perceive heat or cold, thirst or hunger, pleasure or pain of some kind or other. Of this impression there is a copy taken by the mind, which remains after the impression ceases; and this we call an idea. This idea of pleasure or pain, when it returns upon the soul, produces the new impressions of desire and aversion, hope and fear, which may properly be called impressions of reflexion, because derived from it. These again are copied by the memory and imagination, and become ideas; which perhaps in their turn give rise to other impressions and ideas. So that the impressions of reflexion are only antecedent to their correspondent ideas; but posterior to those of sensation, and deriv'd from them. (*A Treatise on Human Nature*, Book I, Part I, Section II)

In the final part of this passage, Hume makes it clear that all ideas ultimately are derived from images, which are the "bedrock" of internal representations. There can be no doubt that images are seen as "surrogate percepts" here, as witnessed by the following quote from the same source (Book I, Part I, Section I):

> The first circumstance, that strikes my eye, is the great resemblance betwixt our impressions and ideas in every other particular, except their degree of force and vivacity. The one seem to be in a manner the reflexion of the other; so that all the perceptions of the mind are double, and appear both as impressions and ideas. When I shut my eyes and think of my chamber, the ideas I form are exact representations of the impressions I felt; nor is there any circumstance of the one, which is not to be found in the other. In running over my other perceptions, I find still the same resemblance and representation. Ideas and impressions appear always to correspond to each other.

Hume goes on to underline further the importance of the resemblance between an image and percept:

> . . . every simple idea has a simple impression, which resembles it; and every simple impression a correspondent idea. That idea of red, which we form in the dark, and that impression, which strikes our eyes in sun-shine, differ only in degree, not in nature. That the case is the same with all our simple impressions and ideas, 'tis impossible to prove by a particular enumeration of them. Every one may satisfy himself in this point by running over as many as he pleases. But if any one should deny this universal resemblance, I know no way of convincing him . . .

Hume's notions are mirrored by Hartley, usually heralded as the founder of British Associationism. Hartley also emphasized the notion that images are the elements from which all thought (not merely memories of things past) is composed.

> . . . the most vivid of these ideas are those where the corresponding sensations are most vigorously impressed, or most frequently renewed; whereas, if the sensation be faint, or uncommon, the generated idea is also faint in proportion, and, in extreme cases, evanescent and imperceptible. The exact observance of the order of place in visible ideas, and of the order of time in audible ones, may likewise serve to shew, that these ideas are copies and offsprings of the impressions made on the eye and ear, in which the same orders were observed respectively. And though it happens, that trains of visible and audible ideas are presented in sallies of the fancy, and in dreams, in which the order of time and place is different from that of any former impressions, yet the small component parts of these trains are copies of former impressions; and reasons may be given for the varieties of their compositions. (*Observations on Man*, Section II, Prop. VIII)

2.3 The Trouble with Treating Imagery as the "Mother of All Internal Representations"

The above-noted conception of imagery seemed to satisfy the first two conditions for a "basic" representation, as follows: The first condition is met because an image is a mental entity that can also be related to physical entities. That is, because an image resembles the percept, and the percept is engendered by physical properties of the perceived object, the image can be related to the referenced object. Further, imagery satisfies the second requirement: Because an image is purportedly derived from the same neural states that register the percept, it is not arbitrarily related to the things it represents (recall my discussion in chapter 3 of how images depict). An image of a Boeing 747 does not appear like a three-toed sloth. The other obvious candidate for the role of internal representation, language, falls short in regard to this second point: It is arbitrarily related to the thing represented.

But what about the third requirement, that a representation specify the objects being represented (that is, dictate its extension)? At first glance, images seem to do the job; after all, they resemble the represented object —by definition. However, there are in fact major problems with trying to use resemblance this way. Probably the most obvious difficulty is that of representing abstract ideas with images. This problem was pointed out so well by Bishop Berkeley:

Whether others have this wonderful faculty of abstracting their
ideas, they best can tell; for myself I find indeed I have a faculty
of imagining, or representing to myself, the ideas of those particular things I have perceived, and of variously compounding and
dividing them. I can imagine a man with two heads, or the upper
parts of a man joined to the body of a horse. I can consider the
hand, the eye, the nose, each by itself abstracted or separated
from the rest of the body. But then whatever hand or eye I
imagine, it must have some particular shape and color. Like-
wise, the idea of man that I frame to myself must be either of a
white, or a black, or a tawny, a straight, or a crooked, a tall, or a
low, or a middle-sized man. I cannot by any effort of thought
conceive the abstract idea above described. (*Principles of
Human Knowledge*, section 10)

This property of image representation may just be a special case of a
more general characteristic: Images must be ''under description'' in order
to represent *anything*, even a particular object (see Goodman, 1968;
Fodor, 1975; Wittgenstein, 1953). That is, we must know what is
important and what is irrelevant to attend to in an image. As Fodor (1975)
points out, for example, a picture or an image of a sitting man could represent John, John's head, a sitting man, bent knees, and so on. This point
seems to have been made, in one form or another, repeatedly in the past.

In *On Memory and Recollection*, Aristotle seems to have appreciated
the fact that images are not identical to ideas, but rather are vehicles in
which ideas occur, vehicles which must be regarded in the proper way to
devine the correct meaning:

Now we have already discussed imagination in the treatise *On
the Soul* and we concluded there that thought is impossible
without an image. For we find in thought the same conditions as
in drawing figures. In the latter without needing a triangle of a
definite magnitude, we nevertheless draw a triangle of definite
size. So, too, the thinking mind, even if it does not think a magnitude, still places a quantitative body before its eyes, although it
does not think it as such. If it is the nature of the quantitative in
an indefinite sense with which the mind is concerned, then
thought represents it under the form of a definite quantity, but
thinks it merely as quantity. (450a 5,6)

Locke pointed out that images, not being objects, do not really ''resemble'' the represented object. Thus, some more sophisticated method of
''reading'' the idea embodied in an image would seem necessary.

To discover the nature of our *ideas* the better, and to discourse
of them intelligibly, it will be convenient to distinguish them *as
they are ideas or perceptions in our minds,* and *as they are modifications of matter in the bodies that cause such perception in us:*

that so we may not think (as perhaps usually is done) that they
are exactly the images and resemblances of something inherent in
the subject; most of those of sensation being in the mind no more
the likeness of something existing without us, than the names
that stand for them are the likeness of our ideas, which yet upon
hearing they are apt to excite in us. (*Essay Concerning Human
Understanding,* Book II, Chapter VIII, 7)

Kant's analysis of this problem emphasizes that images must be interpreted in the context in which they occur. The final two sentences of this
passage from his *Critique of Pure Reason* fit well with the way in which
information is extracted from images in our model. In this case, Kant's
"schema" might correspond to the PRP file from which the descriptive
procedures (used by FIND) are drawn; recall that these procedures provide the interface between material in the surface matrix and the propositional files.

Indeed it is schemata, not images of objects, which underlie our
pure sensible concepts. No image could ever be adequate to the
concept of a triangle in general. It would never attain that univer-
sality of the concept which renders it valid of all triangles,
whether right-angled, obtuse-angled, or acute-angled; it would
always be limited to a part only of this sphere. The schema of the
triangle can exist nowhere but in thought. It is a rule of synthesis
of the imagination, in respect to pure figures in space. Still less is
an object of experience or its image ever adequate to the empirical concept; for this latter always stands in immediate relation to
the schema of imagination, as a rule for the determination of our
intuition, in accordance with some specific universal concept.
The concept "dog" signifies a rule according to which my imagination can delineate the figure of a four-footed animal in a general
manner, without limitation to any single determinate figure such
as experience, or any possible image that I can represent *in con-
creto,* actually presents. This schematism of our understanding,
in its application to appearances and their mere form, is an art
concealed in the depths of the human soul, whose real modes of
activity nature is hardly likely ever to allow us to discover, and
to have open to our gaze. This much only we can assert: the
image is a product of the empirical faculty of reproductive imagination; the *schema* of sensible concepts, such as of figures in
space, is a product and, as it were, a monogram, of pure *a priori*
imagination, through which, and in accordance with which,
images themselves first become possible. These images can be
connected with the concept only by means of the schema to
which they belong. In themselves they are never completely
congruent with the concept.

There seem to be two basic ways in which we could deal with this problem. The classic way was to introduce an interpretive function that se-

lected the important aspects of the image. Locke, Berkeley, Hume, Descartes, Kant, and others attempted to salvage a role for imagery in this way; "stage directions" were introduced to determine the referent of (the thing represented by) an image. For example, the class of triangles could be represented by an image of a triangle plus some directions to attend only to the fact that three straight lines meet to form an enclosed space. The problem is, how are these stage directions learned? If they are in fact an integral part of the representation, they too must satisfy the aforementioned three requirements. We seem to run into problems in positing a nonconventional way of representing the stage directions. These representations are not imagistic, and hence do not represent via the property of resemblance. If a nonconventional way of representing the stage directions exists, then why do we need images in the first place? Our other option is to posit that an innate interpretive function and/or selective kinds of experience determine resemblance, determines which aspects of an image will be attended to by the mind's eye. Then, a particular image will represent only a particular object—even though it logically could have represented others. So, for example, different images will represent John's knees, his head, and so on. The following quote from Wittgenstein is suggestive:

> I see a picture; it represents an old man walking up a steep path leaning on a stick.—How? Might it not have looked just the same if he had been sliding downhill in that position? Perhaps a Martian would describe the picture so. I do not need to explain why *we* do not describe it so. (1953, p. 54)

The problem here is that because we do not have a theory that specifies exactly how an image is represented and processed, we allow ourselves a degree of freedom: We can fiddle around with either the representation or the process and probably get things to come out right. The lack of an explicit theory of image representation and processing allows one to postulate an image for *everything*; let us take a few examples from Tichner:

> Come back now to the authorities: to Locke's triangle and Huxley's composite animal. My own picture of the triangle, the image that means triangle to me, is usually a fairly definite outline of the little triangular figure that stands for the word "triangle" in the geometries. But I can quite well get Locke's picture, the triangle that is no triangle and all triangles at one and the same time. It is a flashy thing, come and gone from moment to moment; it hints two or three red angles, with the red lines deepening into black, seen on a dark green ground. It is not there long enough for me to say whether the angles joining to form the complete figure, or even whether all three of the necessary angles are given. Nevertheless, it means triangle; it is Locke's general idea of triangle; it is Hamilton's palpable absurdity made

real. And the composite animal? Well, the composite animal strikes me as somewhat too even, too nicely balanced. No doubt, the idea in Huxley's mind was of that kind; he, as an anatomist, was interested to mark all the parts and proportions of the creatures before him. But my own ideas of animals are sketchier and more selective: horse is, to me, a double curve and a rampant posture with a touch of mane about it; cow is a longish rectangle with a certain facial expression, a sort of exaggerated pout. Again, however, these things mean horse and cow, are the psychological vehicles of those logical meanings.

And what holds of triangle and horse and cow holds of all the "unpicturable notions of intelligence." No one of them is unpicturable, if you do but have the imaginal mind. "It is impossible," remarks a recent writer, "to ideate a meaning; one can only know it." Impossible? But I have been ideating meanings all my life. And not only meanings, but meaning also. Meaning in general is represented in my consciousness by another of these impressionistic pictures. I see meaning as the blue-grey tip of a kind of scoop, which has a bit of yellow above it (probably a part of the handle), and which is just digging into a dark mass of what appears to be plastic material. I was educated on classical lines; and it is conceivable that this picture is an echo of the oft-repeated admonition to "dig out the meaning" of some passage of Greek or Latin. I do not know; but I am sure of the image. And I am sure that others have similar images. (1909, pp. 17-19) . . . just as the visual image may mean of itself, without kinaesthetic accompaniment, so may the kinaesthetic image occur and and mean of itself, without assistance from vision. I represent the meaning of affirmation, for instance, by the image of a little nick felt at the back of the neck,—an experience which, in sensation, is complicated by pressures and pulls from the scalp and throat. (1909, p. 22)

Even if we could show how images represent particular objects via some form of "resemblance," we would have a long way to go before we could claim that images play a central role in cognition. Consider the most elementary logical operations, like negation, quantification, disjunction, and so on. How would one represent such things using only images? Let us try these few examples: Negation could be represented as two images, one containing a number of things and one containing all but one of them; this might work for picturable objects, but what about classes of objects? If we have a single image represent a class, how do we represent the thing that single image is an image of? (Maybe the image is dimmer when it represents the class?) But what about concepts with no easy referent? Take "furniture" as an easy example. Perhaps a sequence of images (a desk, a sofa, a chair, and so on) can represent the class. So, to represent the concept "no furniture" we will need first a sequence of objects, perhaps of a certain brightness to tell us not to worry about the particular details, which are embedded in another class of objects, and then an image of only the second class in isolation. But wait, how do we know this doesn't mean to add *more* furniture to the first class? Yes, what if we *do* want to say "all the furniture" or "some of it," what now? Well, perhaps we can present only a subset of the images we use to represent the class, and then present the rest for contrast. But how do we know that this isn't just a particular *kind* of furniture, and how do we know how to read the sequence—are we adding some or taking some away? Is the contrast supposed to indicate "some" or "all"? It depends on which image is the "baseline," say, which is the first image of the set. Okay, but how do we distinguish quantification from addition and subtraction? Let alone the *scope* of quantification? Disjunction is no easier. Perhaps we could represent "or" by two images flashing in alternation, one might suggest. Fine. But how about the difference between an "exclusive or" and an "inclusive or"? And how are we going to distinguish this from "x is followed by y" or "x alternates with y"? Whenever we use a sequence to represent something beyond the face value, we then have trouble representing the face event (alternation, in this case) itself. And if we are going to get this fancy with sequences of images and the like, we run into trouble with what was once simple: conjunction, the stock in trade of the Associationists. Two images together do not necessarily represent "and," but may be a part of a context used in representing some more complicated relation. In addition to problems with simple function concepts (like "of"), what are we going to do about tenses? We just blew our chance to use alternation, how about fuzzy images for future events (or past ones)? But we already used that to distinguish a class from a particular . . .

As if all this isn't bad enough, the killer is yet to come: If there is anything that ought to characterize a theory of concepts, it is an account of the combinatorial properties of "meanings." The representations of the concepts of "furniture" and "multicolored" must allow us to derive the meaning of the concept "multicolored furniture." But what if the furniture was multicolored to begin with? Don't let it be, you say. Okay, pick *any* color—or any characteristic—for your images of furniture per se, how do we represent the conjunction of that color or characteristic and furniture? Think about what an image of, say, "not the brand new or the very small multicolored furniture, but all the modern furniture we bought last year" would look like. If images occur in the visual cortex, as some (for example, Hebb, 1968) propose, such an image would tie up visual processing so much that it might be dangerous to think and walk at the same time without a guide dog.

I suspect that with enough sweat, tears, and worn-out erasers some kind of imagery logic could be concocted. But compared to the standard predicate calculus, an imagery calculus would be unwieldy and awkward in the extreme. Further, this logic would be *concocted*, not *reported*; if we really use such a system, presumably we should have some firm intuitions about it.

3.0 CONCLUSIONS: IMAGERY IN PERSPECTIVE

It seems, then, that in psychology, imagery fell into disfavor for three main reasons: First, the original agenda overreached itself; imagery was saddled with too much of the theoretical baggage. It seems unreasonable that all "ideas" should correspond ultimately to images or sets thereof. Second, the data were too slippery. If someone disagreed with one's introspection or analysis, what could be done? Watson seems honestly to have believed that imagery was simply talking to oneself. Tichner never had an "imageless thought" problem; to hear him tell it, *all* of his thoughts were accompanied by rich (albeit sometimes subtle) images. But did anybody believe him? Why should they have? Third, the imagery metaphor was too shallow. It was not clear exactly what it meant to have an image, nor was it clear exactly what sort of an explanation of mental processing one had when appealing to images. The behaviorist movement held glittering promises in this regard: It offered a positivistic hard-headed method for testing hypotheses and a set of more or less transparent theoretical constructs—both of which were all the more appealing after the imageless thought controversy had run on for awhile.

Interest in imagery has revived in part because it is being considered in a more humble, unassuming role than before. Even if images are not the "mother of all internal representations," they may be important as an "engineering" feature of the mind which is not necessary or fundamental so much as just convenient. In particular, recent attention has focused on the role of imagery as a memory aid and as a computational tool. Further, given that there is no obvious necessary reason for people to have imagery at all, or for images to have particular properties, much effort has been devoted simply to demonstrating that mental images are in fact a functional form of internal representation and to studying their nature. The logic of this book has been first to understand some of the basic properties of images, some of the ways in which they serve as repositories of information and some of the ways in which they may be processed, prior to speculating about the role of imagery in cognition. Indeed, it *may* be that imagery has some role in representing word-reference, even if it is not centrally involved in linguistic meaning; we will be in a much better position to study this kind of cart once the horse is placed firmly and properly up in front.

I believe the research program described in this book avoids each of the problems that have historically plagued the study of imagery in the following ways:

Assumptions. On the present view, imagery is a way of representing information that may be especially perspicuous for performing some tasks. Not all thought processes involve imagery, nor is imagery in a privileged position as a form of internal representation. The information represented in an image is defined only vis-à-vis the interpretive procedures that can be satisfied when applied to an image. That is, if there were no description of a rear tire, for example, an image could not serve to represent the information that a car has a rear tire; an image represents some information only by virtue of the fact that interpretive procedures exist to "read" a given spatial configuration as corresponding to an exemplar of some class. Thus, we have attempted to study imagery in the context of a processing system, the whole of which defines how images can represent information. We will not fall into Tichner's trap; the theory must ultimately specify exactly how images represent particular pieces of information. A vague notion of "resemblance" simply will not do.

In addition to representing information about objects in the world in a static form, images also allow one to transform information, to mimic dynamic aspects of our environment. Because of the kinds of transformations we can bring to bear and the kind of representation an image is, we can use our imagery as a "simulation" of possible (and, perhaps, of impossible) transformations in the world. Thus, imagery is an aid to thinking about the consequences of given actions, is a crutch to help us devise a plan for reaching some desired state of affairs. The purposes to which information in an image can be put are undoubtedly wide and varied, and the present theory only begins to outline them. In addition to possibly serving some role in concept learning, reasoning, and pattern recognition, imagery may well serve to make unconscious thoughts and desires manifest in consciousness, as Freud and others have maintained. But it is a long road from the present fragment of a theory to one that specifies how this kind of "symbolic" representation operates.

Methodology. In our research project, we have not taken people's descriptions of their introspections at face value. We listen, and ofttimes empirically test ideas inherent in our (and our subjects') introspections, but we take the reports themselves with a grain of salt. We can think about introspective processes by analogy to perception. Consider Neisser's (1967) notion that a perceiver is like a paleontologist trying to reconstruct a dinosaur from some assorted bone chips. In this case, the actual input is impoverished and incomplete, and only with active processing is it "synthesized" into a meaningful pattern (see Kant, *Critique of Pure Reason*). In the case of introspection, we can draw a similar distinction between the bone chips and the rearranging of them into the dinosaur. The bone chips are the actual data that percolate up from hidden memory processes to consciousness. Importantly, there are no instructions inherent in these fragmentary data that tell one how to interpret them, how to arrange them into a meaningful pattern. We have absolutely no reason to expect people to be authorities on the workings of their images, any more than we should expect them to be authorities on the perceptual processing of objects they see. We need to design tasks that remove, as much as possible, the interpretation of the introspectively accessible data from the subjects. As scientists, we need to isolate the bone chips, so that we can try our hand at arranging them for ourselves. Only with a theory of imagery *plus* a theory of beliefs will we be able to explain people's verbal descriptions of their imagery.

Depth of explanation. We do not try to explain cognitive processing simply by appealing to "imagery." Instead, we are striving to formulate a theory and general model of image representation and processing that has behavioral, process, and explanatory adequacy. The attempt to specify the structures and processes that comprise the imagery system reduces the freedom with which one can appeal to imagery in accounting for some data, and in so doing it expands the possible depth of imagery-based explanations in psychology.

12. Reflections and Refutations

Numerous and varied criticisms have been made of this research project over the course of its development. In this concluding chapter I will reflect on the more fundamental and/or frequently occurring issues and questions.* Following this review and discussion, I will conclude with a few broad comments about the metatheoretical and metamethodological ramifications of the present project.

1.0 CRITICISMS AND RESPONSES

1.1 On Demand Characteristics and Task Demands

During the summer of 1978 I spoke at the TINLAP-2 conference in Urbana-Champaign, and was asked the following question from the floor (roughly paraphrased): "If people rotated an image of an elephant more slowly than an image of a rabbit, would this show that the elephant had more inertia because it weighed more?" The point of this query, as I paraphrased it for the inquisitor, was that one obviously would not account for such a hypothetical finding by appeal to the weight of the image, but that such an effect might show that subjects simply cooperate with what they take to be the experimenter's desires. Similarly, I often have been asked whether subjects might take longer to see parts of smaller images because they know it would be more difficult actually to see parts of smaller objects. This criticism, then, is that "demand characteristics" or "task demands," imposed either by implicit cues from the experimenter or implications inherent in the instructions, are actually responsible for our results. I have four points to make in response.

First, in chapter 9 I described two kinds of experiments in which sub-

*The Kosslyn, Pinker, Smith, and Shwartz (in press) "target article" was in fact written prior to completion of this book, but the response to the commentaries on that paper was written after this book. Thus, a number of new points are raised there, and some of the present ones are developed further. In particular, see this paper for a detailed discussion of Richman, Mitchell, and Reznick's (1979) arguments about possible demand characteristics in imagery experiments.

jects were never told to use images, but nevertheless their response times showed the hallmarks of imagery use when we expected spontaneous use of imagery. In one sort of experiment subjects were asked to begin with a normal or small image before comparing the sizes of two named objects. Even though subjects were never told to *use* their initial images, decision times were slowed down in the latter case when we predicted that imagery should be used. In another experiment, we showed that distance from the point of focus on an image to a queried property affected the time to verify an object's properties *only* for items rated (by other subjects) to require imagery. In this case, subjects were never told to scan an image, nor could they tell when an imagery property was about to be presented, since the different types of items were intermingled. But distance to be scanned affected time when we expected imagery to be used—and only then. It is not clear what sort of task demands or demand characteristics would produce such selective effects of the initial size of, or location of focus on, an image.

Second, we often have predicted rather complex patterns of data, which presumably would be difficult to produce intentionally in response to demand characteristics. Consider three examples: (1) Recall the experiment (chapter 3, section 2.4), in which we used the visual angle of the mind's eye calculated from one group of subjects to predict the time other subjects would require to scan the longest possible nonoverflowing image of a line. The people in the two image-scanning groups would have required a host of paranormal abilities to deduce the expected results in their experiments. (2) The size of a queried property had similar effects on image inspection time for first graders, fourth graders, and adults, as discussed in chapter 10, section 4.0. It seems unlikely that the children could have inferred the hypothesis (and in fact none of the youngest had the slightest inkling of it when I talked with them afterward), and the individual-difference post hoc analysis of the first graders—where children who claimed to use imagery spontaneously showed effects of size, but children claiming not to use imagery did not—does not seem to fit a demand characteristic explanation: In this condition, imagery was not even mentioned, let alone required. (3) In some of the experiments on generation time different people imaged patterns of different complexity, but times nonetheless increased linearly for items of increasing complexity. Certainly clairvoyance is an oft-discussed possibility, but I think we should avoid invoking it if at all possible (but see Anderson, 1976, p. 9).

Third, subjects are always debriefed after the experiment, and only data from those who have not deduced the hypotheses are included in the analyses. In fact, we often obtain mistaken hypotheses when we query subjects after the experiment. For example, in the map-scanning experiment described in chapter 3, section 2.1, several subjects later claimed that they had to slow down when scanning among the closest objects, but there was no evidence of this in the times themselves. True, the fact that subjects seem unaware of the correct hypothesis does not mean that they did not "unconsciously" deduce the point of the research, but this is a last-resource argument, possibly one that in principle can never be eliminated by appeal to empirical findings. It is not surprising, however, that some subjects did realize what was happening upon being asked to introspect about their performance. To say that subjects have conscious access to some aspects of their internal processing, however, is a far cry from saying that the internal processing is itself dictated by the subjects' understanding of task demands.

My fourth point is that in our theory we have not claimed that physical properties of images or image processes are "free." Rather, the properties of apparent rigidity under rotation and the like have received explicit attention in the theory proper. Since we claim that some aspects of these processes—like transformation rate—are under strategic control, it should not be surprising that subjects *can* mimic certain physical properties, like the effects of inertia on rotation rates, if they want to. After all, one of the purported purposes of imagery is as a "simulation" of possible operations on objects in the world. Thus, it should not be surprising that the imagery system is able to mimic certain physical properties. This sort of "task demand" is not only interesting, but totally consistent with our theory.*

1.2 On Methodology

I have sometimes been criticized because my experiments often rely on the subjects actually introspecting and cooperating with the instructions. Most psychologists seem to wish they could create methodologies that treat the subject as an inert hunk of matter that must respond in some fashion regardless of its mental state or the like. I agree that it would be ideal not to have to rely on our subjects' good intentions, but I do not see this as a fatal criticism: If we had failed to obtain meaningful and reliable results, the failure of subjects to perform the task might be one reason for this state of affairs. But given that subjects claim to follow the instructions, and that the data consistently are interpretable, this does not seem a source of major worry. This defense has ample precedent in studies of perception and psychophysics, which often rely on self-reports that may be more demanding than those required here. In psychophysics subjects are commonly asked to assign a number to a given intensity of sensation. These data are taken seriously because they are well behaved and conform to expectations derived from a theoretical framework—as do our data.

---

* See Pinker's discussion in Kosslyn et al., in press, for new data that speak against the claim that our results merely reflect "demand characteristics."

1.3 On Ecological Validity

Neisser (1976) and others have argued that psychological theories should have something to do with what people do in the real world. I take this as axiomatic. The issue is how one should best approach this goal. One school emphasizes studying phenomena as they naturally occur. But this is rather like trying to dig one's teeth into a giant apple; one runs the risk of dying from lack of nourishment. It seems clear we cannot study the "whole man" all of a piece, but must adopt a divide-and-conquer strategy. And this seems difficult to do in "natural" field settings. All of the data reported in this book were obtained in very "artificial" situations, which do not resemble those where imagery occurs naturally in the course of everyday experience. Thus, the results of this project, it has been argued, are not "ecologically valid." I make no apologies for my approach to studying cognition. In fact, I see no alternative if psychology is ever to become a mature science. Only in the "artificial" situations created in the laboratory can we control enough variables to allow us to collect data that bear on specific issues; in the real world, too many factors are conflated to allow easy inferences about cause/effect relations. There is a reason why physicists do not try to study leaves falling off real trees, but turn instead to highly artificial environments (including those having no air at all) in testing alternative hypotheses. In my project I have tried to ensure that my experiments bear on general issues, and are not simply exercises in manipulating variables. We have examined the capacities of the imagery system, which should structure imaginal thinking in all contexts. And we have taken care to avoid studying laboratory-specific phenomena. In chapter 9, for example, I commented about the necessity of being able to generalize to cases where "natural categories" were presumably encoded prior to the subject entering the lab. I am sympathetic with the concern that we study imagery as it is actually used in everyday experience, but have seen no other way to approach this topic than that taken here: Only after we know something about imagery per se can we even identify situations in which imagery occurs, let alone begin to understand why it is used in such contexts.

1.4 On Spontaneous versus Instructed Use of Imagery

In most of my experiments subjects are asked to use imagery to perform tasks that do not seem to require imagery. A proper study of imagery, one complaint stresses, would begin by studying tasks in which imagery must be used. My response to this is straightforward: First, we need a theory to know in which tasks imagery will be required. But such a theory will be taken seriously only if it is rooted in a substantial body of research about imagery. So, Catch-22: We need a theory before we can predict when imagery is used, but we must know when imagery is used before we can formulate the theory in the first place. The only way we can break this circle, it seems to me, is to instruct subjects to use imagery. Then we at least can have some confidence that a given behavior reflects the properties of image processing. Second, even if we had a theory or some other means (patterns in tea leaves, say) that directed our attention to tasks where imagery should be used, how could we then verify this fact unless we knew the "hallmarks" of imagery use (see my discussion in chapter 10)? That is, in order to know whether imagery is in fact being used in some situation, we first must know what behavioral consequences ought to be contingent on imagery use. Again, this is a "Catch-22" situation; only by first studying situations where we know (with some degree of certainty) that data reflect the properties of image processing can we learn enough about imagery to study it "in the field," as it were. Chapter 9 reported some of the fruits of this approach, where we were able to use both the theory and the methodologies developed earlier to study when imagery was used to answer questions about relative sizes and about properties of objects. In future work we hope to apply our methodologies to the study of the really interesting uses of imagery in creative thinking and problem solving, but the systematic study of these processes necessarily —to my mind—must rest on a firm foundation of more basic knowledge about imagery per se.

1.5 On Topics

Thus far in this project we have given relatively short shrift to the major question about imagery that has absorbed previous researchers, namely the role of imagery as a mnemonic. Bower (1978), for example, has complained that I have failed to relate my work to the bulk of the research in the field. As was apparent in chapter 7, this claim is not far off the mark. Some of my reasons are apparent in the discussion in chapter 7: I am not entirely convinced that much of the work on the role of imagery as a mnemonic really has much to do with imagery, as opposed to the effects of "depth of processing" (Craik, 1973) or the like. Further, in order to discuss this function of imagery in a meaningful way, the theory must specify how images are re-encoded into memory. Presumably, images formed from memory can be remembered in a fashion similar to the way actual percepts are encoded. Our theory does not specify how this "front end" operates; we do not yet have a perceptual parser and encoding device. This is a major deficiency. There are many other interesting questions about imagery that we have not yet examined, partly because on my view the prior question, the central problem, is how images serve to represent information in the human mind, and other questions seem to be derived from this central concern. We must start somewhere: Rome wasn't built in a day, and even a journal of a thousand volumes must begin with a single page. We plan to consider a host of topics in imagery, and feel we are better off approaching them from the foundations laid in this book.

1.6 On Imagery and Perception

I have often been asked whether I have performed the analogous experiments using an imagery condition and a condition in which the stimulus is actually perceptually present. My answer is usually in the negative, which is sometimes taken as a failing of my work. This complaint is usually founded on the idea that imagery is to be understood by analogy to perception, which has not been my approach. Instead, I have tried to study how images serve as data-structures in memory that may be processed in various ways. Thus, I have been led to explore the nature of these data-structures in their own right. Although showing that imagery and perception are alike in some regard is often interesting in and of itself (for example, see Finke and Schmidt, 1977, 1978; Shepard and Judd, 1976), and serves to implicate the same system in both kinds of processing, it may not help specify the actual mechanisms involved. For example, similar data could have been produced because both the percept and the image were represented and processed propositionally. I have tried to investigate the properties of the imagery system per se; how much of this system is also used in processing like-modality representations during perception is a separate, albeit related, question. Certainly, many of my tasks (such as those in chapter 3) resemble perceptual tasks, since I was examining spatial properties of images (which are shared by percepts), but the answers to the questions at hand in no way depended on the answers to the corresponding questions about perceptual processing. Whether or not it takes more time to scan across longer distances on a physically present object, for example, is irrelevant to our use of scanning as a kind of "tape measure" to demonstrate that images depict spatial extent. However, in the context of our theory there are many interesting reasons to compare imagery and perceptual processing. For example, I have claimed that the same structure, the visual buffer, is used in imagery and in perception. And now that we have a characterization of the visual buffer used in imagery we know *which* perceptual comparisons will bear on the theoretical claim (for a beginning see Finke and Kosslyn, 1980; Pinker, in press). Further, it would be of interest to investigate the role of the deep representations of images in pattern recognition.

In a slightly different vein, it has been pointed out to me that if perception and imagery really do share the same medium, then the notion of a "visual buffer" is highly implausible. This criticism is based on the prevailing views of visual perception, namely that we analyze stimuli either via a hierarchy of features or by performing something like Fourier transforms on the stimuli (see Kaufman, 1974). I have two responses to this:

First, the visual buffer is a structure that has certain functional properties, as outlined in this book. Whether those properties are derived by aggregating over collections of feature and location detectors or by some complex processing of a Fourier transform is not to the point: At the cognitive level, the functional capacity to represent information in a "visual buffer" seems to exist. It will be important to discover exactly how the properties of this functional capacity are related to the underlying physiology if the theory is ever to have explanatory adequacy, but a failure to specify this reduction in no way negates the process adequacy achieved by positing a functional structure with the properties of the visual buffer. Second, the prevailing views of perception in psychology have not proven very useful as guides to how to program a computer to recognize objects. Rather, the best work in computer vision, to my mind, is that of Marr and Nishihara (1978). They posit a stage in information processing they call a "2-1/2-D Sketch." This representation is functionally similar to the surface representations discussed here (except that it is far too primitive and unorganized; a parsed 2-1/2-D Sketch would more closely approximate our surface representation if we also included information about the relative distance of points on an object from the viewer), and it is not implausible —given our data—that something like it can be generated from long-term memory.

1.7 On Pictorial Properties

Various people have taken issue on various grounds with the claim that images are quasi-pictorial. One claim is that we have used a picture to model a picture, which makes no sense. In fact, we have taken pains to point out that a mental image is *not* a picture, but is a depictive representation, as described earlier. But even this has been criticized, on the grounds that the simple fact that the experience of imagery resembles the experience of seeing a picture does not show that images are pictorial entities, of one sort or another. This is correct, and is why we empirically studied the "privileged properties" of imagery. The fact that images do evince quasi-pictorial properties is a genuine finding, which was not guaranteed by raw introspections. Further, although numerous sorts of representations *could* account for the data, a quasi-pictorial image representation seems the most straightforward. I have not, then, posited the properties of the surface image merely to mimic the properties of a picture, but because they provide perspicuous accounts of data and have led to fruitful new predictions.

Other people have asserted that their images are sketchy and quite abstract, which purportedly violates the claims we have made about the surface representation. This introspection, if valid, is not really damaging: Our model and theory do not make firm commitments regarding the contents of the IMG files. It is possible that some skeletal images, for example, are in fact very schematic. The contents of the deep IMG files are determined by the parsing and encoding processes, which have not been specified in the present theory. In fact, it is open at present whether all types of images are the same: It is possible that one's images of particular exemplars seen only a few times are more sharply delineated than images of very familiar or "prototypical" exemplars (although we have not specified how such prototypical images would be encoded). In addition, it could be that there is a "spatial" representation that is quite distinct from the kind of image examined here, perhaps being represented propositionally or containing motoric components.

In a different vein, our model has been faulted for being too tied into a propositional system. Some purists would seem to prefer that imagery be entirely distinct from discursive representation. Such people often want to identify imagery with one hemisphere of the brain, and find it disquieting that there is no reason to expect this if the present model is correct (recall that both PRP and IMG deep representation are used in image generation). More generally, the model has been criticized for not making enough use of pictorial representation per se. It has been claimed that much image generation, for example, depends on an interplay between what is already in an image and what is subsequently placed there. That is, the image itself serves as a "visual prompt" that leads one to add particular new parts to it. This sort of introspection, if valid, falls in Class 3 of our taxonomy (theory supplementation), requiring not alteration of the present theory but elaboration of it. If such processes do occur (and I strongly suspect they do), it will prove somewhat challenging to model them. For one thing, this scheme requires a "bottom up" pattern recognition procedure that recognizes parts without specifically looking for them (in contrast to our FIND procedures). And it is not obvious how such processes operate.

I make no pretenses that this book is an exhaustive study of imagery, let alone of internal representation in general. In part, I have been trying to develop a way of raising questions of a form that will result in cumulative progress in theorizing. The fact that our model raises numerous additional possibilities not only is not detrimental, but is a point in its favor.

1.8 On Subject Populations

One of the most common questions I am asked when I speak publicly about this work is, "Have you done these kinds of experiments with X," where X is "mental retardates," "people with brain damage," and so on. The answer is no, and the justification parallels my remarks in chapter 9 about the study of individual differences. That is, the prior question is the nomothetic one. I first wish to develop a species-general framework

within which different individuals will vary. And it has seemed most profitable to begin to formulate such a general theory by studying more or less
"normal" populations. (If one were interested in music perception, one
would not start by studying the tone-deaf.) Once we have a reasonable
framework of a normative theory, we can then ask the interesting questions about abnormal subject populations. In particular, the theory will
guide us in (1) locating the sources of individual variations and (2) forming
expectations about the consequences of a given malady. I believe our theory is now well enough formulated that interesting experiments can be
done on aberrant subject populations not only to answer further questions
about the theory (for example, about the physiological locus of different
representations), but to address questions about the nature of a malady
itself (that is, to more precisely delimit the deficits in functional capacities
that underlie a disability). Given that something is known about given
aberrations, the theory will help us decide in which populations it is
worthwhile to conduct special studies of imagery.

1.9 On Disprovability

I recently described our model in detail and was told, "Your model has
so many parameters it can account for anything." There are three points
to be made here: First, insofar as this claim is tantamount to saying that
the theory makes no predictions, it is simply not true (see chapters 5
through 10). Second, the mind is undoubtedly complicated and there is no
reason to expect a model of it to be simple. To be sure, a theory of cognition should clearly specify the lawful relations underlying a model, and
these principles will, it is hoped, be relatively few and easily apprehended
—but even this is not a certainty. Nobody said cognitive psychology
would be easy. Third, the present theory is in fact disprovable, in the way
that any theory worthy of its name is. At this stage of development, no
single experiment will pull the rug out from under the theory taken as a
whole, nor should this be possible given the amount of work that went
into developing the theory. Particular aspects of the theory and model are
disprovable, however; for example, I will not be surprised if it turns out
that images are not refreshed from the surface. If enough cases are encountered that require backtracking and revision of the general assumptions of the theory, or if enough "special cases" are introduced, then the
theory should be regarded with increasing suspicion.

1.10 On Precision

In a complaint related to the foregoing one, I have sometimes been
faulted because the model often offers more than one explanation of a
given result. This complaint reveals a fundamental misunderstanding of

the purpose of our model-building exercise. We are using the model as a means of raising questions of a certain form, namely questions whose answers will foster increased specification of a cognitive theory. That is, we are using the model to drive the empirical program of research by looking for cases where additional experiments need to be conducted to distinguish between alternative accounts (as is found with a Class 2 result) or to motivate extension of the theory (as is found with Class 3 results). We do not simply rest on the fact that the model can explain data in more than one way, but use this observation to motivate empirical investigations, the results of which place further constraints on the theory proper. The five-class taxonomy developed in chapter 6 is a tool used to this end. Numerous examples of this use of the model appear in the second half of this book; in many other instances we have posed the question but have not yet conducted the research. As long as we attempt to distinguish between alternative accounts, and ask our questions within a framework motivated by prior research and conceptual clarification, we have some assurance that progress will be forthcoming.

1.11 On Quantification

Occasionally someone will complain that the model does not predict the numbers, does not make quantitative predictions. I have two responses to this complaint: First, qualitative effects seem to have necessary precedence over quantitative ones; until we can understand the pattern of some data, there seems little sense in trying to account for the precise values of each presumed parameter. Second, it simply is not clear to me what we stand to gain by formulating the model in more quantitative detail at present. Certainly, it makes sense to check for internal consistency by obtaining separate estimates of the different parameters, and I have occasionally done this in the latter part of the book. But we are only beginning to approach the point where alternative theories will be distinguished by the size of predicted effects. Ultimately, we will want the theory to be explicit enough to generate unambiguous quantitative predictions, but at the present juncture we are simply not ready to ask the kinds of questions that require quantitative predictions in order to be answered.

1.12 On Computer Simulation

I have repeatedly been asked exactly what the value of the computer simulation per se has been in the project. In chapter 5 I offered, in the abstract, a number of reasons why computer simulation is a useful technique for constructing models in cognitive psychology. One of the oft-cited uses of actually programming the computer, as opposed to merely conceiving the flowcharts or the like, is that the computer helps one discover the actual consequences of some claim and helps one discover and study complex interactions among separate components. Let me now offer a few concrete illustrations of this claim: (1) We initially made no provisions for scanning to the inactivated region of the surface matrix. Only when the program was asked to find the front tire in the image illustrated in figure 5.8, and received an error message, were we reminded of the problems due to overflow. (Steve Shwartz actually spent some time trying to find the bug when he first received an error message in this situation.) (2) The finding that rate of expansion accelerated with increasing size in our first simulation of the transformation procedures was unanticipated (and wrong, as it turned out) but followed from our implementation of the ZOOM transformation. (3) In an earlier version of the program there was no attempt to keep track of the identity of overprinted points; expansion did not clarify parts of the image in this model. Somehow, this fact escaped our attention until after the model was implemented, at which point we realized quickly that the model was in need of revision. (4) Upon altering the implementation to fill in more information as an image was magnified, we were surprised to discover that resolution was no longer indexed by simple dot density because more dots were now filled in as the image expanded. Thus, an earlier technique of using decreased dot density as a direct index of increased resolution failed to work; the program faltered in assessing whether to zoom in or pan out. We solved this problem by indicating where cells of the activated partition buffer were overprinted (by using capital letters). Thus, as more dots, including those overprinted, appear in a given area, resolution tends to decrease (because contours are obscured). Overprinting is taken to correspond to increased density and brightness, a claim which seems potentially testable. (5) In an earlier version REGENERATE was called every time FIND operated. This resulted in nonlinear increases in the number of operations performed for each additional part added to the image, which was not anticipated or realized until tracings were in hand. The usefulness of the program as a kind of "notepad" should be apparent from the complexity of some of the interrelationships among the different components evident in chapters 6 through 10.

1.13 On Sophistication

Occasionally a genuine, dyed-in-the-wool computer scientist will poke fun at our model, pointing out how primitive it is and that there are better ideas in the artificial intelligence literature. I admit that our simulation is simple, as such things go, but this is hardly a drawback—rather, it is a distinct virtue. We have tried to motivate our model with data, and have not indulged our intuitions or imaginations in a programming exercise. Until there is good evidence that our structures or processes are not good models of human structures and processes, we will not abandon them for another scheme with no supporting data. If another scheme is developed that is as simple as ours and accounts for more data than ours can, we of course will revise as necessary. In particular, it seems likely that the IMG literal file representation is inadequate. Although I have yet to do the experiments, I am convinced that people often image objects reversed, as in a mirror, from the way they actually saw them—especially if the actual orientation of the object violates some strong convention. I am thinking in particular of a painting by Rembrandt, The Man with the Golden Helmet. I repeatedly find myself imaging this man facing to the right, when in fact he faces to the left. This sort of effect would never be expected from our r, Θ representation: Here active computation is required to produce a mirror image; orientation is implicit in the underlying representation, and is not apt to be confused. In addition, if the underlying IMG representations are also used in pattern recognition, as seems reasonable, then the current scheme is even less appealing. We would like to extend the present theory to deal with how the long-term memory files are encoded, which involves studying certain aspects of pattern recognition within the context of the model. Thus, it is a definite drawback that the number of r, Θ pairs encoded varies with the distance of an object from the subject and the like. The most viable alternative representation, the generalized cone or cylinder (see Marr, 1978) is inappropriate in that it does not encode information about the appearance of the outside of an object, but encodes only its general shape. This is clearly inadequate if surface images are to be generated. Other aspects of the simulation are also clearly in need of improvement, notably the surface representation. For example, it seems clear that some nontrivial modifications (of a supplemental nature, however) will be necessary to account for the representation and transformation of information in three dimensions (see Pinker, in press, for a discussion).

1.14 On Definitions

At one point in writing this book I included a section entitled, "A Preliminary Definition of a Mental Image." This was in response to the criticism that I never define what I am talking about. I removed this definition for two reasons: First, it is not necessary to begin with a crisp definition of an entity in order to study it; physics seems to have done reasonably well in studying "electrons," although there is not to this day a precise definition of this term. It is hard to define something one knows little about; if one knew enough about imagery to define it, it is doubtful that a research program such as this one would be necessary in the first place. Second, "image" may resemble a proper name in that it is not really definable, but simply is anchored to some entity in the world. Kripke (1972) and Putnam

(1978) have recently argued that all "natural kind" terms resemble proper names in not having a definition, in not having a meaning that corresponds to a set of defining features or the like. This argument is based on the observation that we would be loath to say that the meaning of a word, like "gold" or "cat," had changed if we discovered that what we took to be a defining property of the object (atomic number, flesh and bones, respectively) was in fact incorrect (if we discovered, say, that gold really has atomic number 73, or that cats are in fact Martian robots). One can apply this argument to the term "image" and claim that it simply indexes a certain class of mental events; it certainly seems true that our study of imagery will not change the meaning of the term itself, and the word itself will probably never be satisfactorily defined (along with most other nouns).

1.15 On Metaphysical Concerns

Probably the most peculiar question I have ever been asked about my project went something like this: "You have shown that one can account for all of your data with a computer simulation. Presumably, computers have no minds and hence have no mental images. Given that you can produce your data without use of mental images in the computer, what makes you think that your data reflect anything about human mental images?" This struck me at the time as either a very deep question or a very misguided one. If a simulation is written to predict weather patterns, we do not say that this shows there is no wind in the world because the computer has no wind in it. A model is not a *copy*, but embodies the essential elements (as defined by a theory) of the modeled entity. The elements of the model may be very different from the corresponding ones of the modeled entity, as long as there is a proper mapping function between the two. As Putnam (1960) has argued, a computer program bears the same relationship to the computer hardware as mental states bear to the brain. Thus, the model specifies the functional states on a computer that are hypothesized to be analogous to ones that occur in the brain. The fact that we can establish this kind of analogous relationship does not establish (or require) an equivalence; the brain is not a digital computer.

The metaphysical worries that apparently haunted my inquisitor strike deep into what we mean by "mental phenomena." Most people on the street probably identify the "mind" with a set of experiences; mental states are characterized by certain qualia, certain sensations. In the present project we have not addressed the mind in this phenomenological framework, but have adopted a "functionalist" approach (see Fodor, 1968; Block, 1980). It seems inappropriate to speak of "inspecting," "transforming," or otherwise operating on an *experience*. This seems a classic case of a Rylian "category error." But experience must have some role in imagery. We obviously cannot reach to the heart of this question without a more general theory of the role of experience in cognition, but —alas—even the *form* that such a theory would take eludes me. Nevertheless, it is of interest to note that the presumed properties of the underlying functional representation of a surface image are remarkably like those evident in our experience of images (spatial extent, resolution, and so on). The problem of explaining qualia is in part a problem of accounting for why certain underlying functional states give rise to, or are accompanied by, certain qualia (that is, why functional states and perceived sensations are paired as they are). The interesting correspondences we find here seem unlikely to be merely coincidental and probably are not trivial.

1.16 On the Imagery/Proposition Debate

The fact that we are able to simulate our results on a digital computer, I have been told, shows that we are in fact making use of "propositional representations." My usual response to this remark is to point out that there are different *levels* of representation involved. One would not say that a picture on a TV screen is propositional merely because it can be described by a set of coordinates with associated gray levels. This would be to confuse the "parent" of the functional representation with the representation itself (see chapter 2, section 2.2.4); the actual picture makes use of "emergent" properties, like contour, that arise when the points are simultaneously present in a particular spatial configuration. Similarly, although there is no actual matrix in the computer and points are stored "propositionally," the *functional* representation that is used by FIND is not propositional; it depicts rather than describes. When you get right down to it, all the representations used in human cognition ultimately involve brain cells. The important point is the way a representation functions in the context of a total processing system, and that is what I have tried to specify here.

1.17 On Pretheoretical and Metatheoretical Commitments

It has been pointed out to me that the present approach rests on a number of background assumptions which are themselves controversial. In particular, I have bought the standard "information processing" approach, positing a system of representations and processing capacities. The Shaw and Bransford (1977) "neo-Gibsonian" school seems to reject these assumptions in favor of a "resonance" metaphor. That is, the mind is likened to a tuning fork, which automatically responds appropriately given a particular stimulus configuration—without the necessity of a series for intervening processing stages. Not only do I reject this approach because it does not lead one to formulate what I take to be process or explanatorily adequate psychological explanations, but I propose that the

present work is the strongest source of argument against this "nonrepre-
sentation" view. I do not believe one can propose a satisfactory theory of
imagery without positing some kind of internal representations and processes that act on them. After all, what could be more of a "re-presenta-
tion" than a mental image? And to the extent that our results indicate that
mental images are bona fide psychological entities, they also vindicate the
entire representational approach in the broader sweep of things.

1.18 On the Uniqueness of a Theory

Anderson (1976, 1978) has argued that we can in principle never formulate theories that are distinguishable from other alternatives. This research
project was singled out in Anderson's 1978 paper as an example of this,
pitting our kind of model against a propositional one. I do not find Anderson's formal proof very interesting, however, as he merely showed that
given a theory, one can always formulate a second, *more complicated* theory that will make the same predictions. His one interesting example of
equivalence, using models of mental rotation, was quickly dispatched by
Shwartz's finding that subjectively smaller images are rotated more
quickly than larger ones—as expected if a surface image is manipulated
and not expected if Anderson's model were correct. In essence, my reactions at the present time are twofold: First, this worry strikes me as tre-
mendously premature. I would like a demonstration that an alternate theory can be formulated to mimic the present one, and I would like to see
whether it differs from ours in any interesting respect vis-à-vis claims
about representations and processes. Second, if such a theory is formulated, one that is at least as general and simple as the present one, my bet
is that it will be possible to conduct a number of experiments to distinguish empirically between the two theories. This is a statement of faith,
but not a wild-eyed one: after all, other sciences have progressed, and
they too have faced the problem that alternative theories can always be
formulated. (The interested reader is referred to the critiques offered by
Hayes-Roth, 1979; Keenan and Moore, 1979; and Pylyshyn, 1979b; but see
also Anderson, 1979.)

1.19 On Practical Applications

There has been a recent move in cognitive psychology toward concern
with the real-world applications of our work. I think this is a worthy
concern, but it should not be a central one of a contemporary cognitive
scientist (as opposed to a technician). On my view if we simply concen-
trate on discovering the truth about how the mind works, applications will
emerge in the natural course of events. This seems to be the basic pattern
in other sciences, where the most dramatic applications (such as with

lasers) were never foreseen by the researchers laying the foundations. I have given some thought to the possible domains of application of our present theory, however. The following areas have come to mind.

Relevance to education. If we come to understand how people represent and use information, we may be able to devise optimal ways of presenting information, ensuring that it will be optimally encoded into memory. Further, it may turn out that the way in which one should be taught certain information depends on the uses to which one will later put it; a pictorial format, with instructions to encode images, might be optimal if one is later to try to solve spatial problems, for example, but less good for other sorts of calculations. The importance of the imagery work is especially clear if the representational-development hypothesis is true; if it is, then not only should early education be geared toward the fact that most information is stored imaginally, but when a propositional format is more effective the translation of information to this format might be promoted to maximize mastery of new material.

In addition, it has long been hypothesized that imagery has a special role in creative thinking and problem solving. If we could study this claim in detail, and it had some substance, the theory should have ramifications for how creative thinking could be facilitated. Consider the following approach to studying this topic, which is a straightforward extension of the present research program: Let us begin by defining a dimension of ways of using imagery in thinking, one pole of which can be called "simulation mode" and the other "notation mode." In simulation mode, one is imaging the things one is interested in and performing transformations to discover the effects of performing the analogous transformations on the actual objects (as would occur, for example, if one were imaging how furniture would look if rearranged in given ways). In notation mode, the image is being used to represent things that themselves are not depicted. For example, in solving three-term series problems subjects sometimes represent the relative intelligence of three people by imaging a line with three dots along it, the line representing the dimension of intelligence and the dots standing for the different people (see Huttenlocher, 1968; Huttenlocher, Higgins, and Clark, 1972). In this case not only must the image be maintained, but the interpretation of the image must also be stored. Between the poles of this dimension are a host of intermediate cases in which schematic elements of various kinds are imaged. Now, the present theory leads me to consider four components in any use of imagery in visual thinking: image generation, maintenance, transformation, and inspection. That is, one must select what image to form, must hold this image, perhaps must update it as new information comes in or transform it in other ways, and must "read off" the results. We now know a fair amount about each of these components, and hopefully can devise ways of organizing images so they are most effectively used. This probably will be easier in simulation mode (such as is used in molecular biology). The problem of *what* image to use in notation mode is not trivial. In particular, a number of the properties of the imagery system are in tension, trading off against each other; for example, images that are easy to maintain (perhaps being composed of stimuli containing "integral" dimensions) may be difficult to transform or update. Thus, some ways of using imagery in notation mode will probably be better for given tasks than others, and it clearly would be beneficial to discover the principles that will guide one in choosing the best representation for a given problem. The present theory gives us a way of structuring questions about visual thinking, and hopefully will lead us not only to study it, but to devise ways of using it more effectively.

Relevance to AI. There exists a proof that the major problems in AI are solvable: the human mind. People can be viewed as the "product of a million-year research project," as Minsky has remarked, and the way we accomplish certain tasks is one workable way a computer might do the same. If people really do use more than a single format in representing and utilizing information in memory, there are probably good reasons for this—and there is no reason why these same factors should not also affect machine intelligence. Unlike improving education, however, one can argue that furthering AI is not necessarily a good thing (see Weizenbaum, 1976). Like most other major advances (such as the industrial revolution), AI is a two-edged sword, but the potential benefits of its success are awesome.

Relevance to therapy. The application of the present work to the therapeutic setting is twofold. First, for relatively mild maladies, "neuroses," the most effective therapy may be equivalent to a form of education. In this case, one would diagnose the patient's unhappy "construct system" (to use Kelley's 1955 term) and effect a change in this way of viewing the self and the world. An understanding of how information is represented and organized will help us learn how to reorganize and reintegrate information in ways more comfortable to the afflicted person. Further, it may turn out that much of the data-base underlying a neurosis is not accessible to conscious processes, but would be malleable if we had a theory of how performing different tasks engaged and affected these underlying structures. The present theory includes a partial specification of how "unconscious knowledge" (in the deep representation) is stored and processed, and there is no reason this part of the theory cannot be expanded to deal with situations that are more interesting from a clinical point of view. Second, for more severe disorders, the root may often be biochemical. In this case, a program of re-education may be inappropriate and ineffective, but we can provide a service in devising more precise diagnostic tests. The theory presented in this book specifies a number of the functional capacities of an imagery representation system, and some of them may characteristically be selectively affected by certain underlying biological disorders.

Relevance to understanding the brain. Our theory is cast on the level of functional capacities of the brain. But this characterization now places some constraints on theories of brain structure and operation. Just as one cannot fully understand the nature and uses of bricks until one has seen walls and the like, our theory casts light on what neural structures must be for—and hence poses constraints that must be met by any theory of brain structure aspiring to something like explanatory adequacy. In fact, one could take patient populations that have specific localized brain damage and see which components of image processing—as specified by our model—seem to be affected. This project might help us understand what particular parts of the brain do, or at least what kinds of activities they affect.

Relevance to human engineering. Given the current theory, one can now ask questions about the "grain" of the visual buffer and the like. The answers to these questions will affect how one will design a map, say, so that the key elements are easily "visible" in an image. Further, the full realization of our theory will specify exactly what kinds of tasks will be likely to involve imagery, and it will then be possible to design equipment for performing these in such a way as to maximally utilize (as defined by the theory) the imagery representation and processing system. For example, in some cases auditory feedback may be optimal, if visual imagery is in fact selectively disrupted by visual input.

Relevance to furthering self-knowledge. I believe that the kind of work cognitive psychologists are engaged in will help us better to "know ourselves." If nothing else, we may be able to characterize individual differences more precisely, and one may become better aware of one's strengths and weaknesses when armed with this kind of information about oneself. I am reminded of an ancient Chinese parable (originally told to me by Eleanor Rosch, who had forgotten the source and told it much better than I can): Once upon a time the adult animals in the forest got together and lamented the state of the younger generation. They were hanging around clearings, loitering on the trail corners, and just generally Not Developing Their Potentials. So the adults decided to start a school. When the question of a curriculum arose, the bears promptly insisted that digging be included; it is an absolute necessity to dig, they pointed out—can't hibernate without it. And the birds chirped in that flying was definitely not to be overlooked—nor was climbing, said the squirrels, gotta learn to climb . . . and so on. They gathered the young animals together and began their education. Soon there were young birds with broken wingtips from trying to dig, baby bears with broken backs from trying to fly, and so on. The moral of this story should *not* be that some people are best fitted for some kinds of jobs or tasks, that some of us are birds and others bears, that some ought to fly and others to dig. Rather, once one knows what sort of animal one is, one then knows how to approach a particular task: If you're a bird and you want to dig you use your beak and claws; if you're a bear and you want to fly—you get in an airplane. I hope that the systematic study of individual differences within the framework of a theory like the one I have outlined in this book will make it possible to learn who is a bird and who is a bear, and how one should take advantage of one's proclivities in learning, making it easier, more efficient, and more enjoyable to acquire new skills, new information or new ways of thinking about things.

2.0 PROGRESS AND PROJECTIONS

I argued earlier that simply accounting for behavioral data is not good enough. We want general models that provide an account of the internal operations that take place when one performs tasks in a given domain. And this account should be mechanistic; knowing a given initial state should allow one to specify the factors that will determine the next state. In addition, even if we attain a correct description of internal processing, we should not stop, but should go on to ask why it is *that* description rather than some other one. Only at this point will we formulate truly deep "explanatory" theories. Following Chomsky (1967), I suggested three criteria of adequacy, which I dubbed behavioral, process, and explanatory, as an aid to assessing whether we were on the right track in our model-building and theory-constructing enterprise. Have we been successful in progressing toward a fully adequate theory? Let me begin by acknowledging that the theory and model are incomplete, and hence cannot be fully adequate by any of the three measures. But this is not to say that we do not have a respectable fragment of a theory in hand, one that can sensibly be evaluated in terms of the three kinds of adequacy. We have come far enough that the present model and theory should be showing signs of being developed into fully adequate versions; if they do not, we have reason to take pause.

It seems to me that the general model and theory get relatively high marks on grounds of behavioral adequacy. The general model allows us to formulate specific models for a wide range of tasks, and these models account for the major qualitative trends in the data. It is true that we have often found the general model to be in need of further development (faced with a Class 2, multiple interpretation, or a Class 3, theory supplementation, finding), but this is as it should be. Each time we did develop the model to account for some data, we also further specified the theory itself. And this in turn further constrained how we could account for additional data. The consequences of earlier commitments became increasingly apparent in the work described in the second half of this book. Importantly, in no case did we encounter a Class 5 (disconfirmation) finding, requiring backtracking and revision of the core theory. In addition, the predictions derived from the model fared well when tested, further assuring us that the model adequately generalizes beyond the data-base upon which it was originally built.

The general model and the theory also do reasonably well on the second criterion, process adequacy. Both have process adequacy insofar as the functional capacities posited by the theory and instantiated in the general model are correct descriptions of those which characterize the human mind. There is some reason to believe we are doing a reasonable job on this score, given our success in generating specific models that account for patterns of data by reference to underlying processing components. In addition, we have found some evidence that the same functional capacities are in fact recruited in different tasks, as the general model specifies. The FIND procedure, for example, did seem to be invoked when images were generated and inspected, and the same factors seemed to affect it in both cases (notably, smaller images were more difficult to inspect when one was trying to integrate additional units and when one was searching for a named part or property). Further, components of the model developed for entirely different reasons were easily and sensibly invoked in accounting for image transformations and question-answering processes. The way the model hangs together across the different kinds of tasks is a source of real encouragement.

In addition, because we strove toward process adequacy from the outset we defined certain processes in particular ways, which are now testable. For example, PUT originally did far less than it does in the current model, but was developed as it now is because it needed those capabilities in order to perform its function in all the different circumstances in which it was called. On the face of things, some of these capabilities may seem better ascribed to a higher-order executive, like IMAGE. But if PUT is correctly characterized, then selectively disrupting it should have specifiable effects that one would not expect otherwise.

Finally, the general model does reasonably well by the criterion of explanatory adequacy, given that the functional capacities instantiated in it were motivated by a theory. The theory gave us prior reasons for positing that particular representations (with specific properties) would be processed in particular ways when one performed a given imagery task. Thus, the accounts derived from our general model have explanatory adequacy in that they were formulated within the constraints posed by the theory. But does the theory itself have explanatory adequacy? Sorry to say, I fear not. We do not have deep reasons why the mind should have the set of functional capacities we have posited. It is hoped that some day theories of brain structure, computational efficiency, and environmental impact on the organism will provide us with the basis of such a rationale (see chapter 5, section 1.4). I wish to emphasize again, however, that cognitive theories are *not* simply parasitic on brain theories. The study of schools of architecture is distinct from the study of bricks, boards, mortar, and nails, although the two domains of study are obviously interrelated.

In summary, although the general model and theory are by no means complete, they seem on the right track. It seems unreasonable to suppose, however, that any model or theory of imagery developed at this point in time will ultimately prove correct. In fact, the three criteria discussed above might best be regarded as "inadequacy" criteria, in that their main function is to tell us when we have gone awry. Given the likelihood that any theory posed at this point will be far too simplistic and perhaps misguided at root, it seems important to introduce yet another way of evaluating the worth of a theory. Namely, we are led to ask, what residue will be left after the theory is gone? Two things, I think: First, a good theory and general model should have led one to discover interesting facts about the mind, facts about systematic phenomena that must be accounted for by any theory in the domain. Second, in the best possible case these facts will implicate given functional capacities and lawful relations among them with such force that even if the theory is wrong at least some of its components will survive in its descendants. On my view, our theory has accomplished both ends reasonably well, and will place important constraints on any future theory of visual mental imagery.

2.1 The Broader Sweep of Things

I have been struck time and time again by how our model-building enterprise has forced us to expand the range of our inquiry in selective ways. I have noted repeatedly in this book that a "front end," a perceptual processor, is necessary to fill in many of the details in our model. And I have found it increasingly desirable to know more about perception per se (including the physiological substrata). What is interesting here is that I started off thinking about the present project as one about the nature of *memory*, and worried that I would be forced to explain ever increasing amounts of data about memory processing in general in order to address imagery in particular. This did not happen. Reflecting on this I have begun to entertain a somewhat radical idea. Thinking of "memory" as an area of cognitive psychology may be like thinking of "the first two feet back from the front bumper" as a part of a car. If we tried to study cars in this way, we would get nowhere. On the other hand, if we studied the frame of the car, its steering mechanism, its engine, and so on, we would soon know everything we ever wanted to know about the car, including what goes on at different distances from the bumper, without ever expressly worrying about the first two feet back. Similarly, it seems to me that cognitive psychology parses neatly into three main areas: language, perception, and reasoning. If we study each of these systems, and how they interact, we may well end up knowing everything we want to know about memory without ever studying it per se. Imagery is interesting because it recruits all three of these "primary faculties," and thus studying imagery illuminates the nature of each of them. Note that since imagery utilizes these faculties in special ways, it makes sense to study imagery as a distinct domain. But if a theory is ever to have explanatory adequacy, we must understand the relevant aspects of the primary faculties it recruits. Similarly, "memory" may draw on the three primary faculties, and the properties of memory may depend on which faculty or faculties are recruited. There is no reason to expect that there will be one set of "laws of memory" (or laws of learning, the flip side of the coin). The laws of memory may vary depending on the properties of the special-purpose memories developed for perception, language, and reasoning and how these properties interact.

This analysis is appealing to me when I reflect about the nature of the "visual buffer" we have posited. It seems unreasonable to suppose that the visual buffer is a partition of a separate memory component, and thus is distinct from the structures used to support the representations underlying the experience of seeing itself. In fact, evidence to the contrary is accumulating (see, for example, Finke and Kosslyn, 1980; Finke and Schmidt, 1977, 1978; Podgorny and Shepard, 1978). If this is true in vision, why should it not be true in other sensory modalities as well? Auditory images may recruit part of the neural structures used in hearing, tactile images may occur in central structures used to represent sensation from the skin, and so on. Given this, why should there be a distinct, special short-term memory structure at all? All short-term memory representations may occur in structures that do double duty in sensory processing. If this is true, then most of the verbal learning work on short-term memory may actually be studies of auditory and motor imagery representation. The tradition in mainline cognitive psychology may have led us astray by encouraging a too-literal reading of the computer metaphor. There is no reason to presuppose that the mind has anything like a "central core" or that it represents information in only one "language of thought."

References

Abelson, R. P. 1963. Computer simulation of "hot" cognition. In *Computer Simulation of Personality: Frontier of Psychological Research*, ed. S. S. Tomkins and S. Messick. New York: Wiley.

Adams, J. A. 1967. *Human Memory*. New York: McGraw-Hill.

Anderson, J. R. 1972. FRAN: A simulation model of free recall. In *The Psychology of Learning and Motivation*, Vol. 5, ed. G. H. Bower. New York: Academic Press.

Anderson, J. R. 1976. *Language, Memory and Thought*. Hillsdale, New Jersey: Erlbaum Associates.

Anderson, J. R. 1978. Arguments concerning representations for mental imagery. *Psychological Review* 85:249–277.

Anderson, J. R. 1979. Further arguments concerning representations for mental imagery: a response to Hayes-Roth and Pylyshyn. *Psychological Review* 86: 395–406.

Anderson, J. R., and Bower, G. H. 1973. *Human Associative Memory*. New York: V. H. Winston and Sons.

Anderson, J. R., and Reder, L. M. 1974. Negative judgments in and about semantic memory. *Journal of Verbal Learning and Verbal Behavior* 13:664–681.

Angell, J. R. 1910. Methods for determination of mental imagery. *Psychological Monographs* 13:61–107.

Anoosian, L., and Carlson, J. S. 1973. A study of mental imagery and conservation within the Piagetian framework. *Human Development* 16:382–394.

Antrobus, J. S., and Singer, J. L. 1964. Visual signal detection as a function of sequential variability of simultaneous speech. *Journal of Experimental Psychology* 68:603–610.

Ashton, R., and White, K. 1975. The effects of instructions on subjects' imagery questionnaire scores. *Social Behavior and Personality* 3:41–43.

Atkinson, R. C., and Juola, J. F. 1973. Factors influencing speed and accuracy in word recognition. In *Attention and Performance*, Vol. IV, ed. S. Kornblum. New York: Academic Press.

Attneave, F., and Olson, R. K. 1967. Discriminability of stimuli varying in physical and retinal orientation. *Journal of Experimental Psychology* 74:149–157.

Atwood, G. E. 1971. An experimental study of visual information and memory. *Cognitive Psychology* 2:290–299.

Audley, R. J., and Wallis, C. P. 1964. Response instructions and the speed of relative judgments. I. Some experiments on brightness discrimination. *British Journal of Psychology* 55:59–73.

Aulhorn, R., and Harms, H. 1972. Visual perimetry. In *Handbook of Sensory Physiology: Visual Psychophysics*, ed. D. Jameson and L. M. Hurvich. New York: Springer-Verlag.

Baird, J. C. 1970. *Psychophysical Analysis of Visual Space*. New York: Pergamon Press.

Banks, W. P. 1977. Encoding and processing of symbolic information in comparative judgments. In *The Psychology of Learning and Motivation: Advances in Research and Theory*, Vol. 2, ed. G. H. Bower. New York: Academic Press.

Banks, W. P., Clark, H. H., and Lucy, P. 1975. The locus of the semantic congruity effect in comparative judgments. *Journal of Experimental Psychology: Human Perception and Performance* 1:35–47.

Banks, W. P., Fujii, M., and Kayra-Stuart, F. 1976. Semantic congruity effects in comparative judgments of magnitudes of digits. *Journal of Experimental Psychology: Human Perception and Performance* 2:435–447.

Banks, W. P., and Hill, D. K. 1974. The apparent magnitude of number scaled by random production. *Journal of Experimental Psychology Monograph* 102:353–376.

Banks, W. P., Yu, H., and Lippincott, W. 1978. Semantic coding in comparative judgments of serial order. Unpublished manuscript, Claremont College.

Baylor, G. W. 1971. A Treatise on Mind's Eye. Ph.D. Dissertation, Carnegie-Mellon University.

Baylor, G. W., and Simon, H. A. 1966. A chess mating combinations program. *AFIPS Conference Proceedings, Spring Joint Computer Conference* 28:431–447. Washington, D. C.: Spartan Books.

Beech, J. R., and Allport, D. A. 1978. Visualization of compound scenes. *Perception* 7:129–138.

Betts, G. H. 1909. *The Distribution and Functions of Mental Imagery*. New York: Columbia University Press.

Block, N. 1980. *Readings in Philosophy of Psychology*, Vol 1. Cambridge, Mass.: Harvard University Press.

Boden, M. 1977. *Artificial Intelligence and Natural Man*. New York: Basic Books.

Boring, E. G. 1950. *A History of Experimental Psychology*, 2nd edition. New York: Appleton-Century-Crofts.

Bower, G. H. 1970. Imagery as a relational organizer in associative learning. *Journal of Verbal Learning and Verbal Behavior* 9:529–533.

Bower, G. H. 1972. Mental imagery and associative learning. In *Cognition in Learning and Memory*, ed. L. Gregg. New York: John Wiley and Sons.

Bower, G. H. 1978. Representing knowledge development. In *Children's Thinking: What Develops?*, ed. R. Siegler. Hillsdale, New Jersey: Erbaum Associates.

Bower, G. H., and Glass, A. L. 1976. Structural units and the redintegrative power of picture fragments. *Journal of Experimental Psychology: Human Learning and Memory* 2:456–466.

Brooks, L. 1967. The suppression of visualization by reading. *Quarterly Journal of Experimental Psychology* 19:289–299.

Brooks, L. 1968. Spatial and verbal components of the act of recall. *Canadian Journal of Psychology* 22:349–368.

Bruner, J. S., Olver, R. O., and Greenfield, P. M. 1966. *Studies in Cognitive Growth*. New York: Wiley.

Buckley, P. B., and Gillman, C. B. 1974. Comparisons of digits and dot patterns. *Journal of Experimental Psychology* 103:1131–1136.

Bugelski, B. R. 1970. Words and things and images. *American Psychologist* 25:1002–1012.

Bundesen, C., and Larsen, A. 1975. Visual transformation of size. *Journal of Experimental Psychology: Human Perception and Performance* 1:214–220.

Byrne, B. 1974. Item concreteness vs. spatial organization as predictors of visual imagery. *Memory and Cognition* 2:53–59.

Carey, S. 1978. A case study: face recognition. In *Explorations in the Biology of Language,* ed. E. Walker. Montgomery, Vermont: Bradford Books.

Chomsky, N. 1965. *Aspects of the Theory of Syntax*. Cambridge, Massachusetts: MIT Press.

Chomsky, N. 1967. *Current Issues in Linguistics*. The Hague: Mouton.

Church, J. 1961. *Language and the Discovery of Reality*. New York: Random House.

Clark, H. H. 1972. On evidence concerning J. Huttenlocher and E. T. Higgens' theory of reasoning: a second reply. *Psychological Review* 79: 428–432.

Clark, H. H. 1973. The language-as-fixed-effect fallacy: a critique of language statistics in psychological research. *Journal of Verbal Learning and Verbal Behavior* 12: 335–359.

Clark, H. H., Carpenter, P. A., and Just, M. A. 1973. On the meeting of semantics and perception. In *Visual Information Processing,* ed. W. G. Chase. New York: Academic Press.

Clark, H. H., and Chase, W. G. 1972. On the process of comparing sentences against pictures. *Cognitive Psychology* 3:472–517.

Collins, A. M., and Quillian, M. R. 1969. Retrieval time from semantic memory. *Journal of Verbal Learning and Verbal Behavior* 8:240–247.

Collins, A. M., and Quillian, M. R. 1972. Experiments on semantic memory and language comprehension. In *Cognition in Learning and Memory,* ed. L. Gregg. New York: Wiley.

Conrad, C. 1972. Cognitive economy in semantic memory. *Journal of Experimental Psychology* 92:149–154.

Conrad, R. 1971. The chronology of the development of covert speech in children. *Developmental Psychology* 5:398–405.

Cooper, L. A. 1975. Mental rotation of random two-dimensional shapes. *Cognitive Psychology* 7:20–43.

Cooper, L. A. 1976. Demonstration of a mental analog of an external rotation. *Perception and Psychophysics* 19:296–302.

Cooper, L. A., and Podgorny, P. 1976. Mental transformations and visual comparison processes: effects of complexity and similarity. *Journal of Experimental Psychology: Human Perception and Performance* 2:503–514.

Cooper, L. A., and Shepard, R. N. 1973. Chronometric studies of the rotation of mental images. In *Visual Information Processing,* ed. W. G. Chase. New York: Academic Press.

Cooper, L. A., and Shepard, R. N. 1975. Mental transformation in the identification of left and right hands. *Journal of Experimental Psychology: Human Perception and Performance* 1:48–56.

Corsini, D. A. 1969a. The effect of nonverbal cues on the retention of kindergarten children. *Child Development* 40:599–607.

Corsini, D. A. 1969b. Development changes in the effect of nonverbal cues on retention. *Developmental Psychology* 11:425–435.

Corsini, D. A. 1970. The effect of type of redundancy on retention in preschool children. *Psychonomic Science* 19:117–118.

Craik, F. I. M. 1973. A "levels of analysis" view of memory. In *Communication and Affect: Language and Thought*, ed. P. Pliner, L. Krames, and T. M. Alloway. New York: Academic Press.

Craik, F. I. M., and Lockhart, R. S. 1972. Levels of processing: a framework for memory research. *Journal of Verbal Learning and Verbal Behavior* 11:671–684.

Crovitz, H. F., Rosof, D., and Shiffman, H. 1971. Timing oscillation in human visual imagery. *Psychonomic Science* 24:87–88.

Davis, F. C. 1932. The functional significance of imagery differences. *Journal of Experimental Pschology* 15:630–661.

Dean, A. L. 1976. The structure of imagery. *Child Development* 47:949–958.

Denis, M. 1979. *Les Images Mentales*. Paris: Presses Universitaires de France.

Dennett, D. C. 1969. *Content and Consciousness*. New York: Humanities Press.

Dennett, D. C. 1978. *Brainstorms*. Montgomery, Vermont: Bradford Books.

Descartes, R. 1911. *The Philosophical Works of Descartes*, Vol. 1, tr. E. S. Haldane and G. R. T. Ross. Cambridge, Eng.: Cambridge University Press.

Ducharme, R., and Fraisse, P. 1965. Etude génétique de la mémorisation de mots et d'images. *Canadian Journal of Psychology* 19:253–261.

Fairbank, B. A., and Capehart, J. 1969. Decision speed for the choosing of the larger or the smaller of two digits. *Psychonomic Science* 14:148.

Farley, A. M. 1974. VIPS: A visual imagery and perception system; the result of protocol analysis. Ph.D. Dissertation, Carnegie-Mellon University.

Fechner, G. T. 1966. *Elements of Psychophysics*. New York: Holt, Rinehart and Winston (originally published 1860).

Fernald, M. R. 1912. The diagnosis of mental imagery. *Psychological Monographs* 58.

Finke, R. A., and Kosslyn, S. M. 1980. Mental imagery acuity in the peripheral visual field. *Journal of Experimental Psychology: Human Perception and Performance* 6:126–139.

Finke, R. A., and Schmidt, M. J. 1977. Orientation-specific color aftereffects following imagination. *Journal of Experimental Psychology: Human Perception and Performance* 3:599–606.

Finke, R. A., and Schmidt, M. J. 1978. The quantitative measure of pattern representation in images using orientation-specific color aftereffects. *Perception and Psychophysics* 23:515–520.

Flavell, J. H. 1970. Developmental studies in mediated memory. In *Advances in Child Development and Behavior*, Vol. 5, ed. H. W. Reese and L. P. Lipsitt. New York: Academic Press.

Flavell, J. H. 1977. *Cognitive Development*. Englewood Cliffs, New Jersey: Prentice-Hall.

Fodor, J. A. 1968. *Psychological Explanation: An Introduction to the Philosophy of Psychology*. New York: Random House.

Fodor, J. A. 1975. *The Language of Thought*. New York: Crowell.

Fodor, J. A. In press. Methodological solipsism considered as a research strategy in cognitive psychology. *Behavioral and Brain Sciences*.

Forisha, B. D. 1975. Mental imagery verbal processes: a developmental study. *Developmental Psychology* 11:259–267.

Funt, B. V. 1976. WHISPER: a computer implementation using analogues in reasoning. Ph.D. Thesis, University of British Columbia.

Galanter, E., and Galanter, P. 1973. Range estimates of distant visual stimuli. *Perception and Psychophysics* 14:301–306.

Galton, F. 1883. *Inquiries into human faculty and its development*. London: MacMillan.

Garner, W. R., Hake, H. W., and Eriksen, C. W. 1956. Operationism and the concept of perception, *Psychological Review* 63:149–159.

Gibson, E. J. 1969. *Principles of Perceptual Learning and Development*. New York: Appleton-Century-Crofts.

Gibson, E. J., and Bergman, R. 1954. The effect of training on absolute estimation of distance over the ground. *Journal of Experimental Psychology* 48:473–482.

Gibson, E. J., Bergman, R., and Purdy, J. 1955. The effect of prior training with a scale of distance on absolute and relative judgments of distance over ground. *Journal of Experimental Psychology* 50:97–105.

Gibson, J. J. 1966. *The Senses Considered as Perceptual Systems*. Boston: Houghton Mifflin.

Gips, J. 1974. A syntax-directed program that performs a three-dimensional perceptual task. *Pattern Recognition* 6:189–199.

Glanzer, M., and Clark, W. H. 1964. The verbal-loop hypothesis: conventional figures. *American Journal of Psychology* 77:621–626.

Glass, A. L., and Holyoak, K. J. 1975. Alternative conceptions of semantic memory. *Cognition* 3:313–339.

Goodman, N. 1968. *Languages of Art: An Approach to a Theory of Symbols*. Indianapolis, Indiana: Bobbs-Merrill.

Green D. M., and Swets, J. A. 1966. *Signal Detection Theory and Psychophysics*. New York: John Wiley and Sons.

Hagan, J. W. 1972. Attention and mediation in children's memory. In *The Young Child: Reviews of Research*, Vol. 2, ed. W. W. Hartup. Washington, D.C.: National Association for Education of Young Children.

Hampson, P. J., and Morris, P. E. 1978. Unfulfilled expectations: a criticism of Neisser's theory of imagery. *Cognition* 6:79–85.

Hayes, J. R. 1973. On the function of visual imagery in elementary mathematics. In *Visual Information Processing*, ed. W. G. Chase. New York: Academic Press.

Hayes, J. 1978. Children's visual descriptions. *Cognitive Science* 2:1–16.

Hayes-Roth, F. 1979. Distinguishing theories of representation: a critique of Anderson's "Arguments concerning mental imagery." *Psychological Review* 86:376–392.

Hebb, D. O. 1949. *The Organization of Behavior*. New York: Wiley and Sons.

Hebb, D. O. 1968. Concerning imagery. *Psychological Review* 75:466–477.

Hesse, M. B. 1963. *Models and Analogies in Science*. London: Sheed and Ward.

Hochberg, J., and Gellman, L. 1977. The effect of landmark features on "mental rotation" times. *Memory and Cognition* 5:23–26.

Hock, H. S., and Tromley, C. L . 1978. Mental rotation and perceptual uprightness. *Perception and Psychophysics* 24:529–533.

Hollan, J. D. 1975. Features and semantic memory: set-theoretic or network model? *Psychological Review* 82:154–155.

Hollenberg, C. K. 1970. Functions of visual imagery in the learning and concept formation of children. *Child Development* 4:1003–1006.

Holyoak, K. J. 1974. The role of imagery in the evaluation of sentences: imagery or semantic factors? *Journal of Verbal Learning and Verbal Behavior* 13:l63–166.

Holyoak, K. J. 1977. The form of analog size information in memory. *Cognitive Psychology* 9:31–51.

Humphrey, G. 1951. *Thinking*. London: Methuen.

Huttenlocher, J. 1968. Constructing spatial images: a strategy in reasoning. *Psychological Review* 75:550–560.

Huttenlocher, J., Higgins, E. T., and Clark, H. H. 1972. On reasoning, congruence, and other matters. *Psychological Review* 79:420–432.

Jastrow, J. 1888. The dreams of the blind. *The New Princeton Review* 5:18–34.

Jaensch, E. R. 1930. *Eidetic Imagery and Typological Methods of Investigation*. New York: Harcourt Brace.

Jamieson, O. G., and Petrusic, W. M. 1975. Relational judgments with remembered stimuli. *Perception and Psychophysics* 18:373–379.

Jones, N. R. 1973. The use of visual and verbal memory processes by 3 year old children. *Journal of Experimental Child Psychology* 15:340–351.

Jonides, J., Kahn, R., and Rozin P. 1975. Imagery instructions improve memory in blind subjects. *Bulletin of the Psychonomic Society* 5:424–426.

Jorgensen, C. C., and Kintsch, W. 1973. The role of imagery in the evaluation of sentences. *Cognitive Psychology* 4:110–116.

Just, M. A., and Brownell, H. H. 1974. Retrieval of concrete and abstract prose descriptions from memory. *Canadian Journal of Psychology* 28:339–350.

Just, M. A., and Carpenter, P. A. 1976. Eye fixations and cognitive processes. *Cognitive Psychology* 8:441–480.

Kahneman, D. 1973. *Attention and Effort*. Englewood Cliffs, New Jersey: Prentice-Hall.

Kaufman, L. 1974. *Sight and Mind: An Introduction to Visual Perception*. New York: Oxford University Press.

Kaufman, L., and Richards, W. 1969. Spontaneous fixation tendencies for visual forms. *Perception and Psychophysics* 5:85–88.

Keenan, J. M., and Moore, R. E. 1979. Memory for images of concealed objects: a reexamination of Neisser and Kerr. *Journal of Experimental Psychology: Human Learning and Memory* 5:374–385.

Kelly, G. A. 1955. *The Psychology of Personal Constructs*, Vols. I and II. New York: Norton.

Kenny, A. 1968. *Descartes*. New York: Random House.

Kerst, S. M. 1976. Interactive visual imagery and memory search for words and pictures. *Memory and Cognition* 4:573–580.

Kerst, S. M., and Howard, J. H. 1978. Memory psychophysics for visual area and length. *Memory and Cognition* 6:327–335.

Kirkpatrick, E. A. 1894. An experimental study of memory. *Psychological Review* 1:602–609.

Koffka, K. 1912. *Zur Analyse der Vorstellungen und ihrer Gesetze.*

Kosslyn, S. M. 1973. Scanning visual images: some structural implications. *Perception and Psychophysics* 14:90–94.

Kosslyn, S. M. 1975. Information representation in visual images. *Cognitive Psychology* 7:341–370.

Kosslyn, S. M. 1976a. Can imagery be distinguished from other forms of internal representation? evidence from studies of information retrieval time. *Memory and Cognition* 4:291–297.

Kosslyn, S. M. 1976b. Using imagery to retrieve semantic information: a developmental study. *Child Development* 47:434–444.

Kosslyn, S. M. 1978a. Measuring the visual angle of the mind's eye. *Cognitive Psychology* 10:356–389.

Kosslyn, S. M. 1978b. Imagery and internal representation. In *Cognition and Categorization*, ed. E. Rosch and B. B. Lloyd. Hillsdale, New Jersey: Erlbaum Associates.

Kosslyn, S. M., and Alper, S. N. 1977. On the pictorial properties of visual images: effects of image size on memory for words. *Canadian Journal of Psychology* 31:32–40.

Kosslyn, S. M., Ball, T. M., and Reiser, B. J. 1978. Visual images preserve metric spatial information: evidence from studies of image scanning. *Journal of Experimental Psychology: Human Perception and Performance* 4:47–60.

Kosslyn, S. M., and Bower, G. H. 1974. The role of imagery in sentence memory: a developmental study. *Child Development* 45:30–38.

Kosslyn, S. M., Heldmeyer, K. H., and Locklear, E. P. 1977. Children's drawings as data about internal representations. *Journal of Experimental Child Psychology* 23:191–211.

Kosslyn, S. M., Heldmeyer K. H., and Glass, A. L. 1980. Where does one part end and another begin? A developmental study. In *Information Integration in Children*, ed. J. Becker, F. Wilkening, and T. Trabasso. Hillsdale, New Jersey: Erlbaum Associates.

Kosslyn, S. M., Holyoak, K. J., and Huffman, C. S. 1976. A processing approach to the dual coding hypothesis. *Journal of Experimental Psychology: Human Learning and Memory* 2:223–233.

Kosslyn, S. M., and Jolicoeur, P. In press. A theory-based approach to the study of individual differences in mental imagery. In *Aptitude Learning and Instruction: Cognitive Processes Analysis of Aptitude,* Vol. I, ed. R. E. Snow, P. A. Federico, and W. E. Montague. Hillsdale, New Jersey: Erlbaum Associates.

Kosslyn, S. M., Murphy, G. L., Bemesderfer, M. E., and Feinstein, K. J. 1977. Category and continuum in mental comparisons. *Journal of Experimental Psychology: General* 106:341–375.

Kosslyn, S. M., and Nelson, K. E. 1973. Imagery use in the verification of sentences. *Proceedings of the 81st Annual Convention of the American Psychological Association* 8.

Kosslyn, S. M., Pinker, S., Smith, G. E., and Shwartz, S. P. In press. On the demystification of mental imagery. *The Behavioral and Brain Sciences*.

Kosslyn, S. M., and Pomerantz, J. R. 1977. Imagery, propositions, and the form of internal representations. *Cognitive Psychology* 9:52–76.

Kosslyn, S. M., Reiser, B. J., Farah, M. J., and Fliegel, S. Generating visual images. Unpublished manuscript. Harvard University.

Kosslyn, S. M., and Shwartz, S. P. 1977a. A simulation of visual imagery. *Cognitive Science* 1:265–295.

Kosslyn, S. M., and Shwartz, S. P. 1977b. Two ways of transforming visual images. Paper read at the 18th annual meeting of the Psychonomic Society, Washington, D.C., November.

Kosslyn, S. M., and Shwartz, S. P. 1978. Visual images as spatial representations in active memory. In *Computer Vision Systems*, ed. E. M. Riseman and A. R. Hanson. New York: Academic Press.

Kowler, E., Benson, G. E., and Steinman, R. M. 1975. The role of small saccades in small decisions. Paper read at the 16th annual meeting of the Psychonomic Society, Denver, Colorado, November.

Kripke, S. 1972. Naming and necessity. In *Semantics of Natural Language*, ed. G. Harmon and D. Davidson. New York: Humanities Press.

Kuhlman, C. K. 1960. Visual imagery in children. Ph.D. Dissertation, Radcliffe College.

Kulpe, O. 1909. *Outlines of Psychology*, tr. E. B. Tichener. New York: Macmillan.

Larsen, A., and Bundesen, C. 1978. Size scaling in visual pattern recognition. *Journal of Experimental Psychology: Human Perception and Performance* 4:1–20.

Lea, G. 1975. Chronometric analysis of the method of loci. *Journal of Experimental Psychology: Human Perception and Performance* 2:95–104.

Leask, J., Haber, R. N., and Haber, R. B. 1969. Eidetic imagery in children: II. Longitudinal and experimental results. *Psychonomic Monograph Supplements* 3:25–48.

Lindsay, P. H., and Norman, D. A. 1977. *Human Information Processing: An Introduction to Psychology*, 2nd ed. New York: Academic Press.

Lippman, M. Z., and Grote, B. H. 1974. Processing of verbal and visual information by young children. Paper read at the 15th annual meeting of the Psychonomic Society, Boston, Massachusetts, November.

London, P., and Robinson, J. P. 1968. Imagination in learning and retention. *Child Development* 39:803–815.

London, P., and Robinson, J. P. 1971. Labeling and imagining as aids to memory. *Child Development* 42:641–644.

Marks, D. F. 1972. Relative judgment: A phenomenon and a theory. *Perception and Psychophysics* 11:156–160.

Marks, D. F. 1973. Visual imagery differences and eye movements in the recall of pictures. *Perception and Psychophysics* 14:407–412.

Marks, D. F. 1977. Imagery and consciousness: a theoretical review from an individual differences perspective. *Journal of Mental Imagery* 1:275–290.

Marmor, G. S., and Zaback, L. A. 1976. Mental rotation by the blind: does mental rotation depend on visual imagery? *Journal of Experimental Psychology: Human Perception and Performance* 2:515–521.

Marr, D. 1978. Representing visual information. In *Computer Vision Systems*, ed. E. M. Riseman and A. R. Hanson. New York: Academic Press.

Marr, D., and Nishihara, H. K. 1978. Visual information processing: artificial intelligence and the sensorium of sight. *Technological Review* 81:2–23.

McGlynn, F. D., and Gordon, B. C. 1973. Image latency and reported clarity as functions of image complexity. *Psychological Record* 23:223–227.

McGlynn, F. D., Hofius, D., and Watulak, G. 1974. Further evaluation of image latency and reported clarity as functions of image complexity. *Perceptual and Motor Skills* 38:559–565.

McKellar, P. 1965. The investigation of mental images. In *Penguin Science Survey*, ed. S. A. Barnett and A. McLaren. Harmondsworth, England: Penguin Books.

McKellar, P. 1977. Autonomy, imagery, and dissociation. *Journal of Mental Imagery* 1:93–108.

Meyer, D. E. 1970. On the representation and retrieval of stored semantic information. *Cognitive Psychology* 1:242–300.

Milgram, N. A. 1967. Verbal context versus visual compound in paired-associate learning by children. *Journal of Experimental Child Psychology* 5:597–603.

Miller, G. A. 1956. The magical number seven, plus or minus two: some limits on our capacity for processing information. *Psychological Review* 63:81–96.

Minsky, M., and Papert, S. 1972. *Artificial Intelligence Progress Report*. Cambridge, Massachusetts: MIT, Project MAC, Artificial Intelligence Laboratory Memo 252.

Moore, T. V. 1915. The temporal relations of meaning and imagery. *Psychological Review* 22:177–215.

Moran, T. P. 1973. The symbolic imagery hypothesis: a production system model. Ph.D. Dissertation, Carnegie-Mellon University.

Morris, P. E., and Reid, R. L. 1973. Recognition and recall: latency and recurrence of images. *British Journal of Psychology* 64:161–167.

Morton, J. 1969. The interaction of information in word recognition. *Psychological Review* 76:165–178.

Moscovitch, M. 1973. Language and the cerebral hemispheres: reaction time studies and their implications for models of cerebral dominance. In *Communication and Affect: Language and Thought*, ed. P. Pliner, L. Krames, and T. Alloway. New York: Academic Press.

Moyer, R. S. 1973. Comparing objects in memory: evidence suggesting an internal psychophysics. *Perception and Psychophysics* 13:180–184.

Moyer, R. S., and Bayer, R. H. 1976. Mental comparison and the symbolic distance effect. *Cognitive Psychology* 8:228–246.

Moyer, R. S., and Landauer, T. K. 1967. The time required for judgments of numerical inequality. *Nature* 215:1519–1520.

Moyer, R. S., and Landauer, T. K. 1973. Determinants of reaction time for digit inequality judgments. *Bulletin of the Psychonomic Society* 1:167–168.

Muller, G. E. 1917. Zeitschrift Psychologie Erganzbd 9 (cited in Woodworth, 1938).

Nappe, G. W., and Wollen K. A. 1973. Effects of instructions to form common and bizarre mental images on retention. *Journal of Experimental Psychology* 100:6–8.

Narasimhan, R. 1969. On the description, generation, and recognition of classes of pictures. In *Automatic Interpretation and Classification of Images*, ed. A. Grasselli. New York: Academic Press.

Neisser, U. 1967. *Cognitive Psychology*. New York: Appleton-Century-Crofts.

Neisser, U. 1972. Changing conceptions of imagery. In *The Function and Nature of Imagery*, ed. P. W. Sheehan. New York: Academic Press.

Neisser, U. 1976. *Cognition and Reality*. San Francisco: Freeman.

Neisser, U. 1978. Anticipations, images, and introspections. *Cognition* 6:169–174.

Neisser, U., and Kerr, N. 1973. Spatial and mnemonic properties of visual images. *Cognitive Psychology* 5:138–150.

Nelson, K. E., and Kosslyn, S. M. 1975. Semantic retrieval in children and adults. *Developmental Psychology* 11:807–813.

Newell, A. 1972. A theoretical exploration of mechanisms for coding the stimulus. In *Coding Processes in Human Memory*, ed. A. W. Melton and E. Martin. Washington, D.C.: Winston.

Newell, A., and Simon, H. A. 1972. *Human Problem Solving*. Englewood Cliffs, New Jersey: Prentice-Hall.

Nickerson, R. S. 1972. Binary-classification reaction time: a review of some studies of human information-processing capabilities. *Psychonomic Monograph Supplements* 4:275–318.

Nielson, G. D., and Smith, E. E. 1973. Imaginal and verbal representations in short-term recognition of visual forms. *Journal of Experimental Psychology* 101:375–377.

Norman, D. A., and Rumelhart, D. E. 1975. *Explorations in Cognition*. San Francisco: Freeman.

Paivio, A. 1971. *Imagery and Verbal Processes*. New York: Holt, Rinehart and Winston.

Paivio, A. 1975a. Imagery and synchronic thinking. *Canadian Psychological Review* 16:147–163.

Paivio, A. 1975b. Perceptual comparisons through the mind's eye. *Memory and Cognition* 3:635–648.

Paivio, A., Yuille, J. C., and Madigan, S. 1968. Concreteness, imagery, and meaningfulness values for 925 nouns. *Journal of Experimental Psychology Monograph Supplement* 76.

Palmer, S. E. 1975. Visual perception and world knowledge: notes on a model of sensory-cognitive interaction. In *Explorations in Cognition*, ed. D. A. Norman and D. E. Rumelhart. San Francisco: Freeman.

Parkman, J. M. 1971. Temporal aspects of digit and letter inequality judgments. *Journal of Experimental Psychology* 91:191–205.

Pear, J. J., and Cohen, R. G. 1971. Simple and complex imagery in individual subjects. *Psychological Record* 21:25–33.

Perky, C. W. 1910. An experimental study of imagination. *American Journal of Psychology* 21:422–452.

Piaget, J. 1970. *Structuralism*. New York: Harper and Row.

Piaget, J., and Inhelder, B. 1971. *Mental Imagery in the Child*. New York: Basic Books.

Pinker, S. In press. Mental imagery and the third dimension. *Journal of Experimental Psychology: General*.

Pinker, S., and Kosslyn, S. M. 1978. The representation and manipulation of three-dimensional space in mental images. *Journal of Mental Imagery* 2:69–84.

Podgorny, P., and Shepard, R. N. 1978. Functional representations common to visual perception and imagination. *Journal of Experimental Psychology: Human Perception and Performance* 4:21–35.

Postman, L. 1974. Does imagery enhance long-term retention? *Bulletin of the Psychonomic Society* 3:385–387.

Postman, L., and Burns, S. 1973. Experimental analysis of coding processes. *Memory and Cognition* 1:503–507.

Potts, G. R. 1972. Information processing strategies used in the encoding of linear orderings. *Journal of Verbal Learning and Verbal Behavior* 727–740.

Potts, G. R. 1974. Storing and retrieving information about ordered relationships. *Journal of Experimental Psychology* 103:431–439.

Potts, G. R., Banks, W. P., Kosslyn, S. M., Moyer, R. S., Riley, C. A., and Smith, K. H. 1978. Encoding and retrieval in comparative judgments. In *Cognitive Theory, Vol. 3,* ed. N. J. Castellan and F. Restle. Hillsdale, New Jersey: Erlbaum Associates.

Putnam, H. 1960. Minds and machines. In *Dimensions of Mind: A Symposium,* ed. S. Hook. New York: New York University Press.

Putnam, H. 1973. Reductionism and the nature of psychology. *Cognition* 2:131–146.

Putnam, H. 1978. *Meaning and the Moral Sciences.* London: Routledge and Kegan Paul.

Pylyshyn, Z. W. 1973. What the mind's eye tells the mind's brain: a critique of mental imagery. *Psychological Bulletin* 80:1–24.

Pylyshyn, Z. W. 1975. Do we need images and analogues? In the Proceedings of the Conference on Theoretical Issues in Natural Language Processing, MIT.

Pylyshyn, Z. W. 1979a. The rate of "mental rotation" of images: a test of a holistic analogue hypothesis. *Memory and Cognition* 7:19–28.

Pylyshyn, Z. W. 1979b. Validating computational models: a critique of Anderson's indeterminacy of representation claim. *Psychological Review* 86:383–394.

Pylyshyn, Z. W. In press. The symbolic nature of mental representations. *Objectives and Methodologies in Artificial Intelligence,* ed. S. Kaneff and J. F. O'Callaghan. New York: Academic Press.

Reed, S. K. 1974. Structural descriptions and the limitations of visual images. *Memory and Cognition* 2:329–336.

Reed, S. K., and Johnsen, J. A. 1975. Detection of parts in patterns and images. *Memory and Cognition* 3:569–575.

Reese, H. W. 1970. Imagery in children's learning: a symposium. *Psychological Bulletin* 73:383–384.

Reid, L. S. 1974. Toward a grammar of the image. *Psychological Bulletin* 81:319–334.

Richardson, A. 1969. *Mental Imagery.* New York: Springer Publishing Company.

Richman, C. L., Mitchell, D. B., and Reznick, J. S. 1979. Mental travel: some reservations. *Journal of Experimental Psychology: Human Perception and Performance* 5:13–18.

Rieffert, J. 1912. Uber die Objektivierung und Subjektivierung von Sinneseindrucken. *Kongress für Experimentelle Psychologie* 5:245–247.

Rock, I. 1973. *Orientation and Form*. New York: Academic Press.

Rock, I., Halper, F., and Clayton, T. 1972. The perception and recognition of complex figures. *Cognitive Psychology* 3:655–673.

Rock, I., and Heimer, W. 1957. The effect of retinal and phenomenal orientation on the perception of form. *American Journal of Psychology* 70:493–511.

Rohwer, W. D. 1970. Images and pictures in children's learning: research results and educational implications. *Psychological Bulletin* 73:393–403.

Rothstein, L. D., and Atkinson, R. C. 1975. Memory scanning for words in visual images. *Memory and Cognition* 3:541–544.

Rumelhart, D. E., Lindsay, P. H., and Norman, D. A. 1972. A process model for long-term memory. In *Organization and Memory*, ed. E. Tulving and W. Donaldson. New York: Academic Press.

Ryle, G. 1949. *The Concept of Mind*. London: Hutchinson and Co., Ltd.

Schacter, S., and Singer, J. 1962. Cognitive, social and physiological determinants of emotional state. *Psychological Review* 69:379–399.

Schwartz, S. P. 1979. Natural kind terms. *Cognition* 7:301–315.

Scripture, E. W. 1896. Measuring hallucinations. *Science* 3:762–763.

Seamon, J. G. 1972. Imagery codes and human information retrieval. *Journal of Experimental Psychology* 96:468–470.

Segal, S. J. 1971. Processing of the stimulus in imagery and perception. In *Imagery: Current Cognitive Approaches*, ed. S. J. Segal. New York: Academic Press.

Segal, S. J., and Fusella, V. 1970. Influence of imaged pictures and sounds on detection of visual and auditory signals. *Journal of Experimental Psychology* 83:458–464.

Sekuler, R., and Nash, D. 1972. Speed of size scaling in human vision. *Psychonomic Science* 27:93–94.

Shaw, R., and Bransford, J., eds. 1977. *Perceiving, Acting and Knowing*. Hillsdale, New Jersey: Erlbaum Associates.

Sheehan, P. W., and Neisser, U. 1969. Some variables affecting the vividness of imagery in recall. *British Journal of Psychology* 60:71–80.

Shepard, R. N. 1975. Form, formation, and transformation of internal representations. In *Information Processing and Cognition: The Loyola Symposium*, ed. R. L. Solso. Hillsdale, New Jersey: Erlbaum Associates.

Shepard, R. N. 1978. The mental image. *American Psychologist* 33:125–137.

Shepard, R. N., and Cermak, G. W. 1973. Perceptual-cognitive explorations of a toroidal set of free-form stimuli. *Cognitive Psychology* 4:351–377.

Shepard, R. N., and Chipman, S. 1970. Second order isomorphisms of internal representations: shapes of states. *Cognitive Psychology* 1:1–17.

Shepard, R. N., and Feng, C. 1972. A chronometric study of mental paper folding. *Cognitive Psychology* 3:228–243.

Shepard, R. N., and Judd, S. A. 1976. Perceptual illusion of rotation of three-dimensional objects. *Science* 191:952–954.

Shepard, R. N., and Metzler, J. 1971. Mental rotation of three-dimensional objects. *Science* 171:701–703.

Shwartz, S. P. 1979. Studies of mental image rotation: implications for a computer simulation of visual imagery. Ph.D. Diss., The Johns Hopkins University.

Simon, H. A. 1972. What is visual imagery? an information processing interpretation. In *Cognition in Learning and Memory*, ed. L. W. Gregg. New York: John Wiley.

Simon, H. A., and Barenfeld, M. 1969. Information processing analysis of perceptual processes in problem solving. *Psychological Review* 76:473–483.

Simon, H. A., and Feigenbaum, E. A. 1964. An information processing theory of some effects of similarity, familiarity and meaningfulness in verbal learning. *Journal of Verbal Learning and Verbal Behavior* 3:385–396.

Smedslund, J. 1961. The acquisition of conservation of substance and weight in children: II. External reinforcement of conservation of weight and the operations of additions and subtractions. *Scandinavian Journal of Psychology* 2:71–84.

Smith, E. E. 1978. Theories of semantic memory. In *Handbook of Learning and Cognitive Processes*, Vol. 5, ed. W. K. Estes. Hillsdale, New Jersey: Erlbaum Associates.

Smith, E. E., and Nielson, G. D. 1970. Representation and retrieval processes in short-term memory: Recognition and recall of faces. *Journal of Experimental Psychology* 85:397–405.

Smith, E. E., Shoben, E. J., and Rips, L. J. 1974. Structure and process in semantic memory: A feature model for semantic decisions. *Psychological Review* 81:214–241.

Smith, I. M. 1964. *Spatial Ability: Its Educational and Social Significance*. San Diego: Knapp.

Spearman, C. 1927. *The Abilities of Man: Their Nature and Measurement*. New York: Macmillan.

Sperling, G. 1960. The information available in brief visual presentations. *Psychological Monographs* 74.

Sternberg, S. 1966. High-speed scanning in human memory. *Science* 153:652–654.

Sternberg, S., Monsell, S., Knoll, R. L., and Wright, C. E. 1978. The latency and duration of rapid movement sequences: comparisons of speech and typewriting. In *Information Processing in Motor Control and Learning*, ed. G. E. Stelmach. New York: Academic Press.

Stevens, S. S. 1975. *Psychophysics: Introduction to Its Perceptual, Neural, and Social Prospects*. New York: Wiley.

Stricker, S. 1880. *Studien über die Sprachvorstellungen*.

Taylor, D. A. 1976. Stage analysis of reaction time. *Psychological Bulletin* 83:161–191.

Teghtsoonian, M., and Teghtsoonian, R. 1969. Scaling apparent distance in natural indoor settings. *Psychonomic Science* 16:281–283.

Thurstone, L. L. 1938. Primary mental abilities. *Psychometric Monographs* 1.

Tichner, E. B. 1909. *Lectures on the Experimental Psychology of the Thought Processes*. New York: Macmillan.

Toulouse, E. 1897. *Review Paris* 6:88–126.

Townsend, J. T. 1971. A note on the identifiability of parallel and serial processes. *Perception and Psychophysics* 10:161–163.

Townsend, J. T. 1972. Some results on the identifiability of parallel and serial processes. *British Journal of Mathematical and Statistical Psychology* 25:168–199.

Townsend, J. T. 1974. Issues and models concerning the processing of a finite number of inputs. In *Human Information Processing: Tutorials in Performance and Cognition*, ed. B. H. Kantowitz. Hillsdale, New Jersey: Erlbaum Associates.

Trabasso, T., and Riley, C. A. 1975. The construction and use of representations involving linear ordering. In *Information Processing and Cognition, The Loyola Symposium*, ed. R. L. Solso. Hillsdale, New Jersey: Erlbaum Associates.

Tulving, E. 1972. Episodic and semantic memory. In *Organization of Memory*, ed. E. Tulving and W. Donaldson. New York: Academic Press.

Tversky, A. 1977. Features of similarity. *Psychological Review* 84:327–352.

Tversky, B. 1973. Pictorial and verbal encoding in preschool children. *Developmental Psychology* 8:149–153.

Vanderplas, J. M., and Garvin, E. A. 1959. The association value of random shapes. *Journal of Experimental Psychology* 57:147–154.

Wallis, C. P., and Audley, R. J. 1964. Response instructions and the speed of relative judgments. II. Pitch discrimination. *British Journal of Psychology* 55:133–142.

Watson, J. B. 1913. Psychology as the behaviorist views it. *Psychological Review* 20:158–177.

Watson, J. B. 1928. *The Ways of Behaviorism*. New York: Harper and Brothers.

Watson, J. B. 1930. *Behaviorism*. New York: W. W. Norton.

Weber, R. J., and Bach, M. 1969. Visual and speech imagery. *British Journal of Psychology* 60:199–202.

Weber, R. J., and Castleman J. 1970. The time it takes to imagine. *Perception and Psychophysics* 8:165–168.

Weber, R. J., and Harnish R. 1974. Visual imagery for words: The Hebb Test. *Journal of Experimental Psychology* 102:409–414.

Weber, R. J., Kelley, J., and Little, S. 1972. Is visual imagery sequencing under verbal control? *Journal of Experimental Psychology* 96:354–362.

Weber, R. J., and Malmstrom, F. V. 1979. Measuring the size of mental images. *Journal of Experimental Psychology: Human Perception and Performance* 5:1–12.

Weizenbaum, J. 1976. *Computer Power and Human Reason*. San Francisco: Freeman.

White, K., Sheehan, P. W., and Ashton, R. 1977. Imagery assessment: A survey of self-report measures. *Journal of Mental Imagery* 1:145–170.

Williams, T. 1965. Some studies in game playing with a digital computer. Ph.D. Dissertation, Carnegie-Mellon University.

Winston, P. H., ed. 1975. *The Psychology of Computer Vision*. New York: McGraw-Hill.

Wittgenstein, L. 1953. *Philosophical Investigations*. New York: Macmillan.

Wolpe, J. 1958. *Psychotherapy by Reciprocal Inhibition*. Stanford: Stanford University Press.

Woocher, F. D., Glass, A. L., and Holyoak, K. J. 1978. Positional discriminability in linear orderings. *Memory and Cognition* 6:165–173.

Woodworth, R. S. 1938. *Experimental Psychology*. New York: Holt, Rinehart and Winston.

Woodworth, R. S., and Schlosberg, H. 1954. *Experimental Psychology*. New York: Holt, Rinehart and Winston.

Wundt, W. 1894. *Lectures on Human and Animal Psychology*, tr. S. E. Creigton and E. B. Tichner. New York: Macmillan.
Wundt, W. 1912. *An Introduction to Psychology*, tr. R. Pintner. London: G. Allen and Company.
Yates, F. A. 1966. *The Art of Memory*. Chicago: University of Chicago Press.
Yin, R. K. 1970. Face recognition: a special process? Ph.D. Dissertation, MIT.

Index

DATE DUE

DATE DUE			
FEB 8 1982			
APR 1 2 1989			
APR 2 6 1989			
5-23-96 ILL# 6275009			
6·21·96 ill 6275009			
APR 3 0 1997			
		PRINTED IN U.S.A	
GAYLORD			

Image and Mind